Wealth
and Democracy

ALSO BY KEVIN PHILLIPS

THE COUSINS' WARS (1999)

ARROGANT CAPITAL (1994)

BOILING POINT (1993)

THE POLITICS OF RICH AND POOR (1990)

STAYING ON TOP (1984)

POST-CONSERVATIVE AMERICA (1982)

MEDIACRACY (1974)

THE EMERGING REPUBLICAN MAJORITY (1969)

WEALTH
AND DEMOCRACY

A POLITICAL HISTORY
OF THE AMERICAN RICH

KEVIN PHILLIPS

BROADWAY BOOKS • NEW YORK

Broadway Books titles may be purchased for business or promotional
use or for special sales. For information, please write to: Special Markets Department,
Random House, Inc., 1540 Broadway, New York, NY 10036.

PRINTED IN THE UNITED STATES OF AMERICA

BROADWAY BOOKS and its logo, a letter B bisected on the diagonal,
are trademarks of Broadway Books, a division of Random House, Inc.

Visit our website at www.broadway.com

First edition published 2002

Designed by Fearn Cutler de Vicq
Charts and graphs by Mark Stein Studios

Library of Congress Cataloging-in-Publication Data
Phillips, Kevin P.
Wealth and democracy: the politics of the American rich/Kevin Phillips.—1st ed.
p. cm.
Includes index.
1. Wealth—United States. 2. Political corruption—United States.
3. Representative government and representation—United States.
4. United States—Politics and government. I. Title.

HC110.W4 P484 2002
305.5'234'0973—dc21
2001052656

ISBN 0-7679-0533-4

9 10 8

For every city {state}, however small, is in fact, divided into two, one the city of the poor, the other of the rich; these are at war with one another.

Plato, *The Republic* IV

Thus, it is manifest that the best political community is formed by citizens of the middle class, and that those states are likely to be well-administered in which the middle class is larger, and stronger, if possible, than both other classes.

Aristotle, *Politics,* Book IV,
Chapter 11

The only thing new in the world is the history that you don't know.

President Harry S. Truman

PREFACE

The genesis of this book over the last decade is twofold. In part, it grew out of the great interest in the topic of my 1990 book, *The Politics of Rich and Poor,* but other roots lay in my increasing turn to history, not least economic history, during the 1990s. It is hard to imagine that the excesses bred in that decade—the technology mania and bubble, the money culture, the belief that economic cycles were over, the policies of market extremism, corruption, and a politics ruled by campaign contributions—could have developed so destructively if so much knowledge of the past had not slipped away in stock market and "new era" triumphalism.

As previous periods of excess crested or crashed, books emerged to flesh out the historical context of wealth and its wayward pursuit. Gustavus Myers published *The History of the Great American Fortunes* just as the Gilded Age was ending under the whip of Theodore Roosevelt and the Progressive Movement. Matthew Josephson published *The Robber Barons* in 1934, just when mid-depression Americans were blaming another generation of commercial and financial leaders for the speculative bubble and crash of 1929. This book was begun in 1999 for much the same purpose: to inform public understanding and aspirations to reform with a sweep of history—the history of wealth, democracy, and their tensions—that goes back to 1776 and before. The stock market mania, the technology bubble, and Enron all have precedents aplenty.

Obviously, these points are easier to make in 2002 than in 1999. In 1999, with the stock indexes reaching for the moon and upscale consumer spending surges correlating with major Nasdaq rallies, history seemed on hold. In January 2000, with the first stages of the crash just weeks away, the movement to draft Ralph Nader to run for president—not, admittedly, a mainstream crowd—held a rally at Washington's Lincoln Memorial at which they read from a letter of November 21, 1864, allegedly written by Abraham Lincoln. Looking beyond the war, he said, "I see in the near future a crisis approaching that unnerves me and causes me to tremble for the safety of my country. As a result of the war, corporations have been en-throned, and an era of corruption in high places will follow, and the money power of the country will endeavor to prolong its reign by working upon the prejudices of the people until all wealth is aggregated in a few hands and the Republic is destroyed. I feel at this moment more anxiety for the safety of my country than ever before, even in the midst of war." Amid the excitement of the rising Nasdaq, hardly anyone paid attention.

Many scholars doubt the genuineness of this letter, and it is a very blunt statement of sentiments that our sixteenth president usually expressed with more restraint. My point, though, is that such viewpoints—which now get one read out of the Republican Party—have a surprising and dis-tinguished history within them. When Theodore Roosevelt was in the White House, his attacks on corporations far exceeded Lincoln's; and at one point, TR specifically repeated and endorsed Lincoln's oft-quoted remarks about labor being superior to and more deserving of support than capital.

Some of this GOP skepticism lingered on in the years of Eisenhower and Nixon. Back in 1990, when I published *The Politics of Rich and Poor,* some of its success was owed to the two lead endorsements on the back of the book jacket. One was from New York Governor Mario Cuomo, then widely expected to be the 1992 Democratic presidential nominee. The sec-ond was from former President Richard Nixon, who gave it with full knowledge that the book was critical of the Reagan and Bush administra-tions for favoring the rich. Nixon's streetcar-worker father had left Ohio for California after getting a name as labor agitator, and he thereafter in-terrupted his McKinley Republicanism to support third-party progres-sives like Theodore Roosevelt in 1912 and Robert La Follette in 1924. As president, Nixon himself supported national health insurance, income maintenance for the poor, and higher taxation of unearned than earned in-come. The 1972 Republican platform actually criticized multinational corporations for building plants overseas to take advantage of cheap labor.

Because my own background is Republican, and I now know much more of GOP history on these subjects, it is hard to avoid the conclusion that the Republican economic policies and biases of the 1990s and early 2000s are a narrow-gauge betrayal of the legacy of the two greatest Republican presidents, Lincoln and Teddy Roosevelt. But that is a debate I will leave to the elections.

Kevin Phillips
West Goshen, Connecticut
January 2002

CONTENTS

INTRODUCTION

Ill fares the land, to hastening ills a prey
Where wealth accumulates, and men decay
—Oliver Goldsmith

The terrorist attack on New York City in September 2001 came only a year after serious candidates in America's millennial presidential election had described how money and wealth in the United States were crippling democracy. Politics, they had said, was being corrupted as the role of wealth grew.

Other critics had found a reemergent plutocracy—defined as government by or in the interest of the rich—challenging popular sovereignty as it had in the late nineteenth century. Scholars also pointed out that the reigning theology of domestic and global markets *uber alles* bore disturbing resemblance to the survival-of-the-fittest canons of that earlier Gilded Age.

None of these circumstances were changed by the destruction of the World Trade Center. The increasing reliance of the American economy on finance is an even more obvious vulnerability. If September's stock market decline briefly shaved another trillion dollars from U.S. financial assets, national politics continued to wear its "for sale" sign. The United States remained what comparisons had clearly shown: the most polarized and inequality-ridden of the major Western nations.

In 2002, as in 1999 and 2000, these predicaments did not represent the American political and economic norm, which has been for such developments to be restrained by suspicions of the rich. Deviations from such wariness mostly have come during optimal periods of broad-based prosperity in which economic opportunities far outweighed these qualms. The early nineteenth century, for example, in the frontier settlement decades humming with bargain-priced government land sales—"doing a land office business" became a common phrase in the 1830s—empowered millions of new small landowners. New World openness in acreage or jobs became a beacon, drawing millions of emigrants from European embarkation ports. Stephen Girard and John Jacob Astor, America's richest men, were two immigrants who had built fortunes with the help of Jeffersonian politics. Wealth in their hands symbolized opportunity.

The other great example came in the quarter century after World War II when the middle class pushed its share of national wealth and income to record levels. The skepticism of the rich imprinted by the Great Depression guided politics and public policy through the 1960s.

These were the two eras in which wealth and opportunity clearly nurtured democracy. Yes, the top 1 percent of Americans had a very large slice, but it was smaller than the share commanded by the aristocracy of Europe.

The last two decades of the twentieth century, by contrast, echoed the zeniths of corruption and excess—the Gilded Age and the 1920s—when the rich in the United States slipped their usual political constraints, and this trend continued into the new century. By the 1990s data showed the United States replacing Europe at the pinnacle of Western privilege and inequality. This, of course, is part of what made the United States the prime target of terrorism in much the same way as the Europe of czars, kings, and grand dukes was during the period of 1880 to 1920. Finance itself had been a target before—in 1886, an anarchist flung acid and fired shots at the stockbrokers of the Paris Bourse, and in September 1920, terrorists set off dynamite on Wall Street in front of the offices of J. P. Morgan. Thirty-four people were killed and more than two hundred injured.

Given these extraordinary wealth-related circumstances, provocations, and stakes, a political history of the American rich must inquire far beyond the predictable concentration of assets, inequality, and conspicuous consumption. It must also pursue troubling and crippling side effects: high levels of political corruption, the arrogance of global economic power, the twisting of the U.S. tax code, and the voter belief in the captivity of government to private interests.

The inroads on American democracy in the 1980s and 1990s have many philosophical as well as political patrons: think tanks, university chairs, and publications joined in praise of economic elites, corporate predators, Darwinian competition, the claims of political moneygiving to be free speech, uninhibited markets, global policing on behalf of investment, and "free" enterprise (however reliant on friendly government). Allied pundits and promoters, in turn, have repeatedly undercut popular programs ranging from Social Security to business regulation. Unelected judges, central bankers, trade regulators, and global economic organizations have been encouraged in taking over powers earlier enjoyed by elected national leaders and legislatures. Critics counter with charges of a growing "democratic deficit."

These trends are closely related to—indeed, many of their conservative protagonists are funded by—America's deepening wealth and income concentrations. Between 1979 and 1989 the portion of the nation's wealth held by the top 1 percent nearly doubled from 22 percent to 39 percent. By the mid-nineties, some economists estimated that the top 1 percent had captured 70 percent of all earnings growth since the mid-seventies.

In 1999 the *New York Times* reported that within the most prosperous fifth of U.S. households, national income growth was shared so unevenly that *some 90 percent of that fifth's gain went to the top 1 percent.* No one, then, should regard the $90,000-a-year accountant or $125,000-a-year lawyer—members of the top 5 or 10 percent—as fellow riders on the same glittering escalator as the investment banker making $1.5 million or the corporate CEO collecting $40 million in annual compensation. Many, many households in the top 5 percent of the population have seen their own status and access to luxuries shrink in the backwash of these new top wealth levels.

Shrewd Republicans and conservatives have long understood their political danger from public outrage over such imbalances. Lee Atwater, the 1988 campaign manager for George H. W. Bush, summed it up: "The way to win a presidential race against the Republicans is to develop the class warfare issue [as 1988 nominee Michael Dukakis belatedly did at the end]. To divide up the haves and have nots and to try to reinvigorate the New Deal coalition."

"Class warfare," however, is a false description, a perverse conservative borrowing from Karl Marx. In the United States, the pro-wealth policies of the right have enjoyed substantial low and low-middle-income support, particularly among religious voters enlisted by cultural facets of conservatism. Moreover, "upper-class" men like Thomas Jefferson, Theodore Roosevelt, and Franklin D. Roosevelt have been the most effective leaders against what TR called the "malefactors of great wealth." When avarice and speculation have run amok, considerable elements of upper-bracket Americans usually joined the political reform camp. Economic class lines simply do not hold, which is part of why wise progressives attack privileges, malefactors, elites, and corruption.

In the millennial presidential election of 2000, the most vehement critic of the developing plutocracy was the reform Republican presidential contender, Arizona senator John McCain III, whose father and grandfather were both distinguished four-star admirals in the U.S. Navy. The reformist Democratic contender, former senator Bill Bradley, was a Princeton-educated millionaire. The Green Party presidential nominee, Ralph Nader, was himself a multimillionaire with $4 million in investments.

Most of the successful U.S. political mobilizations against abusive elites, in short, have appealed to a reform-minded portion of rich Americans. Instead of evidencing class warfare, a fake bugaboo, the historic confrontations have come from a broad-based national arousal against an abusive sector or stratum and its corrosive-seeming concentrations of wealth and power.

The glaring assemblages of wealth during the Gilded Age, the 1920s, or the 1980s and 1990s have themselves come from assertiveness, not passivity. Laissez-faire is a pretense. Government power and preferment have been used by the rich, not shunned. As wealth concentration grows, especially near the crest of a drawn-out boom, so has upper-bracket control of politics and its ability to shape its own preferment. The public has reason to be aroused, because the cost to ordinary Americans has been substantial—in reduced median family income, in stagnant wages, in a diminished sense of community and commonweal, in fewer private and governmental services, and sometimes in poorer physical and mental health amid money-culture values, work hours, and competitive consumption.

Early in his pursuit of the 2000 Democratic nomination, former senator Bradley made the point that "When politics becomes hostage to money, as it did in the late nineteenth century, and as it increasingly is today, people suffer. Neither economic opportunity nor economic security is given the place it deserves in our national ambitions. There is still a very tangible relationship between the level of opportunity and security available to every American family and the extent to which we can keep our democracy secure and separate from the force of money."

Not a few of these circumstances were emerging eleven years ago when I published *The Politics of Rich and Poor.* Its detailing of wealth concentration and policy favoritism during the eighties wound up playing a role in the 1990 and 1992 elections. That book, however, dealt with the transformations of the 1980s and with policies launched under the Reagan administration. The collective changes over two decades turned out to be much more sweeping—a global upheaval in finance, communications, and technology—and the greatest wealth increases came with the new technology fortunes of the late nineties.

This volume, then, is *not* an update of *The Politics of Rich and Poor.* *Wealth and Democracy* ranges much farther afield, pursuing the political and economic history of U.S. wealth, the U.S. record of speculative finance, the Anglo-Saxon proclivity for technology manias, the overlap between watershed technological innovation and economic inequality, and the connections between wealth concentration and the corruption of politics, government, and public policy. Whereas *Rich and Poor* profiled those who made the big wealth gains in the United States during just one decade, *Wealth and Democracy* pulls together the top wealth lists from the 1790s to the turn of the twenty-first century, relating them not just to politics but to the ups and downs of the economy and the size of the rich-poor gap.

By and large, the twentieth-century periods that most increased top wealth did little for median family income—the twenties, eighties, and nineties. Conversely, the decades of progressivism and recoupment by ordinary Americans under Franklin D. Roosevelt and through the sixties involved keeping a lid on the rich. This unfortunate connection weakened in the fifties and sixties, but regained its relevance from the late seventies to the nineties.

This book's larger portrait, over three centuries, of who assembled the great fortunes, how and why and with what effects, stands as the first political history of the American rich. Gustavus Myers's *History of the Great American Fortunes* is now a century old. This updated backdrop is essential for comparing the political, government, and financial effects of previous wealth excesses with those of the 1980s and 1990s.

For example, by 2000 the United States could be said to have a plutocracy, when back in 1990 the resemblance to the previous plutocracy of the Gilded Age had not yet fully matured. Compared with 1990, America's top millennial fortunes were three or four times bigger, reflecting the high-powered convergence of innovation, speculation, and mania in finance and technology. Moreover, the essence of plutocracy, fulfilled by 2000, has been the determination and ability of wealth to reach beyond its own realm of money and control politics and government as well. In America, explains political scientist Samuel Huntington, "money becomes evil not when it is used to buy goods but when it is used to buy power . . . economic inequalities become evil when they are translated into political inequalities." Political inequalities, in turn, lead to more dangerous economic inequalities.

The morphing of politics into a marketplace with barely hidden price tags reached critical mass in the 1990s. Escalating monied control of politics provoked a stream of new studies and volumes about the "Buying of the Presidency" and the "Buying of Congress." Elizabeth Drew, a serious author, employed a suitably stark title: *The Corruption of American Politics.* Pundits labeled pre-2000 presidential fundraising as a "wealth primary" that distilled the new electoral essence: big contributor sponsorship. Others derided the contest itself as our "national auction." Senator McCain dismissed the U.S. system of campaign finance as "an elaborate influence-peddling scheme in which both parties conspire to stay in office by selling the country to the highest bidder."

With Americans of the early twenty-first century confronting plutocracy's *second U.S.* emergence, it is only moderately comforting to know that the first emergence was eventually curbed a century ago by a pair of progressive presidents and the Sixteenth and Seventeenth Amendments to the U.S. Constitution, which authorized an income tax and required popular election of U.S. senators. The victories under Theodore Roosevelt and Woodrow Wilson, however, came after four decades. The measure of the Gilded Age, beginning in the 1870s, was that by the 1890s the goliaths of U.S. business, railroading, and finance had gained de facto control over many state legislatures, the federal judiciary, and the U.S. Senate. Looking back from the 1930s, historian Arthur Schlesinger Sr. observed how "America, in an ironical perversion of Lincoln's words at Gettysburg, had become a government of the corporations, by the corporations and for the corporations."

Schlesinger's analysis has a contemporary ring. While this book confines itself to a brief opening portrait of the George W. Bush administration, reformers like public television's Bill Moyers were proclaiming Gilded Age déjà vu within two months of the Bush inaugural. "Big money and big business, corporations and commerce," Moyers commented, "are again the undisputed overlords of politics and government. The White House, the Congress and, increasingly, the judiciary, reflect their interests. We appear to have a government run by remote control from the U.S. Chamber of Commerce, the National Association of Manufacturers and the American Petroleum Institute. To hell with everyone else."

The public seemed to agree. Late spring 2001 polling by the *New York Times* found 57 percent of Americans indicating that administration policies favored the rich; only 10 percent thought they favored the middle class or the poor. The bias was not hard to explain. A liberal organization, Citizens for Tax Justice, looking at six men—the new president, vice president, and the secretaries of state, treasury, defense, and commerce—

added up their levels of reported 2000 income (a range between $130 million and $191 million) and overall wealth (a range between $185 million and $624 million). The effects were soon visible across a broad range of announced policies. The Enron Corporation collapse and scandals of 2001–2 reawakened and enlarged the concerns of the 2000 presidential campaign.

What has changed from Theodore Roosevelt's day, however, is that we can no longer measure the interplay between U.S. wealth and politics in a purely national context. In consequence, this book also profiles the United States as a leading world economic power at or past its zenith, and does so against the warning backdrop and decline-symptoms of its three predecessors—Britain, Holland, and Hapsburg Spain. Unfortunately, the millennial juxtaposition of shrinking prospects for U.S. manufacturing workers and the lower middle class with the golden zenith of a small elite in finance, investments, and international commerce follows the earlier Dutch and British patterns all too well. Historians freely used the term "plutocracy" in describing the similar phases in those nations' life cycles.

The Republican Party has its own recurring role in partial democratic erosion. Republicanism began its presidential cycles circa 1860, 1896, and 1968 with centrist economics, some concern for labor, and skepticism of capital—first under Lincoln, then under McKinley and Theodore Roosevelt, and later under Richard Nixon and Gerald Ford. Once these crisis-era beginnings gave way to more normal times, the Republican compass has swung toward Wall Street, private profit, market utopianism, and the demanding politics of money. Interest-group insistence and ideology took over. The third and current GOP shift of attention from Middle America to Upper America is no coincidence.

The new U.S. war against terrorism adds a further possibility: that a U.S. government concerned with protecting wealth may do so at the expense of democratic procedures and may try to blame terrorism rather than flawed policy for hard times. There is also the possibility that the "financialization" processes of the 1980s and 1990s—securitizing so many income and debt streams, becoming electronically dependent, exalting the stock market as the center of commerce—have made possible a new manner of economic terrorism and warfare prior great powers never faced.

The middle chapters of this book deal in greater detail with how American wealth nourished itself on government influence and power, how politics has often pivoted on banks, corporations, and the rich, and how eras of money worship and speculation have brought corollary corruptions of government, public policy, and even ideas. To begin with these

chapters, though, would be like a roofer going to work without the spec-
ifications and measurements of the house. Chapters 1 and 2 show how
great wealth in the United States gathered and behaved over more than
two centuries. The nation's biggest individual fortunes grew from $5 or
$6 million in the 1830s to John D. Rockefeller's first billionaire status in
1907, and then lagged behind inflation through about 1980 before jumping to $50 or $100 billion in 2000. This has utterly dwarfed the growth
in median household or worker wealth and income. In just a little over
two centuries the United States went from being a society born of revolution and touched by egalitarianism to being the country with the industrial world's biggest fortunes and its largest rich-poor gap. It is a
transformation that Americans will have to start thinking about.

Those chapters detail not just who had the biggest U.S. fortunes, but
from whence this boodle came—from earlier Revolutionary War finance
and privateering in the 1790s, real estate in the 1830s, railroads in the
1870s, a triumvirate of steel, oil, and railroads in the 1890s, autos and oil
in the 1920s, oil, commodities, and real estate amid the inflation spike of
the early 1980s, and technology, of course, in the late 1990s. For each era
we will see how median households or earners were doing in comparison
to the rich, how the South fared relative to the North, agriculture relative
to manufacturing, the middle quintile of the population relative to the
top 1 percent, and so forth. Several of the major U.S. wealth realignments
actually came in the wake of electoral realignments, notably after the
Revolution, after 1800, then after the Civil War and after the New Deal.

Chapter 3 concludes Part I with a portrait of U.S. fortunes and misfortunes at the turn of the twenty-first century. It begins with a look at
the critical disparity of the 1980s and 1990s: how the unprecedented percentage gains made over those decades by the top strata of 2000—the 400
richest Americans, the 3,000 to 5,000 U.S. centimillionaires (assets of
$100 million or more), and 270,000 decamillionaires (assets of $10 million or more)—occurred alongside a relative stagnation of the middle class
and a decline in the net worths of the bottom 60 percent of Americans.
Real disposable (after-tax) income for nonsupervisory workers peaked in
the late 1960s. Debt taken on by the bottom two-fifths of the population
rose so sharply that by 1995 their inflation-adjusted net worths had fallen
below 1973 levels. I found this evidence especially boggling.

The chapter's next cluster describes the segments of the American
economy that both led the boom and profited so disproportionately: finance, corporations, and technology. By 2001, of course, some of the large

technology fortunes had imploded to degrees not seen since the 1929 Crash.

The last theme grouping of chapter 3 returns to the misfortunes of ordinary American households. Two-breadwinner household pressures, longer work hours, lengthier commutes, deteriorating job benefits, and the troubling shift to temporary employment exemplify an obvious dimension of stress. Beginning in the late 1970s, however, even as gross domestic product figures continued to rise, several indexes showed the net decline of the social health of the United States during the 1980s and 1990s. Prosperity lost its early and mid-twentieth-century correlation with social as well as economic gain.

For an international historical context, chapter 4 turns to the lessons for U.S. politics and economics to be found in the little-appreciated precedents of the three previous leading economic powers: Britain, the Netherlands, and, even earlier, the Spanish Hapsburg Empire (which included Flemish and Italian commercial centers). Their trajectories had some striking late-stage similarities, notably a tendency to dangerously elevate finance while turning away from more humdrum industry and commerce.

Power and money represent one of the world's enduring covert partnerships, and even in the twenty-first century, government backstopping critically underpins success for both finance and technology. Chapter 5, "Friends in High Places: Government, Political Influence, and Wealth," looks at this centrality of government in wealth creation from ancient times down through the nineteenth century as well as at its continuing great importance. Without the intervention of the Federal Reserve Board and the U.S. Treasury during the eighties and nineties, for example, through floods of liquidity, loan rescues, bank bailouts, and transfusions for foreign currencies, the Dow-Jones Industrial Average might never have crossed 5000. Federal assistance, especially by the military, also played a decisive role in advancing technology, from the nineteenth-century revolution of interchangeable parts and the rise of the telegraph to radio and aviation and most recently semiconductors and the Internet, which began in 1968 as the Arpanet under the Defense Department's Advanced Research Projects Agency.

If government has often been the early patron of advanced technology, in the United States and Britain excesses of private finance and citizen enthusiasm have led to technological manias and destabilizing speculative bubbles. The examples are railroads in the nineteenth century; autos, radio, and aviation in the 1920s; and high technology and the Internet in the 1990s.

Chapter 6, "Technology and the Uncertain Foundations of Anglo-American Wealth," pursues these effects. It also illustrates how the great technological revolutions—from the Renaissance and the rise of capitalism to the Industrial Revolution and now the age of the microchip and Internet—worked initially, for several generations, to favor those with capital, skills, and education at the expense of the masses, increasing economic inequality rather than easing it. As the twentieth century became the twenty-first, this same effect was visible from the United States and Scandinavia to Israel and Japan.

Taken together, these three chapters of Part II are meant to underscore how the present wealth of the United States is tied not only to government assistance, public policy, and technology, but to the protective umbrella spread by more than a half century of American global economic hegemony. Eventually, however, the previous world economic leaders proved vulnerable not only to excesses of financialization but to transfer of technological advantage. These can dissipate a global industrial primacy in as little as a single generation. War and terrorism add to the risk.

Part III returns our focus to the interrelation of wealth and "politics," the latter broadly construed to include everything from electoral behavior to government corruption, recurrent expressions of Darwinism, and the tendency of U.S. reform waves to follow speculative collapses. Of the six major realignments of presidential politics, five—those in 1800, 1828, 1860, 1896, and 1932—involved voter backlashes against economic elites that ranged from the southern slaveocracy to the money changers and economic royalists challenged by Franklin D. Roosevelt.

Chapter 7, "Wealth and Politics in the United States," begins with a chronicle of these combats and how criticisms of the excesses of capitalism, Wall Street, banks, multinational corporations, the "money power," or the military-industrial complex have come from many of America's best-known presidents, including such representatives of the conservative party as John Adams, Abraham Lincoln, Theodore Roosevelt, and Dwight Eisenhower. Genuine class warfare is almost impossible in the heterogeneous United States, but stalwart popular opposition to self-serving economic elites is as American as apple pie.

Because eras of private interest in the United States put so much emphasis on the pursuit of money and wealth, they have brought more overt corruption of government—the buying of favors and laws—than have so-called public interest eras. However, chapter 8, "Wealth, Money-Culture

Ethics, and Corruption," goes beyond the venality of government and politicians to weigh parallel distortions in ideas, policymaking, and fashion.

Whereas liberal eras often fail through utopias of social justice, brotherhood, and peace, the repetitious abuses by conservatism in the United States in turn involve worship of markets (the utopianism of the Right), elevation of self-interest rather than community, and belief in Darwinian precepts such as survival of the fittest. Bill Clinton, like President Grover Cleveland during the Gilded Age, showed how a Democratic chief executive can coexist with and largely accept these values during a boom era in which corporate and financial interests predominate.

From the first days of the republic, Americans, like the Dutch and British, were described as a speculating people. If this bent for commerce and risk-taking aided all three nations, it also sowed seeds of excess. Indeed, since the eighteenth century, most of the major financial panics have had a Dutch, British, or American component. Chapter 9, "The Cup Always Runneth Over: Greed, Speculative Bubbles, and Reform," as part of its interplay between greed, speculative implosions, and reform, reminds us that financial markets have their roots in medieval carnivals and fairs—in gambling and the mood swings of human nature, not in cool rationality.

In the U.S. more than elsewhere, the political economy has moved to such rhythms; the major periods of progressivism and reform have followed burst speculative bubbles or other severe economic disillusionment. Speculative heydays pull in large middle-class participation, fueling themes about the democratization of money and investment, at least until the bubble pops. Then comes the disillusionment.

Chapter 10, "Great Economic Power Decline and the Politics of Resentment," frames this politics on two levels: the domestic rhythm and the larger, international angst of a leading economic power in decline. As a world economic power begins to slip—ordinary folk are usually the canaries in the coal mine, because the financial elites keep gaining for a generation or two—popular politics edges into frustration. The early stages can be what historians call a reactionary revival, as in the British heyday of popular imperialism in the 1890s. Only as the gap between the stagnating or declining half or two-thirds of the population and the richer-than-ever cosmopolitan elite becomes inflammatory does politics embrace antielite economics—intensified, of course, by any major slump or speculative implosion.

In the United States between the late 1960s and the end of the century, one can argue that something resembling reactionary revivalism dominated in the Reagan era, but that a specific color of populist frustration followed economic weakness in 1973–74, 1979–82, and 1990–92. Although the boom between 1997 and 2000 submerged these psychologies in a new optimism, chapter 10 looks at the last third of the twentieth century for electoral signs and signals of how subsequent U.S. politics could follow in some earlier Dutch and British footsteps.

The likelihood of U.S. overdependence on finance being a particular Achilles heel is an early-twenty-first-century corollary of global terrorism and could also be a factor in politics and popular response. Manufacturing, the earlier U.S. strength, was less vulnerable.

The Afterword, in a separate Part IV, is a look ahead—a rumination on how history, politics, and the circumstances of American wealth and inequality may play out in the first quarter of the new century. Better that its interpretations await the full presentation of the ideas and circumstances on which they rest.

A word on terminology. A half century has passed since Americans used many of the words that entered the U.S. lexicon during the angry years of the Gilded Age. Terms like *plutolatry* (the worship of wealth), *plutology* (the scientific study of wealth), and *plutomania* (the abnormal or excessive desire for wealth) rarely appeared in American dictionaries published after 1950. The triumph of U.S. power and democracy through the New Deal and World War II, it was thought, had eliminated both the threat of plutocracy and any need for its secondary vocabulary. The novelist Tom Wolfe describes his own novels as "plutography," but he has little company.

This mistake has its own Gilded Age precedent. Early-nineteenth-century Americans, for their part, were convinced that the Revolution of 1776 and the subsequent elimination of primogeniture and entail—both British inheritance devices—had eliminated the threat of an aristocracy in the United States. Change came only after the public's rude post–Civil War awakening to the rise of railroads and other giant corporations. By the 1880s the idea of a nation in the grip of plutocracy was widespread, supported by a flowering descriptive vocabulary.

The eleven chapters that follow use these words only rarely. Beyond "plutocracy," twenty-first-century issues will probably yield a new phraseology of concern and dissent. History tells us that—and much more.

PART I

THE GREAT WAVES OF AMERICAN WEALTH

CHAPTER ONE

THE EIGHTEENTH AND NINETEENTH CENTURIES: FROM PRIVATEERSMEN TO ROBBER BARONS

The people who own the country ought to govern it.
—John Jay, first chief justice of the United States, 1787

Many of our rich men have not been content with equal protection and equal benefits, but have besought us to make them richer by act of Congress.
—Andrew Jackson, veto of Second Bank charter extension, 1832

Corruption dominates the ballot-box, the Legislatures, the Congress and touches even the ermine of the bench. The fruits of the toil of millions are boldly stolen to build up colossal fortunes for a few, unprecedented in the history of mankind; and the possessors of these, in turn, despise the Republic and endanger liberty.
—National platform of the Populist Party, 1892

The debate over the compatibility of wealth and democracy is as old as the republic. From the start, concern that the egalitarian-seeming United States of the late eighteenth and early nineteenth centuries might develop wealth concentrations to match Europe's was a worry for many but also the guarded hope of an important few.

Alexander Hamilton, who favored both a financial class and an aristocracy, would have cherished the possibility of such an elite. John Adams, who thought aristocracies inevitable, would not have been surprised. Thomas Jefferson brooded that such a danger could flow all too easily from urban growth, finance, and commerce. Richard Price, the British reformer friendly to the American Revolution, warned the new nation against foreign banks and finance; and Alexis de Tocqueville, in 1837, hedged his praise for democracy in America with concern that the new industrial elite, "one of the harshest that ever existed," would bring about the "permanent inequality of conditions and aristocracy."

By the beginning of the twenty-first century, when the first clocks along the international date line struck midnight, the United States had met, at least broadly, the hopes of Hamilton and the fears of Jefferson and de Tocqueville. The transformation was hardly linear, given the interruptions of the populist and progressive eras and the New Deal. By 2000, however, the United States was not only the world's wealthiest nation and leading economic power, but also the Western industrial nation with the greatest percentage of the world's rich and the greatest gap between rich and poor.

To make this transformation from agrarian republic to financial aristocracy fully come alive—to fill in its enormous achievement, recurrent corruption, amazing technological innovation, and political pretense—the best course is to begin in the Massachusetts seaports of Adams and John Hancock, the Virginia plantations of Jefferson and George Washington, and the Manhattan financial district of Hamilton, taking nineteenth-century turnpikes and canals to the railroads, stock exchanges, Civil War battlefields, and William Jennings Bryan's angry farm belt and moving on to Hollywood, the World War II defense industries, and Silicon Valley, and always keeping an eye on two principal centers of influence, Washington and Wall Street. By the end of the period covered by this first chapter, from the 1770s to 1900, wealth had enjoyed a glorious century and a quarter. The largest fortune in the United States had grown from an ambiguous $1 million to somewhere in the $300 to $400 million range.

Democracy, in her allegorical garb, was by then wandering around Washington more than a little woebegone, muttering about "the shame of the Senate," watching a U.S. Supreme Court unabashedly hold for railroads in fifteen of sixteen cases, condemning New York City tenements that matched the worst of East End London, and glooming about the lost world of Jefferson, Jackson, and Lincoln.

The unusual political freedom in the U.S., to be sure, was part of what made wealth more openly controversial than it was in Europe. Suspicion of aristocracy, officialdom, and inherited riches was a legacy of the Revolution. Like the earlier citizenry of the Greek and Roman republics, Americans could and did take issue with the abuses of the rich and powerful. Voters could even expect, in some matters, to bring the upper classes to heel. That was part of what republicanism was all about.

Other facets of democracy, however, made wealth in the early United States *less* controversial. Those from poor backgrounds had a chance, sometimes a better one, to share, as along Cornelius Vanderbilt's scrappy, cut-throat New York waterfront or in John Jacob Astor's rough-and-tumble frontier fur business. Self-made men were the best-known standard-bearers of wealth. A humble immigrant could become the richest man in America, because two did—French-born Stephen Girard, who came to Philadelphia as a merchant ship officer, and Astor, son of a poor German butcher.

The egalitarian-minded working classes of New York and Phila-delphia, as we will see, quickly rallied against the Federalist merchants and financiers of the 1790s, with their predilection for British manners and contempt for the common man. Neither of these self-made business-men had such vulnerabilities: Girard, besides being a supporter of the antiaristocratic French Revolution, was ugly; Astor was uncouth, with relatively little social pretense. Most of the Frenchman's clerks dressed better than he did, and Astor and his son handled and "beat" their own furs well into their second decade of business. Neither put on aristocratic airs or offended republican sensibilities.

In such hands, riches symbolized the New World's promise, not some vague prospect of oppression. In contrast to stratified Europe, the more fluid society in America offered a double opportunity: both to make money and to criticize its abuse by the rich, pointing out how excess wealth and stratification undercut the democracy that had nurtured them.

How this duality evolved during the eighteenth, nineteenth, and twentieth centuries provides an essential backdrop to the circumstances of the twenty-first. And our saga can begin, fittingly, amid the distrust and suspicion rife in Philadelphia during the famous July of 1776, mere blocks from the very birth chambers of the new nation, where hot and tired delegates were just putting the finishing touches on the Declaration of Independence.

Many of the declaration's signers were representatives of America's richest families—a Massachusetts Hancock, a New York Livingston, a Carroll of Maryland, a Lee of Virginia, and a South Carolina Rutledge. Theirs was a *revolutionary* document with respect to Britain, but not in matters domestic. King George III might be charged with repeated in-juries, usurpations, and tyrannies and with sending a swarm of officers to harass Americans and "eat out their substance," but not even Jefferson thought to condemn him for setting the rich above the poor. Hierarchy was a fact of life in the eighteenth-century American colonies.

And so only a few hundred yards from Carpenters' Hall, where the declaration's signers met, disgruntled artisans, storekeepers, and militia-men could be found plotting their own cause in small, sparsely furnished homes and unfashionable taverns like the Four Alls on Sixth Street or the Wilkes and Liberty on Arch Street.* Pennsylvania's July 8 selection of delegates to its state constitutional convention was just days away, and they aimed to be in control.

Only supporters of independence were allowed to vote, Tories being barred, and with prewar property requirements also set aside, radicals dom-inated. Part of what goaded those who were about to give Pennsylvania a state constitution was the increasing concentration of Philadelphia wealth and power among a small capital city elite. At the beginning of the eigh-teenth century, middling artisans claimed 17 percent of Philadelphia's recorded wealth. By 1720 this had dropped to 12 percent and in the decade before the Revolution to just 5 percent. During the same period the assets of the most prosperous 4 percent of Philadelphians jumped from 25 percent of the citywide total to 56 percent, luxury proclaiming itself in everything from new mansions and expensive carriages to glittering dinner parties.

The radical architects of the new state constitution took indirect aim at these disparities by expanding the franchise, limiting the terms of state legislators, and opening sessions to the public. They even specified that final passage of bills should be delayed until their contents could be pub-lished in the state's newspapers and debated by the general public. But in the Declaration of Rights attached to the Constitution, they were more direct, declaring that government existed for the "Common Benefit, Protection and Security of the People, Nation or Community, and not for the particular Emolument or advantage of any Single man, family or Set of Men, who are only part of that community." This was bold talk for the eighteenth century, and many delegates had supported an even stronger Sixteenth Article, narrowly rejected, which stated that "an Enormous Proportion of Property vested in a few Individuals is dangerous to the Rights, and Destructive of the Common Happiness of Mankind; and therefore, every free State hath a right by its Laws to discourage the Possession of Such Property."

These complaints had an element of prophecy. Similar resentments have burst forth at frequent intervals in U.S. history. And if grumbles about economic unfairness are not quite as American as the Fourth of July,

---

* The Four Alls was a mechanics' tavern, and its sign depicted four figures: a king with the motto "I govern all," a general with the motto "I fight for all," a minister labeled "I pray for all," and a laborer with the legend "I pay for all."

one may suggest that they are as American as the eighth of July, the day Pennsylvania activists chose their radical constitutionmakers. We will see these angers in clash after clash, sometimes as a bold banner, sometimes as a subtext of unrelieved frustration.

It would be a mistake, though, to imply that such confrontations were a staple of prerevolutionary America. They were not. The British North American colonies, outside New England, being ethnically and religiously mixed, had more of *these* kinds of disagreements. What scholars now call class tensions might throb in New York's feudal landed estates along the Hudson, Philadelphia's artisan precincts, or in the North Carolina backcountry, where an insurgency against the corrupt impositions of the royal governor and the tidewater gentry was bloodily crushed in 1771 at the Battle of the Alamance. But for the most part, once the Revolution broke out, economic disagreements were generally subordinated to the larger struggle against Britain. Patriots agreed on an *external* target: far-off imperial wealth and power.

Within the empire of 1775–76, the center of hauteur and wealth was in England itself, among the royal family and the landed aristocracy, with an addendum among planters from the rich sugar islands of the West Indies. King George III, sighting a particularly ornate coach one day, exclaimed, "Sugar, sugar. Eh! All that sugar." There were also some "nabobs" enriched by India, like Robert Clive, who had made away with half of the coin and jewels of greater Bengal. The hundred or so great landowners of England predominated, although their estates, being entailed to pass automatically to one heir, were never really measured. Estimates from rent rolls suggest that the lands of the richest, the dukes of Bedford and Sutherland, the earl of Derby, and the Grosvenors (soon-to-be dukes of Westminster) could have been worth as much as £5 million each. The half-dozen largest nonlanded British fortunes, by contrast, were in the £600,000 to £1 million range, which by the late 1780s would be some three to five million new American dollars.

Nothing in the thirteen colonies came close, so the American sense of injury and outsidership was economic as well as political. Commerce and industry in North America—even the availability of currency—were all crimped by various acts of Parliament. Had a British journal ventured a list of the twenty-five richest men in the empire in 1775, the American mainland probably could not have claimed any, except possibly the Penns because of their huge Pennsylvania landholdings. Few in London would have thought to check.

George Washington, one of the richest Americans, was no more than a wealthy squire in British terms. His large house at Mount Vernon paled alongside the new showplaces of the British rich like Holkham Hall, Syon House, and Strawberry Hill. The great English estates would have been worth thirty to forty times as much as Mount Vernon. Before the Revolution, the earl of Shelburne, a major landholder in England and Ireland, had spent ninety-seven thousand pounds simply to buy a Gloucestershire borough with three parliamentary seats he could hand out to supporters. Washington's entire net worth at the time may not have matched Shelburne's single outlay. Samuel Powel III, thought to be the richest man in Philadelphia, North America's largest city, lived in a Georgian town house on South Third Street, elegant locally, that would have gone unremarked in London. Chart 1.1 shows the relative per capita incomes in England circa 1774 versus those of the American southern, middle, and northeastern colonies as well as the slow growth of wealth in the future United States.

CHART I.I **Wealth in the Thirteen Colonies**

A. Per Capita Wealth by Region, 1774		
	ALL WEALTH	NONHUMAN WEALTH
South	£93	£36.4
Middle	£46	£40.2
NE	£38	£36.4
Britain (1688, G. King)		£55
Britain (1770, A. Young)		£135

B. Per Capita Wealth (excluding slaves) in the U.S., 1650 to 1774		
YEAR	IN POUNDS	IN 1976 DOLLARS
1650	£24	$1,148
1700	£28	$1,340
1725	£30	$1,435
1750	£35	$1,579
1774	£37.4	$1,782

Source: Per Capita Wealth by Region, *The Statistical History of the United States,* p. 1175; British and other data from Alice Hanson Jones, *Wealth of a Nation To Be,* pp. 301–302.

The southern colonies were the richest in North America because of slaves. Britain, however, was much richer than the thirteen colonies on a per capita basis because of its landed gentry and upper classes. The richest thousand Britons probably had eight or ten times the landed and personal wealth of the richest thousand in the thirteen colonies. On one hand, this concentration at the top made the median Briton less well off than the median American. On the other, the huge gap between the American merchant class and gentry and the British elite helped explain how the prerevolutionary resentments of the Chesapeake tobacco planters against Britain resembled the later agrarian populist outrage at eastern capital and commerce. The architects of the new United States—Washington, Jefferson, all of them—were middle-class bourgeoisie or minor gentry on the larger playing field of the empire, and passed their angry mind-set into the Revolutionary legacy.

The newly independent United States of 1783 may not even have had a *single millionaire* in dollar terms. Elias Hasket Derby of Salem, Massachusetts, flush at war's end from the sale of British vessels and cargoes captured by his privateers, is generally counted the first, although Philadelphia had several (and perhaps better) claimants. Derby himself may not have reached the million-dollar mark until 1786, when his converted privateer *Grand Turk* returned heavy with tea, porcelain, and cassia (Chinese cinnamon) from the first journey by a New England ship to Canton. Possibly he did not reach a million dollars until the 1790s, when the Napoleonic Wars opened up so many trading opportunities for neutral American shipping.

In the United States as in Europe, wartime spoils were still among the great ladders to fortune. Few in Britain or America would have found it surprising, as the fighting of 1775 turned into a full-fledged revolution, that the war more than anything else would reshape the new nation's wealth.

1. THE FORTUNES OF WAR IN THE AMERICAN COLONIES AND IN THE NEW NATION, 1776–90

"The fortunes of war" is a two-edged phrase. Victory is one interpretation, personal profit another. Although rape and plunder in the Mongol or Borgia manner were no longer acceptable in the Europe of the Enlightenment, war itself remained the principal pathway to new territory and grandeur for rulers as well as to huge fees and commissions for paymaster-generals, principal contractors and commissaries, naval officers in search of prize money, and commissioned privateers.

In another display of war's economic effects, all six of the major waves of inflation that have swept the United States have come in its wake, from Bunker Hill to the Vietnam buildup. The money in circulation has always had to be increased sharply, and each new flood that sluiced through a wartime economy has left expanded enterprises and huge profits in sectors from transportation and food to munitions.

This pattern began before the Revolution, of course. Estimates of the richest men in Massachusetts following King George's War (1744–48) fell on those who had managed, financed, and supplied the campaigns launched from New England against the French in Canada. Something like a hundred thousand pounds sterling stuck to the collective hands of the governor, William Shirley, the Louisbourg expedition's commander, Sir William Pepperrell, and the three merchants who controlled provisioning—Thomas Hancock, Charles Apthorp, and John Erving.

The French and Indian War (1754 to 1763) produced even greater profits on both sides of the Atlantic. Senior eighteenth-century government officials, British and colonial, were expected to enrich themselves, especially those who had purchased positions. So-called venal offices were an investment. The cost of defeating France roughly doubled the British debt, and the paymaster-general of the British army, Henry Fox, took a great fortune from what passed through his hands. The earlier great wars of 1689–1713 had made the army's then-paymaster, James Brydges, earl of Chandos, among the richest men in England, flush enough to bear losing £700,000 in the South Sea bubble of 1720.

British expenditures in the thirteen colonies between 1754 and 1763 may have totaled three million pounds, a sum almost half the size of one of the Crown's prewar annual budgets. In 1756, only a year after New York's selection as the colonies' "general Magazine of Arms and Military Stores," an envious Benjamin Franklin—his own Philadelphia, run by pacifist Quakers, being unsuitable—was already grumbling that "New York is growing immensely rich, by Money brought into it from all Quarters for the Pay and subsistence of the troops." Manhattan dined as heartily on seaborne commerce-raiding. Both in the 1740s and again during the conflict of 1754–63, New York–based privateers like the *Royal Hester* earned lucrative returns for merchant investors. Historians Edwin Burrows and Mike Wallace, in their magisterial tome *Gotham: A History of New York City to 1898,* noted that between 1739 and 1763, some two million pounds sterling worth of legalized plunder found its way into the pockets of about two hundred local investors, "an immense accession of wealth" that seeded many of the city's emerging gentry, including families like the Beekmans, Bayards, and Livingstons who still enjoy multiple Social Register listings.

Piracy itself had not been beyond the pale until the early eighteenth century. Much as Queen Elizabeth had profitably winked at the exploits of Francis Drake, many a substantial seventeenth-century English family enjoyed occasional sub-rosa proceeds from piracy. Some economists have ranked thinly disguised piracy behind only the East India Company as a seventeenth-century English overseas investment. Drake's own haul from his three major privateering expeditions "may fairly be considered the fountain and origin of British foreign investment," according to John Maynard Keynes. The richest Englishman of the early 1600s was the earl of Warwick, whose ships plundered the Spanish when England was at war, then when England rested flew Dutch flags or those of the duke of Savoy in pursuit of Spanish booty.

Merchants in the American colonies of the 1690s often funded covert expeditions to plunder gold, silks, and ivory in the faraway waters off India, Arabia, and Madagascar. Much of the £100,000 estate of New York's Frederick Philipse was said to have originated in this way, and in 1696, Edmund Randolph, surveyor-general of customs, complained to London that "pyrates" were welcome in most American ports, abetted by governors like Sir William Phipps in Massachusetts, William Markham in Pennsylvania, and Benjamin Fletcher in New York. As of, say, 1763, it is reasonable to suggest that many of the thirteen colonies' richest merchant families owed 30 to 40 percent of their wealth to the fruits of war, privateering, and earlier piracy.

According to the sketchy data available for the seventeenth and early eighteenth centuries, wealth distribution for the entirety of colonies like Massachusetts and Pennsylvania was relatively egalitarian—the top 1 percent held only 10 to 20 percent of all assets. In mercantile centers like Boston, Newport, New York, and Philadelphia, however, the disparities increased as population growth, war, and commerce led to growing fortunes. Frontier districts and areas of subsistence (rather than market) agriculture kept a relative equality. As Chart 1.1 has shown, by 1774 the plantation colonies below the line just drawn by Messrs. Mason and Dixon were simultaneously the richest—wealth per free person was £137, compared to £46 in the middle colonies and £38 in New England—and the most unequal. Half of the southern wealth was in slaves, some 600,000 valued at perhaps $120 million by the 1780s.

The Revolution realigned status and wealth in the thirteen former colonies with a vengeance, literally. The exodus of roughly one hundred thousand loyalists from what became the United States between 1775 and 1784, often after the expropriation of their property, eliminated perhaps one-third of the thousand largest prerevolutionary wealthholders. These exiles, many of whom received British compensation, included the Wentworths from New Hampshire, the Hutchinsons, Gardners, Apthorps, and Olivers from Boston, the De Lanceys and Philipses from New York, the Penns, Chews, and Allens from Philadelphia, the Calverts from Maryland, and so forth. The holdings of the Penns, for example, were later estimated at $5 million; postwar land values would have made them America's richest family. Such was the hole left by these departures, on top of wartime depredations, that demographer Alice Hanson Jones, in *Wealth of a Nation To Be,* concluded that per capita wealth in the new United States was still lower in 1805 than it had been in 1774.

Once again, wartime finance and supply responsibilities fulfilled their lucrative potential. Philadelphia's most notable achiever was Robert Morris, initially head of Congress's procurement committee, then (after 1781) superintendent of finance. From 1775 to 1777 about one-quarter of the contracts Morris awarded went to his own firm, Willing and Morris, and his purse was further fattened by privateering, much of it coordinated by his business associate, William Bingham, named Congress's principal agent in the Caribbean. As we will see, Morris was also involved in the private but quasi-public Bank of North America. Such were his boasts about financial success that Morris might have been America's richest man by 1782–83. It is certainly possible that he had his million before shipowner Derby. Although he is remembered as "the financier of the Revolution," one historian claims that the truth is "the other way around—the Revolution financed Morris."

Another important beneficiary of the war was William Duer, principal supplier of the military in New York. Next door was Jeremiah Wadsworth, chief commissary in Connecticut, the war's "provisions state" from 1775–79. Scholars have placed both men within a "procurement network" that operated out of Morris's office and would collaborate again in postwar finance.

Although later generations have taken a glossier view, the Revolution was another grand intermingling of public purpose and private profit— and as in the French wars, privateering seems to have been the single most lucrative enterprise. The seven years following the autumn of 1775 saw some two thousand vessels—brigs, barks, brigantines, ketches, sloops, and even a few frigates—sail under letters of marque from the United States or one of the thirteen states. Collectively they would capture three thousand British ships, valued—including cargoes—at the then huge sum of $18 million. Of the major ports, New York, Newport, Charleston, and Savannah were idled during long British occupations. Philadelphia's occupation, just seven months, was too brief to interfere with a good bag of British merchantmen, but in any event Morris, Willing, and Bingham ran their privateers out of many harbors. The result was to concentrate rebel privateering (and postwar capital) in Philadelphia and the open ports of New England: Boston (after March 1776), Marblehead, Salem, Gloucester, and Newburyport in Massachusetts; Providence, Rhode Island; Portsmouth, New Hampshire, and New London, Connecticut.

Over 400 of the 2,000 rebel privateers came from Massachusetts, and 300 came from Connecticut. New England as a whole furnished some 1,200. A single Massachusetts port, Salem—in 1775 the colonies' eighth-largest town—sent out 158 letter-of-marque vessels, capturing 458 vessels and the largest prize tonnage of any single port. Three of the most successful raiders, the *Tyrannicide,* the *General Stark,* and the *Robin Hood,* raised hell from the Caribbean to the Skagerrak. Almost a third of Salem's privateers sailed from Elias Derby's own long wharf, and these alone took 144 prizes worth over $1 million.

Booty underpinned postwar preeminence everywhere in New England. Asa Clapp, who had been a privateer, became the richest man in Maine. New Hampshire's most successful commerce raider, John Langdon of Portsmouth, became governor and U.S. senator. Providence boasted John Brown, privateer and slaver, whose family money gave Brown University its name in 1804.

Massachusetts, however, led the new nation in both related phenomena—privateering and its roster of end-of-the-eighteenth-century millionaires. Besides "King" Derby, other Salem privateering and trading families reaching millionaire status by the 1790s (while such wealth was still rare) included the Peabodys, Thorndikes, Grays, and Crowninshields. William Gray was said to be worth $3 million in 1807 before Jefferson's embargo went into effect. Israel Thorndike, onetime captain of the *Tyrannicide,* left a $1.8 million estate in 1832, one of New England's largest. The Cabots of nearby Beverly also made money from fast boats and good luck.

Even the hierarchy of Boston was determined by the proceeds of privateering and kindred wartime relations with the new government. After combing the city's tax assessments for the years 1771, 1780, 1784, and 1790, colonial historian John Tyler two centuries later documented a virtual revolution in the makeup of Boston wealth. In 1780, men with privateering and war supply connections were climbing into the upper ranks. By 1784 they were moving toward the top. And by 1790 they *were* the Boston business elite. The five with the highest 1790 assessments were, in order: Thomas Russell, merchant and privateer; John Hancock, merchant, smuggler, and privateer; Joseph Barrell, contractor to the French fleet; Mungo Mackay, distiller and privateer; and Joseph Russell, merchant and privateer.

This is not simply an aside. In the 1790s, fortunes derived from privateering and government finance represented the biggest pot of money in the United States. Gustavus Myers, in *The History of the Great Fortunes,* commingled the privateering and shipping fortunes because who could know how much came from capturing a sugar-laden British merchantman in 1781 and how much from selling cargoes of imported coffee, calicoes, and Javan pepper ten years later? Neglecting Philadelphia, he concluded that "nearly all the large active fortunes of the latter part of the eighteenth and early period of the nineteenth century came from the shipping trade and were mainly concentrated in New England." Salem itself in 1800 was the nation's richest city on a per capita basis.

Besides finding a "conspicuous" overlap between wartime privateering and subsequent wealth, the analysis of early Boston tax assessments underscored the second ingredient: government contracts and profitable wartime connections. Ex-privateer Thomas Russell, the richest man in Boston, had also been the confidential agent of Robert Morris, the head of Congress's procurement committee and the richest man in Philadelphia. Joseph Barrell received a 5 percent commission—in golden louis (French coins)—for supplies procured for the French fleet. Two others, just below the top five, were Caleb Davis, state agent for the sale of prize vessels and Boston representative for the Continental board of war, and John Bradford, prize agent for the Continental navy. Nathan Appleton, who would be a principal organizer of the Massachusetts textile industry in 1813, "owed much of his rise to his role as the continental loan officer for Massachusetts." In sum, "Government contracts offered perhaps an even surer way to wealth than privateering's wheel of fortune."

Although no careful accounting has ever been managed, it is likely that from the 1780s through the turn of the century, every millionaire—eight or ten perhaps, possibly fifteen—owed a fair part of his wealth to wartime or postwar connections to the new government. In this respect, the most notable book of 1776, Adam Smith's *Wealth of Nations,* in its way friendly to the putative American republic, managed to miss a prime component of what was helping to build that wealth.

This political shake-up of wealth patterns—the combined exodus of loyalists and their replacement by an elite with lucrative connections—was widely remarked upon, especially in New England, where Robert Treat Paine of Boston said that, "The course of the war has thrown property into channels, where before it never was, and has increased little streams to overflowing rivers. . . ." John Jay said the same of New York, and others of Philadelphia. Historian David Ramsey wrote that new men had replaced the old in Charleston and "rapidly advanced their interests." One corollary was to seed misperceptions of the fluidity of U.S. society itself.

Wartime data was sparse and unreliable, but one further ambiguity bears note. Timothy Pickering of Massachusetts, the Continental army's quartermaster general late in the war, insisted that corruption in the purchase of supplies and equipment, which brought repeated curses from George Washington, almost doubled what the new U.S. government owed in debt by 1783. Because the notes of this indebtedness themselves became a treasure trove for speculators, many of the well-connected profiteers who increased (if not doubled) the postwar debt also profited a second time, a subject to which we will return shortly.

Finally, the war also redrew regional wealth relationships. The plantation South, with the richest mainland colonies of the prewar period, was devastated by British military campaigns and slave losses. In addition, the region's most lucrative crops either changed or lost markets (tobacco) or became less profitable without British imperial subsidies (indigo and naval stores). Northern maritime and financial centers became fortune's new spawning grounds. After the war, the middle states of New York, New Jersey, Pennsylvania, and Delaware collectively displaced Maryland, Virginia, and the Carolinas to lead in regional wealth. The ability to raise capital from the war itself gave Philadelphia and coastal Massachusetts their unique portion of millionaires.

2. WEALTH IN THE EARLY REPUBLIC, 1790 TO 1860

New England came out of the Revolution and then the Constitutional Convention of 1787 dominant in maritime affairs, home to a majority of the nation's greatest fortunes, and partner in government with Manhattan, Philadelphia, Virginia, and South Carolina through the ruling Federalist Party, which controlled the presidency until the election of 1800. By the second and third decades of the nineteenth century, however, American thoughts and wagon tongues were pointing westward. New England's commercial eminence was fading.

The commercial faction of the governing Federalist Party, including men like Hamilton, Jay, Duer, Morris, and Bingham, staked the party future on maritime success, banking, and finance and, to an extent, on renewed close ties with Britain. High officials in New York and Philadelphia, the two U.S. capitals of the 1780s and 1790s, held court with a style and manner that the opposition press described as aping London. Radical democrats charged them with trying to create an aristocracy through both the Society of the Cincinnati, a group of former Revolutionary officers in which membership would be hereditary, and emulation of English finance with its favoritisms and speculative tendencies.

On becoming the first secretary of the treasury in 1789, Alexander Hamilton presented Congress with a bold economic program. To secure the creditworthiness of the new U.S. government, he called for redeeming at full face value not only U.S. wartime debts and certificates but the debt instruments of the various states. Many of the latter had been bought up by speculators at very low prices. The second proposal was to establish in Philadelphia a national depository to be called the Bank of the United States, which would also facilitate the financial operations of the U.S. Treasury.

Despite the longer-term merits of Hamilton's proposals, they immediately benefited the wealthy Federalist elites. The Bank of the United States, observers agreed, was modeled after both the Bank of England and the Bank of North America, established in Philadelphia in 1781 by Robert Morris to aid the U.S. government in its wartime currency and debt management. Shareholders in Morris's bank included not only Philadelphians but wealthy members of the wartime "procurement network" from other states. Controversy swirled, and in 1785 the Bank of North America's charter was revoked by the Pennsylvania legislature, if only temporarily, in response to complaints of the bank being controlled by an upper-class clique, giving loans mostly to well-connected merchants in Philadelphia and ignoring the rest of the state.

This is not dusty politics from a hard-to-reach, forgotten cupboard. Kindred charges periodically haunted Hamilton's Bank of the United

States (1790–1811) and then the Second Bank of the United States (1816–36). As chapter 7 will amplify, resentment of these institutions and their alleged favoritism to wealthy elites would agitate national politics for a half century, while individuals' relationships with both quasi-official banks would be a considerable guide to major U.S. fortunes from the 1780s to the 1830s.

"Assumption and funding," as Hamilton's debt redemption provisions were called, provided the nation's first cornucopia for financial speculators. From New Hampshire to South Carolina, cliques of wealthy Federalist supporters and officeholders, using traveling agents, had bought as many of the federal and state debt instruments as possible at cut-rate prices. Massachusetts seems to have had the largest bloc of holders, original and speculative, many from among the privateering, supply, and Continental loan elites. Bingham of Pennsylvania was also prominent. Lesser profit-seekers prowled through the backcountry, buying up old, unpaid certificates from veterans, widows, and storekeepers. A group of New York investors, given early information on Hamilton's plans in mid-1789 by his deputy, William Duer, collected for as little as ten cents on the dollar some $2.7 million worth of South Carolina, North Carolina, and Virginia state Revolutionary debt. This was about one-third of the three states' total.

The government's choice to pay for the refunding through new excise taxes, heaviest on the Appalachian backcountry—whiskey was one of western Pennsylvania's biggest exports—added to the regional bitterness. In Congress, northerners from coastal and commercial districts lopsidedly supported both the bank, debt assumption, and tax provisions. Rural men and Southerners led the opposition. James Madison failed with his compromise to redeem at less than face value paper held by speculative (rather than original) purchasers. Still, the whole arrangement was in doubt until Hamilton made a deal with Jefferson, who later admitted not understanding what was at stake. In return for assumption, the capital would be moved from New York—Jefferson called it "Hamiltonople"—first to Philadelphia and then farther south.

Details are few on who eventually collected what. However, of the $1.2 million paid out in 1795 to redeem federal notes, for which tabulations have been made, almost two-fifths went to the four New England states. Massachusetts alone received more than all the states south of the Potomac River. Of the overall $40–$60 million disbursed by the federal treasury under the debt assumption and funding program, about half is thought to have gone to speculators. To emphasize its enormity, $40 million would have been almost 15 percent of the estimated U.S. gross domestic product of 1790! Just $20 million to speculators would have exceeded the entire $18 million take of Revolutionary War privateering and three thousand captured ships.

These financial wranglings, along with the arguments over the pro-British image of the Jay Treaty of 1794, helped split Washington's original partyless government into the factions that became the Federalists and Democratic-Republicans. Jefferson, who resigned as Washington's secretary of state in 1793, disparaged the Federalists as Tories, aristocrats, merchants who traded on British capital and "papermen" (bondholders, financiers, and investors); and his allies rose to the attack. Land speculation had abounded before the Revolution, but stock promotion and speculation in the securities of the Bank of the United States—in 1791, their value briefly soared from $25 to $170—was new.

By 1794, "speculator" became an effective political epithet. Massachusetts voters were asked to exclude them from the new legislature. Candidates in North Carolina were told to swear that they had never been interested in the funding system. "Archimedes," in Philadelphia's *National Gazette,* mocked the would-be aristocrats: Speculators, he said, ought to be classified by wealth and awarded titles (such as the Order of the Leech, and "Their Rapacities").

However many treasury payments wound up in prominent Federalists' pockets, the party paid a steep price. Hamilton's use of government banking and debt to reward a wealthy elite trespassed on the Revolutionary credo, as did the excise taxes so anathemous to farmers. Prominent Philadelphia and Manhattan Federalists were belabored for eating with golden spoons, serving sixteen wines with dinner, and playing "God Save the King" for President Washington's state entrances. Several mansions from the late eighteenth century still stand in Philadelphia's Fairmount Park, where Morris and Bingham had summer homes. Once called villas, as Morris, an admirer of Palladio, named them in 1795, they commemorate a surer Federalist sense of architecture than politics.

Wealth and aristocracy remained a target through 1800 as the rich-poor gap widened in the major cities. The share of assets held by the top 10 percent in New York City climbed from 54 percent in 1789 to 61 percent by 1795, while much the same thing occurred in Philadelphia. New York and Pennsylvania were also the hotbeds of conspicuous speculation, and Pennsylvania farmers were the angriest over Federalist taxes. When the elections of 1800 gave Jefferson twenty of the two states' combined twenty-seven electoral votes, the Virginian beat John Adams, and no Federalist ever again held the presidency.

New York and Philadelphia would have their financial elites, with Wall Street and Chestnut Street their symbols. However, Alexander Hamilton's own Federalist circle of friends and allies would not preside. One way or another, most toppled. Two of his closest colleagues, Robert Morris and William Duer, must at some point have been millionaires, perhaps even multimillionaires. But speculative excess brought both men down, and each went to debtor's prison, where Duer died in 1799. Hamilton, honest in his own finances whatever he permitted associates, was killed in his famous 1804 duel with Aaron Burr.

Morris's close associate William Bingham, who helped Hamilton plan the Bank of the United States, did well enough from his privateering and speculation to become the richest man in Pennsylvania and then a U.S. senator. His life, in the title chosen by his biographer, was a "golden voyage." Critics called him Count Bingham and his wife Anne the Queen, carping that his fortune had been amassed in "a discreditable way, partly in privateering and speculating in government warrants." One asked:

> But say from what bright deeds dost thou derive
> That wealth which bids thee rival British Clive
> Wrung from the hardy sons of toil and war
> By arts which petty scoundrels would abhor.

Bingham may have been the richest man in the entire United States in the 1790s, and the case was stronger by 1804 when he died, leaving an estate of $3 million. By that point, though, he had moved to England. A staunch Anglophile, Bingham modeled his city home in Philadelphia on the London town house of the duke of Manchester, gave his daughter in marriage to British banker Alexander Baring, the future Lord Ashburton, and departed for London in 1801 after losing his seat in the U.S. senate.

There is a moral in the saga of Morris, Duer, and Bingham. A quarter century after the Declaration of Independence, great wealth in the United States still seemed to flow from closeness to government—and Jefferson himself was about to fail to eradicate that connection.

While Jefferson's now-victorious party, the Democratic-Republicans, consisted of a more homespun and egalitarian crowd, during the new century's first decade they overwhelmed the Federalists in part through equally partisan economic policies. These began with the National Debt Reduction Act of 1802 to repeal all internal taxes, take on no new debt, and reduce the existing national debt through tariff receipts. Bankers were glum, while Democratic-Republican farmers and frontiersmen cheered. The Louisiana Purchase of 1803 tilted U.S. commerce and development westward, in an egalitarian direction away from the Federalist coast. Population flow across the Appalachians accelerated, helping to redraw the political map. The Embargo Act of 1807, in turn, hurt the Federalist maritime centers, especially New England, by confining U.S. vessels to port to protest British and French mistreatment of American ships. Then in 1811 the Madison administration, under pressure from state banks, succeeded in defeating the rechartering of Hamilton's Bank of the United States.

The Jeffersonian preference for state banks mixed hypocrisy with a practical desire to build a new political and wealth elite. To gain allies against the Bank of the United States, Jefferson as president instructed his treasury secretary, Albert Gallatin, that "I am decidedly in favor of making all the [state] banks Republican by sharing deposits with them in proportion to the disposition they show. . . ." Partly through this leverage, the Jeffersonians did succeed in creating their elite. Watershed presidencies have always tried to do so, although not always successfully. Under Jefferson, the locus of the principal fortunes shifted from maritime New England to New York, Philadelphia, and points south. And most of the new wave of top U.S. fortune-holders were Democratic-Republicans.

The richest American from 1810 or so until his death in 1831 was Stephen Girard of Philadelphia. After arriving from France in 1776, he prospered as a shipowner. By the 1790s he was part of the Philadelphia political circle that favored Jefferson and the French party, with such admiration for Voltaire, Diderot, Paine, and Rousseau that he named his best merchant ships after them.

Diversifying his assets into banking and real estate, by 1810, Girard was the principal creditor of the Bank of the United States. After helping to block its charter renewal in 1811, he bought the bank's building and nonfinancial assets, opening his own Girard Bank in its grand marble premises on Third Street. The trustees liquidating the Bank of the United States soon moved millions of dollars in specie (gold) from the defeated institution to the new one smiled on by the Madison administration.

Girard returned the favor with large loans to the U.S. government during the crisis period late in the War of 1812, and in 1816, when Madison bowed to convenience and arranged the chartering of a Second Bank of the

United States, the banker who read Voltaire took three million dollars of its stock. Also successful with major investments in Philadelphia real estate and eastern Pennsylvania coalfields, he left $6.5 million at his death in 1831, the largest estate the United States had ever seen.

William Gray, the aging Massachusetts shipowner thought to be worth $3 million in 1807, was also a Jeffersonian. His support for the embargo was so unpopular that he had to move away from strongly Federalist Salem. But even in that city the power was shifting. Under Jefferson and Madison, the Democratic-Republican Crowninshields—one secretary of the navy and another chairman of the U.S. House of Representatives' Committee on Commerce and Manufacturing—replaced the Federalist Derbys as Salem's most prominent shipowning family.

The new, more egalitarian politics had also drawn in John Jacob Astor, a German immigrant, who succeeded Girard as the nation's richest man. Jeffersonian officials administered the West, where Astor's American Fur Company began trading in 1808—mostly by stealing from drunken Indians, critics charged—to obtain the large quantities of furs resold in New York, London, and Paris. Astor, too, was a supporter of Jefferson and Madison, and when the treasury failed to sell all of its wartime loan, he joined Girard in taking the entirety of the unsubscribed portion. Astor extended $5,000 in low-interest loans to Madison's successor, James Monroe, and sixty years after Astor died, Gustavus Myers, the muckraking historian, discovered in his company ledgers a payment in 1817 of $35,000 (for unstated services) to Lewis Cass. Then governor of Michigan and later U.S. secretary of war, Cass was regularly helpful to Astor's frontier liquor and fur enterprise.

Southern planter wealth, burgeoning after the invention of the cotton gin in 1793, was also generally in the Jeffersonian camp. The leading plantation owner in the early-nineteenth-century South was Wade Hampton I of South Carolina, rich from cotton and sugar. He died in 1835 with assets well short of Girard's. Nathaniel Heyward, whose South Carolina rice holdings made him that state's grandest planter, owned two thousand slaves and left a $2 million estate in 1851. The 1850s, with slave prices 300 percent to 400 percent above 1800 levels, brought the South its highest postindependence share of U.S. capital and wealth, roughly 30 percent. Of the average Deep South slave owner's wealth in 1860, two-thirds was in slaves, and within the five cotton states of Alabama, Georgia, Louisiana, Mississippi, and South Carolina, slaves accounted for nearly 60 percent of all agricultural wealth.

If the South no longer had the nation's greatest assets, as in prerevolutionary days, it still counted the nation's greatest gaps of caste and class. Almost half of the region's personal income total went to just over a thousand families. Somewhat more broadly, of the 7,500 Americans with wealth over $111,000 in 1860, 4,500 lived in the South, and most were major planters and slaveholders. However, despite the scores of millionaires, multimillionaires were few, and hardly any planters stood out economically or nationally. Louisiana's "River Road" of sugar plantations, from New Orleans to Baton Rouge, was thought to be America's richest locale in the 1840s. Yet the individual owners are remembered only in Spanish moss–draped cemeteries, and the names of the great houses alone live on: Destrehan, Oak Alley, Belle Helene, Rosedown. The richest southerner of the antebellum period was in commerce—Judah Touro, whose New Orleans firm sent clippers loaded with rum, sugar, and even ice all over the world. He left $4 million in 1854.

Nor was the plantation South the only area where wealth concentration increased during the first half of the nineteenth century. By most calculations, northern New England, Appalachia, and the Old Northwest (from Ohio to Iowa and Wisconsin) were the least affected. In general, the more rural, but nonslaveholding, the less pronounced the rich-poor gap. The greatest concentrations of assets and levels of economic polarization came where similar trends had been visible in the eighteenth century—in the large commercial centers like New York, Philadelphia, Boston, and Baltimore. By the middle of the nineteenth century, New Orleans, Cincinnati, and St. Louis were catching up.

Here it is worthwhile to pause for an overview. The universal white male franchise assured by the constitutions of Indiana, Illinois, Alabama, Mississippi, and Missouri during the 1816–20 period made the trans-Appalachian New West the cockpit of democracy in the English-speaking world over the next two decades. But in other parts of the nation, especially the mercantile centers, economic inequality, instead of lessening, seems to have increased, contradicting the old Revolutionary credo that aristocracy and its inheritance laws were all that needed fixing. Untrammeled democratic capitalism, it appeared, could breed its own wealth gaps.

The effect of the "market revolution" and the spread of capitalism in early U.S. industry, commerce, and market agriculture, all hallmarks of 1815–60, produced just such a surge of economic growth, wealth concentration, and inequality. Ironically, its "hands off the markets" credo provided an inadvertent philosophic framework for the postwar excesses of laissez-faire and survival of the fittest. In the meantime, practitioners of the just-emerging school of "political economy" failed to delve into sparse wealth data and income trends, leaving the former for economic archaeologists of a later era.

In New York, according to one calculation, whereas the top 1 percent had 29 percent of the wealth in 1828, that had grown to 40 percent in 1845. So, too, in Boston, where the share of the top 1 percent rose from 33 percent in 1833 to 37 percent in 1848. The assumption that the United States would avoid stratification by adopting republican rather than aristocratic institutions and inheritance laws did remain largely true outside the urbanized areas and plantation districts. This partial truth, reinforced by the egalitarian manners of Americans, led foreigners like Alexis de Tocqueville in *Democracy in America* (1837) into exaggeration that became socioeconomic writ. "Nothing," he wrote, "struck me more forcibly than the general condition of equality among the people."

In fact, as Chart 1.2 shows, within the major northern cities most of the rich had upper- and middle-class origins, a change from the more fluid era that followed the Revolution: Within the mercantile centers, the share in the hands of the top 1 percent bespoke a stratification at odds with the tenets of Jacksonian democracy.

CHART 1.2 **Economic Stratification and the Origins of the Richest Persons in the Major Cities, 1828–60**

A. Family Origins of the Rich, 1828–48

CITY	RICH AND/OR EMINENT PARENTS	PARENTS OF MIDDLING STATUS	POOR OR HUMBLE PARENTS
New York	95%	3%	2%
Philadelphia	92	6	2
Boston	94	4	2

Source: Edward Pessen, *Riches, Class and Power,* p. 85.

B. Percentage of Wealth Held by the Richest 1 Percent, 1841–60

Philadelphia (1860)	50%	New York (1845)	40%
Milwaukee area (1860)	44	Baltimore (1860)	39
New Orleans (1860)	43	St. Louis (1860)	38
Brooklyn (1841)	42	Boston (1848)	37

Source: Williamson and Lindert, *American Inequality,* p. 286.

Some have contended that by the 1830s, later men of the status of Girard (born in 1750), Astor (born in 1763), and Vanderbilt (born in 1794) found less fluidity in the big cities and faced greater obstacles. Perhaps so. The caveat is that these arguments gave too little weight to the 80 percent of the population who lived outside the big commercial centers and the chief slave-owning counties. Many of these other milieus exemplified Jacksonian viewpoints and mores. On the other hand, the notion of downward mobility—shirtsleeves to shirtsleeves in three generations—is also far-fetched. As we will see again through later windows, elements of a hereditary upper class have been calcifying and entrenching in Boston, New York, and Philadelphia, at least, over three centuries.

The early-nineteenth-century rivalry of the leading cities, of course, involved government as well as the marketplace. Philadelphia lost the benefits of its claim to be the hub of U.S. banking after Andrew Jackson vetoed the charter extension of the Philadelphia-based Second Bank of the United States in 1832. Stephen Girard was the last of America's richest men to live there. New York's widening edge after the opening of the state-funded Erie Canal in 1825 was quickly mirrored in its accelerating fortunes: Astor's boodle, along with A. T. Stewart's dry goods empire, the Hudson Valley manorland of the Van Rensselaers (in the $5 to $10 million range by the late 1830s), and the holdings of a half dozen old families blessed by Manhattan real estate.

Stephen Van Rensselaer III, in his seventies by the 1830s, had become the sixth lord of the manor of Rensselaerwyck at the age of five. His frequent omission from the lists of America's early-nineteenth-century rich is a great mistake. The first and biggest of the seventeenth-century Dutch land grants, Rensselaerwyck embraced all of (rural) Albany and Rensselaer Counties and part of Columbia. As the Erie Canal helped fill the Hudson Valley, this estate held between 60,000 and 100,000 tenant farmers in 1838. Rising land values probably made Van Rensselaer almost as rich as Girard and Astor, although estimates are vague, and the New York state government began to dismantle unacceptably feudal Rensselaerwyck in the 1840s.

New York City's great assets were its fastest-growing big-city population, fed by European immigration, and the metropolitan hydroponics of how upstate New York's Erie Canal was turning the eastern Great Lakes into a commercial watershed of the Hudson River. As the bigger cities doubled and redoubled their populations, all the while extending their commercial and transportation tentacles outward, land values soared, especially in the prime downtown centers. Most of the major fortunes in New York and Philadelphia between the 1820s and the 1840s had vital real estate components.

Boston tried to keep up with its rival seaport. For a few years in the 1830s it boasted the best rail connections, and the Boston Stock Exchange remained the center of *industrial* stock listings until the Civil War. So fierce was the rivalry for transatlantic steamship routes that in 1844, even leading Boston businessmen went out to help free the Cunard liner *Britannia* from sudden harbor ice. But within a few years, Cunard's shift ratified New York's preeminence. Given the impact of urban growth on commerce, banking, and especially real estate, the shifting population of the major eastern cities is an essential guide to the related migration and evolution of the great fortunes in the 1830s and 1840s, when the origins of wealth were still largely regional. Probably two-thirds of U.S. millionaires lived in what are now the Boston, New York, and Philadelphia metropolitan areas.

CHART 1.3 **Boston-Salem, Philadelphia, and New York: The Comparative Populations as a Context for Wealth Migration, 1760–1860**

	BOSTON-SALEM	PHILADELPHIA	NEW YORK
1760	21,500 (1760)	17,063 (1760)	18,000 (1762)
1770	NA	23,436 (1769)	22,000 (1770)
1775	22,000	29,000 (est.)	25,000
1790	25,959	25,522	33,131
1800	34,394	55,688	60,489
1810	45,863	79,069	96,373
1820	56,029	99,802	123,706
1830	75,277	136,311	202,589
1840	108,465	258,126	312,710
1850	157,144	330,286	515,547
1860	200,092	565,529	813,669

Note: The chart's combination of Boston and Salem populations is useful in showing Massachusetts' importance through the early nineteenth century. By 1820, however, Salem had stagnated while New York and Philadelphia had also left Boston far behind. Beginning in 1800, the population figures for New York are for New York County (Manhattan), and the Philadelphia figures from 1800 to 1850 include the Philadelphia County towns that became part of Philadelphia by 1860. Figures including the then-rural and unincorporated parts of Philadelphia County would inflate its comparison with New York (then including Manhattan but not Brooklyn).

Perceiving New York's munificent rewards, Astor deemphasized his fur monopolies and China trade for Manhattan real estate—farms, houses, and lots up and down the island—and holdings in city banks, especially in the Manhattan Corporation. After 1830 he was virtually out of foreign shipping. James Gordon Bennett, publisher of the *New York Herald,* contended in 1848 after Astor had left an unprecedented $20 million estate, that half belonged to the people of New York. The reason, he argued, was that Astor's wealth "had been augmented and increased in value by the aggregate intelligence, enterprise and commerce" of the city. And, of course, by the quintupling of its inhabitants between 1810 and 1850. Chapter 5 will return to the governmental ties and politics of real estate in more detail.

A pamphlet published by the *New York Sun* in 1847 credited the city with twenty-five millionaire families and individuals, far ahead of any other urban area and representing one-quarter to one-third of the national total. Twentieth-century researchers dismissed the *Sun*'s listings, and one, Edward Pessen, decided to examine the New York City property assessment records in and around Manhattan, real estate being the key to wealth there as it was in and around London. Taking real estate as determinative, he chose to multiply the extremely understated real estate assessments by a factor of ten to identify the local millionaires, and this calculation yielded 113 for 1846. Because others pegged the assessments at 20 percent to 50 percent of actual value, his calculations may be excessive.

What does seem likely, however, is that in addition to well-known names like Astor, department store pioneer A. T. Stewart, and the increasingly rich Cornelius Vanderbilt, the island of Manhattan along with Brooklyn (then the *separate* seventh-largest city in the U.S.) together probably had six or seven other individuals and families worth at least $2–$3 million at midcentury: the Goelets, Lorillards, Stuyvesants, Beekmans, Rhinelanders, and Lenoxes in Manhattan, and H. B. Pierrepont in Brooklyn. An additional fifty or sixty individuals and families would have been lesser millionaires, at least in real estate–weighted calculations. Indeed, the value of prime land in Manhattan is thought to have increased elevenfold between 1815 and 1850; keeping up with its impact on wealth would have been tricky indeed.

Figures like these, in turn, suggest that there were probably 150 to 200 millionaires and millionaire families in the United States of 1845–50, not the 40 to 60 usually guessed. Manhattan and Brooklyn would top the list with 70 or so, and the rest of New York State might have had another six to eight. According to one local compilation, Massachusetts had 26, and the rest of New England perhaps 10. New Jersey and Pennsylvania together may have mustered 25, with a half dozen in Baltimore and another half dozen in the rest of Maryland, Delaware, and Washington, D.C. The South probably had 25 to 30, mostly the biggest plantation owners, and the Middle West 10 to 15. By the mid-1850s, cotton and slave prices might have raised the southern total to 50. Gold rush riches were too new, at least in 1850, for California to have had more than a handful.

On a by-city basis, Philadelphia had some ten or eleven individual millionaires in 1845 according to a local publication—*Some of the Wealthy Citizens of Philadelphia* (1846)—taken more seriously than the *Sun*'s New York effort. The two richest, with $2–$3 million each, were George Wharton Pepper, whose money came from brewing and real estate, and Jacob Ridgway, a merchant and real estate investor.

The New York and Philadelphia surveys were prompted by the expanded focus on city and state data in the federal Census of 1840, and a later examination of Massachusetts produced figures for Boston. Of the twenty-six Massachusetts millionaires in 1851, Boston had half of them, and Salem, rapidly losing importance, just one. Textile manufacturing profits explained the $5–$6 million range of the two largest family fortunes—that of the three millionaire Appletons (Nathan, Samuel, and William) and the slightly bigger accumulation of the three Lawrences (Abbott, Amos, and William). Merrimack Valley factories aside, the Massachusetts fortunes were mostly mercantile.

No other urban centers matched New York, Boston, and Philadelphia. Baltimore and New Orleans, the next biggest, each had three to six millionaires. Cincinnati, the emerging Queen City of the Ohio Valley West, boasted one major wealth-holding: the downtown real estate of Nicholas Longworth, who left $15 million in 1863. He would have been a substantial multimillionaire in 1850, and his 1863 estate suggested he might have been second or third nationally after Vanderbilt.

On the international level, New York's emergence, together with the enormity of Astor's $20 million estate of 1848, signaled another milestone: the converging sizes of the greatest fortunes in Europe and America. The New World was no longer overshadowed. Nathan Rothschild's £3.5 million estate of 1836 (about $15 million) was Britain's largest through 1857, although this comparison does not include the great landholdings, which were still entailed. In Europe as a whole, the richest nonlandholder was almost certainly France's Baron James de Rothschild, who left nearly £8 million ($40 million) in 1868. In America, Vanderbilt by then had as much.

Compared with the United States, wealth in Europe still stood on foundations of greater economic disparities—the setting of ducal palaces, *Les Miserables,* and the revolutionary barricades of 1830 and 1848. Even in Britain, ability to avoid revolution was a close run thing, given the huge working-class demonstrations in London and Manchester in 1831 and the Chartist strikes and city riots of the 1840s. Astor, the press claimed, heard the New York City workmen cheering the French Revolution of 1848 as he lay dying. But in economic terms, the United States was a mind-set as well as an ocean apart.

To be sure, in the 1820s and then again from the Panic of 1837 into the mid-1840s, times had also been difficult in America. The 1820s gave birth to workingmen's parties in New York and Philadelphia, more antibank bitterness, labor movement gains, and strikes. Wealth concentration in the eastern urban centers—the top 1% percentages of the 1840s in Chart 1.2, higher than in the 1790s—had reached levels that mocked Jeffersonian hopes. The New York–based Locofoco wing of the Democratic Party renewed the "Worky" themes in the 1830s; witness this 1834 campaign song:

> Mechanics, Carters, Laborers
> Must form a close connection.
> And show the rich Aristocrats
> Their powers at this election.
>
> Yankee Doodle, smoke 'em out
> The proud, the banking faction.
> None but such as Hartford Feds
> Oppose the poor and Jackson.

Fortunately, the late 1840s and most of the next decade became a *tableau vivant* of New World prosperity, luring unprecedented emigration from Ireland, England, and Germany despite the belowdecks hell of steerage passage. Output on the farms more than doubled in value during the fifties. The sum of all private property in the U.S. expanded by a remarkable 125 percent. Throughout, the Western frontier added its own important political, economic, and demographic safety valve. The year 1848 came and went without much hint of worker barricades.

Even so, it is culturally important that at the top, the great fortunes of 1815–60 were scarcely more genteel than a Philadelphia wharf, a Staten Island ferry slip, or a Michigan fur post. Whatever the backgrounds of lesser merchants, three of the richest men—Girard, Astor, and Stewart—had been immigrants. All were self-made like Old Andy Jackson himself. A fashionable club had rejected Stewart because he was in trade. Astor had once wiped his hands on his hostess's dress. Vanderbilt, the unpolished son of an illiterate Dutch farmer and boatman, even in his thirties and forties was rarely invited to elegant New York dinners because he swore, spat, and pinched the serving girls.

Ordinary New Yorkers seemed to enjoy this lack of couth. Vanderbilt, who replaced Astor as the city's richest man, was an off-and-on popular favorite—the Staten Island ferry boy made good. Unlike the aspirants of the 1790s, he did not play aristocrat. Besides, the mid-nineteenth-century politics of resentment were complicated in America, which is why the workingmen's parties had only transient impact, unable to make the leap from city influence to serious statewide races.

Ethnic and religious diversity particularly distinguished the U.S. from individual European nations. Some of the urban tensions and problems of the 1840s and 1850s—growing poverty, crime, drunkenness, overcrowded tenements, and urban squalor—also showed a strong correlation with the record immigration, Irish and German. Native birth became a basis for a countermobilization, working-class and middle-class alike, behind cultural themes: temperance (antiliquor), anti-immigrant, and anti-Catholic. In New York and Philadelphia, free blacks also drew white working-class ire as job rivals. Some have even theorized about incipient class politics being diverted by new opportunities for the skilled working class to consume—the amusements of vaudeville and P. T. Barnum's spectacles as well as the availability of cheap carpets and furniture unobtainable by Europeans of similar status in 1845 or 1850.

Andrew Jackson and his successor, Martin Van Buren, had played to popular sentiment in attacking both the Bank of the United States and the favoritism to the rich implicit in government chartered corporations. Jackson's antiestablishment fervor made him a democratic symbol, and his supporters also played havoc with banks and chartered corporations in a number of states. But Jackson's rhetoric could reach only so far, and the politics of whupping bank elites was playing itself out by the late 1840s and 1850s, with no similar bogeyman emerging as a replacement. Just a half dozen states had significant factory districts, and only 4 percent of

Americans were employed in manufacturing. The workingmen's parties of the late 1820s disappeared after the Panic of 1837, and decades would pass before any new political movement based on industrial tensions could identify and assemble a national base. Economic inequality might be high and urban wages and working conditions poor, but sectional, cultural, religious, and ethnic cleavages dominated the elections of 1856 and 1860, dividing wealth-holders and laborers alike.

Moreover, the new debate emerging over slavery, like that over the Revolution, directed the anger of ordinary citizens at *external* targets: Free Soil politicians in the North castigated the plantation elites as a "slaveocracy" hostile to free white labor. The orators of the South, which had much less industry, responded with caricatures of the wage-slavery and capitalist oligarchs of the North. Both sides thus scapegoated a wealthy elite, but conveniently that of their rival section. Working-class causes taking shape in the early industrial era—the ten-hour day, improved mechanic's lien laws, better fire prevention, and others—lacked any comparable national or sectional popular traction.

One exception deserves mention, if only to underscore its isolation. Massachusetts in 1850 was the most industrialized area of the world outside Britain, accounting for almost half of U.S. textile production. This was concentrated in the Merrimack Valley cities of Lowell and Lawrence, already stirred by low wages, long hours, and deteriorating working conditions, which neither party addressed. Massachusetts' dominant Whigs represented factory owners and financiers while the Democrats spoke for farming areas and Jacksonian viewpoints. And so in 1854, a year of ferment, a majority of state voters turned to a *new* party, the secretive Know-Nothings, who swept the gubernatorial, congressional, and state legislative races. Swept is an inadequate description: *they won every single race for the Massachusetts House.*

Their image in history is mostly anti-immigrant and anti-Catholic. Yet beyond that, the new party also attacked the Whigs for favoring monopoly and oligarchy, called for a new "citizens" politics, elected workers as mayors in several municipal election upsets, promised to regulate the railroads, and supported legislation to limit the working day to ten hours. Their gubernatorial nominee took 63 percent statewide, a stunning 70 percent in the major industrial towns, and fully 78 percent in Lawrence, the state's poorest and fastest-growing city. When the new Know-Nothing legislature convened, 100 of its 419 members were workers, an unheard-of ratio.

That legislature has been forgotten because of its lack of success and because of the simultaneous rise of the Republican Party, to which most Know-Nothings soon migrated. Industrialism was too powerful a future to be stymied. Even so, the principal historian of the Bay State's brief electoral revolution, John Mulkern, concluded that "the Know-Nothing legislators had bequeathed an unmatched legacy of reform . . . and in their concern with the negative impact of modernization on the quality of urban life, the Know-Nothings anticipated by a half century the Progressive movement."

It did indeed take half a century for the national reaction to industrialism—and with it, to "predatory" wealth—to crystallize. But before grappling with that slow evolution, we must look at the cyclone-like realignment of wealth and power brought about by the crisis that suppressed the economic debate: the Civil War itself.

3. THE CIVIL WAR AND THE REALIGNMENT OF AMERICAN WEALTH

The effects of the American Revolution, in which the South lost its wealth and economic advantage over the other regions, were mild compared to what the North brought about by the Civil War. This must be understood to grasp how the great fortunes of the last third of the nineteenth century, virtually all northern-based, emerged with a momentum and sheer size that old Jeffersonians and Jacksonians could scarcely credit.

The South Carolina merchants, planters, and militia officers watching on April 12, 1861, when Confederate gunners fired on Fort Sumter in Charleston harbor, represented one of the richest strata of antebellum America. Although the eleven states that ultimately seceded lagged far behind the North in manufacturing, bank deposits, schools, shipping, railroads, urban populations, and most other advanced economic yardsticks, there was one category in which they did not trail: *wealth.* Dixie's four million slaves worth $2–$4 billion were property. Counting them, white southerners had about the same per capita wealth as northerners.

This is what split the nation. Neither the North nor the United States government had the resources to free four million slaves by compensating their owners as the British had in 1834 to free 130,000, mostly in the West Indies. Without that possibility, southern options were stark: orchestrate a peaceful secession or win the ensuing war. Defeat by a northern regime committed to freeing the slaves would bring economic and financial disaster.

Which it did. With a great lead in commerce, industry, and population, the North could borrow heavily to build up a huge war machine, conquer in four years, and in April 1865 compel the Confederacy's unconditional surrender. Schoolchildren learn how General U. S. Grant allowed the defeated southern soldiers to keep their horses because they would need them for spring plowing. Less widely known is how thoroughly southern agriculture and the southern economy itself were devastated.

Defeat brought about two results: First, Dixie's own loss of (mostly agricultural) wealth; and second, at least as important, the relentless political transfer of a critical portion of that wealth into the expansion of Northern industry.

The straightforward cost to the South can be easily laid out. The abolition of slavery eliminated about $2 billion of southern capital and reduced southern land values by roughly the same amount. War-related losses by the southern agricultural sector included two-fifths of the livestock and about half of the farm machinery. State taxes imposed by postwar "carpetbagger" governments to finance Reconstruction further aggravated the decline in land values. By 1870, whereas valuations in the old Confederacy had fallen to about half those of 1860, taxes were four times as heavy.

The realignment of wealth and income was massive. The antebellum South of 1860 had enjoyed 30 percent of the nation's assets; its share in 1870 fell to just 12 percent. According to historian C. Vann Woodward, the Northeast in 1880 led the South in per capita wealth by $1,356 to $376, a ratio close to Germany's lead over undeveloped Russia. Just before the war, the per capita income for white southerners had been about the same as that for northern whites. By 1880 it had dropped to half. The South would be home to only a handful of America's fifteen hundred or so millionaires.

Part of the shift away from agriculture simply reflected the advance of the Industrial Revolution. In Britain, too, capital and income were also moving steadily from acreage to factories and railroad yards. In the United States, however, the South's defeat in the Civil War allowed what would have been a more gradual realignment to become the economic equivalent of a typhoon. Politics got to write a new and recriminatory script.

Just months after the war began, northern leaders, now in complete charge of the government, began to push through Congress a neo-Hamiltonian transformation of the U.S. economy that ultimately included 1) a wartime income tax; 2) large-scale borrowing and debt security issuance in excess of $2.5 billion; 3) a new national banking system; and 4) a massive expansion of the currency and a shift from gold to paper money—the famous greenbacks. Had a stalemated North been obliged to negotiate peace in 1864, its own finances would have been precarious, its own postwar economy depressed.

Instead, victory enabled the North to make the South pick up much of the bill for the nation's economic transformation. Tariff duties, raised in 1861 and 1864 to protect northern manufacturing and finance the war, were pushed higher in 1867 and 1869 in part to help meet the huge Civil War debt. Postwar southerners bore federal taxes (mostly excise levies) despite the lopsided distribution of Washington's expenditures to benefit the North—major categories included payments to bondholders, virtually all northerners, and pensions to Union soldiers (Confederate veterans were not eligible). Economic historian Robert Russel has calculated that southerners paid about $1.2 billion to the rest of the Union during the half century after 1865—a de facto indemnity larger than the one Prussia imposed on France following the Franco-Prussian War of 1870–71.

The redistribution of capital was massive. Data from the 1870 census showed southern agricultural and manufacturing capital *declining* by 16 percent between 1860 and 1870 while northern capital *increased* by 50 percent. Inflation had been a vital facilitator. Analyzing the pumped-up U.S. money supply of 1867, economist Milton Friedman found that about three-quarters represented new types of money (greenbacks, national bank notes, et al.) that had originated during the Civil War.

This tidal wave produced a considerable surge in both the U.S. national income and northern manufacturing enterprise during the 1860s. Once the short-term dislocations at the beginning of the war were past, businessmen could see the gravy train coming down the track. Financier William Dodge in early 1863 wrote to an English friend that:

> Things here at the North are in a great state of prosperity. You can have no idea of it. The large amount of money expended by the government have given activity to everything . . . the railroads and manufacturers of all kinds except cotton were never doing so well.

Of course, the near doubling as the price index rose from 100 in 1860 to 196 in 1865 brought problems as well as benefits. One of the most important involved securing the interests of bondholders. However, postwar finance was just as politically attuned as the wartime species, and to safeguard the northern creditors whose loans had financed victory, Congress in 1869 passed the Public Credit Act making all U.S. government obligations

redeemable in gold. The farm sector in particular howled. Wartime speculators who had bought the bonds in, say, 1864 with greenbacks worth just
forty cents to the dollar (in gold) could now savor a bonanza. Besides collecting their interest in gold (which turned the nominal 6 percent yield
into 15 percent), they could now get a profit on capital of from 100 to 150
percent by being able to cash the bonds for gold rather than the cheaper
paper they paid with. Such were the delayed spoils of victory. By contrast,
the farmer selling his hay at Fort Riley or Fort Scott would get only greenbacks—and fewer of them because crop prices were starting to slump.

This boon for bondholders, when paired with the government's off-
and-on retirements of paper currency, did more than stop wartime inflation. Contraction of the currency helped bring about a quarter century of
deflation that took price levels 25 percent *below* what they were in 1860.
Calculated in 1860 dollars, one nineteenth-century consumer price measurement dropped from 171 in 1868 to 144 in 1873, 92 in 1885, and bot-
tomed out at 75 in 1896. Crop prices, if anything, fell faster. Mortgages,
bonds, and many stocks, however, gained value in the deflationary glow,
to the great benefit of creditors (excluding small rural banks), railroaders,
and manufacturers. Upper-bracket wealth soared, although no measurements as we use now existed for the quarter century after the Civil War.

Favored by the war's redistribution of wealth and income and then by
the postwar deflation that rewarded eastern bondholders, the capital put
into manufacturing rose from $1 billion in 1860 to $10 billion in 1900.
This speed and mass of investment, mind-boggling to look back on, enabled the United States to achieve in four decades what had taken the
United Kingdom nearly a century, and by the 1890s the U.S. had passed
Britain as the world's leading industrial power.

But we are getting ahead of ourselves. It is time to go back to the
nerve-racking but exhilarating summer of 1861. The floodgates of
wartime currency expansion, debt expansion, and government purchasing
are just beginning to open. The first generation of American wealth-
holdings that would rank as the world's largest are already taking shape.

4. THE RISE OF THE GREAT AMERICAN FORTUNES, 1865–1900

The surprise Union defeat in the opening hostilities at Bull Run in July
1861 signaled to northern strategists that the war would last long enough
to require a major financial and industrial mobilization. Two months later
Congress passed legislation to impose an income tax and a host of lesser
levies on everything from corporations to dividends and inheritances. The

new tax revenues, however, would take a while to start flowing, while neither tariff receipts nor individual bank loans quickly arranged at 7 to 10 percent could meet soaring military demands. Bonds would have to be issued and sold.

By the winter of 1861–62 the Philadelphia banking firm of Jay Cooke was selling what over three years would total $1.2 billion worth of government indebtedness. Nearly $800 million took the form of three-year notes paying 7.3 percent interest, while $400 million of bonds were redeemable in not less than five years (or more than twenty) and carried 6 percent interest. Other firms marketed lesser amounts, and by 1865 the national debt had soared from $65 million in 1860 to $2.678 billion, the steepest of America's wartime rises.

The money created by this large-scale borrowing helped produce the near doubling of prices by war's end. Indeed, as Chart 1.4 illustrates, each of the six major U.S. inflation waves came out of a war. While the phenomenon seems unavoidable, the economic burdens and benefits have rarely divided evenly, and the divergences—who pays, who profits—have determined the wartime wealth effect, one of the most powerful that politics and government can influence.

For most northern manufacturers and government contractors circa 1861–62, benefits rolled in. The flood of greenbacks and the convergence of military deadlines and supply bottlenecks often combined to make the prices of essential products rise two or three times faster than the broader inflation rate. Pig iron jumped from $20.25 a long ton in 1861 to $59.25 in 1864. Prices per barrel in the spanking new oil industry leaped from 49 cents in 1861 to $8.08 in 1864. Railroad freight and steamship charter rates rose exorbitantly during these years, although no comprehensive index exists. Wages by contrast tended to lag, which hurt worker living standards but improved business profits.

War-related industries, in a word, boomed. So by and large did merchants and (especially) the new national banks, which were given notable privileges, such as note issuance. While rising overall between 1861 and 1865, the stock market fluctuated so much with individual battles and campaigns—dropping after the defeats on the Chickahominy, for example, and rising after the victories at Vicksburg and Gettysburg—that brokers were in clover.

Because the 1860–1900 period divides into two different wealth leaps, one up to 1873 and another thereafter, this section will follow suit. However, we can begin with a few features common to the entire era. Besides being a notable economic watershed, the war was a great incuba-

CHART 1.4 **Effect Of U.S. Wars On Wholesale Prices, 1770–1972**

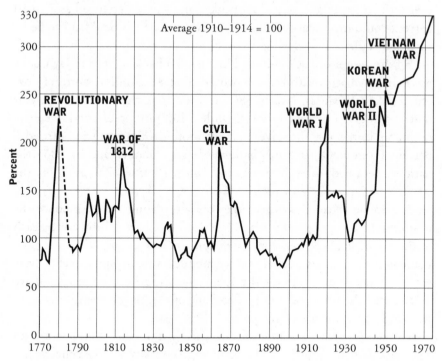

tor of enterprise and entrepreneurs. A surprising number of the commercial and financial giants of the late nineteenth century—J. P. Morgan, John D. Rockefeller, Andrew Carnegie, Jay Gould, Marshall Field, Philip Armour, Collis Huntington, and several other railroad grandees—were young northerners who avoided military service, usually by buying substitutes, and used the war to take major steps up future fortune's ladder. Most existing fortunes also flourished. Vanderbilt's, already some $15 million in 1861, increased fivefold during the war and its immediate aftermath, principally because of railroad profits; and by 1877, when the feisty commodore died, he was worth an almost inconceivable $105 million. But the incubator effect was more important.

Heavy industry shaped all four decades, a notable departure. Between 1805 and 1830, shipping, banking, and ties to government had been key. From 1830 to 1860, real estate, be it southern plantation or northern downtown commercial, outshone shipping, merchandise, and New England's handful of early manufacturing fortunes. The war, however, pushed shipping, merchandise, and even real estate to the side. This era's coming of age rested on railroads, iron, coal, and oil, with their allied finance. New York and Pennsylvania dominated, with increasing competition from Ohio, Illinois, and California.

The war-related realignment also had enduring regional, cultural, and political characteristics. Boston faded in relative terms even while prospering. On the other hand, a telling number of the new fortune-holders spread across the north had Yankee ancestors and cultural roots in New England and small-town upstate New York: Morgan, Rockefeller, Field, Armour, Sage, Gould, Huntington, Stanford, Crocker, Hopkins, Harriman, and others. Their Civil War loyalties were Unionist, their politics lopsidedly Republican. The war that the Yankee creed helped precipitate in turn helped create a grand, new continental stage for Yankee commerce. Some of these nouveaux riches, in keeping with these roots, were frugal or abstemious. Several were unusually religious: John D. Rockefeller later explained his plan to concentrate the fledgling oil industry into the future Standard Oil monopoly as "a matter of conscience. It was right between me and my God." No such pretensions would have come from Girard, Astor, or Vanderbilt.

Later chapters will speak to specific dimensions of nineteenth and twentieth-century wealth creation: the repeating role of technology, the recurring public hostility to banks, Wall Street, and the "money power," the importance of influence in high places, and the repetitious overlap between capitalist heydays and political and philosophic corruption. For now, suffice it to say that the war's awesome forces and ramifications wound up enlarging the largest American fortunes from a $10–$20 million range in the 1840s and 1850s to between $200 million to $300 million in the 1880s and 1890s. Price levels, as we have seen, were about the same or lower in the 1890s. This extraordinary, once-in-a-century enlargement of wealth after the Civil War occurred not through inflation, but as the dollar became worth *more.*

Flush enough to drive English dukes and French princes to wed American heiresses to secure their family estates, the giantizing U.S. economy had a powerful array of engines: a population that quadrupled between 1840 and 1890, the world's biggest network of railroads, a degree of technological innovation that matched or exceeded Britain's and Germany's, and the emergence over five decades of the world's largest industrial capacity. In more or less constant dollars, the U.S. gross national product of 1890 was six times larger than in 1840.

The gains, it goes without saying, were anything but evenly distributed. Great Plains farm incomes in the 1890s were lower than in the 1850s. Skilled workers' wages were somewhat higher (after climbing in the sixties, stagnating in the seventies, and then rising again in the eighties). What truly had done the soaring was the income and wealth of a

CHART 1.5 **The Giantizing of the Largest American Fortunes, 1790–2000**

Between 1790 and early 2000, the size of the largest American fortune jumped from $1 million to $100 billion—Bill Gates in that millennial January. During this period, the chasm between the nation's single largest fortune and the median family income widened from about 4,000:1 to about 1,416,000:1. Here is the portrait:

YEAR	1790	1803	1830	1848	1868
Size of largest fortune	$1 mil.	$3 mil.	$6 mil.	$20 mil.	$40 mil.
Name	Elias Derby	William Bingham	Stephen Girard	John J. Astor	Cornelius Vanderbilt
Median family or household wealth	$250	$300	$350	$400	$500
Ratio of largest fortune to median	4000:1	10,000:1	17,000:1	50,000:1	80,000:1
YEAR	1875	1890	1912	1921	1940
Size of largest fortune	$105 mil.	$200 mil.	$1 bil.	$1 bil.	$1.5 bil.
Name	Cornelius Vanderbilt	William H Vanderbilt	John D. Rockefeller	John D. Rockefeller	John D. Rockefeller
Median family or household wealth	$500	$540	$800	$1,250	$1,750
Ratio of largest fortune to median	210,000:1	370,000:1	1,250,000:1	800,000:1	850,000:1
YEAR	1962	1982	1992	1995	1999
Size of largest fortune	$1 bil.	$2 bil.	$8 bil.	$11 bil.	$85 bil.
Name	Jean Paul Getty	Daniel Ludwig	Sam Walton	Bill Gates	Bill Gates
Median family or household wealth	$7,200	$33,300	$43,200	$45,900	$60,000
Ratio of largest fortune to median	138,000:1	60,000:1	185,000:1	240,000:1	1,416,000:1

small upper portion of Americans. Chart 1.5 illustrates the stunning trajectory in the sizes of the greatest fortunes. Where there had been ten or so U.S. millionaires in 1800, there were some 4,500 by 1900.

Still, it is a mistake to use the term "robber baron" in the slapdash manner of some progressive historians. Besides ignoring the highly relevant seventeenth- and eighteenth-century English and American colonial lineage—"robber" explorers, ship captains, commissaries, and colonial governors—this slights the sheer vitality of the 1860s; the capitalists of that decade simply got too much done. Even the progressive and New Deal era chroniclers could not be entirely critical. Matthew Josephson, who published *The Robber Barons* in 1934, acknowledged three decades later that revisionists were again giving some credit to the late-nineteenth-century capitalists. He added that, "It was not I [in 1934], but the embattled farmers of Kansas, who, in one of their antimonopoly pamphlets of 1880, first applied the nomenclature of Robber Barons to the masters of railway systems."

The distinction is important. The farm belt insurgents attacked the masters—the railroad presidents and speculative capitalists—not the physical builders of the railway systems. Back in 1869, half of Kansas and Nebraska had been cheering the iron trailblazers. Towns clamored to be on their routes, voting subsidies and floating bond issues. Constructing a railroad blended engineering with the ability to secure the aid of federal, state, and local governments, not unlike getting royal approval (and money) for earlier ventures to explore Florida or find the Northwest Passage. The development of North America had always been a cash (or land) proposition. In the post–Civil War years, it could be epic—the stuff of Drake, La Salle, or Lewis and Clark—or several hundred miles of swindling and larceny (the origin of the term "railroaded"). This is the fine if necessarily imprecise line: mountain-girdling iron-rail conquistadores all too soon gave way to corporate hierarchies, achievers to manipulators, empire builders to "papermen."

There is no rigid chronology, no timetable of when these praetorians turned to predators. The Civil War itself had so many dishonest suppliers of horses, guns, ships, shoes, and uniforms that the term "shoddy"—first applied to shredded rags that were rolled, glued, and pressed into ersatz uniforms that fell apart in the rain—grew to describe a whole class of wartime nouveaux riches. "You can sell anything to the government at almost any price you've got the guts to ask," crowed Jim Fisk, one of the wartime profiteers, and so he did, along with many others.

In 1860, New York City had roughly a hundred millionaires. By the end of the war that had tripled. By 1863 the upper 1 percent of Manhattanites (sixteen hundred families), fattened by the nouveaux, counted 61 percent of the city's wealth, up from 40 percent in 1845. Members of the "shoddy aristocracy" were especially likely to have liveried servants and dine at Delmonico's on partridge stuffed with truffles. One historian has estimated that almost one-half of the nearly $1 billion going to private contractors between 1861 and 1865 was pocketed as profit. Lincoln's expressions of contempt matched Washington's cursing of war profiteers eight decades earlier.

The empire builders, however—the Rockefellers, Carnegies, and Huntingtons—built neither of shoddy, nor to produce castles astride passes in Lombardy or cannon commanding the middle Rhine. In peacetime, too, their railroad lines, oil refineries, and steelworks were achievements enough to revolutionize commerce. The citizenry could see the difference. Too caught up in the expansion of the 1840s and early 1850s to worry about the transgressions of the Astors and Vanderbilts, they seem to have equally admired the transcontinental stride of the Iron Horse between 1865 and 1869.

The year 1873, however, marked an important economic and psychological divide. Just four years after the railroads from east and west had linked up in Utah in 1869, the national system had become grossly overbuilt—one mile of track for every 590 Americans. The 33,000 miles added between 1867 and 1873 were more than had existed in 1860. Many of the new lines were unprofitable, and most had "watered stock," named for the practice of Daniel Drew, a Hudson Valley cattle drover turned stock market buccaneer who kept his cattle thirsty on his drives, watering them to raise their weight and price just before market. Watered railroad stock had the same qualities: inflated measurements and phantom value.

The crisis came in September. Jay Cooke & Co. in Philadelphia, the vendor-in-chief of Union war bonds, the largest U.S. bank, drained by financing the Northern Pacific, could not meet a $1 million note coming due. Part of the predicament involved a poorly chosen route along Montana's Yellowstone River through territory contested by an aroused Hunkpapa chief named Sitting Bull. Generations later, the town names along the river still evoke the battles and commanders of some of the bloodiest U.S. Indian wars: Terry, Miles City, Rosebud, Forsyth, Big Horn, and Custer. When Cooke & Co. closed its doors on September 18, a wave of additional railroad and bank insolvencies spread to the stock market. Some leading securities lost half of their value until the New York Stock Exchange suspended trading, which was not resumed for ten days.

The gloomy winter of 1873–74 also marked an end to the North's reasonably broad-based postwar prosperity. Railroad stocks, the mainstays of the exchanges, fell almost 50 percent from their pre-September peaks. For the next six years the financial markets and the general economy remained weak enough that economists applied the term "depression." The daily wages of a skilled worker sank from $2.62 in 1873 to $2.16 in 1879, although consumer prices also fell. Capital investment in manufacturing leveled off, not to begin another major rise until the eighties. The prices received by farmers, weakening since the late sixties, slid further.

The trauma extended to politics. The triumph of Republicanism that followed the Civil War dimmed after 1873. Voters became more sensitive to hard times and corruption. Between 1876 and 1892, the two parties more or less alternated control of the White House and Congress. For five elections, no presidential victor managed a majority of the popular vote. With the presidency weakened, the U.S. Senate, millionaire-dominated and conservative, emerged in the 1880s as the linchpin of national government. Laissez-faire was climbing toward its zenith.

Progressive countercurrents were weak. Massachusetts, still the nation's most industrialized state, finally enacted legislation for a ten-hour day in 1874, but the 1873 downturn crippled fledgling labor unions nationally. Bitter farm discontent did launch the Granger movement to regulate railroads, followed by a series of agrarian third-party presidential candidacies in 1876, 1880, and 1884 (Greenback) and 1892 (Populist).

None of these stalled the growth of America's great fortunes or eased the ever-widening gap between the rich and everyone else. Had the press in 1873 profiled the top U.S. wealth-holders, the list would have included the aging Cornelius Vanderbilt ($100 million), William B. Astor ($100 million), A. T. Stewart ($50–$75 million), railroader and speculator Jay Gould ($30–$50 million), banker Moses Taylor ($30–$40 million), railroader and speculator Russell Sage ($25–$40 million), railroader John Blair ($25–$40 million), and sewing machine magnate Edward Clark ($20–$30 million). Other names in the $20–$30 million range are more debatable. For any selected year, of course, these estimates can only be approximate; wealth data remained sparse.

Seven of the eight above were New Yorkers while Blair lived in nearby New Jersey. Railroad ties now marked the principal track to wealth, in part because of the enormous assistance the railroads received in federal and state land grants and subsidies, roughly $100 million in financial aid and 200 million acres of land between 1861 and 1871. These public lands, alchemized through mortgage finance, provided the lion's share of capital for private railroads, which greatly outweighed other corporations.

As late as 1880, Carnegie Steel had a capitalization of just $5 million. Forty-one railroads, however, had a capitalization over $15 million each, much of it traceable to government largesse. In this respect, the railroad fortunes, too, could be described as heavily if indirectly dependent on real estate. Vanderbilt, (William B.) Astor, Gould, Taylor, Sage, and Blair were all heavily involved in railroads; indeed Astor, with seven hundred Manhattan properties, was also called "the landlord of New York."

John D. Rockefeller, just finished pulling together the framework of Standard Oil in 1873, probably fell short of the $20–$25 million mark. But three men from the Chicago area would have been near: Cyrus McCormick, who turned his invention of the reaper into what became International Harvester, Marshall Field, and meatpacker Philip Armour. This is also the period when U.S. asset holdings moved ahead of those in the United Kingdom, although one British writer has claimed that in overall wealth, the duke of Westminster, owner of much of London's West End, led the richest American, William H. Vanderbilt, until about 1885.

By 1896 the riches of the new top ten had doubled or tripled from 1873. The new wealth no longer rested on railroads alone but on a combination of railroads, coal, steel, and oil. Rockefeller and Andrew Carnegie led with $200–$300 million, William Vanderbilt and William Astor followed in the $100–$200 million category (the collective Vanderbilt and Astor families would each have had $200–$300 million), and Frederick Weyerhaeuser and Marshall Field each commanded around $100 million. Those in the $50–$100 million range, more fluid, probably included J. P. Morgan, Russell Sage, Oliver Payne, Collis Huntington, Marcellus Hartley, John Blair, E. H. Harriman, and H. H. Rogers, along with a half dozen others. Wealth was still New York–centered, but three of the men—Rockefeller, Payne, and Rogers—got their fortunes from the "oil trust" (Standard Oil of Ohio), and Weyerhaeuser and Huntington represented Pacific timber, land, and railroads.

Whether presidents were Democrats or Republicans mattered little in philosophy or management of the economy between the mid-1870s and 1896, because the nation's political culture was in the grip of laissez-faire and social Darwinism—the mock-scientific notion that millionaire capitalists represented a "survival of the fittest" selection process. This was the ultimate reductio ad absurdum of the early-nineteenth-century's market revolution. The Jacksonian notion that government should not interfere on the side of the rich was reworked into the theorem that government had no business interfering on behalf of the downtrodden. Even state child labor laws were overturned by courts as improper governmental interference. The U.S. Senate was the citadel, a House of Industrial Lords. The Gilded Age, a term coined by Mark Twain in his satire of the organization of the "Tunkhannock, Rattlesnake and Youngstown Railroad," ruled unapologetically.

Technological and material progress was steady, witness the rise in the value of manufactures from $1.9 billion in 1860 to $11 billion in 1900, led by steel and oil. Electric power moved out of Thomas Edison's New Jersey laboratory in the late 1880s, substituting amps and volts for steam in factory production, although like the telephone, electricity's commercial leap came after the turn of the century. And by 1900 the United States had an unmatched 193,000 miles of railroad, representing an investment of over $10 billion and bringing in annual revenues of $1.5 billion.

Wealth and incomes, however, were concentrating, mirroring the huge new centralization of the economy through industrial combines, corporate monopolies, and trusts. One analysis in 1890 argued that more than half of the wealth was held by just 1 percent of U.S. families, up from about 29 percent in 1860, and compilations of data at the state level pronounced much the same message. In Massachusetts, where the top 8 percent owned 83 percent of the wealth in 1859–61, they had 90 percent by 1879–81. Thomas G. Sherman, an economics writer, noting that Americans had long believed their nation safe from aristocratic European inequalities, calculated in the late 1880s that whereas one-seventieth of the English population owned about 67 percent of the wealth, in the U.S. the top one-seventieth actually owned between 75 and 80 percent. The numbers are debatable—his U.S. projections seem excessive—but the wry comparison, at least, was apt.

Professor James Huston, in *Securing the Fruits of Labor: The American Concept of Wealth Distribution, 1765–1900,* used a study of newspapers, books, letters, and magazines to date the nation's awakening to corporate and wealth excesses to the late 1880s. More and more citizens were coming to perceive that republican institutions, property inheritance laws, and rejection of aristocracy had been no bar to the emergence of a new elite of giant corporations unacceptable in size and influence. Industrial concentration signaled wealth concentration, they thought, and the extent to which corporate giantism turned labor into a commodity seemed to violate the old concept of labor receiving its due reward for value added.

Henry George published *Progress and Poverty* in 1879, Henry Demarest

Lloyd brought out the articles that became *Wealth Against Commonwealth* in the 1880s, and before the decade closed, magazines were publishing pointed statistical inquiries into wealth levels where none had probed before. A new aristocracy of sorts—this time industrial monopolists, not King George's courtiers or colonial placemen—threatened Americans with an imbalance of power and wealth.

Midwestern and western agriculture, in particular, paid the price, and the most poignant caveat to the nation's hell-for-leather industrialization was the sheer size of the subordinated agrarian population. Farm property still accounted for about one-quarter of national wealth, more than industry. Farm families and dependent small-town folk were still a national majority, although down from four Americans out of five in 1860. In the Great Plains, times were so hard by 1893 that Kansas governor Lorenzo Lewelling issued his famous Tramp Circular, drawing parallels to Elizabethan England and prerevolutionary France. This was no coincidence; declining sector agony was the reverse side of the half century's tenfold enlargement of the greatest industrial fortunes. Just as in the heyday of the Renaissance and the rise of capitalism and then again during Britain's half-century industrial revolution, the peasantry paid for the pleasures of what 1880s critics began to label a plutocracy.

Farmers facing insolvency sat up with kerosene lamps studying pamphlets about money, trying to understand what had gone wrong. Others walked or rode many miles to hear orators lash Wall Street, greedy railroads, and big-city bankers. The swank prosperity of the metropolitan centers—newspapers told of the first electric streetcars in Philadelphia, telephones in Chicago, and garden suburbs in New York—only rubbed salt into the Great Plains' economic wounds as wheat prices plummeted from $1.17 a bushel in 1873 to 91 cents in 1883 and 53 cents in 1893.

This redistribution was not a zero-sum game. Historically, the gains of the great economic transformations outnumber the losses in the long term, if not in the short term. Nevertheless, the policies and forces realigning capital away from the farm regions to the industrial centers were overt and controllable as to degree. By reestablishing gold backing for the dollar, Washington politicians did more than just increase the currency's value. Partial recall of the old nonconvertible paper currency, a companion objective of the back-to-gold movement, shrank the U.S. money supply—and on a per capita basis, with the population growing, the constriction was worse. The per capita money supply fell from $30.35 in 1865 to $17.51 in 1876, rising somewhat in the 1880s and then dropping again in the mid-1890s, which marked the bottom. As crop prices slid for almost thirty years, farmers found their loans ever more expensive to repay.

In addition to currency contraction, the banking system tended to drain away what money the Midwestern or Plains farm districts had to Minneapolis, Chicago, or larger centers in the East to be loaned out there. Also, the railroads, mostly owned by northeastern investors, were hated for plucking the farm districts through localized high freight rates, rebates, and other transgressions. The legacy of Civil War politics was decisive, not just in creating an industrial capitalist party in the North but in keeping the agricultural sector divided along blue-gray lines, crippling any unified political response.

The nonfarm portion of the country was relatively prosperous, led by business and finance, while the urban middle class thrived and expanded. The stock market, which largely reflected the capitalization of the railroads, rose substantially in real terms from the late 1870s through the early 1890s. Corporate profits soared, although no reliable data series is available. On a value-added basis, manufacturing overtook and passed agriculture, as Chart 1.6 shows. Despite the six-year slowdown after 1873, the next two decades—the eighties, in particular—were the vortex of nineteenth-century U.S. economic realignment.

CHART 1.6 **Value Added by Selected Industries, 1859–99**

	1859	1869	1874	1879	1884	1889	1894	1899
Agriculture	58%	53%	47%	49%	40%	35%	34%	33%
Manufacturing	32	34	38	37	47	47	46	49

Source: National Bureau of Economic Research.

Angry agrarians did seem to win a few battles—the Interstate Commerce Commission was established in 1887 to regulate the railroads (at least in theory), and between 1879 and 1893 several laws were enacted for silver purchases or a continued greenback supply. But their effects were minor. When overextended railroad bonds led to a financial collapse in 1893, which widened into a severe depression lasting through 1896, farmers hoped (and investors feared) that a political revolution might finally be at hand. However, this was not to be; the 1896 elections confirmed the agriculture sector's displacement, not its restoration.

The U.S. Senate through the convulsive 1890s remained a citadel of millionaire industrialists, an aptly arrogant metaphor for the late Gilded Age. In those days both senators from each state were chosen by the legislatures, not by the voters. They were, in the words of historians Samuel Eliot Morison and Henry Steele Commager, "Standard Oil Senators, sugar trust Senators, iron and steel Senators and railroad Senators, men known for their business affiliations rather than for their states." The problem no longer lay with grafters like the Tweed Machine or the Whiskey Ring; lawmaking had been institutionally captured at its source, crippling the constitutional balances set up by the framers.

Third-party presidential candidacies like those of the Greenbackers and Populists had stirred farm state discontent that submerged old party lines. Colorado, Idaho, Kansas, Minnesota, Montana, Nebraska, South Dakota, and Washington all elected Populist governors at least once in the 1890s; and when droughts didn't scorch the prairie, anti–Wall Street and antirailroad rhetoric did. William Jennings Bryan's Populist-Democratic presidential bid in 1896 was defeated, although suspense ran high and the race was close.

Especially in July and August that year, the capitalist classes had been scared. Monied Republicans gloomed about Paris communes in Philadelphia and lamppost hangings in Cleveland. But beginning in September, Bryan was undercut, partly by a $16 million Republican war chest ten times his own, partly by employers telling workers not to come back to their jobs if Bryan won, and partly by the Nebraskan's own rusticity, prairie evangelism, and distrust of cities. Ethnic Democrats disliked his Anglo-Saxon Protestant fundamentalism. Too many employees in manufacturing—an ever-growing number in the Northeast and Great Lakes—appreciated both the declining food prices that appalled farmers and the migration of capital into their own workplaces and simultaneously distrusted the hymn-singing countryside. Industry's ascendancy was secure.

Wealth-holders breathed a sigh of relief. The last and greatest of radicalized agriculture's political risings had failed. What few imagined was how its place would soon be taken by a more sophisticated critique of concentrated fortunes and their threat to democracy. Over the next four decades the "malefactors of great wealth" would be opposed by two Democratic presidents and one Republican. The serious challenge to laissez-faire and plutocracy was just over the new century's horizon.

CHAPTER TWO

SERIOUS MONEY: THE THREE TWENTIETH-CENTURY WEALTH EXPLOSIONS

We must abolish anything that bears even the semblance of privilege or any kind of artificial advantage.

—Woodrow Wilson, first message to Congress, 1913

We know now that Government by organized money is just as dangerous as government by organized mob. . . . I should like to have it said of my first Administration that in it, the forces of selfishness and lust for power met their match. I should like to have it said of my second Administration that in it these forces met their master.

—Franklin D. Roosevelt, 1936

That the Great Divide between rich and poor in America has widened is perhaps the most troubling legacy of the 1980s.

—*Business Week*, 1989

The total net worth of average Americans hasn't budged since 1989, despite the bull market. The reason: most families have taken on additional debt, and that outweighs any stock gains. In 1997, the middle fifth of households had a net worth—assets less debts—of $56,000, down from $58,000 in 1989, after adjusting for inflation.

—New York University economist Edward N. Wolff, 1998

The strongest turning away of the United States from great wealth and its abuses in the name of reform and democracy occurred under Theodore Roosevelt, Woodrow Wilson, and Franklin D. Roosevelt in the first four decades of the twentieth century.

The Republican Roosevelt—GOP moneyman Mark Hanna called him "that damned cowboy"—was the first president to seriously grapple with the excesses of the Gilded Age. His predecessor, William McKinley, assassinated in 1901, had been a major of Ohio Volunteers in the Civil War, the last U.S. chief executive to have worn Union blue. Although acknowledged as a friend of the workingman by the American Federation of Labor, McKinley made few speeches in his 1900 reelection campaign, leaving the feistier language to his vice presidential running mate.

Roosevelt, of course, thrilled to a fight. Urban-bred, Harvard-educated, and too young to have been in the Civil War, TR chose foes who, instead of blue or gray, wore the diamond stickpins of "economic man"—the organizers of the great trusts, the stockjobbers, the "malefactors of great wealth," and the "criminal rich." They were people to be scrutinized, not admired. His actions rarely matched his rhetoric, but even mere words from the White House warmed the Progressive climate. In 1899, as governor of New York, Roosevelt had exchanged fears with historian Brooks Adams about the country being "enslaved" by the organizers of the trusts. They talked about Roosevelt's leading "some great outburst of the emotional classes which should at least temporarily crush the Economic Man." And now that he was president, Roosevelt could wield his influence nationally.

The turnabout was extraordinary. Although Bryan had lost his political battle in 1896, within six or seven years many of his ideas and issues were marching forward again—and even winning—under more sophisticated Progressive leadership. Years later, Bryan's widow, editing his memoirs in 1925, claimed as his legacies the federal income tax, popular election of U.S. senators, publicity of campaign contributions, woman suffrage, a department of labor, more stringent railroad regulation, monetary reform, and, at the state level, initiative and referendum. William Allen White, the Kansas editor, aptly remarked that Progressive leaders "caught the Populists in swimming and stole all of their clothing except the frayed underdrawers of free silver."

By 1902–3, four years of rising prosperity and mild inflation had eased the conflict of the mid-nineties. Farmers were less angry—one traveler remarked that "every barn in Kansas and Nebraska has a new coat of paint"—although the old complaints still resonated. And, perhaps most important, the diminishing eastern apprehension of a Bryan victory left middle-class voters freer to act on their own anger at business monopolies and practices, corruption, and extreme maldistribution of wealth. Little in the 1900 elections had suggested the psychological turn, but the new decade would soon scrape some of the gold leaf off the First Gilded Age—and the cyber-fortunes of the second were eight decades away.

1. WEALTH IN THE PROGRESSIVE ERA, 1901–14

The names of the very rich, with few exceptions, were familiar from the 1890s: John D. Rockefeller was becoming America's first billionaire. Andrew Carnegie had begun giving away his half-billion-dollar steel fortune in 1902, and no one else was even close. But except for those two economic whales, Rockefeller and Carnegie, the principal individual fortunes ($100 million to $200 million) and family worths ($200 million to $300 million for the Astors and Vanderbilts) were not much larger in 1910–14 than in the 1890s. The great wave of U.S. heavy industrialization beginning in the early eighties peaked in the 1906–7 period.

Like the Edwardian years in Britain, America in the first decade of the twentieth century was a grand promenade for the rich. Back in the 1880s, William H. Vanderbilt enjoyed the largest U.S. annual income—a stunning $10 million, most of it from interest on U.S. government and railroad bonds. But by 1900, steel magnate Andrew Carnegie was taking in a personal income of over $23 million, and by some estimates John D. Rockefeller's income for 1907 was in the vicinity of $100 million—and there was no income tax to pay. For comparison, the income of the average family was under $500.

The strong economic growth between 1900 and 1907 turned mixed during the next seven years. Overall, and despite the unprecedented great fortunes, a new, mildly inflationary climate also brought a marginally more equitable distribution of the national income. Because of an expanding money supply, based on new gold and silver production, agriculture, still America's single largest industry, saw rising crop prices double the value of midwestern farms between 1900 and 1910. The incomes of those engaged in agriculture rose by about two-thirds during the same period. In the cities and towns, employee wages that had stagnated during the 1890s climbed, lifting average annual earnings from $418 in 1900 to $649 in 1914.

The ranks of ordinary millionairedom also expanded with inflation. The *New York Herald Tribune* had estimated 4,092 in 1890. The surmise for 1900 was closer to 5,000. By 1914 the range was about 7,000.

As Chart 2.1 shows, railroading's share of the principal U.S. fortunes was slipping. Besides railroad owners, the individual net worths that exceeded $60–$75 million at some point during the 1900–14 period—information is vague, and no lists exist for any one year—included the major steel and oil men below Rockefeller and Carnegie as well as the leading copper, tobacco, and lumber magnates and notable financiers like George F. Baker, James Stillman, and the Pittsburgh-based Mellon brothers. Urban utilities and streetcar companies—turn of the century growth sectors—bankrolled three other new entrants. The geography of great wealth still centered on the Northeast and Great Lakes, save for one southerner, tobacco-rich James B. Duke, and three westerners—William Clark, the Montana copper king, Frederick Weyerhaeuser of Pacific lumber fame, and James J. Hill of the Great Northern Railroad.

CHART 2.1 **The Great American Fortunes of 1901–14**

The Thirty Largest Wealth-Holders of the Period

Oil

John D. Rockefeller	$1 billion
Oliver Payne	$100–$150 million
Henry Rogers	$100 million
William Rockefeller	$100 million
Henry Flagler	$75 million
Charles Harkness	$75 million

Steel

Andrew Carnegie	$400 million
Henry C. Frick	$150 million
Henry Phipps	$75 million

Railroads

Russell Sage	$100 million
E. H. Harriman	$100 million
James J. Hill	$100 million
John Jacob Astor III	$87 million*
William K. Vanderbilt	$60 million*

Finance

J. P. Morgan	$119 million
Andrew Mellon	$100 million
Richard Mellon	$100 million
Hetty Green	$100 million
George F. Baker	$75 million
James Stillman	$70 million

Municipal Transit

Peter Widener	$100 million
Thomas Fortune Ryan	$100 million
Nicholas Brady	$75 million

Miscellaneous

Frederick Weyerhaeuser (lumber)	$200 million
Marshall Field (retailing, real estate)	$140 million
William Clark (copper)	$100 million
James B. Duke (tobacco)	$100 million
J. Ogden Armour (meatpacking)	$75–$100 million
William Weightman (pharmaceuticals)	$80 million
Frank Woolworth (retailing)	$60 million

* By this time the Astor and Vanderbilt fortunes were increasingly diffused. These two broader family fortunes would have been in the $300 million to $400 million range.

Gustavus Myers's *History of the Great American Fortunes,* out in 1907, was just one blast among dozens leveled by the so-called "muckrakers"—critics like Lincoln Steffens, Ida Tarbell, Ray Stannard Baker, and Upton Sinclair, who pursued Standard Oil, the meatpackers, trusts, and insurance companies through the pages of new mass circulation magazines like *McClure's, Everybody's,* and *Collier's.* Until 1905 the indexes for the *New York Times* did not list "wealth" or "millionaire" as a subject, but by then discussion was widespread. This was the decade—U.S. manufacturing having already safely established its world lead—when politics, culture, and even the national conscience could catch up with a half century of accumulating abuses. Politely worded reform would no more have shaped a new politics or thrown up a badly needed regulatory framework than soft tactics thirty or forty years earlier would have blasted and hammered railroads over the Sierra Nevadas.

Urban sophistication gave the Progressives another edge over the Populists. The latter had been a rural inflammation, the anguish of a monetarily parched countryside. Bryan's presidential candidacy, for example, seemed to parochialize into a single panacea: free coinage of silver to cure the severe depression. Silver producers and Great Plains farmers were wildly enthusiastic, but the swing states of the 1896 election—Iowa, Minnesota, Wisconsin, Illinois, Indiana, Michigan, and Ohio—had all preferred McKinley. Besides offering little to industrial labor, Bryan's

Democratic platform omitted familiar Populist proposals dealing with railroads, banks, currency, warehouses, and speculators.

Even so, Bryan weakened only a little four years later in his 1900 presidential rematch, and then by remaining a political force through 1914, he bolstered Progressive issues. The Republican Party had its own Western ex-Populist wing as well as a more elite eastern urban reform contingent. Much of this gentry, including Roosevelt, had shunned Bryan in 1896. Now they embraced many of the same ideas. Republican governors like California's Hiram Johnson, New York's Charles Evans Hughes, and Wisconsin's Robert La Follette took Progressive positions—La Follette, moving to the U.S. Senate in 1906, was an especially fierce advocate—and Roosevelt also could frequently count on the reformist wing of the Democratic Party.

The result was a steadily enlarging Progressive record and agenda. As part of the running tide, in 1903 a U.S. Department of Commerce and Labor was established, with a bureau of corporations authorized to investigate corporate behavior. Railroad rate legislation, hitherto ineffectual, was given backbone by the Hepburn Act of 1906. The Pure Food and Drug Act of the same year struck at adulterated or fraudulently labeled products. In 1906, Roosevelt offered a sweeping reform program—income and inheritance taxes, federal licensing of corporations, and prohibition of corporation political funds. And by 1910, no longer in the White House and turning radical, he foreshadowed the even bolder tenor of his imminent independent Progressive presidential bid. "Every man," said TR, "holds his property subject to the general right of the community to regulate its use to whatever degree the public welfare may require it."

The zenith came in 1912. On a new-party platform that ranged from popular recall of judicial decisions to minimum wage standards for working women, Roosevelt split the Republican vote, electing Democrat Woodrow Wilson, also a progressive. The U.S. Socialist Party simultaneously reached its own high-water mark with presidential candidate Eugene Debs garnering almost a million votes and over a thousand Socialists winning state and local office. The irony was that some of Roosevelt's own leading third-party supporters had come from Wall Street—Morgan partners like George Perkins and Frank Munsey, partly committed to restraining the candidate, but also well aware that it might take Progressivism to head off socialism.

Bolstered by these convergences, Wilson's first two years in the White House produced the Sixteenth and Seventeenth Amendments to the U.S.

Constitution, which respectively authorized a federal income tax and required direct election of U.S. senators to replace their selection by state legislatures, as well as the Federal Reserve Act, the Clayton Antitrust Act, and the establishment of the Federal Trade Commission.

More tangibly for ordinary families, the new economic circumstances and mood helped counter Gilded Age wealth and income trends. American statistics were still in their adolescence, but farmers and workers seem to have gained ground between 1900 and 1914. The improvement for agriculture shows best in the average value of an Iowa farm, up almost fivefold by 1914 from its nadir of around $3,800 in 1896.

CHART 2.2 **Average Value (Land and Buildings) Per Farm in Iowa, 1890–1940**

1890	$4,247	1925	$23,207
1900	6,550	1930	19,655
1910	15,008	1935	11,092
1920	35,616	1940	12,614

Inflation that was moderate but ongoing—13 percent from 1897 through 1907, then another 7 percent through 1914—gave family farming some of its sunniest years. Indeed, matching farmers' 1909–14 purchasing power later became the criterion for "parity" in federal support programs. On the wealth front, the more than doubling of the value of U.S. farmland and buildings from $16.7 billion in 1900 to $34.9 billion in 1910 (and probably $45 billion in 1914) must have lessened the Gilded Age concentration of assets. As noted, beyond Rockefeller and the gift-giving Carnegie, the great fortunes listed in Chart 2.1 remained in the $100–$200 million range, even while money lost 20 percent of its worth to inflation between 1897 and 1914. Financial assets also went through several business downturns and stock market slides between 1907 and 1914.

Elsewhere on the ledger, wages in manufacturing and farm income both rose after adjustment for inflation. The period's only estimate of income distribution, by the business-oriented National Industrial Conference Board, attributed 33.9 percent of U.S. personal income for 1910 to the highest tenth and 13.8 percent to the bottom three-tenths, in historic terms a relatively benign number. Economic historians Jeffrey Williamson and Peter Lindert, in *American Inequality,* although leery of the NICB calculation, agreed that farm sector gains might have reduced the gap existing previously. Indeed, the NICB series also squared with agricultural ups and downs by showing a bigger upper-bracket concentration in 1921 or 1929, two poor years on the farm. In those years, nearly 40 percent of income went to the top 10 percent and just 10 percent to the bottom three deciles. Although the data are not Gibraltar-like, they do support a significant probability: that the Progressive Era brought modestly significant changes in wealth and income to match its political rhetoric.

Over the next quarter century, federal data collection itself would improve, enabling a sharper portraiture of America's fortunes and misfortunes. But aside from Henry Ford and a few others, the early twentieth century will not produce new great swashbucklers to match the late nineteenth century's Morgan, Carnegie, and Rockefeller. In the nineteenth century, Thomas Carlyle could describe history as the sum of innumerable biographies. In the twentieth century, economic history, at least, began to exchange statistical drama—the gyrations of median income, the quiet revolutions in income tax, the proliferations of telecommunications, the dimensions of speculative bubbles, the whiplashing of markets, the computerization of the world—for the stalwart personalities. The First World War was an early transition point.

2. WORLD WAR I AND THE GREAT 1925–29 SPECULATIVE BUBBLE

Its outbreak in the summer of 1914 initially unnerved U.S. wealthholders. As the European powers mobilized, the New York Stock Exchange, fearful that foreign dumping of securities might collapse prices, suspended trading and remained shut for almost four months. After trading resumed, however, the Dow-Jones Industrial Average soared in 1915 and reached a new high in 1916 as the U.S. economy began to hum with the profits of producing war material for Europe (not until U.S. entry into the war in 1917 did income taxes, excess-profits taxes, and government regulation begin to bite).

The rate of inflation, war's seemingly inevitable Fifth Horseman, peaked in 1917–19, but the price index continued to rise into 1920, by which point it had doubled. As in the Civil War, workers lost ground because their wages did not keep up. Farm prices, however, rose enough to catapault Iowa farm values to the record high for 1920 shown in Chart 2.2. For business, weighty taxes and regulation kept wartime inflation from being the broad business incubator in 1917–18 that it had been in Civil War days.

War's outbreak in 1914 withered the old Progressive impetus. But once the U.S. declared war and mobilized in 1917, government regulation of agriculture, industry, and railroads proceeded apace, fulfilling a tougher set of interventionist and even Socialist objectives. By years' end Washington was operating the nation's railroads. The War Labor Board, in turn, had forced collective bargaining and the eight-hour day on substantial segments of industry.

Even so, the world war's half decade was lucrative for corporations and the rich. In 1915 and 1916, the lush years before U.S. entry, the top 1 percent had roughly the same share of income and wealth they would register again in 1929. Companies supplying the military had a particular field day. From being just a munitions maker in 1914, duPont profited greatly enough from U.S. wartime seizure of German chemical patents to become a global force in that industry by the 1920s. In the meantime, company profits jumped from $6 million in 1914 to $82 million in 1916. The postwar value to duPont of plants built and governmentally underwritten in wartime was added gravy. Revealingly, some of the biggest drumbeaters for U.S. war involvement and profit-makers from it—J. P. Morgan, the duPonts, Marcellus Hartley Dodge, and Charles Schwab—were from families that had supplied the Northern military during the Civil War.

The stock of Bethlehem Steel, run by Charles Schwab, leader of the Armor Trust, climbed from 33 in July 1914 to a wartime peak of 600. General Motors shares soared from 78 to 750. Copper profits went over the moon. An index of nine ordnance stocks jumped 311 percent in eighteen months. Stuart Brandes, in his history of U.S. war profits, recalled volatile profits and "tumultuous days on Wall Street and on regional commodity exchanges as fortunes were made and occasionally lost. Successful stock and commodity speculators became known, if male, as 'warhogs' and, if female, as 'warsows.' "

War, the reformers complained, was restoring the fortunes of capitalists that the Progressive era had put on the defensive, and subsequent investigators cataloged some egregious examples—over $1 billion spent for combat aircraft, with none delivered, and so on. Popular indignation faded with war memories, but rekindled after the 1929 Crash returned bank and corporate behavior to the spotlight. In 1935 the popular magazine *American Mercury* portrayed the war as "No. 4" in its series called "Thieveries of the Republic." The "Merchants of Death" became another well-worn phrase.

For all that wartime excess-profits taxes curbed the after-tax gains of the munitions business in 1917–18, a generation later the duPont family fortune would rank by some estimates with those of the Rockefellers,

Mellons, and Fords (and within two generations some calculations put the duPonts ahead). As for mere millionaires, the near-doubling of prices between 1914 and 1919 combined with wartime opportunities increased their ranks to an estimated ten thousand. A new magazine called *Forbes* published its estimate of the top thirty:

CHART 2.3 **The Thirty Top Wealth-Holders of 1918**

John D. Rockefeller (oil)	$1.2 billion
Henry C. Frick (steel)	225 million
Andrew Carnegie (steel)	200 million
George Baker (banking)	150 million
William Rockefeller (oil, banking)	150 million
E. S. Harkness (oil)	125 million
Ogden Armour (meatpacking)	125 million
Henry Ford (automobiles)	100 million
W. K. Vanderbilt (railroads)	100 million
Edward H. R. Green (banking)	100 million
Mrs. E. H. Harriman (railroads)	80 million
Vincent Astor (real estate)	75 million
James Stillman (banking)	70 million
Thomas F. Ryan (utilities, transit)	70 million
Daniel Guggenheim (mining)	70 million
Charles M. Schwab (steel)	70 million
J. P. Morgan Jr. (banking)	70 million
Mrs. Russell Sage (railroads)	60 million
C. H. McCormick (farm mach.)	60 million
J. Widener (transit)	60 million
Arthur James (railroads)	60 million
Nicholas F. Brady (transit)	60 million
Jacob H. Schiff (banking)	50 million
James B. Duke (tobacco)	50 million
George Eastman (cameras)	50 million
Pierre S. duPont (powder)	50 million
Louis F. Swift (meatpacking)	50 million
Julius Rosenwald (mail order)	50 million
Mrs. Lawrence Lewis (oil)	50 million
Henry Phipps (steel)	50 million

Source: *Forbes,* March 2, 1918, p. 635.

Pierre S. duPont was only one of a half dozen new additions. The turn of the century pattern of steel, oil, railroads, urban transit, and banking wealth was already being modified, even before the war, by the rise of a mass consumer market that elevated Henry Ford (automobiles), James Duke (tobacco), George Eastman (cameras), and Julius Rosenwald (Sears Roebuck mail order). Still, the pioneering *Forbes* list clearly had some omissions. Neither of the Mellon brothers were listed, nor several others who left centimillion-dollar fortunes within six or eight years. On their face the *Forbes* calculations would support the argument that the Progressive Era slowed the great fortunes. However, even allowing for the wartime tax bite, many of the under–$100 million estimates seem too small: James Duke, listed at $50 million, left $140 million in 1925, and copper baron William Clark, unlisted by *Forbes,* left a bit more in that same year.

Weary of wartime taxes, wealthy Americans in March 1921 welcomed the inauguration of the new Republican president Warren Harding, whose ten-member cabinet was collectively worth more than $600 million. They hoped that his promised return to "normalcy" meant a year like 1905 or 1909, when federal taxes and regulation had been neglible. The new treasury secretary, Andrew Mellon, second- or third-wealthiest man in the United States, was committed to stripping away the tax system's burden on "wealth in the making." In 1924 he would even publish a book to that end.

Not that the government's wartime role was entirely resented. The interaction of antitrust suspension with federal subsidies, wartime research, and military procurement accelerated the postwar success of industries resting on emerging technologies. The first automobile had been built in the 1890s, the first radio signals dated back to 1895, flight to 1903, the first electric power plant to 1881, and the telephone to 1876. What came together in the 1920s was consumer demand and commercial momentum.

Although technology's role in wealth creation goes back to the Renaissance, its commercial maturity and dependence on science came in the nineteenth century. Railroad securities built up the New York Stock Exchange in the 1840s. The steel industry matured around railroad demand. The turn-of-the-century trusts required a largeness of scale that rested on both the productivity of electric power and the protection offered by tariffs. The world war continued the pattern, speeding the development not just of telephones and electricity but of the new transportation infrastructure—highways, trucks, buses, automobiles, air-ports, and airplanes—that would displace the railroads.

CHART 2.4 **The Technological Coming of Age in the 1920s**

	AUTOMOBILE REGISTRATIONS (THOUSANDS)	HOUSEHOLDS WITH RADIO (THOUSANDS)	NET PRODUCTION OF ELECTRIC ENERGY (IN MILLIONS OF KILOWATT HOURS)	SCHEDULED AIR TRANSPORT REVENUE MILES FLOWN	NUMBER OF TELEPHONES (MILLIONS)
1900	8.0	—	—	—	1.4
1910	458.3	—	14,121 (1907)	—	7.6
1920	8,131.5	—	56,559	—	13.3
1922	10,704.0	60	61,204	—	14.3
1924	15,436.1	400	75,892	—	16.0
1926	19,267.9	4,500	94,222	4,318	17.7
1928	21,362.2	8,000	108,069	10,528	19.3
1929	23,120.8	10,250	126,747	22,729	20.0

More than any other innovation, automobiles dominated the 1920s, relocating everything from residential patterns to prostitution (sociologists Robert and Helen Lynd, in their famous study "Middletown," reported that of thirty girls charged with "sex crimes" in the local juvenile court in 1924, nineteen had been in cars). The hierarchy of U.S. wealth underwent its own transformation. Automaker Henry Ford joined John D. Rockefeller as the second U.S. billionaire, and when the federal government published the top income taxpayers of 1924—the first and only time it did so—Ford and his son Edsel ranked second and third (see Chart 2.5). Mrs. Horace Dodge, whose family company made Dodge popularity second only to Ford's in the early 1920s, was ninth. The upper list was a virtual oil and automotive fiefdom.

Like railroads, automobiles brought their own huge ripple effect. Steel profited again, this time along with the oil, plate glass, tire, and highway construction industries. New enterprises of a lesser scale included service stations, auto dealers, taxi fleets, and highway maintenance. The rise of automobiles, by one 1929 calculus, created over four million jobs that had not existed in 1900, or roughly one-tenth of 1929's average workforce.

These foremost taxpayers, especially the top ten, were also the major wealth-holders. However, because many of the rich were arranging their affairs in order to sidestep the income tax—Secretary Mellon himself said so—the list has intriguing omissions. Three not present yet probably among the nation's twenty richest were William Clark, also omitted by *Forbes*, publishing magnate Cyrus Curtis, who left $174 million in 1933, and Campbell Soup founder John T. Dorrance, who left $130 million in 1930.

CHART 2.5 **The Top Fourteen Federal Income Taxpayers of 1924**

John D. Rockefeller (oil)	$6,278,000
Henry Ford (autos)	2,609,000
Edsel Ford (autos)	2,158,000
Andrew Mellon (finance, oil)	1,883,000
Payne Whitney (oil)	1,677,000
Edward Harkness (oil)	1,532,000
Richard Mellon (finance, oil)	1,181,000
Anna Harkness (oil)	1,062,000
Mrs. Horace Dodge (autos)	993,000
Frederick Vanderbilt (land, railroads)	793,000
George F. Baker (finance)	792,000
Thomas Fortune Ryan (urban transit)	792,000
Edward J. Berwind (coal)	722,000
Vincent Astor (land, railroads)	643,000

In wealth terms, the twenties ironically started with a groan, not a roar, when the inflationary wartime boom ended with a major 1920 collapse in price levels, jobs, and stock quotations. The price index decline from 240 in 1920 to 200 in 1922 stands as its sharpest two-year drop, worse than any paired Depression years.

Indeed, the depths of 1920–21 help explain why the early stages of the 1929–32 Crash didn't seem so unprecedented. From $8 billion in 1919, business profits buckled to just over $1 billion in 1920. Foreign trade plummeted by 40 percent, the Dow by 47 percent (from its November 1919 high), and farm prices by nearly 50 percent. Bankruptcies tripled, 453,000 farmers lost their farms, and unemployment jumped to about 15 percent. The number of millionaires probably dropped from ten thousand to six thousand. Despite the bottom in 1921, voters were still angry enough in 1922 to hand the new Republican administration a huge midterm election loss of eighty-three House and Senate seats.

The great twenties boom itself arguably began in late 1924. Construction was surging, the Dow-Jones Industrial Average punched through the previous high (116 back in 1919), and Calvin Coolidge, who became president after Harding's death in 1923, won his own landslide election in November, putting the Republicans back in solid control of Congress and the Washington agenda.

The years after the Civil War had ushered in a rare convergence of favorable circumstances for northern industrialists, and so did the 1920s. However, the attention that the Civil War era merited in chapter 1 as a revolution in wealth and capital, the twenties require as a major economic bubble—a revolution of wealth and capital too speculative and thus aborted. The ingredients are important, and many would repeat again in the 1980s and 1990s. As chapter 7 will amplify, periods of war-generated inflation have often been followed by disinflationary booms—the Gilded Age, the 1920s, and the 1980s and 1990s—in which many Americans are left out, but heyday psychologies dominate until a major bubble breaks.

This pattern was vivid in the twenties. Conservatism held sway over both major parties, and when Wisconsin senator Robert La Follette ran for president as a third-party Progressive in 1924, his 16.6 percent of the national vote—concentrated in farm, mining, and urban labor districts—was taken as proof of no great appeal amid a prevailing bipartisan conservatism.

Tax cuts were the first pillar of boom-era politics. In 1921 the GOP Congress had repealed the excess-profits tax and reduced the maximum income surtax from 60 percent to 40 percent. Then the Tax Act of 1926 in turn repealed the gift tax and reduced the income surtax and estate-tax maximum rates from 40 percent to 20 percent. In addition, Secretary Mellon's massive combination of upper-bracket tax cuts, refunds, and remissions, legal and otherwise, threw kerosene on what were still small speculative fires.

Reduced federal spending, a second encouragement, took shape as Woodrow Wilson's wartime budget deficits morphed into peacetime surpluses big enough to reduce the federal debt from $24 billion in 1920 to just $16 billion in 1930.

Deflation, the third fuel, replaced wartime inflation. The happy combination of mild deflation and a large budget surplus, a first since the 1890s, allowed the Federal Reserve System and the banks to pursue precisely the expansive monetary policy—abundant credit at relatively low interest rates—businessmen and investors craved.

Easy consumer and private mortgage lending, the fourth tinder, fed the boom by more than doubling from $17.3 billion in 1922 to $38.3 billion in 1929. The siren song of advertising (especially through the new radio broadcasts), paired with the new temptations of installment credit, served to convince millions of Americans to buy Dodge coupes, Frigidaires, oil heating systems, and Chris-Craft mahogany speedboats. With 1927–29 wage levels only slightly higher than in 1919–20, many people bought the new semiluxuries with money diverted from necessities. The Lynds, in their study of Middletown, found telling examples. Of twenty-six working-class families lacking bathroom facilities, twenty-one had automobiles. Companies like Beneficial Finance and Household Finance, small potatoes in 1920, grew 30 percent a year. Buying on time soared from several hundred million dollars a year in 1920 to $7 billion by 1929, by which time extending credit to consumers had become the nation's tenth biggest business.

Rising industrial productivity and accelerating corporate, bank, and utility mergers added more combustion. Productivity rose through the rapid spread of electric power and machinery as well as through new forms of communications—autos, trucks, highways, proliferating telephones, office machines, and suchlike. Output per man-hour for manufacturing workers rose from 44.6 in 1920 to 72.5 in 1929, most of which went into profits, not wages. The average year-to-year increase of 5.6 percent exceeded that of any other twentieth-century decade. The gains in the automobile industry, 1,300 percent between 1900 and 1926, anticipated those in computers seventy years later.

Corporate restructuring through mergers and holding company formations, sometimes good for productivity, also helped investment bankers and promoters to price up assets and stock offerings. In 1919, 89 mergers had involved 527 concerns; in 1928, 201 mergers repackaged 1,259. So many family businesses were pulled into the corporate orbit that nearly 20 percent of U.S. national wealth shifted from private to corporate hands. So enlarged, the corporate share of national wealth rose to about 30 percent, and the largest 100 corporations came to command about half of the total U.S. industrial net income. Holding companies were another highlight of twenties restructuring. According to the New York Stock Exchange, of the 573 companies whose stock was traded actively in 1928, 395 were both holding companies *and* operating companies, and 92 did nothing but hold other companies' securities.

In retrospect, of course, the blaze of opportunity was turning into a speculative conflagration. Paper entrepreneurialism helped make the boom of the twenties much more stock market–driven than even the booms of 1898–1901 and 1904 to 1907, which had also accompanied re-structurings—the rise of the great trusts and the Morgan-orchestrated rationalization of industry after industry. As a greater share of the national economy came under the corporate umbrella, more of its components and transactions were also being financialized—pulled within the (rapidly expanding) purview of bank loans, securities, or financial markets.

The mania for common stock was also telltale. Until the twenties, the preferred stock of corporations had been just that—senior securities preferred by investors over common stock because of their cash dividends. Trading volume in common stock was constrained accordingly. Then, in 1920, the U.S. Supreme Court ruled that corporate dividends paid in stock were not taxable. Thereafter, the twin psychologies of sidestepping ordinary income tax rates and speculating for capital gains instead of seeking cash dividends pushed common stock to the forefront. New offerings grew from $30 million a month in 1926 to $800 million a month in early 1929 and a billion dollars a month by late summer.

New investment vehicles and devices also helped to heighten the speculation. Investment trusts, introduced in 1921, by 1929 had taken in $8.5 billion from four and a half million Americans. Other new techniques and devices ranged from Ponzi schemes to bucket shops (outlawed in 1935) and telephone-equipped boiler rooms. The leading commercial banks pumped millions into stock pools, whose objective was to pump up stock values and then unload them on a misled public.

Despite the importance of the Federal Reserve, it was not the only source of the boom's essential fuels—money and liquidity. The short-term, day-to-day "call loans" available to speculators at 5 percent or 10 percent interest rates in 1921 also grew like a spring flood. Their volume climbed from a billion dollars or so in 1923 to about $8 billion in the autumn of 1929. Near the peak, as call money rates touched 15 or 20 percent, banks like J. P. Morgan & Co. and New York's National City as well as corporations led by Standard Oil, Electric Bond & Share, and Bethlehem Steel vied to provide more funds.

Stockowner ranks expanded from under one million in 1914 to a plausible estimate of six to nine million individuals and some five to six million households (out of 29 million households in the nation) in 1929. "Ma Bell" alone—the American Telephone and Telegraph Corporation—had 139,000 shareholders in 1920 and 567,000 in 1930. This influx helps explain both the editorials about the new "democracy" of share ownership and the Dow-boosting expansion of annual volume on the New York Stock Exchange from 143 million shares in 1918 to 1.125 billion in 1929.

Such were the unprecedented economic underpinnings—the pillars and beams, kindling and kerosene—of the first of the great twentieth-century wealth constructions (the fortunes of 1900–1914 must be considered extensions of the 1880s and 1890s). Each year brought a more splendid facade. Corporate profits rose by an average of 9 percent a year from 1923 to 1928. The Dow-Jones Industrials soared from 63.90 in August 1921 to 381.17 in September of 1929. Individual income and wealth shot up like Jack's beanstalk. Millionaires multiplied from something like 5,000–7,000 in 1921 to 15,000–20,000 in 1927, and, finally, to 25,000–35,000 at the bull market peak. Where 75 persons had paid taxes in 1924 on annual incomes over a million dollars, 283 did in 1927, and 519 for 1929, even after Black Thursday and autumn's other dark and gloomy days.

While the markets were setting records and economists talked about a new plateau of permanent prosperity, businessmen, financiers, and Republicans vied with each other in taking credit. Skeptics, though, were identifying weaknesses and inflammabilities. In one of 1929's most percipient books, *Prosperity: Fact or Myth,* author Stuart Chase laid out the sectors where fast cars, bootleg gin, margin accounts, and rising hemlines were most in evidence—the financial markets, major corporations, emerging technology enterprises, the rapidly growing suburbs, urban silk stocking districts, the Middle Atlantic states, the Great Lakes, and California. On the other hand were those whom fortune had bypassed: the Farm Belt, much of the South, the mining districts and railroad towns, the bleak mill canyons of New England, the poor big-city districts and racial ghettos, and the ranks of the unskilled labor force. Poverty was rampant.

The boom's base, Chase contended, was simply too narrow, which echoed the complaints of farm and labor leaders. The farm districts, where nearly one-third of the U.S. population still lived, had staggered in 1920–21 when crop prices fell by half and never regained their footing. The 15 percent of national income going to farm families in 1920 declined to 9 percent in 1929. Farm production dropped from a value of $21.4 billion in 1919 to $11.8 billion in 1929 even as manufacturing revenues and stock market indexes soared. Elsewhere in the workforce, carpenters, plumbers, and electricians thrived, but not miners, railwaymen, or unskilled laborers.

Detailed federal jobs data was still lacking, but the impact of technology seems to have been devastating to many workers, however cheering it was to investors or middle-class householders. Wesley Mitchell, one of the decade's best-known economists, reported in 1929 that "the supply of new

jobs has not been equal to the number of new workers plus the old workers displaced. Hence there has been a net increase in unemployment between 1920 and 1927, which exceeds 650,000 people." Even in 1928, a
municipal survey in Baltimore found unemployment near 42 percent. The
AFL-CIO estimated that nearly 18 percent of union members were out of
work, and one congressional estimate set joblessness at eight million nationally, which would have been close to 15 percent of the workforce.

Although the national income grew by 20 percent during the decade,
the top 5–10 percent of U.S. families absorbed about half of the gain. The
two-thirds of U.S. households living on annual incomes below $2,000—
the supposed budget required for health and decency—might have gotten
a quarter of the increase, but Chase speculated that little was used for better food, housing, or education. Instead, it was "applied to appease the
clamoring salesmen of the new standard of living with their motor cars,
radios, tootsie-rolls, silk-stockings, moving pictures, near-fur coats and
beauty shoppes."

His prophetic skepticism, published as the Crash was beginning, identified how the weakness of rising productivity lay in eliminating jobs and
overrewarding the wealthy. This, in turn, led to twin hazards: a greater
supply of goods than underpaid Americans could long consume and speculative excesses by the wealthy. This boom-era architecture, more vaulting than careful, helps explain why wealth levels collapsed so far from
their artificial 1929 heights.

The Crash itself hardly came without warning. As stock mania grew
in the spring of 1927, President Coolidge sent for Professor William Z.
Ripley of Harvard, who had just brought out a critique entitled *Main
Street and Wall Street*. The two spent almost a day together, and after
Ripley described the "prestidigitation, double-shuffling, honey-fugling,
hornswoggling and skulduggery" behind the soaring Dow, Coolidge
asked what he, the president, could do. Ripley replied that it was a state
matter: New York, not the White House, had authority over the New
York Stock Exchange. In late July, Coolidge gave a speech in Indiana commenting on the low wages of unskilled workers amid stock market rock-
etry, and a few days later he announced that "I do not choose to run for
president in 1928." One can only speculate whether he feared what might
be coming.

Jitters increased with each of 1928's minicrashes—one in June, and
then another in mid-December that followed November's big "Hoover
market" celebrating the GOP's presidential landslide. As 1929 clocked in,

the financial editor of the *New York Times* predicted that the bull market would end that year in a stupendous crash. Herbert Hoover, right after his March inauguration, urged newspaper publishers to editorialize against speculation, shared his worries with the Federal Reserve Board, convinced Treasury Secretary Mellon to caution investors, and sent Vice President Charles Curtis to the New York Stock Exchange to call for moderation.

In the 1980s, conservative tax-cut theorists and market utopians would call for the reenactment of the twenties as an economic triumph botched only by government mishandling, but their grandfathers knew better. Even the Republican Congress of 1929 was part of a wall of worry. In February the Senate had passed a resolution asking the Federal Reserve to provide advice should legislation become necessary to curb speculation. Up in Manhattan, Benjamin Strong, president of the New York Federal Reserve Bank, in mid-1928 just months before his death, had been worried about "a calamitous break in the stock market." This was well before the Federal Reserve Board in Washington warned in March 1929 that stock prices were highly inflated. However, after one interest-rate increase in 1928, nothing more was done until August 1929, when the Federal Reserve jumped the rediscount rate from 5 percent to 6 percent.

Part of the speculative mania reflected assurances that a New Economy was in place and that the establishment of the Federal Reserve System in 1913 had all but abolished the old business cycle. John Moody, founder of the credit ratings agency, had made the same point. Yale economics professor Irving Fisher offered his famously mistaken analysis that stock prices had reached "what looks like a permanently high plateau." In 1932 financier Bernard Baruch, an embarrassed Pollyanna, recalled that, "In the lamentable era of the 'New Economics' culminating in 1929, even in the presence of dizzily spiraling prices, if we had all continuously repeated 'two and two still make four,' much of the evil might have been averted."

The Dow-Jones Industrial Average, after spending the first part of 1929 in a range slightly above 300, put on a summer sprint to September's peak of 381. Over the next three years, and predicted by hardly anyone, the Dow tumbled 340 points, bottoming in July 1932 at 41.

The term "Crash" is also a bit of a misnomer. Despite unfolding into the biggest economic downturn in U.S. history and a grim reaper of net worth from Bangor to San Diego, the events of 1929–30, unlike previous panics, caused no major investment firm to fail during that time. Pynchon & Co. was the first in 1931. From September 1929 to August 1932 the market averages took almost three years to fall the distance climbed in the previous eight. After a winter rally following the brutal first autumn, there was no new precipice, just a long downhill slope.

Commentators usually explain the market's descent as a blend of several causes. One involved how the 1928–29 overproduction of goods, which the public could not afford to keep buying, was already hinting a recession, so that autumn 1929 weakness in construction and auto and steel production helped prime the stock market for scared selling. A second blamed Federal Reserve willingness to let the money supply shrink in 1930–32 for turning a bad recession into a depression. Nor was there any other global "lender of last resort."

By a third explanation, stock market tremors had scared overextended banks in the U.S. and abroad into cutting back loans and international trade financing, which deepened the economic crisis. A fourth factor was the collapse in the mid and late twenties not just of U.S. crop prices but of international commodity prices—in rubber, coffee, sugar, and tin, among others. And most experts concurred that souring business and consumer confidence and the widening 1930–33 failures of U.S. and foreign banks fed one another.

The economist J. Kenneth Galbraith put more emphasis on the ripple effect of the stock market itself. The initial autumn free fall, which knocked the Dow down by some 40 percent, spread into the real economy—as, for example, declines in freight-car loadings, commodities, and steel ingots. And once the stock slide resumed in spring 1930 following the late-November to March rally, the market slump remained a relentlessly negative psychological backdrop through mid-1932.

In his *America in the Twenties,* Geoffrey Perrett tied the early innings of the depression in 1930 to a less-examined causation: the year's sharp falloff in demand for consumer durables. Cars and houses led the decline, demand having been sated by the huge purchases of 1923–29, which buyers managed by taking on record levels of debt. Consumers, who accounted for 92–94 percent of national spending, began shutting their wallets in reaction to the layoffs and the stock market panic. Consumer spending finished 1930 at $70.5 billion, down from $78 billion in 1929.

Wholesale and retail prices joined the retreat, and by late 1930 unemployment was rising sharply. Corporate profits were beginning to implode, as Chart 2.6 shows. Such was consumer debt hangover after the boom's spending binge that in 1932, interest payments consumed 20 percent of national income. Many people simply walked away from their cars, houses, or debts between 1930 and 1932, handing the keys to already wobbly banks.

If the Depression has many explanations, the details of its wealth destruction are surprisingly sketchy. No magazine profiled 1929's big losers. *Forbes* published no 1931 "top thirty" follow-up to its solitary measurement back in 1918.

However, because the rich of the 1920s and 1930s got about three-quarters of their income from dividends and capital gains, the corporate and securities debacles had to be devastating. The market value of the stocks traded on the New York exchange alone dropped from $89.6 billion on December 1, 1929, to $15.6 billion on July 1, 1932. The ranks of millionaires slimmed almost in proportion, from 25,000–35,000 in 1929 to some 5,000 in 1932–33.

Not a few fortunes simply slid off the market's cliff. Most had their belts taken in substantially. The Fisher brothers, who sold their coachwork business to General Motors, saw their $300 million shrink to $100 million. Utilities magnate Samuel Insull's net worth collapsed from $150 million in 1929 to nothing. Even the bluest of blue-chip industrials lost 60 to 80 percent of their value between 1929 and 1932. Heirs to a $4 million estate in the summer of 1930 might well have seen the assets halved before distribution to legatees.

Among the very rich, the holdings of the automotive Fords, chemical duPonts, petroleum Rockefellers, and diversified Mellons survived, especially where tied up in trusts. But because of the stock market collapse and consumer retrenchment, new technologies like radio, aviation, movies, and telephones failed to launch the usual new great fortunes. Joseph P. Kennedy, whose new fortune included the RKO theater chain, was the principal exception. Eldridge Johnson of Victor Phonograph was a lesser one.

Technology stocks epitomized the collapse as they did the bubble. The Radio Corporation of America (RCA), one of the decade's most-traded stocks, became a symbol of its excesses. Selling at $2.50 a share in 1921, it went to 85 in 1928 and then 549 in 1929 before crashing to peanuts in 1932. General Motors plummeted from 73 in 1929 to a paltry 8 in July 1932. Ryan Aeronautic, another favorite of speculators, surged from 69 to 289 during 1928 and then crash-dived in 1929. American Telephone and Telegraph sank from 304 to 72. Shares in Samuel Insull's ill-fated personal utility holding company went from $7.54 each in early 1929 to $150 by August and then to bankruptcy three years later.

So extraordinary, so golden, was 1929, despite autumn's setback, that the top 1 percent of Americans (making over $5,000 a year) wound up flush with 15–17 percent of that year's national income, and the top 5 percent received 32 percent. In terms of holdings, the top 1 percent had between 37 percent and 44 percent of overall U.S. wealth in 1929, depending on the calculation. An economist formerly at the National Bureau of Economic Research appended a few additional nuances: the top 1 percent had 83 percent of the liquid wealth, while the top one-twentieth of 1 percent—38,889 persons—accounted for 30 percent of U.S. savings. All of these shares, highly abnormal, would go unmatched for another seven decades. As for millionaires, their implosion was enormous, but no nationwide count was ever attempted.

The digits 1929 became a quick, unadorned shorthand for disaster. Industrial production and corporate profits did not regain those highs until 1940. And during the disenchanted 1930s, a citizenry digging out from the debris of broken promises and shattered assumptions would rally round a president ready to point a finger of blame. The 1920s' admiration for wealth would become 1930s' distrust.

3. THE NEW DEAL, WORLD WAR II, AND THE "GOOD BOOM" OF THE FIFTIES AND SIXTIES

To adults who had experienced the short but deep slump of 1921–22, the downturn of mid-1930 was as yet no shattering event. The Republicans lost congressional seats that year, but not as many as in 1922. It was in 1932, 1934, and 1936 that voter recriminations finished the Republicans as the nation's governing coalition. The depth of political realignment matched the depth of economic depression.

By Roosevelt's inauguration in March 1933, pig iron production had dropped back to 1896 levels. Farmers were killing their hogs, dumping milk, and burning grain for fuel because prices had collapsed. Unemployment was close to 25 percent, and the failure of five thousand banks wiped out nine million savings accounts. Even as the new president took office, governors all over the United States were declaring bank holidays. The gross national product had shrunk from $103 billion in 1929 to $90 billion in 1930, $75 billion in 1931, and $58 billion in 1932 before bottoming out in 1933 at $56 billion. Thereafter it rebounded to $65 billion in 1934, $72 billion in 1935, and $83 billion in 1936, only to slide again in late 1937 and early 1938, briefly rekindling queasiness about another deep descent.

The blow to America's wealth-holders came from many directions—slumping confidence, crumbling banks, and a depressed economy. Yet, as in the 1890s and 1900s, rising and falling corporate stock market valuations were the principal vehicles. Chart 2.6 shows the striking correlation between the collapse and slow resurrection of corporate profits and the movements of the principal stock market index.

CHART 2.6 **The Collapse in Corporate Profits and the Collapse of the Dow-Jones Industrial Average**

	CORPORATE PROFITS ($ BILLIONS)	DOW-JONES INDUSTRIAL AVERAGE
1929	10.0	Peak: 381
1930	3.7	Range: 260–160
1931	-.4	Range: 190–80
1932	-2.3	Bottom: 41
1933	1.0	Range: 50–110
1934	2.3	Range: 85–110

After making its summer 1932 low, the Dow-Jones Industrial Average quickly bounced off its brief bottom and spent much of 1933 and 1934 in the 80–110 range. This brought the total value of the shares listed on the New York Stock Exchange back up to $20–$30 billion from their $15.6 billion nadir. Much of America's old money, enmeshed in trusts, remained in blue-chip securities that almost all rebounded with the markets. However, only a few of the big new 1920s fortunes—Joseph Kennedy's, Clarence Dillon's, Floyd Odlum's, and some still-growing East Texas oil money—made the major leagues of longevity. With so many erstwhile middle-class Americans eating toast and beans in the mid-1930s, the *concentration* of wealth and income at the top, despite its slimmer count in actual dollars, may have remained close to the ratio of 1929.

Such top-heaviness was unsustainable, though, because of chilling national attitudes toward the rich and the old northern Republican and Yankee business and financial elites and, for that matter, skepticism about the acceptability in a democratic society of million-dollar incomes. This mood, captured by Roosevelt's New Deal in 1935 and 1936, lasted perhaps two decades. Yet its aftereffects lingered through the late sixties and into the early seventies, years that remain the zenith of twentieth-century American egalitarianism. In the meantime, FDR's triumph, like all of America's major political watersheds, was shaping a new economic elite.

For seventy years after the Republican capture of the presidency in

1860, just two Democrats reached the White House, Grover Cleveland and Woodrow Wilson. Both barely won second terms, and two years after each man's tenuous reelection, the GOP regained Congress. In 1936, by contrast, FDR's second-term landslide, bigger than his first, cut back Republican presidential support to the Yankee bare bones of the old Civil War coalition. This transformation of the GOP into a minority based in the northern countryside, small towns, and suburbs left the party's old northern industrial elite politically shorn. A new upstart Democratic economic coalition, soon to displace the nineteenth-century alliance of heavy industry and corporate finance, began to be visible in that election.

Its core, mirroring the pre-1932 inner councils of the 1920s Democratic Party, was capitalist: the Democratic minority of commercial and investment bankers (mostly southern, western, or Jewish) at odds with the Morgan axis, plus dozens of southern and western cotton, oil, mining, and tobacco moguls along with top executives and businessmen from antitariff industries such as farm machinery, agribusiness, and copper. Other enlistees included entrepreneurs in retailing, communications, housing, and construction, who saw their fortunes linked to Keynesian stimulus and middle-class growth, as well as corporate leaders in emerging technology (from aviation to General Electric and International Business Machines). In sectional terms, the new winners were the South and the big cities, both of which benefited from government spending and much-increased influence in Washington. Labor unions, in turn, rode New Deal favor to membership gains and higher wages for workers.

Few of the emerging Democratic capitalists appeared in top national wealth ranks before the 1940s and 1950s. However, the grassroots economic benefits to old outsider constituencies like the South, the major urban centers, labor, and, to a lesser extent, farmers, showed up more quickly in census data. Between 1933 and 1949, a near doubling of national price levels was more than offset by the near tripling of the average manufacturing wage—from $1,086 in 1933 (after dropping from $1,523 in 1929) to $1,363 in 1939, $2,515 in 1945, and $3,095 in 1949. And these wage gains augured still more to come. Whereas only 15.5 percent of the private-sector workforce had been unionized in 1933, the figure by 1939 was 22.8 percent, and by 1945, 33.9 percent, close to the 35.7 percent high reached in 1953. Unionization and blue-collar prosperity rose together.

Benefits to the cities and the middle classes were huge, and the Old Confederacy's share of U.S. personal income rose from 11 percent in 1929 to 15 percent in 1940 and to 18 percent in 1950. Farm income, middling through the thirties, soared as usual from wartime demand. Rare was the New Deal constituency that did not benefit.

The relative (short-term) loser of the 1930s and 1940s was *wealth*—the share of the top 1 percent of Americans who had soared in the twenties and lost headway in the aftermath. Their portion of U.S. personal income, excluding capital gains, dropped from 17.2 percent in 1929 to 12.3 percent in 1941 and 9.6 percent in 1946. To some observers, Roosevelt's 1932–33 attacks on "the moneychangers" and excess wealth concentrations seemed politically at odds with his more conservative predilection for balanced budgets. In fact, as we have seen, this old Democratic mix, originally premised on suspicion of public debt as well as banking elites, traces easily back to the policies of Jefferson and Jackson. In November 1933, Roosevelt echoed those antecedents in a letter to Col. E. M. House, a former adviser to Woodrow Wilson:

> The real truth . . . is, as you and I know, that a financial element in the larger centers has owned the Government ever since the days of Andrew Jackson—and I am not wholly excepting the Administration of W.W. The country is going through a repetition of Jackson's fight with the Bank of the United States—only on a far bigger and broader basis.

Roosevelt did indeed triumph over what Wilson era Democrats had called the "money trust" through a spate of 1933–35 measures creating the Securities and Exchange Commission, mandating separation between banks and investment companies (the connection that built the House of Morgan), reforming the Federal Reserve System, and prohibiting public utility holding companies. What the new president was less willing to tackle was wealth itself, as opposed to a rival Republican political and economic power structure. This became clear in the Second New Deal of 1935, during which the so-called Wealth Tax Act raised taxes on the rich, but not as much in practice as in rhetoric.

Many historians have regarded FDR's 1935 attack on "an unjust concentration of wealth and economic power" that had been abetted by the tax code as partly reluctant and largely a response to the rise in the polls of populist Louisiana U.S. senator Huey Long, whose "Share the Wealth" Clubs were claiming seven million members. Democratic polls suggested that Long's threat to run as an independent in the 1936 presidential race could jeopardize Roosevelt's reelection prospects. As things turned out, Long was assassinated and Roosevelt won in a landslide. In 1937, FDR sought to reemphasize balanced-budget economics, although he was obliged to embrace Keynesian spending stimulus again by the unanticipated recession of 1937–38.

The case against an excessive concentration in the major U.S. wealthholdings of the thirties—that this was an elite of power and inheritance, not of achievement—can be found in FDR's own tax message. However, it was more substantially fleshed out by the report of the Senate Temporary National Economic Committee of 1939–40 and by latter-day muckrakers like Ferdinand Lundberg in his 1937 book *America's Sixty Families.* In 1940 the Securities and Exchange Commission concluded that in about 40 percent of the two hundred largest U.S. nonfinancial corporations, "one family, or a small number of families, exercise either absolute control . . . or working control." Lundberg, in a similar vein, charged that the United States "is owned and dominated today by a hierarchy of its sixty richest families, buttressed by no more than ninety families of lesser wealth." Based on published 1920s tax data and other research, and using his own calculations, he came up with the following (imprecisely dated) calculations of the thirty richest families:

CHART 2.7 **The Top Thirty Wealth Concentrations of the 1930s**

FAMILY AND NUMBER OF TAX RETURNS	PRIMARY SOURCE OF WEALTH	GROSS CALCULATED FORTUNE (MILLIONS)	MAXIMUM ESTIMATED FORTUNE (MILLIONS)
Rockefellers (21)	Standard Oil	1,007	2,000
Fords (2)	Ford Motors	728	—
Harknesses (5)	Standard Oil	450	800
Mellons (3)	Alcoa	450	1,000
Vanderbilts (22)	New York Central RR	360	800
Whitney (4)	Standard Oil	322	750
duPonts (20)	duPont	238	1,000
McCormicks (8)	International Harvester	211	—
Bakers (2)	First National Bank	210	500
Fishers (5)	General Motors	193	500
Guggenheims (6)	American Smelting	190	—
Fields (6)	Marshall Field & Co.	180	—
Curtis-Boks (5)	Curtis Publishing	174	—
Woolworth/Hutton (7)	Woolworth & Misc.	165	—

Dukes (3)	American Tobacco	156	—
Berwinds (3)	Berwind-White Coal	150	—
Wideners (3)	Public Utilities	118	—
Reynolds (7)	R. J. Reynolds	117	—
Astors (3)	Real Estate	114	300
Morgans (*)	J. P. Morgan	110	—
Ryans (*)	Utilities	108	—
Dorrances (*)	Campbell Soup	100	—
Winthrops (6)	Miscellaneous	104	—
Stillmans (3)	National City Bank	102	500
Timkens (3)	Timken Roller Bearings	111	—
Pitcairns (4)	Pittsburgh Plate Glass	99	—
Metcalfs	Rhode Island Textiles	91	—
Clarks (3)	Singer Sewing Machines	90	—
Phippses (16)	Carnegie Steel	89	600

Source: Ferdinand Lundberg, *America's Sixty Families* (1937). The chart above modifies Lundberg's list by removing four investment banking groups—the Morgan partners and the Lehmans, Warburgs, and Kahns of Lehman Brothers and Kuhn Loeb because Lundberg's calculations were based on income, not assets. On the addition side, J. P. Morgan has been put back in, as have the heirs—an indeterminate number marked with an asterisk—of the Thomas Fortune Ryan and John Dorrance estates.

While this chart is adapted from Lundberg's book, his partial use of 1920s tax data means that it can only approximately represent the circumstances of 1937 or 1939, although few new fortunes were big enough to have pushed their way in. Of the twenty largest U.S. corporations in 1937, eight were railroads and seven were utilities. The other five were oil, steel, and automobile companies. However, because new technology and new fortunes were well down the list, Lundberg was almost likely correct in the role he assigned to family concentrations of wealth and influence. Political events and debates of the 1920s and 1930s also gave him evidence to draw on.

In 1925, Professor Pitrim Sorokin of Harvard had completed and published a study showing that the most recent generation of millionaires, in contrast to the previous post–Civil War generation, were largely sired by merchants, manufacturers, financiers, or businessmen. "The percentage of living millionaires whose fathers followed 'money-making' occupations," he found, "is much higher than that of the deceased group. This . . . gives a basis to state that the wealth class of the United States is becoming less and less open, more and more closed, and is tending to be transformed

into a castelike group." Some 38.8 percent of the post–Civil War generation had started out poor, but only 19.6 percent of the living millionaires.

The congressional debate over Secretary Mellon's 1926 tax proposals
also shed light. In response to his claims that an inheritance tax could end
private property in two or three generations, Senate liberals had pointed
out how the Guggenheim, duPont, Harkness, and Pratt fortunes had doubled or trebled in the hands of multiple heirs. Among the duPonts, for example, a dozen members of the fourth generation had assets of $30
million or more; Edward S. Harkness, in turn, left an estate of under $50
million, yet his two sons later left $270 million between them. A decade
later, during the 1935 hearings before the Senate Finance Committee on
the Roosevelt administration's proposed Wealth Tax Act, U.S. Internal
Revenue Service counsel (and future U.S. Supreme Court justice) Robert
H. Jackson testified that whereas fortunes could once be spent by the next
generation, "now they not only perpetuate themselves, they grow. . . .
Furthermore, such estates are largely perpetuated in trusts, and every legal
and economic obstacle to their dissipation is employed. . . . Most of the
large estates as at present managed, we find, not only perpetuate themselves but are larger as they pass from generation to generation." The persistence and growth of inherited fortunes over the remainder of the
twentieth century would make Jackson's words prescient.

The downturn that began in 1937 reversed as war clouds formed over
Europe. The thicker they grew over Poland, Austria, and Czechoslovakia,
the brighter were the skies for America's own economy. The year 1939 was
better, 1940 better still, and then Pearl Harbor turned on the lights in
factories, warehouses, and dockyards from Maine to California. Recovery
came fastest along the two coasts, producing remarkable upsurges in the
average income per family between 1938 and 1942: in Boston ($2,455 to
$3,618), Hartford ($2,207 to $5,208), New York ($2,760 to $4,044),
Washington, D.C. ($2,227 to $5,316), Los Angeles ($2,031 to $3,469),
and San Francisco ($2,201 to $3,716).

Good *economic* reasons, at least, underpinned war nostalgia. Few conflicts have spread so much money so widely. Ready for a giant jobs program, Americans got one—in the first six months of 1942 federal
procurement officers placed orders for $100 billion worth of equipment,
more than the U.S. economy had ever produced in a single year. By the
end of 1943 money was being spent at five times the peak rate of World
War I. Engineers, technicians, specialists, and skilled workers seem to
have been the biggest gainers, along with farmers—the unfailing benefi-

ciaries of wartime food needs—and those of the untrained able to develop skills. Workers able to shift to a war production job often found their wages climbing by 20, 30, or 40 percent. The pay of women factory operatives, for example, rose 50 percent just between 1941 and 1943. Between 1939 and 1945 wages in manufacturing industries went up by 86 percent while the estimated cost of living rose only 29 percent because of price controls. Many who were unemployed as of 1937 six or seven years later found themselves able to buy war bonds.

Wartime taxes on the rich were close to punitive. The bite on family heads earning the average $40 to $50 a week was not. After the deprivations of the thirties, wartime rationing, not taxes or lack of money, was what limited public buying. Purchases of expensive clothing and jewelry soared. Used cars were at a premium. And despite food rationing, the number of supermarkets climbed from 4,900 in 1939 to 16,000 in 1944.

At war's end, Americans were rolling in cash. Average weekly pay had been boosted from $24.20 in 1940 to $44.39 in 1945, not just by high wage rates but by huge overtime and the earnings of 6.5 million women, mostly middle-aged and married, new to the workforce. Many families had their first discretionary income. Between mid-1943 and mid-1945, Americans stashed about a quarter of their take-home pay. By Japan's surrender, an amazing $140 billion was in liquid assets (mostly in small savings accounts and war bonds)—*twice the entire national income for 1939!* By one estimate, this was enough to buy three times the amount of consumer goods that could plausibly be produced during the first year of peace.

For the rich, wartime economics were more complicated. The revenue acts between 1935 and 1943 clearly shrank the top brackets' share of national income. If large corporations reined in their dividend payments in part because they remembered the furor over excess profits in 1918, these undistributed profits conveniently worked to push up stock prices in the 1942–45 bull market. The diaries and letters of military officers from wealthy families contain pleased comments—brief asides from the race across France in the summer of 1944 or island-hopping in the Pacific—on the welcome upward movement of their stocks. The Dow-Jones Industrial Average's leap in nominal dollars from 93 in April 1942 to almost 200 by the end of 1945 nearly twinned the Dow's early bull run from late 1924 to late 1927, save that rising prices weakened the parallel. People living off dividends alone lost ground, but sales of stock were yielding handsome capital gains.

Yet with the official definition of income still excluding capital gains, the income distribution charts of 1944 were dominated by the effects of rising wages, plentiful worker overtime, and the take-home pay of working wives. Economists Claudia Goldin and Robert Margo later gave this narrowing of the gap between the rich and the ordinary population an appropriate name: the Great Compression. As a response to the 1920s speculative bubble and Great Crash, the Great Compression and its egalitarian zenith marked the peak of the democratic counterforce.

Back in 1939, the top fifth of male wage and salary recipients had collected 48.7 percent of the total while the three middle fifths got only 47.8 percent. By 1949 the top group's share had slimmed to 40.1 percent and the middle three were receiving 55.3 percent. Family income distribution over the full decade showed much the same: a shrinking share at the top (and to a lesser extent in the highest 10 percent). The improvement in compensation concentrated in the 50th to 89th percentiles: the middle class, blue-collar as well as white-collar.

The Great Compression, so favorable to the middle class and labor at the (seeming) expense of the top 1 percent, continued into the 1950s. Politically, at least, the middle-class ethos ruled. To commentators like Frederick Lewis Allen, Robert Heilbroner, and David Riesman, the rich had become "inconspicuous consumers," either suffering from a guilt complex or afraid of giving visible offense. Their big houses had been sold off to become orphanages or old-age homes, and fewer upper-income families had servants. In 1953 the new Republican administration of Dwight Eisenhower, far from imitating the deep tax cuts of Treasury Secretary Andrew Mellon after the First World War, decided against seeking a reduction in the 91 percent top income tax rate, which had been kept in effect after World War II.

The take-home pay of America's best-compensated corporate chief executives was only a shadow of the $20 million and $50 million net proceeds widely reported a half century later in the Second Gilded Age. Frederick Lewis Allen, in *The Big Change: 1900–1950,* calculated the disposable income of the best-paid CEO of 1950, Charles E. Wilson of General Motors: "Let us suppose that it had all been handed to him in cash in 1950, and that he had had to pay a federal income tax on the whole $626,300, and on nothing else—and without any exceptional deductions. The government would have taken some $462,000 of it, leaving him only some $164,300."

Beneath this democratic imagery, however, another contrary sea change was gathering. U.S. technology and manufacturing had been revolution-ized by wartime demands. Executives in company after company found themselves selling products commercially unfeasible before Pearl Harbor. Petroleum, in particular, had been made to yield a rainbow of profitable wonders: synthetic rubber, plastics, fibers, and petrochemicals. Victory over Germany and Japan, besides ending domestic constraints, also gave U.S. corporations and banks new global opportunities and markets. In June 1949, the Dow-Jones Industrial Average ended two years of mud-dling in the 165–190 range (1927 levels), transcended postwar depression fears, and began what would be a two-decade leap. The top 1 percent of Americans, who owned about half of the stocks, enjoyed quiet gains that dwarfed those of ordinary wage earners.

With capital gains excluded, the income statistics for 1947–57 con-firmed the continuation of the Great Compression into peacetime. The greatest share of a rapidly expanding national income went to Middle America, the slimmest gains to the top 5 percent. But critics began to point to widely overlooked contrary signals.

One set were the intermittent annual declines, during the 1940s and 1950s, in the reported number of incomes over $100,000. Superficially, previous recipients appeared to be slipping into a lower bracket. More was afoot, though, than met the untutored eye. In the face of wartime and postwar income tax rates, many wealthy Americans either postponed their realization of income or arranged its shift into 1) tax-free vehicles (expense accounts or municipal bonds) or 2) capital gains, which were taxed at a much lower rate. Business expense accounts, notorious during the war, flourished enough in peacetime for novelist John O'Hara to christen "the new expense account society." As for municipal bond interest, which en-tirely avoided federal taxes, by 1957 the amount going to the top 5 per-cent totaled almost $600 million.

Capital gains grew like Topsy during the 1950s, with about half flow-ing to the top 1 percent. In 1955, *U.S. News and World Report* noticed that "in the past five years, (stock) options have produced a whole new crop of millionaires." Corporations that retained rather than distributed their profits, in turn, allowed shareholders to look for capital gains (taxed at 25 percent) in lieu of dividends (often taxed at or near the top rate of 91 per-cent). During the 1923–29 period, according to economic historian Gabriel Kolko, corporations had retained only 27 percent of their net profits. For 1946–59 they held back 51 percent. Putting the capital gains and municipal bond interest into the income share of the top 1 percent would, by Kolko's estimate, have added several percentage points, canceling about one-third of the decline officially reported.

This does not, on balance, rebut the democratic thrust or credentials of the quarter century that began in 1933. Rich citizens were forced into evasions of a sort they would not have imagined a decade or a generation earlier. Literally hundreds of protections for middle-income and poor Americans came into being through programs ranging from housing subsidies to small business loans. Besides, the breadth of national prosperity from the forties through the sixties is indisputable, especially the great gains of blue-collar workers and the middle class. Of the 74 percent increase in the disposable income of all Americans between 1929 and 1950, the bulk came in the 1940s and concentrated among the fortieth to ninetieth percentiles. Between 1952 and 1960, under Republican president Eisenhower, the average family's real income climbed by another 30 percent, and then added the same percentage again under Democratic administrations between 1960 and 1968.

Yet by the late 1950s the postwar egalitarian climate, with the rich described as "inconspicuous consumers," was dissipating. Tax avoidance was on the rise, abetted by ever more loopholes in the Internal Revenue Code. Consumption was edging back into its pre-1929 pattern of keeping up with the Dow-Joneses. In 1955, B. Altman's in Manhattan caused a flurry by quickly selling out of mink-trimmed beer-can openers. General Motors bestirred itself to offer—for $13,074 (the annual salary of a mid-range business executive)—a new Cadillac Eldorado Brougham, which included on its dashboard a tissue-box, vanity case, lipstick, and four gold-finished drinking cups. That same year, *Fortune* concluded that "rich Americans have begun to build big houses again," and in 1958, *Business Week* quoted a fashionable designer saying, "The rich have been hiding for twenty years. They are coming out of their holes. They are having a ball."

Capital gains were the punchbowl. From 160 in mid-1949, the Dow neared 300 during 1953, vaulted the 1929 high bar of 381 by late 1954, cracked 500 in early 1956, stopped only a little short of 700 in 1959, and then oscillated in the 550–725 range for three years. By May 1965, just before Lyndon Johnson's massive commitment of U.S. troops to Vietnam, the Dow was well above 900. Wall Street was exuberant. Even in constant dollars that allowed for inflation, the Dow had regained its 1929 peak in early 1959. Volume on the New York Stock Exchange finally reached 1929 levels in 1961. Capital gains might not be included in income, but their fruits fattened wealth tabulations, and the share of the wealth held

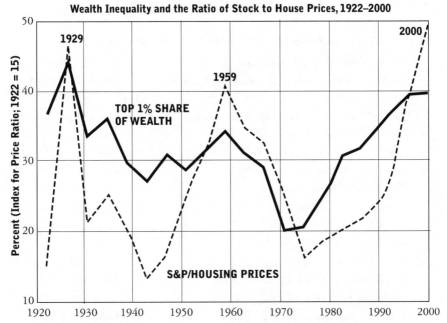

CHART 2.8 **Wealth Inequality and Stock Market Peaks**

Wealth Inequality and the Ratio of Stock to House Prices, 1922–2000

Source: Edward Wolff, *Top Heavy*, (New York, 1995), p.30. Data from Appendix, Table A–1; U.S. Bureau of the Census, *Historical Statistics of the United States*, Part 1 (1975); U.S. Council of Economic Advisors (1992). Data and estimates for 1990s added by author.

by the top 1 percent, which had fallen from roughly 40 percent in 1929 to 22 percent in 1949, was now climbing back to 27 percent in 1953, and 30 percent in 1958. Trust funds brimmed over. Small wonder the rich were coming out of their "holes" and building big houses again.

Stock market peaks, in turn, are closely related to the peaks of wealth inequality and in the number of U.S. millionaires. Chart 2.8 profiles the strong family resemblance between wealth inequality tops and stock market high points. As for the market's relationship with the millionaire totals, the latter—some 7,000 in 1914, 10,000 in 1919 to 6,000 in 1921, 15,000 in 1927, 30,000 in 1929, and 5,000–6,000 in 1932—fit very well with the ups and downs of the Dow-Jones Industrial Average.

Many of the richest Americans of 1957 owed their rank to the stock market's fulsome treatment of their inheritances. Others, however, not a few of them Democrats or Roosevelt backers in 1936, had newer entrepreneurial origins. The oil operators, fresh from the East Texas fields, tended to operate through small private companies, flipping them around like cards in a deck. Because several publications sought to chart the top U.S. wealth-holdings of the late 1950s, the following is a hybrid:

CHART 2.9 **The Twenty-Five Richest Families and Individuals of 1957**

The Mellon Family (oil, aluminum, finance)	$1.6–$2.8 billion
The Rockefeller Family (oil, real estate, finance)	$1.0–$1.9 billion
J. Paul Getty (oil)	$700 million to $1 billion
The duPont Family (chemicals, automobiles)	$600 million to $1.2 billion
The Ford Family (automobiles)	$425–550 million
H. L. Hunt (oil operator)	$400–700 million
Amy (Phipps) Guest (steel, inheritance)	$200–400 million
Howard Hughes (aerospace)	$200–400 million
Joseph P. Kennedy (liquor, real estate, finance)	$200–400 million
Daniel K. Ludwig (shipping)	$200–400 million
Sid Richardson (oil operator)	$200–400 million
Alfred P. Sloan (automobiles)	$200–400 million
The Whitney Family (oil, inheritance)	$200–400 million
The Houghton Family (Corning Glass)	$200–400 million
Vincent Astor (real estate, inheritance)	$100–200 million
Doris Duke (inheritance)	$100–200 million
James Abercrombie (oil operator)	$100–200 million
Stephen Bechtel (construction)	$100–200 million
William Blakley (airlines, express)	$100–200 million
Jacob Blaustein (oil)	$100–200 million
Clarence Dillon (finance)	$100–200 million
William Keck (oil operator)	$100–200 million
William McKnight (3M Co.)	$100–200 million
John Mecom (oil operator)	$100–200 million
C. W. Murchison (oil operator)	$100–200 million

"The Fifty-Million-Dollar Man," *Fortune*, November 1957; "The World's Richest Men," *New York Times Magazine*, October 20, 1957; Ferdinand Lundberg, *The Rich and the Super-Rich* (New York: 1968), pp. 40–42, 159–162.

So many of America's richest men and women were inheritors that to list the qualifying members of the Mellon, Rockefeller, and duPont families would have commanded a dozen of the top twenty-five places, squeezing out much of the new Texas money. Clustering the individuals from the six richest clans into family concentrations permits the list to include more new entrants. It also echoes the inherited wealth persistence of the 1840s and 1930s, trends that will grow in importance through the rest of the twentieth century.

Despite the lack of a comparable list for 1929, the changes over the next three decades were clearly enormous. In addition to the older petroleum geology underlying the Rockefeller, Mellon, and Whitney fortunes, new pools of crude—Texan and Californian, for the most part and still close to the derricks and oil fields—were added with Getty, Hunt, Richardson, Abercrombie, Blaustein, Keck, Mecom, and Murchison. Sun Belt wealth also came of economic age with Hughes (aerospace, movies), Bechtel (construction), and Blakley (transportation).

The wealth realignment hinted at in 1936 is now obvious. No Morgan nor any major New York banker allied to the House of Morgan appears in the top twenty-five. The two self-made financial operators who do, Joseph P. Kennedy and Clarence Dillon, both supported FDR in 1936; Dillon's investment firm produced several New Deal officials, and Kennedy served as Roosevelt's first chairman of the Securities and Exchange Commission. The oil industry leaned Democratic during the New Deal years, partly because so many operators came from one-party Texas, but more tangibly because Democratic Washington enlarged and protected the oil depletion allowance. The New Deal's single biggest tax break for industry, this petroleum sector version of a depreciation write-off allowed the new oil fortunes to sidestep the sharp scythe of that era's income tax. The Sun Belt aerospace, construction, and airline fortunes also traded on governmental connections, beginning with their reliance on New Deal and war-spurred regional growth. Many Texas Democrats, especially rich ones, were souring on their party by the forties and fifties, although multimillionaire "Dollar Bill" Blakley accepted a Democratic appointment to the U.S. Senate as late as 1961.

That same year the Democrats inaugurated a new, young president, John F. Kennedy, whose father was one of their new rich. His wife Jacqueline was a debutante from another wealthy family. All of a sudden America had a multimillionaire president with a whole string of fashionable connections—Newport, Hyannisport, and Palm Beach—closer to the F. Scott Fitzgerald aura of the twenties than the middle-class ethos of the Great Compression. Indeed, the sixties began to display many symptoms of the twenties: youthful iconoclasm, the sexual revolution, "newness" terminology, short skirts, substance abuse, exciting technology, merger mania, and new "conglomerates" put together by "go-go" financiers. And in the background was another stock market boom in which the Dow-Jones Industrial Average hurtled toward a mark that ten or fifteen years earlier had been unthinkable: *One Thousand.*

As the market indexes quintupled, the years from 1949 through the late 1960s became the twentieth century's second great wealth explosion. Millionaire ranks swelled from 27,000 in 1953 to about 80,000 in 1962 and 90,000 by 1965, although in constant 1929 dollars they probably didn't regain their pre-Crash high until 1959 or 1960. Blue-collar workers and the white-collar middle class still shared in the economic gain, witness that 30 percent increase in the average family's real income between 1960 and 1968.

Yet the postwar era was already moving toward closure. Like other U.S. wars, the one spreading in Vietnam in 1965 had brought inflation in tow—3–4 percent a year in 1966 and 1967. Early 1968 even saw a major run on the dollar that left Washington policymakers worried about the currency's future. That same year, in retrospect, brought the twentieth-century crest of the Gini index of income equality. It also marked the purchasing power peak of the federal minimum wage and, according to some computations, the postwar peak of real disposable income.

The long business cyclical upturn of the 1960s officially turned into a recession in late 1969. Indexes of the social health of the nation, in turn, all show declines beginning at various points in the seventies. The year 1974, when inflation broke into a gallop, was a clear marker on the downside.

The overlapping political shift fit a similar chronology. The New Deal coalition ended in 1968 with the Nixon victory that ushered in Republican presidencies for twenty of the next twenty-four years. Liberal ideology had a brief Indian summer because of the Watergate scandal, but this was short-lived. The evolution of the U.S. role in Vietnam from major escalation (1965) to shaky peace (1972) and embarrassed final withdrawal (1975), spans the entire transformation, and the war helped bring on the economic problems.

This chapter, however, will treat the "good boom" as ending in 1965–66, partly because of the near national nervous breakdown over the next decade—from big-city riots and looting and political assassinations to dollar crises, double-digit inflation, and the trauma of military defeat in Southeast Asia. Both the political and economic disarray of 1966–82 and the related stalling of wealth formation make the most sense taken as a separate era.

4. THE HIDDEN CRASH, 1966–82

The aptness of this description is a foundation for understanding not just these sixteen years but the shaky foundations on which subsequent decades were built. The taproots of the 1966–82 failure were sunk in the delusion-threaded 1960s boom, especially the high-borrowing, high-spending, rising hemline, conglomerate-merger "go-go" era and "Great Society" years in which Lyndon Johnson thought he could end poverty in the United States while winning a land war in Southeast Asia. Washington's late sixties economic fine tuning, overambitious sociology, and Asian military commitment all miscarried amid speculation that the postwar U.S. heyday was ending. The implanting of the basic civil rights revolution was the era's principal success.

For ordinary citizens the effects of America's worst bout of peacetime inflation—the Consumer Price Index essentially tripled between 1966–82—began with a median family income shrinkage. Between 1970 and 1982, it was some 8–10 percent in constant dollars. This is less than the 25 percent decline of 1929 to 1938, but useful in making the point that a comparison is in order. By the 1980s, economists like Lester Thurow foresaw middle-class erosion making the United States a society divided between rich and poor.

To others the nation was on the brink of declining great economic power status, much like Britain in the early twentieth century. Wilbur Mills, chairman of the House Ways and Means Committee, opined that the United States could no longer afford its previous global role. Richard Nixon and Henry Kissinger brushed up on the theories of decline laid out by Arnold Toynbee and Oswald Spengler.

Corporate optimism was a related casualty. A sampling of 1,844 *Harvard Business Review* readers in 1975 found nearly three-quarters extremely pessimistic about the U.S. commitment to private property and limited government surviving the next decade. At a series of meetings held by the business-sponsored Conference Board in 1974–75, the corporate executives in attendance agreed that the future of the American free enterprise system was extremely problematic.

Senior political officeholders had their own institutional uncertainties. The Nixon administration's embattled Watergate political espionage was one obvious trespass, while some senior Republicans were equally convinced that the Central Intelligence Agency had a role in trying to overthrow the president. Ronald Reagan briefly weighed the possibility of turning to a third party in 1974. Seven years later, President Reagan and Treasury Secretary Donald Regan were frustrated enough to discuss trying to abolish the Federal Reserve Board.

No satisfactory label has yet captured these years. In his 1987 book *Dollars and Dreams,* economist Frank Levy called the decade and a half after 1972 the "quiet depression." But he later withdrew the phrase as excessive, given the intensity of "depression" in common parlance. As we will see in chapter 4, British economists and economic historians have long used the term "Great Depression" to describe the price deflation and slowed (but only intermittently negative) growth in the United Kingdom over the two decades after 1873. No sharp downturn occurred, but this is the period in which scholars perceive Britain's world economic leadership beginning to wane, despite the still-to-come prewar boom and crest of 1910–14.

A similar transitional role for the 1966–82 period in the United States awaits twenty-first-century clarification. However, that era's discomfort and malaise—culturally, politically, economically, and financially—warrants a dour label regardless. Before turning to the effects on wealth, we should identify those sixteen years as a stock market debacle much closer to that of 1929–32 than most Americans realize.

As with profiling the 1966–82 erosion of median family income, the key is to set aside the ever-inflating numbers in current dollars and recalculate in real or inflation-adjusted numbers. Do that, and the decline from the Dow's 1966 high to August 1982 stops being a mild drop from just under 1000 to 775 and becomes a swan-dive to 260, a loss of almost three-quarters. Between September 1929 and July 1932, during the Great Crash, the Dow's inflation-adjusted decline was a bit less than 80 percent. The roughly comparable decline between 1966 and 1982 justifies the idea of a hidden or silent crash.

In wealth terms, 1968, close to the cyclical peak, was probably when the number of millionaires in the U.S. leaped the 100,000 mark. And the thirty richest Americans in that year's *Fortune* list represented not only old money but quite a bit of new money, including four of the early computer and technology fortunes.

If anything, these figures, which have been adapted, somewhat understate the overall wealth of the established families. This is because they combine the net worths of only those members rich enough to appear in that year's *Fortune* list individually. The chart below also leaves out families that might have reached $200–$300 million because of including,

CHART 2.10 **The Thirty Richest Americans and Families of 1968**

The Mellon Family (oil, finance)	$1.9 billion to 3.6 billion
The Rockefeller Family (oil, finance)	$1.2 billion to 1.8 billion
J. Paul Getty (oil)	$1 billion to 1.5 billion
Howard Hughes (aircraft)	$1 billion to 1.5 billion
H. L. Hunt (oil)	$500 million to $1 billion
Edwin H. Land (Polaroid)	$500 million to $1 billion
D. K. Ludwig (shipping)	$500 million to $1 billion
The duPont Family (chemicals)	$500–700 million
The Ford Family (automobiles)	$450–600 million
The Whitney Family (oil, investments)	$400–600 million
The Houghton Family (Corning Glass)	$350–500 million
N. Bunker Hunt (oil)	$300–500 million
J. D. MacArthur (insurance)	$300–500 million
W. L. McKnight (conglomerate)	$300–500 million
Charles S. Mott (automobiles)	$300–500 million
R. E. Smith (oil)	$300–500 million
H. F. Ahmanson (banking)	$200–300 million
Charles Allen (banking)	$200–300 million
Mrs. V. W. Clark (cosmetics)	$200–300 million
John T. Dorrance (Campbell Soup)	$200–300 million
Charles W. Engelhard (mining)	$200–300 million
Sherman Fairchild (technology)	$200–300 million
Leon Hess (oil)	$200–300 million
W. R. Hewlett (computers)	$200–300 million
David Packard (computers)	$200–300 million
Joseph P. Kennedy (investments)	$200–300 million
Eli Lilly (pharmaceuticals)	$200–300 million
Forrest Mars (candy)	$200–300 million
S. I. Newhouse (media)	$200–300 million
Marjorie M. Post (food)	$200–300 million

say, five $30–$40 million holdings and another dozen in the $5–$15 million range.

In another vein, it is revealing to compare this 1968 compilation against the list of 1901–1914 fortunes on p. 50. With allowance for the price index being quadrupled by inflation, the thirty largest fortunes of 1968 occupy roughly the same terrain as those of sixty years earlier.

Technology was creeping onto the list, but old-line manufacturing was not yet being displaced.

Indeed, looking back at the economic revolution of the postwar quarter century, it came in the unprecedented gains and well-being of the average American family, not in any bold new industrial contours. But this legacy began to blur in the sixties when the three middle quintiles stopped dominating the gains in real family income. Momentum was shifting to the two top quintiles, and by the 1990s the reemerging edge of the top quintile alone over the combined middle three would be a metaphor for the abandonment of postwar commitments to the middle class.

The hints of the late sixties became the acute problems of the seventies. As we have seen, inflation showed real teeth for the first time since 1946–47, sharpened by Washington's Vietnam War outlays and deficit finance. The incipient parallel to Britain's late Victorian weakness grew with the slippage of the U.S. share of world trade and manufacturing, as chapter 4 will develop. Whereas in the late 1940s the United States had produced 60 percent of the industrial world's manufactures and 40 percent of its goods and services, both portions were halved by the late 1970s. The U.S. share of the manufactured exports of the Western industrial nations, almost 30 percent in 1953, had fallen to just 13 percent by 1976. The convergence of inflation and weaker U.S. trade balances in turn undercut the dollar, encouraging foreign governments to trade in their greenbacks for gold. In 1971, President Nixon finally "shut the gold window," triggering a major decline in the U.S. currency.

Inflation would have surged, save that the government simultaneously imposed wage and price controls. Prices had climbed 22 percent between 1965 and 1970, and by early 1971 inflation had reached 6 percent a year. Politically, the controls kept prices handcuffed during the presidential election of 1972, abetting Nixon's landslide. Economically, once they were removed in 1973, inflation broke free again, reaching 6 percent again that year, 11 percent in 1974 (spiking with the OPEC oil price increases), and 6 percent in 1975.

By 1976 the 1973–74 recession had curbed prices again. However, the Federal Reserve Board and new Democratic administration of Jimmy Carter, both embracing economic stimulus, pushed inflation back up to 6.6 percent in 1977 and 7.6 percent in 1978. OPEC thereupon decided on another oil price increase, bringing inflation to its late-twentieth-century crescendo—11.3 percent in 1979, 13.5 percent in 1980, and 10.4 percent in 1981—before a retreat to 6.2 percent in 1982.

Although this was the largest burden weighing on family incomes and securities markets alike, while also warping wealth formation, the characterization of the seventies as a decade of "stagflation" is too sweeping. During three years (1970, 1973, and 1974), U.S. economic performance was bled white by recession. Four other years, however, saw high growth: 1972, 1976, and 1977–78. However, with the median family income flat to down, the postwar quarter century of growth ended. The nadir came in 1980, 1981, and 1982, when cresting inflation broke under a high interest rate counterattack by the Federal Reserve and the economy slid into a deep trough. For the public the bottom came in late 1982 with the first double-digit unemployment figures since before World War II.

Remedies from Washington provided foretastes of the future, including federal economic bailouts of a magnitude not seen since the Reconstruction Finance Corporation of the Great Depression. Companies like Penn Central, Lockheed, and Chrysler obtained individual governmental rescues. Dozens of other U.S. corporations including Braniff, Johns-Manville, LTV, Storage Technology, Texaco, and White Motors took advantage of tailored new provisions in the Bankruptcy Law of 1978, filing for structural and debt reorganization under its permissive Chapter 11.

We cannot attribute any new wealth axis to the purely partisan shift after 1968. Some commentators tried to read one into the politico-economic war between the "Yankees"—the old establishment—and the "Cowboys," the cabal of Texan, Californian, and Floridian nouveaux riches allied with Barry Goldwater, Richard Nixon, and Ronald Reagan (or all three). The geography, of course, was unmistakable. Every passing year gave the principal Sun Belt states of California, Texas, and Florida a steadily higher ratio of the major U.S. fortunes, especially in oil, aerospace, real estate, construction, technology, and "conglomerate" money.

Regional clout, however, greatly outweighed partisan sculpting. Richard Nixon did hope to build a new U.S. elite during his second term, and during his first he had sought support from companies with "Middle American" symbolism: Reader's Digest, TV Guide, Marriott (Hot Shoppes), Holiday Inns, and so forth (Walt Disney, who died in 1966, was another Nixon backer). Yet the Watergate scandal ruined these and other ambitions. More to the point, all four of the presidents elected between 1964 and 1982—Lyndon Johnson (Texas), Richard Nixon (California), Jimmy Carter (Georgia), and Ronald Reagan (California)—hailed from the Sun Belt, so that its rising influence transcended partisanship.

Nor was technology ready to furnish a new wealth axis, given the sliding stock market that played havoc with both capital formation and net worth. In 1968, for example, market gyrations kept several Sun Belt technology centimillionaires—Ross Perot of Electronic Data Systems, Tex Thornton of Litton Industries, and James Ling of Ling Temco Vought—from making *Fortune*'s top list. The seventies prolonged this uncertainty about the coming fortunes.

When economic recovery and transformation began in 1982 under the Reagan administration, conservative theorists claimed a Midas touch for their uncommon mix of tight monetary policy (to kill inflation) and loose fiscal policy (sweeping tax cuts and stepped-up defense outlays, both embraced despite the vast enlargement of federal deficits). However, there was also a convenient politics in managing to blend three streams of conservative thinking: Cold Warrior commitment to defense spending; monetarist insistence that inflation is braked by money supply tightness, not government economic manipulation; and "supply side" emphasis on tax cuts that spur investment, rather than demand. The result was a stock market that more than trebled between 1982 and 1992, producing a boom with prominent imbalances—a widening rich-poor gap, ballooning debt and luxury consumption, and a minimal component of technological advance and productivity improvement.

In part, these years were a prelude to the greater wave of high-tech wealth to come in the nineties. Even so, despite the important political and economic linkages between the eighties and nineties, in several other ways—notably empathy with technology and attention to the poor—the two booms were separate and distinctive.

5. The "Greed Decade": The 1980s and the Aggrandizement of Financial Assets

Like the booming twenties, which President Reagan sought to imitate with tax cuts and permissive regulation, the eighties began slowly in the uncomfortable bowl of a deep downturn caused by the high interest rates needed to squelch inflation. Thus, when *Forbes* magazine, following irregular compendia elsewhere, published its first annual list of the four hundred richest Americans in 1982, the debut made no great splash. Circumstances were not particularly celebratory. In historical terms, neither was the makeup of the new list, so much a product of oil price inflation, and showing a high ratio of inheritance to new industrial achievement.

Next to the titans of the Gilded Age, the individual billionaires of 1982, five of them children of Texas oilman H. L. Hunt, represented a telling slippage in both real wealth and political and economic stature. To make the wealth comparison requires turning the dollars of, let us say, 1910 into their 1982 equivalents (Appendix A sets out year-by-year inflation figures since 1790 and furnishes the yardstick).

Multiplying the estimated fortunes of 1900–1914 by eleven, we find John D. Rockefeller with a 1982 equivalent of $11 billion, Andrew Carnegie next with $4.5 billion, and so on. The actual 1982 list, by contrast, included thirteen individual billionaires, led by little-known shipowner Daniel Ludwig, with $2 billion. Parenthetically, the list of thirty below has been reconfigured from the original list by combining members of the same family, notably Rockefellers, duPonts, Hunts (5), Basses, and Mellons.

Like the bottom-scraping Dow-Jones Industrial Average, the first *Forbes* list, with its unprecedented number of oilmen and oil families as well as timber, commodity, and real estate magnates, portrayed an economy in the stagflationary doldrums. The only technology fortunes in the top thirty were those of computer makers David Packard and William Hewlett. The prominence of so many families also reflected the lack of new fortunes or new wealth-creating forces beyond inflation. Speculation in the press ran more to the death of shares or equities—the theme of a famous *Business Week* cover—than to the birth of a new wealth generation.

Policy and politics were also in disarray. The supply-side economists advising the Reagan White House, unhappy in 1982 as Congress and the White House negotiated legislation partly rescinding the 1981 tax cuts, gloomed through the year about their advice being ignored, their great fiscal experiment undermined. The Farm Belt was in trouble, and the Great Lakes industrial region was smarting under its new, dismissive nickname: the Rust Belt. Only a short time after the *Forbes* list appeared, U.S. unemployment topped 10 percent. By the end of the year, median family income had slipped back to its 1974–75 lows.

As in the early twenties, however, the darkness soon brought a dawn. Although this volume splits the eighties and the nineties into partly separate booms, one can point to them jointly as decades of capital markets generous to new enterprise. Supply-side author George Gilder, among the few conservative thinkers to foresee the fruits, preached endless assurance that microprocessor, laser, and microbiology companies—small, entrepre-

CHART 2.11 **The Petroleum Club of the United States: The Thirty Richest Families and Individuals of 1982**

DuPont Family (chemicals, inheritance)	$10 billion
Hunt Family (oil, inheritance)	6.6 billion
Rockefeller Family (oil, inheritance)	3.3 billion
Daniel Ludwig (shipping)	2.0 billion
Cullen Family (oil, inheritance)	2.0 billion
Bass Family (oil, inheritance)	2.0 billion
Mellon-Scaife Families (oil, inheritance)	1.6 billion
Gordon Getty (oil, inheritance)	1.4 billion
The Phipps Family (steel, inheritance)	1.2 billion
S. I. and Donald Newhouse (media)	1.2 billion
Philip Anschutz (oil)	1.0 billion
Forrest Mars (food)	1.0 billion
David Packard (computers)	1.0 billion
Marvin Davis (oil)	1.0 billion
Pritzker Family (real estate)	1.0 billion
Hearst Family (media)	1.0 billion
Cargill-MacMillan Family (grain)	1.0 billion
Cox Family (media)	1.0 billion
Annenberg Family (media)	1.0 billion
Bechtel Family (construction)	950 million
Koch Family (oil)	800 million
Harry Helmsley (real estate)	750 million
Sam Walton (retailing)	700 million
William Hewlett (computers)	650 million
Weyerhaeuser Family (timber)	650 million
William Caruth (real estate)	600 million
Cyril Wagner (oil)	550 million
Jack Brown (oil)	550 million
Alfred Taubman (real estate)	525 million
E. DeBartolo (real estate)	500 million

Note: The wealth of the duPonts relative to that of other rich families may be skewed by *Forbes'* reach in tabulating an especially extended duPont family. Also, eight billionaires in the oil-rich Bass and Hunt families who would have been among the top thirty as individuals have been only counted within their *family* groupings.

neurial foxes already running circles around the staggering elephants of the Dow-Jones—would justify giving capitalism a new political mandate.

Technology was gathering force in the eighties, dropping hints of greater things to come. Sector firms were among the stock market high-fliers of 1979–82: Tandy, Teledyne, Wang Labs, Prime Computer, Datapoint, Rolm, MCI, and many more. A decade earlier the stock market's "Nifty Fifty" had also had a high-technology vanguard: Polaroid, Xerox, Electronic Data Systems. Breakdowns of manufacturing spending during the 1979–83 slump and turnaround showed high-tech industries alone performing in a steady uptrend.

At the same time, Gilder's technological enthusiasms considerably exceeded those of the White House. Ronald Reagan had been speaking more broadly in saying, "What I want to see above all is that this remains a country where someone can always get rich." He and his treasury secretary, Donald Regan, a former chairman of the giant stockbrokerage firm Merrill Lynch, talked about replicating some of the moods and policies of the 1920s. Their most conspicuous inattention was to the earlier decade's technological underpinnings.

No Henry Ford or Thomas Edison, leading lights of the twenties, stood out in the eighties. Productivity gains were still in their Santa Clara and Palo Alto adolescence. The entrepreneurialism admired and understood by President and Mrs. Reagan was that of their four-decade Southern California acquaintances: movies, real estate, television syndication, publishing, retailing, fashion, and wholesaling. The products that Wall Streeter Regan knew best were financial: stocks, options, and deals. So when high-tech groups like the American Business Conference and the Semiconductor Industry Association looked to Washington for help against foreign business-government collaboration, the president and his advisers were scarcely more attracted to helping high-tech than to pushing a labor-backed "industrial policy" on behalf of embattled Rust Belt industries. Under both Reagan and Bush, conservative governments declined to "pick winners."

Thus, while the Reagan years brought economic growth, especially in 1984–85, technology made no great leap forward, either in stock market capitalization or in productivity, as Chart 3.25 will illustrate. Looking back from the nineties, many Silicon Valley venture capitalists dismissed the eighties as a weak prelude. Most of the nation's economic growth came in the services sector. And too much, critics quipped, was financed by a credit card.

Four engines powered the expansion of the economy that began in 1982. Military spending increased enormously, pouring money into defense contractors and military installations. Corporate investment grew, favored by 1981 tax legislation, putting substantial money into computers but far more into office buildings and construction. The third engine was debt, which ballooned as governments, corporations, and individuals borrowed as rarely before, plowing most of that back into the economy. Fourth, much like the 1920s, financial activities accelerated—from stock market gains and their wealth effect to mergers and leveraged buyouts, dealmaking, and the steady growth of bank and investment sector employment. Expanding debt and the profits of innovative finance, both frequent boom companions, also stimulated luxury consumption.

Beyond applauding markets, the economic ideology of mainstream Republicanism during the twentieth century was to promote wealth in general rather than specific industrial sectors. Not surprisingly the disinflation, deregulation, and tax cuts of the Reagan and Bush administrations favored financial assets, the principal repositories of serious wealth. Between 1982 and 1992 the Dow-Jones Industrial Average trebled in nominal dollars, which meant a doubling even after inflation. Paper entrepreneurs, a term coined by political economist Robert Reich, took an unusual share through merger and leveraged buyout activities. Thanks to stocks, tax changes, real estate, and buyout opportunities, inherited wealth held its place, bolstered by the lack of any major new challenges to the status quo.

The noted economist Charles Kindleberger, in a mid-1990s analysis, capsuled his qualms about the eighties. Much of the money individuals received from the 1981–86 reductions of the top income tax bracket from 70 percent to 28 percent, said Kindleberger, "seems to have been spent on consumption: second and third houses, travel, luxury apparel, cars, jewelry, yachts and the like, rather than being saved and invested. Some savings were held in liquid form to take advantage of 'investment' opportunities in funds for mergers and acquisitions, takeovers, or arbitrage in the securities of companies possibly subject to takeovers; in other words, held liquid for trading in assets rather than being invested in capital equipment for production."

Between 1979 and 1989 the portion of the nation's wealth held by the top 1 percent nearly doubled, skyrocketing from 22 percent to 39 percent, probably the most rapid escalation in U.S. history. Chart 3.14 in the next chapter, uses Congressional Budget Office data to show the extraordinary extent to which the Reagan and Bush administrations of 1981 to 1993 benefited the top 1 percent rather than the rest of the population. Economist Edward Wolff, noting the nineteenth-century distinction between Europe as the continent of hierarchy and the United States as the seat of opportunity, commented that "by the late 1980s, the situation appeared to have completely reversed, with much higher concentration of wealth in the United States than in Europe."

By 1992, twelve years of Republican presidents had brought little new *direction* in wealth save for an end to oil domination. Just three of that year's thirty richest Americans represented technology: Bill Gates and Paul Allen of Microsoft, and Ross Perot. Otherwise, the economic strategy of 1920s replication, of bolstering corporations and expanding financial assets, had been a roaring success. Wealth had ballooned, making the top individual and family fortunes of 1992 two to three times the size of their 1982 counterparts. The gap between the rich and everyone else was yawning to widths unseen since the 1920s and 1930s.

Conservative rhetoric about leaving everything to the marketplace was misleading. Laissez-faire, as we will pursue in chapter 5, had been a myth in the Gilded Age and was again in the eighties. Simply to imprint a new bias on the federal government required a calculated politics—an effective use of Washington, not marketplace, policy levers. This activism was visible across a wide range of issues, from tax legislation and blueprints for conservatizing the judiciary to economic deregulation, labor policy, trade, and the increasing federal role in bailing out shaky banks, savings and loans, corporations, currencies, and Latin American debtors.

From the 1790s forward, effective national regimes in the United States, as we have seen, have almost always *employed* rather than *disestablished* federal power. Jefferson himself sought to build a political and economic power structure around state banks. Madison, his heir, began promoting commerce after the War of 1812. Conservatives of the 1980s, for their part, rarely balked at using authority to promote economic goals, even if many changes required a new role for government. The most important new functions and layers involved the collectivization of financial risk. Liberals, for their part, had built much of their 1932–68 politics around collectivizing the risks of old age and indigence through programs like Social Security, welfare, and Medicare. Conservative government, especially in the eighties, undertook to collectivize a different set of risks, this time the perils to investors of seeking high returns by putting money in precarious financial institutions, currencies, or overseas investments.

No gain in power or prestige exceeded that of the Federal Reserve Board. Much of its expanded responsibility was necessary, first to deal with the complications after currency rates were untied from gold in the early 1970s, and a second time after inflation forced federal deregulation

CHART 2.12 **The Thirty Richest Individuals and Families of 1992**

Walton Family (retailing)	$25.3 billion
Mars Family (food)	9.0 billion
DuPont Family (chemicals, inheritance)	8.6 billion
S. I. and Donald Newhouse (media)	7.0 billion
Bill Gates (software)	6.3 billion
Bass Family (oil, inheritance)	6.2 billion
Mellon-Scaife Family (inheritance)	5.6 billion
Rockefeller Family (oil, inheritance)	5.5 billion
John Kluge (media)	5.5 billion
Warren Buffett (investments)	4.4 billion
Cox Family (media)	4.2 billion
Sumner Redstone (media)	3.5 billion
Pritzker Family (real estate, investments)	3.4 billion
Dorrance Family (food)	3.3 billion
Koch Family (oil)	3.0 billion
Hunt Family (oil)	3.0 billion
Hearst Family (media)	2.9 billion
Ron Perelman (investments)	2.9 billion
Ted Arison (shipping)	2.9 billion
Paul Allen (software)	2.8 billion
Laurence and Preston Tisch (media)	2.8 billion
Rupert Murdoch (media)	2.6 billion
Richard DeVos (marketing)	2.5 billion
Jay Van Amdel (marketing)	2.5 billion
Phipps Family (inheritance)	2.5 billion
Annenberg Family (media)	2.5 billion
Ross Perot (computer services)	2.4 billion
Edgar Bronfman (liquor and investments)	2.4 billion
H. L. Hillman (investments)	2.4 billion
Ted Turner (media)	1.9 billion

Source: "The Forbes 400," *Forbes*, October 1992.

of bank interest rates in 1980. The dollar stakes of money supply and interest rate regulation now soared. At the same time, this elevation of an institution managed by an unelected board of governors and commingling official authority with private banking industry participation became a sectoral Magna Carta of sorts. It empowered the banks and facilitated the disproportionate growth of wealth tied to capital and the financial markets. Nineteenth-century favoritisms akin to those of the First and Second Banks of the United States were creeping back into place.

Strict free-market conservatives were as disapproving of Fed links to banks as left-leaning liberals. In a mid-1980s interview, Milton Friedman criticized the lessening of competition and the dismissal of moral hazard, calling banking "a major sector of the economy in which no enterprise ever fails, no one ever goes broke. The banking industry has been a highly protected, sheltered industry. That's because the banks have been the constituency of the Federal Reserve." The direction of overall U.S. economic growth—warmed and watered by federal favoritism and protection—was beginning to twist toward finance.

James Grant, an irreverent financial publisher, called the process a "socialization of credit risk," and suggested that the "attempted suppression of the corrective phase of the business cycle" was distorting the domestic and global economy. Cycles and failures, he argued, were necessary, even indispensable: "By suppressing crises, the modern financial welfare state has inadvertently promoted speculation."

The most egregious skews, which led the *Economist* of London to observe wryly in 1991 that "socialism" had at last come to America, showed up during the mammoth S&L bailout of 1989–92. This was the rescue by federal deposit insurance, under the auspices of the newly created federal Resolution Trust Corporation (RTC), of several thousand misbehaving savings and loan associations and banks. Their jeopardy or insolvency arose out of permissive, laissez faire-minded federal regulation on one hand, and on the other, the greed of negligent or criminal managements, many with friends in the Democratic Congress or the Republican White House.

On this unfortunate foundation, the S&Ls mixed speculative banking with parvenu flair—Dallas-based Sun Belt Savings and Loan, to pick one, threw a party at which guests were fed lion and antelope meat while the bank's chief executive, "Fast Eddie" McBirney, presided in the garb of Henry VIII. Wholesale insolvencies eventually moved the problem to Washington, into the lap of federal deposit insurance and the hands of the RTC. By 1990 the latter had the largest assets of any corporation in the United States: $210 billion, including everything from shopping malls, junk bonds, and mortgages to a chunk of the Dallas Cowboys, 40 percent of the land in Colorado Springs, and two-thirds of the thrift assets in Arizona.

The rescue was financed by floating hundreds of billions of dollars' worth of U.S. bonds, to be paid for by the public over forty years. Not all of the rescue was necessary. Big depositors were completely paid off in disregard of the $100,000 ceiling of federal depositor insurance, and many of

CHART 2.13 **The Middle Class and the Rich, 1948–1992**

A. The Great Tax-Rate Turnaround, 1948–90: Median Families versus Millionaires or the Top 1 Percent		
	MEDIAN FAMILY'S EFFECTIVE FEDERAL TAX RATE (INCOME AND FICA)*	MILLIONAIRE OR TOP 1% FAMILY'S EFFECTIVE FEDERAL TAX RATE (INCOME AND FICA)†
1948	5.30%	76.9%
1955	9.06	85.5
1960	12.35	85.5
1965	11.55	66.9
1970	16.06	68.6
1975	20.03	
1977		35.5
1980	23.68	31.7
1981	25.09	
1982	24.46	
1983	23.78	
1984	24.25	
1985	24.44	24.9
1986	24.77	
1987	23.21	
1988	24.30	26.9
1989	24.37	26.7
1990	24.63	

*The data in the column originates as follows: the 1948 figure comes from *The Statistical History of the United States, 1976;* the figures for 1955 to 1983 come from Alan Lerman of the U.S. Department of the Treasury Office of Tax Analysis. The calculations after 1983 come from Eugene Steuerle and Jon Bakija, *Right Ways and Wrongs Ways to Reform Social Security* (Washington, D.C.: Urban Institute Press, 1993).

†The figures for 1948 to 1970 represent the effective tax rates for those earning $1 million a year and come from U.S. Treasury Department unpublished data set forth on p. 1112 of *The Statistical History of the United States, 1976.* FICA is not included, but the rates would not even be affected by a percentage point. The rates from 1977 onward are for the top 1 percent of families as computed by the Congressional Budget Office tax simulation model and include all federal taxes. Source: the 1992 Green Book of the House Ways and Means Committee, p. 1510. The effective rate on millionaires would be close to the rate on the top 1 percent.

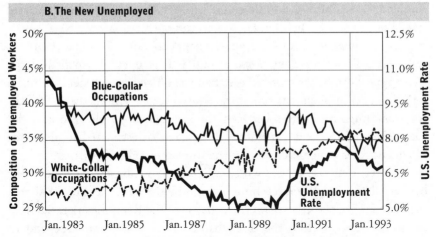

B. The New Unemployed

Source: *New York* magazine, December 6, 1993 (data from Morgan Stanley).

the assets were sold in attractive packages to the politically well connected, sometimes with agreed-upon federal subsidies to sweeten the pie.

The industrial policy debate of the early 1980s had long since ended. But in retrospect, the United States *did* adopt a kind of "industrial policy," one that bowed to the mounting national importance of both private finance and the treasury and Federal Reserve Board. Instead of seeking to restore the older manufacturing industries or build the new technological sector, Washington authorities steadily protected and advanced banking and finance, providing rescues from perils, insolvencies, and crises hitherto regarded as being hazards of the marketplace. The continued eminence of both the treasury and the Federal Reserve furnished a central continuity between the eighties and the nineties and the Republican Bush and Democratic Clinton eras. Finance was in a bipartisan catbird's seat.

Average Americans were losing ground overall from the late seventies through the mid-nineties. Chart 2.13a juxtaposes the painful Reagan era convergence of the effective federal tax rates of median families and millionaires. Chart 2.13b profiles the increasingly white-collar makeup of U.S. unemployment. The very rich, as we saw in the 1992 top-wealth list, were gaining even more than the top 1 percent. By 1992 the political debate had crystallized, with Democratic presidential nominee Bill Clinton charging that "the rich got the gold mine and the middle class got the shaft."

The Republicans were especially unlucky that the downturn of 1990–92 fell disproportionately on white-collar employees and middle-income families, sensitizing them to economic policies' new edges. Business magazines spoke of the first white-collar recession. From New

England to California, middle-class children started qualifying for free school hot lunches. Their fathers sometimes operated lawnmowers, weed-cutters, or snowplows for local governments to work off property tax assessments. The *Philadelphia Inquirer* noted that "unemployment in large cities appears to be far more severe than the official government numbers indicate. . . . Employment statistics released recently from the 1990 census show huge differences between the number of people who consider themselves jobless and the numbers reflected in estimated local unemployment rates issued monthly by the Bureau of Labor Statistics."

The ten-year rise in the white-collar composition of unemployment between 1983 and 1993, reaching fruition by the 1992 election, as shown in Chart 2.13b, helped explain the collapse of the Republican presidential coalition. Support from the disenchanted bulked large in independent Ross Perot's 19 percent backing, reversing President Bush's 53.6 percent majority of 1988 into a losing 37.7 percent and handing Clinton a six-point victory.

6. THE GREAT TECHNOLOGY MANIA AND BUBBLE
OF THE 1990S

Technology was not the only missing face of the 1980s economic boom. The stock market surge, while aggrandizing the rich, also lacked any watershed aspect. The rise of the Dow-Jones Industrial Average from 775 in 1982 to 3200 in the summer of 1992, once adjusted for the 830 percent change in the Consumer Price Index since 1929, was just regaining the earlier heights of the Hoover era. The Clinton years brought the new era advance.

But as chapter 6 will amplify, the United States has a long history of stock market advances and tumbles linked to large and small technology manias. The mid-to-late 1990s produced a whopper. By 2000, when this bubble formed by the Internet and the Nasdaq finally popped into the sharpest and deepest one-year decline of a major U.S. stock average, the mania had enjoyed roughly a three-year run. This was approximately the duration of the earlier grand delusions—the Dutch Tulipmania of 1635–37, the South Sea and Mississippi bubbles of 1719–20, the Great British Railway Mania of 1844–48, the 1925–29 bubble stage of the Roaring Twenties, and the Japanese stock and real estate bubble of 1986–89. All were milestones in national wealth formation and destruction, and several echoed on a global level.

The Internet mania, at least, might not have been able to gather under

Republican auspices. Unlike golf courses and bass boats, the Internet was not culturally Republican. Neither were the sort of people who founded companies named Yahoo, Google, or Ask Jeeves. Indeed, the key swing constituencies in the national GOP coalition, wooed by Nixon and Reagan alike, were the South and the northern ethnic groups variously known as hard hats, Middle Americans, and Reagan Democrats. Part of the Republican appeal had been in its criticism of the vocational seedbeds of the future Internet: the media, education, and the "knowledge" industries. Moreover, beyond a few small-scale research projects, the Reagan and Bush administrations ignored the agendas for improving U.S. competitiveness in the high technology industry urged on them by Silicon Valley and Massachusetts' Route 128 complex. In 1992, John Young, the Republican chairman of Hewlett-Packard and prior chairman of President Reagan's Commission on Competitiveness, bolted to support Democratic nominee Bill Clinton.

The Democrats, by contrast, reproached during the GOP years for proximity to the liberals of academe, education, communications, and entertainment, now found themselves with better links to the nineties' emerging technologies. When Massachusetts governor Michael Dukakis had won the Democratic presidential nomination in 1988, his backers included the Massachusetts High Technology Council and companies like Raytheon and Analog Devices.

Four years later, technology's disillusionment with the GOP found a more successful double expression. In badly splitting the GOP coalition, Perot, the formerly Republican computer services and software billionaire, made particular inroads into high-tech sections from Massachusetts to the Pacific. Bill Clinton, in turn, expanded the usual Democratic backing in the communications and entertainment industries by adding support among technology executives. In 1996, with a record to point to, Clinton consolidated his support in high-tech areas by taking 50 to 70 percent of Perot's previous voters and enlisting the checkbooks of dozens of the Silicon Valley and Los Angeles new rich.

The increasing openness to Democrats extended to Wall Street. Part of it reflected the financial sector's own increasing emphasis on computerization, research, mathematics, mass marketing, and international markets and organizations. Grinds and globalists were replacing Groton and Skull and Bones men. But soon after taking office, Clinton had shifted toward the Wall Street and bond market view under the tutelage of chief economic adviser Robert Rubin, the former Goldman Sachs cochairman. This in turn led to closer collaboration with Federal Reserve chairman Greenspan, who was then reappointed in 1996.

That same year, a reelection-primed Clinton gave his policy of deficit reduction credit for the stock market setting records—a new one every year, with the Dow almost doubling between the summer of 1992 and the end of 1996. The increments in the *Forbes* list, stagnant from 1989 to 1992, grew again. The combined wealth of the *Forbes* 400 jumped from $392 billion in 1994 to $432 in 1995 and $477 billion in 1996. The number of technology fortunes included rose steadily, and in 1996 Bill Gates of Microsoft took first place with $18 billion.

The full speculative context, however, had still to unfold. Never before had a Democrat in the White House presided over a great technology mania and bubble. America's one previous world-class mania and bubble, in the late twenties, had come under the Republicans. Nor did Democrat Grover Cleveland's two terms during the Gilded Age count. Despite the intensity of U.S. railroad speculation, the true, wild-eyed railway mania that resembled the dot.com obsession had occurred between 1844 and 1848—and done so, quite fittingly, in Britain, where railroading had begun.

However, if the Democrats were the more important incubators of the Internet mania, the underpinning *economic* spirit was the market-deifying, tax-cutting, and assets-aggrandizing conservatism given its head in the eighties. This part of the framework was more Republican.

Besides the influence of Federal Reserve chairman Greenspan and treasury secretary Rubin, Democratic policy was powerfully pulled by the Republican capture of Congress in the anti-Clinton revolt of the 1994 elections. Economic compromise between the White House and Congress itself became conservative. A century earlier, the Darwinian ideology of the Gilded Age preached by an entrenched Republican U.S. Senate had imposed much the same conservative framework on willing Democrat Grover Cleveland. Nor did liberals miss the irony as Clinton posed for the cameras signing measures like welfare reform, spending cuts, and the capital gains tax-rate reduction of 1997. One stalwart regretted that "The President embraced major objectives of big business and finance as his own—promoting globalization, further deregulation, the managerial values of efficiency and continued shredding of the old social contract." The unique dual framework of the fin de siècle Internet and market-oriented finance was now in place.

Much as the 1929 Crash had done for its preceding decade, the stock market implosion of 2000–2001 fixed a spotlight on the late nineties as a kind of financial Dr. Jekyll's laboratory, its facilities to be examined ever after for evidence of what stimulants and elixirs had led to such run-amok excess. As late as 1997 many pundits were still underscoring the decade's relatively weak growth—2.3 percent since the business cycle peak in 1989 compared with 2.7 percent in the eighties cycle, 3.2 percent in the seventies cycle, and 4.4 percent in the sixties cycle. Then, all of a sudden . . . mania and surging growth. Silicon Valley publishers Anthony and Michael Perkins, authors of *The Internet Bubble,* a prescient warning published in 1999, suggested 1997 as the transition year when the understandable regional excitement of Silicon Valley—market capitalizations and venture capital outlays were already mushrooming—turned into the full-fledged national mania so obvious by 1998 and 1999. Chart 2.14 shows the emergence of the bubble.

CHART 2.14 **When the Nasdaq Turned into a Bubble**

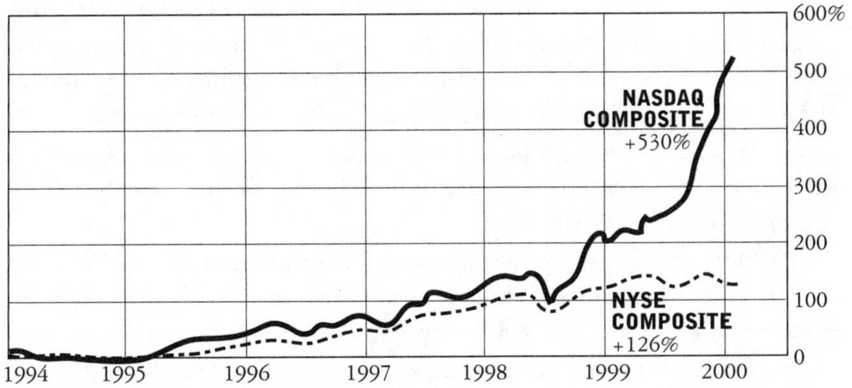

Note: The baseline is January 1995.

The Nasdaq and New York Stock Exchange composite index closely tracked each other until 1995. Some bubbling was apparent in 1996 and 1997, and the major bubble formed in 1998.

Changed Washington economics certainly helped. Clinton's growing emphasis on reining in federal spending and borrowing to free up more private credit at lower rates was popular on Wall Street. And as we will see in chapter 9, the Gilded Age and 1920s booms, like the 1990s bull market, had also profited from federal cheese-paring and debt reduction, common spurs of the expansive *private* credit that speculation requires.

Investors were also reassured by Federal Reserve chairman Greenspan and his record of containing the brief 1987 stock market crash and achieving a soft landing for the U.S. economy in 1994–95. The prestige and puissance of the Fed in the nineties, much like the fledgling presence of the Federal Reserve System in the twenties, provided both psychological and monetary comforts. In this new era of skilled central banking, or so belief went, either speculation could be kept in bounds or the institutions and markets turning shaky would be bailed out. Whatever the chairman's periodic inveighing against irrational exuberance, the public came to believe that he kept liquidity on tap like the average neighborhood barkeep—a tap that was opened wide in 1997 with his three rate cuts to dissolve the Asian currency crises, and once more in late 1999 when the money poured into the system to ease the never-materializing Y2K threat. Instead, it expanded the Nasdaq bubble to its final winter 1999–2000 diameter.

The sense of technology making a vaulting leap also fed investment momentum. The analyses by Austrian economist Joseph Schumpeter that speculative mania usually take shape around important technological breakthroughs, or new financial techniques, institutions, or instruments, or both together, will be pursued in later pages. For the moment, suffice it to say that the slowly gathering economic impact of technology and the Internet went from a relatively flat line in the eighties into a major acceleration between 1993 and 1996.

The epic dream, the techno-financial siren song, swelled in 1997 and 1998 as theories of a new "long boom" mingled with boasts of a New Era economy able to transcend old limits. Pseudoreligious pronouncements of microcosmic faith and insinuations of technology as divinity jostled with dizzy notions of how the Internet would usher in a postpolitical wired world in which government became redundant.

As ever, capital followed cupidity. Serious observers boggled at how Morgan Stanley Dean Witter's index of 73 Internet companies had collectively lost $1.5 billion in 1998 yet sported a combined market value of $115 billion, a perversity that made the bubblings of 1929 appear cautious. But irrational exuberance didn't matter. The carousel of fools was gathering speed. As we will see in chapter 6, the overinvestment and then collapse and disillusionment in the Great Railway Mania was just as insane. By 1848 the two-year decline in British railway shares was £230 million, equivalent to half the national income, more or less the same ratio of implosion and wastage that U.S. technology shares would manage by 2001.

We should also note some of the other new bubbling beakers and sizzling voltages prominent in the financial laboratory of the 1980s and 1990s—the financial deregulation, innovation, speculation, and advanced mathematical moneymaking formulae sweeping the Western world. Centrist and even leftish politicians joined in the applause. In the United States, stock market gains had propelled the growth of the gross domestic product during the eighties, but Bill Clinton gave the bond and stock markets a new level of attention and public commitment.

Under his aegis, bond markets became leading indicators in 1993, monitored for proof that deficit reduction would bring down interest rates and stimulate business investment. *New York Times* correspondent Thomas Friedman developed a genre of mid-1990s articles on Clinton "stock market diplomacy"—policies calculated to reassure and support the financial markets. Soon the rising stock market itself became a touchstone, by 1996 made into a Clinton reelection poster. Then, as the volume of trades on the New York Stock Exchange tripled between 1993 and 1999, ballooning capital gains tax receipts became still another poster: the unexpected foundation of deficit reduction. As receipts jumped from $25 billion in 1991 to $62 billion in 1996, $79 billion in 1997, $89 billion for 1998, and $102 billion for 1999, the deficit became a surplus, hailed as a "virtuous circle" in economic policy which in turn bolstered stock prices.

Where Herbert Hoover had worried in 1929 about speculative excesses, Clinton vacationed in Bubbleland. Steven Gaines, author of the Hamptons tome *Philistines at the Hedge Rows,* told the *New York Observer* in 1999 that the people of Long Island's ultimate Babylon "want desperately for Clinton to be safe. He is the spirit of the bull market."

The escalating federal economic reliance on capital gains payments from the top 1 or 2 percent of the population was accompanied by some other revealing portraiture. Liberals at Washington's Economic Policy Institute, insisting that the 1990s produced only an average level of business investment (inflated by the "quality adjustments" to computer prices made by the Commerce Department), identified a very different economic spur. What really led the recovery parade, they contended, was soaring consumption—much of it on the part of the top percentiles and much of it unleashed by the $8 trillion in new stock market wealth created between 1993 and 1999. The logic became clearer in 1999, when the *New York Times* began a news story with a stunning new truth: "The gap between rich and poor has grown into an economic chasm so wide that this year the richest 2.7 million Americans, the top 1 percent, will have as many after-tax dollars to spend as the bottom 100 million."

Calling it "Stockmarket Keynesianism" skirted the parallel to the pre-Keynesian twenties. But other economists added confirmation: of all the post–World War II business expansions, the one starting in 1991 had by far and away the weakest average annual inflation-adjusted growth in *wages* (0.2 percent) compared with *stocks* (14.2 percent). Clearly, stock profits drove a larger part of the 1990s expansion than of any other since the Coolidge years.

The centrality of stocks was on more and more economists' lips. The Federal Reserve would have to begin weighing assets prices in setting interest rates, some maintained, so as to prevent bubbles from taking shape. Others countered that the Fed was already quietly doing so. One political pundit wondered whether Washington's growing revenue dependence on top-bracket wealth concentration and high stock prices—the orchards producing the economic fruits of high-end consumer spending and soaring capital gains tax receipts—might not fundamentally warp official policies toward supporting stocks and wealth and maximizing market capitalizations for big corporations.

There were even more profound implications. Long ago, European governments pursued mercantilist policies, centered on exports, in order to accumulate wealth as defined by gold. The U.S. domestic and international policies of the eighties and nineties, slowly expanding their reach and sophistication, nurtured U.S. banks, securities markets, and investors, promoted U.S. corporations and exports, and bailed out most of them when necessary—a combination that can be described, with no great reach, as neo- or financial mercantilism on behalf of U.S. corporations and financial assets. This made it a far cry from the free enterprise of the storied variety.

Such candor was rare in the financial press, but in 1996 an article in *Foreign Policy* entitled "Securities: The New Wealth Machine," explained how "securitization—the issuance of high-quality bonds and stocks—has become the most powerful engine of wealth creation in today's world economy." Whereas societies used to accumulate wealth only slowly, they can now do so quickly and directly, and "the new approach requires that a state find ways to increase the market value of its productive assets." In such a strategy, "an economic policy that aims to achieve growth by wealth creation therefore does not attempt to increase the production of goods and services, except as a secondary objective." Given the subsequent profile of the late 1990s and early 2000s, rarely has so large a Washington cat been let out of such a significant economic bag.

The ultimate expression of wealth or financial mercantilism involved the elimination under Reagan, Bush, and then Clinton of so-called "moral hazard" in U.S. and global finance through bailouts and rescues by one agency after another. The deliverance list kept growing: Under Reagan, major banks, a threatened Latin American default on bond payments (1983), and a stock market flooded with liquidity on the day after its October 19, 1987, crash. The S&L financial oxygen tent of 1989–92 stretched over the whole Bush administration. Under Clinton, resurrections were almost biblical: the collapsing Mexican peso, with its threat to U.S. bondholders (1994), shaky Asian currencies and banks (1997), the arrangement by Greenspan for Wall Street to bail out Long Term Capital Management (1998), and the Federal Reserve's late 1999 Y2K miscalculation.

Chart 2.15 amplifies this distinctive hallmark of late-twentieth-century U.S. world economic leadership. Small wonder that so many upper-bracket Americans felt so comfortable in their speculations.

CHART 2.15 **Financial Bailouts and the End of Moral Hazard, 1980–2000**

YEAR(S)	RESCUE	METHODOLOGY
1982–86	Mexico, Argentina Brazil Debt Crisis	Federal Reserve, U.S. Treasury arrange relief package to avoid domino effects on major U.S. banks.
1984	Continental Illinois Bank	Federal Reserve and Treasury orchestrated U.S. aid, including an FDIC purchase of $4 billion of the bank's troubled loans and extension of deposit insurance to the 85 percent of Continental deposits over the $100,000 insurance ceiling.
Late 1980s	Discount Window Bank bailouts	Federal Reserve gave unpublicized loans to 350 banks that later failed, giving big depositors time to flee.
Oct. 1987	Support operation after stock market crash	Federal Reserve flooded the system with liquidity after the big one-day decline, and some have charged that U.S. authorities secretly manipulated the futures market to prevent further declines.
1989–92	S&L bailout	At an ultimate cost of some $250 billion, Washington sets up Resolution Trust Corporation (RTC) to sell off the assets of

		hundreds of S&Ls bailed out after reckless lending and management practices made them insolvent.
1990–92	Bailouts of Bank of New England and Citibank	Treasury deposited $1.8 billion in Bank of New England to allow big and foreign depositors to exit, and then U.S. government stepped in with a $2.3 billion bailout; in Citi's case, the Federal Reserve cut interest rates relentlessly to allow the major banks—Citi most of all—to rebuild their balance sheets and stock prices.
1994–95	Mexican Peso bailout	U.S. Treasury tapped a little-known departmental resource—the Exchange Stabilization Fund—to help Mexico support the embattled peso and to secure U.S. investors in high-yield Mexican debt *(tesobonos)*.
1997	Asian currency bailout	U.S. government—treasury and Federal Reserve—pushed for $200 billion IMF bailout of East Asian nations with embattled currencies, although many of the East Asian excesses grew around the perception, fed by the Mexican rescue, that the U.S. would use the IMF to bail out foreign lenders.
1998	Long Term Capital Management bailout	Federal Reserve Chairman Greenspan, supported by Treasury Secretary Rubin, orchestrated a private sector bailout of the giant hedge fund, ostensibly to avoid the threat to markets from an unwinding of its huge positions, but also because of LTCM's old-boy network and close involvement with other central banks (Italian, Taiwanese).
1999	Y2K Liquidity Surge	Federal Reserve liquidity created to safeguard banks from any Y2K crisis winds up fueling the final stages of the Nasdaq bubble.

Like the twenties, the stock-market tilted boom of the nineties was badly imbalanced. Median household incomes, adjusted for inflation, declined in 1993 and 1994 and stayed about the same in 1995 and 1996. Of the stock market gains between 1989 and 1997, some 86 percent flowed to the top 10 percent of households. Slightly over 42 percent went to the top 1 percent alone. More painfully, according to the Federal Reserve Board's triennial survey of consumer finances, the net worth of the median U.S. household (including home equity) in constant dollars *declined* from $51,640 to $49,900 between 1989 and 1995 because so many Americans had debts growing faster than their assets. Most had little, if any, stock. The decay of net worth worsened farther down the income ladder; poor households were taking on the most debt.

For those in the economic middle, circumstances brightened somewhat in 1998 and 1999 as the boom crested. People in the bottom fifth of the population made relatively larger gains, aided by high employment and Washington policy boons like the earned income tax credit and an increase in the minimum wage. However, much of the upbeat new data for 1998 and 1999 was overtaken by the 2000–2001 downturn before it could even reach the Government Printing Office.

In the meantime, as the millennium approached, the economic and financial stakes had been doubled and redoubled by the reluctance of top economic policymakers in both parties and on the Federal Reserve Board to accept any cleansing recessions, crashes, bankruptcies, or significant bear markets, another symptom of wealth mercantilism. Each time, whether in 1987, 1989–91, 1994, 1997, or 1998, too much of a threat was seen to banks, bondholders, securities markets, financial markets, or—quietly at the heart of all the other rationales—to assets accumulation itself.

On October 19, 1987, the morning of the great one-day, 508-point stock market crash, the *Wall Street Journal* had run a chart showing the eerie resemblance between the stock market trajectory of the twenties and that of the eighties to date. The Federal Reserve, providing liquidity, had contained the damage. A decade later the chart-drawers were turning out new comparisons: the market ascent of 1990–99 once again matched the flight path of the twenties. One precarious resemblance had been piled on another.

Finally, of course, after reaching the extraordinary level of 5048, up 300 percent from the autumn of 1998, the Nasdaq began its crash dive. But we are getting ahead of ourselves. It is late 1999, technology has become a god, and the millennium is about to be celebrated in the shadow of a truly staggering profile of American wealth.

MILLENNIAL PLUTOGRAPHICS: AMERICAN FORTUNES AND MISFORTUNES AT THE TURN OF THE CENTURY

The extraordinary growth in net worth that began when the market took off in 1982 has produced opulence and ostentation on a scale that previous generations never dreamed possible. . . . It's time to start thinking about The Billionaire Next Door.

—*Forbes Magazine*, 1999

Far from being a New Economy that makes the middle class rich and the working class more comfortable, this bull market, with its overvalued stocks, has led to a new inequality from which the knowledgeable insider definitely benefits the most.

—*The Internet Bubble*, 1999

An average middle-class family's income rose by 9.2%, after inflation, from 1989 to 1998, but they also spent 6.8% more time at work to reap it. Without increased earnings from wives, the average middle-class family's income would have risen only 3.6% over the decade. Middle-class families held (just) 2.8% of the total growth in stock-market holdings between 1989 and 1998, but accounted for 38.8% of the rise in household debt.

—Economic Policy Institute, 2000

Caught up in technology as a people and nation, the United States has greeted the advent of new centuries and the millennium with particular enthusiasm. Americans have always tried to hurry up the future—and nowhere was this more evident than in the decision to celebrate the millennial turning at the beginning of 2000 instead of 2001, as most experts insisted was chronologically correct.

The impact of this calendar change on both technology and wealth was striking. A hundred years before, in a less feverish climate of technology worship and stock market speculation, the new United States celebrated the new century on the correct, lagging schedule at midnight on December 31, 1900. This, in turn, affected that era's technology ardor and stock market bubble. Instead of building toward a climax in 1900, it moved toward its crest in 1901.

And what a crest it was. The press was full of speculation about trains that might go 150 miles an hour and automatic changemakers that would replace sales clerks. That was the year Marconi made the first transatlantic radio transmission, and in May, Americans began flocking to the Pan American Exposition in Buffalo, New York. Lit by a 337-foot electric tower powered by current generated at nearby Niagara Falls, the exposition also featured the forerunner of a fax machine and a simulated trip to the moon. The stock market, caught in this same euphoria, made its own peak that June, reaching price-earnings multiples that according to economist Robert Shiller were unequaled until 1929. Then it started sliding, bottoming out several years later.

In America, then, the fin-de-siècle aspect of national plutographics is no coincidence. Technology and the Nasdaq burst a far, far bigger bubble in 2000–2001 after building toward a peak of stock prices and huge new fortunes on an accelerated calendar. Once again a technological euphoria collapsed, bringing the stock market and wealthy at least partway back to reality and again making the century's end a turning point.

The millennial implosion itself staggered economists. Moody's Investors Service pointed out how much the market value of assets held by U.S. households in the first quarter of 2001 had fallen 5.8 percent from the corresponding period a year earlier. The value of stocks and mutual fund shares held by Americans slid by $8.7 trillion or 31.6 percent, but the plunge in financial wealth was partly offset by a 12 percent increase in real estate values. It was the first such year-over-year decline since the much milder 1.4 percent drop registered in the fourth quarter of 1974.

This being said, the measurements and interpretations of turn of the century American wealth—one person's broad-based boom being another's grotesque, undemocratic imbalance—are best discussed a layer at a time. Parts II and III of this book contain greater detail on its origins, controversiality, and politics. This chapter trains its optic on the glitter and the gap: the whos, whys, and wherefores of U.S. income and assets distribution, plus the shortfalls for the larger number of persons left out at the end of one American century and the uncertainty of another.

As we have seen, the transformation of the 1990s and its carryover into the new century was another economic megashift—a rendezvous of innovation, technology, and finance sufficient to increase the top individual and family fortunes tenfold from $6–$10 billion in 1982 to the $75–$100 billion peaks of 1999–2000. The comparable climb from Commodore Vanderbilt's $15–$20 million of 1861 to the $200–$300 million mountaintops of the late 1890s had taken twice as long. Pretense that the non-wealthy were gaining at any comparable rate was as hollow in the 1990s as it had been in the 1890s.

Once again the great wealth-holdings had soared to an extent beyond the ken of the average citizen. Back in 1790 the fortune of America's supposed first millionaire, Elias Hasket Derby, was roughly four thousand times the assets or annual income (in kind) of the average Massachusetts family. Alongside Derby's, the size of their wealth would have been like a cat crouched at the base of Mount Greylock, Massachusetts' highest peak (3,491 feet). That was a scale the citizenry could deal with.

Not so the biggest U.S. technology fortunes of 2000. These towered like 14,000-foot Rocky Mountain peaks over a median family income that by comparison was ant-sized and almost invisible. Over two centuries, the greater the complexity attained by the U.S. economy—in size, technology, and financial sophistication—the loftier the distance between its uppermost and bottom layers. Defenders of fin de siècle wealth concentration said, in effect, so what? Wealth is as wealth consumes. Poor Americans had video games, Nikes, and affordable fast food their grandparents never dreamed of. Their comparative wealth and incomes, by this logic, were unimportant.

We will revisit this debate, but begin by exploring the condition and distribution of wealth and incomes at the end of the twentieth century. Although this chapter has seven subheadings, they bunch into three interpretive clusters. The first is a two-part portrait of the late nineties—of the rich and then ordinary Americans—as an *inversion* of the 1950s in moral, philosophic, and wealth terms. The second ties together the trio of interests that fed most heartily on the eighties and nineties: finance, high technology, and corporations. The last theme links two subheadings—how ordinary Americans are overworked and overstressed, and how U.S. social indicators have slumped since the 1970s as national prosperity tilted toward finance.

The initial focus of chapter and book alike is unappreciated size: the massiveness of U.S. wealth, both old and new, at the century's opening. Skilled financial and legal management has entrenched what after three, four, or five generations of money is becoming a hereditary aristocracy.

The upthrust of the largest U.S. fortunes principally reflected gargantuan increases in stock market valuations, especially technology holdings. Of the top thirty fortunes of autumn 1999, eight were new money, mostly first-generation, in the computer, software, cellular, and Internet sectors. Eight others fell into the related media and entertainment fields; many were second and third generation. Parenthetically, of the *entire Forbes* 400, 140—a full 35 percent—represented technology in some form. Returning to the top thirty, another seven came from finance (three) or management of inheritances (four), the latter including the multigeneration family fortunes: duPont, Rockefeller, Mellon, and Phipps.

This reversal from the democratic late 1940s and 1950s in both attitudes and income distribution had not happened overnight. We have seen how during the fifties, with the rich still on the defensive, the largest proportion of the decade's income gains went to the three middle fifths or quintiles of the population. By the 1990s, in a turned-around economy in which wealth had become the vogue, the three middle quintiles were falling behind while the top fifth, and especially the top 1 percent, regained its Coolidge-era momentum.

The rise of great riches within a nation has usually been a force for inequality—certainly in the Gilded Age and 1920s, then again in the eighties and nineties. Top-tier America, as we have seen, pulled ever farther ahead of the median U.S. household. The latter kept only a little ahead of inflation during the quarter century after 1973, in large measure because of two breadwinners and longer work hours. Worse, official data overstated the small improvement of middle-class wages and incomes by leaving out critical offsets. With federal taxes as well as inflation allowed for, the average income of the median fifth of families actually declined by 1 percent between 1977 and 1994.

Ordinary families gained amid the late nineties boom, but even in 1999, analysts found that the average real after-tax income of the middle 60 percent of the population was lower than in 1977—an extraordinary contrast with the huge gains of the top 1 percent. Some of the first results from a special section of the U.S. Census of 2000 created a stir by showing median family incomes in New York and California, for example, *declining* 5 to 6 percent between 1990 and 2000. Among the major Western industrial nations, it was the United States, its Revolution 225 years distant, that now had the highest levels of inequality.

Going beyond the 1950s–90s inversion, the second part of this chapter weighs three specific sectors—finance, technology, and large corporations—that concentrated wealth and accelerated economic inequality. Bluntly put, the "financialization" of America and its values, even more pervasive in the 1990s, reached critical mass in the two decades with the deregulation of banks and securities markets and the application of technology—the financial sector bought 30 percent of the computers sold to U.S. business—in bringing even remote nooks and crannies of the economy within the electronic marketplace. Other indicia of the financial triumph included the soaring incomes of the Wall Street community, the emergence of trillion-dollars-a-day global cyber-markets in currency and bonds, and the remodeling of corporations to fit institutional investor demands and calendars.

For technology the nineties brought a golden mutual embrace with capitalism, the confirmation, first communion, and bar mitzvah of both the Internet and the Nasdaq. The Microsofts, Intels, and Ciscos strutted on the heights of stock market valuation. Profit centers from Manhattan to Silicon Valley swayed to Latin American–type wealth disparities. The effects of technological innovation have often been thus, as we shall see in chapter 6. Its late-twentieth-century culpability in the retreat of the older U.S. manufacturing sector recalled the casualties of past economic upheavals. Part of the widening income gap reflected erosion in the fading sectors, part reflected the rewards showered on the developers of the critical new technology.

The large transnational corporations, for their part, achieved record earnings while hiring fewer Americans than ever before—and the two often seemed related. As the five hundred largest U.S. corporations eliminated almost five million U.S. jobs between 1980 and 1999, they tripled their assets and their profits and enlarged their market value eightfold as measured by stock prices. Pillars of this success included growing ratios of profitable overseas investment and earnings, the declining percentage of the total U.S. tax burden paid by corporations, large productivity gains from labor-saving technology, and the ability to confine worker compensation gains to only a small share of the productivity gain.

Communities and workers howled, but government acquiescence in the shutting down of older manufacturing followed in the footsteps of the earlier Dutch and British reorientations toward finance. U.S. manufacturing workers being so exposed, their hourly compensation dropped below that of a dozen European labor forces, while imported goods as a share of GDP jumped from 3 percent in 1970 to almost 15 percent in 1999. Capital rode the transnational trends; labor suffered them.

These portraits of finance, technology, and corporations mostly examine the boom's benefit to wealth. The chapter's last subsection, by contrast, turns to the dark side of the boom—the overlap between stressed and overworked Americans and the shift to financial rather than broadbased prosperity as well as the declines shown by broader social indexes beginning in the 1970s.

In contrast to the financial statements of the *Forbes* 400 and the *Fortune* 500, ordinary families pressed to maintain their purchasing power sent new waves of women into the labor markets. This gave the United States the world's highest ratio of two-income households, with its hidden, de facto tax on time and families. Whereas back in 1960 only 19 percent of married women with children under six had worked, by 1995 fully 64 percent did, exceeding the other industrial nations. Work pressure grew. Back in the 1950s and 1960s, U.S. workers had put in shorter hours than similar employees elsewhere. By 1999, over one decade, the average work year had expanded by 184 hours. The Bureau of Labor Statistics reported that the typical American worked 350 hours more per year than the typical European, the equivalent of nine work weeks.

Wage earners in the United States collectively ended the decade with less pension and health coverage as well as with the Industrial West's least amount of vacation time, shortest maternity leaves, and shortest average notice of termination. Small wonder the United States had one of the world's highest death rates from hypertension. Work-related stress provided a further caveat to household incomes.

" Buffeted by these downcurrents—longer work hours, two-earner households, personal strain, and the increasing cultural and philosophic subordination of median households—the broad U.S. quality of life indexes began to decline in the 1970s. Until the seventies, social health and progress indicators in the United States had climbed upward alongside the gross domestic product. But once having turned, they continued to fall, continuing on a downslope through the eighties and most of the nineties as federal policy remained preoccupied with capital rather than with workers or social conditions. Middle-class Americans increasingly noticed the haste of banks, home builders, airlines, and others to provide high-priced services to the rich and bare bones to everyone else. "

Thus our chapter heading: American fortunes *and* misfortunes at the turn of the century. Now for the amplifications, charts, and details.

1. THE RAW PLUTOGRAPHY OF WEALTH

Just seventeen years after *Forbes* began listing the four hundred wealthiest Americans, the largest individual fortune in the United States had climbed from $2 billion to $85 billion. The best introduction to the stark plutography of the millennium is a simple juxtaposition: the levels of the top individual and family fortunes of the autumn of 1982—the names don't matter—set alongside those of the autumn of 1999. As Chart 3.1 (below) shows, the average increase was more than tenfold, more than five-fold even after inflation. Previous U.S. economic history offers no parallel, not even the Gilded Age peak.

A bit lower down, the four hundred richest Americans between 1982 and 1999 increased their average net worth from $230 million in 1982 to $2.6 billion, also more than tenfold in nominal terms and over 500 per-cent in constant dollars. The entire top 1 percent, over one million fami-lies, gained about 150 percent (nominal) and 75 percent (real). By contrast, the net worth (including home equity) of the middle quintile of the U.S. population, adjusted for inflation, *declined* 10 percent between 1983 and 1995, but then rose in 1998 and 1999, only to slide again in 2000–2001. As we will see, the comparison with the gains for the richest Americans shown in Chart 3.1 could not be more striking.

Besides the sheer size of upper-bracket gains, other changes stood out. Technology billionaires, of whom there were two in 1982, Messrs. Hewlett and Packard, had become fifteen of the top thirty by 1999, counting communications (with its increasing cable television and tech-nology components), telecommunications, software, networking, and computers. Of the ten biggest fortunes, five were now technology-based: Bill Gates, Paul Allen and Steve Ballmer of Microsoft, Michael Dell of Dell Computer, and Gordon Moore of Intel.

The decline of the old families, whose assets appeared to pale by contrast, was deceptive. Dismissals of the inheriting rich have been com-mon in United States, especially during eras of preoccupation with sud-den new magnitudes of wealth. Alexis de Tocqueville, for example, had observed years earlier that "in no country in the world are private fortunes more precarious than in the United States. It is not uncommon for the same man in the course of his life to rise and sink again through all the grades that lead from opulence to poverty." Still, "not uncommon" and "typical" are different concepts. The Rockefellers, duPonts, Mellons, and Phippses, albeit well down in the top thirty of 1999, still increased their holdings pretty much throughout the twentieth century, as Chart 3.2 shows.

CHART 3.1 **The Top Thirty Family and Individual Fortunes: A 1982–99 Comparison**

The Thirty Richest Families and Individuals of 1982 (Amounts Only)	The Thirty Richest Families and Individuals of 1999	
$8.6 billion	Bill Gates (Microsoft)	$85 billion
6.6 billion	Walton Family (Wal-Mart)	80 billion
3.3 billion	Paul Allen (Microsoft)	40 billion
2.0 billion	Warren Buffett (investor)	31 billion
2.0 billion	Steve Ballmer (Microsoft)	23 billion
2.0 billion	Fisher Family (The Gap)	20 billion
1.6 billion	Michael Dell (computers)	20 billion
1.4 billion	Cox Family (media)	19 billion
1.2 billion	Mars Family (candy)	16 billion
1.0 billion	Gordon Moore (Intel)	15 billion
1.0 billion	McCaw Family (cell phones)	13 billion
1.0 billion	duPont Family (inheritance)	13 billion
1.0 billion	The Bass Family (oil)	13 billion
1.0 billion	The Dorrance Family (food)	11 billion
1.0 billion	Johnson Family (Fidelity Inv.)	11 billion
1.0 billion	Philip Anschutz (fiber optics)	11 billion
1.0 billion	John Kluge (media)	11 billion
1.0 billion	The Pritzker Family (real estate)	10 billion
950 million	Mellon Family (inheritance)	10 billion
800 million	Sumner Redstone (media)	9 billion
750 million	Newhouse Family (media)	9 billion
700 million	Koch Family (oil)	8 billion
650 million	Rockefeller Family (inheritance)	8 billion
650 million	Jeff Bezos (internet)	8 billion
600 million	Kirk Kerkorian (entertainment)	7 billion
600 million	Ted Turner (media)	7 billion
550 million	Rupert Murdoch (media)	7 billion
550 million	Charles Schwab (finance)	7 billion
525 million	Phipps Family (inheritance)	7 billion
500 million	Hearst Family (media)	7 billion

Source: *Forbes* 400, 1982, 1999.

CHART 3.2 **The Successful Enlargement of Old Money, 1900–2000**

Estimated Wealth per Family							
	1930s[1]	1957[2]	1968[3]	1982[4]	1992[4]	1999[4]	2000
Rockefeller	$1bil.	$1–2bil.	$1.2–1.8bil.	$3.3bil.	$5.5bil.	$8bil.	$8.5bil.
duPont	$0.4–1bil.	$0.6–1bil.	$300–700mil.	$10bil.	$8.6bil.	$13bil.	$14.6bil.
Mellon	$0.4–1bil.	$1.6–2.8bil.	$1.9–3.6bil.	$1.6bil.	$5.6bil.	$10bil.	$10bil.
Phipps	$90–600mil.	$200–400mil.	NA	$1.2bil.	$2.5bil.	$7bil.	$7bil.

Sources: Lundberg[1], *Forbes* and *Fortune*[2], *Fortune*[3], *Forbes*[4]. The $200–$400 million Phipps estimate in 1957 is for Amy (Phipps) Guest alone.

In his 1937 book, *America's Sixty Families,* Ferdinand Lundberg had estimated the combined wealth of these five dozen in the $9 billion range. A little more than sixty years later, four of the richest—the Rockefellers, duPonts, Mellons, and Phippses—had increased their combined $2–$4 billion of 1937 to roughly $38 billion without owning a dominant piece of any emergent industry. Elaborate trusts, well-staffed family offices, and professional financial management had combined into the U.S. equivalent of the entail and primogeniture that kept landed wealth intact and concentrated in eighteenth and nineteenth-century Britain. "By establishing a family office," said *Forbes,* "you hope to protect heirs yet unborn against economic misfortune long after you are dead. Six generations after Commodore Cornelius Vanderbilt made his fortune, it [the Burden family fortune of a half-billion dollars] continues to grow. By pooling their money and following an aggressive investment strategy, 43 of the descendants of the Commodore's great-great grandson, William A. M. Burden . . . remain individually and collectively wealthy."

Besides family offices, other favored top 1 percent money management vehicles include hedge funds, which generally require an investment of at least $1 million and which, in contrast to mutual funds, are virtually unregulated. Some six thousand were thought to be operating worldwide, with the biggest concentration—over one hundred—in Greenwich, Connecticut, just minutes from piles of wealth (and from the best French restaurants north of Manhattan). One local magazine story quoted Wall Streeters saying that the "intellectual capital" of New York was moving to the Greenwich area, and senior executives at Fidelity investments complained that hedge funds, by luring the hotshot managers, were reducing the quality of money management available to middle-class investors in funds like Fidelity's.

Still another option for wealthy families was to form their own private trust companies. Under the laws of permissive states like South Dakota, Wyoming, and Delaware, these operations can pool small trusts into a common trust fund invested collectively (with little crimping regulation and access to hedge funds). According to one 1998 analysis, families recently forming captive trust companies included the Bells of General Mills, the grain-trading Cargills, the Ziff publishing dynasty, and the Pratt family of Standard Oil. The latter, with a family office serving 250 kin, found that many of the youngest Pratts couldn't access high-quality management and had their money in mutual funds. A captive trust company solved the problem.

Some one hundred fifty to two hundred years earlier, the pre–trust fund slippage of many of the earliest wealthy families—the Hancocks, Derbys, and Van Rensselaers, for example—coming on the heels of the huge upheavals of the Revolution, helped create a framework for the nineteenth century's exaggerated folklore of shirtsleeves to shirtsleeves in three generations. The disruptive effects of the Civil War on the South also added some examples. But many claims have verged on the absurd. One chronicler of the 1990s recounted that "when 120 of his [Commodore Vanderbilt's] descendants met at Vanderbilt University for the first family reunion in 1973, there was not one millionaire among them." Strange, because two generations earlier, twenty-two Vanderbilt multimillionaires had a collective fortune estimated at about $350 million. Perhaps the millionaire Vanderbilts simply thought better of meeting cousins in (relative) need of funds. Perhaps the Vanderbilts should have invited their Burden cousins.

In 2000, *Forbes* magazine, besides noting that 137 of the *Forbes* 400 had inherited their wealth or built their fortune from inheritance, listed forty families each having collective fortunes of between $1.2 billion and $14 billion. Here, too, inheritance or assets transfers would have been important. Of these forty families, the four richest—duPont, Rockefeller, Mellon, and Phipps—put five individuals into the top 400, but only a handful of the other clans did. Combining the lists, it seems reasonable to conclude that about 400 American families, from large clans to just the close family of a top 400 member, had at least $1 billion in the autumn of 2000. Probably another 400–500 families had between $500 million and $1 billion.

Below this, national wealth portraiture blurs down to the decamillionaire level—the 274,600 American individuals or families estimated to have had fortunes of $10 million or more in 1998. As for the U.S. individuals or families with assets of over $100 million but less than $500 million in that year, five thousand was a conservative estimate. Probably another twenty thousand to thirty thousand individuals or families had between $50 million and $100 million.

Another calculus is to build forward from the past. Some five hundred to a thousand families inherited or amassed $25–$50 million or more between the Civil War and the 1920s and survived the 1929 Crash. By 2000 at least half would have had upwards of $100 million. Their various family branches, twigs, and tree-grafts, probably some 15,000 to 25,000 heirs, constituted the mainstays of what was quietly becoming an American hereditary aristocracy. Had the United States had a British-type peerage, dozens in the fourth or fifth generation of descent would have been second earls or third viscounts.

A second newer stratum, favored by the greening of smaller pre-1960 fortunes of $5–$20 million in the hothouse climes of late-twentieth-century bull markets, probably contributed another several thousand extended families and 25,000 to 35,000 heirs. Combined with 50,000 new rich of at least $25 million net worth, these yield at least a rough approximation of America's richest 100,000 families, the millennial top one-tenth of 1 percent identified from time to time as the high-income core of the larger 1 percent measurement.

Tomes of the late 1990s like the *Millionaire Next Door* dwelt upon a different and somewhat misleading face of U.S. wealth: the unchic owner of a chain of small dry cleaners, a Coca-Cola distributorship, or 4 percent of a minor technology IPO. His or her net worth might be $2.6, $4.1 million, or even $7.9 million, but the family taste, residence, and cars were middle-class. True enough, but in a late-1990s United States with 274,000 decamillionaires, including some 5,000 centimillionaires, and 40,000 with at least $25 million, second-rank entrepreneurs with $2, $4, or $8 million could hardly be called rich.

Besides overstating ordinary-family stock ownership, proponents of a misleading democratization of wealth thesis stressed the social mobility themes repeated over and over during the nineteenth and twentieth centuries. Inherited wealth, they insisted, was always being overtaken, eroded, or broken up in the democratic chaos of the American economy. Hard-charging *nouveaux riches* relentlessly displaced the worn-out gentry. De Tocqueville was only one of many foreign travelers who spread this notion, refurbished periodically by the rags-to-riches tales of Horatio Alger in the 1880s and similar parables in the 1920s and 1960s. To be sure, as we will see in chapter 9, speculative bubbles, as well as luring in a suddenly incautious middle class, invariably produce a very visible unmannered coterie of *nouveaux riches*. The lasting democratization, however, has been *de minimus*. A second flawed premise of elite vulnerability—that not even large fortunes can support large blocs of heirs—came from Professor Andrew Hacker in 1997: "With each new generation, a limited supply of silver spoons must be divided among a greater number of heirs."

A limited supply? Not for the Rockefeller, Mellon, duPont, and Phipps fortunes, and similar, if smaller-scale, gains have cushioned many other families. The Burden family office referred to was but one example. The downward portraiture of 200 Richardsons emptying the Vicks Vapo-Rub pot or 300 Weyerhaeusers clear-cutting the ever-generous forest—all set against a backdrop of Boston Cabots, Chicago McCormicks, and Philadelphia Pews dropping off the charts into upper-middle-class privation—must bring bemused smiles at dozens of trust company offices from Maine to La Jolla and Newport Beach. In fact, the family fortunes of the top one-tenth of 1 percent by and large doubled, trebled, or quadrupled between 1982 and 1999. Clans delisted by *Forbes* because of the even bigger gains of new money had for the most part notably increased their figurative supply of silver spoons. Chart 3.3 sets out the escalating average net worths of the top 400 and the rise in the number of decamillionaires and families with *incomes* over $1 million.

Like a proverbial iceberg, the bulk of this family wealth mass sat below the surface of public examination, too small for the *Forbes* and *Fortune* investigators and kept from scrutiny by inaccessable trusts and estates departments of major law firms and private client sections of little-known banks. Back in 1937, a look-see at just sixty families, with another 150 in a supporting tier, might have sufficed for Lundberg to introduce the American rich. A similar ambition for 2000, however, would cover at least ten thousand families without getting below $60–$75 million in assets. Their entrenchment, through the offices of U.S. Trust, Bessemer Trust, Northern Trust, the Trust Company of the West, and so on, was a little-told story of the 1990s. Through Bessemer, originally a private vehicle, the Phipps family enlarged its collective wealth from under $1 billion in 1982 to $7 billion in 1999.

Staid Bessemer, greeting the new millennium with the motto "Enhancing private wealth for generations," claimed in advertisements that its private client investments had annualized returns of 37.93 percent between 1987 and 1999, partly by pursuit of venture capital and buyout opportunities not available to the run-of-the-suburbs millionaire. Taken at its face value, this suggests that the lesser rich families did more than

CHART 3-3 **Wealth at the Gallop, 1982–2000**

	1982/83	1985	1989–90	1995	1996	1997
Mean net worth of *Forbes* 400 ($ millions)	396	516	896	1,090	1,218	1,621
Thousands of U.S. Decamillionaires (Assets over $10 Mil.)	66	NA	65	190	NA	NA
Thousands of Households With Annual Incomes Over $1 Mil.				87	111	142

NA: Not Available

Source: The mean *Forbes* net worth data comes from Broom and Shay, *Discontinuities in the Distribution of Great W* Levy Economics Institute, June 2000. The decamillionaire data comes from Wolff, *Recent Trends in Wealth Ownership,* Institute, April 2000. Several marketers published estimates for 1999 and 2000 that put decamillionaire numbers in the 250,000 number of households with adjusted gross incomes of $1 million or more comes from the Internal Revenue Service.

entrench; dozens must have bumped the half-billion mark. In the nineties, Bessemer undertook tortuous research projects to chart the locations of the U.S. rich, presumably enrolling an additional number. Other families chose the family investment office approach. Few of these were the "millionaire next door," save to persons living in Jupiter Island, Atherton, or Old Westbury.

Chart 3.3, in profiling the ascent of the rich, left out two categories. Billionaires rose from 13 in 1982 to 298 in 2000 and then fell to 260 in 2001. The number of assets millionaires, meanwhile, climbed high enough—four to five million in 1999, perhaps fewer in 2001—and became so upper-middle-class that private bankers have amended the term "millionaire" to fit just those *earning* over $1 million.

Were the ratio of millionaires to be adjusted for the century's huge inflation and a trebled U.S. population, obviously it would be smaller. The movement, however, would still be strikingly upward. For example, back in 1900, that year's approximately 5,000 millionaires represented one for every 18,000 Americans. In 2000, even translating assets back into 1900 dollars, over 200,000 persons would still have crossed that million-dollar assets line. This notably higher ratio, one for every 1500 citizens, reflected the polarization of assets attendant on economic complexity, the opportunities of technology, and a cultural acquiescence in massive inequality.

Of one thing we can be sure: the portion of U.S. personal income going to the top 1 percent of Americans (over one million households) steadily increased during the eighties and nineties. Moreover, within that broad upper-bracket category, the expansion was led by the top one-tenth of 1 percent (100,000 households). Both groups regained their 1929 income shares.

CHART 3.4 **The Expanding Income Share of the American Rich**

	1981	1985	1989	1991	1993	1995	1997
Top One Percent Share of U.S. Income, Including Capital Gains	9.3%	11.3%	12.5%	11.1%	11.8%	12.5%	15.8%

Calculations from Congressional Budget office data by Lawrence Mishel of the Economic Policy Institute. For fuller detail on top-tier income trends, see Appendix B.

In weighing the roughly 40 percent of assets and 12 to 20 percent of U.S. income commanded by the top 1 percent of Americans in 2000, a brief historical recapitulation is in order. Back in the mid-eighteenth century, this same stratum's share of assets in towns like Boston and New York was only 10 to 15 percent, although just before the Revolution the figure climbed toward 20 percent. By the 1820s the share of the top 1 percent in the mercantile cities reached 30 to 35 percent, climbing to 40–50 percent by 1845. Because Appalachia and the lands to the west were less stratified, for the nation as a whole by 1860 the share of wealth in the hands of the top 1 percent has been estimated at 29 percent.

As chapter 2 discussed, the high-water mark of U.S. wealth concentration and inequality occurred during the quarter century before World War I, but precise official markers do not exist. A somewhat informed guess would put the zenith around 1901 or 1902. By this point the heyday of the trusts and great industrial combines had bestowed huge wealth on a small handful while the farm holdings of rural America were still near the beginning of a recovery from their mid-nineties nadir.

The argument against wealth concentration peaking in 1905 or 1906 is that although railroad and industrial stock prices would have ridden the expansion just cresting, by then farm values were rising at least as fast. Nationally the value of farm property, with its broader distribution, still outweighed that of industrial property. Perhaps the top 1 percent of Americans briefly had 50 to 60 percent of all U.S. wealth in 1905 or 1906 (in the big cities alone they certainly did). However, there is no reliable data, and a 45–50 percent national share seems more likely. By 1914, business cyclical ups and downs and the first bite of the new progressive income tax were slowing wealth concentration until the extraordinary 1915–16 European war-related profits surge noted in chapter 2.

Because collection and tabulation of wealth data improved after World War I, Chart 3.5 is a reasonably reliable portrayal of the top 1 percent's subsequent share. By the end of the 1990s that share had returned almost to the post–World War I record set in 1929. This was less than the imprecise Gilded Age highs, but not by much. The late Gilded Age, late twenties, and late nineties mark the peaks.

Wealth's geography, meanwhile, was shifting. New York's hegemony, lopsided in the 1920s and still easily documented in the 1950s, ended in the 1990s as technology and entertainment lifted California into the lead. The movement from East to West cemented in the 1990s. By 2000 the states with the largest number of the 400 richest Americans were

CHART 3.5 **Millennial Wealth Concentration: The Return to 1929**

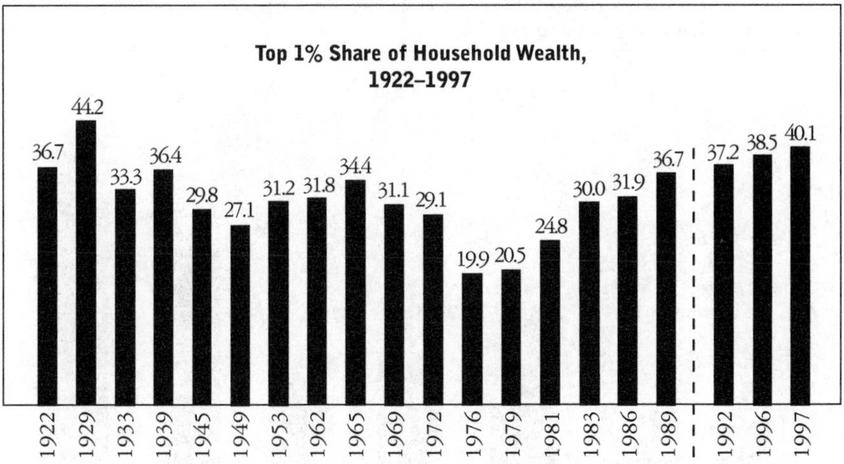

Top 1% Share of Household Wealth, 1922–1997

Year	Value
1922	36.7
1929	44.2
1933	33.3
1939	36.4
1945	29.8
1949	27.1
1953	31.2
1962	31.8
1965	34.4
1969	31.1
1972	29.1
1976	19.9
1979	20.5
1981	24.8
1983	30.0
1986	31.9
1989	36.7
1992	37.2
1996	38.5
1997	40.1

Source: Edward Wolff, *Top Heavy*, 1996, New Series Households data, pp. 78–79 (for years 1922–89) and "Recent Trends in Wealth Ownership," 1998 (for years 1992–97).

California (107), New York (46), Texas (34), Massachusetts (17), and Washington State (15). The technology crash dropped California back to 92 in 2001, but the underlying realignment stuck.

The larger result as the new millennium unfolded was a United States long shed of its revolutionary outlook that had become home to greater economic inequality than any other major Western nation, including erstwhile aristocratic France and Britain. Chart 3.6 shows the international comparisons prepared with data from the World Bank. Other data shows inequality in the U.S. exceeding that of any of the nations in the Organization of Economic Cooperation and Development (OECD).

As British colonies, several of the future United States had once courted an aristocracy. Seventeenth-century South Carolina created baronies of forty-eight thousand acres to be held by hereditary landgraves, while Virginia governor William Berkeley, during the English Civil War years, had induced some younger sons of the English gentry to emigrate. Titles being rare, leading Virginia families employed numerals: William Byrd III, Philip Ludwell III, and so forth. In the 1930s, wealth chronicler Lundberg updated the numerical ostentation—John Jacob Astor VII, George F. Baker III, August Belmont IV, Pierre duPont III, Marshall Field V, John D. Rockefeller IV, Cornelius Vanderbilt V, and so on—of names he said would fill any American *Almanach de Gotha.*

CHART 3.6 **The United States Leads in Inequality**

How Many Dollars Those in the Richest Fifth Earn for Every Dollar Earned by the Poorest Fifth

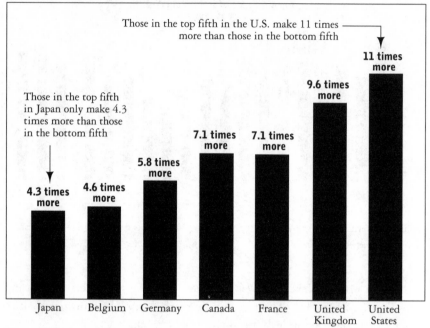

Source: Data from the World Bank as prepared by Public Agenda (1996).

Any U.S. analogy to foreign aristocracy would have seemed foolish in the 1880s despite that era's wealth. Amid the New Deal, the rich were targets. The early-twenty-first-century United States, however, not just the world's richest major nation, had also become the West's citadel of inherited wealth. Aristocracy was a cultural and economic fact, if not a statutory one.

The postmillennial crash of the technology-heavy Nasdaq, so devastating to the new Internet, software, and telecom fortunes, had much less effect on old money tied up in trusts and family holdings and widely diversified among investment sectors. But for technology, a debacle worse than 1973–74 and approaching 1929–32 grew out of springtime carnage, followed by autumn's bruising, winter's further chill, and the second spring consummation of the worst-ever Nasdaq decline—some two-thirds from March 2000 to April 2001. Company valuations and fortunes alike imploded. From a peak of 5048 in March, Nasdaq's average fell to 1650 a year later, the largest one-year decline for a major stock market average in U.S. history.

Between September 1929 and July 1932, as we have seen, the value of all the securities traded on the New York Stock Exchange fell from $85 billion to just $15.6 billion. Between March 2000 and April 2001 the value of the securities traded on the Nasdaq dropped from $7 trillion to near $4 trillion. The value of all U.S. stocks collapsed from roughly $15 trillion early in 2000 to just over $10 trillion in April 2001. In late September 2001, the *Economist* of London, pondering the blow to the U.S. economy posed by that month's terrorist attack, noted that the 14.3 percent fall in the Dow-Jones Industrial Average in the five days to September 21st was its biggest one-week loss since 1933, and went on to add that "America's broadest share index has fallen by almost 40% from its 2000 peak. That sounds modest compared with the 85% plunge in the three years after 1929, but the stockmarket plays a bigger role in the economy today. The loss of equity wealth over the past 18 months is equal to 75% of GDP, a bigger proportionate loss than after the 1929 crash."

Leading technology firms like Microsoft, Cisco, and Intel figured prominently in the valuation implosion, and Chart 3.7 shows the decline of the leading technology fortunes between 1999 and 2001. Hundreds of other stocks lost 90 to 100 percent of peak market capitalization values ranging as high as two or four billion. The crash dives of much-traded securities like Ariba, Broadcom, Nortel, JDS Uniphase, and PMC Sierra paralleled the plummets of the twenties. Back in 1999, *Forbes* magazine had divided that year's four hundred richest Americans into tech-bubbling categories like Microsoft Money, Cable Guys, Hard Drivers, Kings of the Code, Webmasters, and Bandwidth Boys. By 2000, however, seventeen of the 1999 tech listees, from Red Hat to Compuware, had lost their places; and in 2001 the triage got even bloodier with forty-four casualties, major owners of companies from Aether, Ariba, Avanex, and Blue Martini to Uunet Technologies, Vitria, and Yahoo.

Clever analysts had charted how, in the giddy months of the boom, retail sales patterns had spiked and sagged with the upward zigs and downward zags of the technology index. By 2001, not surprisingly, a negative wealth effect was visible on the downside, contracting what had earlier expanded.

The wealth list exits and realignments were staggering, a sequence of convulsions, collapses, and vivid exits unprecedented in the previous half century of increasingly serious *cinema plutostatistique*. Ross Perot had become the first person to suffer a billion-dollar one-day paper loss decades earlier when his EDS stock plummeted in 1969, but Bill Gates lost $12

CHART 3.7 **The Decline of the Leading Technology Fortunes, 1999–2001 (in $ billions)**

FORTUNEHOLDER	1999	2000	2001
Bill Gates (Microsoft)	85	63	54
Paul Allen (Microsoft)	40	36	28
Steve Ballmer (Microsoft)	23	17	15
Michael Dell (computers)	20	16	9.8
Gordon Moore (Intel)	15	26	5.3
McCaw Family (cell phones)	13	14.5	5.7
Philip Anschutz (fiber optics)	11	18	9.6
Jeff Bezos (Internet)	8	4.7	1.2

billion in one day when the value of his Microsoft stock toppled on Black Friday in April 2000. The net worth of the combined four hundred richest Americans, as measured by *Forbes,* dropped from $1.2 trillion in 2000 to 950 billion a year later, a decline of 21 percent, the largest year-to-year drop in the magazine's chronicling.

While technology and communications had taken a huge hit, other categories had come on strong by 2001. Oil was one, along with retailing and another grouping that could best be described as food, beverages, and consumer products like cosmetics and greeting cards. Not only did this favor the old economy, but it favored family holdings, not a few of older money like the Wrigleys of chewing gum fame. Chart 3.8, instead of mixing the individual and family fortunes of 2001 as portrayed by *Forbes,* shows the top thirty of each in two separate columns. The Walton family had pulled far ahead of Bill Gates, and the older money once again outweighed the first-generation crowd, although not by nearly as much as in the 1930s.

CHART 3.8 **The Changing American Wealth Landscape of 2001**

The Thirty Richest Families		The Thirty Richest Invididuals	
NAME	WEALTH ($ BILLIONS)	NAME	WEALTH ($ BILLIONS)
Walton (Wal-Mart)	91.8	Gates (Microsoft)	54
Mars (candy)	27.0	Buffett (investments)	33
Cox (media)	22.6	Allen (Microsoft)	28
Johnson (mutual funds)	13.7	Ellison (Oracle)	21
DuPont (inheritance)	12.0*	Kluge (media)	10.6
Bass (oil)	11.2	Redstone (media)	10.1

Pritzker (real estate)	11.0	Ballmer (Microsoft)	10.0
Newhouse (media)	10.0	Dell (computers)	9.8
Mellon (inheritance)	8.5*	Anschutz (fiber optics)	9.6
Koch (oil)	7.7	Murdoch (media)	7.5
Rockefeller (inheritance)	7.3*	Ergen (media)	7.1
Fisher (retailing)	7.3	Soros (finance)	6.9
Bechtel (construction)	7.0	Turner (media)	6.2
Dorrance (food)	6.8	Broad (real estate)	5.5
Bronfman (liquor)	6.8	Moore (Intel)	5.3
Lauder (cosmetics)	6.5	Kerkorian (investments)	5.3
Hearst (media)	6.4	Lerner (banking)	4.9
Phipps (inheritance)	6.0*	Knight (footwear)	4.9
McCaw (cell phones)	5.7	Arison (entertainment)	4.6
Simplot (potatoes)	5.0	Goodnight (software)	4.6
Tisch (diversified)	4.7	Omidyar (Internet)	4.6
Johnson (floor wax)	4.5	Davis (oil)	4.5
Getty (oil)	4.3	Annenberg (media)	4.0
Smith (manufacturing)	4.3*	Bloomberg (media)	4.0
Lupton (beverages)	4.0	Bren (real estate)	4.0
Hunt (oil)	4.0**	Schwab (finance)	4.0
Scripps (media)	3.8	Warner (toys)	4.0
Hall (greeting cards)	3.8	Geffen (media)	3.9
Wrigley (chewing gum)	3.5**	Greenberg (insurance)	3.9
Chandler (media)	3.3	Perot (investments)	3.9

Source: *Forbes* 400 Richest Americans for 2001; *Forbes* 400 Richest Americans for 2000.

* Forbes family wealth calculations for 2000, reduced by 15 percent to allow for stockmarket decline; **personal calculation based on *Forbes* listing for one individual plus allowance for other family members not listed.

2. ORDINARY AMERICANS: LEFT BEHIND

By 2000, the increasing distance between the median family and America's top 1 percent elite—a million households now enjoying an average income of almost $1 million and an average net worth of $8–$10 million—had been a point of national discussion for over a decade. Rare was the newspaper or magazine reader who had not seen some extremely graphic presentation of the economic polarization of America, two of which are adapted in Chart 3.9a and 3.9b.

In 1988, eleven years before becoming U.S. Treasury secretary,

CHART 3.9a **The Economic Polarization of America, 1967–1997**

Average Inflation-Adjusted Annual After-Tax Income of Poor, Middle-Class and Rich Households

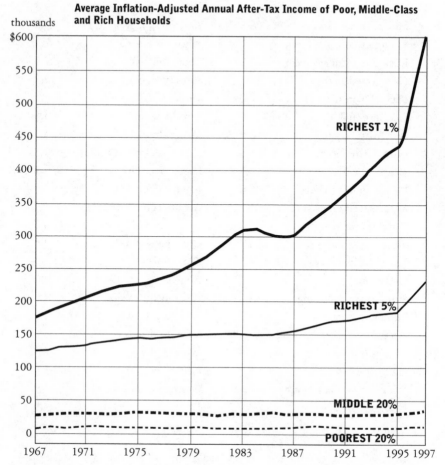

Source: Doug Henwood, *The Nation*, March 29, 1999, modified to include the top 1% and to include 1997 figures based on Table 1-1C of the Congressional Budget Office study "Effective Federal Tax Rates," October, 2001, p. 128.

Lawrence Summers, the Democratic economist, had charged that "the U.S. today is in the midst of a quiet depression in living standards. The median income of the typical American family is right now the same as it was in 1969." The Republicans, infuriated by such language during the Reagan-Bush years, returned fire in 1994 by employing updated data to stir middle-class frustrations against the Clinton administration. Two years later, GOP presidential nominee Robert Dole accused Clinton of "reigning over the first recovery since World War Two to leave American workers behind." The Democrats, predictably, claimed that everyone was gaining, not only the rich.

CHART 3.9b **A Growing Income Disparity**

The top one-fifth of American households with the highest incomes now earns half of all the income in the United States. Their share has risen since 1977, while the share of the one-fifth with the lowest incomes has fallen. Figures have been adjusted for inflation.

Household Groups	Share of All Income		Average After-Tax Income (Estimated)		Change
	1977	1999	1977	1999	
One-fifth with lowest income	5.7%	5.2%	$10,000	$8,800	12.0%
Next lowest one-fifth	11.5%	9.7%	$22,100	$20,000	9.5%
Middle one-fifth	16.4%	14.7%	$32,400	$31,400	3.1%
Next highest one-fifth	22.8%	21.3%	$42,600	$45,100	5.9%
One-fifth with highest income	44.2%	50.4%	$74,000	$102,300	38.3%
1 Percent with highest income	7.3%	12.9%	$234,700	$515,600	119.7%

Figures do not add to 100 due to rounding.

Source: *Congressional Budget Office Data Analyzed by Center and Policy Priorities.* Reprinted in the *New York Times,* September 5, 1999.

A few business and financial publications were candid in describing the underlying trends. "The revolution in office technology has broken the back of the market for secretaries and clerks," said *Barron's.* "Robotics has destroyed whole categories of factory work. These seismic shifts have meant that millions of people who might otherwise have gotten the blue- and pink-collar positions in these sectors must now chase what jobs remain. And an increased labor supply generally brings a lower wage."

"What's happening," explained *Business Week,* "is that a new class of left-behind workers is being created, encompassing a large portion of the workforce. They have jobs, sometimes with high salaries, but while their New Economy counterparts' earnings soar, the left-behinds are struggling to post small real gains in income. That's why, despite the overall prosperity, many households keep taking on more debt. . . ."

By the decade's end, thanks to earned income tax credits and a long overdue minimum wage increase, the second Clinton term produced a slightly less skewed income distribution than the previous GOP regimes. The gap between top and bottom, still widening from 1993 to 1996, was mitigated by gains for the two bottom fifths during the peak of the business cycle from 1997 to 1999. The widening crevice between the top 1 percent and the beleaguered middle, however, was untouched.

Official (Census Bureau) U.S. household and national income data did have weaknesses, and criticism clustered around two poles. Conservatives, eager to mute criticism with statistical portraits able to show low incomes rising alongside those of the rich, argued that the official definition should include public assistance dollars: welfare, food stamps, and the like. Progressives, for their part, countered that the annual cash intake of the rich was understated by how the official definition of income excluded capital gains. Didn't the Internal Revenue Service, by contrast, *include* them in each year's taxable income?

Both had a point. The effect of federal public assistance dollars on the overall U.S. income pattern was considerable—$50–100 billion a year (mostly to the lower fifth). The omission of capital gains, 40 to 50 percent of which (by value) accrued to the top 1 percent, was a much more concentrated cornucopia. Their growth was elephantine, as Chart 3.10 shows. Enlarged by such inclusions, the top 1 percent income figures several pages back taken from Congressional Budget Office data considerably exceeded Census-derived calculations. Between 1980 and 1998, tax-reportable capital gains jumped from $75 billion to $446 billion, vaulting so high that their 1995–98 revenues did much to overcome the federal budget deficit.

CHART 3.10 **The Explosion of Capital Gains Income, 1980–2000**

(In billions of current dollars)								
	1980	1985	1990	1995	1996	1998	1999	2000
Net capital gains minus net capital losses on IRS returns	74.6	170.6	124.2	170.4	237.1	446.1	507.0	
Capital gains tax receipts	16.9	30.8	34.8	44	62	84	98	118(E)

Source: IRS, CBO for end-of-decade capital gains revenue and estimates. A wide range of estimates has been in circulation.

Practical, as opposed to legal, definitions of income should also include other factors: taxes, debt, and, for the poor, perhaps even the ups and downs of government human resources outlays. Disposable income figures, for example, usually have been variations on after-tax income, taxes being the centerpiece of what an individual or a household cannot spend. Unfortunately, the Reagan administration discontinued official publication of these figures in 1981, so it is necessary to use nonofficial series. However, while the effects of the major federal taxes—income and FICA (Social Security and Medicare)—can be assembled, excise taxes (principally on tobacco and alcohol) are often left out, and because state and local exactments vary from jurisdiction to jurisdiction, the latter are almost always omitted. The disposable income series in Chart 3.11, for example, includes federal excise taxes but leaves out state taxes. Because of the acknowledged regressivity of state and local levies, their omission

CHART 3.11 **The Disposable Income Squeeze, 1948–1994**

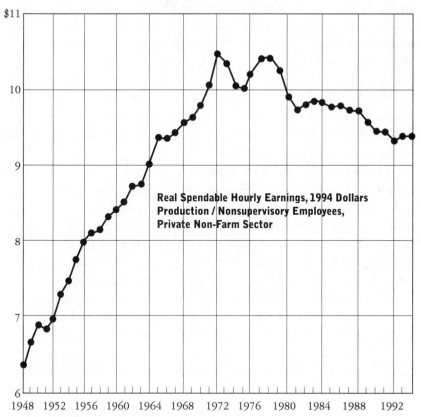

Real Spendable Hourly Earnings, 1994 Dollars
Production / Nonsupervisory Employees,
Private Non-Farm Sector

has typically overstated the disposable income of the lower-income groups.

Looking at both the before-tax and after-tax incomes of each income level leaves no doubt about the real-world blessings of 1981–86 tax reform. Indeed, the after-tax numbers were more revealing than pretax figures. Between 1977 and 1999, according to one analysis of Congressional Budget Office data, the after-tax income of the top 1 percent, adjusted for inflation, grew faster (115 percent) than their before-tax income (up 96 percent). Tax changes, notably those of the 1980s, played a role in their disposable income growth.

By contrast, the inflation-adjusted, after-tax income flowing to the middle 60 percent of households in 1999 was slightly below the same figure for 1977. This upholds the profile in Chart 3.11 that shows the ordinary worker losing ground in disposable income. The bottom fifth of households, most injured, experienced a 9 percent loss. Thus, the downturn in the after-tax income of nonsupervisory workers reflected not just global forces but the dramatic shift in effective tax rates (income and FICA combined) begun in the seventies and crystallized during the several tax overhauls of 1981–90. While the bite of the income tax was reduced, enlarging top-bracket after-tax income, the jump in the regressive FICA tax eroded after-tax income in the lower brackets. The upper middle class, far from benefiting in millionaire style, was actually put in a higher tax bracket than millionaires, as chapter 5 will illustrate.

As a politico-fiscal upheaval, the eighties tax redistribution must rank with the Hamiltonian blueprint of 1789–92 (assumption and funding, internal taxes), the Civil War upheaval (the North-South realignment of power and capital), and the New Deal (tax and fiscal changes that undercut the pre-1929 financial elite and elevated the middle class). Like the first two examples, this one favored the national economic elite, which has been the more frequent beneficiary. Parenthetically, much the same effect was visible next door in Canada, where the Conservative government of Prime Minister Brian Mulroney imposed a regressive and much-disliked "general sales tax" in the early 1990s. In 1997, *Statistics Canada* reported that that year's median family income, after taxes and adjusted for inflation, was 6.7 percent lower than the average household income ten years earlier.

As for the disparate state and local taxes omitted in federal computations, one measurement between 1985 and 1990 found the weight of their increases greatest for the bottom fifth (1.2 percentage points) and least at the top (0.5 percentage points). These changes raised the state and local tax burden to 13.8 percent of income for the average family in the bottom fifth, 10 percent for the average family in the middle fifth, and 7.6 percent for the average family in the top 1 percent. In the late nineties, however, budget surpluses allowed a substantial group of states to give income tax relief to the poorest quarter of the population, reducing although not eliminating the disparities visible early in the decade.

During the 1980s federal budget pressures and changing political priorities shrank "human resources spending" (excluding Social Security and Medicare) from 28 percent of all federal outlays to just 22 percent, which had a considerable effect on the de facto, if not de jure, income of the poor. These effects eased in the late 1990s because of new federal spending in addition to the earned income tax credit.

The worsening dimension of the nineties, especially for low-income and unskilled workers, involved dwindling employee benefits and health coverage. Long perceived as a great equalizer, between 1982 and 1996 they increasingly became part of the architecture of polarization. They were awarded freely—lavishly—in the top echelons and stinted near the bottom, where increasing ratios of employees were temporary or transient and found themselves partially or fully excluded. According to the Bureau of Labor Statistics, only 26 percent of employees in the bottom 10 percent had health insurance provided by their companies, down from 49 percent in 1982. For mid-range employees, 84 percent had coverage in 1996, down from 90 percent in 1982.

Outlays for child care, transportation, health care, and food needed so that a second spouse could work notably reduced two-earner household income in fact, although not by government definition. Every dollar of additional wages, of course, *did* count as income, especially exaggerating disposable incomes among middle-bracket working couples. Because official statistics paid no attention, attempts to deal with these inadequacies were necessarily private. One was the New Misery Index created in 1991 by economist Edward Hyman of the ISI Group, which blended four categories—taxes, medical payments, Social Security levies, and interest payments. From taking 24 percent of U.S. personal income in 1960, these four had climbed to taking 40 percent by 1990. During the 1990s, they reached 42 to 43 percent. For example, between 1983 and 1998, the proportion of individuals whose employers paid the full costs of health coverage fell from 45 to 27 percent, increasing individual burdens.

Debt, the mother of interest payment burdens, tends to grow fastest in booms. This is when financial institutions, advertisers, and salespeople push credit, and when households trying to keep up with the Joneses accept it, escalating debt levels to new highs. For many people in the low and

CHART 3.12 **The Stages of Rising Consumer Debt in the 20th Century**

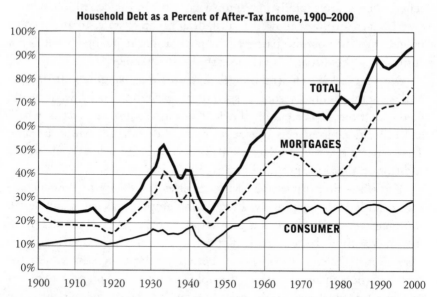

Household Debt as a Percent of After-Tax Income, 1900–2000

Source: Indicators (by Doug Herwood), *The Nation*, July 19, 1999, p. 12 (based on historical statistics and Federal Reserve flow of funds accounts).

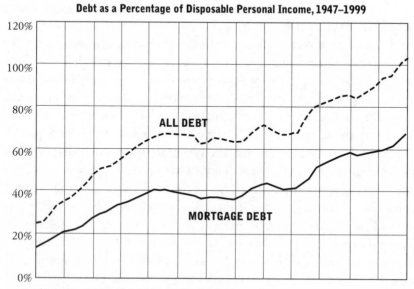

Debt as a Percentage of Disposable Personal Income, 1947–1999

Source: *The State of Working America, 2000–2001*, p. 277 (based on authors' analyses of Federal Reserve Board data).

middle-income groups, debt grew faster than assets, just the reverse of the trend in upper-income persons borrowing to make investments. Between 1989 and 1998, while families in the middle fifth enjoyed just 2.8 percent of the rise in stock market holdings, they accounted for 38.8 percent of the uptick in household debt. Chart 3.12 illustrates the rising debt burden.

As the chart shows, the great surge of the 1980s and 1990s took household debts up to a level that was roughly 90 percent of annual personal income (after tax). The distribution of that increased debt worsened its pressures. Between 1992 and the decade's end, mortgage debts grew some 60 percent faster than income, so that homeowners' equity in their houses in 2000 declined to the lowest level in a half century—54 percent, down from 70 percent in 1982 and 60 percent in 1991. Credit card debt outpaced income growth by an even wider margin, with balances between 1989 and 1995 climbing 398 percent in the lowest-income fifth of the population, 108 percent in the next lowest and much less among the more prosperous. Net worths in the bottom 60 percent of the population fell between 1989 and 1995 because the buildup in debt exceeded any growth in assets. In the bottom fifth, cancerous debt growth turned its net worth negative.

From the eighties through 1997, according to Professor Edward Wolff, a respected wealth watcher, this debt-triggered stagnation (or worse) of net worth had several negative effects. First, for median-income families, it meant that few shared in the financial boom—even the minority with personal stock holdings. At the same time, so few blacks and Hispanics participated in the financial arena that, even while nonwhite *incomes* went up, the *wealth* gap between whites and nonwhites widened. Chart 3.13 illustrates both problems.

CHART 3.13 **Median Net Worth Stagnation and the Racial Wealth Gap, 1983–1997**

A. Stagnating Median Household Net Worth (in 1995 dollars)					
	1983	1989	1992	1995	1997
Median Net Worth	$51,100	$54,600	$46,600	$45,600	$49,900
Median Financial Wealth	$11,000	$13,000	$10,900	$10,000	$11,700

Source: Edward Wolff, "Recent Trends in Wealth Ownership," 1998, based on data from successive versions of the triennial Federal Reserve Survey of Consumer Finances. The 1997 estimates were projected by Wolff on the basis of change in assets prices between 1995 and 1997.

B. Median Household Net Worth and Financial Worth by Race, 1995

NET WORTH			FINANCIAL WEALTH		
		$61,000			
$7,400	$5,000				$18,100
			$200	$0	
Black	Hispanic	White	Black	Hispanic	White

Source: Edward Wolff, "Recent Trends in Wealth Ownership," 1998.

The net worth data grew and improved somewhat for minorities and median-income families in the Federal Reserve Board's 1998 Survey of Consumer Finances. But in 2000 and 2001, the stock market crash and economic downturn wiped away much of the brief gain.

Similarly, with respect to income, for those in the middle or near the bottom, the offsets ignored in official figures—tax burdens, benefits and health coverage declines, the interest payments needed to service record indebtedness—mocked their officially published incomes, albeit these were rising from 1997 to 2000. By contrast, for members of the top 1 percent, the major official omission in calculation was *benign*: a definition of income that helpfully understated their cash flow by excluding capital gains.

By the end of the 1990s, as Chart 3.14 illustrates, the upward redistribution of income within the population was striking. Whereas for four decades after World War II, the combined three middle quintiles had more of U.S. personal income than the top quintile, its resurgence marked the eighties and by the late 1990s the upper fifth recaptured the lead. The resubordination of the middle class reflected a powerful confluence of market economics, shifting ideology, and a boom weighted toward capital and finance, not wage earners. What no one knew was how much it might reverse.

CHART 3.14 **The Great Compression — and The Great Inversion**

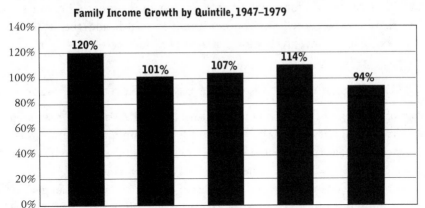

Family Income Growth by Quintile, 1947–1979

Source: Economic Policy Institute.

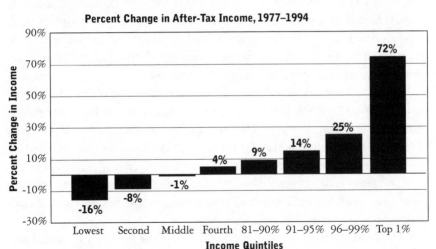

Percent Change in After-Tax Income, 1977–1994

Source: Congressional Budget Office.

The sharp contrast in the two halves of the chart attests to the upheaval in biases and policies. The basic framework of the 1947–79 evenness with a middle- and lower-income edge came from the New Deal and Great Compression, especially in the forties and fifties. As for the flagrant 1977–1994 favoritism to those at the top, the chart may overimply its Republican genesis in that Democrats held the White House in 1977–80 and 1993–94. However, beginning in 1978, the tenor of economic policy was increasingly conservative, and the "Great Inversion" partly reflects that.

At this point it makes sense to leave the contrast between the wealthy and other Americans for a look at three increasingly potent economic sectors that have keynoted the concentration of wealth and the widening rich-poor gap: finance, technology, and corporations.

3. THE FINANCIALIZATION OF THE UNITED STATES, 1980–2000

Part of what gave finance new momentum in the 1990s, as we have seen, was its congeniality with other expansive forces: computer programming, advanced mathematics, global deregulation of capital movement, global trading, and a Noah's Ark of new speculative instruments.

If the underlying avaricious imperative of finance hadn't changed, its size, sophistication, and influence certainly had. From thirteen British colonies lacking an autonomous currency or a stock exchange, the United States had taken less than 175 years to become the cockpit of world finance. And in the last quarter of the twentieth century, through deregulation, floating currencies, state-of-the-art computers, and electronic search-and-profit programs, finance was transformed from yesteryear's somewhat patient capital to organized impatience.

Of the trillion dollars of currency trades made daily in the global markets of the late 1990s, only 2 to 3 percent had to do with actual trade in goods or services. Early in that decade the annual trades of CS First Boston, a major bond house, by themselves exceeded the size of the U.S. GDP. "Since the mid-1980s," noted the *Financial Times,* "securities houses and investment banks have increasingly pursued the shorter-term rewards of trading profits more rigorously than they have the longer-term rewards from client relationship banking."

The United States, in the forefront, became the first leading world economic power to see its "real economy," the usual workaday one represented by GDP, surpassed fortyfold in nominal dollar volume by the "financial economy," with its electronic trades. Partially real and partially unreal, with the day-to-day balance simply guesswork, the profits of these digital dances seeped into the real economy, and by the mid-1990s the financial sector— finance, insurance, and real estate—for the first time moved ahead of the manufacturing sector in U.S. national income and GDP measurements.

Historically, an Icarus tendency, an overambitious national wingspread for finance, has been a problem, not an asset, for leading world powers. During the finance-dominated eras of Dutch and British global economic primacy, the "real economy" retreated and wealth concentration grew. The United States, too, has seen a broad correlation between the principal expansions of banking, financial innovation, and the stock markets—the 1790s, the 1830s and 1840s, the Gilded Age, the 1920s, the 1960s, and the 1980s and 1990s—and the most notable enlargements of wealth and economic inequality.

All of these six expansions, each one a building block of slow financialization, logically favored the people who owned the banks, investment firms, and the bulk of the stocks.

The 1790s saw the creation of the Bank of the United States, followed by the first speculative fevers over federal bonds and bank stock in New York and Philadelphia as well as the expansion of maritime commerce.

The 1830s and 1840s, remembered for the triumph of market capitalism, also marked the beginnings of serious volume on the New York Stock Exchange, the first U.S. stock boom (in railroad securities), the creation of stock exchanges in a half dozen U.S. cities, the introduction of the telegraph, and the sharp increase in the number of banks in the United States from 208 in 1815 to 901 in 1840 and 1,562 in 1860.

The Gilded Age, for its part, rose with the Civil War–created national banking system and a massive currency expansion, fed heartily on wartime speculation in stocks and gold prices as well as the advent of the ticker-tape, and then gorged on the great postwar buffet of watered railroad securities. Its waning years witnessed the pro-creditor zenith of the gold standard, the advent of telephones on the New York exchange (1878), the first million-share day (1886), and the securities bonanza from the turn-of-the-century organization of the great industrial combines by J. P. Morgan and the so-called Money Trust.

The 1920s roared with the surging volume of the stock market and its attendant mergers, holding companies, investment trusts, call loans, boiler rooms, bucket shops, and stock pools. New York banks led in the distribution of speculative Latin American debt securities, the forerunners of junk bonds.

The mergermanic, go-go years of the 1960s were powered by easy money, the rise of mutual funds, and the advent of "conglomerate" corporations. Almost by nature, bull markets, financial innovation, and speculative heydays have furthered wealth concentration—at least until a major bubble pops—by disproportionately rewarding the investor class, notably the top 1 percent of the population.

The 1980s and 1990s, it must be said, pushed earlier innovation and speculation into the shade. Had the U.S. financial sector, as part of its less-than-onerous regulatory compliance, been required to pass in review before Washington's Federal Reserve Building in late 1999 or early 2000, the spectacle would have been Roman. The hugely expanded securities business would have marched under ten thousand flags, one for each of the multitude of exchanges, investment firms, mutual funds, hedge funds,

CHART 3.15 **The Financialization of America, 1980–2000**

Over the three decades from 1970 to 2000, the United States slowly substituted the securities sector for the banking sector as the linchpin of the overall financial sector. This, more than anything else, allowed finance to make a megaleap in economic importance similar to that of manufacturing in the U.S. of the late nineteenth century—a process this book describes as financialization. Here are the obvious measurements of the change that took place in the 1980s and 1990s.

	1970	1980	1985	1990	1995	1996	1997	1998	1999	2000
Average daily volume of shares traded on New York Stock Exchange	12m	45m	109m	157m	346m	412m	527m	674m	809m	1.041b
All mutual fund assets		$48b	$135b	$495b	$1.1tr	$2.6tr	$3.1tr	$4.5tr	$5.5tr	$6.8tr	$7.8tr
Value of U.S. stocks (Wilshire Total Market Index) in trillions (as of December 31)	NA	$1.4tr	NA	$3.1tr	$6.1tr	$7.2tr	$9.2tr	$11.3tr	$13.8tr	$12.2tr
Percentage of Americans owning stocks individually or through mutual funds and pension plans	10	NA	12	28	41				48	

Note: In 1988, bank deposits were three times as large as mutual fund assets, but as stock indexes rose, the assets of mutual funds (including money market funds) overtook bank deposits in 1995 and bank assets in 1998. More stock purchases by mutual funds pushed stock indexes up, which then attracted even more money into funds, which pushed the stock indexes further. The two-decade interaction between the five trends is obvious. With demand increasing the value of stocks well beyond the growth of corporate profits, the net effect was a massive, expansionary recapitalization of America around the securities sector—both those who ran it, shorthanded as Wall Street, and the 10 percent of Americans who owned 85 percent of the stock (and especially the top 1 percent who owned 42 percent). The result was a huge increase in the role of the securities industry, its influence, and its techniques.

Source: New York Stock Exchange, Investment Company Institute, Wilshire Associates.

and the like. Then the ever-more-concentrated banking industry, under the shimmering silver and gold emblems of famous credit cards (heraldic symbols of authorization to charge 15 percent interest when depositors' accounts earned 3 percent). Further cheers, had shareowners been on hand, would have come from the pass-by of U.S. corporations, most ever more tributary to finance, each under a ticker-symbol banner, with precedence by stock market capitalization. Less than a century after Harriman, Carnegie, and Ford, the broad financial sector now dwarfed railroads, steel, and automobiles.

Although the new century brought some reversal, Chart 3.15 details the incredible 1982–2000 momentum of rocketing mutual fund assets, annual trading volume up tenfold on the New York Stock Exchange and more on the Nasdaq, burgeoning hedge funds, the Himalayan upthrust of the market capitalization of listed U.S. corporations, and the worth in cumulating trillions of all U.S. stocks, which peaked near $15 trillion in early 2000. Trying to extend comparisons to decades before the eighties is pointless because even next to those of 1981 and 1982, the volumes and levels for 1999 or 2000 were ten, twelve, or fifteen times higher, a fair explanation of the parallel jump in the great fortunes.

By way of context, the unprecedented billions pouring into stocks and mutual funds, besides dwarfing any previous totals, marked a historic shift—the overtaking by the hitherto speculative securities sector of more sedate and long-dominant banking institutions in total assets managed. In reaching $2.6 trillion in November 1995, mutual fund assets for the first time exceeded deposits in the U.S. commercial banking system. By 2000 their margin had widened to several hundred billion dollars, in retrospect a leading indicator of vulnerability. At the same time, sweeping deregulation was further blurring the lines between the banking and investment sectors. To flesh out the transformation, the percentage of U.S. individual wealth committed to stocks jumped during the 1990s from 12 percent to 26 percent. Individual *financial* wealth, a narrower category, went from being 20 percent in stocks to 50 percent. More than ever before, wealth itself was being securitized—traded on exchanges rather than lived in, minted, worn as jewelry, or ridden in leagues and miles.

As we have seen this did not give Mr. and Ms. J. Q. Public the new and weighty stake so often attributed to them. Indeed, the nation's collective private wealth had become so heavily concentrated in the hands of the top 1 percent (40 percent)—or at best, the top 10 percent—that expansion of these holdings accounted for most of the increase. Talk about the shareholdings of the "average American" greatly misled because that average was pulled up by the huge top-tier ownership.

"For all the talk of mutual funds and 401 (k)s for the masses, the stock market has remained the privilege of a relatively elite group," observed the *Wall Street Journal* in 1999. "Nearly 90% of all shares were held by the wealthiest 10% of households. The bottom line: that top 10% held 73.2% of the country's net worth in 1997, up from 68.2% in 1983. Stock options have pushed the ratio of executive pay to factory worker pay to 419 to 1 in 1998, from 42 to 1 in 1980." As already noted, middle-class families—specifically the middle quintile—had accounted for just 2.8 percent of the total growth in stock market holdings between 1989 and 1998.

Given the stagnation of median family net worth, talk about the United States becoming a Republic of Shareholders hardly applied to a family whose miniscule stock "portfolio" or pension fund interest had grown by $2,600 or even $6,100 while its debt load for college, health insurance, day care, and credit cards had jumped by $12,000. Still less did it apply to the majority of Americans who didn't own any stocks, even indirectly through pension funds or mutual funds.

The bias to the affluent that permeated the 1982–2000 financial revolution paralleled the financial sector's own profile and orientation. Strategic light years beyond its midcentury era of bond coupons and passbook savings, U.S. finance was becoming a network of computers, mathematical equations, and skilled, highly-compensated professionals reaching from global command centers to humdrum peripheries like ATM and credit card machines. High-earners required expensive equipment and research to provide expensive services to others, the preferred among whom also had high earnings or wealth. Tenements, trailer parks, and even lower-middle-class suburbs were not a relevant constituency.

Computerization mothered a new dimension of financialization: almost any business pursuit could be comprehended and kneaded into a stock offering; almost any loan category could be securitized and sold in bulk like mortgages; and almost any definable economic trajectory could be sold piecemeal as a future earnings stream. Corporate goals and mental processes also financialized. Corporate chief financial officers, rare before the eighties, now often had to supervise risk managers, options traders, and currency arbitrageurs. Senior executives fixated on types of stock options and compensation packages. More retiring high-level politicians gave up law firms for financial groups and investment banks. Former presidents became traveling investment bank promoters: George H. W. Bush for the Carlyle Group in China and Saudi Arabia.

Corporate diversification showed kindred traits. American Can Company turned itself into a financial services firm named Primerica, which several incarnations later merged with Citicorp. General Electric sold off its consumer appliance division, preferring to emphasize the huge financial profits of its General Electric Credit Corporation. By 2000, GE Credit Banks could be seen as far afield as the Czech Republic. Ford Motor Company came to depend on high profits from a subsidiary, Ford Credit Corporation, heavily involved in global hedging. Making things became unfashionable, as the *Wall Street Journal* reported in a November 1999 front-page article. Enron, the Houston-based energy firm, financialized it-

CHART 3.16 **The Evolution of Risk Management Techniques**

	1992 —— Differential swaps
Portfolio swaps —— **91**	
Equity index swaps —— **90**	
Three-month Euro-DM futures ⌐ **89**	⌐ Ecu interest-rate futures
Captions ⌐	└ Futures on interest-rate swaps
88	
Average options ⌐ **87**	⌐ Bond futures and options
Commodity swaps ⌐	└ Compound options
86	
Eurodollar options ⌐ **85**	—— Futures on US dollar &
Swaptions ⌐	municipal-bond indices
84	
Interest-rate caps and floors —— **83**	⌐ Options on T-note futures
	├ Options on currency futures
82	└ Options on equity-index futures
Equity-index futures ⌐ **81**	⌐ T-note futures
Options on T-bond futures ┤	├ Eurodollar futures
Options on Bank CD futures ┘ **80**	└ Interest-rate swaps
Currency swaps ┘ **79**	
78	└ Over-the-counter currency options
T-bond futures —— **77**	
76	
T-bill futures —— **75**	—— Futures on mortgage-backed bonds
74	
73	—— Equity futures
Foreign currency futures —— **1972**	

Source: Chase Manhattan.

self into a company that traded energy like stock options, becoming "more akin to Goldman Sachs than to Consolidated Edison"—at least until its 2001 collapse became a symbol of nineties excess. By 2002, Enron had joined the Nasdaq bubble as a metaphor for financial excess.

Just as rocket science took men into space in the 1950s, another exotic mathematics—in this case, capital asset pricing, options theory, and price and volatility models—took finance into a hitherto unexplored galaxy of profits. Turning money into equations and digital impulses—shifting to the megabyte standard, in economic journalist Joel Kurtzman's term—allowed it to jump time and geography, creating the transnational netherworld in which traders in New York, London, and Paris warred electronically over Belgian francs and Thai bahts and global arbitrage fed on shoals of cyberdecimals.

Two developments of the 1970–80 period—the delinking of currencies from gold and the deregulation of banking and interest rates—unleashed speculative and arbitrage opportunity just as breakthroughs in computers and microchips produced almost unimaginable trading capacities and tools. The innovations in financial derivatives between 1972 and 1979 had been significant, as Chart 3.16 shows, but the 1980s gave financialization its spectacular new digital toolbox.

Finance, in a nutshell, was the first major U.S. economic sector to benefit from a computer-driven productivity revolution, which equipped it to gain its national preeminence. Just how much is not always realized. Back in chapter 1 we saw how U.S. manufacturing passed agriculture in value-added during the 1880s. The finance, insurance, and real estate sector overtook manufacturing during the 1990s, moving ahead in the national income and GDP charts in 1995. By the first years of the next decade, it had taken a clear lead in actual profits. Back in 1960, parenthetically, manufacturing profits had been four times as big, and in 1980, twice as big. The overtaking by finance, enabled by a dozen federal rescues and preferences, began in the eighties and consummated in the nineties.

Because finance boomed before the other sectors in the 1980s, the decade's early wealth movements registered most prominently in the Wall Street compensation charts. Chart 3.17 listing the ten top Wall Street moneymakers for 1986, 1991, and 1996, illustrates their stunning take-off after the bear-market finale of mid-1982. By 1986 the best-rewarded were making six to eight times as much as the stalwarts of 1982. By 1996 their compensation had quadrupled again.

As the Dow-Jones doubled from 3500 at the end of 1992 to 7000 in 1997, and then stretched on its toes to peak at 11,722 in January 2000,

CHART 3.17 **Soaring Wall Street Earnings in the Great Bull Market**

(The top ten from 1985–1996 *Financial World* Annual Survey of Wall Street's Top 100 Earners)

CALENDAR YEAR, 1986	
Michel David-Weill, Lazard Frères	$125 mil.
George Soros, Soros Funds	$90–100 mil.
Richard Dennis, C&D Commodities	$80 mil.
Michael Milken, Drexel Burnham	up to $80 mil.
J. M. Davis, D. H. Blair	$60–65 mil.
Jerome Kohlberg, KKR	$50 mil.
George Roberts, KKR	$50 mil.
Henry Kravis, KKR	$50 mil.
Ray Chambers, Wesray	$45–50 mil.
William Simon, Wesray	$45–50 mil.

CALENDAR YEAR, 1991	
George Soros, Soros Funds	$117 mil.
Julian Robertson, Tiger Mgt.	$65 mil.
Paul Tudor Jones, Tudor Mgt.	$60 mil.
Bruce Kovner, Caxton Corp.	$60 mil.
Michael Steinhardt, Steinhardt Partners	$55 mil.
John Henry, J.W. Henry Co.	$50 mil.
Henry Kravis, KKR	$45 mil.
George Roberts, KKR	$45 mil.
Michael Ovitz, Ovitz Agency	$40 mil.
Robert MacDonnell, KKR	$35 mil.

CALENDAR YEAR, 1996	
George Soros, Soros Funds	$800 mil.
Julian Robertson, Tiger Mgt.	$300 mil.
Henry Kravis, KKR	$265 mil.
George Roberts, KKR	$265 mil.
Stanley Druckenmiller, Soros Funds	$200 mil.
Robert MacDonnell, KKR	$200 mil.
Sam Fox, Harbour Group	$190 mil.
Thomas Lee, Thomas H. Lee Co.	$130 mil.
Nick Roditi, Soros Funds	$125 mil.
Jerome Kohlberg, KKR	$112 mil.

Source: *Financial World.*

volume on the New York Stock Exchange hit 100 million shares a day in 1982, crossed the billion-share mark in 1997, and passed 2 billion in early 2001. An even more explosive increase by the Nasdaq put its volume ahead in the mid-1990s. In a startling portrait of how the real economy was affected, the New York State comptroller in mid-1998 issued a report

CHART 3.18 **The Technology Spurt of the Late 1990s and the Making of the Stock Market Bubble**

Note: The Hambricht and Quist Technology Index (now Chase Hambricht and Quist) included leading technology stocks from both The New York Stock Exchange and the Nasdaq. Sharp growth began during the Clinton years.

contending that a surprising 56 percent of New York City's total income growth since 1992 had been provided by securities firms, more than double the rate of the previous decade.

Speculative eras have often birthed new exchanges or trading arenas—the London Stock Exchange in the "bubble" years of 1690–1720, the New York Stock Exchange in 1790 amid Hamilton's controversy, the spurt of U.S. and British regional exchanges in the railroad boom of the 1830s and 1840s, the emergence of the U.S. commodity markets in the Gilded Age, and the importance of Manhattan's informal Curb Exchange in the reckless 1920s. The upsurge of the 1980s and 1990s elevated the Nasdaq, and its 1999 crescendo brought online an estimated five to seven million day traders, who for a while accounted for 25–33 percent of all retail trading. Chart 3.18 recapitulates the mid-1990s rise of technology stocks after the relative placidity of the 1980s. Ultimately, the Nasdaq itself suffered an eighteen-month peak-to-trough decline of over 70 percent in the 2000–2001 crash.

The Nasdaq implosion, obviously, was a comeuppance for both technology and finance, which have fed each other in most of the great Anglo-American boom-bust cycles. However, before turning to technology, we must note the escalating role of corporations—ambition's preeminent route to a stock exchange listing—in the late-twentieth-century realignment of American wealth.

4. THE ROLE OF CORPORATIONS AND THE ECONOMIC REALIGNMENT OF THE UNITED STATES

Over two centuries corporations have become the underpinning of U.S. finance and wealth, also serving as an important, although rarely central, touchstone of American political controversy. As we will revisit in greater detail, four periods stood out in which corporations incited Americans through overconcentration of power and wealth, neglect of national interests, or outright corruption: the 1830s, when Andrew Jackson attacked specially chartered corporations and their ties to wealth; the Gilded Age, with its furor over monopolies and trusts; the New Deal years; and the late 1960s and 1970s, when corporations came under renewed attack for giantism and inattention to consumers, racial discrimination, and the environment. Between 1968 and 1977, the percentage of Americans crediting businesses with pursuing a fair balance between profits and the public interest dropped from 70 percent to 15 percent.

Ralph Nader in his mid-1970s book *Taming the Giant Corporation* had summed up part of the complaint: "In 1955, it was estimated that 44.5% of those working in manufacturing worked for the top 500 companies; by 1970 it was 72%. Between 1948 and 1968, the largest 200 U.S. industrial firms increased their share of all industrial assets by 25%. Today (1976), these 200 control two-thirds of all industrial production." However, as the late seventies mired in stagflation, the electorate wearied of consumerist, environmental, and anticorporate reformers. Corporate power rebounded toward what, by the 1980s and 1990s, became a new Gilded Age, with geographical and financial expansions to match.

The biggest U.S. firms grew enormously in size, assets, profits, and international investment and orientation. But as a striking concomitant, they came to employ fewer and fewer U.S. workers, pay an ever lower share of the total federal tax burden, shift more of their production overseas, and consider themselves as international rather than U.S. companies. For all that corporation after corporation put the U.S. flag in its TV commercials after September 11, 2001, the fashion in the 1990s was otherwise. Boeing CEO Philip Condit said he wanted to get rid of his company's American image, and Dow Chemical CEO Carl Gerstacker yearned for Dow to have its headquarters on an island owned by no nation. Few were the major multinational firms that did not favor international governmental arrangements like the World Trade Organization, an expanded International Monetary Fund, and the controversial Multinational Investment Agreement.

In 1961 the 100 largest U.S. industrial firms had 22 percent of the total assets of all nonfinancial corporations. By 1977 that had climbed to 24 percent, by 1995 to 30 percent, and by 2000 to about one third. Their assets more than doubled between 1980 and 1990, and then again in the nineties. The biggest were country-sized; in 1998, Exxon-Mobil was as big as the Saudi Arabian economy, and General Electric a match for Colombia. General Motors, having passed Hong Kong, was closing in on Turkey. Bill Gates and Paul Allen, the cofounders of Microsoft, together with Berkshire-Hathaway's Warren Buffett, had a 1999 net worth larger than the combined GDP of the 41 poorest nations and their 550 million people.

As corporate profits doubled in the nineties, with stock option–laden corporate executives working to squeeze out every last dollar, one result was the general downgrading of home-nation employee and community interests. Peter Capelli, professor at the Wharton School of Business, put it bluntly: "Today, a CEO would be embarrassed to admit he sacrificed profits to protect employees or a community."

One well-rewarded strategy was to cut costs by moving operations and production to foreign locales with cheaper labor and less regulation. Overall profits of the largest 500 corporations climbed as the percentage derived from overseas facilities rose from 3.4 percent in 1950 to 6.1 percent in 1960, 9.9 percent in 1970, 19.3 percent in 1980, and 19.7 percent in 1990. Wages dropped from 66 percent of corporate revenues in 1992 to 62 percent in 2000.

In another variation, one of the most effective corporate players, California-based Seagate Technologies, the leading computer disk-drive maker, with 80 percent of its workforce in Asia, all but avoided U.S. taxes by a strategy it was obliged to disclose in its 1999 annual report. With the help of tax holiday deals in Singapore, Malaysia, Thailand and China, its subsidiaries in these nations had amassed $1.6 billion in undistributed earnings as of that year. If that money had been earned in the U.S.—or if it were to be repatriated—the U.S. tax bill would be $565 million. Seagate's stock price, however, reflected the overseas assets.

Corporations also drove down their tax liability by securing federal and state rate changes and specific tax breaks in the U.S. Internal Revenue Code as well as by skill in rearranging income, production and transactions between their facilities in different nations. As a result, whereas back in 1950 and 1970 corporations had paid 26.5 percent and 17 percent of the total U.S. federal tax burden, that dropped to 12.5 percent in 1982 and 9.1 percent in 1990. In virtually any year, a considerable number of corporations weren't paying any federal income tax. Chart 3.19 shows the shift of the federal tax burden away from corporations and onto the backs of low- and middle-income individuals through FICA taxes.

Besides some $60 billion a year in industry-specific tax breaks, the Cato Foundation, a Washington think tank hostile to corporate largesse, has estimated that at the turn of the century the federal government provided business some $75 billion a year in subsidies. Ralph Estes, professor of business administration at the American University, has hypothesized the broader annual social costs of corporations—everything from corruption to injury, stress, lobbying, pollution, waste, and overcharges—that go unreimbursed and are thus borne by communities, employees, customers, and society at some $2.6 trillion in 1994. This seems too sensationally drawn, but Estes' larger point is that *nobody knows:* in the present system, corporations are largely unaccountable.

CHART 3.19 **The Declining Share of the Federal Tax Burden Paid by Corporations and the Rising Share Represented by Payroll Taxes**

	CORPORATE TAXES AS A % OF TOTAL RECEIPTS	PAYROLL TAXES (SOCIAL SECURITY AND MEDICARE)
1950	26.5%	6.9%
1960	23.2	11.8
1970	17.0	18.2
1980	12.5	24.5
1990	9.1	35.5
2000	10.2	31.1

Source: Federal Receipts and Outlays, Economic Report of the President 2001; 2001 OASDI Trustees Report; Operations of the HI Trust Fund, 1970–2010.

Reduction at the state level was just as rewarding. In 1957 corporations had provided 45 percent of local property tax revenues in the states,
but by 1987 their share had plummeted to some 16 percent. By the
nineties, more and more companies demanded economic concessions from
cities or states either to relocate to the new locality or remain in place after
threatening to leave. Tax abatements became widespread strategies.

The convergence of tough tactics and multiple opportunities produced
striking profits growth. Chart 3.20a displays the striking increase in profits for all U.S. corporations between 1980 to 2000, with the big surge
coming in the nineties. The principal beneficiaries were the shareholders
as opposed to the lower-ranking stakeholders—employees and communities. And inasmuch as Americans with top 1 percent incomes owned
about 45 percent of the privately-held stock, we can now identify another
major pillar of their prosperity: the steady aggrandizement of corporations
and rising profits as shown in Chart 3.20a. Chart b shows the percentage
of corporate-related assets in the hands of that small top 1 percent elite.

CHART 3.20 **Top 1% Shareholders and the Ballooning of Corporate Profits,
1980–2000**

A. The Rising Profits of U.S. Corporations, 1980–2000

	1980	1985	1990	1995	1996	1997	1998	1999	2000
Profits (billions)	209	255	389	650	729	801	775	814	930(E)

B. The Ownership of Corporate and Business Assets (1992)

	BUSINESS ASSETS	STOCKS	BONDS	TRUSTS
The top 1%	61.6%	49.6%	62.4%	52.9%
The next 9%	29.5	36.7	28.9	35.1
Everyone else	8.9	13.6	8.7	12.0

Source: Profits—*Economic Report of the President, 2001,* Table B-91; ownership—Wolff, *Top
Heavy,* p. 64.

In this milieu, pressure to maximize profits and stock prices by cutting
employees came from both top management and from Wall Street and institutional investors, the latter responding to yardsticks that a single layoff
added $60,000 to future-year bottom-line earnings. If layoffs and downsiz-
ings continued even as profits set records in the nineties, that was because the
layoffs and downsizings—13,000 employees here, 9.2 percent of the workforce there—were often the *reason* for the profits. In 1996 the Democratic
Policy Committee of the U.S. House of Representatives responding to that

year's brief furor over corporate compensation, produced a report including details of the one-day personal stock gains of the chief executives of Mobil Oil, AT&T, and Chase and Chemical banks following layoff announcements.

A year earlier, the American Management Association had published a

CHART 3.21 **Declining Employment at the Top 500 U.S. Industrial Corporations**

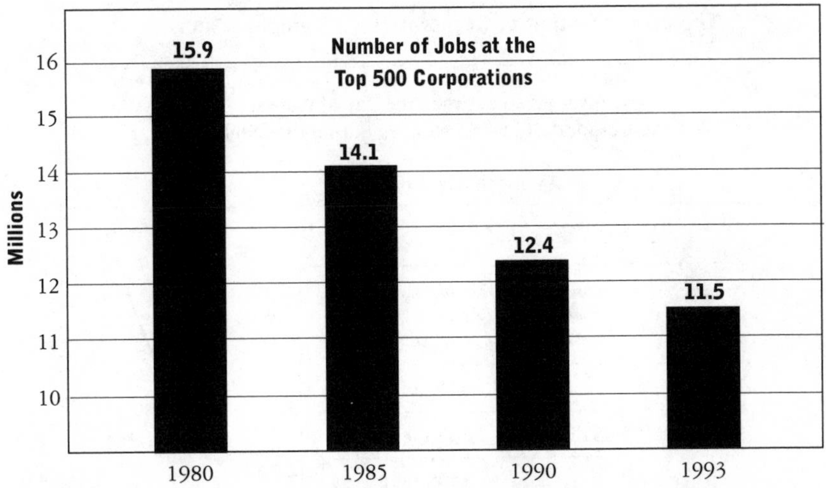

Source: U.S. Department of Commerce, Bureau of the Census, *U.S. Statistical Abstract,* various years, and "The Fortune 500. The largest U.S. Industrial Corporations," *Fortune*, April 18, 1994.

book by Alan Downs, a senior corporate consultant, entitled *Corporate Executions: The Ugly Truth about Layoffs: How Corporate Greed Is Shattering Lives, Companies, and Communities.* His thesis was that partly out of management avarice and partly because of pressure from Wall Street, corporations were using downsizing as a tool for short-term stock manipulation. Based on an examination of twenty-two companies that announced large layoffs during 1994, Downs found a strong (.31) correlation between the size of the layoff and the compensation of the CEOs.

In the meantime, the number of jobs within the United States offered by the top 500 ratcheted downward. From time to time the sheer volume of job reductions produced protests from elected officeholders. However, these largely pro forma objections had little effect. The readiest data is for the Fortune 500 top corporations. Chart 3.21 illustrates the sharp decline in their U.S. labor force between 1980 and 1999.

Whatever pangs corporate chief executives might have felt, stock price growth let them wash away the sour taste with champagne. Financialization itself was central to the metamorphosis that overtook large corporations during the 1980s and 1990s. As the stock market of the 1980s threw off the memories of 1966–82, corporations attuned themselves to the increasing omnipotence of the $15 trillion-under-management (by the late nineties) U.S. investment community—money managers, brokerage firms and ana-

CHART 3.22 **The Disconnection of Corporate CEO Compensation**

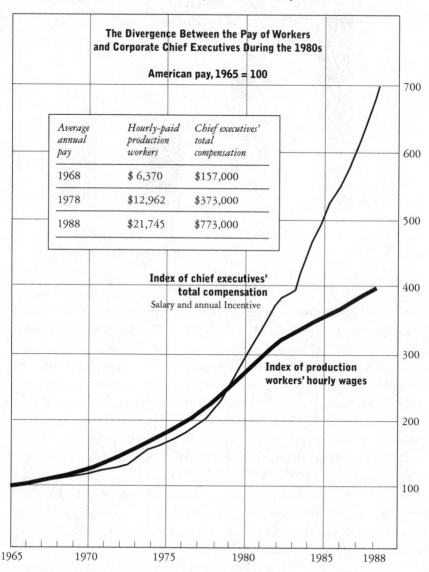

The Divergence Between the Pay of Workers and Corporate Chief Executives During the 1980s

American pay, 1965 = 100

Average annual pay	Hourly-paid production workers	Chief executives' total compensation
1968	$ 6,370	$157,000
1978	$12,962	$373,000
1988	$21,745	$773,000

Index of chief executives' total compensation
Salary and annual Incentive

Index of production workers' hourly wages

Source: Sibson & Company and *The Economist*, June, 1989.

lysts, investment banks, and the increasing ranks of mutual funds and other institutions. Top corporate executives found themselves in a golden vise: keep stock prices moving up as required in their own incentive packages or run the risk of perishing. On the other hand, those who had watched financial operators and investment bankers feast royally during the first half of the eighties now reveled in their own seat at capitalism's high table.

Compensation for corporate CEOs, like the top wealth lists, began to reflect the stock market. *Business Week* reported average compensation more than doubling between 1983 and 1988. However, as late as 1987, *Forbes* found that the average pay among the 800 chief executives of the largest corporations was $762,000, about the same as the average for a similar number of top partners in the major Manhattan law firms. Going back to the late 1960s, the pay of corporate CEOs had been only twenty-five times that of hourly production workers. Then in the mid-eighties, as Chart 3.22 shows, CEO compensation decoupled from its old relationships and opened up a yawning gap. Between 1981 and 1989 the ten biggest corporate CEO compensation packages increased 500 to 700 percent, a bit less than financial sector behemoths, but symptomatic of the new values taking over America's boardrooms.

The nineties, in turn, broke all records. The ratio of the pay of corporate CEOs to the hourly wages of production workers soared from 93 times that of workers in 1988 to 419 in 1999. While the wages of ordinary workers barely kept up with inflation, the average compensation among the top executives of the largest corporations vaulted 481 percent between 1990 and 1998 to an average of $10.6 million. Corporate profits, by contrast, rose only 108 percent. Chart 3.23 shows the ten largest CEO compensation packages for 1981, 1988, and 2000. Those of 2000 are forty to fifty times higher than those of 1981. Declines were not significant until 2001.

The increasing importance of money management and stock markets to U.S. corporations is hard to exaggerate. Most companies named chief financial officers during the 1980s, especially firms inclined to undertake restructurings or deal in futures, currency arbitrage, and risky derivative instruments. Investor relations became a growth area, and by 2000 the typical corporate CEO was presenting at ten to fifteen investor conferences a year, talking with the company's biggest institutional investors, and occasionally taking calls from his industry's most important Wall Street analysts. Whereas back in 1960 only 12 percent of shares of the typical publicly-listed company turned over each year, by 1998 the figure was 76 percent—a hyperactivity that required careful attention. The compensation committees of large corporate boards grew in importance as top ex-

CHART 3.23 **Up, Up and Away: The Rise of Top Corporate Executive Compensation, 1981–2000**

(The top ten from the annual *Business Week* survey of the highest-paid U.S. executives)

1981

NAME/FIRM AND COMPENSATION (IN MILLIONS)	
R. Genin/Schlumberger	$5.7
F. Hickey/Gn. Instrument	5.3
J. Kluge/Metromedia	4.2
J. Riboud/Schlumberger	3.0
H. Gray/United Tech	3.0
R. Adam/NL Industries	2.9
R. Cizik/Cooper Industries	2.8
D. Tendler/Philbro	2.7
A. Busch/Anheuser-Busch	2.6
F. Hartley/Union Oil	2.3

1988

NAME/FIRM AND COMPENSATION (IN MILLIONS)	
M. Eisner/Disney	$40.1
F. Wells/Disney	32.1
E. Horrigan/RJR Nab.	21.7
F. Johnson/RJR Nab.	21.1
M. Davis/Gulf & West	16.3
R. Gelb/Bristol-Myers	14.1
W. Stiritz/Ralston-Purina	12.9
B. Kerr/Pennzoil	11.5
J. Liedtke/Pennzoil	11.5
P. Fireman/Reebok	11.4

2000

NAME/FIRM AND COMPENSATION (IN MILLIONS)	
John Reed/Citigroup	$290
S. Weill/Citigroup	225
G. Levin/AOL T-W	164
J. Chambers/Cisco	157
H. Silverman/Cendant	137
L. Koslowski/Tyco	125
J. Welch/GE	123
D. Peterschmidt/Inktomi	108
K. Kalkhoven/JDSU	107
D. Wetherell/CMGI	104

Source: *Business Week,* May 10, 1982; May 1, 1989; and April 16, 2001.

ecutive pay packages, golden parachutes, loans, benefits, and incentives became ever more lucrative and complex.

As the bear market took hold in 2001, the huge portions of stock reserved for employees, especially in technology companies, became controversial. According to one major survey, technology firms had on average 23 percent of their stock set aside in employee (largely management) options. Preoccupation with personal option–related time frames often led management to riskier strategies like adding debt and making high-priced stock buybacks, thereby lowering returns to (other) shareholders as well as producing market instability and volatility.

Other companies, like Microsoft, found the business of selling put options on their own stock a terrific way to make money. Through the late nineties, with Microsoft shares rising steadily, the options expired worthless so that the company kept the premiums, which in the second half of 1999 alone added $472 million to its profit statement. Dell, in some fiscal quarters, made more money selling options than computers. Other tech firms all but put themselves in the venture capital business, sometimes so successfully that realized investment gain exceeded operating income. Intel, Microsoft, Cisco, and Compaq were all big players in the in-house stock portfolio game through 1999.

Because quarterly earnings reports were stock market milestones, transactions and deals were often tailored to investment-related calendars. Business buyers of technology, in particular, were advised to negotiate major purchases late in a quarter, when companies faced harsh Wall Street scrutiny: "Companies who don't make their earnings forecasts are punished terribly, so that . . . the deal window opens the first or second week."

Management of employee pension funds shed its dull blue-collar image by adding major gains to corporate bottom lines. Not only did a number of companies switch to so-called cash-balance pension plans to reduce their pension liabilities, but in 1999 a number of major corporations—General Electric, Bell Atlantic, IBM, and Lucent—were able to use excess pension fund income (from the stock market gains of pension assets) to substantially increase operating profits and thus elevate their stock prices.

Simultaneously with technology's boost to financialization, the new corporate and money management tools available insured that the technology-based rewards of corporate productivity gains in the mid- and late-nineties went lopsidedly to capital—to management and shareholders. Chart 3.24, a candid philosophic capsule of the late 1980s and 1990s, shows how the productivity gains of that era, like those of the Gilded Age

CHART 3.24 **Productivity Gains, Profit Surges and Wage Stagnation, 1987–1995**

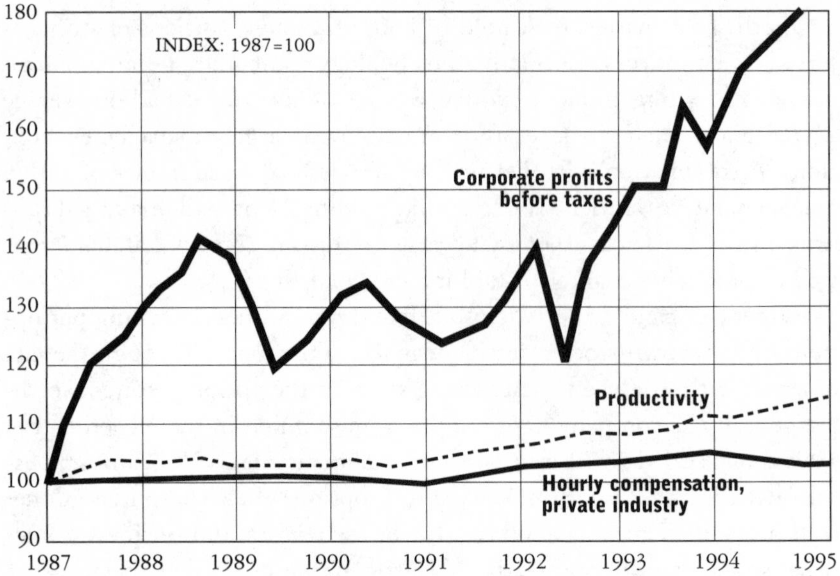

INDEX: 1987=100

Corporate profits
before taxes

Productivity

Hourly compensation,
private industry

Source: *Washington Post*, June 23, 1995.

and 1920s, bolstered capital through company profits rather than elevating workers through wage gains.

The lucre of productivity gains, however, brings us to the next leg of the triangle. Even the largest corporate compensation packages—the summa cum laudes of CEO graduation from hired managers to crypto-owners—came up small next to the biggest money of the 1990s. These were the stockmarket fruits of the fin-de-siècle technology mania and speculative bubble enjoyed—if in some cases, not for long—by several hundred founder-owners of the major technology companies in the heady years from 1997 to 1999. Like nineteenth-century railroads that barely existed, young technology companies, Internet start-ups in particular, found themselves ending the twentieth century with no earnings but absurdly high share values. In an age of excess, technology and finance joined to lead the way.

5. TECHNOLOGY, WEALTH, AND INEQUALITY

Innovation, to paraphrase the Austrian economist Joseph Schumpeter, has been the mother of speculation. The important innovations can be in finance, in technology, or in both. Indeed, some of the biggest bubbles have come from simultaneous pioneering.

The fuller intermingling of technology, speculation, and wealth distribution, healthy and unhealthy, will be developed in chapter 6. What this section profiles is technology's role as an influence-in-waiting during the 1980s, followed by a mid-nineties upsurge that turned into one of history's rare manias around 1997, producing a massive wealth increase that proved to be more than half bubble as the Nasdaq collapsed.

Sectors like biotechnology and computers enjoyed small booms during the turnabout years in the early 1980s, displaying more verve than the *Fortune* 500. Still, market watchers, venture capitalists, and productivity specialists agree that few great things happened in high-tech funding in the early eighties or during the four years between 1987 and 1991. Supposedly hot prospects like artificial intelligence, robotics, and pen computing quickly cooled. A few soon-to-be-well-known companies went public—Microsoft, Sun Microsystems, and Amgen in 1986, Cisco in 1990. However, as indicated by both the technology stock index earlier and the technology trends that follow, the impact on U.S. wealth remained relatively flat through the eighties until 1992.

Chart 3.25 includes a half dozen principal yardsticks for the 1980–2000 period ranging from the growth of available venture capital to the increases in Internet usage, the technology sector's share of stock market capitalization, productivity, the percentage of business capital investment going for technology purchases, and the volume of trading on the Nasdaq. Politically, although the sector's threshold of startling growth overlapped with the partial transformation of national politics taking shape in 1992–93, the identification of a high-tech era with the Democrats may wind up no clearer than the Republicans' earlier loose identification with the new Sun Belt.

The Internet, which went from catalyst to mania, took wing in 1992 and by 1994 over a million Americans were already on-line. Investors soon saw networking as a bigger growth (and productivity) sector than personal computers had been ten to fifteen years earlier, and in financial circles, 1995, the year Morgan Stanley actually took Netscape public, became "Year One in the on-line era." Semiconductor, networking, and computer firms did soar. The bubble emerged in 1997, grew large in 1998, huge in 1999, and swelled at maximum circumference just before popping in 2000. Chart 3.26, as metaphor, shows the spectacular rise and equally spectacular fall of the Internet fortunes within the *Forbes* 400 from 1997 to

CHART 3.25 **The 1990s and the Coming of Age of Technology**

A. Broad Measurements

	1990	1995	1996	1997	1998	1999
Business infotech spending as a share of total business equipment/buildings outlays*	28%	32%	32%	33%	33%	34%
Nasdaq Composite Stock Index (12/31)	374	1052	1291	1510	2192	4069
Annual productivity gains (percentage)	1.3%	0.7%	2.8%	2.3%	2.7%	2.5%
Technology share of total S&P 500 capitalization	5%					30%

*This data comes from Bureau of Economic Analysis (Commerce Department) Table 5.4, *Private Fixed Investment by Type.* A higher rate of increase is shown by Table 5.5, *Real Private Fixed Investment by Type,* which is computed in chained 1996 dollars.

Source: Commerce Department, Nasdaq, Bureau of Labor Statistics.

B. Computer, Internet, and Software Sectors

	1970	1980	1990	1999
U.S. households with computers	0	1%	22%	53%
Market value of publicly traded U.S. computer and related devices companies (billions of $)	43	47	57	415
Market value of publicly traded U.S. software companies (billions of $)	1	6	33	440
U.S. households connected to Internet	0	0	0	38%
Market value of publicly traded Internet companies (billions of $)	0	1	5	138
Number of worldwide Internet hosts	13	213	313,000	56 mil.

Source: Annual Report of the Federal Reserve Bank of Dallas, 1999.

CHART 3.26 **The Rise and Fall of the Internet Billionaires, 1997–2001**

Name (Company)	Wealth by Year				
	1997	1998	1999	2000	2001
James Clark (Netscape)	700 mil.	NL	NL	875 mil.	740 mil.
Richard Adams (Uunet)	560 mil.	750 mil.	1.4 bil.	1.0 bil.	NL
Jeffrey Bezos (Amazon.com)	NL	1.6 bil.	7.8 bil.	4.7 bil.	1.2 bil.
David Filo (Yahoo)	NL	840 mil.	3.7 bil.	6.5 bil.	625 mil.
Jerry Yang (Yahoo)	NL	830 mil.	3.7 bil.	6.4 bil.	625 mil.
Naveen Jain (InfoSpace)	NL	NL	730 mil.	2.2 bil.	NL
Pierre Omidyar (Ebay)	NL	NL	4.9 bil.	4.6 bil.	4.6 bil.
Jay Walker (Priceline.com)	NL	NL	4.1 bil.	1.6 bil.	NL
Mark Cuban (Broadcast.com)	NL	NL	1.4 bil.	1.9 bil.	1.4 bil.
Todd Wagner (Broadcast.com)	NL	NL	675 mil.	1.2 bil.	800 mil.
Michael Robertson (MP3.com)	NL	NL	1.0 bil.	NL	NL
Meg Whitman (Ebay)	NL	NL	960 mil.	900 mil.	850 mil.
Andrew McKelvey (Monster.com)	NL	NL	700 mil.	2.1 bil.	1.3 bil.
Robert Glaser (RealNetworks)	NL	NL	2.4 bil.	2.4 bil.	NL
Steve Case (America Online)	NL	NL	NL	1.5 bil.	1.1 bil.
David Wetherall (CMGI)	NL	NL	NL	1.7 bil.	NL
Joseph Ricketts (Ameritrade)	NL	NL	NL	1.8 bil.	850 mil.
J. Stuart Moore (Sapient)	NL	NL	NL	1.4 bil.	NL
Jerry Greenberg (Sapient)	NL	NL	NL	1.4 bil.	NL
Timothy Koogle (Yahoo)	NL	NL	NL	1.1 bil.	NL

NL: Not Listed

Sources: Annual *Forbes* 400 listings, 1997–2001.

2001. Many of those who survived were bought out early or made timely use of their high-priced stock to buy other non-Internet enterprises.

The Internet at its summit of flattery gathered romantic kudos for ostensibly giving humankind a new participatory democracy and breaking the hold of commercial, financial, and governmental elites, much the same naivete to which telegraphs, railroads, and steamships had led the pens of Walt Whitman and Alfred Tennyson. Microsoft chairman Bill Gates was sober enough in saying that "the information highway will change our culture as dramatically as Gutenberg's press did in the Middle Ages." It was claims like that of Nicholas Negroponte in *Being Digital* that "digital living" would close the generation gap and contribute to "world peace" that amounted to warmed-over railway Pollyannaism spread on a silicon wafer.

Like the Internet, Britain's Great Railway Mania had spawned pop philosophers and a multitude of clubs and special publications. The railways had led to new stock exchanges from Liverpool to Cincinnati—even to railroad banks on both sides of the Atlantic. The Internet, in turn, elevated not just Charles Schwab & Company, but on-line finance—after-hours trading, e.trade, e.bank, and the cleverly named My Discount Broker.com. The two implosions were also similar.

Besides technology's enlargement of the reach of the investment business, the new launches of stratospherically successful technology securities flotations in the late nineties boom increased the already notable economic inequality in high-tech districts. In citadels of the new *digirati,* from New York to Silicon Valley, nannies, servants, and gardeners became among the fastest-growing occupations. Small-home prices doubled, lifting them way beyond the reach of families with median incomes. Ordinary workers languished.

A second polarizing effect was indirect and global. American chip and computermakers, by giving portions of the Third World the technology to displace older U.S. manufacturing and then by outsourcing much of their own simpler forms of production, helped during the eighties and nineties to send overseas millions of high-paying and hitherto unionized jobs. Some of them had given the blue-collar workers of Pittsburgh and Toledo, San Jose and Sunnyvale, their middle-class incomes, cars, and lakeside fishing cabins of the 1950s and 1960s. Chart 3.27 shows the contrast between the many jobs the best-capitalized U.S. manufacturing company had once offered and the relatively small amount of employment that Microsoft, Cisco, Oracle, Intel, Apple, and Sun Microsystems mustered in the mid-1990s. The six firms' growth since then has not begun to make up for the U.S. jobs lost at companies like GM.

Some of the major companies did have large employment rolls, but for wage and tax reasons, they were mostly overseas. Seagate Technologies, for example, in 1999 had 65,000 of its 82,000 workers in Asia.

CHART 3.27 **The New Economy: High Technology, Low Employment**

Employees, 1995			
Intel	32,600	General Motors	709,000
Oracle	19,000		(predominantly
Microsoft	15,500		in U.S.)
Apple	14,400		
Sun Microsystems	13,300		
Total	94,800		

The somewhat higher employment of the high-tech corporations in 2000, before the implosion, was also more deceptive. Few firms had highly paid unionized production lines; most had sizable ratios of well-paid professionals and even more temporary workers. Of the skilled professionals, many were not Americans but foreigners on H1-B visas—at Cisco, for example, 45 percent of the workforce was noncitizen. And the high ratio of employees hired as temporaries and contract workers, who generally did not get stock options and other benefits, fueled commentaries on two-tier cultures and class tensions in Silicon Valley and in Redmond, Washington, the home of Microsoft.

Technology publishers Anthony and Michael Perkins, describing the peak years as a high-technology Gilded Age in their prophetic 1999 book *The Internet Bubble,* pointed out that as venture capitalists and Internet entrepreneurs grew fabulously rich, the gap between the haves and have-nots only grew wider in Silicon Valley and the world. They were not the only insiders who had philosophic qualms. Michael Moritz, a former *Time* reporter turned venture capitalist, was caustic more than a year before the bubble burst: "Look at our [high-tech] companies. Maybe they've produced 100,000 jobs or 150,000. But what kind and for whom? Jobs that 250 million people in this country aren't qualified for. Jobs for guys out of MIT and Stanford. Jobs that in many ways gut the older industries in the Midwest or on the East Coast. What are we investing in? Companies that enable people to work harder and longer—anytime, anyplace. You can be reached on a ski lift, on a beach or on a plane. What good is that for people's lives?"

By 2001 such questions had been mooted in many parts of California, New York, and elsewhere by the 1929-like collapse of many of the Internet and telecommunications companies hailed only months earlier. For aspects of biotechnology, new philosophic doubts were also setting in. The forward march of technology would continue, but the debris of periodic speculative manias has always caused a pause.

6. OVERWORKED AND STRESSED AMERICANS

Over the long run of history, technology has been prosperity-building, time-saving, and labor-saving. The twofold meaning of the latter goes to the heart of the problem. Back in the 1920s, glib advertising copy shouted the blessing of innovations like electric vacuum cleaners, washers, and refrigerators. Household labor-saving devices, they were called.

The second semantic interpretation produced little advertising copy. Fewer could wax eloquent about the new electrical machinery of the twenties that allowed companies to save labor in the sense of being able to discharge workers. Economists published lists of those areas where the cuts were deepest: tobacco, coal, lumber, and shoemaking.

Pressures like these helped curb pay, and many women went to work because husbands' wages were not enough and they and their families craved the new consumer goods. This raised the female percentage of the workforce to about a quarter, but in the 1923 case of *Adkins v. Children's Hospital*, the U.S. Supreme Court had struck down a minimum wage for women so that pay was low and hours were long. Family stress was high. The disproportionate share of the decade's income gains went to the 6 percent of the gainfully employed who made over $3,000 a year. Of the remaining families, it was estimated that about a quarter were chronically destitute.

Beneath a greater abundance and glitter, the eighties and nineties yielded similar angst. Among women with children under six, the percentage who worked rose from 19 percent in 1960 to 64 percent in 1995. In some households, two workers had three or four jobs. In Atlanta, a hub of notable urban sprawl, the average resident in 1999 lost 53 hours to traffic delays, up from 25 hours even in 1992. Survey data showed the percentage of Americans complaining about always being rushed climbing from 25 percent in 1965 to 28 percent in 1975, 32 percent in 1985, and 38 percent in 1992. With real nonsupervisory wages declining for much of the population during the period, householders met this strain by wives going to work, by new magnitudes of borrowing as we saw earlier, and by working longer hours.

International comparisons underscore the discomfort. During the decades after 1945, when the unionized percentage of the workforce peaked and workers on the production line at Ford or General Electric lived better than European bank managers, the average annual hours worked by Americans were below those of the Japanese and many Europeans. By 1980, Americans still worked fewer hours than the Japanese, but put in more time on the job than the British, French, and Germans. Between 1990 and 1995 the average annual hours worked in the United States finally passed those of workaholic Japan, leading the International Labor Organization to report in 1999 that Americans toiled the longest hours in the industrial world.

CHART 3.28 **Average Annual Hours Worked, 1950–98**

	1950	1960	1990–92	1997–98
Japan	2166	2318	2031	1889
United States	1867	1795	1919	1966
Britain	1958	1913	1773	1731
Germany	2372	2136	1616	1560
France	1926	1919	1668	1634

Source: The data for 1990–98 are from the International Labor Organization (ILO) or the OECD and have been widely cited. Those for 1950 and 1960 are from a University of Groningen/Conference Board series taken from OECD publications. Most papers comment on the general lack of comparability between nations and between separate measurements within nations.

To fully assess the U.S. work burden against the backdrop of relatively stagnant nonsupervisory wages, American pay must be placed alongside its inflation-adjusted equivalents in more relaxed Britain, France, Germany, and Japan. Wages in those places *rose* in the eighties and nineties while working hours *shortened.*

What U.S. economists disagreed on was how to compute the foreign comparisons: Should we use the actual currency exchange rate, which

CHART 3.29 **U.S., European, and Japanese Wage Trends, 1960–2000**

Relative hourly compensation of manufacturing production workers, 1979–96 (using market exchange rates, U.S. = 100)			Relative hourly compensation of manufacturing production workers, 1979–96 (using purchasing power parities, U.S. = 100)		
COUNTRY	1979	1989	1998	COUNTRY	1979	1989	1998
United States	100	100	100	United States	100	100	100
Germany	125	124	151	Germany	86	111	132
France	85	90	98	France	66	86	87
Britain	63	74	89	Britain	62	76	81
Canada	87	103	85	Canada	81	92	107
Japan	60	88	97	Japan	49	61	78
Denmark	116	102	122	Denmark	71	78	96
Netherlands	126	105	111	Netherlands	87	101	107
Norway	114	128	128	Norway	70	90	105
Sweden	125	123	119	Sweden	78	88	97
Switzerland	117	117	131	Switzerland	75	87	96

Source: Economic Policy Institute.

often showed European and Japanese wages overtaking or leading America's, or was it more accurate to use "purchasing power" adjustments premised on the idea that the U.S. dollar really bought more at home than its exchange rate suggested? Chart 3.29 shows the comparative wage trends for the U.S., Britain, France, Germany, Japan, Canada, the Netherlands, Switzerland, Sweden, Norway, and Denmark using both methods.

Currency nuances notwithstanding, the evidence illustrates the transformation of the United States from its high-wage and best-working-conditions status during the quarter century after 1945 to a society that, for the bulk of its workforce, was increasingly middling in wages, harsh in hours worked, and more stinting in benefits. The rebuttal—that this approach contributed to a U.S. economy with only 4 percent unemployment versus the 8 to 11 percent rates in Europe—was debatable at the core of its employment assumptions.

From 1948 to 1996, the percentage of males over the age of sixteen counted in the workforce dropped from 87 to 75 percent. Especially in the eighties and nineties, large numbers of previously employed men after awhile stopped looking for a job, but this kept them out of the workforce and thus out of U.S. unemployment ranks.

The Wall Street Journal reported in 1996 that during the previous year 852,000 men between twenty-five and fifty-four lost jobs but weren't looking for work because of circumstances ranging from clinical depression to pride and inflexibility. MIT economist Lester Thurow said that the total of "missing men," some 5.8 million that year, put the true unemployment number in the range of 14 percent. *Get America Working,* a reputable Washington-based group, contends that the real jobless rate in 2000 was 35 percent because the seventy million healthy adults not actively seeking jobs should have been counted. The male dropout rate is the crux, however. A similar pattern in the UK, where official statisticians ignored a growing (one million men under fifty) bloc of "economically inactive" in the 2001 jobless count, prompted the *Financial Times* to query whether an official British unemployment rate of 5 percent was really any better than European Union figures twice as high.

One can also question the true status of the forty million Americans working only part-time. Persons in that category seeking full-time work, yet counted as unambiguously employed, are better described as half-employed. Other countries, without so many part-timers or "temporaries," differ in how they relate them to the workforce. Together, the two caveats suggested a plausible alternative U.S. jobless count not unlike the 10 percent figures of Western Europe.

Boasts of a truly low unemployment rate, then, seem a spurious justification for the U.S. middling wage patterns, weak job benefits, and greater number of hours worked. The better explanation is unofficial U.S. embrace of a controversial model—a commitment to globalization, especially in services, that accepts corollaries of diminished manufacturing, accelerating wealth stratification, higher than acknowledged levels of joblessness, contained wages, and high levels of imports.

This much resembled the Britain of 1910 and the Holland of 1740. Both were leading world economic powers in which national elites preoccupied themselves with success in finance and services, generally unconcerned that the old fabric of well-paid skilled workers, the British "nation of shopkeepers," or Dutch *brede middenstand* (broad middle) was beginning to fray. Whereas Dutch workers had once been highly paid, by the mid-eighteenth century their working conditions had deteriorated. The same was true of Britain in 1900–1914 where, as men's real wages fell, more and more women went to work, as the next chapter will discuss.

The probable slippage of U.S. wages below those of Holland, Denmark, Switzerland, Sweden, and Norway by the end of the 1990s was only part of the story. The yearly hours worked in those five nations, for example, were so much less than the 1,966 put in by Americans in 1997—just 1,399 in Norway, 1,552 in Sweden, 1,643 in Switzerland, 1,689 in Denmark, and 1,679 in the Netherlands—that data showing the five's better health coverage, lower stress and hypertension, vastly longer paid vacations, serious job retraining programs, and lengthier dismissal-notice requirements burnished already strong comparisons. The bottom economic two-thirds of the population in these countries had overtaken their American counterparts.

7. FINANCIAL PROSPERITY AND SOCIAL DECLINE

Too little data exists to easily compare the changes in social conditions, health, and education that accompanied the U.S. economic booms of the 1850s, Gilded Age, and 1920s with well-documented indicia of the 1980s and 1990s. Most of the time, improvements in education and health were thought to have accompanied the earlier surges in economic growth, although social workers like Jane Addams and Jacob Riis believed that deteriorating conditions in such big city slums as Manhattan's

CHART 3.30 **The Paradox of a Rising Gross Domestic Product and Declining Indexes of Social Health**

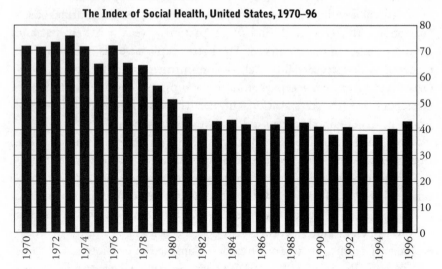

The Index of Social Health, United States, 1970–96

Source: Fordham Institute of Innovation on Social Policy.

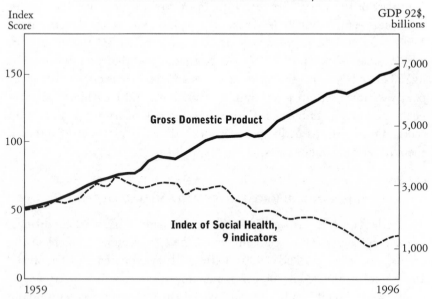

Index of Social Health and Gross Domestic Product, 1959–96

Source: Fordham Institute of Innovation on Social Policy.

Lower East Side in the 1880s and 1890s matched or exceeded the worst sections of London.

There is little doubt that circumstances in a range from years of school attended and levels of nutrition to mortality and live-birth rates broadly improved. During the 1980s and the 1990s, by contrast, the two most widely watched U.S. indicators, the Fordham University Index of Social Health and the Genuine Progress Indicator (GPI) published by San Francisco–based Redefining Progress, showed a more or less steady decline from the high-water marks of the 1970s. The Index of Social Health, for example, included ongoing downtrends in measurements like child poverty, health care coverage, and youth homicide.

Upticks in both of these indicators came during business cyclical peaks in 1985–88 and 1995 to 1999. In the latter period, about one-third of the losses since the late 1970s were regained. However, as Chart 3.30 below shows, the overall trendline for both the eighties and the nineties remained down. The two measurements used somewhat different criteria, although most components in each drew scoffs from believers that the economy should be measured by economic transactions and dollars alone. It was striking, though, that both indexes had been rising along with the gross domestic product until they began diverging in the 1970s. Chapter 8 will pursue the most likely causation: that market- and wealth-focused financial booms have too narrow a base, benefit, and commitment.

Beyond these indexes, the finance-centered boom of the late twentieth century ignored other social criteria and goals. Despite general prosperity between 1997 and 2000, poverty and demand for food and housing assistance grew in many middle-class areas of affluent high-technology and financial centers like California and greater New York City. Besides steep apartment rents and home prices, blame was also put on declining employee benefits, low-income debt payment burdens, and the numbers of officially "employed" who could not make ends meet as part-time or temporary workers.

For the middle class there were other costs as the huge money flows to the rich increased the price tags of affluent forms of consumption enough—not just first-class airline seats, but the cost of health clubs, sports admissions, symphony tickets, museum admissions, good restaurants, private schools, banking services, and big-city automobile maintenance—that many in the eightieth and even ninetieth percentiles could no longer afford what their similarly situated parents in the 1950s and 1960s had often managed. As one observer put matters, wherever space and attention were limited, more was going to the rich, while the services still available to the middle class became automated, digitized, and sparser. From baseball games and golf courses to school admissions, flooding upper-bracket cash ratcheted up prices. "Extra spending at the top," said Cornell University economist Robert Frank, "raises the price of admission."

As the federal, state, and municipal budget surpluses of the late 1990s stalled and shrank in 2001, where the future compass needle would point was hardly discussed. However, the ups and downs of U.S. economic history offered no true parallels. Late-twentieth-century financialization had no meaningful precedent, while previous American boom decades, as noted, had not been marked by diverging social and economic indicators. To pursue such precedents, it is time for our story to shift from wealth to another set of circumstances, this time foreign, that beckon across the years. These are the late stages of the trajectories of the three previous leading world economic powers: sixteenth-century Spain, seventeenth and early-eighteenth-century Holland, and nineteenth and early-twentieth-century Britain.

Comparison is best for the latter two, not surprisingly. Yet all three displayed parallel symptoms during the late stages given to increasing emphasis on finance and services overproduction. Polarization of wealth and income set in along with some measurements of social decay. The top percentiles became richer than ever while the lower portions of society lost ground. In many ways, Americans at the beginning of the twenty-first century might think themselves looking in a mirror.

PART II

THE ORIGINS, EVOLUTIONS, AND ENGINES OF WEALTH

GOVERNMENT, GLOBAL LEADERSHIP, AND TECHNOLOGY

CHAPTER FOUR

THE WORLD IS OUR OYSTER: THE TRANSFORMATION OF LEADING WORLD ECONOMIC POWERS

As societies consolidate, they pass through a profound intellectual change. Energy ceases to vent through the imagination, and takes the form of capital.
—Brooks Adams, *The Law of Civilization and Decay*, 1896

History repeats itself, but only in outline and in the large. We may reasonably expect that in the future, as in the past . . . that new civilizations will begin with pasture and agriculture, expand into commerce and industry, and luxuriate with finance.
—Will and Ariel Durant, *The Lessons of History*, 1968

The seed of imperial ruin and national decay—the unnatural gap between the rich and the poor . . . the exploitation of boy labor, the physical degeneration which seems to follow so swiftly on civilized poverty . . . the swift increase of vulgar, jobless luxury—are the enemies of Britain.
—Winston Churchill, 1908

Wealth exists in an *international* rather than just a national context, although the elite classes of leading world economic powers in modern times have always thought of themselves and their nation as exceptional, unique, sui generis. Cocksure Americans were hardly the first to think themselves immune from prior history. Spaniards, Dutch, and British believed much the same, especially as their hard-won national unifications, conquests, or commerce led them toward world primacies. The inevitable tide of disarray and disenchantment that eventually followed in each country, instead of striking the population all at once, lapped first at the poor and the ordinary citizenry even while the elites were still reaching their giddiest heights.

These internal divergences have become little more than subchapters and footnotes of history. The *desengaño,* or national disillusionment of early-seventeenth-century Castile, the Spanish heartland, reflected its stricken industry, emptying cities, poverty, plague, rising mortality rates, and refeudalization. The malaise of mid-eighteenth-century Netherlands came as textile towns withered, once spic-and-span streets became filthy, fewer ordinary folk could afford the old bread, meat, and dairy-based diet, retreating hygienic standards and poverty brought epidemics and rising mortality rates, gin and migration became workers' escapes, and neighboring German and Flemish towns grew to fear marauding bands of Dutch beggars. In Britain, the dark side of pre–World War One opulence was one in which ebbing industrial competitiveness forced down wages, household consumption of meat and sugar declined, emigration crested with two million English, Welsh, and Scots leaving for the U.S. or the dominions, slum housing became a national scandal, and working-class ill-health was revealed when huge numbers of Britain's young men were examined for military service and found medically unfit. In each nation such were the disparities, while elites enjoyed peaks of conspicuous consumption and financial smugness.

Inasmuch as the Spanish-centered Hapsburg Empire, the (Dutch) United Provinces, and Great Britain were the three leading world economic powers preceding the United States, the increasing economic polarization of their later stages of world leadership was an ill omen for a somewhat similarly placed successor state. As we look at the trajectories over several centuries of the four successive leading world economic powers, we will see the degree to which great individual wealth-holdings, a troubling mix of national fortunes and misfortunes, and widening internal gaps between the rich and the poor often reflect a point well past the zenith.

Great powers in particular have found history full of meaningful repetition, especially in broad outline. What Americans were asking themselves at the end of the twentieth century and the beginning of the next was what the Dutch had asked in 1750 and many British had pondered in the decades leading up to the world war: Was their increasing national reliance on finance and services rather than physical commerce and goods production the secure and reliable evolution of a genuinely new economy—or was it a familiar and vulnerable twilight stage of a great economic power?

Historians on both sides of the Atlantic had chewed on the subject for over a century. In *The Law of Civilization and Decay,* published in 1896, historian Brooks Adams—of the Boston Adamses—related a nation's decline to the rise of financiers and their values, a breed he saw everywhere in the U.S. of his era. Theodore Roosevelt, reviewing the book, disagreed in part—Adams was certainly premature in assessing U.S. vulnerability—but added that "with Adams' contempt for the deification of the stock market . . . all generous souls must agree." Having just attended the Republican celebration dinner following success in the 1896 election, a dismayed TR admitted that he was "personally realizing all of Brooks Adams' gloomiest anticipations of our gold-ridden, capitalist-bestridden, usurer-mastered future," although it would be six years before he could point fingers from the White House.

Despite Adams's detours to the silver content of Roman coinage under Nero and the unpopularity of the Marwari moneylenders of northern India, the basic connection he drew between excessive finance and national peaks and declines advanced previous thinking. Mid-nineteenth-century political economists like Germany's Friedrich List had set out five simpler stages of national evolution: savage, pastoral, agricultural, agricultural-manufacturing, and manufacturing-commercial. Since Adams's day, twentieth-century historians and economists have added overpreoccupation with banking and financial services as a threshold-of-decline stage for Holland and Britain. Fernand Braudel and others have written how Venice and Genoa, too, displayed these rhythms, but the lack of pre-sixteenth-century detail limits any comparison.

What this chapter will call the financialization of the leading world economic powers has usually been a late and downward-edging stage of their international leadership. A national focus on financially generated wealth accompanied by an erosion in the relative well-being of ordinary citizens, most strikingly those in declining industrial pursuits, has been inauspicious. This is a cautionary backdrop to the kindred transformation of America and the unfolding of the extraordinary gap between the rich and everyone else portrayed in the previous chapter.

Late-twentieth-century concerns about the maturation of America typically dwelt on individual rather than national aging—on what it would mean to have a steadily growing share of the population above sixty. A few historians, however, have offered various arguments for national life cycles—Carlo Cipolla in *The Economic Decline of Empires* (1970), Richard Hutch in a 1991 address to the Economic History Association, and Charles Kindleberger in *World Economic Primacy: 1500 to 1990* (1995)—although they do not focus on finance. Still others have argued that nations themselves can have hardening arteries, interest-group calcifications that bring political and economic sclerosis. The "end of history" thesis, by contrast, acclaimed liberal capitalism as a fulfillment transcending clogged economic blood vessels, a benign end of evolution. This chapter probes leading world economic powers in a different manner, more like a psychologist cataloging the sequential stages of adulthood, and finding the preference for finance over physical effort a later passage.

We could pose yet another counterpoint: the notion that the transformation of the United States from agriculture to railroads and steel, then through automobiles and early computers to megafinance and the Internet is really more of an escalator ride through a hall of centuries than a national aging process. So viewed, the expansion of finance, record wealth concentration, and rising inequality in the U.S. at the beginning of the third millennium principally reflect the effects of uniquely intensive globalization and the new economy of rapid technological change.

The similar trajectories of the previous leading economic powers, however, present a powerful argument for stages of development that the U.S. itself is following. Despite being too complicated to put in a single neat chart, the considerable parallels in the ups and downs of Spain in the 1500s and early 1600s, Holland in the 1600s and early-to-mid 1700s, and Britain in the 1800s and early 1900s resonate across five very different centuries.

Some observers have employed caricature. One eighteenth-century Dutch burgomaster confronted dinner guests with the "courses" of Dutch history—red herring and cheese (the simplicity of infancy), followed by plain puddings and roasts (the straightforwardness of prime), and then French wines and delicacies (the sophistication of decay). Late Victorians, with so recent an example, simply worried about Britain becoming another Holland. After the United States conducted its first serious debate on "decline" in the late 1980s, even the palmy days of the late nineties brought restatements of historical-decline analogies and fears of persisting U.S. vulnerabilities from disparate analysts like Harvard economic historian David Landes, theorist Edward Luttwak, and former *Business Week* editor William Wolman. Disquiet, although muted, had not gone away.

Through the prior centuries the most reliable signals of full-fledged or relative decline came when a leading power, its leaders overconfident from a generation or two at the center of world commerce, embraced global finance and services as the political economy of the future, allowing production or seafaring to fade. The ancient and medieval examples need not concern twenty-first-century Americans; the precedents of Spain, the Netherlands, and Britain should.

1. Three Cautionary Tales: Spain, Holland, and Britain

Leading economic powers are not made or unmade overnight. Each of the three that preceded the United States gained that status over roughly a half century, always amid a powerful convergence of commercial, political, geographic, and cultural forces.

Greater Spain became the world's most important political and economic force by the 1540s and 1550s. Shipments of gold and silver from the New World, only a trickle in the decades following Columbus's explorations, now arrived on a large enough scale to help bring on what scholars have called the "sixteenth-century price revolution." Dynastic upheaval also extended Spain's reach. Ferdinand and Isabella had ruled Castile and Aragon. Their Hapsburg son-in-law, Charles V, by 1520 would not just be king of Spain, but ruler of Austria, southern Italy, Burgundy, and Flanders as well as the elected Holy Roman Emperor.

Imperial economics gained sophistication in the late 1550s as the Spanish Crown, already sovereign over Antwerp and the Low Countries, allied itself with the merchant bankers of the rich, maritime republic of Genoa. Besides the Flemings and Augsburgers, the Hapsburgs ruling in Madrid had now enlisted another financial elite with an influential network across Europe. After these convergences, Greater Spain was not displaced as Europe's leading power until the drain of the Thirty Years' War (1618–48) and the full-fledged emergence of an independent Holland.

The United Provinces of the Netherlands, born of a late-sixteenth-century revolt against Hapsburg authority, started their own extraordinary climb to commercial leadership while Spain's might was still in place. The engines of Dutch advance were maritime, commercial, and even religious. The expulsion of Protestants in 1585 from the Spanish Netherlands (later Belgium) sent so many bankers, merchants, and artisans fleeing to the Protestant north that in the words of one refugee, "Antwerp became Amsterdam." Mushrooming from 30,000 residents in 1580 to 105,000 in 1622 and 201,000 by 1662, Amsterdam replaced Antwerp as Europe's commercial capital.

Frugal and commercially adept, the Dutch, only a million or so in contrast to 16 million Frenchmen and 20 million Spaniards, soon boasted the world's largest merchant fleet—some 6,000 ships in 1669, virtually as many as the rest of Europe—as well as its largest pool of investment capital. The Dutch also developed Europe's most advanced technology, and through it large and successful textile, shipbuilding, fishing, and specialized industries. In the 1600s, Dutch shipping jumped from regional importance to lucrative control of the so-called "rich trades" to the Baltic, the Levant, and the Indies, an edge they held for another hundred years. By the 1700s, although Amsterdam remained Europe's great lending center, the Dutch elite had begun to shift their own investments to the next great economic power: Britain.

The precise timing of Britain's own emergence is a continuing debate. Defeat of the French in 1763 gave the British a huge global empire, to say nothing of diplomatic precedence over the representatives of King Louis. Besides launching the Industrial Revolution, Britain also controlled the world's largest navy and verged on replacing Holland as Europe's principal pool of investment capital. Defeat of Napoleon in 1815 made British industry, capital, and empire paramount. But after a mid-Victorian heyday, large portions of British manufacturing were becoming obsolescent by the early twentieth century even while finance and national wealth were still reaching a zenith. Two world wars completed Britain's decline and transferred global economic leadership to the United States.

Even these short capsules preview some striking recurrences. The early decades of each emerging economic primacy—Greater Spain in the 1520s and 1530s, Holland in 1600 or 1615, late Georgian and regency Britain—were fat years for each nation's economic elite. But it was the subsequent heydays, the golden ages, that brought the flood tide of commercial opportunity, new markets, and wealth that produced the broadest benefit for the largest number. Thereafter, each nation's relative distribution of wealth and income would narrow. Stratification would set in. But for now we will examine the relative breadth of opportunity and wealth of each nation's best years.

For all that Spain's economic data is least reliable, these years stretched from the 1530s, when the gold and silver began pouring in, to the 1580s, after new techniques had further increased New World silver output, bringing what Spaniards called the *largueza*—the abundance of money. Besides restoring national confidence, shaken by periodic royal bankruptcies, the *largueza* also underwrote the ill-fated armada against England. Commercial and manufacturing towns like Toledo, Segovia, and Burgos grew through the 1570s or 1580s. Seville, principal base of the American trade, increased its population from 70,000 in 1530 to about 150,000 in

1588, the Armada year. A turning point is often found in 1596, when yet another royal bankruptcy from overspending produced a wave of national pessimism.

The golden age of the United Provinces, in turn, came between 1647, when Dutch ships were readmitted to seaports under the Spanish Crown, and the French invasion of 1672. Some historians have stretched it further, from the 1630s up to 1702 and the economic disruptions of the War of the Spanish Succession. Dutch commercial success in the first half of the seventeenth century was middle-class and relatively unpretentious. This cultural conservatism is still apparent in the cautious, calculating faces painted by Rembrandt or Hals and the sober facades of their great houses on Amsterdam's Heerengracht.

If thrifty Holland had Europe's first industrial proletariat, it was a relatively well-paid one—wages were two or three times higher than in Switzerland or nearby Germany. Dutch municipal neatness and sanitation was the wonderment of visitors. Commercial centers like Amsterdam, Leiden, Haarlem, Delft, and Zaandam doubled and trebled their population in the first half of the seventeenth century (even while Castilian towns far to the south were *shrinking* by almost the same ratios). Yet the Dutch prosperity and wealth that most impressed foreign observers was that of the *brede middenstand*—the broad middle of the population whose ratios were unmatched elsewhere in Europe. In the words of one historian, "The Republic was an island of plenty in an ocean of want. Its artisans, even its unskilled workers and its farmers (for it seems a misnomer to call them peasants), enjoyed higher real incomes, better diets and safer livelihoods than anywhere else on the continent."

The third golden age, Britain's, stretched from the great railway boom of 1846–47 through the symbolic Crystal Palace Exposition of 1851 and into the 1870s. R. F. Delderfield set his most famous novel, *God is an Englishman*, in the Kentish Weald of the heady 1850s. His metaphor was the success of a small provincial transport entrepreneur in an era that saw England become a vibrant grid of factories, railroads, and canals. These sped manufactured goods—textiles especially, but also ironware and machinery—to docksides in London, Liverpool, and Bristol for shipment around the world.

Up 30 percent between 1800 and 1830, international trade then jumped fivefold between 1840 and 1870, with British vessels and manufactured exports accounting for about half of the total. London's population climbed from just over 2 million in 1841 to just under 5 million in

1881. Metalworking Sheffield swelled from 111,000 to 285,000 and textile-based Salford from 53,000 to 176,000. Coal mining centers in Wales and northeast England quadrupled their smaller head counts. Industrial slums also thickened their gloom and squalor—tenements untouched by daylight, rivers like dye vats—but the wages of ordinary Britons, adjusted for inflation, rose by about one-third in the quarter century between 1850 and 1874–75. Skilled Britons became the wage elites of European labor.

The British middle and lower middle classes, 15 to 25 percent of the population depending on one's calculus, gained even more rapidly. Suburbs began spreading around London. Household sugar consumption soared in the 1850s and 1860s, and more middle-class families could afford at least one servant. Elements of the middle class became a leisure class. By 1871, out of a British population of 26 million, 170,000 "persons of rank and property" without visible occupation, mostly women (many widowed or unmarried), lived on the interest and dividends from a half century of commercial and railroad expansion.

Let us underscore this next point: *What all three "golden ages" involved, first and foremost, was a wave of success that brought broad enough status and prosperity to set the generality of Spaniards, then Dutch and Britons, ahead of their peers elsewhere.* At first God was Spanish, which the banners of the sixteenth-century galleons more or less proclaimed. To Holland's favored *brede middenstand,* the Almighty must have been a Dutch burgomaster. And on Delderfield's bustling mid-nineteenth-century Kentish plain southeast of London, God *was* an Englishman.

The equivalent heyday in the United States, as we have seen, spans the years from World War II to some point in the 1960s or the early 1970s—the "good years" following the Good War, the era of the Great Compression, when income growth was high and the distance between bottom and upper wage levels was at its narrowest.

The next stage for each leading power began to erode this relatively broad prosperity. Developing weaknesses in production or older forms of commerce—the Spanish wool industry, Dutch fisheries, or British ironware—were recurring early symptoms, as were an emerging disproportion of financiers and rentiers coupled with an ever-greater inclination to invest in government bonds or send money out of the country for a better return. Adverse international developments, from the fiscal burdens of a drawn-out war to foreign tariffs or trade restrictions, were another menace. At some point, incipient or relative decline gave way to the painful actuality. From each economic peak, the ebbs seem to have taken fifty to eighty years to become obvious and bring on a new leader.

Spain's decline resembled a setting for Don Quixote and Sancho Panza, replete with economic policy windmills at which Spanish leaders tilted unsuccessfully. Miguel Cervantes lived and wrote during this frustrating period, which haunts his novel. Pitfalls for the economy were everywhere, not least in the roles played by gold and finance.

The annual flow of bullion from the Americas, while close to its fabulous peak, was no longer much of a barometer by 1600. Successive kings had mortgaged future treasure shipments to finance their imperial ambitions. Nuggets from Peru and Mexico paid for siege guns before Maastricht and musketeers on the Rhine, and far too many of them, given how two-thirds of Spain's revenues went to service debt. Even so, the cascade of precious metal—New World production merely enlarged Europe's gold coin and plate by 20 percent, but tripled its silver trove—served to enervate the Spanish economy even as it inflated prices. In the words of one seventeenth-century Spaniard, "The possession and abundance of such wealth altered everything. Agriculture laid down the plough . . . trade put on a noble air, and exchanging the work-bench for the saddle, went out to parade up and down the street. The arts disdained mechanical tools. . . ."

The lure of easy money, in short, undermined what modern observers would call Spain's "real economy." The kingdom of Ferdinand and Isabella had a successful wool-growing industry in Castile as well as two established commercial centers (Burgos and Medina del Campo) and several known for manufactures: Segovia (textiles) and Toledo (textiles and steel). By the 1580s their midcentury growth reversed as Spaniards left the hitherto more prosperous north for Madrid, the new capital, and Seville, arrival port for the American treasure. The textile industry, middling in size but Spain's largest, peaked in the 1570s and then lost markets. When it was unable to meet New World demand, other sources had to be found. The bullion inflow in the meantime had so inflated Spanish wages and prices that foreign imports, cheaper and often better, undercut much of Spain's own domestic production.

Historians have generally blamed the Spanish government for not strengthening domestic industry. Northern Castile, they agree, had the necessary commercial skills and infrastructure, and development funds could have been found—over the last half of the sixteenth century, the Spanish Crown's revenues doubled and then redoubled. However, besides facilitating extravagance, Spain's incessant borrowing led to an elaborate infrastructure of debt instruments and arrangements as well as a horde of domestic and foreign bankers.

Their Most Catholic Majesties, the rulers of sixteenth-century Spain, took their revenues and funds from taxes, banker loans, and issuance of credit bonds. Peasants, artisans, and merchants paid most of the taxes because hidalgos (gentlemen) were exempted by law. In addition to borrowing from bankers, mostly Genoese, the Crown also issued credit bonds called *juros,* typically paying 5 to 7 percent but sometimes as much as 12 to 14 percent depending on the revenue source specified. Originated in the fifteenth-century war against the Moors in Granada, the later *juros* issued by Charles V and Philip II were bought by merchants, hidalgos, and grandees, or indeed by any Spaniard with money. "The result," according to a leading historian, "was the growth of a powerful rentier class in Castile, investing its money not in trade or industry but in annuities."

Merchants and successful artisans particularly felt the squeeze. As rising taxes destroyed Castilian enterprise, their burden (and the circumventions available) "induced wealthy merchants and businessmen to abandon their businesses and buy privileges of *hidalguia* in order to escape the burden of taxation."

As the sixteenth century ended, a group of economic commentators known as *arbitristas* (projectors) offered a perceptive if slightly oversimplified indictment. Their principal voice, Martin Gonzalez de Cellorigo, wrote in 1600 that all proper proportion between the classes had been lost, and that Spain had "come to be an extreme contrast of rich and poor, and there is no means of adjusting them to one another. Our condition is one in which we have rich who loll at ease, or poor who beg, and we lack people of the middling sort, whom neither wealth nor poverty prevents from pursuing the rightful kind of business enjoined by natural law." Treasure fleets had dulled the willingness to work, and the bourgeoisie had been lured away by easy money from investments and hunger for social prestige.

Then, speaking from the depths of frustration, Gonzalez de Cellorigo argued that "Money is not true wealth," the latter coming only from increased agricultural and manufacturing production rather than from precious metals. Spanish wealth was being "dissipated on thin air—on papers, contracts, *censos,* and letters of exchange, on cash, and silver, and gold—instead of being expended on things that yield profits and attract riches from outside to augment the riches within." An ambassador from Venice and others echoed these observations.

As discontent grew, the Spanish government of the 1620s proposed banking reforms, a 5 percent interest rate cap, prohibitions on the import on foreign manufactures, curbs on extravagant dress, and a two-thirds reduction in the number of municipal offices. But very little of this became law. Meanwhile, the Thirty Years' War drained Spanish coffers; the gold and silver arriving in Seville in 1625 was only half of what had come in 1600; maritime trade passed to other nations, and by the mid-1600s the tonnage of merchant shipping between Spain and the Americas had shrunk by two-thirds.

By the early seventeenth century, as decline became irrefutable, cities like Burgos and Toledo contained only half their population of 1561. People went back to the countryside in a "refeudalization" akin to that of Italy. Seigneurial agriculture grew again, with many lords the richer for owning large holdings of government bonds. By 1650, Spain's historical sun, at least, had set. The imaginary Don Quixote is better known than any Spanish leader these paragraphs might have mentioned.

Retrospection on the Dutch Republic's eighteenth-century ebb has matched historians over absolute versus relative decline, with an edge to the former. Output in the major Dutch textile center of Leiden started slipping in the 1670s. One index of Dutch industrial production showed a peak in 1667. Workers' wages stagnated after 1671, although purchasing power sometimes improved because of declining food prices. Finance began to displace hands-on commerce. As early as the 1650s, traders in Amsterdam had complained that the ruling burgomasters and regents, once themselves in trade, now "derived their income from houses, land and money at interest."

Such observations only grew. By 1688 the English consul in Amsterdam, William Carr, observed that, "The old severe and frugal way of living is now almost quite out of date in Holland; there is very little to be seen of that sober modesty in apparel, diet and habitations as formerly. Instead of convenient dwellings, the Hollanders now build stately palaces, have their delightful gardens and houses of pleasure . . . nevertheless, the grave and sober people of Holland are very sensible of the great alteration."

Changes in the Dutch economy were deepened by two great military conflicts—the Nine Years War from 1688 to 1697, and the War of the Spanish Succession from 1702 to 1713. Jonathan Israel, in his magisterial 1995 volume *The Dutch Republic: Its Rise, Greatness, and Fall, 1477–1806,* employed "The Later Golden Age: 1647–1702" as a chapter title, but asserted separately that, "The permanent, irreversible decline of Holland as a maritime and industrial power commenced only in, or around, 1688 with the onset of the Nine Years War and its many harmful consequences for the Dutch economy."

The continuation of war in 1702–13 strained Dutch maritime strength and credit to the breaking point. The navy, which under Tromp and De Ruyter had outsailed England's, was broken. Trade with the Mediterranean and Levant ebbed. Dutch interest rates were forced up to 9 percent in 1709 (versus 6 percent for Britain) and by 1713 the republic's national debt had tripled over 1688's. This pushed high taxes steadily higher, even as other European nations felt free to raise protective walls against Dutch textiles. Shipbuilding joined fisheries in the doldrums, and the Zaandam industrial district, Europe's most intensive, peaked in the 1720s and then declined in the face of growing protectionism elsewhere on the Continent.

Dutch mechanical skills continued to lead the world and Amsterdam's entrepôt kept a number of high-value-added industries—tobacco processing, sugar refining, sail canvas, silk, and linen—prosperous through the 1740s. By the 1750s, however, the plight of large sections of the United Provinces was beyond denial. James Boswell's notes from a 1764 visit are often cited: "Most of their principal towns are sadly decayed, and instead of finding every mortal employed, you meet with multitudes of poor creatures who are starving in idleness. Utrecht is remarkably ruined. There are whole lanes of wretches who have no other subsistence than potatoes, gin and stuff which they call tea and coffee. . . ."

Towns that had grown with industry now hemorrhaged. Leiden's population fell from 70,000 in 1688 to 60,000 in 1732 and 36,000 in 1749, Haarlem's from 50,000 to 40,000 and then 26,000. Zaandam dropped from 20,000 in 1688 to 12,500 in 1749. Three of the urban centers that were still expanding exemplified the Periwig Age: Amsterdam managed the money; The Hague grandly housed much of the diplomatic corps and nobility; and Schiedam distinguished itself—if that is the word—as the principal Dutch manufactory of gin, the new craving of the masses. Visitors found it hard to remember that this same nation a century earlier had bustled with middle-class prosperity.

Food and tax riots were common in the disillusioned 1760s and 1770s. Meanwhile, spokesmen for the so-called "Patriotic" movement charged— shades of the Spanish *arbitristas*—that the once great Dutch Republic had become a society split between rentiers and beggars, the two groups least useful. Even the principal latter-day historians of the Netherlands—those writing in English like Jonathan Israel, Simon Schama, and C. R. Boxer, along with many Dutch—have echoed these pejoratives.

Schama, in his *The Embarrassment of Riches,* noted that "historians have found it possible to speak of an 'aristocratization' of the Republic around this time. Certainly, by 1730, the culture which had once transected social divisions had split into subcultures which corresponded to them . . . even by the 1740s, writers in the 'spectatorial press' were equating cosmopolitanism with excessive remoteness from the *brede middenstand* [the middling sort] and both as a betrayal of national patrimony."

Israel, in his comprehensive survey of the Dutch rise and fall, emphasized the financial preoccupation—the shift by the Dutch upper classes to the passive economics of holding bonds and securities. By 1742, those who remained active merchants and manufacturers were falling from the upper-income echelons in Leiden, Haarlem, and other major towns. The typical mid-eighteenth-century family of the governing or regent class had 57 percent of its assets in States of Holland bonds, over 25 percent in shares, obligations, and foreign funds, and just 12 percent in land and houses. Isaac Pinto, a Dutch economic writer, had found it worrisome in 1771 that bonds, shares, and foreign funds "were the linchpin of civic wealth and status, the principal pillar of the social system, a situation quite unlike that existing in other countries."

"A further symptom of the economic collapse," according to Israel, "was the astounding increase in the transfer and depositing of Dutch capital abroad. Amsterdam banking houses with foreign connections plied a roaring business throughout the eighteenth century in exporting the capital the United Provinces had accumulated during the seventeenth." Mid-eighteenth-century estimates credited the Dutch with owning about a quarter of Britain's public debt and roughly one-third of the shares of the Bank of England and the (British) East India Company. As a measure Dutch of financial power, even as late as 1766 an observer noted that, "If ten or twelve businessmen of Amsterdam of the first rank meet for a banking (i.e., a credit) operation, they can in a moment send circulating through Europe over two hundred million florins in paer money, which is preferred to cash. There is no sovereign who could do as much." This while a growing part of the population was jobless.

The mass of Dutch overseas assets, about 80 percent of them in England, was so large that Dutch officials insisted that the sum of foreign earnings made up for the decline in other sectors of the national income. However, the unacceptable polarization of income and wealth involved in such a calculus drew reformers' ire, and in the words of Professor Charles Boxer, "whether Dutch capital was invested at home or abroad, it was lent to bankers and to brokers of commercial bills, rather than in developing home industries or fostering Dutch shipping."

Because Britain owed part of her own rise to the Dutch, some aware-ness of the United Provinces' mistake cautioned the leadership classes of the United Kingdom through the 1850s and 1860s. But in the 1900s, when these lessons were most relevant, Britons mostly ignored them. Americans, in turn, noted British precedents during the debate over the possibility of U.S. decline in the late 1980s and early 1990s, but largely neglected them as the millennium approached, despite U.S. parallels to the Britain of 1910–14.

In 1865, Matthew Arnold was one of the first to worry about England "declining into a sort of greater Holland." The *Annual Register* for 1866–67 expressed concern that "there may be signs already, though not precisely the same that have appeared before the decadence of other great empires." What this pessimism amid unprecedented prosperity reflected was evidence that the *unchallenged* period of British industrial supremacy was ending. The new circumstances were indeed less favorable—an eco-nomic slump after 1873, rapid and rival industrialization in the U.S. and Germany, renewed European protectionism (rising tariffs in Germany, France, and Russia), and a leveling-off of British exports.

To the man in the street, however, the disquiet of the 1860s was pre-mature. Just as the American public would not feel negative consequences for a quarter century after the mid-twentieth-century zenith of the U.S. share of world production, the technical evidence of Britain's apogee in the 1860s or early 1870s meant little to the average Briton. Working-class gains would continue for several decades, and popular opinion would eventually place Britain's imperial peak in the glittering years before 1914.

Still, concerns about competitiveness were hardly misplaced. Chart 4.1 puts the sharp 1870–1900 decline in Britain's share of world manufac-tures alongside the gains for the U.S. and Germany:

CHART 4.1 **Comparative National Shares of World Manufacturing Production**

PERIOD	BRITAIN	GERMANY	U.S.
1870	31.8%	13.2%	23.3%
1881–85	26.6	13.9	28.6
1896–1900	19.5	16.6	30.1
1906–10	14.7	15.9	35.3

Source: Friedberg, p. 36.

By the 1890s, nervousness had spread to the general populace. The inroads of German machines, tools, household goods, and children's toys came alive in a mid-decade book entitled *Made in Germany.* Then a second publication pointed at *The American Invaders: Their Plans, Tactics, and Progress.*

After 1900 the combination of rising prices in Britain and increasing foreign tariffs made exports produced in the U.K. more expensive abroad, pressuring British industrialists anxious to retain endangered markets to hold down their home wage costs. Between 1899 and 1913, inflation-adjusted wages in Britain dropped by about 10 percent, a shrinkage of purchasing power quickly evident in lower consumption of meat, sugar, and beer. By 1914 women were 41 percent of the workforce in manufacturing—twice the level in the United States—partly because more families needed two incomes to survive.

Thus did Britain slip into circumstances akin to those in the United States in the 1980s and most of the 1990s—slumping nonsupervisory wage levels and declining basic industries on one hand, and at the other end of the scale a heyday for banks, financial services, and securities, a sharp rise in the portion of income coming from investment, and a stunning percentage of income and assets going to the top 1 percent. Because of these considerable parallels, early-twentieth-century Britain is treated in this chapter with more detail than the other periods.

The share of British capital in the hands of the top 1 percent probably peaked in 1911–13, when that segment commanded a stunning 69 percent. The largest fortunes in the United Kingdom, while well below those of Rockefeller and Carnegie, had nevertheless doubled or trebled in the decades surrounding the turn of the century. The duke of Westminster led the lists with holdings valued at £14 million ($70 million). George Dangerfield, in *The Strange Death of Liberal England, 1910–1914,* described 1911 as a year of London "climbing towards its peak of plutocratic splendor, and tales of ballrooms banked high with the loot of hothouses, of champagne flowing like a sea, of bare backs, jeweled busoms and fabulous expenditure."

The island kingdom had almost always imported more goods than it exported, making up the merchandise trade deficit with the proceeds of so-called invisible exports—shipping, banking, insurance, and the like—as well as with the earnings on British investments overseas. Upper-income Britons had long been investing abroad—a total of £160 million by the early 1840s, £250 million by the early 1850s, and £1,000 million by 1873. By 1900 a full £2,000 million had made its way to destinations from Argentina to Zanzibar. The more Britain's own industry lost its edge, the greater the ratio of funds migrating in search of better yields. By 1910–14 the impressive £200 million *annual income* on these huge investments coupled with strong overseas earnings from shipping, banking, and insurance more than covered Britain's merchandise trade deficit. On the eve of war in 1914, then, whatever the conditions in East End slums and Welsh mining towns, it was equally true that the British Isles boasted the most important banks and merchant banks, the center of world finance (the City of London), the hub of world insurance (Lloyd's), and about 90 percent of the world's tramp steamers.

With Britain controlling so much of the international economy, well might her substantial investing class regard the world itself as their oyster. If Chilean railroads, Malayan rubber plantations, or Ohio utility bonds yielded better returns than factories in Warwickshire, so be it. During the prewar half-decade—a crescendo of finance as well as politics—almost twice as much investment flowed abroad as stayed at home, boosting the British overseas total from £2,000 million in 1900 to £3,000 million in 1907 and £4,000 million in 1914. Some 43 percent of *all* global investment was theirs. Critics felt that, in the words of one British historian, "At the very moment when creativity and capital were needed for industrial renewal at home, resources were being siphoned away." Much the same complaint was made about the eighteenth-century Dutch investment pattern.

The one notable attempt to assist heavy industry occurred during the 1901–6 Conservative government of Prime Minister Arthur Balfour. Foreign tariffs were climbing, and to combat them the Conservatives took a program for limited trade protection and tariffs into the general election of 1906 and suffered overwhelming defeat. Protection's most ardent exponent, Colonial Secretary Joseph Chamberlain, repeatedly invoked the Spanish and Dutch analogies, warning that preoccupation with finance was making Britain more divided between rich and poor and less self-sufficient: in short, "richer and yet weaker." The nation, he insisted, could not survive as "clearing house of the world" or merely a "hoarder of invested securities" unless it also created wealth through production. Like Gonzalez de Cellorigo in 1600 and Isaac de Pinto in 1770, Chamberlain's caution, although spurned, was more correct than wrong.

Financialization and the concentration of income and wealth proceeded in tandem. Downward wage pressures that cost working families their meat and beer also spurred trade union membership and politics during the years before 1914, electing a growing contingent of MPs from the new Labour Party to Parliament. The lifestyle of the prewar upper class, in turn, became a stereotype that echoes into the twenty-first century: imperial pomp and circumstance, huge yachts, the pheasant shoots of empty-headed marquesses, and new luxury hotels from Biarritz to Marienbad all ready to welcome English milords. As Britain's economic center of gravity shifted from smoke-stained provincial industrial centers to the City of London and the Sussex-Surrey stockbroker belt, George Bernard Shaw had a character in his play *Misalliance* predict that, "Rome fell, Carthage fell; Hindhead's time will come." Winston Churchill as home secretary in 1908 made some of the pithiest comments of all on the explosiveness of the rich-poor gap—one serves as an epigraph at the beginning of this chapter.

The financial, shipping, and export interests rarely lost battles, and in a match with the cosmopolitanism of Lombard Street, Swinton machine shops and Birmingham ironworks had no chance. As late as 1900, British wealth remained concentrated among the landholding nobility (although their portion was starting to slip) as well as among financiers like Rothschild, Baring, and Cassel, trading magnates like Lipton, Lever, Cadbury, and Selfridge, and the brewing dynasties of Guinness and Whitbread.

The wealth-holders in the industries needing protection, by contrast, were much less rich or influential. Important in Warwickshire or Northumberland, they counted for little in London. Of the nobility who were company directors, roughly one-third, most of them sat on bank, railroad, insurance, and overseas trading boards. Hardly any industrial firms had titled directors and only 7 percent had bankers. The orientation of upper-middle and upper-class investors added to the bias. According to L. H. Jenks in *The Migration of British Capital,* preoccupation with dividends from Penang, the Pampas, and the Transvaal nurtured "the growth of a rentier governing class whose interests lay outside the community in which they lived and exerted influence."

Endangered manufacturing, in short, lacked friends in high places. Besides losing the 1906 election debate among voters (who thought protection would make food prices climb), old-line manufacturing lost as decisively among the elites. Moreover, the halfhearted views of smokestacks among London's financial, mercantile, and professional elites were hardly unique. One European historian has concluded that of the old centers of commercial capitalism from Genoa to Antwerp and Amsterdam, none played a leading role in the advent of modern industrialization.

Well into the 1920s, memories of London's prewar glories at the center of world finance still convinced governments that Britain could return to the belle epoque of P&O liners and a pound sterling as unassailable as the Royal Navy. Small matter that the war had forced Britain to liquidate £500 million of its overseas assets, extend huge and possibly uncollectible loans to France and Russia, and borrow £1,000 million from the United States. If textiles and steel might never regain pre-1914 production and export levels, the City of London and financial services could and would. This hope was reinforced by changing 1920s wealth patterns in which commerce and finance (merchants, bankers, shipowners, merchant bankers, stockbrokers, and insurers) accounted for almost 40 percent of British millionaires.

To bet on this financial future, British policymakers chose in 1925 to return to a highly valued pound to reestablish sterling's global role, rejecting a cheaper valuation that might have produced an export-led manufacturing revival. Such were the realities of interest group pressure. However, that year's evidence of British overseas investment returns topping prewar figures was a delusion. Bloated price levels in 1925 relative to 1914 explained the seeming gain. Measured as a percentage of national income, gross return from foreign investment came to only half its prewar level, and fell further after the 1929 stock market crash.

Adjusted for inflation, the wages of ordinary Britons actually rose during the 1930s, the worst pain having come in the postwar industrial dislocations. Not so for the upper classes, who saw their taxes climbing and disposable income slipping. The share of British wealth in the hands of the top 1 percent began a half century of decline—from two-thirds in 1914 to just one-third by the 1960s. During the "long weekend" of the twenties and thirties, elements of the upper class could pretend that times had not changed, but the six painful years of World War II would all but eliminate overseas investments, force the postwar devaluation of the pound, and complete the collapse of British world economic leadership.

The embarrassments of the late 1940s—liquidation of overseas assets, the perils of sterling, and financial dependence on the U.S.—made Edwardian prowess ancient history despite the passage of little more than three decades. The size of the principal British fortunes continued the shrinkage visible in the 1930s. In 1947, a trying year when the British current account deficit of £600 million represented a brutal 6 percent of

GNP, the economy was so austere—food and clothing were strictly rationed—that Princess Elizabeth got no waiver for her wedding, just an extra hundred ration coupons.

Such were the postwar tax levels on British wealth that dukes opened their ancestral castles to well-paying tourists. Other formerly affluent Britons simply gave up. John Harris, a British writer, "discovered a situation that had no parallel elsewhere in Europe: a country of deserted country houses, many *in extremis*, most in surreal limbo awaiting their fate." He wrote—and also captured by camera—their embarrassing portrait in a book called *No Voice from the Hall.*

The caution of the three tales and the abandoned mansions, of course, is for the United States.

2. GLOBALIZATION AS THE PROJECTION OF A LEADING ECONOMIC POWER

Ironically, an earlier round of selling or abandoning country houses in England and Ireland had taken place after World War I, an apt but little-known local parallel to the gathering international retreat of Pax Britannica. One vital component of that ebbing pax, the openness of the world economy from 1870–1913—reexamined with interest as the debate over the next great globalization heated in 2000—was less a phenomenon of global fraternity than a projection of British power and its demand that investment and export opportunities remain open.

Indeed, some economists believed that "globalization" of trade and investment had achieved slightly higher percentages under British auspices in the late Victorian and Edwardian years than it had again by 2000.* This was chiefly because of the Royal Navy and the City of London, but also because much of Africa, Asia, and the Caribbean had been carved into

---

* The notion that Britain did this through laissez-faire rather than government activism is a Victorian fairy tale. From 1845 to 1870, laissez-faire dominated British domestic policy in the sense of denying any role for government in aiding the masses or ameliorating poverty. Globally, however, Britain spent huge sums on the principal supervisory force that watched its world commerce—the Royal Navy. Steel development had more than a little to do with the navy; India was run by mercantilist precepts; the Bank of England was charged with maintaining the pound sterling; and the British government subsidized transatlantic steamers and telegraph cables and bought half the shares in the Suez Canal Company. With that kind of laissez-faire, Britain built an empire and projected the globalization regime of open sea-lanes, open ports, and (relatively) free movement of investment.

British, French, Dutch, Belgian, Iberian, and German empires-cum-trade areas. Money, investment, and goods moved relatively freely, albeit economic nationalism and armaments spending were parading together more and more loudly from the 1890s through the outbreak of war in 1914. The world war, of course, proved the reversibility of that globalization as its British underpinnings crumbled and nationalism redoubled across Europe.

Putting the dates of 1870 to 1913 around this earlier era of openness, as millennial discussants did, leaves little doubt about its British origins. The United Kingdom, after all, led during that period on five relevant dimensions: world trade and shipping, visible and invisible exports, banking and finance, colonial expansion, and weight of overseas investment. Ideology added a sixth: a crusading ardor for free and open markets. Other Europeans, however, took British free trade piety with a large grain of salt. Britain itself had been protectionist from the seventeenth century to the 1840s, very conspicuously in the eighteenth century while wrestling commercial and finance leadership away from the Dutch.

Before 1870–1913, to find the previous period of relative economic openness, we must go back to those same Hollanders shrewd enough to make Amsterdam the world entrepôt and implant commercial outposts from Japan and the Indies to Manhattan and the Caribbean. This era ran from 1648, when the Thirty Years' War ended, to the 1670s, when Dutch commerce began to suffer from the new French mercantilism (government economic and trade management) under Louis XIV and his famous minister, Jean Baptiste Colbert. According to the principal historian of Dutch trade and industry, "The basic reason for the decline of the Dutch world trading system in the 1720s and 1730s was the wave of new-style industrial mercantilism that swept practically the entire continent." As barriers went up, Dutch profits weakened and Dutch technology diffused: "The key decades for the spread of systemic interventionism in northern Europe, the 1720s and 1730s, were the same as the decades of the decisive decline of the Dutch world trade system, and for a very good reason: the phenomena are two sides of the same coin."

The Spanish and Portuguese in turn had captained the first great globalization wave from the late fifteenth century to the first decade of the new seventeenth century. However, Dutch and British precedents alone suffice to suggest a general rule—that periods of openness and globalization tend to reflect the sponsorship of a self-interested leading economic power— which leads to the circumstances of the United States and the world trading system of 2000.

In the 1920s, when World War I and growing British economic weakness had eroded pre-1914 globalization, the United States had no interest in taking up its sponsorship. Fresh from another wartime triumph in 1945, however, it chose to do so—and by the seventies and eighties, Washington was shaping a new international elite and globalization process around the multiple stages of the General Agreement on Trade and Tariffs (GATT), the increasing importance of international financial agencies, and the collaboration of the major central banks, especially within the Group of Seven (the U.S., Japan, Germany, Italy, France, Canada, and Britain).

By the 1990s the U.S. wealth and opinion-molding elites, professing a commitment to free trade and capital movement similar to Britain's, also had a roughly comparable profile of economic self-interest. As we have seen, the concentration of American wealth at the top—from finance, technology, and services, not basic manufacturing—rode with the winners, not the losers, in the globalized survival of the fittest.

One important question at the millennium, then, was whether globalization was still dependent on a leading world economic power—and if so, whether that American foundation was solid. Certainly the escalating U.S. reliance on finance was something that British, Dutch, and even Spanish precedents judged shaky. Still, careful comparison suggests that the U.S. trajectory as the leading world economic power circa 2000 was no more complete than Britain's had been in 1900–14. The critical later stages were still unfolding, with a world hegemony in the balance.

3. The Incomplete U.S. Ascendancy as the Leading World Economic Power

To be specific, the United States of 2000 was roughly as distant from its post-1945 peak share of world production as the Britain of 1910–14 had been from her own. The evolution of the American republic over that star-spangled half century had also, like Britain's, seen eventual stagnant wages, the shrinkage of behemoth industries—textiles, steel, automobiles, and consumer electronics—and an outpouring of population from old industrial cities: Pittsburgh, Detroit, Cleveland, and dozens smaller. Women entered the workforce in large numbers to keep their families' heads above water (just as in 1900–14 Britain).

What had once been the world's highest manufacturing pay scales faded to memory, while soaring investment income going to the top 1 percent of Americans evoked both the Dutch and British pasts. So did the value of U.S. overseas holdings, which principally through new investment swelled from about $2.4 trillion in 1989 to $7.4 trillion in 2000. Upper-bracket Americans, at least until September 2001, were as enthralled by the other delights of globalization—travel, low-priced imports, the profits of investing in low-wage production, and affordable servants—and just as captivated by the idea of finance and services as the key to the future.

In New York and California, particularly, the concentration of the top U.S. fortunes amid hunger and beggars reflected the highest inequality ratios in the industrialized West. The expanding ranks of nannies, gardeners, housekeepers, cooks, and personal trainers, especially before the Nasdaq collapse, also smacked of Dutch and British precedents. Even amid the bull market, rising poverty in lower-middle-income sections of New York City, often within sight of Manhattan's penthouses and office building canyons, recalled the literature of prewar British dismay over the huge gaps between London's East and West Ends.

Also like Edwardian Britain, the United States was coming to worry less about trade with other Western industrial nations and more about access to low-wage countries (in several cases, U.S. quasi-dependencies) like Mexico, Latin America, Taiwan, China, and Korea. The UK of 1914, after a similar reorientation, sold over two-thirds of its exports to Latin America, Asia, and the empire, directing much of its overseas investments to these same places. India, well and truly the Star Sapphire in the imperial crown, became the principal market for British cotton goods and the largest source of investment returns flowing back to Britain. The Raj also served as a lucrative, low-wage platform from which wholly or partly owned British companies produced textiles, pig iron, and other goods cheaply enough to sell in China and Japan.

Thus the parallel to the importance of Mexico, China, and other cheap-production locales to the early-twenty-first-century United States—as export markets, as places where investments (factories or bonds) yield a pleasing return, and as vital external platforms for inexpensive production of goods, be they parts and components bound for the U.S. or finished manufactures bound elsewhere. As Britain had India, the U.S. has Mexico, Taiwan, and China to buoy corporate and investor profits while indirectly pushing down U.S. wage levels.

The economic, ideological, and military triumphalism of the United States at the millennium resembled the behavior of prior powers near or passing their peaks, when ruffles and flourishes seem to maximize. The state trumpets of Queen Victoria's golden and diamond jubilees in 1887 and 1897 and the coronations of Edward VII in 1901 and George V in

1910—cavalcades of imperial might in which Indian rajahs marched with Burmese mandarins and Zulu chiefs—sounded their most regal notes as the figurative bell was starting to toll for British industrial and economic hegemony. The Spanish were no less cocky in 1588, nor were the Dutch in 1688 when their prince, William of Orange, sailed to take up England's crown. Hegemony nurtures pride and illusion.

On the positive side of the ledger, the United States of 2000 opened the new century with counterindicators of youthfulness and innovation, not least the new U.S. global primacies in biotechnology, electronic finance, and computer networking via the Internet. Optimists also held up U.S. success in balancing its federal budget and beginning, ever so slightly, to reduce the enormous debt taken on since 1941.

Technological revolutions to be sure have vulnerabilities and dark undersides as well as huge benefits. Chapter 6, in its examination of technology and wealth, will amplify this chapter's brief references to the threats posed by technology transfers, speculative manias and bubbles, and surging foreign industrial rivals to the earlier leading economic powers. Suffice it to say in this discussion that by 2001 the two-year Nasdaq crash had significantly dented earlier U.S. technological assuredness—as had the low tech, but appallingly successful terrorist destruction of the World Trade Center.

Moreover, despite the reassurance of the return of U.S. federal budget deficits to surpluses during the late 1990s stock market boom, skepticism about the fiscal future reawakened in 2001. The turn-of-the-century deterioration of the current account deficit—the net of exports, imports, and U.S. overseas income—set out in Chart 4.2 raised another specter. British currency perils, current account deficits, and economic decline had rubbed against one another with unhappy effects in the 1930s, the 1940s, and then again in the 1970s. The millennial current account deficit of the United States, however, was worse in percentage of gross domestic product than any experienced in Britain before the inglorious crisis of 1947.

CHART 4.2 **The Rise of the U.S. Current Account Deficit, 1975–2000**

(Definition: Net of exports, imports, and U.S. overseas income)										
	1975	1980	1985	1990	1995	1996	1997	1998	1999	2000
Amount in billions of current U.S. dollars	+27	+20	–89	–42	–64	–71	–82	–155	–265	–445

Not that leading powers' ups and downs are ever fully explained or settled. British and Dutch historians of the late twentieth century were still battling over the origins, severity, and long-term meaning of the British ebb nearly a hundred years back and the Dutch decline a hoary 250 years ago. The trajectory of the United States—no nation of the maritime periphery but a large continental power blessed with resources and a huge, rich home market—should stay higher longer and fuel generations of debate.

4. INTERNATIONALISM: THE MIND AND SOUL (AND EVENTUAL ACHILLES' HEEL) OF LEADING WORLD ECONOMIC POWERS

The United States of the early twenty-first century, like the other leading powers before, had become so internationalized—in political thinking, interest-group weight, culture, investment, wealth dependence, and even internal population changes—that few opinion-molders had any interest in reversing the process. Here, moreover, the roots go back to the very convergences of people and opportunity that pushed each nation onto the global stage.

Instead of nationalist origins, some economic invocation of *volkisch* fulfillment, the birthing of leading economic powers is essentially international—a blend of geographic unification and annexation, successful overseas exploration and conquest, and the in-migration of skilled and well-capitalized refugees and cosmopolitan elites. Spain rose in the half century after 1492 because of Genoese explorers, American gold and silver, a Hapsburg inheritance that stretched from Burgundy to Vienna, Flemish advisers, Italian bankers, and Jews who became Christian converts *(conversos)* to avoid expulsion.

The emergence of the United Provinces, in turn, was hugely helped by aid from the Protestant powers of northern Europe. It also profited from three sixteenth and seventeenth-century streams of refugees whose membership had high ratios of commercial skills: some 150,000 Protestant Flemings, fleeing Antwerp, Bruges, and Ghent after 1585, doubled Amsterdam in size and turned it into Europe's new commercial capital; 10,000 Sephardic and German Jews, some of them bankers and merchants, brought family and religious networks; and 15,000–20,000 Huguenots fleeing the France of Louis XIV came later with other talents and connections.

Even seventeenth-century England owed much to Flemish weavers,

Dutch engineers and financiers, and Jewish and Huguenot merchants and bankers. In the 1690s, after Dutch *stadholder* Willem of Orange became King William III of England, the English quickly made over their finances—modeling the new London Stock Exchange after the Amsterdam Bourse, the Bank of England after the Amsterdam *Wisselbank,* and England's new long-term funded public debt on the successful Dutch practice. As we have seen, by the middle of the eighteenth century, Dutch investors had shifted enough capital to own an estimated 20 to 30 percent of the British public debt and comparable portions of the stock of the Bank of England and the East India Company.

Was all of this a coincidence? Of course not. Only part of each world economic leadership—probably not the major part—grew out of the Castilian *meseta,* Dutch polders, or English coal and iron country. The exodus of Protestant Flemings, French Huguenots, and Jewish refugees, so entrepreneurially and financially minded, first undercut the architects of their initial persecution—Catholic Spain and France—and then helped shift Europe's economic and commercial leadership to tolerant Holland and afterward to relatively tolerant England. Kindred in-migrations to the United States during the eighteenth and nineteenth centuries were undoubtedly important to the U.S. commercial bent. The nation-switchings of five commercial peoples at least once and even two or three times—Flemings, Jews, Dutch, Huguenots, and English Puritans—give the saga a recurring human face.

Each golden age, however, typically saw each power edge into nationalism and triumphalism. Internationalism took on elements of ethnic pride. Historians cite this cocksureness of a sixteenth-century Spaniard: "Let London manufacture those fine fabrics. . . . Holland her chambrays, Florence her cloth; the Indies their beaver and vicuna; Milan her brocades; Italy and Flanders their linens . . . so long as our capital can enjoy them. The only thing it proves is that all nations train journeymen for Madrid and that Madrid is the queen of parliaments, for all the world serves her and she serves nobody."

The most conspicuous Dutch boast, given its sculpting on the exterior pediments of the huge Amsterdam town hall begun in the glory year of 1648, showed that city receiving the tribute of the four continents—Europe, Africa, Asia, and America—while a Dutch Atlas, unassisted, held up the globe on his back. In Britain, W. S. Jevons, the mid-Victorian economist, caught the equal self-assurance of the 1860s: "The plains of North America and Russia are our cornfields; Chicago and Odessa our granaries; Canada and the Baltic are our timber forests; Australasia contains our sheep farms, and in Argentina and on the western prairies of North America are our herds of oxen; Peru sends her silver, and the gold of South Africa and Australia flows to London; the Hindus and the Chinese grow tea for us, and our coffee, sugar and spice plantations are all in the Indies. Spain and France are our vineyards, and the Mediterranean our fruit garden. . . ."

In a few more decades polarization set in, widening the gap between the cosmopolitans and large chunks of the workforce. But far from flagging, the new internationalism, in contrast to the earlier one, took on a smug, satisfied, center-of-the-world urbanity tied to huge wealth and royal courts—to some extent, the Madrid of 1610; more compellingly the Holland of Amsterdam and The Hague circa 1720; and most of all, the London of 1890–1914. Each became a magnet for those seeking power, money, or a good place to enjoy what they already had, and many of the arrivals were foreigners.

How could London not draw the English-speaking wealthy from everywhere, asked one Briton, "with ships from all the world calling at her ports, with an old and well-ordered society, a secure government, an abundance of the personal service desired by the wealthy, a land of equitable climate, pleasant if not grand scenery, a large and ample life organized to sport, amusement and the kind of enjoyments pleasing to the leisured classes?" Indeed, Park Lane, in London's West End, was invaded by American millionaires, Argentine beef barons, and South African gold and diamond kings.

Foreign capital came, too—sometimes to places named Lombard Street and the Old Jewry from earlier waves—working both to internationalize London and to think, speak, and grow in British pounds. Of the city's great merchant banking houses, the Rothschilds' eighteenth-century beginnings in Frankfurt (under the sign of the *rot schild,* or red shield) are legendary. The first Baring had arrived from sea-trading Bremen two generations before the Rothschilds, in 1717. The founder of Hambro's, Carl Joachim Hambro, came from Copenhagen in the nineteenth century; the Schroeders came from Hamburg and the Lazards from Alsace. Morgan Grenfell was built up before the U.S. Civil War by two Americans, George Peabody and Junius Morgan, the father of J. Pierpont. Of the later-arriving German Jews, Sir Ernest Cassel became the personal banker to Edward VII.

As for British industry circa 1900, it was not altogether British. Far from attending Eton or Harrow, many notable entrepreneurs had been born abroad or were members of religious minorities. The principal enterprise in British chemicals was German-run—Brunner-Mond, later Imperial Chemical Industries. Americans played a significant role in Britain's automated machine tool industry, and U.S. capital, in particular Westinghouse, provided much of the voltage in the UK electrical industry. Thus the 1890s book about *The American Invaders.* Indeed, Britain's first tram (1860) had been American-built, and when the London underground was electrified and the first "tube" constructed in 1907, the engineering and financing were largely American.

In steel, although Britons pioneered most of the late-nineteenth-century developments, much of the benefit migrated. Americans, Germans, and French thronged Middlesbrough, site of the first major British open hearth steel plant, and went home to incorporate the new processes in larger and better plants. Skilled British workers left in droves, mostly for America.

Which brings us to the Achilles' tendons exposed by the internationalization of each leading economic power, of which three stand out. The first, almost inevitable, has been the enlarged vulnerability that comes with financial preoccupation and a rentier culture—nonchalance toward humdrum-seeming production, tendencies to acquire buildups of debt, and increasingly transnational loyalties.

Next comes the aging of the nation's early-stage technology and industrial base and its susceptibility to technology transfer, foreign scientific innovation, and the migration of key industries. The third precarious exposure is to war—the ruination and debt brought on by great-power diplomatic and military overreach. The Thirty Years' War (1618–48) was Spain's undoing, the European conflicts of 1688–1713 were Holland's, and World Wars I and II wrote Britain's leadership obituaries. When late-stage internationalism ignores its rising debt, financial vulnerability, pockets of technology weakness, and resource constraints, overstretch makes wars especially costly.

In both the Dutch and British cases, international exposure diffused the prowess that earlier connections had assembled. The increasingly finance-dominated Holland of the later eighteenth century was wracked by bank-connected panics in 1763, 1772, and 1780. Firms like Hope & Company, Clifford & Co., Neufvilles, or Hornica, Hoguer & Co., uninterested in industry, speculated in commodities and Dutch East India Company stock and competed to make loans to Catherine of Russia, the kings of Denmark and Sweden, and German princes. Technological skill and invention petered out, and in the words of Jonathan Israel "many highly skilled artisans emigrated to Britain, Scandinavia, Prussia or Russia. Dutch shipbuilding workers and carpenters were in heavy demand throughout northern Europe. Soon the highly skilled were also leaving Amsterdam. When Sweden banned imports of processed tobacco, in the 1740s, entire workshops, with their men and machinery, removed to Stockholm." What internationalization had helped to give, it helped take away.

Britain's unfortunate example is scarcely cold. The earlier record of British scientists and inventors pioneering nineteenth century developments in chemistry, steel, and electrical machinery could not keep the United States or Germany from seizing the lead in each by 1900 because of superior schools and research facilities, better-trained workers, and the scale of management and resources made possible by monopolies and cartels. Progress has little respect for prior-generation laurels, and obsolescence can build quickly. Nineteenth-century U.S. steel pioneer William Metcalf observed that "the steelworks of Sheffield were hermetically sealed . . . the holders of the keys being apparently unconscious that their best workmen were swarming over to the States." Britain's overbuilt, first-in-the-world railway system added to the problem by including too many unprofitable, useless, or duplicative lines, running small and inefficient freight cars, and anchoring aging industries to obsolete works and outdated economic geography.

Besides which, pre-1914 anxiousness to maintain export levels prompted Britain to sell large quantities of coal and advanced machinery to Germany and other rivals who used it to challenge British output. Many merchant banks, in turn, were more interested in loans to Imperial Russia or "Gaucho banking" in Argentina than in rebuilding home industry. The eventual long list of technologies at least partially pioneered in Britain yet lost to serious commercial development elsewhere—aniline dyes, vanadium and silicon steel, radio, penicillin, jet engines, radar—testifies to how much and how quickly inventiveness can diffuse. By 1945 the concerns of 1865 and the fears of 1895 had been realized—and worse.

However, if British financial, industrial, and technological leaderships had followed the nineteenth-century flood of British capital, skilled workers, and technology to the rising United States, the new millennium offered no further successor in the four-century-old Dutch-British-American continuum. A technology and leadership transfer would have to be more wrenching.

5. WORLD ECONOMIC LEADERSHIP AND
ITS EXTENSIONS OF WEALTH

Rare are the Spanish, Dutch, or British economic histories that do not, at some point and context, discuss how each nation, in its later stages of world leadership and beyond, settled into a pattern of partly living off accumulated political, military, commercial, financial, and linguistic proceeds, connections, and power. Zenith decades had concentrated capital, along with expertise in banking and financial services, insurance, shipping, and communications, and continuing access to the remainders of empire and spheres of influence. After a century or more in the international sun, substantial portions of each nation's elite, at least, could enjoy a golden sunset, taking advantage of these opportunities.

As seventeenth-century Spain woke up to her decline, a major part of its effort by the early eighteenth century went toward reestablishing the imperial profitability of Mexican silver, Cuban sugar, and wheat from the Rio Plata. From providing only one-eighth of the imports of Spanish America in 1700, Spain sent fully half by the 1780s. As Dutch difficulties in turn worsened in the 1740s and 1750s, the East Indies remained near peak profitability, with Moluccan spices and Javan sugar and coffee bulking larger in Amsterdam's thinking than before. Other opportunities survived in Dutch colonial Curaçao, the Suriname plantations, and in trade with the Americas in sugar and tobacco. By then most of the wealthiest Dutchmen were landowners, investment bankers, high government officials, or rentiers living off government bonds, interest, or the earnings of the quasi-official Dutch East India Company.

Britain's policy after the 1890s, in turn, relied on the earnings of overseas investments, on City of London financial services, and on exports to India and the dominions and to quasi-colonies like Argentina, Chile, and Uruguay. Economic historian E. J. Hobsbawm, after reviewing late Victorian critiques, summed up the process as Britain "living off the remains of world monopoly" while opting "to retreat into her satellite world of formal and informal colonies," and to export "her immense accumulated historical advantages in the underdeveloped world, as the greatest commercial power, and as the greatest source of international loan capital." The British fortunes of the 1920s and 1930s reflected this reorientation more than those of the 1890s and even 1910.

There are obvious continuities with the United States at the beginning of the twenty-first century. Like Britain a hundred years earlier, the favorable U.S. balance in a broad category of service exports—insurance, stock brokerage, banking, travel, transportation, global construction and engineering, law and advertising, music and entertainment, news and communications, computer services and software—can be thought of as fruits of its post–World War II commercial, political, military, and linguistic supremacy. The North American Free Trade Agreement (NAFTA) together with the American emphasis on East Asia can be taken as a commercial focus on hemispheric and post–World War II spheres of influence.

The differences are also important. The merchandise trade deficit of the United States circa 2000 was too large, and the earnings on overseas investment too small, to keep the nation in the overall global creditor status Britain enjoyed even after World War I. On the contrary, the United States, gorging on imports, let itself become the largest international debtor to the tune of some $1.7 trillion and entered the new century obliged to count on foreigners continuing to send money—to buy U.S. bonds or purchase U.S. companies or stocks through the New York Stock Exchange or the Nasdaq.

In the late nineties many economists, entirely willing to call that money-flow dependence precarious, took assurance from the technological innovation wave of that decade. The United States appeared to have reemerged as the center of world technology. And with English becoming the world's technological and communications age lingua franca, the United States in this view had jumped back to the head of the industrial line, the historical equivalent of a Houdini escape. Nor was any obvious successor power emerging to replace the United States at the center—the other English-speaking nations being collateral beneficiaries—of a techno-linguistic hegemony stretching from North America to Britain, Ireland, Holland, and Scandinavia and thence through Israel and India to Singapore, Hong Kong, and Australasia.

The millennial technology crash drew this self-assurance into question, and besides, economic history rarely preserves a turn-of-the-century status quo. Two of the forces affecting wealth and its shifts demand particular attention: technology (and its transfer), which is the subject matter of chapter 6, and the vital role and influence of government, to which we now turn.

CHAPTER 5

FRIENDS IN HIGH PLACES: GOVERNMENT, POLITICAL INFLUENCE, AND WEALTH

All wealth is power, so power must infallibly draw wealth to it by some means or another.

—Edmund Burke, 1780

The mischief springs from the power which the monied interest derives from a paper currency which they are able to control, from the multitude of corporations with exclusive privileges which they have succeeded in obtaining . . . and unless you become more watchful in your states and check this spirit of monopoly and thirst for exclusive privileges you will in the end find that the most important powers of government have been given or bartered away. . . .

—Andrew Jackson, farewell address, 1837

A bold and aggressive plutocracy has usurped the Government and is using it as a policeman to enforce its insolent decrees. It has filled the Senate with its adherents, it controls the popular branch of the legislature by filling the Speaker's chair with its representatives, and it has not hesitated to tamper with our Court of last resort.

—James B. Weaver, 1892 Populist presidential nominee

W hether five hundred years ago or now, power and wealth have rarely been far from one another. Truly private enterprise, had the term existed in the fifteenth or sixteenth century, would have been on a small-to-middling scale. Those whose fortunes were large had ties to officialdom, even if much of their income came from Spanish wool, Hungarian mines, or Umbrian farmlands. Government held the keys: high offices, commissions, fees, licenses, monopolies, and from time to time the bloodier benefits of war, confiscation, and pillage. The great rich were rulers or popes. Or, as the Peruzzi, Medici, and Fugger families proved, bankers to rulers and popes. Financiers of that era sought rela-

tionships with power, government loans, and great ventures, not the humdrum beginnings of industry.

The Dutch, as we have seen, began as thrifty traders and clever sailors.
Yet as Holland matured, power and wealth intertwined. Many of the rich
became part of the regent class—the governing elite of councillors, mag-
istrates, and senior officials. Holding office was itself a route to wealth,
and the municipal and provincial elites invested much of their worth in
the securities of the governments they served. By the eighteenth century
the ruling class lived well on the income from British and Dutch bonds
and shares of both nations' East India companies.

The path to preferment in the France of Louis XV took a lascivious
route through Paris's fashionable gambling rooms and royal bedchambers. The richest man in France in 1720, in whose heyday the term
millionaire was coined, was John Law, a Scottish-born banker. Some years
earlier, in the gaming dens both men frequented, he had met the rakish
regent of France, the duke of Orleans, who ruled for his young cousin
Louis. Through that connection, Law was authorized in 1716 to establish a bank, which before long became *la Banque Royale.* In 1717 he
received the trading monopoly with French Quebec, Louisiana, and
the West Indies. Control over French trade with China, Africa, and the
East Indies followed as well as the profitable responsibility of collecting the king's indirect taxes—the *tabacs,* the *gabelles* (salts), and the *aides.*
Law lumped them all together—colonial management, banking, and
trade—in the Mississippi Company, of which he was the principal shareholder.

Gullible investors heard Louisiana described as a mountain of gold
studded with diamonds and emeralds, graced by a fine capital—in fact,
little more than a few streets, a rampart, and a basin—named for its distinguished royal patron, Orleans. Shares in *Le Mississipi,* as Parisians called
it, rose fortyfold. Upper-class Parisians talked of little else. Law, by now
the king's comptroller general of finances, during this period held France's
biggest fortune. But by 1720, when thin revenues failed to justify either
the gauzy descriptions or the share prices, the *Mississipi* bubble and then
the bank collapsed, producing riots in the Rue Quincampoix, the Parisian
stockjobbing center. Law fled to London.

Orleans died in 1723, immortalized in W. S. Lewis's biography as the
"libertine Regent." His esprit survived, though, and in the 1740s two
banker brothers named Paris-Duverney, old rivals of Law, became the new
financial powers by introducing the attractive young niece of their stew-

ard into King Louis's household. The young woman, whose charms did the rest, was Jeanne Antoinette Poisson, better known to posterity as Madame de Pompadour.

Even in the English-speaking countries, wealth and government cohabited well into the eighteenth century, although with less joie de vivre. The major joint-stock companies of Queen Anne's day, chartered by Parliament or the Crown, were intimately connected to the two political parties. The Bank of England and the New East India Company wore Whig colors, the South Sea Company and the Old East India Company Tory blue. What the twentieth century would label corruption in the eighteenth was business as usual.

Reform grew in the nineteenth century, especially in America, as part of a larger transformation in which ordinary folk gained the vote as well as broadened legal protection while new ethical obligations descended on government. But it was a slow process. City councils could still assess property and taxes arbitrarily; members of legislatures could vote lucrative charters to their employers and benefactors. Canal companies raised funds through lotteries; railroads in some places could double as banks.

Ethical as well as commercial lines remained fuzzy. President James Monroe, holding loans from John Jacob Astor, blithely signed a law on his behalf. U.S. Senator Daniel Webster could routinely dun a bank for a retainer that had not been paid. And in the late 1860s, James G. Blaine, speaker of the U.S. House of Representatives, who sometimes appeared to double as a securities salesman, could try to push Arkansas railroad shares on financier Jay Cooke even as he, Blaine, advanced that same railway's cause before the House.

Venality in government remained a given. Thirty members of the New York state legislature known as the Black Horse Cavalry could be had en bloc. Until its partial reform in 1871, the Tammany Hall–controlled New York City Board of Aldermen was worse, a transatlantic version of the famously corrupt eighteenth-century Parliament of Ireland.

The corsair past was barely subdued. The richest man in British North America at midcentury, Enos Collins of Nova Scotia, began by supplying British troops and capturing U.S. merchant ships during the War of 1812. As late as the Civil War, U.S. naval officers still received prize money for capturing an enemy vessel, and in 1863, Lincoln and his war cabinet debated whether to resume commissioning privateers, finally deciding not to. During the period when cotton taken on Southern rivers was a lawful prize, Northern naval officers spent more time prowling for bales than fighting Confederates. Booty's memory died hard.*

We have seen how wars produced the major inflationary waves in the U.S., with new fortunes usually riding high on the crest. To show how much partisan politics also mattered to the rich, this chapter will argue that several major U.S. political watersheds—those of the immediate postindependence period as well as those in 1800, 1860, and 1932—spilled over into four realignments of America's leading wealthholders, as touched upon in chapters 1 and 2. Friends or benefactors in high places, more than just convenient, often remained a necessary fulcrum of success.

To be more specific, this chapter will also catalog the principal techniques by which levels of government in the United States over the years have been harnessed to shift wealth from one group, sector, or region to another. The opportunities of debt management, currency inflation or deflation, central banking, tax and tariff policy, whatever their societal debits and credits, have always been good pickings for a select minority. So, too, for favoritisms to corporations and railroads as well as government subsidies to industry and technology from the telegraph to the Internet. Few of America's great fortunes have not been so abetted, despite the rhetoric of pristine markets and unaided enterprise.

The relationships to government in more recent centuries, especially the twentieth, have lost the directness of plundering khans or royal mistresses. Bedchambers have been replaced by antechambers and lobbies. Power and authority, however, have not become less important. This chapter's story is of that evolution—from pillage or confiscation of church assets to a more subtle reliance on presidencies, central banks, international organizations, and the latter-day help of officials in legislatures and regulatory bodies rather than in commissaries or palaces.

---

* The elder J. P. Morgan, who joked about tracing his ancestry back to Henry Morgan, the seventeenth-century pirate, named his yacht *Corsair* (a Turk or Saracen pirate) and painted it pirate-flag black. This further underscores how little need there is to trace the predatory side of the nineteenth-century American rich back to the medieval robber baronage of the hills and rivers of central Europe. Railroaders or moneymen alike would have found sufficient inspiration in the sixteenth, seventeenth, and eighteenth-century conquistadores, land-grabbers, war profiteers, pirates, and privateers of the Western hemisphere alone.

1. SWORD AND SCEPTER: GOVERNMENT AND WEALTH UP TO THE INDUSTRIAL REVOLUTION

Naming the wealthiest persons of the eleventh, thirteenth, or fifteenth centuries is a fool's game. Contenders like Tenkaminen, Enrico Dandolo, and Nyatsimba are sparse entries even in the thickest encyclopedias. However, the listees in a millennial compilation by the *Wall Street Journal* of "Fifty of the Wealthiest People of the Past 1,000 Years," set out in Chart 5.1, prove an important generalization: political and governmental power underlay fortune. Of the fifty named, thirty were rulers or major government officials; nine were bankers or financial agents to governments or traders under official license. Through the late 1700s, important moneymen were the only ones outside high officeholders to be named— Florentine Filippo de Peruzzi, banker for popes and monarchs; Jacques Coeur, moneyman to King Charles VII of France; Cosimo de Medici, banker to the papacy; Jacob Fugger, manager of the pope's money and collector of cash for the remission of sins; Sir Thomas Gresham, financial agent for Queen Elizabeth I; and the flawed but brilliant John Law.

CHART 5.1 **Fifty of the Wealthiest People of the Past 1,000 Years**

NAME	PERIOD	OCCUPATION	SOURCE OF WEALTH
Al-Mansur	938–1002	Moorish regent of Cordoba	Plunder
Basil II	958–1025	Byzantine emperor	Land confiscation, silk trade
Machmud	971–1030	Ruler of Afghanistan	Plunder, slave trade
Tenkaminen	11th century	Caliph of Ghana	Gold, ivory and salt trade
Al-Mustansir	1029–1094	North African ruler	Gold and trade
Suryavarnan II	12th century	Khmer ruler	Gold and trade
Enrico Dandolo	1107–1205	Ruler of Venice	Trade, plunder
Innocent III	1160–1216	Pope	Taxes, indulgences
Genghis Khan	1162–1227	Mongol conqueror	Loot
Kublai Khan	1215–1294	Ruler of China	Inheritance, confiscation
Filippo Peruzzi	13th century	Florentine banker	Banking, trade
Mansa Musa I	14th century	Ruler of Mali	Gold and trade
Jacques Coeur	1395–1456	French Royal financier	Banking, finance, and trade
Cosimo Medici	1389–1464	Banker to papacy	Finance, trade
Nyatsimba	15th century	Zimbabwe emperor	Loot, gold, trade
Alexander VI	1431–1503	Pope	Graft, embezzlement
Liu Jin	1452–1510	Court eunuch of Ming China	Graft
Montezuma II	1466–1520	Aztec emperor	Taxation, tribute
Jacob Fugger II	1459–1525	Banker	Finance, papal money manager

Atahualpa	1502–1533	Inca emperor	Gold and silver
Henry VIII	1491–1547	King of England	Taxes, confiscation
Suleiman	1494–1566	Ottoman emperor	Taxes, governance
Thomas Gresham	1519–1579	English royal financier	Merchant banker
Philip II	1527–1598	King of Spain	Taxes, governance
Shah Abbas	1571–1629	Persian ruler	Silk monopoly, exports
Albrecht von Wallenstein	1583–1634	Governor of Bohemia	Marriage, governance
Nicholas Fouquet	1615–1680	French royal treasurer	Embezzlement, governance
Y. Tatsugoro	17th century	Japanese merchant	Silk, rice, trade
Aurangzeb	1628–1707	Moghul ruler of India	Inheritance, governance
Osei Tutu	1670–1712	Ashanti emperor	Slave trade, governance
John Law	1671–1729	French royal controller	Banking, finance
Sir Robert Clive	1725–1774	British conqueror in India	Loot, payoffs
Richard Arkwright	1732–1792	British textile magnate	Inventions, textile factories
Ho-Shen	1750–1799	Chinese court official	Graft, kickbacks
Stephen Girard	1750–1831	U.S. financier	Trade, finance
Nathan Rothschild	1777–1836	British banker	Finance, loans to governments
Howqua	1760–1843	Chinese merchant	Moneylending, trade with West
John J. Astor	1763–1848	U.S. financier, trader	Fur trade, banking, Manhattan real estate
Cornelius Vanderbilt	1794–1877	U.S. shipper, financier	Ships, trade, railroads
Cecil Rhodes	1853–1902	British magnate	Diamond mines
Hetty Green	1835–1916	U.S. investor and miser	Financial markets
Andrew Carnegie	1835–1919	U.S. industrialist	Steel industry
J. D. Rockefeller	1839–1937	U.S. industrialist	Oil refining
Simon Patino	1860–1947	Bolivian tin magnate	Mines, tinfoil
Calouste Gulbenkian	1869–1955	British oil magnate	Oil royalties, brokerage
Mir Osman Ali Khan	1886–1967	Nizam of Hyderabad	Jewels, gold, governance
T. V. Soong	1894–1971	Chinese finance minister	Banking, finance, investments
J. Paul Getty	1892–1976	U.S. oil magnate	Oil and investments
Sultan Haji Hassenal Bolkiah	1946–	Ruler of Brunei	Beneficiary of Brunei's oil wealth
William Gates II	1955–	U.S. software executive	Stock ownership in Microsoft

Source: *Wall Street Journal,* January 11, 1999.

The Industrial Revolution put a seal on several transformations.*
English textile pioneer Richard Arkwright was the first to build a fortune
around manufacturing, although he had connections to government and

---

* Not until the Industrial Revolution did Europe have the largest fortunes. The richest man
in the late seventeenth century, the Moghul emperor Aurangzeb, was thought to have had annual revenues of $450 million, ten times those of Europe's richest potentate, Louis XIV.

received a knighthood. The subsequent early-nineteenth-century fortune-holders among the fifty—U.S. banker Stephen Girard, British banker Nathan Rothschild, Chinese trader Wu Bingjian (Howqua), and American fur monopolist John Jacob Astor—were all businessmen who, while not royal bankers or government paymasters, exemplified a transition period in which intimate relations with officialdom remained vital.

Girard, as we have seen, was a close ally and benefactor of the Jefferson and Madison administrations. Rothschild, first credentialed as the financial agent of Prince William of Hesse-Cassel, became rich and famous as the great London-based loanmaker to governments. Wu Bingjian (Howqua), perhaps the richest man in China, was the senior of the hong merchants in Canton, one of the few authorized to trade silk and porcelain with foreigners. Portraits of the pigtailed Howqua in his robes still hang in Salem and Newport mansions built by U.S. merchants grateful for Howqua's assistance.

Astor, too, traded on closeness to power. Besides the bribes and connections that built his fur empire and the loans he made to the government during the War of 1812, the rich New Yorker had helped organize the Second Bank of the United States in 1816, serving as one of its first directors. He held stock in five of New York City's better-known banks—the Manhattan Company, the Merchants' Bank, the Bank of America, the National Bank, and the Mechanics' Bank—and helped several obtain their official charters.

Municipal favoritisms greatly enhanced Astor's Manhattan real estate holdings, like those of the Goelets, Schermerhorns, and Brevoorts. These boons ranged from the city's cheap sales to well-connected investors of valuable "water plots"—shoreline, swamp, and pond tracts easily and profitably reclaimable for development—to vastly understated assessments that kept their property taxes low. Part of Astor's shrewdness was in picking investments that would profit from the state-financed Erie Canal, city-financed municipal improvements, and Manhattan's extraordinary population growth.

Astor and Girard themselves, along with Cornelius Vanderbilt in his younger days, represented what the principal historian of the nineteenth-century transportation revolution, George R. Taylor, aptly labeled "metropolitan mercantilism"—the fiercely competitive alliances of businessmen and local governments in New York, Philadelphia, Boston, Baltimore, and Charleston to maximize and develop each city's commercial and transportation hinterlands. Rails, waterways, and banks were the municipal weaponry, less destructive than the crossbows and siege cannon used by earlier Italian city-state rivals. The edge gained by New York City from the fabulously successful Erie Canal—a $7 million project funded by New York State—spurred Boston and Philadelphia to push their own canal, pike, and rail networks westward, although with less success.

Early-nineteenth-century U.S. merchant capitalism, in sum, remained a milieu in which a late-eighteenth-century Briton or American would have felt at home. Government still had greater gravitas than business. In his *History of American Law,* Lawrence Friedman explained how, in the special charters granted by state legislatures of that period, "franchise was a key legal concept. The franchise was a grant to the private sector, out of the inexhaustible reservoir of state power . . . in the first place, many corporations were chartered to do work traditionally part of the function of the state. The jobs included banking, roadbuilding, and the digging of canals. Secondly, since each franchise was a privilege and favor, the state had a right to exact a price, which might include strict control or even profit sharing." In many places, especially through the 1830s, state or local governments continued to build and operate the turnpikes or canals (and even a few banks and railroads).

The metropolitan wealth elites—most fortunes remained local—took repeated advantage, finding these alliances profitable. Besides his banks, Pennsylvania's Girard helped get state approval for the Schuylkill (pronounced "skookle") Canal and the Pottsville & Danville Railroad. Astor was another major shareholder in specially chartered transportation companies—the Mohawk & Hudson Railroad, the Delaware & Raritan Canal, and the Camden & Amboy Railroad, among others.

The prominence of rich beneficiaries whetted public suspicions of the privilege that clung to the word "corporation." Daniel Raymond, in his *Thoughts on Political Economy* (1820), the first general text on economics written in the United States, called corporations "detrimental to national wealth. They are always created for the benefit of the rich, and never for the poor. . . . The rich have money, and not being satisfied with the power which money itself gives them, in their private individual capacities, they seek for an artificial combination, or amalgamation of their power, so that its force may be augmented." William Leggett of the Workingmen's Party called the chartering elites a state-supported "order of American barons" and advocated a general incorporation law to replace the government cronyism. Andrew Jackson, in his 1837 farewell address, also lashed "the multitude of corporations with exclusive privileges."

In Pennsylvania, Ohio, and elsewhere, popular demands for "equal distribution of costs and benefits" to replace charter favoritism convinced state governments themselves to undertake much of the canal building and early railroad construction. This petered out in the voter anger over governmental involvements and state insolvencies that followed the economic crisis of 1837. Even so, the dollar outlays of cities and states for canals, turnpikes, and railroads were already enough to exceed anything else the peacetime government did during the first half of the nineteenth century. The cities—not least their private property owners—thrived.

This familiar world of private wealth nestling close to government authority changed quickly in the 1840s and 1850s. Cities were getting much bigger. Immigration was soaring. Ironworks, engine works, machine shops, and railroads heralded the U.S. version of the Industrial Revolution. Burgeoning commerce meant more and more new business on a scale that compelled modification of the economic roles hitherto played by government.

The sheer volume and legislative burden of special charters, for example, called out for replacement by easy, uncomplicated incorporation under a general statute. New York had passed such a law for small industrial corporations in 1811, but persisting popular distrust limited its use and blocked attempts elsewhere until the climate changed in 1837. Although companies specially chartered by legislatures remained numerous through the Civil War, after 1845 more and more states required that incorporation be under the *general* statute. Supervision of business by the state shrank accordingly, foreshadowing a further hands-off philosophy after the Civil War.

The rise of stock exchanges provided milestones in capital formation as well as chess pieces of metropolitan competition. The New York Stock & Exchange Board, established in 1817, overshadowed its Philadelphia rival despite the latter's imaginative but desperate (pretelegraph) use of signal stations to keep in touch with Manhattan. The Boston exchange, in turn, dominated trading in industrial stocks. Volume on the New York exchange rose from 1,000 shares a day and listings for several dozen corporations in 1830 to 50,000 shares a day and several hundred listings by 1850. This enlargement of exchanges, particularly New York's, would soon make them capital markets marshaling enough resources to let entrepreneurs seek private investors rather than government as a partner.

As government's hold slackened, with easy incorporation permitted by statute, private companies, markets, and industrial enterprises grew like mushrooms. Federal power would expand again from 1861 to 1865, but the underlying momentum of laissez-faire currents after the war worked a reversal of the old relationship of wealth and the state. For roughly three decades beginning in the 1870s, government would be subservient to corporations and financiers, its role usually that of servant and police force, not senior partner as of yore. However, before we turn to the details of how government in the United States favored or rearranged wealth, it is useful to begin with a broader context: how the principal U.S. electoral realignments have often changed the arrangement of U.S. wealth.

2. U.S. Political Watersheds and Wealth Realignments

Discussion of wealth and property as shapers of politics harks back to Plato and Aristotle. Other thinkers followed, from Plutarch to John Locke. The most-quoted American pronouncement is James Madison's, that, "The most common and durable source of factions [parties] has been the various and unequal distribution of property. . . . A landed interest, a manufacturing interest, a mercantile interest, with many lesser interests grow up of necessity in civilized nations and divide them into different classes actuated by different sentiments and views." Charles A. Beard, the Progressive historian, posed a grander thesis in his book *The Economic Basis of Politics*: that economics drove the great realignments of American political parties.

In some cases, yes, in others, no. Yet even believers in the greater sway of factors like wars or regionalism, race, and religion must give economics great weight. Moreover, as we have seen, several of the major U.S. electoral watersheds have been accompanied by the leadership of new regions and economic sectors and followed by upward or downward asset and income redistributions. Turning points of politics have become turning points of wealth.

Thomas Ferguson, a Massachusetts political scientist, has offered a related "investment theory" of U.S. politics. Realignments, in this scheme of things, "occur when cumulative long-run changes in industrial structures (commonly interacting with a variety of short-run factors, notably steep economic downturns) polarize the business community, thus bringing together a new and powerful bloc of investors with persisting interests." Investors in politics, by this view, include the larger financial contributors to parties and candidates.

While this equation is too narrow to explain the periodic realignments of the larger national electorate, Ferguson's attentions to "realignments" of economic sectors and political contributors identified important behavior. This chapter will frame a different but related theme: the varying extents to which watershed electoral realignments have been followed by related shifts within the ranks of the richest Americans. Four instances stand out: the years of independence and the beginnings of the republic along with the recognized national political watersheds of 1800, 1860, and 1932.

The wealth realignment arising out of the American Revolution and the Constitution of 1787 was manifestly political. Between 1775 and 1783 over 100,000 loyalists left the future United States, mostly for Britain, Canada, or the Bahamas. Many forfeited estates that prior to 1775 had been among the colonies' largest. In virtually every state, postwar observers spoke of new riches turning prewar hierarchies topsy-turvy. The first U.S. presidential election in 1788, in turn, ushered in a new government centered on George Washington. Included were a group of men who had made money out of the Revolution and now sought, in the style of the late-seventeenth-century English Whigs, to entrench a new monied elite around the financial management of the new nation.

This Federalist elite, as we have seen, was a transient one. The New Englanders enriched by wartime privateering did furnish many of America's richest families through the War of 1812. However, the New York–Philadelphia axis of wartime financiers and procurement officials stumbled during the 1790s, with William Duer and Robert Morris going to debtors' prison. Government connections could make millionaires, but not necessarily always rescue them.

The second of America's political wealth realignments followed the electoral watershed of 1800, after which the victorious Jeffersonians trapped the defeated Federalists in New England–centered minority status while electoral power shifted to the South and Middle Atlantic cities. The War of 1812 hurt Yankee commerce, and the region's several shipping fortunes in the $2–$3 million range lost their national preeminence—not that reliable measurements exist—to Stephen Girard and John Jacob Astor, whose closeness to the Jefferson, Madison, and Monroe regimes needs no repetition.

No parallel shift followed the rise of Jacksonian democracy and the electoral watershed of 1828. Jackson, after all, basically extended the common man courtship and anti–Bank of the United States politics of the Jeffersonians. His 1832 veto of the Second Bank's rechartering, ending as it did Philadelphia's claim to being the U.S. banking center, boosted Baltimore and iced the cake of New York's financial preeminence. After Stephen Girard died in 1836, Philadelphia never again commanded one of the nation's top two or three wealth-holdings.

Yet on the large wealth-holder level, of the South's several dozen millionaires from rice, cotton, sugar, and mercantile activities, most were Whigs, not Jacksonians. Perhaps half of the millionaires of the 1840s called New York home, including Astor, but their politics, too, shaded toward the Whigs. Of the twenty-five millionaires in Massachusetts in 1850, over 85 percent were Whigs, and the figure for Philadelphia was at least two-thirds. Jackson was a powerful president, but he did not create a new national economic elite.

The Civil War, of course, did—a huge realignment under the aegis of wartime and postwar Republican policy. The principal wealth flows were from South to North and from agriculture to railroads and industry. As we have seen, many of the northerners climbing highest on the ladder had Yankee antecedents, even if they hailed from upstate New York, Ohio, or Michigan, and had gotten their commercial running start during the war years. Once again the imprint of politics and policy was unmistakable.

The election of 1896 became an electoral watershed when a victorious new industrial Republican coalition arose out of twenty years of a close party balance. However, the election's effect on the great fortunes was to *secure* rather than *realign* them. In July wealthy Clevelanders had worried, in the words of one, about being "hung from lampposts on Euclid Avenue." Spared from such fate at the hands of William Jennings Bryan's rural Jacobins, upper-class Americans breathed a sigh of relief with Republican William McKinley. Wealth-holders settled back to enjoy the stock market's run-up to the new century of electricity, telephones, automobiles, and even flying machines.

During the two-decade stalemate of 1876–96, U.S. millionaires had been perhaps two-to-one Republican, less proportionately than in the 1860s. This reflected some reformist support for Democrats Tilden (1876) and Cleveland (1884, 1888, and 1892) as well as the antitariff sympathies of both many wealthy merchants and exporters. In the ideological maelstrom of 1896, though, U.S. millionaires may well have been eight or ten-to-one against Bryan and for McKinley, some of which stuck. The existing elite continued, but more Republican than before.

Notwithstanding his fierce rhetoric, Theodore Roosevelt's time in the White House caused no more wealth realignment than Jackson's.

Progessivism principally slowed wealth's earlier unhindered increase by discrediting survival-of-the-fittest viewpoints, reducing political corruption, and reestablishing government as a regulatory force. The neo-laissez-faire industrial GOP regimes of the 1920s for their part, despite ambitious tax cuts and reductions in government, failed to shape any new wealth configuration, largely because of the 1929 Crash.

This left the Democratic watershed election of Franklin D. Roosevelt in 1932 to achieve the first definite political realignment of great wealth since the Civil War. Profiles of the 1930s showed the older rich families still ascendant, and the great bulk of them remained Republican. Several old names like Astor, Vanderbilt, and Harkness had appeared on the list of 1932 Roosevelt support, but their interest cooled. However, business and financial support for Roosevelt's reelection in 1936 included new increments—in oil, agribusiness, finance, multinational corporations, and technology—that foreshadowed changes visible in the top wealth lists by the 1940s and 1950s. These included Texas oilmen who were Democrats at least through World War II, pro-Roosevelt financiers like Clarence Dillon and Joseph P. Kennedy, and aviation magnates with Democratic ties (William Blakley and Howard Hughes).

The launching in 1968 of a quarter century of Republican presidencies, overlapping with the large realignment of wealth to the Sun Belt, sparked rhetoric about Yankee and Cowboy wars, Dallas conspiracies, and status-hungry Orange County new rich. But although the movement of Florida, Texas, and California into a GOP presidential pattern from 1968 to 1988 buoyed the regional shift, it was not Republican-engineered. The Roosevelt years had laid the groundwork for the huge demographic expansion through prewar federal largesse and then the World War II influx of military and defense installations. Richard Nixon was hungry to create a new establishment in the 1970s, but Watergate foreclosed any possibility, and in any event the Sun Belt–based presidents during the 1968–92 GOP era came from both parties: Democrats Johnson and Carter as well as Republicans Nixon, Reagan, and Bush.

In the 1990s the overlap between a new top U.S. wealth elite based on technology, software, entertainment, and Internet money and a collaborative new Democratic regime in the White House suggested another possible watershed. None of the World War II generation Republican presidents elected between 1968 and 1992 had any particular interest in "high" technology. Nixon is remembered for being unable to erase an audiotape; Reagan's fascination ended with movie cameras; and apolitical

Silicon Valley executives joked to visiting journalists that George H. W. Bush didn't know a computer chip from a potato chip.

It's at least plausible to relate Democratic White House tenure and the nineties emergence of a wealth realignment tied to technology. Holding national power during an economic, technological, or regional emergence and working to bring it to fruition can be enough to claim credit. The basic hegemony of industrial Republicanism from the Civil War through the 1920s (despite the stalemate of 1876–96) depended on being present and ardent at *both* creations: the new political era and the postwar economics that took modern shape around railroads, steel, and oil.

In sum, if national politics can shape new wealth elites from time to time, then small wonder that government has been—and undoubtedly still is—one of the most powerful forces shaping the creation and distribution of wealth within the United States.

Each of this chapter's final three sections will examine one stream of this influence: First, the powerful wealth-shaping dimensions and nuances of U.S. fiscal and monetary policy over two centuries, next the acceleration in the 1990s of efforts by multinational banks and corporations to create a friendly *international* regulatory framework for investment and profit, and then the role played by levels of government in the United States—both as policy architect and political captive—in the emergence of technology, industries, and corporations.

3. WEALTH AND GOVERNMENT ECONOMIC POLICY IN THE UNITED STATES

From the nursery years of the Republic, U.S. government economic decisions in matters of taxation, central bank operations, debt management, banking, trade and tariffs, and financial rescues or bailouts have been keys to expanding, shrinking, or realigning the nation's privately held assets. With the operating politics of economic gain following these principal pathways, wealth-holders have sometimes steered government decisions toward a group benefit and sometimes simply taken individual advantage. Occasionally public policy tilted toward the lower and middle classes, as under Jefferson, Jackson, and Franklin D. Roosevelt. Most often, in the United States and elsewhere, these avenues and alleyways have been explored, every nook and cranny, for the benefit of the financial and business classes.

The politics and management of government debt, to begin with, produced many of the large personal European and American fortunes of the eighteenth and early nineteenth centuries. The earlier Dutch, having seen the periodic bankruptcies of Spanish kings, built a very different and successful system around a funded debt supported by reliable revenue streams; and by 1694 the Bank of England was established after the Dutch model, along with a new and fast-growing English funded debt. Both banks and both funded debts quickly created prospering groups of "moneymen"— bankers, jobbers, and speculators—as well as a pair of debtor classes committed to the Dutch regents and England's King William III.

Ancient as these events may seem, they were living, breathing examples worthy of emulation to the three men who made their late-eighteenth-century names bringing similar practices to the United States: Robert Morris (born in England), Alexander Hamilton (born in Nevis in the British West Indies), and William Duer (born in England and educated at Eton). Well acquainted with the theory, practice, and speculative opportunities of Anglo-Dutch finance, all three rejected the typical "country party" views of the Virginia planters, who mostly echoed the concerns of William Blackstone and Adam Smith that funded debts led to executive tyranny and the eventual insolvency of the state, or both.

Funded debt, to Hamilton, was an engine of state and even a "national blessing." He and his allies sought to create a private class of "moneymen." It was also a first-class factional opportunity in addition to binding creditors to the interest of the new U.S. government, as earlier lenders had been to the political success of Dutch and English loan-issuers.

The mechanisms put in place from 1790 to 1792—the Bank of the United States, funded long-term U.S. debt, federal assumption of state and local debt, and the forerunner of the New York Stock Exchange—became the playground of the incipient speculator class. If these arrangements generally fulfilled Hamilton's promise of nation-building, they also justified Thomas Jefferson's sweeping condemnation of national banks and funded debt as agents of corruption. The first American wave of securities speculation came in New York and Philadelphia in 1791, as Bank of the United States shares climb from $25 to $60, peaking at $170 in some three months. Similar speculation developed in the new U.S. bond issues, and when the bubble around Bank of the United States and other bank stocks popped, Hamilton ordered the treasury into the market in March and April of 1792 to support the price of government debt. His allies sighed with relief over what by some accounts was the first U.S. financial bailout.

The profits to be made were large. Four men who may have constituted a succession of America's richest individuals between 1783 and 1848— Robert Morris, William Bingham, Stephen Girard, and John Jacob Astor—built at least part of their wealth on the proceeds of investment or speculation in state and federal debt and Bank of the United States stock. Government finance also produced the largest personal net worths in early-nineteenth-century France and Britain, those of Nathan Rothschild, James Rothschild, and Gabriel Julien Ouvrard, the French wartime paymaster and financier. Public debt in those days was arguably the principal *private* financial opportunity.

As the mass of government debt grew, it lent itself less to producing nations' leading personal fortunes. The principal financier of the North's triumphant road to Appomattox, the great bond-seller Jay Cooke, went bankrupt in 1873, pulled down by overextended railroad underwriting as well as by the scheming of the House of Morgan to gain the preeminent role in U.S. government finance. J. P. Morgan and a second financier also much involved in underwriting and supporting government bonds, George F. Baker of New York's First National Bank, both appear among the wealthiest for 1901–14 in chapter 2, although the top of the list was dominated by oil and steel.

Post–Civil War era debt management, like its postrevolutionary predecessor, had substantial elements of a political reward system. Confederate bonds became, literally, not worth the paper they were printed on; wartime federal bonds, conversely, became something of a treasure trove. As Washington began its large-scale borrowing in 1862, Treasury Secretary Salmon P. Chase thought in the earlier vein of Dutch regents, London Williamites, and Alexander Hamilton. Banks that bought the new federal bonds in order to be able to issue federal banknotes, Chase wrote, would bind themselves politically to the Northern cause.

Once victorious, Washington delivered handsomely for the Northern banks and individuals who had purchased most of the war's $2 billion issuance of notes and bonds. Many had paid for the securities in greenbacks, which typically traded at a considerable wartime discount to gold. Treasury interest, however, had been temptingly payable in gold from the start, a good return. Then in 1869, Congress passed and President Grant signed the Public Credit Act, providing that federal debt securities, whether or not bought with below-par paper money, be redeemed in gold. While less egregious than the early 1790s speculative gains from assumption and funding, this windfall was on a much larger scale.

As both government and the national debt giantized in the twentieth century, the effects of debt had less to do with personal fortune and more to do with public spending and broader economic redistribution. Woodrow Wilson, Franklin D. Roosevelt, Harry Truman, and Lyndon Johnson all tolerated or could not stop wartime and postwar inflation that undercut the real value of many financial assets, especially mortgages and bonds, even as it supported domestic production and spending. Although this Democratic brand of wealth and income redistribution struck hard at certain assets and after-tax incomes, it usually produced enough economic growth and increased consumer spending to create new business opportunities and markets.

By contrast, the upward redistribution patterns of conservative governments in the 1920s and then again in 1980s and 1990s generally followed the contours of economic policy after the Civil War. This involved cutting some taxes and trying to abolish others, emphasizing deficit reduction or budget balance as a priority (if not always achieving it), and working to stymie farm price supports, block easy money, and reduce what later generations would call human resources spending. The genesis and recurrence of this GOP political economics is pursued in chapter 7.

Managed this way, the outcomes in the Gilded Age, the 1920s, and the Reagan and Bush administrations were highly favorable to financial assets, which were lopsidedly owned by the top 1 percent of the population. The benefits to upper-bracket wealth that flowed from these financial booms and their varying contractions of government debt, taxation, and spending were broad, more widely distributed within the top tier than the concentrated debt repayment to loyal creditors and supporters after the wars of 1775–83 and 1861–65.

Federal debt politics and management took on a new nuance in the 1990s after the tax cut, defense spending, and budget deficit buildup of the 1980s. This flowed from the famous advice given to just-inaugurated President Clinton in 1993. Your success or failure, chief economic adviser Robert Rubin told Clinton, lies in the hands of a bunch of bond traders. Like many other national leaders during the 1990s, he had to submit to two new power centers: central bankers and increasingly global bond markets. Almost by definition, their influence, as we will see, worked to favor finance, the stock market, and continued concentration of wealth.

Ironically, Thomas Jefferson, Andrew Jackson, and several other early-nineteenth-century presidents had more or less predicted that a national debt buildup would ultimately mean loss of control to bankers and "papermen," although they erred in seeing it just around the nineteenth-century corner. Like the Dutch and British, the United States could never have achieved its global trajectory without a central bank and a funded national debt, but there was a price. Adam Smith had warned in 1776 that "the practice of funding [has] gradually enfeebled every state which has adopted it," citing Spain and Holland as cautions for Britain. The latter's own debt, in turn, did become a punishing weight by the 1930s and 1940s, and the international, national, and consumer debt levels of the United States were points of uncertainty as the twenty-first century opened, 1990s homage to the bond markets not withstanding.

Taxes, in some form, provide the revenue stream funded debt requires. This had been central to Dutch and English success, and Hamilton also knew revenues would be essential. The Federalist levies put into effect—principally the excise tax on whiskey, but also land taxes and stamp taxes—were unpopular enough in the 1790s to help defeat Hamilton's party in 1800. Revenue tariffs levied on thirty items from molasses and hemp to nails were better accepted. Jefferson quickly repealed all internal taxes in 1802, leaving tariffs as the principal revenue source of the U.S. government until 1911, save for the high tax emergency of the Civil War.

At the federal level, in short, taxes as opposed to tariffs were rarely a key to enlarging or redistributing wealth until the establishment of the permanent income tax in 1913. Tariffs, while also indirect taxes on consumers, were also tools for protecting and stimulating U.S. companies and industries and their wealth effects will be examined in that connection shortly.

Taxation during the nineteenth century, as we have seen, was principally local and property-based, which lent itself to favoritism. In many jurisdictions, not least New York City, the rich were widely able to convince officials to set extremely low assessments of real estate, personal property, or both. While the burdens sidestepped were not huge, full assessments would have slowed the real estate boom. This, in turn, would have somewhat reduced the property-based Manhattan and Philadelphia fortunes of the 1830s, 1840s, and 1850s.

Critics complained about another redistributionist aspect. Some jurisdictions increased ordinary citizens' real estate, personal property, and other local and state taxes in order to fund interest payments on bond issues and subsidies to canals, railroads, and other enterprises. Raising money this way helped build the great railroad fortunes, dependent as many were on railroading's lucrative underpinnings of federal, state, and local land grants, subsidies, tax abatements, and the like. One-third to one-half of the $4.6 billion U.S. railroad capitalization circa 1875 was thought to have such public-source origins. Not only did many successful railroad barons assemble more public than private financing, but for several decades railroad attorneys thrived fighting ongoing efforts to make the railroads give back public lands and financial aid in cases where the line was never or only partially built.

From the sixteenth to the eighteenth centuries it was widely held in Europe that taxes should fall heavily on the lower orders to make up for the feudal obligations from which the peasantry had been or were being relieved. Such views were unacceptable in the United States. However, as a practical matter, Federal tariffs fell heavily on consumers and were often bitterly opposed in agricultural states and districts. Tariff-fixing was dominated by commercial interests during the industrial era. Thereafter, in the early twentieth century as the federal income tax and FICA (Social Security and Medicare) taxes grew to become the major revenue sources, the lobbying and interest-group scheming once reserved for the great tariff bills refocused on tax legislation.

Tax law, its loopholes, and exceptions obviously bulks large in any twentieth-century examination of what classes, industries, and individuals in the United States got wealth and how. Hundreds of books have been published with titles using every verb, adjective, and noun form of words like rob, steal, and thieve. These next few pages can only identify some highlights (and lowlights).

After the Sixteenth Amendment to the federal Constitution in 1913 authorized an income tax, which Congress passed that same year, the First World War sent the top rates paid by individuals and corporations climbing to a level needed in wartime but obviously excessive once peace came. The Republican strategy on taking office in 1921 was to dismantle this as much as possible, while attempting to replace it with Treasury Secretary Mellon's own blueprint: a regressive national sales tax on all articles in retail trade. Progressives in Congress blocked the switch, but a series of four tax cuts between 1921 and 1928 lowered the top individual income tax rate from 77 percent to 25 percent, reduced corporate income and excise taxes, and repealed the excess-profits and gift taxes. One critic estimated that up to 1926, the Mellon tax cuts had saved wealthy individuals and corporations over $4 billion a year, huge amounts in years when the federal budget was some $3 billion.

Feeling thwarted even so, Mellon undertook an unusual program of refunds, rebates, and remissions totaling another $6 billion during his nine years in office. Many were determined by Assistant Treasury Secretary S. Parker Gilbert and his aides on little more than a whim, according to a

U.S. Senate investigation led by Michigan progressive James Couzens. Some of the givebacks, including one to the Mellon banks in Pittsburgh, were held to be illegal. Thousands of lawyers, accountants, and tax experts were busy submitting and handling tens of thousands of requests and submissions to the treasury, and as the money was paid out, much went to fuel the speculative boom and stock market bubble.

Franklin Roosevelt and the New Deal raised the top individual tax brackets, eliminated Mellon's fiscal favors, tightened inheritance taxes, and eliminated the personal holding companies through which some of the rich had deducted the expenses of their estates, stables, horses, and planes. They were mad enough to prompt Manhattan jokes about dinner parties in evening dress going down to the Trans-Lux to hiss FDR in the newsreels. Even the New Deal, however, gave tax favors to the biggest industry run by Democratic supporters: oil. The oil depletion allowance, begun in the twenties, took on its great importance during the high-tax-rate years of the thirties, forties, and fifties.

In the fifties and thereafter, the perfection and enactment of tax loopholes, credits, and exemptions became one of Washington's principal cottage industries, partly because this time the top individual income tax bracket (91 percent) remained long after the end of World War II. The Republican Eightieth Congress reduced it in 1948, only to lose control of both the House and Senate that year in a landslide repudiation influenced by Democratic charges of GOP favoritism to the rich. This convinced the GOP to leave the nominal top rate alone through all eight years of the Eisenhower administration. Democrat John Kennedy would bring it down in 1963 to 77 percent.

The difference between the decade after World War I and the decade after World War II deserves emphasis: the first had seen the resources of a victorious United States poured into a speculative 1920s bubble; the second saw taxes on the rich remain high, upper-bracket excess restrained, and the growth of a healthier and happy working class and middle class extended. In retrospect, it was an uncommon achievement.

By 1978–80, however, the federal tax system had developed a new Achilles' heel: the impact of 1970s inflation on the tax-rate tables, widely nicknamed bracket-creep. Local property taxes had also expanded painfully. The outcome was another uncommon phenomenon: a middle-class tax revolt. However, in a politics increasingly dominated by contributors and corporations, the middle three-fifths of the nation had little say in the actual resculpting of the tax code carried out between 1981 and 1990. In some ways the spirit of Andrew Mellon had returned.

The Economic Recovery Tax Act of 1981, soon followed by a recession and the first double-digit unemployment since the Depression, ballooned the federal deficit partly because of the revenues that Democrats and Republicans competed to give away to corporations. It became as of that date the single biggest cut in the history of the federal income tax. The most notorious provision, so-called "safe harbor leasing," allowed companies that could not themselves use the act's extravagant depreciation allowances and investment tax credits to *sell them to other companies.* General Electric, according to one business history, touched off a furor by disclosing that it had used the provision not only to wipe out most of the company's 1981 tax liability but to pick up $110 million in refunds for previous years. The sum of corporate-claimed depreciation for 1982–87 totaled an extraordinary $1.65 trillion. Although the provisions of the 1981 act were only part of the architecture, huge sums of potential corporate income liability were lost to depreciation excesses.

In 1983 a presidential commission headed by future Federal Reserve chairman Alan Greenspan decided that while corporate and individual income tax rates were coming down, especially in the top brackets, Social Security and Medicare (payroll) taxes on lower and middle-income Americans had to be increased, and to an extent that would make them more onerous than income taxes for an ever-growing portion of the population. In 1985, for example, a two-earner family making $25,000-a-year paid more in FICA taxes than in income taxes; by 1995, expanding FICA earnings coverage and higher rates made them the greater burden for two-thirds of U.S. families.

The "Tax Reform" Act of 1986 was hailed by persons in or near the highest income tax bracket, which dropped to 28 percent. However, national polls showed that its reform label was not taken seriously by most others. Behind the facade of eliminating "tax preferences for the rich and powerful," the act had some 650 special provisions usually called "transition rules" or "technical corrections" invariably disguised, albeit thinly, in dense language.* Mellonism was back, indeed.

The 1986 act, furthermore, established a rate structure that peaked for

---

* The exemption for a single Beverly Hills securities dealer was phrased this way: "Special Rules for Broker-Dealers—In the case of a broker-dealer which is part of an affiliated group which files a consolidated Federal income tax return, the common parent of which was incorporated in Nevada on January 27, 1972, the personal holding income (within the meaning of Section 543 of the Internal Revenue Code of 1986) of such broker-dealer, shall not include any interest received after the date of enactment of this Act. . . ."

the upper middle class, not millionaires. Federal taxwriters came up with an unusual device called the "bubble" through which a 33 percent marginal rate applied to households in the $70,000 to $170,000 range, but fell to 28 percent for those with higher earnings. Another was created in the overhaul of 1990 when, because of what tax expert Emil Sunley of the accounting firm of Deloitte & Touche called George Bush Senior's "passion for subterfuge," the president rejected any new nominal top rate higher than 31 percent. This small increase, by itself, was not enough to replace the revenues brought in by the previous bubble, so a second had to be implanted. *The Economist* of London distilled the effect as follows: "True marginal tax rates in the United States are at their peak for two-earner couples making between $50,000 and $100,000 a year—precisely the middle-income people who would best respond to the incentive of lower rates. America has one of the world's least progressive tax structures . . . the payroll tax wreaks havoc with marginal tax rates."

Chart 5.2 shows the old and new effective-rate bubbles as calculated by a leading accounting firm. It should also be considered alongside the

CHART 5.2 The New Tax Rate Bubble

Figures are based on average gross income for a family of six under the old and new tax laws.

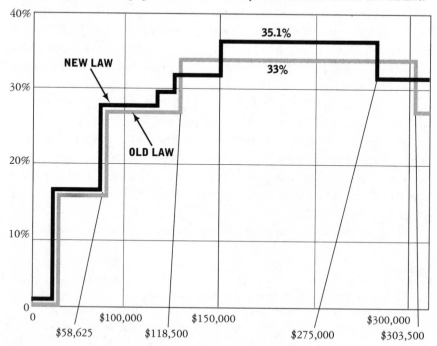

Source: *Investors's Daily,* 11/21/90. Source: Coopers & Lybrand.

portraiture in Chart 2.13a of the extraordinary convergence over nearly a half century of the effective tax rates of the median American family and the millionaire or top 1 percent family.

The Clinton administration, while imposing a new 39.6 percent top rate in 1993, still declined to pursue reestablishing the wide gap between the top bracket and those affecting middle incomes so unmistakable in 1940, 1960, and even 1980. Congress would not have gone along. In late 1999, when the Republican Congress proposed massive tax relief for corporations, maverick GOP senator John McCain condemned his party for breaking its commitment to eliminate "corporate welfare," adding, "Now we're going to see this big thick tax code on our desks, and the fine print will reveal another cornucopia for the special interests, and a chamber of horrors for the taxpayers."

Not even a full book—perhaps not even a shelf of them—could begin to do justice to the role of federal income-type taxation in shaping, favoring, and from time to time even helping to realign wealth in the United States. These previous pages have simply tried to convey the spirit and some of the techniques.

Besides managing debt and taxation, government has powerfully affected the economy through contraction or expansion of the currency, once simply describable as inflation and deflation. Rising prices have been one of the snarling dogs let slip by war, as Chart 1.4 illustrated. Chapters 1 and 2 discussed their effects on industry, with wage earners usually wartime losers because their real purchasing power shrank. The exception was the inflation surrounding World War II, which was controlled by wage and price controls and excess-profits taxes so that the working and middle classes did as well (or better) than everyone else.

Deflation was often pursued by government within a few years of the end of hostilities to restore the wartime erosions of purchasing power and financial assets. To some degree it is legitimate. Its abusive form, exemplified by the per capita currency squeeze of the Gilded Age, came as a continuing quarter-century overcorrection that shrank price levels below outbreak-of-war levels, whittled the assets of a vulnerable borrowing class (agriculture) and made more capital available to the expanding sector (manufacturing). This deflation was a major ingredient in the enormity of the U.S. industrial fortunes and the realignment of wealth they entailed.

The last of the major twentieth-century inflation waves, stirred by Vietnam era fiscal mistakes and the follow-up oil price increases of 1973–74 and 1979–80, produced the abnormal oil and Texas-bias in the top U.S. wealth list for 1982 as well as the parallel erosion of financial assets and the stagnation of U.S. median family income. Commodity, timber, and real estate fortunes were other beneficiaries.

The two political parties have risked inflation for different reasons. The Republicans did so in 1861–65 to save the Union. Then during the Reagan years they tolerated 4 to 6 percent inflation as the price of cutting upper-bracket and business taxes and increasing defense outlays, the wishes of two key constituencies. The Democrats have been even more accepting, not simply because the four major twentieth-century wars the U.S. has entered began during their tenures, but also in response to urban, education, labor, and minority constituencies anxious for more spending (and little concerned about the effects on inflation or financial assets).

Mildly inflationary federal spending, as in the New Deal, has been a means for *downward* redistribution by liberals and progressives of some of the wealth and income that conservative politics has redistributed *upward* through deflation, tax cuts, and budget constriction. Some of the largest twentieth-century U.S. fortunes built by consumer spending—in retailing, footwear, department stores, apparel, real estate, entertainment, food, and tobacco—owed their size to these expansive economic biases, and Democratic party loyalties were common among wealth-holders in these industries.

By the 1980s, however, the politics of monetary orchestration was ascending to a new inscrutability. Three once fairly simple U.S. economic yardsticks—currency exchange rates, the size of the money supply, and the measurement of inflation—had given way to multiple series, elaborate equations, and opaque pronouncements by unelected regulators, central bankers especially. The early seventies' unhooking of currencies from gold and the 1980 deregulation of finance and interest rates opened two new game fields, enlivened by the new strategic trading reach that computer electronics gave to financiers and speculators. Once-remote and even arcane regulatory institutions took on steadily more influential roles, especially the Federal Reserve Board as shepherd of the U.S. banking system and controller of the U.S. money supply spigot. Their power to define the trends and formulas became the power to decide in which directions what increments of money would flow.

With currencies no longer tied to anything but paper, what was the money supply? What was the dollar's value in 2000, say, as opposed to 1990?—or, for that matter, what was its value for determining whether American workers earned more than German workers? Currency market outcomes were accepted for the general valuation. In the second instance, however, the actual exchange value for dollars versus *deutsche marks* was rejected by U.S. officials in favor of an equation purporting to reflect the comparative domestic purchasing power of the respective currencies as determined by international bureaucrats. Rightly or wrongly, this brought a higher value for the dollar that made the U.S.-German wage comparison look better to ordinary Americans.

As for whether the U.S. currency was expanding or contracting, watchers and central bankers had a choice of dozens of measurements. The relatively simple money supply yardstick, M1—not to be confused with the famous weapon—had been outdated by the fecundity of bank and financial deregulation in creating all kinds of new accounts, funds, deposits, and derivatives. Some of the M variations covered the entire monetary waterfront, others just the main piers and terminals; a few even included the ferries in the harbor. As the market squalls raged, M2 and M3 were sometimes pushed aside by a newer acronym—MZM (money of zero maturity: currency and all checking-type assets, including money-market funds). In short, how much the "money supply" was expanding and where became a matter for experts and exotic equations, not Main Street—or even Congress.

Price measurements themselves had become more subjective and political, as in the 1990s debate over whether the Consumer Price Index had overstated inflation. During the 1920s and 1960s, two other eras when new technology crowded the U.S. economy, the fact of automobiles and radios, and later jet passenger aircraft and computers getting better and cheaper was not used to adjust the measurement of prices actually paid. By 2000, however, "quality"—a term just as subjective as dollar "purchasing power" and the ambiguous "money supply"—had become an approved modifier of the Consumer Price Index. "Better" goods brought an adjustment that you really paid less: improved computers, less inflation.

In 1996 the CPI was also adjusted to correct a supposed prior overstatement of inflation. *Barron's,* the U.S. financial weekly, later mocked both the quality adjustments and political opportunism, rejecting any conspiracy theory but saying they had "helped to create a palpable gap between the cost of living in the real world that we poor souls inhabit and the cost of living in the Land of Oz fashioned by statistical fancy."

The federal government was not neutral. It profited from understatement of inflation, as did holders of financial assets. By contrast those who received pensions or cost-of-living increases, or who depended on bank interest or benefited from indexed tax brackets, preferred price increases to be fully scorecarded. The Federal Reserve Board was not neutral, either. It had no problem with soaring CEO compensation based on stock prices or profits; it routinely worried about fast-rising wages for workers, an ill omen to its inflation-sensitive financial constituency.

Befuddled voters and confused elected officials let more and more decision-making flow to unelected "experts"—courts, regulatory agencies, and most of all the Federal Reserve. Because the latter's perceptions of the dollar, inflation, and the money supply were backed up by the ability to implement them, the Fed's power ballooned, first under Chairman Paul Volcker (1979–87) and then into the nineties and new century under Chairman Greenspan. And the United States was by no means alone; central bankers were also taking the economic wheel in other advanced nations.

What made the late-twentieth-century aggrandizement stand out in the United States was how its nineteenth-century politics had rejected this sort of powerful, elite central bank. After Andrew Jackson vetoed the rechartering of the Second Bank of the United States in 1832, the Whigs failed to get a new one established because Van Buren, Tyler, Polk, and other pre–Civil War Democratic presidents were unwilling to accept central banks tied to private interests. Even post–Civil War Republicans left well enough alone. Indeed, the United States enjoyed some of its best economic growth following the 1830s and 1840s rejection of a central bank in favor of the so-called independent treasury approach. During most of the years between Van Buren's administration and Wilson's, subtreasury units operating independently of banks and private business served as federal depositories and currency distributors.

However, in the early 1900s, the leaderless array of national banks, state banks, and trust companies grown up under the subtreasury system proved unable to mobilize emergency reserves or currency to deal with two successive eastern-centered crises—the so-called Rich Man's Panic of 1902–3 and the bank-linked Panic of 1907. Some centralized coordination was imperative, bankers said. Populists and Progressives meanwhile nursed their own complaint: that over the previous decade, control over U.S. finances had passed to a dangerous private "money trust" of banks, corporations, and insurance companies in the orbit of J. P. Morgan.

Both camps had a point. The Morgan network *did* have enormous power. Yet under the independent treasury system, banks had twice been unable to marshal the currency and reserves needed for the stress-points of twentieth-century finance. Each side leaned toward a new system able to exercise national control, albeit from different perspectives. The resulting Federal Reserve System, launched in 1913, maintained ostensible banking decentralization through twelve separate Federal Reserve districts, but was headed by a new Federal Reserve Board in Washington, part financial regulator and part agency-designate for the crisis mobilization of currency and bank reserves.

The decisive planning of the new system, however, was that begun by bankers in meetings on Georgia's Jekyll Island in 1908 and carried into the National Monetary Commission deliberations that shaped the 1913 enactment. As the Federal Reserve System found its peacetime feet in the 1920s, its dual statutory relationship to the banking industry as well as government pulled its loyalties towards the former. The framework was in place, even if the immediate politics were not, for a de facto third Bank of the United States.

This time, the impact on wealth would exceed anything Hamilton or Biddle might have dreamed. We have seen how heavy stepping on the monetary brakes in 1920 brought a deep recession that cut the Dow-Jones Industrial Average roughly in half and probably did the same for million-airedom. The Fed botched an even bigger series of challenges in the 1925–32 period, losing particular stature in 1931–32 for its disastrous aversion to lowering interest rates. Constituency biases were at work. Had rates been driven down in 1931–32, major money-center banks would have suffered precariously reduced earnings from their large portfolios of government securities.

Following this mix of ineptness and bank-tied parochialism, the Fed kept a relatively low profile from the mid-1930s to the 1960s, regaining credibility in the fifties and sixties and gathering power steadily thereafter. In the eighties it increasingly assumed the proactive and central role that it had failed to grasp in the late 1920s and early 1930s. Power flowed accordingly.

Parts of this story, which began in 1979 with Paul Volcker's appointment as chairman, have already been told. The brief reiteration in this chapter is to underscore the Fed's arguable emergence—in the name of the government—as the principal U.S. wealth-shaping institution and to amplify its financial-sector biases, its proclivity to bailouts, and the Rumplestiltskin-like ability of its chairman, Alan Greenspan, to weave a half-trillion-dollar increase in stock values with congressional testimony or to doom hopes with a raised eyebrow.

By the spring of 2001, with the Nasdaq registering a two-thirds decline from its prior high, the Fed chairman's role in creating liquidity or its lack—and therefore new wealth or its contraction—became a national discussion. First, had the Fed blown up a fair part of the late-nineties speculative bubble through monetary expansiveness as well as bailouts and tailored liquidity surges? Second, had the Fed then popped the bubble with its series of interest-rate hikes in 2000?

Even the debate had aspects of an institutional coronation. A minority of economists suggested that the Fed would have to find some way of openly relating its money-supply management to stock market movements. Others waved transcripts of 1994 Fed Open Market Committee meetings, including frank comments by Greenspan on how to use monetary policy to affect stock and bond prices and deal with assets bubbles. Financial mercantilism was busy evolving guidelines. Writer Bob Woodward revealed in 2000 that back in 1987, the Fed's options book for dealing with a stock panic included organizing stock purchases by major securities firms and "targeted Fed lending specifically designed to support stock values." E. Gerald Corrigan, president of the New York Federal Reserve Bank, actually had a contingency plan for directly guaranteeing the payments between brokerage firms. If the United States, as seems arguable, had quietly embraced a "financial strategy" in lieu of an "industrial strategy," the Fed had quietly become its guarantor—and long before the securities market and terrorist traumas of 2001.

Chapter 9, in examining the politics of speculation, will amplify the contributory roles that various central banks have had in the major financial speculative bubbles of the last four centuries—from John Law and the South Seas Bubble in 1720 to the Crash of 1929 and the Great Depression and the implosion of the Japanese stock market and real estate bubble in the 1990s. Ironically, *Forbes* magazine, as the Nasdaq crash was just beginning in 2000, pointed out that these same events, the three biggest bull markets of previous history—the South Seas Bubble (up 729 percent from 1706 to 1720), 1929 Crash (up 394 percent from 1921 to 1929), and Japanese bubble (up 694 percent)—just happened to be followed by the biggest crashes: 83 percent (London, 1720–22), 86 percent (New York, 1929–32), and 64 percent (Tokyo, 1989–95).

Even so, the divergences among the three implosions' effects on wealth were also notable. The collapse of the South Sea Bubble halved some of England's most notable personal fortunes and wiped out many smaller ones, but it did not spread far into that era's real economy. The U.S. Crash of 1929 wiped away much of the decade's wealth formation and devastated the real economy as well.

In Japan, however, various government rescue attempts to bail out or support the tumbling stock and property markets made the 1990s a decade of economic stagnation—a contained depression, in some accounts—but avoided any 1930s-type result for ordinary Japanese and propped up most of Japan's billionaires. By 2001, whatever the economic dismay among ordinary Japanese, Japan still had twenty-nine of the world's five hundred or so billionaires, with banking and finance boasting four of the top five.

In Mexico, 1990s bank privatization created some twenty-eight billionaires and the mid-decade U.S. bail-out of the shaky peso with a $50 billion loan kept that inflated financial sector afloat. Ordinary Mexicans paid the price of economic damage. As for the effects of the International Monetary Fund and its global financial rescues, mostly in less developed countries, analyses by Columbia University economist Charles Calomiris found a recurring reinforcement of economic inequality. Financial elites were propped up; fiscal stringency requirements like spending cuts and tax increases applied more broadly.

Ultimately, the degree to which U.S. economic policy during the eighties, the nineties, and the bear markets of 2000–2001 was so heavily influenced by neo-mercantilism and bail-outs may serve as a historical warning. But in a nearer time frame, this bias—and the example of Japan's spread-out dislocations after its 1990 crash—may provide the benchmark for measuring U.S. Federal Reserve achievement during the post-millennial decade.

4. BEYOND THE UNITED STATES: U.S. WEALTH AND TRANSNATIONAL GOVERNMENT

Before turning to the role of government in advancing industry and technology and fortunes built around those sectors, it is worthwhile to briefly explore the high international plateau of twenty-first-century regulation represented in finance by central banks but in global trade and loan matters by the World Trade Organization, International Monetary Fund, and World Bank. Once again a new layer of government became a new framework of opportunity.

Over some two centuries, banks, railroads, and industrial corporations have proved their skill at playing the multiple levels of government within the United States. The opportunities of state banks versus national banks have been judged, the best state regulatory frameworks, tax structures, or aid packages shopped for, and federal legislation invoked to preempt state supervision. And as we will see shortly, late-nineteenth-century corporations, railroads in particular, used the power they were able to gain over state legislatures—which then elected U.S. senators—to take effective control over the federal Senate and federal judiciary.

The 1980s and 1990s brought another such intergovernmental opening. We have seen how the unelected Federal Reserve emerged as a governmental powerhouse, playing international as well as domestic U.S. management roles. Central banks also enlarged their independent authority elsewhere, especially in early-nineties Europe, where the Maastricht Treaty required the national central banks of countries participating in the European Union to meet a prescribed standard of political independence.

By 2000, Europe had its own European Central Bank, and together with the Bank of Japan and the U.S. Federal Reserve, the three dominated the global financial system, controlling upwards of 80 percent of growth in the developed world. "Governments have largely ceded to these three institutions the responsibility of controlling world inflation, and to do this they must necessarily influence the near-term path for GDP and unemployment," noted Goldman Sachs economist Gavyn Davies. "Rarely, if ever, can so much power have been wielded by such a small number of institutions sitting outside the direct democratic process."

The International Monetary Fund, in turn, was the global agency to which nations, usually poor or embattled ones, turned for loans and assistance in economic crises. The conditions of those loans usually involved austerity and measures to make the local economy safer for foreign investors. The U.S. Treasury Department was influential in IMF decisions, and one economics professor, Rudiger Dornbusch of MIT, stated simply that the IMF was "a tool of the United States to pursue its policy offshore."

In collaboration with U.S. multinational banks and corporations, the U.S. government, on a bipartisan basis, was indeed closely involved in writing the rules of the new global investor economy, especially through two new frameworks brought into existence in the 1990s: the North American Free Trade Agreement (1993) and the World Trade Organization (1995). The bottom line, from the standpoint of American multinational banks and corporations, was that the U.S. market had lost its old importance. Investment opportunities, production facilities, workers, and markets also had to be sought elsewhere, which would require the creation of a protective international legal and regulatory framework, one able to secure investment by overriding contrary local parochialisms and procedures.

Although criticism had forced the tabling in 1998 of a proposed Multilateral Agreement on Investment, the enactment of the North American Free Trade Agreement and the World Trade Organization included sections authorizing similar protections. Both agreements were pushed through Congress under so-called "fast track" procedures. When fast track was in place, the House and Senate were required to consider major trade legislation on a take-it-or-leave-it basis, with amendments prohibited. Otherwise, amendments—including ones to strike provisions thought to trespass on U.S. sovereignty—might well have passed.

However, new transnational enforcement procedures helped to explain why the World Trade Organization was superseding the General Agreement on Trade and Tariffs. NAFTA, too, had a section that established a system of arbitration under which investors from one of the other two nations could bring claims against the U.S., Canadian, or Mexican governments. Investors were allowed to demand compensation should the profit-making potential of a venture be injured by national, state, or local government decisions. The broader WTO, in standards for members that former director-general Renato Ruggiero called "a new constitution for a single global economy," permitted governments to bring actions against other nations before special WTO tribunals for interfering with the flow of goods and capital.

Several decisions by these three-member panels—routinely operating behind closed doors and generally staffed by former government or corporate trade officials—illustrated the transfer of power. One ruling against the United States required amendment of the Clean Air Act to permit the entry of Venezuelan gasoline that did not meet federal standards. Thailand, for its part, was told to give up manufacturing a cheap AIDS drug after the U.S. threatened a WTO suit on behalf of an American pharmaceutical firm. Critics in the U.S. Congress pointed to the large potential for WTO panels to overturn state and local laws in the United States. Each year, they said, Japan, the European Union, and Canada publish lists of American laws that each considers WTO-illegal. In 1999, according to the Georgetown University Law Center, ninety-five such laws were tentatively identified in California alone.

In terms of procedure, no appeals to other bodies were allowed from tribunal decisions based on criteria that free trade, economic growth, and enhanced financial returns outranked different local values. This fueled critics. Journalist William Greider, a latter-day muckraker, charged that, "The WTO aspires, in effect, to create a Bill of Rights for capital, crafted one case at a time by the corporate lawyers filing their confidential pleadings in Geneva. It is not hyperbole when critics say the system defines property rights and common social concerns as irrelevant to trade."

To the AFL-CIO, the rules of the new global economy were being "created by government muscle, wielded behind closed doors, largely on behalf of the most powerful corporate and financial interests." Democratic U.S. senator Fritz Hollings of South Carolina, who became chairman of the Senate Commerce Committee in 2001, charged that "the WTO puts our social contract in jeopardy; its one-size-fits-all capitalism threatens to destroy America's standard of living."

Even corporations had some second thoughts when a WTO tribunal ruled in 2001 that a $4 billion U.S. tax break for exporters was in violation of the new international rules, and affected U.S. companies howled. By and large, though, the new framework was one that U.S. multinational corporations promoted and favored. So did investors who understood that American wealth principally rested on stock market valuations tied to corporate profits.

But before we move away from government's role in shaping modern American wealth, it is necessary to look at one further pivot: promotion of industry and technology.

5. INDUSTRY, CORPORATIONS, TECHNOLOGY, AND THE ROLE OF GOVERNMENT

Since America's first decades the federal government has played a powerful role in encouraging industry and technology through ways other than debt and credit, taxation and money supply management, important as those encouragements have been. Vital political and judicial help was also given to the evolution of corporations. The amplification is that for three or four decades during the Gilded Age, corporations and railroads took their favors—enormous ones that helped produce the world's biggest fortunes—by all but seizing key portions of federal and state government. The legitimate encouragement of industry and technology aided U.S. growth and democracy; these political usurpations fundamentally threatened it.

The government's own aid to industry and "mechanics" began at the Constitutional Convention in 1787. And from the first days of the Republic, federal, state, and municipal authorities accomplished much to promote fisheries, forges, and factories, and perhaps most of all, new technologies.

The Constitution of the United States, at Thomas Jefferson's urgings, specifically called for the new government to encourage patents. Besides being aware of the practices of Anglo-Dutch finance, he was also mindful of what both nations had achieved by emphasizing patents and patent protection as a foundation of scientific and commercial success. The British reciprocated in a peculiar way. After the burning of Washington in 1814, Congress was able to meet in the building that had housed the patent authorities, spared by the British invaders out of respect for invention, if not for American government.

Agreement by economic historians on the vital role played by the unusually effective patent systems of Holland and Britain—by protecting invention, they stimulated investment—has even produced time lines. Half of all the Dutch patents granted between 1590 and 1790 came during the 1600–40 period, the country's all-important early maturity period. As for the British, before the 1760s fewer than a dozen patents a year were typically issued, then in 1766 there were thirty-one, then thirty-six in 1769, and sixty-four in 1783, these eighteen years being more or less the period of the inventive foundation of the Industrial Revolution. Another quantum leap came in 1824 and 1825, the threshold of the two decades that gave Britain the name "workshop of the world."

The U.S. Patent Law of 1790, followed by the establishment of a full-fledged patent office in 1836, gave inventors exclusive rights for fourteen years and made the United States a well-run market for ideas as well as goods. New England, with its mechanics, tinkerers, and metalworkers, quickly achieved the highest per capita number of patents, and by the 1840s the three-winged patent office building, a Greek temple on F Street, was so full of models of Yankee inventions—prototypes of everything from Alfred Vail's printing telegraph to Elias Howe's sewing machine—that it became a principal Washington tourist attraction. The acerbic Charles Dickens admitted that it was "an extraordinary example of American enterprise and ingenuity."

The most important early American convergence of inventiveness and practical industrial achievement flowed from another federal stimulus, a War Department contract given to Connecticut inventor Eli Whitney in 1798 to produce ten thousand muskets. To make them, Whitney devised molds, dies, and templates to produce interchangeable parts. To reassure nervous officials inquiring about delivery, "Whitney went to Washington, taking with him ten pieces of each part of a musket. He exhibited these to the Secretary of War and diverse army officers as a succession of piles of the several different parts. Selecting indiscriminately from each of the piles, he put together ten muskets, an achievement which was looked upon with amazement." Not long afterward he helped set up the U.S. arsenals at Springfield, Massachusetts, and Harper's Ferry, Virginia. There his methods were improved upon, opened to inspection, and borrowed by other industries, launching the "American System of Manufactures."

This system, in turn, led to the United States pioneering not just in guns, clocks, sewing machines, and farm implements but in the larger machine tool industry through still-famous company names like Pratt & Whitney and Brown & Sharpe. Connecticut gunmaker Samuel Colt, worth $5 million at his death in 1862, was another major beneficiary of these innovations, to say nothing of Civil War contracts. The prominent mid-nineteenth-century fortunes of Isaac Merrit Singer and William Clarke (sewing machines) and Cyrus McCormick (farm machinery) also grew out of Whitney's innovation.

The War of 1812, for all its military mismanagement, sparked a huge new commitment, even among Jeffersonians, to the manufactures and internal improvements able to avoid the unpreparedness so embarrassing during the war. In a late 1815 message to Congress, President Madison called for a second Bank of the United States, government encouragement of turnpikes, riverways, and canals, and tariff protection for war-bred "manufacturing establishments, especially of the more complicated kinds." All of these, he thought, were "undertakings conductive to the aggregate wealth . . . of our citizens."

The states and cities made larger outlays, but Washington, too, spent substantial sums on turnpikes, canals, and railroads. Between 1815 and 1840 some 4 million acres of public domain land were granted to canal projects in the Great Lakes states and $3 million was subscribed to the stock of canal companies, principally the Chesapeake & Ohio. The port city of Baltimore, doubly benefited by the federally subsidized C&O Canal and by several million dollars of municipal aid for the Baltimore & Ohio Railroad, jumped from a population of 30,000 in 1800 to 360,000 in 1860. This surge incubated two of America's $2–$3 million fortunes of the 1850s, those of Johns Hopkins and Alexander Brown and his family (of the merchant bankers Brown Brothers of New York, Philadelphia, and Baltimore).

The help that railroads received from Washington is especially striking. At federal expense, government engineers made surveys for railroads, estimated their costs, and helped supervise their construction. From 1830 to 1843, Congress suspended the tariff on iron used in railroad construction, effectively a $6 million subsidy. The first of the federal land grants to railroads followed in 1850, some 3.7 million acres in Illinois, Alabama, and Mississippi to support the construction of the Illinois Central. Of the $23 million the Illinois Central had spent by 1857, most was raised from mortgages on the federal lands and only a sixth from shareholders, underscoring the centrality of the federal contribution. Prior to 1861, four other acts granted 18 million acres to forty-five additional railroads. The U.S. Military Academy at West Point was a particular boon, with one expert contending that "up to 1855, there was scarcely a railroad in this country that had not been projected and in most cases managed by officers of the Corps (of Engineers)." Of the 2,218 graduates of the U.S. Military Academy before 1867, 124 became presidents, chief superintendents, or chief engineers of U.S. railroads.

The federal government had been subsidizing northeastern fisheries since the 1790s, but in 1816 the region's nascent textile industry got more critical aid from tariff legislation. While purporting to set the import duties on cheap British calicoes from India at 20 percent, the bill's small print pointedly added that whatever their actual cost, cheap textile imports would be valued at twenty-five cents per yard for duty purposes. That meant that cloth costing fifteen cents would be valued at twenty-five cents so as to pay a duty of five cents (33 percent), all but prohibitive. Protected in this way, the revenues of the Boston Manufacturing Company increased tenfold between 1817 and 1825, securing and multiplying the fortunes of the mill-owning Appletons and Lowells.

Passage of the Navigation Act of 1817 completely closed the American coastal trade to foreign shipping, a commercial blessing for many of the shipping fortunes named in chapter 1. Under a second approach, designed to promote U.S. trade with China and the East Indies, federal authorities generally allowed merchants returning to U.S. ports from those places six to twelve months to pay their tariff duties. This meant huge, interest-free loans; Astor alone at one point had a float of $5 million.

Last but not least, because private investors held back, a $30,000 appropriation from Congress in 1844 funded the development of Samuel F. B. Morse's experimental installation of the first telegraph from Washington to Baltimore. Besides sparking a newspaper boom, the telegraph spurred the operation of railways and steamboats, catching on so quickly that by 1852, 23,000 miles of line had been put up and by 1860,

50,000. Andrew Carnegie got his start with telegraphy before going into railroads, iron, and steel. Western Union, the dominant telegraph firm, was for awhile in the hands of the Astor and Vanderbilt interests until control passed to Jay Gould.

When the Civil War made the federal government the country's single largest purchaser of goods, the effects on the iron and steel, textile, shoe, and meatpacking industries were huge. As we have seen, many of the century's most famous business names got their start amid wartime opportunity: Besides Carnegie and Morgan, Armour and Swift emerged in packing. The mechanical reapers and mowers Cyrus McCormick turned out in record number, besides securing his own fortune, permitted the North to produce record crops even with so many men away in the armies. By 1864 the overall manufacturing index for the North alone was 13 percent higher than the index for the entire nation in 1860. Federal authorities built arms factories and pharmaceutical plants, chartered and financed the Union Pacific and Southern Pacific railways, and established the National Academy of Sciences to help harness science for the war effort.

It was a great fallacy for the period after 1865, when not described as the Gilded Age or the Great Barbecue, to be called the era of laissez-faire out of belief that government during these years shrank and reduced its role in the nation's affairs. Its size, payroll, and activity remained well above prewar levels. The change was the willingness of many institutions and officeholders to mobilize behind a neo-Darwinian "survival of the fittest" credo. While this minimized some aspects of government, it maximized others. So emphatic was this new domestic activism—by courts, monetary authorities, the military and quasi-military private police, and state legislatures captured by corporations to send millionaire business stalwarts to the U.S. Senate—that any description of laissez-faire might be better replaced by a variation on the unofficial motto of the Mardi Gras: *laissez les bons temps rouler.*

Portions of government, in fact, were at least periodically reform- or regulation-minded, including some state legislatures, state constitutional conventions (especially in the Midwest and West) and the U.S. House of Representatives (especially during economic slumps). To neutralize such threats, the business and financial communities and their political allies countermobilized an even weightier portion of official authority. The "fittest" could not have survived without using government, and on a magnitude that went far beyond captive state railroad commissions or bribed city aldermen.

Federal and state courts took on a strongly conservative and pro-business bias by the 1880s after decades of appointment of judges from business and commercial practices. By the end of the nineteenth century their interpretations sent the law in pursuit of one innovation after another, without which the fortunes of the Gilded Age would have been considerably slimmer. Take the humdrum sounding issue of judicial review by state courts of legislative acts. State judicial decisions voiding laws as unconstitutional, rare before 1850, became common between 1861 and 1885. Then between 1885 and 1899 over a thousand such rulings were delivered. The Minnesota Supreme Court alone struck down seventy-seven.

Many of these decisions came under the statement in Article V of the U.S. Constitution that citizens may not be deprived of life, liberty, or property without due process of law. In 1877, U.S. Supreme Court justice Samuel Miller observed that from 1789 to 1868, when the due process constraint applied only to the *federal* government, cases were few and far between. But after 1868, when the Fourteenth Amendment applied Article V protections to the states, all of a sudden the dockets of the high court became crowded. The Fourteenth made the due process guarantee into a sword conservative judges could use to cut down state and federal legislation for "unreasonably" interfering with property or contracts.

Judicial activism was further expanded in the 1880s by the Supreme Court's far-reaching holding that corporations, not just individuals, were "persons" within the protection of the due process clause. This, too, was an enormous stretch. It soon meant, for example, that railroads and utilities would be protected against states empowering regulatory commissions to make final determinations on the reasonableness of rates. Finality could only come from the courts.

The judicial inventions of the late nineteenth century were so laden with specious property rights theory that U.S. Supreme Court justice Oliver Wendell Holmes was driven to his famous protest: that the Constitution did not embody laissez-faire or any other economic theory, and that "the Fourteenth Amendment does not enact Mr. Herbert Spencer's *Social Statics.*" Holmes also pointed a stern finger at the supposed "dogma, Liberty of Contract . . . which is not specifically mentioned in the text [the Constitution] which we have to construe."

Labor, too, ran afoul of judicial innovation. During the 1880s, U.S. courts began to turn the old chancery remedy of an injunction into a weapon to be used against labor leaders and strikes. Angry Populists charged in their 1892 national platform that "Corruption dominates the

Ballot Box, the Legislatures, the Congress and touches even the ermine of the bench." Henry Demarest Lloyd, author of *Wealth Against Common-wealth,* accused the conservatives of a "revolution which is putting the attorneys of corporations into . . . the bench to be attorneys still."

The conservative revolution also paraded federal troops, state militia, legally sanctioned state forces like Pennsylvania's Coal and Iron Police and private organizations like the Pinkertons, whose ties to industrial and Republican interests dated back to Civil War days. After the Homestead strike of 1892 and the Chicago Pullman strike of 1894, broken by federal troops despite the opposition of Illinois governor John Altgeld, the rhetoric of farm Populists and labor radicals hardened. The Populists of 1892, speaking of the three hundred Pinkerton agents who fought strikers at the Carnegie steel mills in Homestead, Pennsylvania, near Pittsburgh, condemned the "hireling standing army, unrecognized by our laws, which is established to shoot them [workers] down."

The U.S. steel industry had its own backdrop. Carnegie needed to break the Amalgamated Association of Iron and Steel Workers at Homestead in order to mechanize that plant (which made naval armor) as he had others, by bringing in new technology, laying off high ratios of workers, imposing twelve-hour days, slashing wages, and, as a result, tripling production in eight years. One chronicler of the Homestead strike has insisted that "it was common knowledge that the monumental profits earned by Carnegie Steel in the 1890s grew directly from the defeat of unionism." At the very least, Carnegie made a calculated decision to retain the profits of technology rather than distribute them as wages.

However, besides the judiciary, there was a still more extreme example of corporations and wealth seizing one level of government to control another. This was the takeover of state legislatures by corporations, railroads, and mining companies, partly to dominate their legislation but just as important, to get a lock on the U.S. Senate, the members of which (until 1913) were chosen by those very legislatures.

Robert and Leona Rienow, authors of one of the few books about the process, called the lack of attention "all the more astonishing because the Senate was the heart and core of all this 'roaring, clanging commercialism'—as Theodore Roosevelt described it—and in the Senate chamber every great fortune was incubated, every new commercial empire was sanctioned, every reform was circumvented. . . ." It was also the body in which every senior government appointment, every federal judicial nominee, had to be confirmed.

In any event the overlap between the Senate's rise within the governmental structure and the parallel ascent of corporations within the U.S. economy was unmistakable. The two fed on each other from the late 1860s to the early 1900s when corporations—indeed, wealth itself— began to be curbed. A half century earlier, during the post–Civil War decade, businessmen had been extorted by the more simplistic forms of government corruption—New York's Tweed Ring, the Whiskey Ring, the Customshouse Ring, and suchlike. This produced the half-reformism wryly summarized by New York's Horatio Seymour: "Our people want men in office who will not steal, but who will not interfere with those [in private enterprise] who do."

The solution, which endured for some forty years, was the "state boss" system, through which key leaders brokered the relationships between the corporations and railroads on one side and the state legislatures, the U.S. Senate, and Washington officialdom on the other. Presidents usually had less clout, and were often nominated by cabals of state bosses. Samuel Eliot Morison and Henry Steele Commager in *The Growth of the American Republic* listed twenty-five of these "real rulers"—from Simon Cameron to Mark Hanna—who stood behind the "titular" leaders (presidents), and all save one of them had served in the U.S. Senate. The capture of the Senate by business and finance represented the crippling of any populist or progressive role for government.

It also represented an extraordinary fusion of politics and American millionairedom. The names in Chart 5.3 come from several magazine compendia for 1902–3, and the peak may have come a few years later in 1906, when 25 to 28 senators—one-third of the entire membership— were counted among Theodore Roosevelt's "malefactors of great wealth." All of the Senate's millionaires of 1902–3 were Republicans, save for two Democrats who represented Rocky Mountain silver and copper mining interests. Anyone wishing to compare these fortunes with those of early-twenty-first-century senators should multiply the 1902–3 figures by about eleven to adjust for inflation. The resulting figures dwarf those for any Senate in the 1990s or early 2000s.

In capturing the one segment of the federal government chosen by the states, the business and financial community struck at a constitutional Achilles' heel perceived by at least one of the architects of 1787, Hugh Williamson of North Carolina. He had warned that "Bribery and cabal can be more easily practiced in the choice of the Senate, which is to be made by legislatures composed of a few men, than of the House of Representatives, which will be chosen by the people."

If anything, Williamson underestimated. Spurred by the largesse of

CHART 5.3 **The Millionaires of the U.S. Senate, 1902–3**

SENATOR	PARTY AND STATE	FORTUNE	SOURCE/INDUSTRY
Nelson Aldrich	Republican, RI	$12 mil.	Public utilities, finance
Russell Alger	Republican, MI	$15–20 mil.	Lumber
Levi Ankeny	Republican, WA	$2–4 mil.	Banking
William Clark	Democrat, MT	$100 mil.	Copper
Chauncey Depew	Republican, NY	$5–10 mil.	Railroads
Charles Dietrich	Republican, NE	$1–2 mil.	Mining
John Dryden	Republican, NJ	$50 mil.	Insurance (Prudential)
Stephen Elkins	Republican, WV	$30 mil.	Railroads, coal
Charles Fairbanks	Republican, IN	$2–4 mil.	Law, railroads
Mark Hanna	Republican, OH	$7–10 mil.	Street railways, coal, iron
John Kean	Republican, NJ	$5–10 mil.	Railroads, banking
Thomas Kearns	Republican, UT	$5–10 mil.	Mining, freight
Henry Cabot Lodge	Republican, MA	$2 mil.	Inheritance
Joseph Millard	Republican, NE	$2–4 mil.	Banking
Francis Newlands	Democrat, NV	$2–3 mil.	Mining
Redfield Proctor	Republican, VT	$10–15 mil.	Quarrying
Nathan Scott	Republican, WV	$2–4 mil.	Glass manufacturing
Reed Smoot	Republican, UT	$1–2 mil.	Banking
John Spooner	Republican, WI	$2–3 mil.	Law, railroads
William Stewart	Republican, NV	$5 mil.	Mining
Francis Warren	Republican, WY	$1–3 mil.	Ranching
George Wetmore	Republican, RI	$10 mil.	Inheritance

Note: The list is from the *Financial Redbook of America of 1903* and the *World Almanac of 1902*, with the addition of John Spooner as suggested in Rienow, op. cit. The vocational data comes from *Who Was Who in American Politics* (1974), with miscellaneous sources used for wealth data and estimates.

competition for U.S. Senate seats, the typical legislature fulfilled Mark Twain's words that, "I think I can say and say with pride that we have legislatures that bring higher prices than any in the world." From Jackson, Mississippi, to Columbus, Ohio, from Madison, Wisconsin, to Dover, Delaware, when U.S. Senate vacancies were to be filled, capital after capital became a cross between a carnival and a feeding trough. Satchels were filled with crisp new currency, brothels were rented for entire weeks, judicial vacancies were filled en masse, all for the cozening of "hapless wretches from the hamlets, fields and backwoods, struggling against the glitter of such money as they had never seen before."

Sufficient proof of bribery was hard to come by, because it was not enough to show that money changed hands in the candidate's suite—he had to have been there. Nor was it enough to show that *some* voters were bribed; enough had to be involved to determine the election. In the waning days of the nineteenth century, Sen. George Sutherland, a future president of the American Bar Association, naively proposed a bill to unseat those senators whose places were found to be purchased. This prompted Sen. Weldon B. Heyburn to reply, in all seriousness, that, "We might lose a quorum here, waiting for the courts to act."

Sometimes the hassle of legislative selection stretched over 60 or 85 ballots; the militia occasionally had to be called out (Kentucky in 1897), and from time to time greedy factions simply stalemated. Over a ten-year span, thirteen seats in the U.S. Senate were vacant because of home-state inaction. By 1900 the House had voted five times on a constitutional amendment for the direct election of senators, but the Senate never assented.

Here, too, the Progressive era spurred reform. Within the Republican Party a small but growing minority broke ranks, symbolized by the private comments of Iowa senator Jonathan P. Dolliver, later set down by Wisconsin progressive Robert La Follette in his diary. Lamenting his actions of a quarter century, Dolliver said, "I do not propose that the remaining years of my life shall be given up to a dull consent to all those conspiracies which . . . use the lawmaking power of the United States to multiply their own profits and to fill the marketplace with witnesses of their avarice and greed. . . . I want to look my Maker in the face. . . . I want to meet him with a clear conscience." Finally, in 1912, after many states had adopted popular advisory referendums to guide the legislatures in their choices, the Senate itself belatedly accepted what became the 17th Amendment in 1913.

We have already mentioned the textile provisions of the tariff of 1816 and what they did for New England textile fortunes. Many other tariff acts followed, some famous like the Tariff of Abominations in 1828 and the Morrill Act of 1861, others with only a date, not a name. But two of the acts that became law during the Senate's three-decade corporate captivity, the McKinley tariff of 1890 and the Dingley tariff of 1897, stood out not only for unusually high rates but for grand motivation. Greed in these situations took on a new dimension. More was involved than revenue; much more was at stake than protection for American workers and industries.

The last fifteen years of the nineteenth century and the first decade of the twentieth represented the peak of the merger movement that put together the industrial combines called trusts. To maximize the value of these new assemblages, a monopoly or partial monopoly was important. Protection of the organizations' products against possibly cheaper foreign imports was a related necessity. Thus the gloating comment by sugar magnate Henry O. Havemeyer that, "The mother of all trusts is the customs tariff." Of the forty-four monopoly combinations that *Chicago Tribune* editor Horace White counted in 1888, all but three, he said, were made possible by tariff protection, although others thought this exaggerated.

Chronicles of the putting-together of the McKinley and Dingley tariffs portray some of the Gilded Age's most unrestrained avarice: this provision for Senator Quay and the Iron and Steel Association, another for the textile people, that for Havemeyer and the sugar refiners, and so on. In the evolution of the major combines, of fortunes that still live on, special tariff provisions ranked with the wide-open Corporation Law of the State of New Jersey and the inadequacy of federal antitrust legislation.

For two or three decades, then, democracy was corrupted at its constitutional core. Control of the Senate secured not just that chamber but the federal courts, the U.S. Supreme Court, and the U.S. Army to the service of American industry and finance. A century after the fact, memoirs have made it clear that both the Interstate Commerce Act of 1887 and the Sherman Antitrust Act of 1890 were virtual empty shells, legislation designed to appear to respond to public demands.

Railroads were the hub of private interest domination of the federal government. Their principal assistance from Washington in the decades after the Civil War—a period economic historian Carter Goodrich labeled the "era of national subsidy"—took the form of loans and public domain lands deeded to the railroads at a rate of twenty square miles for every mile of track. By 1871, when grants to railroads ended, they had received a total of 130 million acres. So commonplace was fraud, however, with many railroads never completing their plans and some never even laying track, that those involved looked for protection to Congress and the courts. Many succeeded, although some 20 million acres had to be returned.

By 1885, when John Spooner, one of the legal architects of an 1872 U.S. circuit court ruling which protected railroads that had never laid track from automatic forfeiture of their lands, became a U.S. senator from Wisconsin, railroads were by far and away the nation's leading industry. Yet such were the ethics of those years that Spooner could one day be a paid lawyer for the railroads in the Supreme Court and then the next day speak for them on the floor of the U.S. Senate.

The famous Kansas editor William Allen White recalled an election of a U.S. senator by that state's legislature in which the Missouri Pacific struck a bargain with the representatives of the Rock Island and Santa Fe. Having given up their man in 1903 for the other railways' choice, the Missouri Pacific would get the next senator. Iowa governor Albert B. Cummins, in turn, described a Washington hearing of the U.S. Senate Commerce Committee on railroad rebates: "I was the only man in that large room crowded to the doors who had not gone there on the invitation of the railroads and on a free pass. While the chairman was probing, there sat by his side the general attorney for all the railroads in the United States . . . passing to the chairman question after question to embarrass me. . . ."

It takes but a slight shift of perspective to call U.S. railroad success as much a product of the public sector as of the private sector. No one can say what percentage of the great railroad fortunes amassed between the Civil War and the turn of the century flowed from federal and state assistance and the interlocking political directorate described above, but purely private enterprise seems to have been as rare as genuine laissez-faire.

While most of the twentieth century lacked the de facto seizure of political power by corporations and the financial sector so visible in the Gilded Age, one fundamental similarity did persist: huge levels of government support for industry and technology in research grants, subsidies, wartime expenditures, and policy commitments.

Commercial supplies of electric power, for example, began with the opening of Manhattan's Pearl Street Station in 1882, but by 1900 electric motors were only providing 5 percent of the power used by manufacturing, and by 1914 the figure was still under 40 percent. Then in the 1917–18 war years, according to Thomas Hughes, a leading historian of the electrical industry, the U.S. government built power plants of unprecedented size while a large number of interconnections of electric light and power systems were made. Between 1919 and 1929 the percentage of the horsepower used in manufacturing that came from electricity jumped from 55 to 82%. In 1935 federal subsidies for rural electrification extended large-scale electricity usage into the countryside. During the twenties and thirties, as electric power spread, "such devices as vacuum cleaners, dish-washing machines, and clothes-washing machines (that) had been developed as far back as the 1850s and 1860s" became practical with electric motors. Production soared; new fortunes were built.

Aviation, of course, was an obvious creature of government interest and collaboration. World War I began the first large-scale production, and then output revived in 1926 when the government announced plans to expand its aircraft fleet. The Kelly Air Mail Act of 1925 expanded federal airmail contracts to carry subsidies for the adoption of multiengine aircraft, radios, and navigational aids. World War II provided a huge new commercial and technological impetus, and Washington's role carried over into peacetime with U.S. military expenditures on research and development (R&D) providing more than 70 percent of aviation industry R&D spending in the years after the war.

Radio had its own intertwining with government. During World War I the navy took over all radio patents and speeded radio's development. After the war the navy, General Electric, and Westinghouse set up a new company, the Radio Corporation of America, to hold all the patents and steer technological development. An admiral served as an ex officio member of the board of directors and functioned as a liaison with government. In the words of one chronicler, "Every leading technician or official of RCA was a reserve officer of the Army or Navy, and the company was geared to instant conversion to war duty as an arm of the government." At first it was not clear whether radio and the limited electromagnetic spectrum would be publicly or privately owned—one plan was to set aside 25 percent of the spectrum for public service. However, the end result of the Radio Act of 1927 and the Communications Act of 1934 was to give broadcasters the airwaves. The public service strings attached were scarcely more effective than those attached a half century earlier to the public lands given railroads.

While less romanticized than railroads, each of these achievements— electricity, aircraft, and radio—produced their own Pollyannas, poets, and speculative vehicles, as chapter 6 will amplify. However, as so many experts on technology argue, the slowness of commercial development indicates that innovation rarely creates its own immediate demand. Particularly in electrical power and aviation, government was essential in evolving both the technologies and the demand that let them grow.

Which brings us to the early days of the computer, semiconductor, networking, and Internet developments that figured so prominently in the late-twentieth-century boom. The story, however, is essentially the same: a powerful, even critical early role on the part of the federal government.

Some pages back we saw how "the American System of Manufactures"—mass production made feasible by interchangeable parts—got its start through innovations made by firearms producers under contract to the War Department. Besides which, "historians of technology have long known that a number of fundamentally new machine tools—for milling machines, forging machines, edging machines, to name but four of the most important—first appeared in the firearms industry." All of these inventions and processes were rapidly disseminated within New England, because the War Department required contractors to share their improvements with the Springfield Armory, which in turn made them available to all respectable comers. How telling, then, that a century later, much the same thing took place with computers and semiconductors.

By 1943, as wartime mathematicians at Pennsylvania's Army Ballistics Research Laboratory found themselves falling behind in meeting the military's needs for analyzing trajectories and computing artillery firing tables, Army Ordnance funded a crash program to produce the ENIAC (Electronic Numerical Integrator and Computer). Completed in 1945 and generally described as the first electronic computer, the wall-sized ENIAC, with its 18,000 vacuum tubes, spent only a few weeks calculating firing tables before Los Alamos mathematicians were allowed to use it for calculating the hydrodynamics of hydrogen bombs.

Its follow-up, the EDVAC, was the first stored-memory computer, and its details were disseminated so widely that army lawyers ruled that they passed into the public domain. The next group of computers were funded or commissioned as follows: SEAC (1949) for the Bureau of National Standards, IAS (1951) for the army, navy, and RCA; Whirlwind (1949) for the SAGE strategic air-defense system, Univac (1953) by Remington-Rand for the Census Bureau, other government agencies and business buyers, and the IBM 701 (1953) for the Defense Department. By this point commercial demand was catching hold.

The transistor in the meantime had been invented in 1949 at the American Telephone & Telegraph Company's Bell Laboratories, and AT&T, because of a federal antitrust suit filed that same year, was encouraged to disseminate information, spurring development. In 1954 the silicon junction transistor was produced for the U.S. military for use in radar and missile applications. The invention in 1958 of the integrated circuit (IC)—a leap forward that combined a number of transistors on a single silicon chip—had not been undertaken for the armed forces, but federal military and space applications became the IC's market and proving ground.

Technology specialists Nathan Rosenberg and David Mowery have tabulated the importance of the federal procurement. Chart 5.4A, below, shows the growth of semiconductor production, with the Department of Defense taking over one-third of total semiconductor production until 1963. Chart 5.4B shows the huge initial dependence of IC producers on military sales.

CHART 5.4 **Transistors, Integrated Circuits, and the Importance of the Defense Department Market, 1955–68**

A. U.S. Semiconductor Production 1955–68

YEAR	TOTAL SEMICONDUCTOR PRODUCTION, *millions of dollars*	DEFENSE SEMICONDUCTOR PRODUCTION,* *millions of dollars*	PRODUCTION FOR DEFENSE, *% of total*
1955	40	15	38
1960	542	258	48
1965	884	247	28
1968	1,159	294	25

* Defense production includes devices produced for the Department of Defense, Atomic Energy Commission, Central Intelligence Agency, Federal Aviation Agency, and National Aeronautics and Space Administration.

B. U.S. Integrated Circuit Production 1962–68

YEAR	TOTAL PRODUCTION, *millions of dollars*	AVERAGE PRICE PER INTEGRATED CIRCUIT, *dollars*	DEFENSE PRODUCTION SHARE OF TOTAL PRODUCTION,* %
1962	4†	50.00†	100†
1963	16	31.60	94†
1964	41	18.50	85†
1965	79	8.33	72
1966	148	5.05	53
1967	228	3.32	43
1968	312	2.33	37

* Defense production includes devices produced for Department of Defense, Atomic Energy Commission, Central Intelligence Agency, Federal Aviation Agency, and National Aeronautics and Space Administration.

† Estimated.

Source: Mowery and Rosenberg, *Paths of Innovation,* pp. 129 and 133.

Just as U.S. antitrust officials pushed for diffusion of critical technology, Mowery and Rosenberg emphasize that the Department of Defense did so for its own goal of ensuring a "second source" of the technology DOD was buying. Compliance meant that firms had to exchange designs and share enough process knowledge to ensure that the components would match.

The emergence of the microprocessor in 1971, which led to personal computers and work stations, owed less to Washington. Not so the development of software. Antitrust pressure induced IBM to "unbundle" its hardware and software, opening up space for independent software producers. Mowery and Rosenberg also conclude, despite lack of a single time series, that, "Much of the rapid growth in custom software firms during the period from 1969 through 1980 reflected expansion in federal demand, which in turn was dominated by Department of Defense demand."

The Internet, of course, began as a project of the Defense Department's Advanced Research Projects Agency (DARPA). In a 1968 essay, DARPA computer pioneer J. C. R. Licklider discussed how a few weeks earlier he and others "participated in a technical meeting held through a computer." He correctly predicted in that same essay that being "on line" through a network of multiaccess computers had the potential to "change the nature and value of communication even more profoundly than did the printing press and the picture tube." By 1969 the idea of a network got a $1 million budget at DARPA, and by the early 1970s, ARPANET was wired to twenty-three sites with some connection to government funded computer research.

Taken over after some years by the National Science Foundation, ARPANET had 100,000 sites when it was shut down in 1989, its sites to become part of other networks. Collectively these networks assumed the name Internet, gaining a new potential in 1993 when Marc Andreessen, a codewriter at the federally-funded National Center for Supercomputing Applications, came up with a vernacular protocol for Web access by the multitudes. That year the number of commercial Web sites jumped from fifty to over ten thousand, and Andreessen and his friends helped found Netscape.

Two other new sectors of the 1990s, telecommunications and biotechnology, also owed much to the federal government. However, the story of the latter, at least, is almost repetitious. Penicillin had become a major Washington priority during World War II, and postwar pharmaceutical development in turn owed much to research by the National Institutes of

Health. By 1965, Washington accounted for almost two-thirds of all spending on biomedical research. Even in the mid-nineties, some 40 percent of national biomedical research was still underwritten by the federal government. When the mapping of the human genome was announced in 2000, much of the credit went to the federally-sponsored Human Genome Project, the biotech equivalent of the half-century-earlier Manhattan Project to split the atom.

Telecommunications is another story, bearing some resemblance to how the railroads built their success on being awarded free government land. The telecommunications industry, like radio, received spectrum from the government under pledges of public service but at no serious cost. "The free distribution of the public-owned electromagnetic spectrum to U.S. radio and television companies," according to one critic, "has been one of the greatest gifts of public property in history, valued as high as $100 billion." The Telecommunications Act of 1996 alone, which gave each existing television broadcaster an additional six megahertz of spectrum so that they could start broadcasting simultaneously in digital and cable, drew fire for giving away spectrum worth $40–$100 billion in return for a loose promise of public service programming. But most politicians were silent, too well aware of the power the major media conglomerates exercised over their careers, another parallel to the influence of the railroads a century earlier.

Millennial arguments that technology and science were pushing government to the sidelines faded in 2001 with the Nasdaq and belief in a New Economy. While the abstract potential of the Internet or interactive television to displace the state might exist, the practical prospect lost credibility. Similarly, although the abstract power of the universe—of atomic fusion—may dwarf all others, in practical terms, the acceleration of technology once again looked to depend on politics and society. Indeed, as twenty-first-century research moved toward explosive changes at the intersection with life sciences, altering life and death, even some of those involved expected government to further reassert its decision-making power. In any event, the War on Terrorism in the United States pushed government to the fore again.

However, we are getting ahead of ourselves. Whatever the future balance between politics and government on one hand and science and technology on the other, the role of technological watersheds over six centuries in creating, polarizing, and realigning wealth, both within nations and internationally, demands its own attention. This is the chapter to which we now turn.

CHAPTER SIX

TECHNOLOGY AND THE UNCERTAIN FOUNDATIONS OF ANGLO-AMERICAN WEALTH

The Dutch technician was to the 17th century what the Scottish engineer was to the 19th century, but in even wider fields of economic activity. He was to be found wherever profitable occupation offered and . . . wherever government or private enterprise was in need of technical or managerial skill.
—Charles Wilson, *Holland and Britain* (1945)

The history of the technology industry is always the same: excitement about something new, followed by a speculative mania, then a bust. The size of the Internet bubble may never be repeated, but bubbles are a feature of new markets. For as long as people have speculated, their business sense has declined in proportion to their sense that others were profiting effortlessly. This human tendency is fantastically heightened when people invest in technology—perhaps because the technology industry is so focused on the future, and is so millennarian.
—Anthony Perkins, *Red Herring Magazine,* 2001

In the wake of the past year's litany of horrors, the public's infatuation with all things digital has faded. On Wall Street and on Main Street, a feeling has set in that the information revolution has played itself out, or at least has entered a period of prolonged abeyance.
—John Heileman, *PC Magazine,* 2001

Over more than two centuries of American wealth it is difficult to argue that the effects of technological innovation, from interchangeable parts to the microprocessor, have outweighed the impact of government power and preferment. More experts on technology have found innovation typically *responding* to markets, mobilizations, and consumers—to political and economic society, in short—instead of *leading* them. We can likewise doubt that technology has outweighed representative government, effective markets, and English-speaking freedoms in achieving the economic leadership of Britain and then the United States.

However, this book's discussion of technology after government, besides recognizing its lesser influence to date, also reflects its nineteenth and twentieth-century momentum and the likelihood of more achievement and controversy to come. From a wealth perspective, "technology" became somewhat important with the basic Industrial Revolution, surged with electricity and chemistry during the nineteenth-century Scientific (or Second Industrial) Revolution, accelerated with automobiles and aerospace, and then burst old assets hierarchies open with the computer networking and biotechnology of the 1990s and 2000s. Far from being supplanted by technology, government, as we have seen, has frequently provided the essential impetus and support for notable innovation.

Besides, technological advance has frequently had negative social, economic, and political side effects that have called the influence of government back into play. From early textile machinery to the Internet, the early stages of major innovations have generated rising social and economic inequality almost as a matter of course. The early twenty-first century, in turn, has brought predictions by some technology gurus and observers that the next great scientific revolution coming in molecular electronics—genomics, biotechnology, and robotics—will enable economic elites to artificially (and expensively) enhance their cerebral capacities relative to persons without the money to keep up. Technology (and venture capitalism) may also be at loggerheads with religion, politics, and government in matters of cloning, life extension, and genetic manipulation. Any restraints on technology could spill over onto finance capital.

In short, technology, like finance, is the arena of an elite, not some benign village common. Government may sometimes restrain it accordingly. Moreover, because onrushing science has periodically swelled popular belief that the latest breakthroughs can remold human nature, tame the universe, wither away the state, and suspend the business cycle, technology has led to manias and most of the notable speculative bubbles of the nineteenth and twentieth centuries. Popular and governmental disenchantment have often followed.

The national backdrops of Western technological achievement have a striking continuity. Over the last four centuries the United States and its principal colonial founders, Holland and Great Britain, have been successive leading world powers in technology as well as in broad commerce and finance. The technological flag, however, seems to have transferred before the financial one. Holland and Britain retained their status as financial centers even after manufacturing had shriveled and entrepreneurs and engineers had begun to migrate.

Simply to shape a nation from their half-submerged coastline, the one million Dutch had to reclaim one-third of it from sea, then build the world's best merchant ships and seafaring equipment, both famous successes. These engineering and nautical talents, scientifically enriched by Leeuwenhoek's famous high-powered microscopes, Van der Heyden's street lamps and fire-fighting pumps, and Huygens's pendulum clocks and navigational instruments, upheld Dutch primacy for more than a century. Historians agree that, in the words of one, "The United Provinces, rather than Britain, was still the world's technological showcase down to around 1740."

Even so, the Industrial Revolution was about to crystallize around British attributes and inventions: James Hargreave's spinning jenny (1766), James Watt's steam engine (1768), Richard Arkwright's power loom (1787), and Henry Court's patents for puddling and rolling iron (1783–84), all following on others earlier in the century. Along with other British circumstances, these enabled the United Kingdom between 1760 and 1830 to single-handedly account for two-thirds of the growth of European industrial output. Textiles led, with the mechanization of spinning improving productivity by a factor of 300 to 400. Britons of the Victorian era could fairly call their nation "the workshop of the world."

But this baton, too, was passed. Pioneering nineteenth-century discoveries in steel, chemicals, and electricity could not keep Britain in the forefront of the second science-and-laboratory-dependent wave of industrialization, and by the 1880s and 1890s, Germany and America both pulled ahead. The United States of the mid-nineteenth century, under the spur of its high labor costs and huge, machinery-demanding farmlands, had already taken the lead both in mass production techniques—from assembly lines to the beginnings of scientific management—and in the manufacture of durables like sewing machines, typewriters, guns, machine tools, and farm equipment. American exhibits at Britain's Crystal Palace Exposition of 1851 impressed British manufacturers, and by 1860, English writers like Charles Reade worried that "American genius is at this moment ahead of all nations in mechanical invention," although financial services, overall manufactures, and dominant exports kept the UK well in front economically. By the 1890s, as we have seen, U.S. industrial production exceeded Britain's.

Germany, with its skills in engineering, chemicals, and precision instruments, was a contender for primacy until the two world wars handed Britain's mantle to the U.S. Aerospace, computer, semiconductor, and telecommunications achievements thereafter successively reconfirmed U.S. technological leadership, despite the steady displacement of large parts of the older U.S. manufacturing sector by cheaper imported products.

Hardly comprehensive, these capsules are simply intended to illustrate that various stages of technological preeminence were front and center in the three nations' sequence of global economic and commercial leadership. Each of the three had a particular bent for putting technological and financial innovation together.

1. TECHNOLOGY AND THE MAJOR U.S. WEALTH WAVES

If politics and government had the greatest impact on wealth well into the twentieth century, the century ended with brilliant technological fireworks. As we have seen, index after index showed the Internet, biotechnology, and other sectors bursting forth in the early-to-mid 1990s. In less than two decades, half of the top thirty U.S. wealth positions in 2000 had been seized by the open-collared magnates of Internet, chips, fiber-optics, software, biotech, and bandwidth. Indeed, since textile and railroad days the top wealth lists in the U.S. have had a history of such entry.

Even in landed Britain the technological innovation of the Industrial Revolution did produce several of the dozen or so British fortunes of over one million pounds left to heirs before 1856. Richard Crawshay, the Welsh ironmaster, amassed one as did Richard Arkwright, the textile machinery patent holder and cotton manufacturer. The richest among them was the cotton magnate Sir Robert Peel, father of the later prime minister of the same name. He left £1.5 million (U.S. $7.5 million) in 1830.

In the 1820s and 1830s, manufacturers (of textiles) begin to appear among the wealthiest Americans, albeit with smaller holdings than Peel's. Samuel Slater, who came to the U.S. with the details of Arkwright's machinery memorized, built the first U.S. cotton spinning mill in Rhode Island in 1790 and had a fortune of $1–$2 million at his death in 1835. Fifteen years later surveys in Massachusetts estimated the wealth of each of the two leading textile-making families, the Appletons and Lawrences, in the $5–$6 million range. This was the last period in which Britain boasted the larger industrial fortunes.

The American railroad, steel, and oil fortunes, as we have seen, dwarfed those on the other side of the Atlantic. Textiles had fallen off the map of top wealth. The four biggest U.S. fortunes of the 1890s were in the $100–$300 million range—Rockefeller (oil), Carnegie (steel), Vanderbilt (railroads), and Astor. No private British estate had yet exceeded the £3–4 million range ($15–$20 million), although the landed wealth of the duke of Westminster was at least £14 million.

Britain's railroads were on too small a scale to produce a Vanderbilt, Gould, or Harriman. Travel from Manchester to Liverpool or London to Brighton was small cheese next to the route of the Union Pacific and even the New York Central. For that matter, British coal, iron, steel, and metalworking businesses were mostly small to midsized family affairs rather than large industrial combinations in the U.S. or German manner. Thus, a practical reason for the much greater size of U.S. fortunes, especially in the 1890s and 1900s, was how many rested on near-monopolies and combinations, some of them tariff-supported. Many industrial behemoths were created to command huge valuations in the stock market, which assumed an ever-expanding role.

If the partnership of technology and finance took on serious scale in the mid-nineteenth century with railroads, lesser precedents went back considerably farther. In England the Convex Lights Company was founded in 1684 to produce a new kind of street lighting, followed in 1687 by dozens of companies to build diving engines to reach wrecked treasure ships (one had just been found that year by Sir William Phipps). This was the first decade of a major speculative boom, and scores more mechanical proposals came in the 1690s, then another wave in 1720, the year of the South Seas bubble. Two of the least disreputable were Puckle's Machine Gun Company and Sir Richard Steele's "fish pool" scheme for a boat designed to transport live fish (underwater) to the London market. Even during the Napoleonic Wars the new gas lighting in central London—first developed to keep war-related factories producing at night—had society buzzing about "the famous shares" of the Light and Heat Company, supposed "to make the fortune of all who hold them."

The railroad manias of the 1830s and 1840s, vastly bigger, produced investment flows huge enough to mushroom the listings and importance of the stock exchanges in London and New York and prompt new ones in Boston, Manchester, Liverpool, Leeds, and Glasgow. On both sides of the Atlantic, but in Britain first, railroads dwarfed all previous public works, paraded technology that seemed generations ahead of the rest of the economy, inspired poets, and became synonyms for ultramodernity.

Unfortunately, this made them vehicles for manias unmatched since the South Sea and Mississippi bubbles. According to one British estimate, "only a small fraction of the £240 millions invested in [British] railways by 1850 had any such rational justification . . . and much of it was sunk without trace." As a measure, that £240 million was equal to 40 percent of Britain's annual GDP and exceeded the capitalization of the nation's biggest industry, cotton textiles. The fervor repeated in America, where the money flow was so great—a third of it from Europe—that by 1860, U.S. railroads had a capitalization of $1.2 billion, about the equivalent of Britain's ten years earlier. By 1900, U.S. railroad capitalization had increased to $10 billion and railroad listings remained the largest group on the New York Stock Exchange, even though the great industrial combinations were passing them in clout.

The excesses of railroad proliferation are an issue to which we will return. The great benefit of railroad construction on both sides of the Atlantic, manifestly, was its extraordinary stimulus to coal, iron, and steel production and to exports, communications, and economic growth in general. Its detriment—the sooty cloud that often hid the stimulative silver lining—came in how U.S. railroad stock and bond difficulties wound up being ingredients or triggers of virtually every nineteenth-century panic and depression, beginning in 1837. As we will see, these downturns, tied to speculative overvaluation and implosion, ushered in periods of enormous hardship for many average Americans, even as railway securities—well-watered, manipulated, or both—remained the mainstays of two-thirds of the great U.S. fortunes into the 1880s.

As that decade began, forty-one railroads boasted a capitalization of $15 million or more, while Carnegie Steel's was only $5 million. Over the next quarter century, organization of the great new industrial combinations and trusts became the fashion in moneymaking. Industrial or metallurgical technologies were spun into figurative gold by the alchemy that investment bankers like J. P. Morgan performed in circumstances of weak antitrust laws, protective tariffs, and enthusiastic capital markets.

Standard Oil of Ohio had a capitalization of only $1 million when John D. Rockefeller organized it in 1870. A decade later, Standard became the Oil Trust, refining 95 percent of the nation's oil. By the new century the value of its well-organized petroleum monopoly had climbed to $300 million or so. Elsewhere on the technology front, the Morgan interests in 1892 packaged a number of smaller electrical concerns into the General Electric Company, greatly reducing competition, and the combination was said to quadruple the separate capitalization of the parts. A decade later the House of Morgan amalgamated the major farm machinery companies, transforming premerger assets of $10.5 million into a corporation (International Harvester) valued at $120 million.

This golden harvest of over 300 monopolies, combinations, and trusts between 1894 and 1900 still left the biggest prize uncombined and unmerged: *steel*. From that $5 million capitalization of 1880, Carnegie Steel grew to be worth $200 million in 1898, and finally fetched $492 million in 1902 when it was merged into a new trust, U.S. Steel, which became America's first billion-dollar enterprise. In the end most of Morgan's major designs succeeded. With the collaboration of politics, law, finance, and government, technology's imprint on wealth during this period miniaturized any European comparisons.

The next big technological cavalcade of the 1920s featured automobiles and lesser economic phenomena like radios, moving pictures, and airplanes. But as we have seen, these stocks, bid up to wild heights, plummeted as the Crash unfolded from 1929 to 1932. Until the early 1950s, twenties-based memories of where mania might lead kept the public from again making technology an icon.

Caution finally ebbed in the late fifties and sixties. Growth stocks like IBM, Polaroid, Xerox, Texas Instruments, Hewlett-Packard, and Electronic Data Systems soared but zigzagged, moving their founders in and out of the 1966–70 lists of the richest thirty or fifty Americans. The lure of technology accounted for some one-third of the Nifty Fifty, many of their stratospheric valuations crashing to earth in the market breaks of the early seventies.

The point of this recapitulation is simple: the Anglo-American fascination with technology has figured in—and been lavishly rewarded by—six wealth waves. The late-eighteenth-century Industrial Revolution, as we have seen, visited Britain three or four decades earlier than America. The railroad boom began in Britain and affected both nations, but its greatest comparative fortunes were those of United States from the late 1860s to the 1890s. Oil and steel powered the late Gilded Age wealth wave in the United States, and automobiles drove wave number four, again American-centered. The fifth, more multidimensional, rested on the post–World War II coming of age in aerospace, pharmaceuticals, chemicals, computers, and office equipment (U.S.).

Revealingly, only two of the wealth waves in the United States lacked a major technological component: the financial and real estate escalators of the Hamilton, Girard, and Astor periods, and the inflationary surge of the 1970s and early 1980s with its benefits to oil, commodities, and real estate. Otherwise, the centrality of technology in U.S. wealth creation— from railroads onward—clearly exceeded industrial Britain's, where land ownership remained economically, socially, and politically dominant until Queen Victoria's last years.

By this numerology the high-tech crest of the 1990s—global, but led by the U.S.—was the sixth wave. Each has overshadowed its predecessor, and the surge built around the microprocessor and Internet revolution was no exception despite the chastening it received in 2000–2001.

Not that any of these waves, including the *tsunami* of the 1990s, rested on technological breakthroughs alone. Each, as we have seen, also involved a parallel increase in the instruments, velocity, and volume of the financial markets. New financial formulae and techniques heightened—arguably inebriated—the markets' exuberance in valuing the emerging technology. The Austrian economist Joseph Schumpeter, in particular, viewed speculative excesses as tending to cluster around *both* phenomena—major developments in technology, but also financial and other innovations that "transformed the economic structure and upset the pre-existing state of things."

At their millennial peak the new technology fortunes clearly enjoyed another such synergy. By the late 1990s the financial sector, for its own avid use, had become one of the largest purchasers of computers and software. These had become the essential electronic brain cells and motor neurons of arbitrage, relentless securitization (of everything from bundled snowmobile loans to the expected lifetime earnings of sports figures), and derivative instruments formulated to hedge this or that hazard. Like earlier waves, the nineties also required ample credit and surges of liquidity, imprecise stimuli that jumped the usual fence-lines of money-supply definition.*

Technology and finance had flirted with de facto merger before. Back in the 1840s, new railroads in some states were permitted to issue their own banknotes. Mississippi, for one, was crisscrossed by self-promised "railroads" that laid only engraved paper tracks. Railroads and canals both

---

* Liquidity itself is one of the more socially discerning forms of money. As furnished in recent years, it is almost always found hovering fondly around foolish bankers, clumsy speculators, and stock markets gashed by rampaging bears. It is rarely found in ruined farm districts or cities where giant corporations have laid off 20,000 employees.

helped finance themselves with lotteries. The virtual merger apparent in the twenty-first century, however, differed by involving the technology itself. The Internet had become part of the stock market. So had opportunity-scanning software. Heads of Internet brokerage firms doubled as financiers and technology entrepreneurs. Steamboat Road in well-heeled Greenwich, Connecticut, housed dozens of hedge funds, some full of Nobel Prize winners, math geniuses, and computer nerds, all seeking to squeeze megaprofits from short-term market pricing aberrations.

One upshot of technology and finance operating in tandem was yet another round of grossly overvalued companies, this time with names that exuded technopresence or cyberspaciality—Abgenix, Cytogen, Novadigm, Polycom, Informatica, and hundreds more—and on a scale of capitalization previously unimaginable. Back in 1982–83, broadcast and print media had begun running lists of multimonth gains or losses in the value of the shareholdings of prominent corporate founders—a $1.2 billion gain for David Packard between August 1982 and July 1983, a $1 billion decline for Leslie Wexner of The Limited between September 15 and October 23, 1987. Such were the fevered markets and overvaluations of 2000–2001, however, that a volatile week or even day could fatten or slim a technology magnate by $3 billion, $4 billion, or in the case of Microsoft's Bill Gates, a loss of $20 billion.

Every few weeks in 2000 brought a new species of stock market record: the first, second, third, or fourth-largest single-day loss of market capitalization by a U.S. corporation. Vaunted Cisco, for example, plummeted from $550 billion in early 2000 to $111 billion in March 2001, one hundred times the largest 1929–32 implosion and ten times bigger even allowing for inflation.

This is the technology-wave backdrop to American wealth creation and loss. However, a dark side of technological upheaval also showed itself in the late nineties—harder times for many ordinary households. Alongside the era's huge fortunes, the loss of purchasing power among large portions of the citizenry recalled not only previous American stresses but the sort of polarization that had disfigured the two previous great world economic transformations.

2. TECHNOLOGICAL UPHEAVAL AND ECONOMIC POLARIZATION

Disproportionate gains by the rich, big enough to enlarge the gap between them and most of the rest of the population, had been hallmarks of the Renaissance and the Industrial Revolution. No one has doubted the greatly increased wealth of both eras' elites. The caveat to the wage inadequacy of the lower orders, however, is said to be their offsetting consumption: in both periods, the argument goes, poor and ordinary folk gained through new pleasures and consumer goods—salt and spices, cheap clothing, trains to ride, fresh fruit. But fact remained fact: that each upheaval nevertheless widened the economic gap between those with capital and skills and those less favored. Increases in the cost of living and taxes frequently eroded the latter's real income or purchasing power.

The analogy to the late twentieth century is already filling in. However, to revisit the first two modern economic transformations, we have to return to Europe. The Renaissance and the rise of capitalism, between roughly 1450 and 1625, hummed with technological and commercial innovations. These ranged from Gutenberg's invention of the printing press, with its massive diffusion of knowledge, to a host of new mercantile instruments and practices. At sea, improvements in maritime design and construction combined with Copernican astronomy and spherical trigonometry and new aids to navigation. Together with advances in ships' cannon, they extended Western trade from nearby seas to far-off oceans, opening up the globe to European explorers, merchants, and colonializers. In the words of Sir Walter Raleigh, "He that commaunds the sea, commaunds the trade, and hee that is Lord of the trade of the world is Lord of the wealth of the world."

The increasing complexity of commerce, technologically aided, in turn demanded more sophisticated calculations. The first printed European mathematics textbook, the *Treviso Arithmetic* of 1473, sought to educate merchants and the "reckoning masters," who aided them. Treviso itself was just outside of Venice, the center of commercial reckoning, which established Italy's first university chair of navigational mathematics (1444) and Europe's first endowed public lectures on algebra. Many terms still used in commerce—*credito* (credit), *valuta* (value), *netto* (net), and *arithmetica* (arithmetic)—come from fifteenth-century Italian.

The most sweeping economic descriptions of the Renaissance—W. W. Rostow's label of "the commercial revolution" (after 1488) and economic historian John Nef's thesis of "the first industrial revolution"—go beyond scholarly acceptance but they do distill important changes. Maurice Dobb, R. H. Tawney, and others viewed this period through an economic lens and spotted "the rise of capitalism." The years from the late 1400s to the early 1600s have also been called the "price revolution" because of high inflation, which magnified the losses of the poor and uneducated.

Commerce, invention, and finance intermingled and soared. Population grew, especially in the cities. Luxury flourished. Merchants became indispensable middlemen, coordinating the new world network of suppliers and markets needed to support the huge 600 to 800 percent increase between 1450 and 1625 of trade carried in European ships. Grain, food, and then fuel prices in particular began to rise. The increases were slow at first, but as they speeded up, wages fell behind, often sharply. Peasants and tenant farmers staggered under rent increases that outran their crop receipts. Diets everywhere had less meat and grain, and peasants spoke with envy of grandparents who had eaten decently from farming the same plot of land.

The view of Fernand Braudel, the French economic historian, is that price rises were greatest in the places most pervaded by sixteenth and seventeenth-century commerce: Venice, Spain, and the Netherlands. In the late-eighteenth-century England of the Industrial Revolution, similarly, the inflated costs of renting a carriage or staying in a hotel were often prohibitive for foreigners. High English prices, Braudel observed, were also a burden to that nation's own poor and middle classes.

One useful explanation for both inflation and increasing polarization of wealth comes from considering these great transformations as surges of *complexity*—waves of economic, political, and commercial change—profound enough to break down old vocational and price relationships, greatly favoring persons with position, capital, skills, and education. To most mid-sixteenth-century Europeans in poor urban districts or country villages, by contrast, the new techniques of printing, mining, navigation, and shipbuilding—Venice's extraordinary *arsenale* had the assembly lines and standardized parts from which a seagoing galley could be built in a single day!—were incomprehensible and scarcely mattered next to inflation's all-too-obvious reduction of their living standards.

Professor David Hackett Fischer in his study of price revolutions and the rhythm of history found the losers to be the tenants and workers who had few skills and no capital, so that "the growing gap between returns to labor and rewards to capital was one of the most important social consequences. . . ." For all that the Medici Bank might boast branches in London, Geneva, Bruges, and Avignon, according to another historian "the momentous social effect of the price revolution was to open the chasm between the haves and the have nots—in essential things like diet and housing—wider than it had been for a thousand years." Braudel concluded that during the two centuries of capitalist excitement from 1450 to 1650, "the progress made by the upper reaches of the economy and the increase in economic potential were paid for by the mass of the people whose numbers were increasing as fast or faster than production."

The Industrial Revolution, for its part, was a grand phenomenon of late-eighteenth-century Britain. Besides waterpower, coal and iron resources, new canals, turnpikes, and inventions, the United Kingdom of Great Britain and Ireland had other relevant attributes: a strong commercial and capitalist impetus, the world's preeminent colonial expansion (in India and America), maturing finance, and the stimulus of mobilization for the global Seven Years' War (1756–63). Industrialization was only one facet; indeed the grand description awaited the 125-year retrospect of Arnold Toynbee's 1881 lectures on "The Industrial Revolution of the 18th Century in England."

The revolutionary aspect of change between 1763 and 1790 was threefold: The substitution of machines for human skill; cheap enough power to justify assembling workers in a factory or collective production area; and a portability of that power (coal or wood-run steam engines) that allowed production to be located strategically and away from animals or water. Thus the contrast with the earlier large-scale production centers like the *arsenale,* the English potteries, Holland's great Zaandam industrial district. None had combined advanced processes with portable power.

Part of the stress for British workers reflected how agriculture, hitherto the economy's largest sector, had also embraced scientific management and mechanical aids in the late eighteenth century. As a result large numbers left or were thrown off the land just as the emerging textile mills and ironworks needed cheap labor, so that pay suffered accordingly. In a time of rising prices, real wages in Britain declined from 1750 through the Napoleonic Wars. Few historians disagree.

The postwar downturn following Napoleon's defeat in 1815 saw prices drop rapidly while wages fell as fast or faster. Entrepreneurs, bondholders, and landlords profited at labor's expense. Interpretive disagreement begins with the 1820s and 1830s, which saw some improvement for labor. Then real wages sagged again in the late 1830s and early 1840s. What can be said with reasonable certainty is that from 1760 to 1845, the era when British industry came of age, the preponderant and overall although not uninterrupted trend in real wages was *down.*

As a postscript, where wages did gain, the increases were often mocked or outweighed by worsening social and working conditions. In the coal industry, real wages advanced between 1790 and 1840, "but at the cost of longer hours and a greater intensity of labor, so that the breadwinner was 'worn out' before the age of 40." Child labor, socially acceptable in earlier parent-supervised home industry, became a scandal under the pressures of the factory system despite what may have been better pay.

The return of sixteenth-century wealth and income disparities in new garb was almost literal: the fashion preoccupations of Britain's Regency period matched the symbolic extravagance of Medici Florence. Owners, landlords, and capitalists took the lion's share of Britain's gains from increasingly productive technology of farms, mills, and factories. Grand new houses were their *palazzi,* pavilions in Brighton their Tivolis. So huge was the pool of capital from mechanically tended estates and well-worked looms that the British upper classes in the quarter century after Waterloo invested—gambled—extravagant sums on high-paying bonds of the new South American nations and individual U.S. states, then plunging into railroads. Halcyon years for the agricultural gentry, the 1750–1830 period also served the new industrial middle class. Not so for unskilled laborers or those who had lost their familiar world of dinner at the farmer's table and access to village greens and commons.

Not surprisingly, some workers and farm laborers reacted violently to the technology that seemed to explain their job losses or wage declines. Arkwright's water frame was loathed, and in 1779 his mill in Lancashire was destroyed by a mob. The Luddites, famous for smashing textile machinery during the Napoleonic Wars, reached their peak of destructiveness in 1826. Handloom weavers, their once-decent wages reduced to starvation levels, turned out to smash the hated power looms in Manchester and Blackburn. In farm districts, too, threshing machines were broken, and the hayricks burned at night into the 1840s.

By 1851, the year of the famous "Great Exhibition of the Works of Industry of All Nations" at London's Crystal Palace, the wages of labor had begun what would be a sustained rise. Even radical critics found themselves impressed, both by the achievements of the Industrial Revolution and by what it seemed to augur for British prosperity. The "workshop of the world" was about to pay Europe's—and in some cases, the world's—highest wages, especially to skilled men. Yet for three earlier generations the bottom half or two-thirds of the population had lost ground in the manner of the Renaissance peasantry. Capital, not labor, harvested innovation's early fruits.

U.S. industrialization generally followed suit, with a lag of several decades. We discussed in chapter 1 the Lancashire-like anger of the textile-producing Merrimack Valley of Massachusetts in 1854, together with how the Civil War growth of railroads and industrialization was accompanied by real pain in the agricultural sector. The peak years of the U.S. Industrial Revolution were no simple transformation of America into a humming "new economy" of machine tools, electric turbines, and giant trusts. Farm machinery manufactured in the United States, especially the reaper, played a major role in turning less-developed regions of the world into rival export granaries: South America, Australia, and Russia. This additional production—in some ways the fruit of the American system of manufactures—helped lower crop prices to levels that put American family farms out of business.

Here again new consumption opportunities were no offset. Nor would they be again during the 1920s when few embattled farmers in Kansas or Minnesota felt assuaged by watching silent movies, listening to the radio, buying automobiles (perhaps, as in Middletown, in lieu of indoor plumbing), or waving at airplanes barnstorming over Topeka. Coal miners, unskilled workers, and many more shared the pain, the twenties being when "technological unemployment" entered the jargon of economics. Some 200,000 workers a year lost jobs to new machinery, and in 1929 the economist Wesley C. Mitchell calculated that the ranks of the jobless grew by more than 650,000 between 1920 and 1927. Productivity gains were hogged by business and minimally distributed to labor, repeating Britain's Regency and the U.S. Gilded Age, and a major advance in economic inequality reflected these priorities.

The gathering high-technology emergence from 1970 to 2000 showed many similarities. Chronologically, this third of the great transformations arguably began in the years between 1959, when Jack Kirby and Robert Noyce invented the integrated circuit chip—the microchip—and 1971, when Silicon Valley got its name and Intel, Noyce's firm, built the first microprocessor. This was the "computer on a chip," the tiny piece of silicon that could be programmed for anything from controlling industrial processes to monitoring the flight of a missile. The next major evolution, the first personal computer, appeared in 1975, the year Bill Gates and Paul Allen founded Microsoft. The public, however, was as yet unaware of significant economic effects.

The economist Fritz Machlup had pointed out an earlier, related changeover during the 1960s. What he called the Knowledge Industry—education, the media, computermakers, management gurus, consultants, and others who merchandise ideas, not goods—had raised its share of U.S.

GNP from 25 percent in 1955 to one-third in 1965. This trend also affected politics, producing in the sixties and seventies what conservatives attacked as a liberal elite—a supposed "new class" of educators, performers, analysts, and communicators. However, if this phenomenon further establishes the sixties and seventies as a revolutionary threshold, the economic impact of high technology, as opposed to the status gains of the cognitive class, unfolded slowly in the 1980s and then accelerated in the 1990s.

Chapter 3 has set out the related wealth effect—the rise of the Nasdaq, the nineties takeover of the *Forbes* 400 list by technology magnates, the tenfold 1982–2000 increase in the size of the largest fortunes, the ballooning of high-technology stocks from just 5 percent of total U.S. market capitalization in 1980 to 30 percent in 2000 before the Nasdaq crash. This chapter embellishes some of the dark side of the upheaval: the hemorrhage of older manufacturing industry, the expansion of imports to account for 35 to 40 percent of all manufactures purchased, the decline of real manufacturing wages, the stagnation of median household income, the technology-related escalation of economic inequality. Capital migrated overseas, taking with it production hitherto based in the United States and leaving basic manufacturing in the loser's role that agriculture filled during the nineteenth century.

In short, the analogy of the late-twentieth-century technological revolution to the two previous great transformations is compelling. As to the converging effects of technology and globalization at the turn of the millennium, few if any indexes exist, which is logical enough. Upheavals of this magnitude have usually also entailed revolutions in what needs to be measured. Many of the federal data series still used in 2000—gross domestic product, national income, unemployment, consumer price index, et al.—were legacies of the 1930s and mid-twentieth century. By 2000 new challenges had emerged, but new measurements had not—akin to a similar statistical dearth that even British Cabinet ministers had complained of a century earlier.

The U.S. lack of effective measurements of the global interplay of trade, technology, capital, labor, and wage levels was a predicament. No one doubted that during the 1980s and 1990s a widening wage gap had opened up between Americans who enjoyed education and skills and those who did not. Technology had to be a factor. Still, the wage and job losses by the least proficient and less educated came *before* computerization of the workplace accelerated in 1983–84. And if technology in U.S. offices and assembly lines was so determinative, why had the nation's productivity gains of the eighties and early nineties been so minimal?

For the 1979–93 period as a whole, not a few technologically-skilled job categories—engineers, architects—lost rather than gained real wages. Indeed, entry-level offers to new college graduates working in information technologies, including computer programmers, stagnated during most of the 1990s, climbing only in the end-of-decade boom. Better education was at best a partial answer; other economic effects seemed to moot its benefits.

Determining the job or wage effects of trade or globalization (including technology transfer) was also complicated by both terms' vagueness and imprecision. "Trade" included exchanges between facilities of the same multinational company in two different countries. Globalization was less a useful definition than a political and cultural Rorschach blot. Studies rarely found single, trade-type explanations providing more than 20 to 40 percent of the job or wage effects. What the available measurements could *not* encompass was critical: the extent to which new technology enabled and accelerated the use of cheap, relatively unskilled labor in foreign and domestic manufacturing facilities, with the result of eroding U.S. wages and equality indexes.

Besides which, few doubted that U.S. domestic policies and governmental biases also contributed. The subordination of manufacturing to finance was one; another was the weaknesses that made labor unions less able to protect wages. Moreover, the presidents of the eighties and nineties permitted corporations to raise profits and stock prices by slashing workforces and trimming wages and benefits. In the early eighties the competitiveness of U.S. manufactures had also been crippled by Federal Reserve policies that drove the dollar to abnormally high values.

Still another effect of trade and globalization lay in the weapons they gave to management against employees and unions. A Cornell University study of labor organizing drives determined that in 62 percent of the cases examined, management fought back by threatening to shift production to a lower-wage area. Enough companies had already done so to make the threat itself work in a larger number of instances.

These all worked to increase economic inequality. So did the proliferation of international business and commercial lobbies in Washington as well as the enlargement of business influence permitted by the loophole-ridden federal election laws. None of these circumstances lent themselves to measurement in a statistical series.

Perhaps the most intriguing turn-of-the-millennium analysis of globalization and its effects came from academicians Jeffrey G. Williamson and Kevin O'Rourke in a 1999 book entitled *Globalization and History.* Williamson, coauthor of *American Inequality: A Macroeconomic History,* cited in chapter 2, applied a wealth-and-income lens to the current globalization and the previous example prior to World War I. In a nutshell, he and O'Rourke concluded that the 1870–1914 globalization of trade, migration, and capital flows increased inequality in the countries like the United States, Canada, and Australia and stabilized it in open European

CHART 6.1 **Seven Major Characteristics of the Great Economic Revolutions**

CIRCUMSTANCE	RENAISSANCE AND RISE OF CAPITALISM	INDUSTRIAL REVOLUTION	HIGH-TECH REVOLUTION
Critical new technology	Shipbuilding, aids to navigation, metallurgy	Steam engine, power loom	Silicon chip, computer and microprocessor, human genome
Communications developments	Printing press, books, advanced mathematics, global exploration	Telegraph, popular newspapers, railroads	Telecommunications and the Internet
Finance, Banking and Investment	Commerical banks, bourses and bonds	Regional stock exchanges, beginning of popular securities markets	Electronic finance, 24-hour trading and derivative instruments
Commercial and competitive philosophies	Machiavellianism and Calvinism	Laissez-faire and Social Darwinism	Rule of the marketplace and globalization
Economic complexity	Greatly increased	Greatly increased	Greatly increased
Economic imperialism	Venetian, Portuguese and Spanish empires	Rise of the British Empire (and other European empires)	U.S. economic hegemony implemented through GATT, NAFTA and WTO
Economic wealth concentration and polarization	Pronounced in the centers of the transformation	Pronounced in the centers of the transformation	Pronounced in the centers of the transformation

industrial nations like Britain. Inequality helped breed a backlash that brought globalization to an end. The relevance for the twenty-first century, the two contend, is that the rise in inequality in the OECD nations since the 1960s, after four previous decades of egalitarian trends, again overlapped with a new wave of globalization, which could also be cut short.

Thus the appropriateness of viewing the previous great transformations and the late-twentieth-century high-tech upheaval through a larger lens—as a series of economic, demographic, political, and technological complexities beyond capture in statistics but roughly describable in recurring circumstances, attitudes, and effects. The chart on page 265 shows seven important shared characteristics. Such was the imprint of polarization and inequality in the third great transformation, with evidence that stretched from Tokyo and Hong Kong to Silicon Valley and from Manhattan to Finland and Bangalore.

3. America and the World: Technology and Inequality at the Millennium

For a number of interrelated reasons, from the impact of technology to the effects of financialization and new trading patterns, the worsening global rich-poor gap of the last three decades of the twentieth century stands out. Not only did it match the two earlier great upheavals, but a much larger portion of the world's population was affected.

To begin with a global overview, the 1990s drew attention to a sub-technological "Fourth World"—the weakest of undeveloped nations, mostly in Africa, unable for want of advanced technology or technological competence, to raise productivity or living standards. From a ratio of 30:1 back in 1960, the disparity between the poorest and richest quintiles of the world's population had climbed to 75:1 by 2000. Per capita income in the United States, nine times that of Chad or Ethiopia back in 1900, led by 45:1 in 2000. Between 1980 and 1996, per capita GNP actually declined in some sixty countries. Technology—construed as computers and the changes they made possible—helped enlarge this chasm.

If the technologically advanced countries left the rest of the world in the economic dust, their internal wealth effects also evoked past excesses. Polarization and inequality grew in tandem. In some cultures erosion of democratic traditions was seen as a real problem. Besides the United States, rich nations dislocated by digitalization included Japan, Israel, Britain, and Scandinavia, particularly Sweden and Finland.

Earlier post–World War II commercial successes in Japan—in particular, the successful 1965–85 manufacture of consumer electronics—had left relatively undisturbed the egalitarian society and income distribution established after 1945. Government subsidies and favoritism to small shopkeepers, rice growers, fishermen, and other groups persisted. The fin-de-siècle Internet revolution, by contrast, came as Japan was already under pressure to move toward deregulation, competition, and the greater social and economic inequities these entailed. Software, Internet, and wireless companies led in the movement away from traditional job protection, paternalism, and compressed salaries toward greater inequality, pay for performance, and star-system hiring. Tax policy also conformed as the Japanese government reduced the highest income tax rate from 65 to 50 percent while increasing burdens at lower levels.

Until Japanese high-tech stocks crashed with the Nasdaq in 2000, their skew of the nation's wealth was striking. Ponytailed instant millionaires abounded in Tokyo's Shibuya district as fledgling stock issues soared, becoming the city's principal source of new wealth. The collapse of net worths shown in Chart 6.2 moderated but did not reverse this pattern.

CHART 6.2 **Japanese New Rich Billionaires and the Technology Crash**

NAME/BUSINESS	PEAK VALUATION OF STOCK, JAN.–MARCH 2000 (IN $ BILLIONS)	JUNE 2000	JULY 2001
Masayoshi Son/Softbank	78.6	29.7	5.6
Yasumitsu Shigeta/Hikari Shushin (wireless Internet)	42.0	2.3	NL
Toshihiro Maeta/MTI (mobile phones)	3.9	0.6	NL
Koki Okuda/Trans-Cosmos (information systems)	3.4	1.0	NL
Masatoshi Kumagi/InterQ (Internet provider)	3.8	1.0	NL
Kagemasa Kozuki/Konami (electronic games)	2.4	1.4	1.1
Tetsuro Funai/Funai Electric (audiovisual)	4.7	3.3	1.6
Hiroshi Fujiwara (Internet research)	3.0	0.7	NL

Source: *Forbes,* June 11, 2000; 2001. NL means "not listed" in the July 9, 2001, *Forbes* survey of world billionaires.

Scandinavia was another prime example, having already passed the United States in 2000 as the world's most intense information economy based on the percentage of citizens with access to computers, the Internet, wireless phones, or other information technologies. According to research by the International Data Corporation, Sweden led, with the United States second, followed by Finland, Norway, and Denmark.

Home to two of the world's three largest wireless phone makers, Finland's Nokia foremost and Sweden's Ericsson in third place, Scandinavia took the smart wireless handset as its information technology of choice, leaving computers behind. So committed, the Nordic countries also pioneered in m.commerce, the mobile variety, which used wireless handsets for everything from paying for parking or theater tickets to mobile dating services. In terms of wealth and income distribution, the results included a mobile-phone elite, especially in Finland and Sweden.

Most large wealth in Finland involved Nokia. In December 2000 its sales accounted for 4 percent of Finnish GDP and its shares made up 70 percent of the value of the Helsinki stock market. Of Finland's top fifty income earners in 1999, all were past or present executives of Nokia. Their wealth, lacking any official tabulations, was fattened by a 245 percent jump in Nokia stock in 1999 alone. Data compiled by the Luxembourg Project on Finnish and Swedish wealth and income distribution showed inequality rising in both nations in the nineties, although the wealth effect faded in 2000–2001 as the stocks of both Ericsson and Nokia collapsed by 75–85 percent from their bubble highs.

In Britain, where income and wealth polarization had been rising since the 1980s, the Internet, in particular, drew attention for its embellishments. Deregulated finance had already revolutionized the City of London, and as in Wall Street, the city's high comfort with technology spilled over into the Internet sector. Some initial placement offerings traded on names and connections, and following the IPO of lastminute.com, which involved a relative of the marquess of Anglesey, the *Financial Times* observed that "the Internet, which was supposed to be a great leveler—cutting through class and traditional networks—has instead quickly become a platform for the rise of a new/old moneyed elite. The names of some individuals read like an excerpt from Debrett's [the reference book on the aristocracy]." London's millennial boom in maids, gardeners, cooks, butlers, and nannies also drew on the new technology money, as well as on the profits of communications and financial services.

Hong Kong, the former British colony, was home to kindred circumstances. Two of the major Internet companies, Tom.com and Pacific Century Cyberworks, were owned by the region's richest tycoon, Li-Ka Shing, and his family.

In Israel, older men and women who remembered sand in the streets of Tel Aviv and camel caravans taking oranges to Jaffa told of being stunned in the late 1990s to find burgeoning high-technology and Internet companies destroying their country's legacy of kibbutzim and communalism. High technology accounted for over 40 percent of Israeli exports in 2000. Ten thousand Israelis worked in Silicon Valley, and some 120 Israeli companies were listed on the several New York stock markets, second only to U.S. and Canadian firms. Of ten industrial countries surveyed by Babson College and the London Business School, only the United States and Canada surpassed Israel in key measures of entrepreneurialism, including independent start-up companies, mostly technology-linked.

Salaries among high-tech managers and engineers, most of them fluent in English, had doubled between 1997 and 2000 while wages in other parts of the economy remained stagnant. Buyouts by U.S. companies of Israeli firms fed the trend, especially the $4.5 billion buyout of Chromatis Networks in June 2000. Shali Tshuva, who supervised government studies of the technology sector, told the *New York Times* that, "What bothers me is that it might create an upstairs-downstairs environment here. There is such an enormous difference in income between old-economy employees and new-economy employees, you might wind up with two economies in the same country." The newer one largely left out Arabs and Orthodox Jews, the two large, poor minorities.

So much for the impact on the rich nations of the "First World." In some respects, the more important effects, while also internally polarizing, came in the two giant Asian nations expected to ride the high-tech revolution to an advanced status never achieved during the industrial period. Economists in the IMF, World Bank, and elsewhere who oppose the notion that globalization and technology are widening the gap between the world's have- and have-not nations invariably acknowledge that India and China, with their huge populations totaling over 2 billion, are central to their case. Without China and India, the great bulk of the undeveloped world that is losing ground would dominate the outcome, but when the two giants are included, their considerable economic gains are enough to ease worldwide income inequality by at least a few yardsticks. Strategists in the West can hardly take comfort, because huge portions of the have-not world are losing ground, and the gains by India and China may well represent the early-stage emergence of the two nations and continent most likely to challenge the twenty-first-century technological advantage of the United States.

India boarded the Internet and software express quite successfully in the 1990s, drawing on its 15–30 million-strong English-speaking and well-educated middle class. Even so, one-third of the 900 million population still lived in absolute poverty. Hyderabad, whose Nizam had once been the wealthiest man in British India, led the tech parade, along with nearby Bangalore. Although just 280,000 Indians worked in the technology sector at decade's end, the benefits to India's elite were broader. India's software exports jumped from about $1 billion in 1995 to some $5 billion in 2000, principally to the United States. At the height of the boom, a survey by McKinsey & Company predicted a rise to $50 billion in a decade. John Wall, president of Nasdaq International, enthused that, "There are potentially 100-plus companies in India that could list on the Nasdaq." Indeed, between the start of 1999 and the spring of 2000 the market value of the software sector on the Bombay Stock Exchange rose from $4 billion to a peak of more than $50 billion. Employees of Infosys alone included 270 millionaires in dollar terms, at least before the bubble broke.

India's millions of engineers also became the principal foreign source of skilled technicians for Silicon Valley under the U.S. government's H1-B visa program. In 2000, the total of skilled Indian workers in the U.S. approached 75,000, including more than one-quarter of the workforce at Cisco, the networking giant. Charts 6.3a and 6.3b show the growth of India's software industry and the rising dependence of U.S. companies on Indian engineers as well as an overview of the millennial ups and downs of the leading Indian high-tech fortunes. Thousands more Indians, it should be noted, held lucrative niches in the U.S. financial sector, and roughly a score of U.S. computer, Internet, and software firms had Indian-born chief executives. All of these ties greatly assisted India's fledgling software industry. In wealth distribution terms, the result was yet another glamorous *digirati,* bubbly stock markets, and Western high-rise buildings in a poor and more polarized society.

Still, even though India's software industry and related fortunes suffered from the postmillennial tech crash, few serious observers saw the country as anything but an ascending force in twenty-first-century technology thanks to its large number of English-speaking engineers and low wage rates. Software engineers commanding $75,000 a year in the U.S.

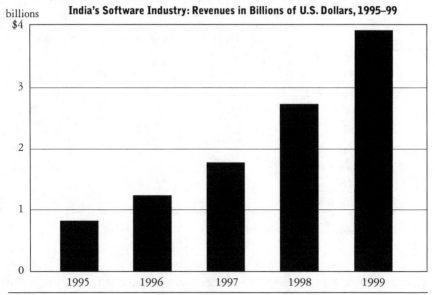

CHART 6.3a **Indian Software: Billionaires and U.S. Visas**

billions   **India's Software Industry: Revenues in Billions of U.S. Dollars, 1995–99**

U.S. H1-B Visas Issued to Indian Workers ...   **As a Percentage of Total H1-Bs Issued**

thousands

Source: India's National Association of Software and Service Companies, U.S. State Department, *Investor's Business Daily*, July 6, 2000, p. A10.

could be hired for one-fifth as much in Hyderabad or Bangalore, and by 2001 the Indian government reported nearly one thousand tech firms—several hundred American—with foreign operations in Bangalore. As we will see shortly, a kindred situation was developing in China: increasing polarization, but amid impressive economic progress and bright prospects.

To return to the United States, the four major technology and financial concentrations—the region including San Francisco Bay and Silicon Valley along with the metropolitan areas of Boston, New York, and Washington, D.C.—all had among the nation's highest wealth and income disparities. California and New York were both among the five states with the most unequal income distribution in the 1990 and 2000 censuses, although California, being home to Silicon Valley, drew the most scrutiny.

CHART 6.3b **Indian Technology Billionaires**

NAME	PEAK VALUATION OF STOCK, JAN.–MARCH 2000 (IN $ BILLIONS)	JUNE 2000	JULY 2001
Azim Premji/Wipro (software services)	37.6	9.3	6.9
Subhas Chandra/Zee Telefilms	10.6	3.3	NL
Shiv Nadar/HCL Technologies (software)	9.0	3.8	2.2
B. Ramalinga Raju/ Satyam Infoways	3.2	1.2	NL
NR Narayana Murthy/Infosys	1.5	0.8	NL

Source: *Forbes,* June 12, 2000; *Forbes,* July 9, 2001.

Longtime residents who remembered the two-lane roads and pear or-chards of the 1950s—or even the Santa Clara County of the 1960s, when high technology still meant smallness of scale and a democratic work-place—described the new Valley of Dollars with the tone of elderly Israelis bemoaning the lost spirit of the kibbutzim. "The technological elite are doing extremely well," said Larry Kimbell, director of UCLA's Anderson Business Forecasting Project. "The spectacular wealth is caus-ing a tremendous sense of anxiety because it's from a process most of us aren't involved with. . . ."

During the last years of the twentieth century, "Siliwood"—clumsy shorthand for the joint ascendancy of Silicon Valley and Hollywood in California's wealth firmament and entertainment and software export ma-chine—joined New York as the most rapidly stratifying major U.S. re-gional economy. According to a study by the Public Policy Institute of California, that state as a whole led the nation in increasing economic dis-parities during the period from 1976 to 1994. Inflation-adjusted income among the poorest 10 percent of Californians fell 30 percent, a sharper drop than the 8 percent national decline. In 1969, twenty states had more inequality than California in men's earnings; by 1989 only Texas and New Mexico did.

Within Silicon Valley the shift to high-value-added technology ex-plained the polarization. For the 1991–97 period, despite a boom, real in-comes for the poorest 20 percent of households in the region fell by 8 percent, compared with a gain of 2 percent for the lowest quintile in the state as a whole. Incomes for the top fifth, by contrast, climbed by an average of 20 percent, more than double the statewide rate. Researchers also began to fault a specific employment practice: the trend among technology companies to hire temporary workers, taken on since the 1980s at twice the pace of overall employment growth. By 2000, part-time workers—for the most part clerks, electronics assembly workers, and technicians—accounted for a third of the total workforce. Tens of thousands were skilled foreign workers with H1-B visas, principally Asians and, in many cases, poorly paid and at the mercy of their employer.

A senior research scholar at Stanford University's Science, Technology, and Society program, Alex Pang, summed up how the bloom was fading from the valley's rose: "Fast money may or may not encourage dealmaking over real company-building, but it has definitely put the squeeze on the Valley's middle and working classes. For every new millionaire shopping at Draeger's, there are dozens of professional families struggling to afford two-bedroom $500,000 homes and many more working families crowded out of the bottom of the market. Indeed, high real estate prices, along with over crowding and traffic, are eroding the area's quality of life and its ability to attract new talent." At the peak of the stock market boom, real estate agents in San Jose admitted to "feeling ashamed of the impact on ordinary house-seekers: The condo in Sunnyvale with 18 offers; the 'nothing special about it' ranch home in Los Altos with the asking price of $999,000 that just sold for $2 million."

Another dimension of regional economic stratification lay in the hollowing out of the regional job profile: high-end professional jobs getting the publicity, lower-end jobs catering to the wealthy actually showing the biggest growth. By one calculation, food store, restaurant and bar, garden supply, and automotive dealer and service occupations accounted for more new jobs in the 1992–99 period than the valley's high-profile computer and office equipment sector. In the busy domestic service sector, the new hires of the year 2000 included twelve butlers dispatched by Ivor Spencer's in London to run the households of busy Internet executives.

In Hollywood, the other linchpin of the state's communications and entertainment megaplex, yesteryear's egalitarianism—the screen version, at least—had also vanished in a cloud of elite values. Entertainment had replaced aerospace as southern California's principal export industry in 1996, and union leaders charged that during the 1990s, Hollywood's "above the line" talent—actors, directors, and writers—demanded and got exorbitant fees for their services, leaving a lower share of the production budget for "below the line" craft and blue-collar workers. Wages and work conditions worsened as unions made repeated concessions, sometimes under threats that production would be moved to Australia, Canada, and other lower-wage, nonunion locations. Between 1990 and 1998 the share of U.S. film and TV production conducted overseas doubled to 27 percent.

Home to the communications capital of the East, albeit with a much higher ratio of broadcast and print media, publishing, and finance, New York State in 1996–98 led the other forty-nine in income distributional inequality. Global nexus of words, images, and money, Manhattan was also a center of glittering polarization. The Community Service Society of New York, in a survey its president termed ominous, reported that the overall rate of poverty in New York City among families with children was up from 19.3 percent in 1986–88 to 32.3 percent in 1996–98. Included were more families in which the head of household had attended college or had a degree—only 11.1 percent of the poverty ranks in the late 1980s, they contributed 23.0 percent on the cusp of the millennium. The shift to temporary jobs with lower pay scales was a factor in New York, too, along with a hollowed-out job profile as clerical and backroom employment moved to Maine and South Dakota (or Ireland and India).

As the millennium turned, whether that took place on January 1, 2000, or January 1, 2001, the proof that technology, trade, and globalization had created wealth was easy to find, especially in the affluent communities lived in or visited by upscale professionals—who were largely willing to take the broader argument on faith. But despite vague, well-intentioned insistences, the evidence farther down the economic ladder was more to the contrary—in the poorest half or two-thirds of the world, and for that matter, in the poorer half or two-thirds of the leading financial and technological nations themselves.

To be sure, past precedents also suggested that average Americans would ultimately benefit from breakthroughs of the new technologies. However, over the first generation or two of the great transformations, painful disparities—working to the detriment of ordinary people who rarely understand what is happening or why—have been the historical rule, not the unfortunate exception.

4. Theories of Progress and the Advent of Technological Manias

Technology is rarely thought to be poetic, but the verse of men like Alfred Tennyson, Ralph Waldo Emerson, and Walt Whitman provide instructive exceptions. Their excitement mirrored society's. In mid-nineteenth-century Massachusetts, Emerson, seeing the steam engine and early electricity grab public imagination, enthused that, "Machinery and transcendentalism agree well . . . stagecoach and railroad are bursting the old legislation like green withes. . . . Our civilization and these ideas are reducing the earth to a brain. See how by telegraph and steam the earth is anthropologized." Whitman agreed that thanks to the steamship, the telegraph, and factories, "never was the average man, his soul, more energetic, more like a God."

Few enthusiasms better document technology's manic propensity. Back in 1792, Erasmus Darwin, grandfather of the famous Charles, had even managed to wax poetic about a future shaped by steam, and some years later William Wordsworth penned tribute to gas lighting. As industry stretched its legs in the late-nineteenth-century United States, even reformers like Henry George swooned over "those muscles of iron and sinews of steel making the laborer's life a holiday . . . realizing the golden age of which mankind have always dreamed. . . . For how could there be greed where all had enough?" The cynical Henry Adams, in turn, reacted to electricity by feeling "the forty-foot dynamos as a moral force, much as the early Christians felt the cross . . ."

By the 1920s, Britain's capacity for such Pollyanna thinking had died in the World War I trenches, and odes to technology became lopsidedly American. Books about the radio age described how many Americans, still undaunted, believed that the new phenomenon would bring world peace, uplift democracy, improve education, and renew religion. Automobiles and aviation unleashed more of the same.

The point to underscore is that technological mania develops from exaggerating rational underpinnings. Before October's great crash, 1929 was the year of the first television broadcast, of movie theaters installing sound equipment, of the first transcontinental airline service, and in New York, of the completion of the Chrysler Building, tallest in the world. Hard-bitten law enforcement authorities in Detroit were predicting that the latest technology—radio-equipped patrol cars—would finally defeat crime. Owen Young, the otherwise practical chairman of General Electric, accepted an honorary degree in June with a speech conjoining physics and poetry. Physical researchers, he enthused, would become the modern counterparts of Shakespeare, Marlowe, Ben Jonson, and Milton. "There may be enough poetry in the whirr of our machines," he said, "so that our machine age will become immortal."

The automobile billionaire Henry Ford, not to be outdone, in early 1929 published a book entitled *Machinery and the New Messiah.* Religion, he wrote, would soon be overshadowed:

Machinery is accomplishing in the world what man has failed to do by preaching, propaganda or the written word. The airplane and the radio know no boundary. . . . They are binding the world together in a way no other systems can. The motion picture, with its universal language, the airplane with its speed, the radio with its coming international program—these will soon bring the world to a complete understanding. Thus may be visioned a United States of the world. Ultimately, it will surely come.

And so it went that year. Dr. Charles Mayo, of the famous clinic, opined that a cancer cure was imminent. Test-tube babies would follow. Even aging would be abolished. Author Warren Sloat in his book *1929,* a fifty-year retrospective, confessed amazement at the mood he found: "Not the least remarkable of the successes of technology was its uncritical, almost hypnotic public endorsement. No philosophers or magazine writers could swerve the public from an enthusiasm for applied science almost religious in its faith."

Elite confidence that technology was remaking human nature—Henry George's naivete about greed, Henry Ford's "peace ship" of 1915, Tennyson's vision of furled battle flags—found a match in the expectations of many academics and market enthusiasts that scientific economics was on the cusp of eliminating the business cycle. Together, and especially in the nineteenth and twentieth centuries, these have been twin pillars of Pollyannaism.

Just prior to the Railroad Mania of 1847, Britain's Bank Act was thought to have legislated away financial crises by limiting the availability of credit for speculation. By 1873 some New York financiers had become convinced that government safeguards barred crises like those of 1837 and 1857. The powers of the secretary of the treasury were such, wrote the *New York Herald,* that "it is difficult to conceive of any condition of circumstances which he cannot control," until the severe downturn of 1873–79 proved otherwise. The heady boom of 1901 was bolstered by confidence in the new trusts as well as by the technological expositions and fanfare that greeted the new century.

Several booms later, in 1927, the head of Moody's Investors Service wrote about civilization in the process of perfecting itself. By 1929 dozens of articles and books had appeared about the new era in technology and finance. Irving Fisher, the Yale economist, lives on in memory for his 1929 prediction that downturns were being replaced by a "permanent plateau of prosperity."

The prosperity of the 1950s brought a mild resurgence of talk about new eras and the greater competence of finance in 1955–56. However, the midcentury peak came with the renewed technological enthusiasm of the 1960s, whetted by space exploration, moon landings, computers, color television, and commercial jet aircraft and exemplified in the stock market by a new wave of pop electronic stock names—Transitron, Dutron, Circuitronics, and the like. As the Dow-Jones flirted with the magic 1000 mark, the sixties also brought a resurgence of belief that the business cycle was passé. The U.S. Commerce Department, venting that optimism in 1968, changed the name of its monthly periodical *Business Cycle Developments* to *Business Conditions Digest.*

Similar bravura was heard again in 1989 and 1990, when the business cycle had run seven years and just prior to the arrival of the mid-1990 downturn. However, the late 1990s saw the next full crest of dual Pollyannaism: on the one hand, the message that technology, led by the Internet, was transcending history; on the other the belief that the business cycle itself was being overcome by new management skills and the extended capacities of the computer networking age. The speaker of the U.S. House of Representatives, Newt Gingrich, himself an acolyte of technology-minded futurist Alvin Toffler, broadened his critique of Washington to decry "the so-called business cycle" as a humbug maintained by Federal Reserve economists and other experts.

Against this backdrop, the excesses of the late twentieth century verged on predictability. Microprocessors and the Internet, in attaining messiah status, had merely replaced steam, railroads, and electric dynamos as chapels in which the newest technologies were worshiped. Magazines like *Wired* and *PC* took over where publications like *Railway Progress* and *Aeronautics* had left off. For every considered statement of what truly constituted a revolution—the impact, for example, of the telegraph on communications, of electricity on factory operations, or of the silicon chip on computers and computer networking—the nineteenth and twentieth centuries have produced dozens of naive visions, some ultimately quite damaging.

5. A LONG WAY FROM HARMLESS: THE ECONOMIC AND SOCIAL COSTS OF TECHNOLOGY MANIAS AND BUBBLES

Technological naivete by itself would have mattered less without the complicity of financial promoters. However, Holland, Britain, and the United States, being not only the successive showcases of world technology but the successive centers of capitalism, joint-stock companies, capital markets, and speculative finance, have usually made too much of a good thing. The architecture of the boom has all too often become the film of an unsustainable excess.

Comments on the speculative tendencies of Dutch, British, and Americans have been legion. As for the repetitive implosions, doubters can consult economist Charles Kindleberger's book *Manias, Panics, and Crashes.* Of his twenty-eight major examples between 1720 and 1975, twenty-one originated wholly or partially in the avid stock market cultures of Holland, Britain, and the United States. Initially, of course, close relations between technology and finance produced benefits by enlisting the capital needed to support innovation. The periodic national bane, alas, was the frequent subsequent distress, most prominently in the United States, from the implosion of technologically-fed speculative bubbles.

Chapter 9 will take a larger approach to the culture and politics of speculation in the United States. But the repetition of eighteenth and nineteenth-century technology booms that bubbled and burst is instructive, especially because it has rarely been pursued. There is no need to revisit the small British speculative booms in diving engines, gas lighting, or canals. However, America's three great technologically-nurtured nineteenth-century boom-bust sequences (1857, 1873, and 1893) can be summed up in one fast-speeding, revolutionary word: *railroads.* None of these matched the opening-round psychological delusion of so many Britons in the Great Railway Mania of 1844–48, but the repetitive damage of the several railroad implosions to the larger U.S. economy was particularly vivid on that side of the Atlantic.

No sooner had the first British railroad opened in 1828 than Americans began planning one. As we saw in chapter 1, the Baltimore & Ohio had thirteen miles of track in 1830, and that same year the tiny Mohawk & Hudson linked Albany and Schenectady. By 1835 rail links spread out from Baltimore, Charleston, Boston, New York, and Philadelphia and joined the last two. New coal mines, iron foundries, machine shops, and locomotive works soon followed. By 1837 a dozen other railways had joined the Mohawk & Hudson on the New York Stock Exchange. State governments, in turn, had subscribed or loaned an estimated $43 million to the iron carriages, and state banks were pumping out paper money with abandon. All of this hubbub fed gathering speculation.

In 1831, when trading on the New York Stock and Exchange Board began in shares of the New York & Harlem, "a frenzied boom in stocks of the new technology got underway. By 1835, at the height of the mania, rail trades had outstripped those in all the NYS&EB's hundred-plus listed stocks and bonds." Total volume increased tenfold, to six thousand shares a day, and U.S. markets also saw their first margin trading—fifty dollars to a broker would suffice to own $500 worth of stocks—and "manipulative short sales."

The bubble popped in 1837, but what started out as a panic in May, when eight hundred U.S. banks suspended payment, seemed to pass by 1838. Then by 1839 it widened into a depression, which lasted until 1843. Before the dust cleared, the states of Indiana, Michigan, Mississippi, Maryland, and Pennsylvania had repudiated their debts. Real estate values collapsed—in Chicago to only 14 percent of what they had been in 1836. Then in the second wave of the downturn, railroad share prices, already decimated in 1837, fell by 50 percent between February 1839 and February 1843. Consumer prices dropped by almost one-half over these four years and wages fell faster. In 1839, New York writer Charles F. Briggs published what was probably the first depression novel—*The Adventures of Harry Franco, a Tale of the Panic of 1837.*

This, arguably, was the first technology-related U.S. bubble and bust. Dozens of railroads failed; Illinois, Indiana, and Michigan sold their state-launched railroads to private purchasers, and railroad construction fell by two-thirds between 1838 and 1843. British investors in U.S. railroads and state bonds took an enormous bath. But as would also be the case in later bubbles, ordinary Americans suffered worst of all. The number of persons receiving relief in New York City jumped from just under 30,000 in 1837 to over 80,000 in 1838—29 Gothamites out of 100. Times remained hard well into the 1840s.

The next speculative collapse came in 1857, after the miles of track laid had jumped from about three thousand to just under 24,000. The investment involved, mostly private (and significantly British), soared from $372 million to nearly $1 billion. The states during the same period borrowed about $90 million to finance railroad construction. But by 1854–55, investors began to realize that many of the new rail projects were not showing the projected profits. New railroad construction shrank. British bankers began withdrawing capital. By the summer of 1857 railroad stocks were 45 percent below their 1853 peaks.

The broad trigger came in August when the failure of Ohio's leading bank toppled others in New York and touched off chaos. Railroad and other stock prices plummeted; loans were called, and many stocks could not be sold for enough to meet the margins. The stronger banks held out, but eventually suspended payments in October. The Erie, Illinois Central, Michigan Central, and Reading Railroads all failed. The damage did not end there, of course. New York's spending boom tied to railroad stock profits imploded. Over 5,100 businesses collapsed, involving liabilities of nearly $300 million. Unemployment in eastern cities was serious enough in 1858 to put a major strain on relief agencies.

The Panic of 1873, even more intertwined with irresponsible railroad management and finances, was more devastating—and longer lasting. Railroad mileage had more than doubled between 1857 and 1873, with 35,000 miles of that track built during the pell-mell 1865–73 period, as much as in the two generations preceding.

Railroad stock prices peaked in March. By late summer the Wall Street bears were clawing in the biggest arena of U.S. finance: railroad stocks and bonds had a combined value of between $3 and $4 billion in a year when the federal budget came to only $290 million. Drexel, Morgan & Company was hammering at the Northern Pacific, financed by the House of Cooke, the biggest investment bank in the United States and Drexel Morgan's great rival. The Northern Pacific, charged the Morgan men, was a second South Sea bubble.

Charles Kindleberger, the eminent historian of panics, has emphasized two circumstances in looking back at the 1873 collapse. The first was political—the nervousness among investors over the growing antirailroad successes of the Granger movement, which favored state legislation to bar discriminatory charges and rebates, establish regulatory commissions, and set maximum freight rates. Illinois had acted in 1867 and 1871, Minnesota in 1871, and Wisconsin and Iowa would follow in 1874. The damage to the stock of the wayward Rockford, Rock Island & St. Louis suggested what could happen elsewhere, and stock prices suffered.

The second and larger catalyst involved the failures of the New York Warehouse & Security Company as well as the Kenyon, Cox & Company and Jay Cooke & Company on September 8, 13, and 18 respectively, because of their advances to the Missouri, Kansas & Texas, the Canada Southern, and the Northern Pacific Railroads. The latter could no longer sell bonds for funds to complete construction or meet debts.

Of the debacle on September 18, one Cooke biographer wrote that, "The news spread like a fire in one of the Northern Pacific's own prairies." The *Tribune* reported that when news of the Cooke failure was announced on the New York Stock Exchange, "a monstrous yell went up" and "dread seemed to take possession of the multitude." A reporter for *The Nation* observed that all that day and the next, a "mad terror" gripped the exchange.

"All about the failure of Jay Cooke," newsboys shrilled across the country, and Matthew Josephson, himself fresh from the Wall Street of 1933, would later chronicle the excitement in *The Robber Barons*: "The largest and most pious bank in the Western world had fallen with the effect of a thunderclap. Soon allied brokers and national banks and 5,000 commercial houses followed it into the abyss of bankruptcy. All day long, in Wall Street, one suspension after another was announced; railroads failed; leading stocks lost 30 to 40 points, or half their value, within the hour. . . ."

The market remained closed for ten days while recriminations flourished. The aging Commodore Vanderbilt blamed the railroad buccaneers: "There are many worthless railroads started in this country without any means to carry them through." Many "went from nowhere to nowhere." Once again, railroad mania had gotten out of hand. The biographer of railroad king James J. Hill wrote years later that states and communities had competed for lines "that could not do anything but a paper business for years to come, and the reckless discounting of these securities for the benefit of promoters and construction companies . . . the hypothecation of the future, built a towering pyramid of hope." Economist Thorstein Veblen in the 1890s, and R. E. Riegle, chronicler of the Western railways, agreed on yet another consequence: that the speculative proliferation of weak railroads delayed for forty years the needed consolidation (in the 1890s) of the U.S. transportation system.

By 1876 half of U.S. railroads, with 21,000 miles of track, were in receivership for bond default. Many fell to the Vanderbilt and Gould interests. But once again the pinch was worse for ordinary Americans. The iron and steel industries, dependent on the railroads, idled through most of the decade. An estimated three million men were unemployed in 1874.

The economy finally recovered in 1879, and by 1882, 11,569 miles of new track produced a boom—the first time that word was used in an economic sense. Once again, much of the building represented speculative construction or rivals out to undo each other, and by 1883 earnings and rail stock prices were falling again. This convinced J. P. Morgan to try to broker an end to the "fever for building and extending competitive lines." But his arrangement lasted only a year, and a second attempt in 1888 dissolved even more quickly. America's railroads were still a disaster waiting to happen.

That struck in 1893, although tremors had been felt in 1890, and some economic historians have viewed the 1890–96 period as essentially one long downturn. The Philadelphia & Reading Railroad, carrying $125 million debt on a capitalization of $40 million, failed in February 1893, which led to concern about other shakily-financed railroads. Follow they did, and companies controlling one-third of the U.S. railroad system were among the nearly sixteen thousand businesses that failed. "Never in the history of transportation in the United States," reported the Interstate Commerce Commission in June 1894, "has such a large percentage of railway mileage been under the control of receiverships." Besides the Reading, the carnage included the Erie, Northern Pacific, Santa Fe, Baltimore & Ohio, Union Pacific, and 149 others capitalized at $2.5 billion. This time Morgan's proposed reorganizations would stick, and by 1900 most of the U.S. track was owned by six major systems.

The bad news was that the 1893 railroad collapse once again helped to usher in a lengthy depression that didn't really end until early 1898. As we saw in chapter 1, rural America, especially the cash grain areas, was driven almost to revolution. The interplay between technological mania, greedy finance, lack of regulation, and the realignment of income and wealth from the U.S. agricultural sector to the railroad and heavy industrial sector was enormous, even if no equation can be made. The extent of misjudgment and recklessness was stated as well by Cornelius Vanderbilt and J. P. Morgan as by any Minnesota Granger or Kansas Populist. The railroad bubbles—metaphors for nineteenth-century U.S. inability to embrace new technology without dangerous excess—can be identified as factors in four downturns, two often called depressions, that lasted for 20–23 out of 60 years between 1837 and 1897.

Obviously railroads were not the only factor in these downturns, although they played a powerful part—in the depth of the damage as well as in the triggering. Railroads had at least collateral significance in the panics of 1901 and 1907, but their long starring role in the cavalcade of speculative excess essentially ended with the nineteenth century. By the 1920s the interplay between emerging technology, a popular mania, and a recklessly innovating financial sector had shifted to new and multiple subject matter: automobiles, radio, aeronautics, telephones, electric utilities, and motion pictures. And as we have seen, once again a boom turned to bust, and with dire effects in the ordinary economy.

CHART 6.4 **Railroad Speculation and the Disruption of the U.S. Economy**

PANIC YEAR	DURATION OF DOWNTURN OR DEPRESSION
1837	1837, 1839, 1840, 1841, 1842, 1843
1857	1857, 1858
1873	1873, 1874, 1875, 1876, 1877, 1878, 1879
1890/93	1890, 1891, 1892, 1893, 1894, 1895, 1896, 1897

The twentieth century also continued the effects of communications innovations in encouraging technological and financial excesses—the convergence of telephones, radio, and movies in the 1920s, to a lesser extent television in the 1950s and 1960s, and then the importance of financial cable television (CNBC) and the multiple excitements of the Internet in the 1990s. When the technological innovation is also a communications watershed—the railroad and telegraph in the 1840s and 1850s, the triple play of the twenties, and then the Internet and telecom heyday of the nineties—the excesses seem to intensify.

Which brings us to the mania and speculative bubble of the late nineties and the implosion of 2000–2001. Both the exuberance and the dream vision of technology matched the other peak irrationalities, the British Railway Mania of the 1840s and the U.S. Roaring Twenties. The damage to the real economy in the early 2000s was first visible in what became a recession in manufacturing, deepened into a crisis for several technology industries, and then began to spread more widely into service industries in 2001.

What would take much longer to clarify was the damage to the future of U.S. economic leadership from the huge overinvestment in the Internet and other technology and the massive U.S. loss of capital and disarray in the 2000–2001 crash, to say nothing of the potential technology-transfer from an unnerved and weakened U.S. technology sector moving more of its production and investment overseas.

6. THE MOVABLE FEAST: GLOBAL LEADERSHIP AND TECHNOLOGY TRANSFER

Twice in modern history, the West's premier center of technology lost that status—Holland by the middle of the eighteenth century, Britain by the end of the nineteenth. The United States, at the beginning of the twenty-first, stood in considerable continuity with both. This was true not just in technological and speculative heritage, but in the same high degree of internationalization that left its predecessors wide open to reversing fortune.

If the Holland of 1740 and the Britain of 1910 stood out as heavily internationalized societies, so did the America of 2000. Some of the change came after the U.S. advance to global leadership after 1945, but more followed the stresses of the 1970s, visible both in finance and in the lowered emphasis on manufacturing. Massive merchandise imports made the United States the world's principal debtor nation in the 1980s and 1990s, accompanied by a steadily enlarging international payments deficit. These numbers, set out two chapters back in Chart 4.2, put the United States in a position that even the British did not assume until the indignities of World War II.

The second side of indebtedness showed in steadily rising foreign ownership patterns within the United States. The share of U.S. manufacturing assets in foreign hands jumped from 3 percent in 1970 to 8 percent in 1980 and 19 percent in 1990. Then a late nineties surge increased foreign ownership from $270 billion of U.S. manufacturing assets in 1997 to $497 billion in 2000, with a parallel access to U.S. industrial research and development. This followed from acquiescing in a ballooning current account deficit that reached $445 billion by 2000. Economist Paul Krugman had predicted in 1987 that "the political issue of the 1990s is going to be the foreign invasion of the United States." He was correct about the phenomenon, but the technology and stock market booms diverted the public attention and delayed the politics.

In fact, a nation grown up under a protective tariff had let itself become the global goods market of last resort, a fin de siècle refuge for the world's poor, tired, and hungry, producers of excess (and often subsidized) steel, automobile parts, consumer electronics, and computer parts. Accepting this transformation was thought to be beneficial to America's larger international economic development and to the U.S. stock market. Services and high value-added exports would be more rewarding. British pride, indeed, had managed a partly similar misappreciation in the early twentieth century. An economist at New York's Bankers Trust, about to be purchased by Deutsche Bank, said in 1999 that, "A burgeoning trade deficit continues to act as a safety valve for the U.S. economy, siphoning production away from potentially overheating domestic industries and thus helping keep inflation tame."

By a strict calculus, of course, the internationalization of the United States could be said to have begun with De Soto, Verrazano, Cabot, La Salle, and Raleigh. However, the stages relevant to our discussion took the spotlight in the 1980s, with a broad range of economic danger signals: industries mired in decline, a mounting flood of manufactured imports, stagnating median wages, an uncertain currency, chronic U.S. international borrowing, a border with Mexico overrun by illegal immigration, the sale to foreign purchasers of hitherto American-owned companies and banks, and even a rising share of U.S. patents being taken out by non-Americans. The relatively self-contained nation of 1920–70 found itself pushed and pulled into many new international relationships, most visible in urban windows on the world like New York, Washington, Miami, Los Angeles, and San Francisco.

By 1990, tabulations showed foreign ownership of between 20 and 40 percent of the downtown office space in New York and Los Angeles. The rich foreigners buying luxury apartments or estates in New York, Florida, and California, albeit uncounted, almost certainly dwarfed the pre–World War I parallel in Britain. For the rich who could manage English, the United States was the place to be, as it also was for the technologically or economically ambitious, the wandering *digirati,* and electronic *cambetistas,* or money-changers.

The District of Columbia had particular attractions for influence- and favor-seekers. From Rome through Madrid to The Hague and London, leading-power capitals have always become magnets, accretions of wealth and parasitism. In the late 1970s some four hundred foreign corporations, organizations, banks, and trade associations already had registered representatives in Washington. By the 1990s, that had trebled. Bashfulness was not an asset. Former Republican cabinet officers signed on as well-paid spokesmen for organizations like the Association for Foreign Investment in America and the Association of Foreign Investors in U.S. Real Estate. Rare was the Washington law office, consulting group, trade organization, or public relations firm, with two or three foreign clients, that did not polish its commitment to globalism accordingly.

California in the eighties was the first big state to watch several major banks pass into foreign hands. By 2000, however, large enough chunks of New York finance had become foreign-owned and internationally refocused to evoke the Edwardian London of Barings, Hambros, and Rothschilds. Deutsche Bank bought Bankers Trust along with the investment firm of Alex Brown. Dresdner Bank purchased Wasserstein Perella. Sumitomo had 15 percent of Goldman Sachs. ING, the Dutch financial giant, owned Aetna Financial Services as well as the once-redoubtable Barings. Zurich Financial took over Scudder Investments. Credit Suisse, having in the 1980s bought and merged First Boston into Credit Suisse First Boston, added Donaldson, Lufkin & Jenrette. S. G. Cowen became Société Générale S. G. Cowen. UBS (Union Bank of Switzerland) Warburg purchased Paine Webber. The munificent prices Wall Streeters received in selling only added to their elite wealth profile.

Meanwhile, so emigrationist were the investment patterns of U.S.-based multinationals that each year, more reported 20, 30, or even 50 percent of their revenues and profits as originating from overseas. As International Pharmaceuticals or Pacific Widget began identifying themselves as *international* firms, even chief executives based in San Francisco or Detroit were increasingly likely to speak English with a German or Australian accent. Silicon Valley built its new plants in Ireland, China, or India. Hollywood looked to wherever people watched movies, listened to compact discs, or flocked to Disneyworlds. The lists could go on, but it seems unnecessary. The United States of 2000, in sum, was as different from the country of 1950 as the imperial Britain of 1910 had been from the shopkeepers' and ironmongers' nation of 1860. American chief executives and proconsuls, in turn, were just as emphatic as their British predecessors in opposing restraints on capital or trade.

Where elites prosper on a political economy of profitable openness, technology and capital move easily—and when the hour of disappointment or adversity comes, it arrives surprisingly quickly. Chapter 4 marshaled some of the evidence. Spain had little manufacturing to safeguard, but its financial and commercial capacities were further drained in the seventeenth century as Genoese, Frenchmen, Flemings, and Portuguese Jews left for greener pastures. Hollanders should have seen the straws in the wind when some of Amsterdam's foreign moneymen followed William of Orange to London in the 1690s. Capital transfer was close behind, and the migrating skills of Dutch carpenters and engineers only another generation or two.

The essence of the successive Dutch, British, and American internationalisms, intensified in the rentier cosmopolitanism that flourished decades beyond each golden age, has been to oppose restraints on the flow of capital, labor, and trade with an insistence that borders on theology and brooks no argument. The self-interest of the prevailing elites has been obvious, however. Leading powers formerly committed to protection and mercantilism back when *that* approach profited them—Britain from the sixteenth century to the early nineteenth, the United States from the 1790s to the 1930s—elicit cynicism with their new insistences.

The changes have been well cataloged. In the Dutch case, its industrial decline, especially in textiles, was closely tied to two waves of European protectionism and new or higher duties on imports. The prohibitive tariffs put by England and France on Dutch cloth and finished textiles in the late seventeenth century were followed by similar measures in Russia, Prussia, Denmark, Norway, and Spain in the first quarter of the eighteenth century. These cumulatively devastated the Dutch industry. The British, in turn, lost hope of spreading free trade and laissez-faire in the late nineteenth century as France, Germany, the United States, and Russia imposed or increased duties on imported goods.

Not a few historians have wondered how the British, in particular, could have so misread the ebb and flow of nations as to dismiss warning signals. The example of Holland was only 40 miles across the Channel and just 150 years in the past. Much of the answer probably lay in the hubris, even self-deception, that attends leading world economic power status—the ideological and geopolitical equivalent of technological mania and irrational exuberance.

The British, as they tried to sell the rest of Europe on their new credo of economic openness, infused their insistence with the moral fervor prominent in Victorian society. The Liberal Party became its unswayable upholder, the City of London its principal interest group, and allied intellectuals its theorists. Moreover, in downplaying the economic jeopardies apparent in the 1900s, party leaders like Lord Rosebery, the former prime minister, and future prime ministers H. H. Asquith and Sir Henry Campbell-Bannerman touched on virtually every argument heard again in the United States of the 1980s and 1990s. Demands for reciprocity would provoke foreign countermeasures. Britain's future lay in finance and services (where we have a favorable balance). Official statistics were not clear enough to act on. And perhaps most of all, the real answer was to achieve "better education, better training, better methods, larger outlooks" (Asquith, 1903) and to "fight them [tariffs] by a more scientific and adaptive spirit—by better education" (Rosebery, 1903).

One is tempted to say that the United States, caught up in a somewhat similar situation, has been no better at marking the British lesson than Britons had been in heeding the Dutch. True, there were important differences. A century after the earl of Rosebery urged "a more scientific and adaptive spirit" on his countrymen, Americans—or at least a higher percentage of them—seemed to still display it, witness the role of Silicon Valley as the Mecca of global technology. Early-twentieth-century Britain boasted nothing so cutting-edge. Besides, the Britain of 1900 had two obvious challengers in the United States and Germany. The United States of the millennium had no immediate rival that kept it looking over its shoulder.

On the other hand, technology and capital were more mobile than ever. A twenty-first-century technology shift might require only half the time of the (for then, rapid) 1875–1900 British loss of stature in the steel, chemical, and electrical industries, three notable technological cockpits of that era. The extraordinary 1914–45 volte-face in Britain's global capital and investment positions might take just one-third of that time a century later. Here we must pick up on the British electrical and chemical industries where chapter 4 left off. Their loss of workers, technology, and leadership to United States and Germany, with a dependence on Americans and Germans in key positions even within Britain, was an early and ill augury.

Economic openness became a drawback. British enlisting of foreigners to aid or run chemical and electrical industries that locals could only half manage solved immediate needs but clouded future prospects. Take Britain's loss, between 1860 and 1881, of the coal-tar dye industry made possible in the late 1850s by the inventions of William H. Perkin. Germany had the schools, laboratories, and trained chemists that Britain did not, and as companies like Hoechst, BASF, and Bayer flourished, many of the Germans manning the fledgling British concerns took attractive offers to return home and "the British organic chemistry industry shriveled." To Harvard economic historian David Landes, this Britain-to-Germany loss represented "one of the biggest, most rapid industrial shifts in history." The British electrical industry was dominated by a U.S. firm, Westinghouse, and despite Britain's earlier midcentury eminence, Americans were also needed by the eighties and nineties in the lagging British machine tool industry.

Steel in particular faced a migration of technology and leadership. Britons kept making many of the leading discoveries: Bessemer's process of 1856, the open-hearth furnace of 1867, and between 1880 and 1906 the development of the specialized silicon, tungsten, and manganese steel metallurgies. However, large numbers of skilled English workmen and engineers had migrated to the United States, beginning in the 1840s and 1850s when the extent of U.S. industrial opportunity became as compelling as the higher level of U.S. wages. One scholar, David Jeremy, has posited a "Transatlantic Industrial Revolution" in which immigrants carried industrial methods and techniques—for quarries, lead mines, and potteries as well as iron and steel—from midcentury Britain to America. U.S. tariffs, in turn, obliged the specialized steel firms of Sheffield—partly dependent on American markets—to set up manufacturing subsidiaries and operations in Pennsylvania, where their technology further diffused (or spread under license). By 1914 success with electric furnaces and high-speed-tool steels gave the United States the same lead in specialty metals that it had achieved in basic steel during the 1890s.

Against this backdrop, the importance of the U.S. technological lead was already hedged by historical precedents even before the 2000–2001 Nasdaq crash. The latter and its implications, however, dropped the percentage of economists banking on the U.S. technological lead from 37 to 28 percent. By this point, moreover, the American inventions of the silicon chip in 1959 and the microprocessor in 1971 were as distant as Britain's pioneering Bessemer, open-hearth, and Gilchrist-Thomas technologies had been to the more precarious steel universe of the early 1900s.

There was also the matter of personnel. The conspicuously limited job creation of the major U.S. technology firms bespoke several warnings. Firm after firm was increasing its reliance on overseas production and software engineers and suppliers, especially, as we have seen, in India, China, Taiwan, and the rest of relatively low-wage East Asia. Even more to the point, many U.S. firms were dependent on foreign nations, mostly Asian, to fill American-based jobs with skilled engineers and programmers unavailable in the U.S. labor pool.

This reliance extended to the highest levels of management. Of the four or five hundred top U.S. Internet, telecom, chip, and networking firms, dozens had Chinese, Indian, or Asian-American chief executives, and Silicon Valley was home to large numbers of Indian, Chinese, and Taiwanese executives and engineers. A group with major representation in the Valley, IndUS Entrepreneurs, estimated that 30 percent of the software engineers there were of Indian origin. An economist at the University of California in Berkeley used a Dun & Bradstreet database to count 750 local companies run by Indians. The workforce at Cisco Systems' San Jose headquarters was 45 percent Asian; Santa Clara County as a whole had a nonwhite majority and a 24 percent Asian population.

The Valley, indeed, seemed to foretell Asia as the next leading world economic region. A *New York Times* profile in 2000 explained that, "The defining character of Silicon Valley today is not the pasty-faced plaid shirt-wearing aerospace engineer, but a young geek from Taipei or Bangalore with an H-1B visa. . . ." American universities, too, were educating hundreds of thousands of foreigners to man rival economies. Others who had come much earlier were going back—thousands of scientists returning to Taiwan alone—drawn by East Asian pride, growth, and prospects. On all counts, partnership arrangements were proliferating.

Moreover, behind the U.S. computer-industry tie to Taiwan, which in 2000 made 39 percent of the world's disk drives, 54 percent of its monitors, and 93 percent of its scanners as well as 53 percent of the laptops and 25 percent of the personal computers, lay the unnerving prospect of Taiwan's manufacturing absorption into the fast-growing Goliath of mainland China. More and more Taiwanese firms were moving production there. Labor on the mainland cost only one-quarter to one-third as much as on Taiwan, and China had two other lures: graduation of new engineers at a rate of 145,000 a year and a domestic computer market growing 40 percent annually. The upshot was that of the computers and laptops sold in the United States by such companies as Compaq, Dell, and Gateway, a growing ratio of the components and even final products came from China, not Taiwan, putting the U.S. into what the *New York Times* described as an "odd position: its main supplier of PC's and other information-technology, or I.T., gear will be its main strategic adversary." Most businessmen just shrugged. Back in the 1990s, the chief executive of Boeing, a major U.S. defense contractor with assembly lines in China, had dismissed technology transfer in aerospace production as something Washington, not Boeing, would have to deal with.

The rate at which U.S.-originated technology was diffusing, relocated, and being pirated was already a subject of concern from Washington and Wall Street to Hollywood. However, it was unduly assumed that the United States and the English-speaking world had a basic protection: that English was not only the lingua franca of global commerce but was also the lingua franca—perhaps lingua anglica had become more apt—of the Internet and global networking. American business publications and meetings of the millennial period hummed with talk of global standards and software protocols, all focused around U.S.-dominated groups like the Organization for the Advancement of Structural Information Standards (OASIS) and the National Industrial Information Infrastructure Protocols Consortium (NIIIPC), the latter working with the U.S. government to establish open industry software protocols through the government-backed Advanced Research Projects Agency, the 1960s birthplace of the Internet.

However, the Asian-based threat to the Dutch-British-American chain of economic and technological hegemony dating back some four hundred years is obvious, even if the time frame of any leadership transferral is problematic. In 2000, Asia was already about to pass the United States in its number of Internet users. Officials talked of China itself pulling ahead by 2005, and one China watcher noted that were China to grow at 7 percent a year, it would surpass a U.S. economy growing at 3 percent sometime between 2020 and 2030. What some scholar may not document until 2025 or 2040 is the broader perspective, far-sighted planning, and unexpected early twenty-first century success stories dug from ministry and corporate files and technical libraries in Delhi, Bangalore, Hyderabad, Singapore, Kuala Lumpur, Taipei, Tokyo, Hong Kong, Shanghai, and Beijing.

PART III

WEALTH AND DEMOCRACY

THE RHYTHM OF POLITICS AND CONFRONTATION

CHAPTER SEVEN

WEALTH AND POLITICS IN THE UNITED STATES

Banking establishments are more dangerous than standing armies.

—Thomas Jefferson

The Bank (of the United States) is trying to kill me and I will kill it.

—Andrew Jackson, 1830

Labor is prior to, and independent of, capital. Capital is only the fruit of labor, and could never have existed if labor had not first existed. Labor is the superior of capital, and deserves much the higher consideration.

—Abraham Lincoln, 1861

There are only two kinds of rich—the criminal rich and the foolish rich.

—Theodore Roosevelt

The moneychangers have fled from their high seats in the temple of our civilization. We may now restore that temple to the ancient truths.

—Franklin D. Roosevelt

Wealth and politics have a long history of intense interaction in the United States. From the 1780s on, foreign visitors remarked about Americans being money-fixated. John Stuart Mill, the English political economist, suggested in 1860 that in America, "the life of the whole of one sex is devoted to dollar-hunting, and the other to breeding dollar hunters." A generation earlier, Alexis de Tocqueville had observed that, "Whenever the reverence which belonged to what is old has vanished, birth, condition, and profession no longer distinguish men, or scarcely distinguish them, hardly anything but money remains. . . . Among aristocratic nations, money reaches only to a few points on the vast circle of man's desires; in democracies, it seems to lead all."

Lacking that hereditary aristocracy to control access to wealth and squelch discussion, the United States has hummed with both: the avid businessman's pursuit and the populist complaint. As we have seen, favors gained through politics—the making and bestowal by government of bank charters, railroad land grants, tariff protection, monopolies, the money supply, oil depletion allowances, bailouts, and tax advantages—played critical, sometimes brazen, roles in creating economic elites. Honoré de Balzac, the French writer, surely exaggerated in commenting that "Behind every great fortune, there is a crime," but relatively few American fortunes seem to have had immaculate conceptions in political or moral terms.

Public opinion for its part has distrusted economic elites and periodically used democratic politics to curb their abuses. Banks, special corporations, railroads, the giant trusts, the "money power," Wall Street, and the "malefactors of great wealth" have all spent decades in the firing zone of angry electorates. A politics in this tradition is unlikely to blink at confronting twenty-first century elites.

Part I of this book has followed the crests and troughs of American wealth, and Part II has pursued the origins and sources of that wealth, especially in government, technology, and under the umbrella of U.S. global economic leadership. Part III now turns to the politics—to the leaders and ideologies of past confrontation, to the governmental and philosophic corruptions of monied eras, to speculative excesses as the leading ushers of national reform, and to the forms of popular resentment visible in the politics of previous leading economic powers during their later years of deepening internal polarization.

A point to underscore: serious U.S. arousal against abuses of wealth and power has always transcended class lines—class warfare is both a rare bird and a dubious term—and many of the notable triumphs have been led by persons with sophisticated and affluent backgrounds: Jefferson of Monticello and the Roosevelts of Oyster Bay and Hyde Park. Indeed, George Washington of Mount Vernon led the earlier opposition to concentrated wealth and hauteur three thousand miles away in London that created the United States.

Also, Americans have given their highest regard to presidents who wove political battle flags from the various threads of popular indignation—a definition that adds the names of Jackson and Lincoln to the four just mentioned. The lesser esteem given to those presidents hailing bankers or proclaiming that "the business of America is business" completes the historical measurement. Politics, as we are about to see, often lends itself to moneymaking, but its higher levels of popular respect—generally missing in the late twentieth century—are reserved for those who have fought the forces of avarice.

1. WEALTH CREATION AND U.S. POLITICS

The fledgling United States of the late eighteenth century had economic elites, but as chapter 1 has explained, many of them were newly made men, pushed up in Boston, Philadelphia, and elsewhere by what were, quite literally, the fortunes of war: money from privateering, provisioning the military, or the profits of wartime finance. Loyalist landowning families like the Penns, Fairfaxes, and Wentworths lost their holdings, and even the rich landowners on the patriot side acquiesced, as we have seen, to ending the laws of entail and primogeniture that allowed property to be passed along intact from generation to generation.

Not only did the various states end the legal institutions of a hereditary aristocracy, most established political systems with a more democratic franchise than existed anywhere in Europe, and within another fifty years, universal (white) male suffrage was widespread. Absent that hereditary aristocracy, politics and government became vital pathways to enrichment, usually through some form of commerce—trading, selling, shipping, or banking.

Favoritism was inevitable, but broad popular voting rights ensured that the more undemocratic or controversial sort of governmental collusion with the wealthy—profit opportunities from elite banks, land deals, tax abatements, tariff provisions, special corporate charters, and the like—could become political issues and often did. No other nineteenth-century electorate was so attuned to such matters, although America's self-made rich managed to get away with sharp practices and the sort of folksy, popular corruption that entrenched aristocracies generally suppressed in Europe.

We will return shortly to the major wealth-related issues that played most often on the American political stage. But first, to underscore the interplay between fortunes and friends in high places, it is useful to recapitulate in a few paragraphs the realignments of top wealth that followed some of the watershed U.S. electoral changes and realignments of governing coalitions. That was part of what American democratic politics was often about.

The first wealth realignment attended the American Revolution itself. Many Tories fled, and war-related profits created a layer of new rich. Jefferson's accession in 1800 led to the second shift of top wealth, which over the next quarter century collected in the hands of political allies like Stephen Girard and John Jacob Astor. The Jacksonian "revolution" of 1828 basically continued the elite of the previous Jeffersonian era.

As we have seen, the Civil War not only expanded but massively realigned wealth-holding away from the slave-owning South to Northern financiers and industrialists. The political watershed of 1896, in turn, confirmed the fortunes of Northern industries and allowed them to expand further in the next decade through mergers, trust formations, and several stock market surges.

The Democratic watershed put in place by the mid-depression election of 1932 affected wealth in several ways: first, by reducing the share of the rich in favor of the rest of the population; second, by slowly creating a new group of top wealth-holders from consumer industries, aviation, and the Texas oil fields along with a small group of politically connected nouveau riche financiers, among them Joseph P. Kennedy.

The Republican presidential supremacy begun in 1968 by itself did not create a new group of wealthy in the Sun Belt. What it did was confirm bipartisan regional gains that also reflected the influence of Sun Belt Democratic presidencies like Lyndon Johnson's.

From these examples, it is clear that while both Republicans and Democrats have presided over significant realignments of wealth-holders, the two parties themselves have played substantially different historical roles. National Democratic watersheds took shape from the defeat of a conservative commercial or financial elite, often one that voters associated with hard times or speculative excesses. The eras begun by Jefferson in 1800, Jackson in 1828, and Franklin D. Roosevelt in 1932 all involved successful confrontations with bankers and "money-changers."

The handful of conservative Democratic presidents, by contrast, included those whose elections, instead of occurring during popularly minded Democratic cycles, came during Republican eras that were on the cusp of or already caught up in conservative capitalist heydays—Grover Cleveland during the Gilded Age, Jimmy Carter on the threshold of the 1980s, and Bill Clinton in the 1990s. Cleveland hobnobbed with Wall Street bankers and lawyers while Carter and Clinton both appointed or reappointed conservatives to chair the Federal Reserve Board and control the U.S. money supply. Clinton probably gloried in stock market gains as much or more than any Republican predecessor—and it's also fair to describe him as the first Democratic president to preside over a technology mania.

The casual observer, noting that each party has conservatives and liberals, may wrongly see little difference. In fact, party nuances and time frames have been important to the eras of the greatest wealth formation. Republican presidential periods launched each of the big three—the Gilded Age, the Roaring Twenties, and the eighteen-year Bull Market of the 1980s and 1990s. Capitalist conservatives, not liberals, have been the ones to put the flint, steel, and spark together with the speculative tinder.

Intriguingly, the Republican cycles that wound up producing market booms and crashes started off in 1860, 1896, and 1968 with a more centrist economics and politics that can reasonably be described as middle-class nationalism. These three transformations are worth understanding because of their centrality in the great booms. Investors would have made especially impressive profits by buying representative stocks near or not long past the midpoints of the three GOP presidential eras—in, say, 1878, 1921, or 1982.

CHART 7.1 **The Twelve Shared Characteristics of the "Capitalist Heyday" Periods—the Gilded Age, the Roaring Twenties, and the Great Bull Market of the 1980s and 1990s**

1. Conservative politics and ideology, with mostly Republican presidents but even Democratic presidents in these eras—Grover Cleveland, Bill Clinton—tend to be economically conservative.
2. Skepticism of government—from laissez-faire to program cuts and deregulation—and emphasis on markets and the private sector.
3. Exaltation of business, entrepreneurialism, and the achievements of free enterprise.
4. Replacement of public interest politics by private interest politics, with high levels of corruption.
5. Aspects of survival-of-the-fittest thinking—from social Darwinism to welfare reform and globalization.
6. Labor union weakness and/or membership decline.
7. Major economic and corporate restructuring—repeating merger waves and the rise of trusts, holding companies, leveraged buy-outs, spin-offs et al.
8. Obstruction, reduction or elimination of taxes, especially on corporations, personal incomes, or inheritance.
9. Pursuit of disinflation—supportive of creditors—in response to prior inflation (from the Civil War, World War I, and the Vietnam era).
10. A two-tier economy with stronger prosperity along the coasts and in the Great Lakes area, and greatest weakness in the commodity-producing interior.
11. Concentration of wealth, economic polarization, and rising levels of inequality.
12. Bull markets and rising, increasingly precarious levels of speculation, leverage, and debt.

Chart 7.1 profiles for each era the recurring convergence under the GOP of selected economic forces and circumstances—disinflation or deflation, unhappiness with government and preference for business, a souring toward labor, tax reductions (especially for the upper brackets), and tightfisted federal budgeting. Each confluence has meant a boom in financial assets, the emergence of a polarized, two-tiered economy, dangerous speculation, and the rise of wealth concentration. The world has no other political party with anything like the same record over a century and a half. As a wealth phenomenon, it is greatly understudied.

Skeptics will say that the Republican presidents before the booms were much the same as the ones who came later. This is simply not true. The early presidents in the three Republican cycles—Lincoln and Andrew Johnson from 1860 to 1868, William McKinley and Theodore Roosevelt from 1896 to 1908, and Richard Nixon from 1968 to 1974—were much more progressive if not populist in their economics, for which there is abundant documentation.

All three GOP watersheds occurred amid a level of national tensions out of which a civil war actually began, in Lincoln's case, or threatened to in the passions of Populism and Bryan in 1896 and the urban riots and Vietnam-fanned violence of the late 1960s. Each time, the Republicans successfully invoked middle-class values, patriotic nationalism, and opposition to forces they accused of being willing to divide the nation in the streets or on battlefields. With the previous party coalitions in flux, each time the last thing GOP strategists wanted was to have the image of bankers or cartoon plutocrats with spats and dollar signs on their waistcoats.

Abraham Lincoln, the Illinois Rail-Splitter, told his audiences that, "Labor is prior to, and independent of, capital. Capital is only the fruit of labor, and could never have existed if labor had not first existed. Labor is the superior of capital, and deserves much the higher consideration." His great strength in the 1860 election came in the Yankee countryside, towns and small cities among yeoman farmers, storekeepers, artisans, and small manufacturers; whereas the silk-stocking electorates and clubgoers of Boston, New York, and Philadelphia were much more suspicious. To finance the Civil War, Lincoln supported the first U.S. income and inheritance taxes. Contemptuous of wartime gold and currency speculators, in 1863 he had Congress pass a law—entirely ineffective—prohibiting trade in gold futures.

The rise of industrial capital during the war years seems to have worried Lincoln. In 1864 he cautioned a workingmen's association against the "effort to place capital on an equal footing with, if not above labor, in the structure of the government" and he warned working people "to beware of surrendering a political power which they already possess, and which if surrendered, will surely be used to close the door of advancement against such as they . . ."

Vice President Andrew Johnson, who moved to the White House in 1865, was an uncouth Tennessean with a strong populist streak. He warned in 1869, as he was about to leave office, that "an aristocracy based on near two billion and a half of national securities has arisen in the Northern states to assume that political control which the consolidation of great financial and political interests formerly gave to the slave oligarchy. The war of finance is the next war we have to fight." Four years later Mark Twain coined his famous term, the Gilded Age.

William McKinley, who beat Bryan in the epic, watershed clash of 1896, would probably have been defeated had not his own record met some concerns of farmers and laborers alike. For farmers, McKinley had earlier supported silver coinage and greenbacks and criticized Democratic president Grover Cleveland for putting gold ahead of men. He reiterated his commitment to bimetallism—minting silver money as well as gold— in his 1897 inaugural address and abandoned a monetary role for silver only when large (and inflationary) new gold discoveries made it unnecessary.

The Ohio Republican had first made his political name defending, successfully and without pay, thirty-three coal strikers; and as governor of the Buckeye State he enacted legislation to fine employers who prevented their employees from joining unions. Many years later, Samuel Gompers, president of the American Federation of Labor, wrote of McKinley: "He would frequently ask me to the White House to see him and sometimes I would ask for the privilege. At no time was I disappointed."

In 1900, with an open vice presidency, McKinley curbed the doubts of his close adviser Mark Hanna and threw the nomination to the GOP convention delegates, who picked outspoken New York governor Theodore Roosevelt. When the latter became president after McKinley's assassination, as we have seen, muted progressivism gave way to the trumpeting Bull Moose variety.

After Richard Nixon won the presidency in 1968 amid cultural wars that were tearing the Democratic Party apart, he, too, sought to avoid the stereotype of mahogany-paneled boardrooms to build a New Majority going beyond traditional Republicans. His own origins, Nixon made clear, were in "cloth-coat" Republicanism, not the mink-coat variety. He backed tax reform that gave a lower top rate to wage earnings than to unearned income, invited labor leaders to the White House, and pushed for a guaranteed income program for the poor (under the influence of his Democratic White House counselor Daniel P. Moynihan). In 1971 he imposed Rooseveltian wage and price controls, partly on the advice of his Democratic treasury secretary, John B. Connally.

It is remarkable, then—in no way a coincidence—that in three Republican presidential cycles, this beginning-stage middle-class nationalism, with its openness to labor and somewhat populist or progressive economics, could be replaced so conclusively by the language of Wall Street, Darwinism and tax-cut worship. The explanation is that partway into each cycle there came a crest of inflation—in the mid to late 1860s, in 1919–20, and in 1979–81—that either elected a new Republican administration or handed one already in office the perfect environment for a favorite alchemy. Inflation was crushed into disinflation, government spending was curbed in favor of exaltation of the marketplace and tax cuts, financial markets surged, and wealth was concentrated.

How these cycles also produced a speculative bubble, which then popped, is a discussion for chapter 9. Suffice it to say that the pursuit of wealth unleashed was stunning. This was true both in the size of fortunes made and in the peak (and unsustainable) price-earnings ratios reached by stock indexes in the Gilded Age, Roaring Twenties, and 2000. The importance of politics in wealth creation and alignment could hardly have a better display case.

Before turning to the dimension of popular hostility—the nineteenth and twentieth-century importance of banks, corporations, and railroads as U.S. political bogeymen—it is useful to discuss how the ancestry of similar indignations goes back to prominent anti-British tenets of the American Revolution. In some ways these tell us more than the debates over domestic political leadership and the issue of "who shall rule at home?," which conservatives generally won.

A surprising radical heritage emerges from the answers to *a second* question of 1776: "What elite shall no longer be permitted to rule our economy and polity from thousands of miles away?" The abuse heaped on distant Britons enlivened the Declaration of Independence and sensationalized its verbs: plunder, ravage, destroy, and desolate. The revolutionaries' willingness to perceive merchants, banks, debt, and credit as tools of alien tyranny, conspiracy, and even "enslavement" took root in the national psyche and bloomed again in the 1790s, 1830s, 1890s, and 1930s.

In economic matters the Declaration cited only the king's (actually Parliament's) taxation without representation, his appointment of a swarm of officeholders to "harass our people, and eat out their substance," and the Crown's arbitrary restraints on colonial trade. However, many opinion-molders had been more blunt in less elevated forums. Alexander McDougall, a prominent patriot in New York, attacked the Tea Act of 1773—the provocation of Boston's Tea Party—by calling the East India Company an "illegal monopoly" obtained by "bribery and corruption" and adding that its wealth "had poisoned the system at home [in Britain] into a system of corruption, which they are now endeavoring to extend to this country."

Virginians in turn complained that the Navigation Acts requiring their locally produced tobacco to be shipped to Britain cost them £500,000 a year and handed over to British middlemen the profits from selling Virginian tobacco elsewhere in Europe. Additional taxation, they fumed, would make them pay the empire a "double contribution."

In addition to tea monopolies and taxation, many colonial leaders had protested Parliament's Currency Act of 1764, which shrank liquidity and constrained agriculture and commerce by prohibiting new provincial issues of paper money. New England shipowners scoffed at the Navigation Acts which (unsuccessfully) prohibited them from trading with most of Europe and the French West Indies, although not even John Hancock thought to assert the right to smuggle. Iron makers, especially in Pennsylvania, chafed under limitations on production imposed by Parliament's Iron Act of 1750.

In retrospect, the most influential incitement lay in requiring proud Virginia and Maryland plantation owners to sell their tobacco only in manipulated British markets—shipments elsewhere were prohibited—for a going rate set by London, Bristol, and Glasgow merchants, whose tactics and inveiglings added insult to Navigation Act injury. For the Washingtons, Jeffersons, and Lees, rancor bloomed in the late 1760s and early 1770s, when British financial and stock panics tightened credit so that London merchants, in turn, squeezed the Chesapeake planters by refusing to accept Virginia paper money and withholding further credit. Thomas Jefferson later summed up that the merchants "gave good prices and credit to the planter till they got him more immersed in debt. . . . Then they reduced the prices given for his tobacco so that let his shipments be ever so great, and his demand of necessities be ever so oeconomical, they never permitted him to clear off his debt." By the 1770s, Chesapeake tobacco growers had run up about half of the debts owed to British creditors within the thirteen colonies. In the words of historian T. H. Breen, planters "spoke of tobacco, merchants and Parliament as if they had all somehow conspired to compromise the planters' autonomy."

In this paranoia-tinged hostility to a remote mercantile and financial elite, debt-burdened Virginia agrarians foreshadowed the late-nineteenth-century outrage of the debt-burdened Prairie. Take the language of the Granger and Populist attacks and substitute Glasgow tobacco factors and London merchants for Chicago railroads, Minneapolis grain traders, and New York bankers, and you have a strikingly similar rancor. George Washington, himself a major tobacco debtor, all but anticipated William Jennings Bryan's complaints about eastern banks in his protest that "our whole substance does in a manner already flow to Great Britain." So, too, for Jefferson's disgruntlement that "planters were a species of property annexed to certain mercantile houses in London." Nor did the growers shrink from radical remedies. Nine months before Bunker Hill, they had persuaded Virginia's counties to close their court systems to British debt proceedings, blocking merchant recoveries.

In short, opposition to British economic elites—be they government ministers, colonial bureaucrats, hated customs agents, Admiralty judges, London bankers, or Glasgow tobacco importers—bulked large in the Revolutionary mind-set, especially in its greatest strongholds, New England, inland Pennsylvania, and the Chesapeake region. For tobacco planters these fears persisted after war's end in 1783 because the peace treaty entitled British creditors to collect on the earlier debts they held. Efforts were made to keep these financial wolves from plantation doors— Virginia's courts remained closed to British suits—but ultimately, following the Jay Treaty of 1794, the planters did have to pay up, in some instances completing ruination.

The Southern landed gentry and yeomanry alike retained their bitterness toward financiers, "papermen," and stockjobbers. According to one historian, "The hard-pressed tobacco gentry took alarm when Hamilton threatened to promote commerce at the expense of agriculture," perceiving in his approach "the funded debt, national Bank, and chartered privileges that commercialized and corrupted Britain." George Washington shared enough of this doubt to be lukewarm about Hamilton's financial plans. Like Adams, Lincoln, and Theodore Roosevelt, Washington's conservative politics transcended fealty to business and commerce.

In sum, while the American Revolution was not about redistributing wealth within Virginia or Massachusetts—even though it wound up doing so—redistributing wealth from British merchants and middlemen back to the thirteen colonies was an early ambition. Wealth and politics in the United States have interacted from the start.

2. BANKING, RAILROADS, MONOPOLY, AND THE MONEY POWER: THE FINANCIAL AND CORPORATE WHIPPING POSTS OF U.S. POLITICS

Small wonder that the Jeffersonians and the Jacksonians, heirs to the mood and animosities of the Declaration, would be aroused enough to take a political whip to official banks and speculators in government debt. Much of this story has already been told in chapters 1 and 5. However, a few additional aspects warrant interweaving at this point.

Banks in one form or another—and this is not limited to the first and second Banks of the United States—were a principal bogeyman of early U.S. politics. Of the ten U.S. presidents to follow Washington, virtually all were occasional or fervent critics of banks, either out of sectional distrust, dislike of banks' mispractices and favoritism, or simply because of partisan politics.

Virginians like Jefferson and Madison were in the vanguard, but Federalist John Adams shared some of the distaste. In an 1811 letter, he wrote, "Our whole banking system I ever abhored, I continue to abhor, and I shall die abhoring." Jackson and Van Buren were prominent in their hostility. Even William Henry Harrison, the only elected Whig among the ten, president for just a month in 1841 before he died of pneumonia, had been obliged, in an 1825 Ohio state senate race, to say that he would like to see all banks destroyed, if that were possible, and their paper banknotes replaced by gold and silver. To placate antibank rioters Harrison had also favored using taxes to drive the local branch of the Second Bank of the United States out of the state. Vice President John Tyler, a Virginian who took office as the tenth president in 1841 on Harrison's death, vetoed three proposals for a new Bank of the United States and was read out of the Whig Party. James K. Polk, the eleventh president, was called "Young Hickory" for standing where "Old Hickory," Jackson, had also stood. No other distaste commanded at least the lip service of so many presidents for so long.

For the Jeffersonian and Jacksonian Southern yeomen and planters, hostility to the Bank of the United States had psychological roots in the eighteenth-century suspicion of Hamiltonian and London finance. However, for economically vulnerable small farmers, especially in the South and trans-Appalachian West, the burgeoning state banks of the nineteenth century—a handful in the 1790s grew to 250 in 1818 and 800 by 1840—also drew suspicion. Besides seeming to cater to the local power structure, some of these banks periodically refused to honor their own banknotes by redeeming them in gold or silver. Described as suspending payment in specie, this practice infuriated local depositors as it made their paper money worth much less than face value beyond the immediate area.

State constitutions adopted by Indiana, Illinois, Missouri, and Alabama between 1816 and 1820 specified the future chartering of only a single bank—and that was to be partly owned and controlled by the state. Kentucky's angry legislature replaced the Bank of Kentucky with a state paper money loan office (with a $200 limit), and Tennessee followed suit. To the east, Pennsylvania lawmakers resolved to shut down the forty-two town banks authorized in 1814 by requiring them to resume specie payments. Other eastern states reacted by forbidding nonspecie banks to pay dividends to investors. Pennsylvania had antibank riots to match Ohio's, and politicians who successfully represented the ordinary citizenry—governors like George Clinton of New York, Simon Snyder of Pennsylvania, Nathaniel Macon of North Carolina, and William Carroll of Tennessee—became invincible enough to hold office for a decade or more. From 1781 to the 1840s banks in their various uses and misuses can fairly be called the longest running objects of grassroots economics resentment.

We will come back to twentieth-century banking and finance, which under the pejorative label "the money power" became highly controversial again from Bryan's day to the New Deal. In the 1830s and 1840s other corporations—ones specially chartered to manufacture iron or build turnpikes, canals, and early railroads—angered Jacksonians and members of the several major-city workingmen's parties. However, no *national* set of economic bogeymen emerged to replace banks until after the Civil War.

Railroads became the first corporate Goliaths, capturing legislatures and buying judges as lightly as they bridged rivers and bypassed uncollaborative towns and counties. The "war" in 1869 between Cornelius Vanderbilt and Jay Gould for control of New York's Erie Railroad involved hired judges, bought legislatures, and tens of millions of dollars, extraordinary stakes for an era when even the largest manufacturing firm was capitalized at $1–$2 million. By the early 1870s the looting of the Union Pacific Railroad through the Credit Mobilier holding company was even more lucrative: the controlling group headed by Massachusetts congressman Oakes Ames was thought to have drained off $44 million. Profits from wheeling and dealing in New York rail lines made Vanderbilt's fortune the first to exceed $100 million by the mid-1870s. Until the heady 1860s opportunities opened by railroads—economic vistas ranged from subsidies to the unprecedented profits to be made from huge government land grants along with watered stock issues, extortionate freight rates, and stock market corners and pools—Astor's $20 million of 1848 had been the high-water mark.

Railroad mass and influence is hard to exaggerate. As late as 1880, as we have seen, seventeen railroads were capitalized at $15 million or more, with just one manufacturer (Carnegie Steel) at $5 million. In 1873, near the peak of the rate wars, Edward G. Ryan, chief justice of the Wisconsin Supreme Court, had America's iron horsemen in mind when he warned the graduating class of the state university that, "The accumulation of individual wealth seems to be greater than it ever has been since the downfall of the Roman Empire . . . vast corporate combinations of unexampled capital, boldly marching not for economic conquests only, but for political power." In his own Wisconsin, the Chicago, Milwaukee & St. Paul and the Chicago & Northwestern controlled state politics for almost three decades.

Despite their practices, rates and corruption becoming major state-level issues, the railroads ruled in a score of other states—the Southern Pacific in California, the Northern Pacific in North Dakota, the Burlington in Iowa, the Boston & Maine in New Hampshire, and many more. Corruption in the East was bipartisan, usually lacking any particular ideological edge, but even in large states with a broad industrial base the raw influence of the major companies was enormous. Charles Francis Adams, who would later become chairman of the Union Pacific, wrote in 1869 that railroad corporations "Bid fair soon to be the masters of their creator" and were "establishing despotisms" in state after state.

In 1888, President Charles W. Eliot of Harvard, in an essay on "The Working of the American Democracy," pointed out how vastly the railroads outstripped the states. In Massachusetts, he said, the major railroad (the Boston & Maine) employed 18,000 persons, had revenues of some $40 million a year, and paid its highest salaried officer $35,000. The Commonwealth of Massachusetts, by contrast, employed only 6,000 persons, had revenues of $7 million, and paid no salary higher than $6,500. And a huge railroad like the Pennsylvania would overshadow its own state regime even more decisively.

In the Farm Belt and West, where voters aroused over the fairness of grain elevators, weights, and freight rates could occasionally prevail at the polls, their battle with the railroads became bitterly ideological. Between 1867 and 1874 the Farmers Alliance and the Grange won victories in Illinois, Wisconsin, Iowa, and Minnesota for what became known as the Granger Laws—legislation to establish elected railroad commissions and regulate grain elevators, weighing practices, and railroad freight and passenger rates.

Railroad issues held a lesser and briefer sway at the national level. The Populist platform of 1892—shorthanded as "the railroad corporations will either own the people or the people must own the railroads"—left the two national parties unmoved. And in 1896, William Jennings Bryan was too preoccupied with silver and money to emphasize railroad reforms. Only between 1900 and 1910 did the debate heat on the Federal level as Bryan flirted with government ownership and Theodore Roosevelt promoted rate regulation (achieved in the Hepburn Act of 1906). TR held out the possibility of government licensing, but called government ownership no more than a last resort.

By the end of the 1880s, however, public concern over the railroads was already being leapfrogged, save in the farm states, by apprehension of an even more potent breed of large corporation—the early oil, lead, sugar, leather, whiskey, and beef combines with $15 and $20 million capitalizations increasingly described as trusts and monopolies. Whereas the reformism of the 1870s had been targeted on railroad rates or blatant graft and corruption (the Tweed Ring, the Whiskey Ring, Credit Mobilier), the new popular indignation accused the "giant" corporation of several trespasses: First that its size and stranglehold, like the royal monopolies of old, was achieved with the collusion or permission of government. Second, that corporate giantism necessarily submerged Americans' cherished early-nineteenth-century "labor theory of value," in which workers merited the fruits of their own industry. And third, that the first two factors—monopoly or near-monopoly plus the downgrading of labor—were combining to produce new fortunes of unprecedented size and power.

Former general James B. Weaver of Iowa, who later became the Populist presidential nominee of 1892, had warned in 1880 that the founders had abolished primogeniture and entail "so that the wealth of the country should diffuse itself among the people according to natural and beneficent laws. They did not contemplate the creation of these corporations. . . ." The more detailed and telling indictments came from writers and scholars. Henry Demarest Lloyd penned an influential series of articles about Standard Oil, the first large industrial trust, later published as a single volume with the ringing title *Wealth Against Commonwealth*. Richard T. Ely and other young economists launched the American Economic Association with a manifesto calling laissez-faire "unsafe in politics and unsound in morals." Thomas Shearman published an article, *The Owners of the United States,* contending that corporate-led concentration of wealth mocked America's revolutionary legacy. "By 1890," as the historian Henry Steele Commager would later recall, "the fight to control big business had become the leading problem of American politics."

Nevertheless, Bryan, in his famous 1896 "Cross of Gold" speech, ignored monopolies and trusts just as he looked beyond railroads. In fairness, the heyday of the trusts did not come until 1897 to 1904, and by 1900 both McKinley and Bryan, especially the latter, were criticizing the tidal wave of reorganization. Just those seven years saw 4,227 firms consolidated into 257. By 1904 a total of 318 trusts held 40 percent of U.S. manufacturing assets and boasted a capitalization of $7 billion, seven times bigger than the U.S. national debt.

Little could be done. The Sherman Antitrust Act of 1890 remained an ineffectual roadblock hamstrung by the courts. But following McKinley's assassination in 1901 the trusts soon found themselves facing an unanticipated problem in Washington: the quirky political opposition of the new president, who used language they had never before heard from the White House.

If Theodore Roosevelt's actions on the trusts rarely matched his words, serious legislative reform in any event had no chance of getting through the business-held U.S. Senate. Besides, the rhetoric launched from his White House "bully pulpit" and his 1912 independent Progressive presidential campaign underpinned much of the reform achieved in 1913–14, including enactment of the Clayton Antitrust Act and the establishment of the Federal Trade Commission. "I believe in corporations," Roosevelt once said. "They are indispensable instruments of our modern civilization; but I believe that they should be so supervised and so regulated that they shall act for the interest of the community as a whole."

The 1912 election results testified to Progressivism's progress. From Populist Weaver's 8 percent of the vote in 1892 and Bryan's 47 percent Democratic-Populist fusion support four years later, the combined totals for progressives Wilson and Roosevelt in 1912 jumped to 68 percent,

with Socialist Eugene Debs, running on a government ownership platform, carving out another 6 percent. This left William Howard Taft, the
incumbent conservative Republican, in third place with just 23 percent.
Business and finance had cause to be nervous.

Chapter 1 has told much of the story of the rise of the "money issue"
in the 1870s, 1880s, and 1890s. The objects of agrarian scorn were eastern finance, Wall Street, and the "money power," more or less in that
order. New York and Philadelphia bankers had been targets since the
1790s; Thomas Jefferson labeled financially-attuned Manhattan
"Hamiltonople" while Andrew Jackson loathed Chestnut Street, the
Philadelphia financial district where Nicholas Biddle and the Second
Bank of the United States had their white marble lair. The insurgents of
the 1870s, 1880s, and 1890s hurled their epithets against "eastern finance"—"the East has placed its hands on the throat of the West," said
Sen. William Allen of Nebraska—until "Wall Street" took over as the preferred opprobrium.

In 1890 the Populist firebrand Mary Ellen Lease, she who had urged
Kansans to "raise less corn and more hell," told her audiences that "Wall
Street owns the country. It is no longer a government of the people, by the
people and for the people, but a government of Wall Street, by Wall Street
and for Wall Street." Two years later Populist presidential nominee James
B. Weaver deplored how "Wall Street has become the Western extension
of Threadneedle and Lombard streets," the London location of the Bank of
England. Eastern finance had grown into what would become an enduring symbol.

For the farm states in particular, trying to separate the various strands
of late-nineteenth and early-twentieth-century discontent may be point-
less for reasons well-summarized by Professor Russel Nye in his classic
Midwestern Progressive Politics:

> The whole inter-related problem of credit, monopoly, currency and
> tariff fused into one major issue in the Midwest—the impoverished
> farmer versus the Eastern "money king." The railroad man, the mo-
> nopolist, the speculator, the banker, the mortgage holder, the manu-
> facturer, all merged into a single composite creature, the "plutocrat,"
> whom the farmer hated and feared. The "plutocrat" planted no corn or
> wheat, built no towns, and battened on the labor of those who did; he
> foreclosed mortgages, raised freight rates, charged high interest, stole
> public lands and bought legislatures.

The "money power" was an old term used by Jacksonians and then Populists. The more conspiracy-minded among them saw the moneymen as the root of all evil: the dragon whose slaying would remove most other problems. Kansas senator William Peffer, for example, promised that, "With the destruction of the money power, the death knell of gambling in grain and other commodities will be sounded."

Hitherto vague, the term took on new (and more specific) meaning during the Progressive era as shorthand for the interlocking groups of banks, investment firms, and insurance companies through which J. P. Morgan was said to control American finance. A congressional (Pujo Committee) investigation in 1912 laid out the supposed interlock. The Morgan interests at the helm of the system held 341 directorships in 112 corporations (insurance, trading, manufacturing, transportation, and utilities) with a capitalization totaling $22 billion. This single network of interests, foes charged, commanded more than twice the assessed value of all real and personal property in the thirteen southern states and indeed more than the assessed value in all twenty-two states west of the Mississippi.

Curbing the money power was one of Woodrow Wilson's ambitions, albeit naive, in pushing the Federal Reserve Act of 1913. In his "New Freedom" speech of 1912, Wilson worried: "We have been dreading all along the time when the combined power of high finance would be greater than the power of the government. Have we come to a time when the President of the United States or any man who wishes to be President must doff his cap in the presence of this high finance, and say 'You are our inevitable master, but we will see how we can make the best of it'?" However, the Federal Reserve did not turn out to be the counterbalance Wilson had sought.

Franklin D. Roosevelt, after the success of his 1933 speech excoriating "the unscrupulous money-changers" who "stand indicted in the courts of public opinion, rejected by the minds and hearts of men," took up related themes through the 1936 elections. New Deal Democrats had passed the Glass-Steagall Act to separate the ownership of banks and investment firms in order to decouple bank profits and lending patterns from the stock market. The Securities Exchange Act, in turn, prohibited stock market pools, insider trading, and market manipulations while creating a new Securities and Exchange Commission to police the markets. The Federal Reserve Act was amended to give the board power to curb margin loans and confine the purchase of U.S. government securities by the regional Federal Reserve banks to what was needed for their performance of open-market operations.

Roosevelt's sense that he was confronting another incarnation of the "money power" jumped out of the private letter he wrote in 1933 regretting that "a financial element in the larger centers has owned the government ever since the days of Andrew Jackson" and characterizing his own reform proposals as "a repetition of Jackson's fight with the Bank of the United States—only on a far bigger and broader basis." Like Wilson's rhetoric, FDR's struck a public chord. The greenback and silver issues, by contrast, had never persuaded a national audience. This time, in the wake of 1929 and its abuses, reform succeeded.

Since World War II awarded the United States clear world economic leadership, the combats of earlier periods have been subdued, with concern about the Federal Reserve Board never approaching earlier hostility to the Bank of the United States or the supposed money power. Large corporations, in turn, became minor issues—bogeymen only during Ralph Nader's emergence in the late sixties and early-to-mid seventies, and then again for several years in the nineties when the public fretted over soaring CEO salaries, brutal job lay-offs, soft-money corruption of politics, and the early vibrations of the globalization issue. Nevertheless, these themes helped outline a potentially serious agenda.

By this point it should be clear that class warfare and a politics of opposition to abusive economic elites are two very different things. Class warfare has been uncommon in U.S. national politics, although readily identifiable in labor and agrarian splinter parties, under Huey Long, and in socialist movements. Nationally the predominantly regional, ethnic, religious, and racial fabric of party loyalties typically blocks class-based alignments while the democratic core of American thinking ensures that important minorities of upper-income wealth-holders and professionals will support persuasive campaigns against an abusive elite.

We have already mentioned Washington, Jefferson, and the two Roosevelts in this connection. Abraham Lincoln, who in 1860 ran on a platform holding free labor above capitalism, was a prosperous railroad lawyer. Significantly, two of the men who sought or won the Reform Party presidential nomination between 1992 and 2000 were maverick billionaires—globalization critic Ross Perot and Manhattan real estate developer Donald Trump, who came out for a wealth tax. Two other prominent billionaires gained attention as prominent critics of U.S. corporate behavior and upper-bracket tax cuts (investor Warren Buffett) and the Darwinian side of American capitalism (financier George Soros).

Even campaigns that came closest to attacking "the rich"—Jefferson's in 1800, Jackson's in 1828 and 1832, Bryan's in 1896, those of TR and Wilson in 1912, and FDR's in 1936—saw a varying minority of

American wealth-holders back each man for regional, personal, party, or parochial economic reasons. Occasionally these nominees made sweeping attacks, but most of their criticisms were targeted to a particular facet, concentration, or abuse of wealth. This particularization, after all, has been the successful approach.

Jefferson's ire was usually at bondholders, "papermen," and speculators, whom he associated with the governmental favoritisms of the rival Federalist Party. In condemning "the aristocracy of our monied corporations," the gentleman from Monticello meant bankers. Many wealthy planters, however, were his allies. Jackson's enmities were not very different. He disliked the government-assistance-seeking Whig commercial elites just as Jefferson had opposed their mercantile Federalist predecessors. His attacks were less on the wealthy per se than on those who operated through government-chartered corporations, most notably the Second Bank of the United States, which he accused of favoring eastern and foreign investors at the expense of the South and West. He, too, had important allies in planter and state bank circles.

William Jennings Bryan, despite his image as a prairie Jacobin, mostly confined his attacks to narrower targets and implied abuses. He spoke about the "encroachments of organized wealth" and "idle holders of idle capital," although in 1896 he went farther by inviting attendees at the Democratic convention to join "the struggling people" against "the money-owning and money-changing class." He also originated the "trickle-down" economics charge by saying, "There are those who believe that, if you will only legislate to make the well-to-do prosperous, their prosperity will leak through on those below. The Democratic idea, however, has been that if you legislate to make the masses prosperous, their prosperity will find its way up through every class which rests above them."

Woodrow Wilson lashed the "money power," described the fight against business monopoly as "a second struggle for emancipation," and worried about the federal government being controlled by the special interests of the rich. "The masters of the government of the United States" he charged, "are the combined capitalists and manufacturers of the United States." But money, monopolies, and special interests, together with the equity of the federal income tax established in 1913, marked off the bounds of his rhetorical comfort.

Theodore and Franklin Roosevelt, from more privileged backgrounds, were more willing to spell out the duties of the rich and what might be imposed on them. TR, always disdainful of the vulgar nouveaux riches, by 1906 was worried enough about deepening U.S. class tensions to stop distinguishing between good and bad fortunes. All great fortunes were "needless and useless." His newly acquired mission, according to one historian, was to forestall "the least attractive and most sordid of all aristocracies," a plutocracy. In 1907 TR blamed that year's panic on "the malefactors of great wealth." He attacked "the reactionaries of the business world" who demanded "immunity from public control."

In 1912, still seeking the Republican presidential nomination before eventually turning to a third party, he argued that "wealth should be the servant of the people, not the master," and that "we hold it to be a prime duty of the people to free our government from the control of money." He expressed agreement with Lincoln that labor was superior to capital, and added that the best protection for capital was the perception of being handled "not only in the interest of the owner but of the whole community."

Franklin Roosevelt's preferred targets in 1932 and 1933 were abusive elites he described as "money changers"—the ones he had talked of being thrown from the temple—and "economic royalists" rather than the merely rich, which included his own family. In his 1936 message to Congress, the Squire of Hyde Park welcomed "the hatred of entrenched greed," later telling a cheering political audience that "I should like to have it said of my first Administration that in it the forces of selfishness and lust for power met their match. I should like to have it said of my second Administration that in it, these forces met their master."

But Huey Long's threat from the Left, which forced Roosevelt to propose the Wealth Tax Act of 1935, also required him to revisit some of the rhetoric of the Oyster Bay branch of the family. In sending the Wealth Tax Act to Congress, FDR declared: "The transmission from generation to generation of great fortunes by will, inheritance or gift is not consistent with the ideals and sentiments of the American people. Great accumulations of wealth cannot be justified on the basis of personal or family security. Such inherited economic power is as inconsistent with the ideals of this generation as inherited political power was inconsistent with the ideals of the generation which established our government."

And while FDR avoided class warfare, he was a master of class theatrics. In 1940, when a prominent Republican sniffed that Democratic supporters were "paupers, those who earn less than $1,200 a year and aren't worth that," Roosevelt replied: "Can the Republican leaders deny that this all too prevailing Republican sentiment is a direct, vicious, unpatriotic appeal to class hatred, to class contempt?" He also followed speakers who minced no words in setting a class-related scene. Here, in the vivid, sympathetic prose of a New Deal era historian, is a description of one such rally in Pittsburgh in 1936:

As the 1936 campaign got underway, the note of class conflict sometimes reached a high pitch. At an excited night meeting at Forbes Field in Pittsburgh, a stern-faced Danton, State Senator Warren Roberts, spat out the names of the Republican oligarchs: Mellon, Grundy, Pew, Rockefeller. The crowd greeted each name with a resounding "boo." "You could almost hear the swish of the guillotine blade," wrote one reporter afterwards. Then came Governor George Earle, their handsome Mirabeau, and he too churned up the crowd against the enemies of their class. "There are the Mellons, who have grown fabulously wealthy from the toil of men of iron and steel . . . Grundy, whose sweatshop operators have been the shame and disgrace of Pennsylvania for a generation; Pew, who strives to build a political and economic empire with himself as dictator; the duPonts, whose dollars were earned with the blood of American soldiers; Morgan, financier of war." As he sounded each name, the crowd interrupted him with a chorus of jeers against the business leaders. Then the gates opened at a far corner of the park; a motor-cycle convoy put-putted its way into the field, followed by an open car in which rode Franklin Delano Roosevelt, grinning and waving his hat, and the crowd, whipped to a frenzy, roared its welcome to their champion.

The reader should not take these profiles as merely the views of a handful of popular presidents. In fact, opposition to a series of regional and economic elites has been a hallmark of the once-a-generation watershed upheavals of U.S. electoral politics. These are uniquely American; no real parallels exist among the other major Western nations.

3. OUR HEROS HAVE (ALMOST) ALWAYS BEEN COMBATIVE

Each of the seven U.S. political watersheds—the American Revolution and the elections of 1800, 1828, 1860, 1896, 1932, and 1968—involved a major party campaign against a national elite. If we include Washington and the pro-Independence "party of 1776," six of the seven won. In four of the insurgencies, the elites and institutions rolled into an attack theme were economic; in the other three instances, including Nixon's victory in 1968, the elite under fire was principally cultural, sectional, or political, but with significant economic overtones. These recurrences are not collateral epiphenomena; they go to the essence of U.S. political behavior and still abide in the national psyche.

The American anger of 1776 at Britain's elite can be reread in the

Declaration of Independence, where it sizzles. The "second revolution" in the watershed election of 1800 had an obvious anti-elite component, given the political and social geography of Jefferson's victory and his attacks on the domestic taxes, financial institutions, and speculator classes of Hamiltonian Federalist economics. So too, for the Jacksonian revolution a generation later, with its common-man emphasis and southern, western, and urban working-class coalition as well as the prominence in Jackson's 1832 campaign of his attack on upper-class finance and the Second Bank of the United States.

Lincoln's Republican watershed of 1860 also fits because of how he represented free white labor, including much of the old northern Jacksonian stream, against the southern "slaveocracy," which was then among the preeminent U.S. elites and had commanded great power in Washington. That the Republican Party later changed the badges of its economic garb from free labor to capital does not detract from its operating dynamics of 1860.

Although Bryan's insurgency against the ruling northern financial and industrial elite was defeated in 1896, that hardly affected the nature of the clash—and if the Republicans had not had a twenty-to-one fundraising edge, the close result might have tipped the other way. In any event, Populism left its mark on the national scene, and the great president of the new GOP era, TR, trained his own verbal guns on much of the same culture of money and business that Bryan had attacked.

The watershed of 1932 came from the success of Franklin D. Roosevelt's mid-Depression landslide in uniting the old Populist and Progressive states of 1896 and 1912 against the redoubts of northeastern industrial Republicanism—the six states sticking with Hoover were four in New England plus industrial Pennsylvania and duPont-dominated Delaware. While campaigning, FDR's frequent targets were the bankers, financiers, and speculators who were much in the news that year during the congressional investigations of stock pools, market-rigging, and insider manipulations.

Students of the 1968 victory of Richard Nixon, which began a run of Republicans in the White House for twenty of the next twenty-four years, generally describe the campaign's elite-bashing as cultural and political. The antiestablishment "outsider" conservatism gaining influence in the Republican Party targeted both the party's "eastern establishment"—the axis of Rockefellers, Scrantons, and Lodges—and a larger "eastern liberal establishment" clustered around the prestige media, foundations, think tanks, and Ivy League universities. The insurgent Right enjoyed mocking the "radical chic" millionaires, lampooned by writer Tom Wolfe, who had held Park Avenue and Southampton parties for Black Panthers and California grape pickers.

Most of the country's millionaires still backed the Republicans, to be sure. Yet Nixon won his 1968 victory in the South, Farm Belt, and West, doing poorly in establishment bailiwicks like the East Side of Manhattan. By the 1970s and 1980s the affluent intelligentsia and the "knowledge industry" criticized by populist conservatives—more or less overlapping with the eastern liberal establishment—became more easily identifiable as being, in addition, an *economic* elite. With the Internet and high-tech boom of the nineties, the broadly defined communications elite would completely overshadow the old Republican railroad, mining, and basic manufacturing axis. But in the late sixties and early seventies, this transformation was hard to grasp, so that most commentators dwelt on the cultural and sectional aspects of Republican elite-bashing.

On the Democratic side of the party system, the accepted presidential heroes are the architects of the anti-elite watersheds: Jefferson, Jackson, and Franklin D. Roosevelt. Wilson, elected in the 1912 high tide of Progressivism, is near the head of the second tier. Some also put Harry Truman in that grouping, partly as FDR's heir and partly out of admiration for his come-from-behind triumph in the 1948 election. His acceptance speech to that year's Democratic convention marked off autumn's boxing ring with Missouri directness: the Republican Party "still helps the rich and sticks a knife in the back of the poor."

Revealingly, the highest-ranked presidents of conservative antecedents (Federalist, Whig, or Republican) are the three—Washington, Lincoln, and TR—who made their own names fighting elites (British, slave plantation, and corporate). Two in the second tier, Adams and Eisenhower, also warned against elites they distrusted. John Adams's disdain for Hamilton's financial circle was well known, and his distrust of banks has already been noted. Eisenhower cautioned, as he retired in 1961, that in "the councils of government, we must guard against unwarranted influence, whether sought or unsought, by the military-industrial complex." Even Ronald Reagan, committed to entrepreneurial wealth, boasted of being a former union leader, privately criticized big business, and discussed the idea of abolishing the Federal Reserve Board.

The two most regarded figures in nineteenth- and twentieth-century British Conservative politics—Benjamin Disraeli and Winston Churchill—reinforce the point. Both were mavericks. Churchill's worry about child labor and luxury in Edwardian Britain appears as an epigraph at the beginning of chapter 4, and Disraeli—proponent of a Tory democracy that included social reforms—was given to tossing off comments like, "as a general rule, nobody has wealth who ought to have it."

As part of the exaggeration that history had ended in capitalist triumph, the 1990s produced not just belief in a New Economy and an end to business cycles, but a kindred naivete that a politics of opposition to elites was also passé. The contrary evidence of middle-class radical spasms in U.S. politics from 1966 to 1980, and then again from 1990 to 1996, will be discussed in chapter 10. However, a larger context, framed in chapter 4, must also be brought into the political equation.

This is the U.S. millennial drift toward a *reassertion* of history: the contradiction of American exceptionalism by growing analogies to the later-stage weaknesses of the previous leading world economic powers. Golden ages, almost by definition, do not lend themselves to successful national insurrections against ruling elites. Even the later decades, with disquieting crosscurrents but nothing more, have not stirred insurgencies.

Belief in exceptionalism dies hard, but when it happens, the evidence is that politics sours. The disgruntled electorate's 1992 search for a charismatic outsider—a potential watershed political leader—was probably a beginning, considering that Democrat Bill Clinton and Reform candidate Ross Perot together took 62 percent of the total vote. By the 2000 election, however, despite the partial unfolding of the Nasdaq crash, the optimism about the economic future renewed in the late nineties remained high. The bogeymen discussed in this chapter were never prominent.

To be sure, roughly one-third of the electorate at some point, either in the primaries or in November, supported the three candidates, McCain, Bradley, and Nader, who spelled out the election year's subtext of indignation and reform. But those arguments themselves were a limited agenda, with McCain and Bradley invoking the analogy of Theodore Roosevelt and his fight against corruption and corporate power—a combat that took place in a very different era, when the United States was on the cusp of world economic leadership, not showing early signs of old age.

However, before we turn to the forms in which the politics of frustration broke out in previous leading world economic powers, it is necessary to sketch two other circumstances: the philosophic as well as governmental corruption that accompanies economic booms and heydays in the United States, to which we now turn, and the hopeful human and political rhythm of speculation and reform, a further chapter ahead.

CHAPTER EIGHT

WEALTH, MONEY-CULTURE ETHICS, AND CORRUPTION

A combination of laissez-faire and political corruption is a common feature of later [speculative] manias.

—Edward Chancellor,
Devil Take the Hindmost: A History of Financial Speculation, 1999

Commercial and financial crises are intimately bound up with transactions that overstep the confines of laws and morality. . . . The propensities to swindle and be swindled run parallel to the propensity to swindle during a boom. . . . And the signal for panic is often the revelation of some swindle, theft, embezzlement or fraud.

—Charles Kindleberger,
Manias, Panics, and Crashes, 1978

The most successful politicians are no longer the best executives or the best legislators, but rather the best fundraisers.

—Elizabeth Drew,
The Corruption of American Politics, 1999

A society which reverences the attainment of riches as the supreme felicity will naturally be disposed to regard the poor as damned in the next world, if only to justify making their life a hell in this.

—R. D. Tawney, British historian

Corruption, like larceny, comes in many forms, some blatant, others more subtle. Booms, speculative heydays, and other periods of money worship bring the highest ratios of both corruptions, the hard and the soft.

It stands to reason that bribery, embezzlement, fraud, swindling, and other "hard"—criminal—forms of avarice rise with the heat of soaring stock indexes, market worship, and the glorification of consumption and gain. The 1980s and 1990s saw political and governmental corruption in the United States recapture the laxity of the Gilded Age and Roaring Twenties. In the late twentieth century, however, venality was also endemic among the other Group of Seven industrial nations—Japan, Germany, Italy, France, Canada, and Britain—a moral convergence to match the contagion of market-driven philosophy.

In the epigraph at the beginning of this chapter, Charles Kindleberger capsuled the practical and philosophic interrelationships of financial booms and unlawful behavior. A megaboom was bound to breed even more. Many, many books and articles have explored the transgressions, and the *Wall Street Journal,* in an ethical retrospective on the nineties, acknowledged that "historians are intrigued by the parallels they see between this era's frauds and those from past periods of financial frenzy." From Kindleberger's research, crashes and panics have often "been precipitated by the revelation of some misfeasance, malfeasance or malversation [the corruption of officials] engendered during the mania. It seems clear from the historical record that swindles are a response to the greedy appetite for wealth stimulated by the boom."

Less obtrusive but at least as important has been the corollary corruption of thinking and writing—the distortions of ideas and value systems to favor wealth and the biases of "economic man."* In this sense, too, the eighties and nineties echoed the Gilded Age and the 1920s.

Unusual corruption amid periods of boom and speculation goes back to ancient times. However, chroniclers of the interplay between speculative finance and corruption in Britain and the United States usually pick up their tale with the "financial revolution" between 1690 and the 1720 implosion of the South Sea bubble. Rules and stock markets were emerging together. Bribes of call options given to members of Parliament to facilitate an East India Company charter in the 1690s led to the expulsion of the speaker of the House of Commons, the impeachment of the lord president of the Council, and the imprisonment of the governor of the East India Company. When the famous South Sea Company stock bubble burst in 1720, crowds outside Westminster howled for retribution against

---

* One person's corruption of policy is another's true wisdom, of course. Liberalism went beyond public acceptance in the 1960s and 1970s by calling welfare recipients "clients," anointing bureaucracies, and appearing to condone violence. On the other side, conservatism's historic excess has been to go too far toward the interests of the rich and the worship of markets.

the stock-owning officeholders—some one hundred lords and three hundred members of the House of Commons had shares—who had cooperated in the laxity that had left the populace "bubbled." Parliament expelled the four MPs who were South Sea directors, and the chancellor of the exchequer was sent to the Tower.

Transgressions were just as grand in the Gilded Age. The Credit Mobilier scandal turned up proof that both the previous and present vice presidents had been given railroad stock to enlist their sympathies. During the Harlem Railroad battles of 1864, members of the New York legislature openly speculated against Vanderbilt's Harlem position, lost, and had to meet their obligations. The old Commodore chortled that, "We busted the whole Legislature, and scores of the honorable members had to go home without paying their bills."

By 1892 the men and women writing the preamble to the Populist platform were seething in recollection: "We have witnessed for more than a quarter of a century the struggles of the two great political parties for power and plunder . . . to secure corruption funds from millionaires."

Of course, the bounds of honesty are always being updated. In 1720 a man could hire a clerk but could not count on his loyalty; the lines between business and theft were imprecise. In the United States the borrowing of bank funds by officials was not definitively ruled illegal until 1799. Insider trading was outlawed in the U.S. in the 1930s, but not until 1980 by Britain and the late 1980s by Japan. In the meantime, new practices, relationships, and gray areas have emerged.

By World War I the face of "corruption" in the United States had been changed by reforms like popular election of U.S. senators, direct primaries, initiatives and referenda, and in some states even voter recall of judges. What muckraker David Graham Phillips had called "The shame of the Senate" was washed away. But criminal activity resurged in war contracts and the loose climate of the twenties; witness the Teapot Dome scandal, the corruption that came with Prohibition and bootleg liquor, and the post-1929 convictions of dozens of financiers. Still, the many New Deal securities and banking reforms enacted between 1933 and 1935 point out just how many abuses had been legal and common practice up to and even through the Crash.

One legacy of the New Deal was to infuse American politics and policymaking with egalitarian and anticorporate biases, which many business leaders and conservatives found offensive. But beginning in the 1970s, as politics turned conservative again, a group of conservative multimillion-

aires and foundations underwrote an ever-growing network of policy journals, university chairs, and think tanks. Originally funded in a small way
to counter the prevailing liberal bias, by the 1980s they had become influential in constraining government and scripting new directions for tax
legislation, monetary policy, business regulation, and even judicial
decision-making.

The result by 2000 was a Washington in which liberals found themselves muttering about "corruption" that was largely legal behavior—
decision-making lubricated by so-called "soft money" political
contributions, and resulting in flagrant tax favoritisms, bank bailouts,
gutted regulations, and see-no-evil administration of the federal election
laws. Little of it was morally defended. In 1996, when the federal government, after little debate, gifted some $70 billion worth of public
spectrum-band to the telecommunications industry, even several conservative U.S. senators decried its resemblance to the freewheeling gifts of
public lands to the railroads a century earlier.

Indeed, through both "hard" corruption—the straightforward, in-
dictable kind—and the "soft" variety, in which bribes wore veils and laws
and regulations were bent to dubious purposes, the domination of politics
by wealth and corporations circa 2000 bore some resemblance to the captivity of the Senate by business a century earlier. Running for president on
the Green Party ticket, Ralph Nader, in the last few days of the campaign,
echoed the latter attacks of the Greenbackers and Populists. "The two parties," he declared, "have morphed together into one corporate party with
two heads wearing different make-up."

Richard N. Goodwin, former speechwriter for John F. Kennedy, had
several years earlier offered a Wilsonian reprise: "The principal power in
Washington is no longer the government or the people it represents. It is
the Money Power. Under the deceptive cloak of campaign contributions,
access and influence, votes and amendments are bought and sold. Money
establishes priorities of action, holds down federal revenues, revises federal
legislation, shifts income from the middle class to the very rich. Money
restrains the enforcement of laws written to protect the country from
abuses of wealth—laws that mandate environmental protection, antitrust
laws, laws to protect the consumer against fraud, laws that safeguard the
securities markets, and many more." But so long as the economy and stock
market remained strong, much of the electorate did not seem to care.

In keeping with our emphasis on both aspects of venality, governmental and philosophic, this chapter's first subsection, on political corruption

and speculative heydays, will lead into a look at how philosophy and public policymaking during such periods has shifted to emphasize markets and Darwinian behavior and to find civic virtue in erstwhile private sins like greed, self-interest, and profligacy. The 1980s and 1990s provide another vivid example. Moreover, the two decades saw an unusual phenomenon: indexes of social well-being declining even as economic growth indexes climbed. But first, the basic context is essential.

1. POLITICAL CORRUPTION AND CAPITALIST HEYDAYS

Lord Acton's famous saying about power corrupting and absolute power corrupting absolutely can be applied with some dilution to the peaks of finance and speculation. No evidence suggests that the United States has been worse than other nations; the causation involved is human nature.

The nineteenth-century railroad manias, as we have seen, intertwined with speculating politicians on both sides of the Atlantic. In 1865, 165 British members of Parliament were serving as railroad directors, and the number remained over one hundred through the 1880s. And during the 1980s and 1990s, venality in the United States was easily exceeded by that in Italy, where literally thousands of businessmen and politicians were accused, and in Japan, where the corruption of banks, corporations, the national legislature (Diet), and the ruling Liberal Democratic Party was intertwined.

During the 1980s the historian Arthur Schlesinger Jr., speaking of the United States, suggested that idealistic progressive administrations have displayed less graft and stealing than regimes dominated by private interest: "Under FDR's New Deal, the national government spent more money than ever before in peacetime and regulated the economy as never before; but there was a notable absence of corruption. Lyndon Johnson had been a notorious wheeler-dealer, but there was much less graft in his Great Society than in the conservative administrations of the 1920s, 1950s and 1980s." When he wrote this, however, the Republicans had held the White House reins during all but a few years of the major twentieth-century booms. Only in the 1990s did Bill Clinton illustrate the ethical similarity of a Democratic administration holding office during a money-culture boom.

The abuses of the Gilded Age, too, were at least as much driven by money culture as by party. In *Devil Take the Hindmost: A History of Financial Speculation,* author Edward Chancellor observed that, "Periods of speculation had always fostered dishonesty, but in the nineteenth-century American stock market, this tendency was even more pronounced. The corruption of speculation was not limited to company promoters and stock operators: it affected the entire political class in the 1860s (even three decades later, the 'reforming' President Grover Cleveland was implicated in a stock market pool arranged by James Keene)." In 1873 the speculator Jay Gould explained his own politics as the head of the Erie Railroad: "In a Republican district, I was a Republican; in a Democratic district I was a Democrat; in a doubtful district I was doubtful; but I was always for Erie." Many of his business and railroading colleagues could have said the same.

What made the corruption of the 1980s and 1990s rank with the Gilded Age was not the individual scandals of the Reagan, Bush, or Clinton years—there was little to match the Customs Ring, the Whiskey Ring, or the shameless Senate. The new crux was the vast, relentless takeover of U.S. politics and policymaking by large donors to federal campaigns and propaganda organs. The S&L scandals showed the corruption in both parties, and junk-bond king Michael Milken claimed in a boast to the *Washington Post* that "the force in this country for buying high-yield securities has overpowered all federal regulation." Indeed, the eighties saw the financial sector take the lead in Washington lobbying outlays and in dollars provided to federal election campaigns. Both cemented a fast-returning relationship: politics was finance, and finance was politics, just as the men with diamond stickpins had said a century earlier.

Statistics help to tell the tale. From relative peanuts in the early eighties, the money contributed to federal politics by the finance, insurance and real estate (FIRE) sector rose almost as fast as the money channeled to finance by federal bail-outs and permissive regulation. According to the Center for Responsive Politics, the totals contributed rose from $109 million in the 1992 cycle to $162 million in the 1996 cycle and a walloping $297 million in the 2000 cycle, by which point the FIRE sector was collectively the largest giver. Of the total, the sector was particularly prominent in contributions from individuals—$148 million that cycle—and in soft money ($108 million), the quietest agent of influence. The congressional tax-writing committees were a particular target, and during the 2000 cycle (which for senators stretched from 1995–2000), the House and Senate committee members received $45.7 million from individuals in all sectors, not just FIRE.

The FIRE sector is also regularly the biggest spender on lobbying of all business sectors. It laid out more than $200 million—again based on Center calculations—in 1998, the year when industry executives and lobbyists led by Citigroup co-CEO Sanford Weill succeeded in convincing Congress to effectively revoke the New Deal era Glass-Steagall Act which among other things separated banks and insurance companies.

While a full portrait of the late-twentieth-century money-culture excesses and their carryover may await 2015 or 2020, one can see a basic resemblance to the four-decade period between 1870 and 1913. In its first stage, corruption took ten to fifteen years to become clear. Then, over the next fifteen, money became all-powerful while reform dawdled. The fourth decade, in each case coinciding with the iconoclasm of a new century, saw popular resentment of money politics and demand for remedies begin to gain the upper hand.

We have seen how the late eighties and nineties were the period of money's late twentieth-century rise to dominate U.S. politics, paralleling the simultaneous ascent of market philosophy and the boom in the financial markets. Besides the likeness to the Gilded Age, there was also a resemblance to the 1920s. Conservative theorists have ignored these overlaps, rarely criticizing money in politics because of their predilection for the example of markets—by definition places where things are bought—and their hope to recast politics in a market mode. The third-party candidacy of Ross Perot in 1992, which attacked corruption and two-party domination in American politics, provided a brief revitalization as money lost centrality and voter turnout jumped to 55 percent from 50 percent in 1988. However, money was back in 1994, fueling the Republican capture of Congress, and then again in 1996 when both major parties' fundraising set records, which were then shattered in the nineties. Chart 8.1 shows the enormous sums coming into what some donors did indeed hope was becoming a marketplace.

To convey some idea of the growth of campaign finance since, say, the late seventies—and with it the pressure on legislators to be able to enlist donors—Common Cause presented the relevant statistics to a 1994 Congressional hearing. In 1976, winning Senate incumbents laid out an average of $610,000 on their races. By 1986, the figure had grown to $3 million. By 2000, the average figure for all Senate incumbents was $4.4 million, while the average winner in all races raised $7.3 million.

As the fundraising chase mounted, critics of the political process focused more and more on the determinative role of money in election outcomes. Reports by the Center for Responsive Politics and Citizen Action contended that in the 1996 congressional races, the candidates who raised the most money won 92 percent of the time in the House and 88 percent of the time in the Senate. In the sixty House districts identified before the election as toss-ups, Republicans had an average of 42 percent more money to spend. By 1999, pundits began describing the initial fundraising of presidential candidates a decisive "wealth primary," pointing out

CHART 8.1 **The Buying of American Politics**

A. Sources of the Money Raised for the Federal Election Cycles of 1996 and 2000 (Including Soft Money)

	1996	2000
Donors giving under $200	$734 million	$550 million
Large individual donors	$597 million	$912 million
Soft money	$262 million	$498 million
PACs	$243 million	$267 million
Public funding	$211 million	$238 million
Others	$200 million	$ 57 million
Candidates' own money	$161 million	$205 million
Total	$2.4 billion	$2.73 billion

Source: Center for Responsive Politics.

B. The Escalating Funding of Congressional and Presidential Elections, 1992–2000

	MONEY RAISED FOR CONGRESSIONAL ELECTIONS	MONEY RAISED FOR PRESIDENTIAL ELECTIONS
1992	$659 million	$331 million
1996	$791 million	$426 million
2000	$1.05 billion	$529 million

Source: Federal Election Commission.

C. The Mounting Sums Needed for Senate and House Campaigns

	1992	1994	1996	1998	2000
Average Senate Winner Spent	$3.93 million	$4.57 million	$4.69 million	$5.23 million	$7.72 million
Average House Winner Spent	$543,599	$516,126	$673,739	$650,428	$840,300

Source: Center For Responsive Politics.

the close correlation between the frontrunners' share of their party's early cash—60 percent for Republican George Bush and 64 percent for Democrat Albert Gore—and their support in the polls. Over the first six months of 1999 the $103 million taken in by all presidential candidates was three times the amount for the comparable period four years earlier.

Television helped create the nexus, being a medium of marketing and entertainment—and an expensive one. As television advertising took over elections, so did communications markets and audience sampling. In 1999 and 2000, the Republican and Democratic parties followed the market message to its logical conclusion: raising ever-larger contributions in soft dollars—ostensibly limited to use for party-building activities—from donors that were overwhelmingly corporate.

The reaction by the Republican and Democratic contenders taking the reform side was angry. Former New Jersey senator Bill Bradley, the Democrat, insisted that "democracy doesn't have to be a commodity that is bought and sold." On the day front-runner George W. Bush announced having raised $37 million, enough so that he could forgo federal matching funds and avoid spending limitations, the reform-minded Republican, Senator John McCain, denounced the campaign finance system as "an elaborate influence-peddling scheme by which both parties conspire to stay in office by selling the country to the highest bidder."

McCain also denounced the House Republicans' big tax bill glutted with provisions favorable to banking and securities firms, oil and gas operators, and insurance and utility companies, thought by some to be the quid pro quo for the many millions in party donations. Charging that it broke the GOP promise to deal with "corporate welfare," the Arizona senator said, "Now we're going to see this big thick tax code on our desks, and the fine print will reveal another cornucopia for the special interests and a chamber of horrors for the taxpayers."

The Democrats, for their part, had pioneered in 1996 on another dimension, raising funds abroad, of which many came from international favor-seekers—apparently including intelligence services of nations like China. President Clinton was embarrassed, and some commentators believed that the preelection White House fundraising scandal in 1996 helped influence voters to keep the Republicans in control of Congress.

As with Mark Twain's writings during the Gilded Age, satire could be devastating. During the 2000 campaign, a group called billionairesfor-bushorgore.com, joining in the market analogy, posted the following on their website:

While you may be familiar with stocks and bonds, currency speculation, IPOs and all the rest, there's a new investment arena you
should be aware of: *legislation.* If a mutual fund returns 20% a year,
that's considered quite good, but in the low-risk, high-return world of
legislation, a 20% return is positively lousy. There's no reason why
your investment dollar can't return 100,000% or more.

Too good to be true? Don't worry, it's completely legal. With the
help of a professional legislation broker (called a Lobbyist), you place
your investment (called a Campaign Contribution) with a carefully selected list of legislation manufacturers (called Members of Congress).
These manufacturers then go to work, crafting industry-specific subsidies, inserting tax breaks into the code, extending patents or giving
away public property for free.

Just check out these results. The Timber Industry spent $8 million
in campaign contributions to preserve the logging road subsidy, worth
$458 million—the return on their investment was 5,725%. Glaxo
Wellcome invested $1.2 million in campaign contributions to get a
19-month patent extension on Zantac worth $1 billion—their net re-
turn: 83,333%. The Tobacco Industry spent $30 million in contribu-
tions for a tax break worth $50 billion—the return on their
investment: 167,000%. For a paltry $5 million in campaign contri-
butions, the Broadcasting Industry was able to secure free digital TV
licenses, a give-away of public property worth $70 billion—that's an
incredible 1,400,000% return on their investment.

Whether or not Twain would have agreed with depicting corruption
itself as a market is impossible to say, but interested readers are referred
to his story of the fictional Tunkhannock, Rattlesnake & Youngstown
Railroad.

Chart 8.2 takes a further look at how the influence of money has directly or indirect corrupted federal and state governance on levels the average person does not appreciate—the fairness and integrity of state courts
and judges and arguably the audit practices of the Internal Revenue Service
(pressured by Congress to focus more audits on the Earned Income Tax
Credit program). Some three-quarters of the individual money that fueled
turn-of-the-century presidential and congressional races came from donors
with incomes over $200,000 a year (in essence, the top 1–1.5%). A cynic
might find some connection with how Washington has abetted the wildly
disproportionate growth of top 1 percent incomes and wealth.

CHART 8.2 **The Money Culture and "Soft Corruption"**

1. State Courts: The Rule of Law—or Money?

* Average amount raised by winning candidates for a seat on the Michigan Supreme Court in 1994: $287,000.

* Average amount raised by winning candidates for seats on the Michigan Supreme Court six years later in 2000: $1.3 million.

* Michigan Manufacturers Association's explanation of what "swayed the Supreme Court election to a conservative viewpoint, insuring a pro-manufacturing agenda": the association's campaign contributions.

* Percent of cases heard by the Wisconsin Supreme Court involving a campaign contributor to a Wisconsin Supreme Court candidate: 75%.

* How often the Ohio Supreme Court ruled favorably for clients of twenty Cleveland-area attorneys who gave the most cash to justices' political campaigns between 1993 and 1998: two-thirds of the time.

* Proportion of Texas attorneys who believe campaign contributions influence judicial decisions "very significantly" or "fairly significantly": 79%.

* Proportion of campaign money the ten Texas Supreme Court justices who faced an election between 1994 and 1998 raised from lawyers, law firms, and litigants who filed appeals with the high court during the same period: 52%.

Source: Public Campaign, Washington, D.C. *Corruption Perception Index* #20, August 3, 2001, including detailed citations.

2. The Shift of Federal Tax Audits from the Wealthy to the Poor, 1988–99

TAXPAYER GROUP	% AUDITED IN 1988	% AUDITED IN 1999
Incomes Over $100,000	11.4%	1.15%
Incomes Under $25,000	1.03%	1.36%

Source: The Center for Public Integrity, Washington, D.C. As the share of U.S. income going to over $100,000 a year households has soared, their share of audits has plummeted. The origins of this and related audit data are detailed in the Center's book *The Cheating of America* (New York: 2001), pp. 13–15.

3. The Dominant Funding of Congressional and Presidential Politics by Top 1% Households

$1,000 and Over Donors in the 1999–2000 Election Cycle		
CATEGORY	NUMBER	AMOUNT GIVEN
$1,000–$9,999	325,747	$619,040,837
$10,000 plus	14,888	$444,617,244
$100,000 plus	719	$151,642,813
$1 million plus	6	$7,770,700
Total	340,345	$1,063,658,141

Source: Center for Responsive Politics, *Capital Eye,* Summer 2001.

Annual Family Income of Congressional Election Donors, 1997	
$500,000 or more	20%
$250,000–$499,999	26
$100,000–$249,999	35
$50,000–$99,999	14
$49,999 or less	5

Source: Random sampling of donors by the University of Akron funded by the Joyce Foundation in 1997.

4. Public Concern About Unethical or Illegal Behavior by Officeholders Obligated to Campaign Contributors

* Percentage of the public that thinks politicians often do special favors for people and groups who give them campaign contributions: 80% *(ABC News,* March 2001)
* Percentage who think this is not a problem: 11%
* Percentage who think those special favors tend to be unethical: 74%
* Percentage who think these special favors tend to be illegal: 46%
* Percentage of candidates for statewide office who report spending at least one out of every four of their waking hours raising money for their campaigns: 55% *(Campaigns and Elections* survey, April 2001)
* Percentage who report spending more than half their time raising money: 23%
* Percentage of the public that thinks unlimited contributions to political parties (soft money) should be banned: 66% (Reuters/Zogby Poll, March 2001)

Source: Public Campaign, Washington, D.C.

In chapter 7 we looked at the ten shared characteristics of the speculative heyday of the Gilded Age, Roaring Twenties, and the eighties and nineties. Corruption, alas, recurred reliably enough to be the eleventh shared characteristic. But now it is time to focus on the philosophies that supported these display cases of greed, ruthlessness, and indulgence—and, in the end, helped trigger popular upheaval and reform.

2. PRIVATE VICES, PUBLIC VIRTUES

The second imprint left by the money culture during eras of unleashed capital and speculation has been cultural and intellectual: the marshaling of thinkers, writers, publications, and academies on behalf of wealth, markets, and corporations. Certain themes keep coming back like homing pigeons.

Human nature itself goes through stages of self-interpretation. Conservative eras rediscover the greed and marketplace, polish the image of freebooters like Jay Gould and after awhile think nothing of drowning politics in money. Liberals rediscover social justice, polish the image of Robin Hood and after awhile, think nothing of drowning policymaking in sociology. But for the millennial context, the open Pandora's Box is "conservative." There is also a relevant literature going back some six centuries that explains how yesteryear's private sins and vices—individual compulsions to self-interest, avarice, luxury, and pride—can and do reemerge from time to time as commercial and civic virtue, indeed props of unusual national success.

Bustling economies from Venice and Antwerp to Manhattan have proved the point. However, if these confluences of sin and success have done stock exchanges and museum wings proud, political histories and corruption records bear a different witness. Far from sharing the gains, ethics and democracy have generally been eroded by the same wash of money that could hang a Bellini portrait in Venice or a John Sargent or Winslow Homer painting or a Saint-Gaudens panel in Gilded Age Boston or New York.

The Renaissance was the first display—a tableau of vice triumphant, building success around the interplay of what medieval thinkers had regarded as the principal human vices. Greed for distant luxuries did help to build oceanic commerce. Pride and vanity stimulated demand for the most expensive architectural design and artistry, fabrics, and even pigment sources (ground-up semiprecious lapis lazuli for ultramarine blue).

Conspicuous consumption became a pillar of statecraft when the ruling doges of late-fifteenth-century Venice poured money into municipal ostentation to hide signs of maritime weakness. Licentiousness stimulated art demand (as with the competition for nude paintings by Titian among the duke of Urbino, Cardinal Farnese, and others). One modern scholar concludes without reservation that, "The world we inhabit today, with its ruthless competitiveness, fierce consumerism, restless desire for ever wider horizons, discovery and innovation . . . is a world which was made in the Renaissance."

Bernard Mandeville, who grew up in the Holland of the Golden Age, argued in *The Fable of the Bees* (1714) that far from owing national success to religion, austerity, and thrift, even the Calvinist United Provinces represented self-seeking and were a nation built on transforming private vices into public virtues. A seventeenth-century Dutch poet had already made part of the point in verse:

> We Amsterdammers journey . . .
> Wherever profit leads us, to every sea and shore
> For love of gain the world's harbors we explore

It smacked of truth. Avarice built Dutch commerce and the Amsterdam Bourse. Prodigality, vanity, and luxury-seeking led to impressive art and architecture as well as a far-flung gathering-in of spices, cloths, jewels, and fragrances. The early-seventeenth-century rivalry of the Dutch and English for the Spice Islands of the East Indies—the coffee of Mocha, the nutmegs of Banda, and the cloves of Ternate—was a study in bloodshed and despoliation as well as greed. The emergence of Amsterdam as the *emporium mundi* stimulated not only trade but luxury crafts (diamond cutting, delftware, chocolates, and liqueurs) and finishing industries (tobacco, sugar, dyestuff, and fine cloths). Licentiousness paired with money-hunger to make Amsterdam a city where sin itself was a profitable adjunct to maritime commerce.

The English-speaking world had its own examples. One English political thinker, Sir Thomas Smith (1513–77), a principal secretary of state under Edward VI and Queen Elizabeth and regius professor of law at Cambridge, won repute for arguing that private avarice could serve the public good. His words were especially timely because Henry VIII, turned Protestant, had earlier dissolved the Catholic monasteries, enriching the Protestant nobility. A number of monastic buildings became mercantile

establishments—Glastonbury Abbey, for example, becam/
manufactory. A century later, according to historian Jo'
England's nouveaux riches moneymen of the 1680s and 16،ـ
duced a theory of economic growth that endorsed competition and acclaimed vanity, ambition and emulation as part of a new market
dynamic."

Coming on the heels of the Industrial Revolution, Adam Smith's famous analysis in *The Wealth of Nations* (1776), explaining how economic
self-interest ultimately served the public good, found a warm welcome
over the next four decades in a Britain experiencing sharp wealth polarization. At the peak of regency-period amorality just after Napoleon's defeat, the discussion of private vices as public virtue was frequent enough
at country house parties to be reported by the novelist Emily Eden.

Over the years, discussion of public virtue being forged from private
interest and indulgence has seemed to concentrate just where a cynic
might expect: in the prosperous settings of fifteenth to nineteenth-century
innovation and capitalism from Bruges, Antwerp, Genoa, and Venice to
Amsterdam and London. If corruption has a locus in money-worshiping
periods of boom and upheaval, so does philosophic tribute to self-interest
and avarice.

By the American Gilded Age, self-justification picked up a new ingredient: a quasi-scientific borrowing from the evolutionary theory of
Charles Darwin. Self-interest, brutal competition, and rapacity could
cloak themselves in Darwinian competition and reemerge scientifically
credentialed as survival of the fittest. And although Herbert Spencer, the
principal adapter of evolution to social theory, was an Englishman, these
ideas—shorthanded in history as social Darwinism—had their greatest
impact in America. The explanation, according to historian Richard
Hofstadter, was that, "American society saw its own image in the tooth-
and-claw version of natural selection."

Scientific phraseology and analogy suited the new age of railroads,
telegraphs, and steamships better than any sixteenth or seventeenth-
century parlance of sin and civic virtue. Reform, in this evolutionary milieu,
could be dismissed as unjustifiable interference with the wisdom of nature.

Thinkers in the United States picked up the beat. By 1871, America's
leading poet, Walt Whitman, wrote in *Democratic Vistas* that, "I perceive
that the extreme business energy, and this almost maniacal appetite for
wealth prevalent in the United States, are parts of amelioration and
progress, indispensably needed to prepare the very results I demand. My

theory includes riches and the getting of riches. . . ." The best-known interpretation came from William Graham Sumner, professor of political and social science at Yale. Dismissing egalitarianism as "survival of the unfittest," he argued that "millionaires are a product of a natural selection, acting on the whole body of men to pick out those who can meet the requirement of a certain work to be done. . . . It is because they are thus selected that wealth—both their own and that entrusted to them—aggregates under their hands. They may fairly be regarded as the naturally selected agents of society for certain work. They get high wages and live in luxury, but the bargain is a good one for society." Albert Jay Nock, a conservative traditionalist, ruefully recalled the ethos of his 1870s boyhood: "The most successful (or rapacious) businessmen were held up in the schools, the press and even the pulpit as the prototype of all that was making America great."

Especially in the 1890s, millionaires like Andrew Carnegie, John D. Rockefeller, Chauncey Depew, and James J. Hill proudly identified themselves as Darwinian selectees. Clawing self-interest had made them the lions of the economic veldt, the commercial chosen ones. Successful over three decades, social Darwinism probably represents the longest-lasting philosophic shield ever held up by American wealth accumulators.

By the end of the century, however, contrary interpretations were catching hold. Thorstein Veblen in his famous *Theory of the Leisure Class* (1899) mocked the idea that the avaricious capitalists were any sort of "fittest." Indeed, the self-interested "pecuniary" man, with his chicanery, luxury, and conspicious consumption, far from turning these private traits into a public virtue, played a predatory and morally delinquent role. Oliver Wendell Holmes likewise turned the tables in a Massachusetts state court opinion, trapping social Darwinism in its own Pleistocene jungle by upholding a strike by organized labor as "a lawful instrument in the universal struggle of life."

By the 1920s the trinity of Darwinism, conspicuous consumption, and economic self-interest were ready for another boom-era revival. "The business of America is business," proclaimed President Calvin Coolidge. Government regulation was curbed and in some circumstances gutted. A few years earlier even the pundit Walter Lippmann had linked democracy to "the right to purchase consumer goods at low prices." Bruce Barton, later a Republican congressman, published a book portraying Jesus Christ as the world's first great salesman. Sinclair Lewis, the iconoclastic novelist, wryly observed that "the Romantic Hero was no longer the knight, the wandering poet, the cowpuncher, the aviator, nor the brave young district attorney, but the great sales manager, who had an Analysis of Merchandizing Problems on his glass-topped desk, whose title of nobility was 'Go-getter. . . .' "

Expansions of merchandising and consumption—the ties to self-indulgence jump out—also tend to correlate with the great economic upheavals, partly because the successful want to put their achievement on display, but also because expansive "can't help ourselves" popular consumption surges can be huge wealth generators. The point is that great economic events and their supporting philosophic justifications cross-fertilize each other. The economic thrust may come first, but supporting ideology, with its deification of self-interest, greed, and consumption, gives boom and bull market circumstances greater momentum and longevity.

After the egalitarian milieus of the New Deal, the Eisenhower years and even the early sixties, self-interest, greed, and consumption made a major comeback during the Reagan years. The new president said that, "More than anything else, I want to see the United States remain a country where someone can get rich," His treasury secretary, Donald Regan, acknowledged their hope of recapturing the 1920s, saying, "We're not going back to high-button shoes and celluloid collars. But the President does want to go back to many of the financial methods and economic incentives that brought about the prosperity of the Coolidge period."

Adam Smith ties appeared all over Washington. New magazines wooed economic ambition with titles like *Inc., Venture, Millionaire, Entrepreneur,* and *Success.* Hostile takeovers, leveraged buyouts, and junk bonds became the jousting lances. Risk arbitrageur Ivan Boesky, one of their paladins, told cheering business school audiences that, "Anyone who thinks greed is a bad thing, I want to tell you that it's not a bad thing. And I think that in our system, everybody should be a little bit greedy."

Fashion industry historians add their insight that the Reagan years outconsumed the twenties. Through a series of opulent New York parties centered on the Metropolitan Museum of Art and several department stores, Nancy and Ronald Reagan, advised by former *Vogue* and *Harper's Bazaar* editor Diana Vreeland, appeared to be favoring a new "aristocracy." Instead of producers, they saluted packagers and promoters: movie stars, Hollywood glitterati, department store chief executives, dress designers, media moguls, and fashion purveyors. Vreeland herself had said, "Everything is power and money and how to use them both. . . . We mustn't be afraid of snobbism and luxury."

The Renaissance had also lionized the Idols of Consumption, the top artists and purveyors of luxury goods—Botticelli, Titian, Michelangelo, Leonardo da Vinci. Even in the middle of the Industrial Revolution, the English regency period, a vanity fair and zenith of profligacy, immortalized its archarbiter of fashion: Beau Brummel, the famous dandy. There was money in it; Master Rundell, principal jeweler to the dissipated prince regent, left one of England's largest fortunes (£1.5 million) on his death.

The research firm of SRI International was among those interpreting the Reagan era in the light of the Medicis. "The seven deadly sins of the Middle Ages—pride, gluttony, avarice and prodigality, lust, sloth, anger and envy—were converted into the driving values of the Renaissance era. With the probable exception of sloth," they said in 1985, "our modern economy could not exist if people were not motivated by these values." The same could be said of the golden age of Holland, the financial revolution of the 1690s, the British Industrial Revolution, the U.S. Gilded Age, and the Roaring Twenties. They all shared these common threads.

In the 1980s, as befitting an age of knowledge industries and communications, the selling of a new political economics was mounted through a well-funded network of foundations, societies, journals, and theories. Broadly, their efforts were designed to uphold corporations, profits, consumption, wealth, and upper-bracket tax reduction and to undercut government and regulation. Some of those involved antedated the 1970s, most notably University of Chicago economist Milton Friedman and the "Chicago School" of free market economics. All together, they would give self-interest—critics substituted selfishness and greed—another philosophic era in the sun.

3. GREED AND CIVIC VIRTUE IN THE LATE-TWENTIETH-CENTURY BOOM YEARS

Milton Friedman had been an adviser to Barry Goldwater and then Richard Nixon before "monetarism" got its name from a sympathetic academician in 1968. Those on the Right liked the downgrading of government in his theory that the money supply itself was the key to both GNP growth and inflation management. Governmental interference in the economy, Friedman advised, was almost always counterproductive. He also excused both the stock market crash and speculators from blame for the Great Depression; that he assigned to the Federal Reserve.

Vice-into-civic-virtue theology had a new set of rostrums. To Friedman, greed was the basis of society. The challenge of social organization, he said, was to "set up an arrangement under which greed will do the least harm: capitalism is that kind of system." Speculators, seeking personal profit, played a useful role. He dismissed the idea of a *res publica*—a public interest apart from individual and group self-interests. One could almost see the ghosts of Mandeville, Spencer, and Sumner snapping off salutes.

The larger "Chicago school," pushed to the forefront by the failures of sociology and liberal "fine-tuning" economics in the 1960s and early 1970s, emphasized a free-market core theology that broadly dismissed the role of governments. A few enthusiasts proved embarrassing with their claims that markets and economics also explained behavior from racial discrimination to divorce, suicide, and drug addiction. One such was Chicago law professor-turned-federal appeals court judge Richard Posner's suggestion of a market for babies to make it easier for couples to adopt. But the school's basic message was unimpaired.

The pervasiveness of self-interest also led economist Arthur Laffer and journalist Jude Wanniski in 1973–74 to place tax cut theology alongside market freedom in the pantheon of the new politics. Republican economist Herbert Stein labeled their work "supply-side fiscalism" because it called for fiscal (tax) policy to strengthen the *supply* (investment) side rather than the *demand* (Keynesian) side of the national economy. This the two shortened to "supply side." They also acknowledged borrowing from French economist Jean Baptiste Say (1767–1832), whose dicta was that "supply creates its own demand." Soon a third supply-side architect, George Gilder, took the idea of supply creating its own demand back to the potlatch ceremonies of the Kwakiutl Indians of the Pacific Northwest.

Potlatches or no, here was a rationale for two important capitalist impulses—the desire to overinvest and overproduce (without running afoul of slumping demand) and to stimulate expansion through tax breaks for (rich) *producers* rather than (relatively poor) *consumers*. The drawback, unfortunately, involved the chastening memories of U.S. overproduction after the Napoleonic Wars, again in the 1880s and 1890s, and then, most conspicuously, in the 1920s. Overinvestment was also recurrent. However, even if the real world had periodically discredited Say's Law, supply-side enthusiasm helped enact the Reagan administration tax cuts of 1981; businessmen were happy to applaud if not altogether believe.

Wanniski's work was funded by a grant from one of the small but influential group of conservative foundations. Many more grants followed to others. By the late 1970s the funder group included the John M. Olin, Sarah Scaife, Harry and Lynde Bradley, and Smith Richardson foundations. Through the seventies and eighties their decisions helped support and fortify American enterprise along a broad front of intellectual engagement.

The Public Choice movement and Law and Economics movement both fed well at the conservative table. Their particular twist to self-interest as public virtue emphasized the subordination of lesser values—politics and abstract legal principles—to the more compelling mechanics of markets.

Public Choice all but dismissed the historic institutions and periodic successes of American democracy. Its practitioners hypothesized a Darwinian world in which politicians thought only of reelection and pursued selfish goals, as did egocentric voters. Such a politics, then, should be kept from interfering with markets, which had their own more reliable dynamics and evolutions.

If this seems like too narrow a viewpoint to flourish, two proponents, James Buchanan and Ronald Coase, won Nobel prizes. The inflation of the seventies and the burgeoning budget deficits of the eighties certainly lent credence to the movement's economic suspicions of interest groups. On top of which, Public Choice profited from its mathematical models, algebraic equations, and quantification techniques appearing "scientific." The analogy here is to the doctrines of William Graham Sumner and Herbert Spencer. Much of social Darwinism's appeal, as we have seen, rested on scientific borrowings—or perhaps more accurately, on a pseudoscientific extension of science.

The basic appeal of Public Choice to businessmen and conservatives, of course, lay in how its message reinforced suspicion of government and its official activities. As for the Law and Economics movement, whereas Public Choice demeaned politics and governmental action, the former—perched on similar University of Chicago foundations—argued that American law as a system of commands, prohibitions, and rules often contradicted and countermanded the "natural logic" of the markets.* The solution lay in cleansing the law of interferences like government economic regulation and making it work to facilitate the freedom of the markets.

---

* This natural logic or natural law of the markets is elusive. In free market eyes, it is benign by definition. To others, markets, while useful and necessary, are seen having a tendency to concentration of wealth and monopoly.

The usefulness to wealth-holders of steering federal judges in this direction was obvious. By the late 1990s, under the auspices of Virginia's George Mason University, some two-thirds of them had attended all-expenses-paid two-week institutes and seminars to expose them to Law and Economics thinking. There was a small parallel to the late-nineteenth-century effort by corporations to put friendly judges—the sort who would search every supportive alcove of the 14th Amendment—on as many courts as possible.

As the Republican early 1990s gave way to the Democratic mid and late nineties, Chicago theory drew rebuttals. Liberal economist Robert Kuttner charged that Law and Economics misdescribed the actual behavior of consumers, falsely pretending that humankind followed the precepts of a Chicago economics textbook. Political scientists at UCLA, in turn, collected evidence that individual voting behavior correlated less with the voter's own perceived economic condition and more with his or her perception of *overall* national conditions.

A telling rebuttal of market-manic thinking came from economic historian Douglas North, the 1993 Nobelist. "The evolution of government from its medieval, Mafia-like character to that embodying modern legal institutions and instruments is a major part of the history of freedom," said North. "It is a part that tends to be obscured or ignored because of the myopic vision of many economists, who persist in modeling government as nothing more than a gigantic form of theft and income redistribution."

Selfishness as civic virtue, however, also renewed its consumptionist drumbeat. Researchers at the Dallas Federal Reserve Bank proffered the thesis that household circumstances were best measured by what the householders consumed, not the mere "proxy" of earnings or income. Consumption, as glorified from the Renaissance and the English regency to the fascination of president and Mrs. Reagan with Oscar de la Renta, Bill Blass, Ralph Lauren, Yves St. Laurent, and Bloomingdales has been an economic mainstay and cultural fascination of heyday capitalism.

The economic utility of promoting consumption is that during heydays the public typically pursues the most popular new innovations and products—automobiles, radios, and movies in the twenties, athletic shoes, video games, and cellular phones toward the millennium—at the expense of such humdrum needs like indoor plumbing, education, and medical care. Consumer spending booms are also profits booms. Besides, using consumption as a gauge works to overstate popular well-being, all the more so because its measurements ignore assets and leave out debt burdens, which climbed most during periods like the 1920s, 1960s, and the 1980s and 1990s precisely for those least able to afford them.

By an even more expansive view, consumption had become part of the new edifice of democracy-as-market. By driving a car, buying a movie ticket, or watching a television commercial, U.S. consumers participated every day in the democracy of the marketplace, or so suggested the editorial pages of the *Wall Street Journal.* What was widely purchased was, ipso facto, democratically approved. Buying and selling, indeed, was a large part of what democracy was about.

Thomas Frank, a cultural critic, collected these musings in a book entitled *One Market under God.* Markets would become the democratic rulers in the nineties, said banker Walter Wriston: "Markets are voting machines; they function by taking referenda." Ultimately even the proletariat would "fight to reduce government power over the corporations for which they work, organizations far more democratic, collegial and tolerant than distant state bureaucracies." Broadcaster Rush Limbaugh, too, wanted to "let the marketplace rule." Former House speaker Newt Gingrich dreamed about the possibility of establishing a "consumer-directed government," once even suggesting that major questions could be resolved by simply asking "our major multinational corporations for advice." Meanwhile, legal scholars working with the business community and its allied think tanks polished arguments that writing a check to a political campaign was a form of free speech protected by the First Amendment. To be sure, a politics that candidly espoused these ideas would not have lasted very long. But it was the private mind-set and ambition of an influential minority.

Religion, too, has had its voice in the conservative economic chorus. From colonial times, preachers had often obliged. During the Gilded Age the Reverend Henry Ward Beecher lauded business for fat speaking fees, and Baptist minister Russell Conwell became a millionaire from the appeal of "Acres of Diamonds," his sermon to large and prosperous crowds that getting rich was a noble aspiration. The twenties had Bruce Barton's story of Jesus as the world's greatest salesman. President Calvin Coolidge even confused religion and economics when he observed that "The man who builds a factory builds a temple. The man who works there worships there." Kindred voices in the nineties were Paul Zane Pilzer, author of *God Wants You to Be Rich,* Catherine Ponder of the Unity Church Worldwide who penned *Dare to Prosper,* and Deepak Chopra, author of the *The Seven Spiritual Laws of Success.*

Social Darwinism, in turn, made a further comeback through the insistence by many political officeholders, financiers, and leaders of multinational corporations that the onrush of globalization was inevitable, although as chapter 4 points out, it hadn't been in earlier periods. This time, the jungle in which the fittest, both individual and corporate, would survive was to be worldwide. "There is no alternative," said British prime minister Margaret Thatcher. In the 1880s and 1890s social legislation had been dismissed as the unwisdom of government meddling with evolutionary inevitability. A century later a similar cloak of unstoppability was thrown over the globalization of labor markets and management of trade markets by corporate-dominated institutions like the World Trade Organization.

A century earlier, reform legislation had finally gathered momentum as social Darwinism was displaced by early-twentieth-century Progressivism; pre-1914 globalization itself was badly wounded in the trenches along the Somme and Marne, dying in the twenties and thirties with free trade and Liberal England. Past "globalizations," as we have seen, were not inevitable, but elite-driven and often related to the heyday of a particular world power.

The 1990s brought a new wave of neo-Darwinian self-assuredness. In 1999 billionaire Philip Hampson Knight of Nike posed for *Forbes'* annual photograph alongside his corporate reflecting pool, sneakered feet extended, with a snarl on his lips against critics who charged him with making his shoes and his profits through low-wage labor in Asian sweatshops. "That isn't an issue that should even be on the political agenda today," said Knight. "It's just a sound bite of globalization." But some of this confidence withered when the new century began with mass rallies against the annual meeting of the World Trade Organization.

In the mid-1980s, the historian Arthur Schlesinger Jr. dismissed the Reagan-era package of conservative economic issues—attacks on regulation, glorification of the unfettered market, and embrace of supply-side (or "trickle-down") tax policy—as being less new ideas than "the boilerplate of every private interest era." Perhaps, but by 2000 the conservative restatement of old-market theology, antiregulatory shibboleths, God-wants-you-to-be-rich theology, and Darwinism had built up the greatest momentum since the days of Herbert Spencer and William Graham Sumner.

Such ideas may gestate, as in the early 1920s and late 1970s, as familiar conservative correctives to antimarket, pro-government, and sociological excess. However, in the United States, and in combination with technological mania, they can develop an extraordinary and ultimately exaggerated force.

4. DEMOCRATS AND THE NEW ELITE

We have seen in chapter 7 how the Republican Party, amid three of America's most divisive periods, briefly embraced a middle-class nationalism or national unity politics that included a surprising openness to labor viewpoints, progressive taxes, regulation of corporations, and skepticism of large-scale capitalism. By the later years of its three national cycles, however, the GOP had put on its full-dress uniform of heyday or aggressive capitalism—a commitment conspicuous again at the end of the twentieth century.

The evolution on the Democratic side has been strikingly different. Party watersheds have involved opposition to financial, mercantile, or speculative elites, often (but not always) crystallized by public reaction to an economic downturn that had begun under a conservative regime. In the middle of conservative or Republican cycles, however, amid boom circumstances, the Democrats tend to lose their bearings and become almost as collaborative with heyday capitalism as the dominant GOP. Examples include the Gilded Age twin conservative administrations of Grover Cleveland, the pro-business economics of congressional Democrats during the 1920s, the policies of the Carter administration of 1977–81, and the money-culture bias of the eight Clinton years with their bond market and Wall Street orientation. The "corruption" here is that the system loses an essential counterbalance.

Cleveland, a sound money Gold Democrat from New York, was the only U.S. president to serve two terms interrupted by four years of a president of the other party. His four year interregnum was spent at the Manhattan law firm of Francis Lynde Stetson, who represented J. P. Morgan. By 1892 the Republican administration of Benjamin Harrison, who replaced Cleveland, had soured many eastern bankers by conciliating inflation-minded silver backers. As the Democratic convention opened that summer, in one historian's words, "the great banking interests of New York" and "a large part of Wall Street" favored Cleveland. They were reassured that his campaign manager was multimillionaire William C. Whitney, well recognized as "a representative of corporate finance in politics." Weighing Cleveland's two terms as a whole, Woodrow Wilson, the next Democratic president, insisted that the New Yorker hadn't been a Democrat at all. "Cleveland," remarked Wilson, "was a conservative Republican."

Jumping ahead to the 1920s, the party presidential nominees of 1920 and 1924, Ohio publisher James Cox and corporation lawyer John W. Davis, were in many ways as conservative as their Republican opponents. Cox and Davis along with the 1928 nominee New York governor Alfred E. Smith would wind up joining the business-dominated Liberty League to oppose Franklin Roosevelt and the New Deal. Smith's principal fundraiser of 1928, John J. Raskob, was a senior adviser to the duPont interests. Historian David Burner also recalled that "in the first session of the Seventieth Congress—the last to meet before the stock market crashed—almost all [congressional] Democrats, in company with the United States Chamber of Commerce, continued to clamor for [tax] reductions beyond the wishes of President Coolidge."

The Democratic presidencies during the post-1968 Republican era continued to fit the pattern. Georgian Jimmy Carter, elected in 1976 in the wake of Watergate, was moderately conservative in his economics, kept on close terms with home state bankers and corporate chiefs (Coca-Cola and Lockheed), undertook financial deregulation before Reagan, and appointed Paul Volcker, a moderate with conservative leanings, as chairman of the Federal Reserve Board. Liberal historian Schlesinger, after citing Carter's conservative views—"Government cannot solve our problems. It can't set our goals. . . ."—charged him with "an eccentric effort to carry the Democratic Party back to Grover Cleveland."

In a number of ways Bill Clinton continued where Carter left off. However, the nineties had also intensified a larger transformation within the Democratic Party. Its internal economic balance of power had shifted appreciably. This change occurred between the 1950s, when the Democrats started showing gains among college graduates and urban and suburban professionals, and the 1990s, when the onetime party of Jefferson and Jackson emerged as the clear choice of many of the new Internet and telecommunications rich headed to the top of the *Forbes* 400.

Much more was involved than the Democrats' familiar practice of conforming to financial booms. The increased party support visible among urban professionals after the late 1950s might have been no more than a new round of Mugwumps and Progressives. What made the transformation deeper and different was the rise of the knowledge sector discussed in chapter 3—the soaring numbers of Americans employed in education, communications, research, and professions from law to psychiatry. In the midst of the liberal political failure of the late 1960s and early 1970s, Democratic responsiveness to this sector was at first a political minus.* However, with the demographics looking far more auspicious, Will Marshall, president of the "New Democrat" Progressive Policy Institute, could argue in 1997 that, "Just as industrial workers formed the backbone of the New Deal coalition, the party needs to attract the knowledge workers emerging as the dominant force in the information economy," the "wired workers" who use computers.

The elites of the knowledge sector were more important, however, both as big-dollar contributors and powerful opinion molders. David Friedman, a fellow at the New America Foundation, argued in the *Los Angeles Times* that a "cleansing of working-class concerns from America's once progressive politics" reflected the emergence of a "new, fabulously privileged elite—including Web-site and computer gurus, actors, directors, media magnates and financial power brokers" who exercised "unparalleled influence" over mainstream liberalism. As chapter 6 has discussed, they were not simply a cultural elite but an important economic elite frequently at loggerheads with the ordinary, nonprofessional workforces of their industries.

Thomas Ferguson, an expert on political fundraising, identified telecommunications as the industry that stood out in its 1996 support for Bill Clinton. This commitment, he explained, congealed around influencing what became the high-stakes Telecommunications Act of 1996: "For years, Hollywood, network and cable television, book publishers, news concerns, radio stations, computer and software makers and phone companies had all been making vast sums of money as individual entities. By 1993, however, changes in technology and regulatory practice were bringing these industries together at an explosive pace, and almost everyone wanted legal rights to get into everyone else's business."

Besides these ties to a specific, hugely wealthy economic sector, the need of Democratic candidates for large-scale campaign funding had its own profound influence. "Unfortunately, we've been cowed into the position of not sticking up for working people," one Democratic strategist told the *Philadelphia Inquirer* in 1995, "because we've been looking increasingly to wealthy interests in order to fund our campaigns. You end

---

* My own book, *The Emerging Republican Majority,* discussed the rise of the knowledge industry, but the media was uncomfortable with the term in 1969. One newsweekly changed my reference to "knowledgeable industry executives."

up spending time with wealthy people who say 'Let's not make this a class thing.'" That many, if not most, Democratic-connected lawyers, consultants, and lobbyists in Washington also worked on behalf of corporations, trade associations, and the wealthy bolstered the reorientation.

The larger pressure, however, arose from the underlying partial transformation of the Democrats into the party of a wealthy cultural and technological elite, indeed one whose fortunes and supporting middle-class numbers in parts of the North matched those of the GOP. The power blocs in Washington lobbying also reflected this reorientation. According to a study entitled *The New Liberalism,* both the congressional agenda and the focus of "liberal" lobbies in Washington had since the 1960s swung away from economic issues—tax fairness, manpower training, and farm supports—to so-called "post-material" issues like the environment, abortion, and the Family Medical and Leave Act. The author, Professor Jeffrey Berry, identified Bill Clinton as the first Democratic president to move away from traditional liberal economics to a "post-materialist" quality of life agenda. If the postmaterialism was premature and exaggerated, the directional shift was real enough.

Holding office during a boom for which it got much of the credit, the Democratic Party of the nineties steered clear of indicting the wealth and income distributions that heyday capitalism had brought. As the first decade in the new century began to unfold with a Republican in the White House, some of those Democratic inhibitions fell away, but a substantial underlying party transformation remained.

5. THE DIVERGENCE OF U.S. ECONOMIC GROWTH AND SOCIAL WELL-BEING

Something unusual happened to American economic growth and social well-being indexes in the 1970s: As chapter 3 has shown, the two began to diverge, although watchers didn't realize how much until the late eighties and early nineties, at which time the social measurement indexes were finally formalized, using comparative databases carried back through 1950 in one case and 1970 in another.

Government and private data in the United States cannot be weighed without their political as well as statistical context. In the Depression-battered thirties, for example, measuring unemployment became a compelling national priority. Until then the jobless numbers had been understated and erratic in Europe and even less organized in the United States. Given the blight of the Depression, a second new emphasis for the

1930s was keeping track of the ups and downs of the business cycle. Data for the gross national product, for its part, evolved to analyze and organize World War II production.

After the 1930s efforts to measure social trends ended with World War II, attention slumbered until the late sixties when the apparent success of economic measurement and micromanagement at the federal level led to a naive hope that social policy also could be statisticized and managed from Washington. Federal publication in 1966 of the first *Social Indicators* was followed in 1967 by Minnesota senator Walter Mondale's proposal for a Council of Social Advisers to be on a par with the Council of Economic Advisers. Both projects soon drowned in the public's disillusionment with experiments like the War against Poverty, school busing, and rent subsidies as well as the underlying skepticism of Republican presidents. The Nixon administration turned the next (1974) volume of *Social Indicators* into a neutral chartbook. In 1981 the Reagan administration discontinued publication altogether. Republican policy intellectuals committed to a market emphasis generally distrusted social yardsticks, which had sometimes been abused.

The serious revival of interest in social indicators in the late 1980s and early 1990s reflected concern over the Reagan era's rising inequality and seemingly shrinking social safety net. The Index of Social Health was begun in 1987 by the Fordham (University) Institute for Innovation in Social Policy under director Marc Miringoff. Of its sixteen criteria, half were economic, ranging from wages, unemployment, and health coverage to child poverty. The others were noneconomic, including infant mortality, high school dropout rates, violent crime, and teenage drug use. From a peak of 76.9 in 1973, the index fell to 40 in 1986 and 38 in 1993, rising slightly to 43 in 1996 and 46 in 1999. Chart 3.29 shows the three-decade pattern.

A second index, quite different in its mechanics, was the Genuine Progress Indicator, begun in 1994 by San Francisco–based Redefining Progress. In many ways this was an alternative gross domestic product calculus in which unproductive activities counted in official-defined "growth"—the cost of commuting, environmental burdens, growth that made incomes more unequal, foreign borrowing, family outlays made to cope with ill-health and so on—were reentered as minuses. On the other side of the ledger, activities not hitherto counted in the official gross product—housework, for example—were added in as pluses.

Surprisingly, the trend, at least, of the Genuine Progress Indicator almost paralleled the Index of Social Health. Both rose with the upward-moving gross domestic product through the early seventies. Then as per capita GDP kept rising, the indicator, like the index, flattened and turned down. Interestingly, the same 1970s downturn occurred in two other less recognized chartings: the Index of Leading Cultural Indicators drawn up by former education secretary William Bennett, and the Index of Sustainable Economic Welfare, an environmentally centered measurement conducted by University of Maryland economist Herman Daly. Obviously, some things were going wrong.

The various samplers agreed less on the whys and wherefores than over the decline. Fordham's Miringoff suggested the loss of well-paying blue-collar jobs might be to blame. However, both the timing of the divergence from mid-to-late seventies and the particular weaknesses demonstrated in Fordham's international social benchmarks by the more individualistic, capitalist English-speaking nations suggested an additional influence: the deemphasis in the U.S. and Britain of social and environmental criteria and the effects of a triumphant conservatism loosely committed to markets, globalization, Darwinism, and distrust of noneconomic criteria.

Indeed, as we have seen, the notion of an ebb barely hides in a half-dozen economic indices. Besides manufacturing, current account deficit, wage and household debt numbers, the Department of Labor admits that if part-timers wanting more work and those wanting jobs but lacking necessary transportation or child care were included, the unemployment level of 2000 would have been twice the official 5.5 million total, or some twelve million. The failure to count as unemployed older men who dropped out of the workforce in large numbers during the last quarter of the twentieth century also kept the jobless numbers down.

According to critics, definitions of poverty in the United States have served as much to hide the problem as to profile it. The Census Bureau, doubting the adequacy of the established—and relatively reassuring—poverty definition, recommended raising the household threshold to $19,500 a year, which would have left 46 million Americans short in 2000.

Miringoff, in his 1999 volume *The Social Health of the Nation,* also included revealing late-1990s individual rankings of the Western industrial nations for over two-thirds of his sixteen yardsticks. What these show is that in inequality measurements, the English-speaking nations, with their greater emphasis on markets and individualism, invariably led. In the percentage of poverty among those over sixty-five, the U.S., Australia, and Britain were the top three. For child poverty, the U.S., Britain, Australia, Canada, and Ireland were the five nations where it was highest. In the percentage of those finishing high school, the U.S. ranked lowest; and in overall inequality, the (negative) ranks were as follows: U.S. (1), Ireland (2), Australia (4), Britain (6), and Canada (8).

In rankings for other facets of the perils of the unfittest, the highest rates of youth homicide came in the U.S., Northern Ireland, New Zealand, Canada, Israel, Switzerland, and Australia. With respect to wage levels, such was the relative downward pressure since the seventies in the English-speaking countries that six—the U.S., Canada, Australia, Britain, Ireland, and New Zealand—were in the bottom eleven. The top eleven nations were all Continental European. It is hard not to conclude that the other English-speaking nations, sharing many of the benefits of U.S. financial and technological prowess, also share some of the accompanying inegalitarian economic and social trendlines.

Parenthetically, university and public health researchers in Britain and the United States also began to report during the 1990s that health and life expectancy were better in states, metropolitan areas, and other jurisdictions with greater community-mindedness and more egalitarian income distributions. One survey, done in 1998 by two researchers at Harvard's School of Public Health, found that among 282 metropolitan areas, mortality rates were more closely linked to *relative* than *absolute* income, with rising inequality meaning higher mortality. Their thesis: that erosion of trust or "social capital" may explain inequality's influence on health.

The United States of the millennium, caught up in the glories of markets and globalization, was scarcely more open to these debates than the Britain of 1900. Two decades of glorifying markets, consumption, and self-interest had taken their toll. However, pressures for change were growing, and as the theorists of "economic man" lost credibility in the stock market crash of 2000–2001, there were new glimmerings of disenchantment with finance and speculation, the subject to which we now turn.

CHAPTER NINE

THE CUP ALWAYS RUNNETH OVER: GREED, SPECULATIVE BUBBLES, AND REFORM

Speculation has come of age; it can sit quite comfortably side by side with investment; and it is as legitimate and necessary as the securities markets themselves.

—Walter Werner and Steven Smith, *Wall Street,* 1991

Speculators may do no harm as bubbles on a steady stream of enterprise. But the position is serious when enterprise becomes a bubble on a whirlpool of speculation. When the capital development of a country becomes a by-product of the activities of a casino, the job is likely to be ill done.

—John Maynard Keynes, *The General Theory of Employment, Interest and Money,* 1936

Those animal spirits aren't limited to the realm of finance. Hitler overstretched; Napoleon overstretched. In fact, in *The Theory of Moral Sentiments,* Adam Smith said that most of the world's troubles come from somebody not knowing when to stop and be content.

—Charles Kindleberger, 1994

I n *Devil Take the Hindmost,* his much-praised history of financial speculation, Edward Chancellor began by pointing out its behavioral roots in gambling, carnivals, and other frolics. Dignity and hierarchy—the sixteenth-century equivalent of pinstripes—were nowhere to be seen.

Of the early Amsterdam stock exchange, Simon Schama observed that, "Such was its reputation as an undignified bazaar that the great lords of capital who themselves enjoyed substantial dividend income from share trading disdained to set foot in the place, delegating the daily business of buying and selling to professional brokers." Indeed, until the London financial boom of the 1690s, the word "broker" itself had referred "simply to a procurer or pimp." "Blue chip" stocks later took their now-prestigious name from the color of the most expensive chip at the Monte Carlo casinos. And so on.

Such are the antecedents of the markets, if not of our own individual fortunes (achieved, of course, by pluck, study, and acumen). The persisting touch of *carnival* can be seen in descriptions of the New York gold market of the 1860s and the Wall Street of the 1920s as "carnivals of speculation." Gambling's psychological kinship has also remained obvious. The balance is unclear. Up to a point, risk-taking has encouraged economic expansion. On the other hand, when bubbles implode they have brought caution and contrition. In the United States, particularly, burst speculative bubbles have done service as the preconditions of major reform waves.

1. The Bacchanalian Connection: Fairs, Carnivals, Gambling, and the Origin of Markets and Speculation

Four centuries of evidence portray the pursuit of stocks as a heated rhythm of life, not a cool display of market rationality. Speculative waves have elements of periodic release, which tie into a larger cyclicality of behavior: the alternations of greed and fear, abandon and regret.

Before Antwerp domiciled the world's first stock exchange, the financial markets of northern Europe circa 1500 followed the seasonal fairs to Antwerp and such other places as Bruges, London, Paris, Champagne, Lyon, Frankfurt, Leipzig, and Medina del Campo. The latter, little remembered, was the de facto financial capital of sixteenth-century Spain, where royal bankers at fair time paid the king's debts and arranged his loans. These popular gatherings, descendants of the fora and bacchanalia of ancient Rome, enjoyed church exemptions from the medieval restrictions on trade and finance. At the famous Leipziger Messe, German mining shares changed hands as early as the fourteenth century. Gambling itself was a commonplace, accompanied by raucous language—the "billingsgate" (after the abusive London fish market) that still persists in trading floors and pits. "Speculation," Chancellor concluded, "grew out of the crowds and bustle of Renaissance fairs and carnivals, and although by the 17th century, the carnival was in a decline and fairs had been replaced by permanent stock exchanges, the carnival spirit lingered in the marketplaces."

As for speculation's kinship to gambling, the epigraph at the start of this chapter in which Keynes likened it to a casino is only one comment among thousands. Cicero described buying shares in Roman *publicani,* the companies of his day, as a gamble to be avoided; Daniel Defoe said of England in the 1690s that wagering had simply moved into the Royal

Exchange. Milton Friedman, in a 1960 defense of speculation, explained its criticism by many economists as a "natural bias of the academic student against gambling," although before long, portions of academe were justifying speculation within the Efficient Market Hypothesis.

Toward the end of the technology bubble of the 1990s, commentators hypothesizing "irrational exuberance" tended to emphasize history over mathematics. Yale professor Robert Shiller, in one critique, sought to correlate U.S. speculative surges to the gambling waves of the 1980s and 1990s and before that, the 1920s. There is a modicum of evidence.

From lotteries and casinos to riverboat gambling, the business of wagering (including associated restaurants, bars, and hotels) surged between 1982 and 1994 from $10.4 billion a year to almost $40 billion. True, no direct proof tied the increased risk-taking in lotteries, video keno, and off-track betting parlors to stock market hubris. Schiller's observances at Yale, however, provided a telling anecdotal documentation: a local Connecticut billboard that touted off-track betting, in big letters, as being "Like the Stock Market, Only Faster."

The stock ticker ballyhoo of the twenties, in turn, had overlapped with a gambling craze heightened when the crime mobs controlling Prohibition-era bootlegging branched out into speakeasies, numbers games, craps, and roulette. The *Reader's Guide to Periodical Literature,* Shiller found, showed growing stock market activity paralleled by rising attention to gambling between 1925 and the beginning of the 1930s.

Earlier, during the first decade of the twentieth century, with its two speculative or "rich men's" panics of 1901 and 1907, gambling was widespread in the men's clubs of the major stock- and commodity-market centers. Manhattan's most fashionable gambling emporium, the Saratoga Club, next door to Delmonico's, was patronized by moneymen and owned by Richard Canfield, himself a speculator who turned a $2 million profit on Reading Railroad stock.

Lotteries in the United States and a reckless fashionability of gambling in Britain provided important backdrops to the securities fevers of the 1790s and the first third of the nineteenth century. Not a few of Britain's daytime speculators spent their evenings gamboling* and gambling at

---

* Dictionaries point out that a gambol—a frolic or dancing about for joy or sport—comes from the same Latin root as a gamble. So does gambado or gambade, meaning an antic or escapade. The line of descent would seem to be from frolic to gamble to financial wager to speculation.

White's, Brooke's, Boodle's, and Almack's, the Card Room at Bath, and local assembly rooms from Plymouth to Edinburgh. Losing a large sum on Peruvian scrip or Mexican mining shares was easier if one frequently lost as much at faro, hazard, or even whist. The seventeenth-century Dutch, in turn, had a penchant for gambling. "Wagers," said historian Simon Schama, "were made on every conceivable opportunity, from the outcome of a siege to the sex of an impending baby . . . the line between casual betting and organized trading in stock was often blurred."

The mathematics of chance—be they laws of probability, Hoyle's rules of games, or Black-Scholes derivative theory—have led keen students to both gambling and finance. If Manhattan club owner Richard Canfield combined roulette with railroad securities, the early career of John Law, the great Scottish-French financier, mingled finance with success in applying advanced probability theory to the dice game of hazard. So fine was the moral line that lottery tickets circulated as currency in the England of the 1690s and into the 1700s in several mainland American colonies. Financial writer James Grant, identifying a latter-day parallel in the Japan of the 1990s, where lottery tickets were "negotiable securities," noted that they had to "be handled by banks." How much this blurring might have encouraged the Japanese speculative bubble of the 1980s cannot be known.

As first cousin to gambling, speculation has involved a fluctuating ratio of rational behavior to human emotion. Its ebbs and flows have had cultural and social as well as economic importance. Thus the interaction with politics. And over the centuries, it has mattered considerably in success and wealth that some cultures were more speculation-minded than others.

2. SPECULATIVE CULTURE AND WORLD ECONOMIC LEADERSHIP

The contribution of such a bent to Dutch, British, and then American ascent to world economic leadership may match their entrepreneurialism, emphasis on patents, inventions, and property laws, and innovation in science, industry, commerce, and finance. (Practically speaking, the Dutch-British-American continuum has also included the Flemings, Jews, and French Huguenots.)

All three nations' speculative inclinations have drawn comment from countless economists, historians, and foreign visitors. As we saw in chapter 4, of the more than two dozen panics and crashes between 1720 and

1975 identified by economist Charles Kindleberger, three-quarters involved a major Dutch, British, or American role. Part of this, to be sure, simply reflected their world economic preeminence. By the 1780s, Dutch and British annals would have provided ample support for Alexander Hamilton's case that a great commercial nation *needed* a class of speculators or moneymen. Before their rise in the 1670s, argued one historian, "there was no stock market in London and England was a weak nation-state. In 1712, only forty years later, the shares of many joint-stock companies were traded on an active and highly organized capital market. . . . Furthermore, Great Britain had become one of the major military powers in Europe." Between 1600 and 1640 a similar transformation had uplifted the Dutch.

The danger, touched on by Keynes, was not just the peril when national enterprise became a bubble on a whirlpool of speculation rather than the other way around. Both Britain and the United States, as we have seen, paired the rewards of speculation with several weaknesses, visible from the railway mania of Victorian times to the millennial technology bubble. One is the tendency to technology-linked speculative manias. Another is the repetitive delusion that new developments in financial, managerial, or governmental capacity have brought about a truly new era, so that previous cautions about speculative excesses and painful recessions can be thrown to the winds.

Few economic historians have pursued how often financial speculation helps bring on a broader economic downturn. This Anglo-American weakness, developed in chapter 6, can be recapitulated in a few sentences. According to Charles Kindleberger, the panics and crises centered in Britain and connected to technology were those of 1772 (turnpikes, canals), 1793 (canals), 1797 (canals), 1836 (textiles, railroads), 1847 (railroads), and 1857 (railroads). Several were seriously felt. A comparable list for the United States would include those of 1837 (railroads) and 1857 (railroads), both linked to Britain, and the downturns of 1873 (railroads), 1890s (railroads), 1929 (autos, utilities, and other technology), and 2000 (Internet, telecommunications, and other technology). In the United States, they seem to have spread more into the rest of the economy.

The longer-term costs of Britain's manic approach to railroad stock and railroading included massive overinvestment, diversion of huge amounts of wasted capital from uses elsewhere, a poorly laid out rail system with massive duplication and undersized freight cars, and perhaps most of all, by 1900 a geography of transportation that anchored British industry to the 1830s and 1840s. The United States, too, had a wasteful, overbuilt railroad system by the 1890s, but the weight of prior downturns linked to speculative railroad excesses fell heaviest on farmers. The irony is that it had compensating effects—economist Joseph Schumpeter's "creative destruction"—in speeding the evolution of the U.S. industrial economy.

The severity of the U.S. Crash of 1929, in turn, partly reflected the sheer size of the bubble blown up or enlarged by speculation. In Schumpeter's terms, however, the weak economy of the 1930s left America uniquely positioned to mount an extraordinary mobilization for the 1938–45 war. The impact of the imploding U.S. technology bubble of 2000–2001 on the industry's profits and prospects, still being felt, surprised observers as weakness spread into the broader economy.

These speculative excesses have been critically supported by the tendency of elites to spin illusions for themselves and the less-sophisticated public about the new capacities of government and private sector management. Manias require convincing siren songs: insistence that things really are different this time, financially as well as technologically.

Unprecedented new financial and managerial capacities always seemed at hand. In the England of 1825, a young Benjamin Disraeli assumed that the boom would not turn to bust because of the era's superior commercial knowledge. Britons watching the great railway mania unfold in 1845 believed that dangers had been removed by the Bank Act of 1844, which required the Bank of England to restrict credit expansions. They were wrong. A leading British railway historian, Adrian Vaughan, described 1847 and another panic in 1866 as situations in which "the supposedly self-balancing system of market forces had been overcome by greedy self-interest."

In the United States of 1873, confidence reposed in the new prowess and reach of the U.S. Treasury—the department had sold bullion in 1869 to quell a major gold speculation and in 1872 had served as a lender of last resort by the innovative method of trotting out retired greenbacks. The stock market panic of 1901, in turn, surprised an American investor class convinced by the new managerialism, Morgan's rationalization of industry, and the rise of the trusts, "that old rules and principles and precedents of finance were obsolete." This description came from Alexander Dana Noyes, later financial editor of the *New York Times*. He recalled 1901 as the first, and the 1920s the second, "of such speculations in history which based its ideas and conduct on the assumption that we were living in a New Era."

Years after leaving office in 1933, former president Herbert Hoover contended that creation of the Federal Reserve Board was part of what had lulled Americans into the "new era" suppositions. Productivity gains, mergers and economics of scale, and scientific management added to confidence levels. By the 1960s, as we saw in chapter 2, rationales for diminished business cyclicality and speculative vulnerability cited the new tools of Keynesian theory and the prospects for successful micromanagement of the national economy.

By the late 1990s, as the cup of speculation ran over, so did the fountains of New Era encouragement. On top of the revolution in productivity, inventory control through the Internet would smooth out business cycles, derivative instruments and electronic finance would hedge any risk, and the Federal Reserve stood ready with unprecedented resources and management tools. Besides which, shaky financial institutions could be bailed out. In late 1999, J. Kenneth Galbraith, in his eighties, proved to have the last word: "The oldest rule in economics, for which I take credit, is that when someone says we have entered a new era of permanent prosperity, you should take cover. That has been said many, many times in the last three hundred years." It is, he might have added, the rhythm of credulence on which speculative mania depends.

In the meantime, the United States of the 1990s had developed one of the most sophisticated global economic management strategies ever deployed by government. The late eighties and the beginning of the nineties had seen the "rise of the traders" to head major Wall Street investment firms. Now Washington economics took a similar direction with the appointment of Robert Rubin, the former currency arbitrageur and cochairman of Goldman Sachs, as chairman of Clinton's National Economic Council in 1993 and as secretary of the treasury in 1996.

From his experience running Wall Street's most sophisticated money-making machine, Rubin, more than any other individual, built a partial governmental equivalent in the Clinton administration: the U.S. economy, like a major Wall Street international investment firm, would be run to make money and attract it from around the world. Leverage and speculation were both givens. The global reach of the Federal Reserve under Alan Greenspan was complementary.

Large policy bets were placed on federal deficit reduction to cheer the bond market, bring down interest rates, and stimulate economic expansion. This would bolster tax receipts, corporate profits, the Dow-Jones, and the Nasdaq. Rising stock prices in turn would buoy consumer spending and expand income and capital gains tax payments, shrinking the deficit further. Business and financial support would strengthen the administration's hand. White House backstopping for U.S. overseas trade, insistence on openings to Mexico and China, persistent leadership on behalf of NAFTA and the WTO, and support of U.S. corporate objectives abroad combined to escalate corporate profits and stock prices alike. Mercantilist tax provisions and export subsidy mechanisms like the Export-Import Bank and the Overseas Private Investment Corporation regained stature.

Whatever bank, investment firm, loan, or currency problems might become serious would be rescued or bailed out, at least wherever possible. Financiers also knew what was becoming *unacceptable*: any recession or major wealth disruption. The Fed and the treasury, in a sense, become joint, proactive managers of the multi-trillion-dollar "USA Fund." Market economics might be the claim, but globalized U.S. government economic management was the game.

Whatever the gambit and degree of calculation, it achieved the longest peacetime recovery in U.S. history, turning the U.S. economy of 1997–99 into the wonder of Asia and Europe. The stock market indexes headed into the stratosphere, bolstering popular confidence even through 2000 as air started to leak out of the balloon.

3. AVARICE, LUXURY, ARROGANCE, AND DEBT: THE FOUR HORSEMEN OF U.S. SPECULATIVE IMPLOSIONS

By many yardsticks, the speculative, wealth-driven, and debt-related vulnerability of the United States of 2000 matched the Gilded Age and Roaring Twenties. But along with the skills of financial mercantilism, some other new characteristics—there are always new ones—nurtured the insistence in the nineties that things were different.

Like kindred excitements from Renaissance Italy to Edwardian Britain, speculative eras in the United States have been carried along by the increasing pace—or perhaps more aptly, the loosened reins—of the erstwhile sins teamed to drive the great wagons of economic expansion. As what had been investment begins to bubble, pride, hubris, and arrogance strain at their harnesses. Greed and avarice toss their heads. Debt steps ever higher. Prodigality, luxury, and gluttony champ at their bits.

Journalists would be more likely to say that crowds begin to infect each other, behavior gets more manic, and asset prices grow more extreme. This is the boom before the bust, which comes when the rush for liquidity —and sanity—takes over.

Still, different U.S. political ideologies have shaped somewhat different booms. Under conservative or "private interest" national regimes, upper-class vanity and self-interest tended to be more open. When liberal or progressive administrations were in power amid a bull market, soaring top-bracket incomes and glutting luxuries, they have been more guarded in approval. Awareness of the many Americans not sharing has been greater.

Of the private sins, pride and arrogance were staples during the Gilded Age, the Roaring Twenties, and the 1980s. Chauncey Depew, president of the New York Central and then a U.S. senator, told Manhattan dinner audiences of the 1890s that they represented the survival of the fittest of those who had come to the metropolis in search of success and power. Treasury secretary Andrew Mellon looked to the Depression to purge farmers and marginal businesses, putting enterprise and capital in firmer hands; and his successor, Ogden Mills, as the economy worsened, dismissed suggestions that a family could live comfortably on $50,000 a year. "On $50,000 a year," scorned Mills, "you can't even keep clean." The 1980s had Leona Helmsley, wife of the real estate billionaire, saying, "Only the little people pay taxes."

Greed and avarice were just as prominent. In 1894 the U.S. Supreme Court struck down an 1893 law establishing a bare-bones federal income tax of 2 percent on the top several percentiles of income by calling it "an assault on capital," a "stepping stone to other, larger and more sweeping, till our political contests . . . become a war of the poor against the rich." Multimillionaires of the twenties, in practices later prohibited by 1930s legislation, avoided taxes by incorporating their yachts, automobiles, airplanes, and racing stables, thereby claiming operating losses on them as charges against personal income. In the 1980s, corporate raider and arbitrageur Ivan Boesky gave Republican and business school audiences the message that "greed is good."

Debt must always come to the feast. Huge borrowings, on a scale never before possible, were necessary for the Hapsburgs, French Valois kings, Medicis, and other rulers of the Renaissance—some of whom periodically declared bankruptcy—to indulge their expensive tastes in architecture, art, and the building of nation-states. So, too, for the nineteenth and twentieth centuries. The massive indebtedness taken on to buy, promote, or construct the railroads was a principal element in nineteenth-century boom-bust patterns on both sides of the Atlantic. The failure of Jay Cooke & Company, investment bankers to the overindebted Northern Pacific Railroad, was the insolvency that ushered in the 1873 depression.

We have seen in chapter 2 how the rampant credit-mongering of the 1920s so expanded household debt that in 1932 some 20 percent of U.S. personal income went for debt service. Chart 3.12 shows America's three large twentieth-century waves of private debt expansion. Their overlap with speculative crests of the 1920s, 1960s, and tandem heights of the 1980s and 1990s leaves little to the imagination.

Prodigality and luxury repeat as forms of self-expression by the rich, especially the new rich. Edgar Allan Poe, writing in the 1840s, observed that because the United States had "an aristocracy of dollars, the display of wealth has here to take the place and perform the office of the heraldic display in monarchical countries." This anticipated Thorstein Veblen's famous premise, set out in *The Theory of the Leisure Class* (1899), that, "In order to gain and hold the esteem of men it is not sufficient merely to possess wealth or power. The wealth or power must be put in evidence, for the esteem is awarded only on evidence."

Display has been most provocative near speculative peaks or after a burst bubble had left a damaged citizenry ready to growl. The acme of the Gilded Age came with the Bradley Martin ball held in 1897 at New York's Waldorf-Astoria, in which guests came dressed as royal courtiers, Martin himself as Louis XV. With every sumptuous detail reported by the Hearst and Pulitzer newspapers, a huge backlash made the Martins flee to England, never to return.

Novelist F. Scott Fitzgerald, looking back in 1931, described the twenties as the "most expensive orgy in history . . . the whole upper tenth living with the insouciance of grand ducs and the casualness of call girls." Such caricatures have thrived in the retrospect of social repentance. The capsules for the eighties seem to be the birthday parties held by gauche wives for financiers Saul Steinberg and John Gutfreund. The first, titled "An Evening of Seventeenth Century Old Masters in Celebration of Saul's Fiftieth Year," was held in a replica of a Flemish tavern with semiclad live models *en tableau vivant* as figures from Rubens and Van Dyck. Mrs. Gutfreund's transgression was to book two seats on the Concorde to fly the birthday cake to Paris, a mere bagatelle, one would think, next to some of the Texas savings and loan galas.

Aware of negative public reaction to the eighties, the Democratic Clinton administration trod carefully in its 1993–2000 coexistence with a level of income polarization, greed, and neo-Darwinism its leaders had lambasted under the Republicans. Over the eight Clinton years the image of White House fundraising and of giving priority to wealthy donors, bond traders, and the stock markets was modified by the administration's push for legislation helpful to low-income groups (minimum wage increases, earned income tax credits, and federal coverage of prescription drug purchases).

Even among self-congratulations for the state of the economy in the 1996 elections, Democrats pursued a careful demeanor. Clinton's treasury secretary, Robert Rubin, though a Wall Streeter, lacked the hauteur of a Mellon or a Mills. Democratic thinkers enthused about money "democratizing"—losing its erstwhile Republican, Wall Street, and Episcopal aloofness—as investment and shareholding spread. A young Democratic writer, Daniel Gross, boasted that whereas in the 1980s, GOP financiers used leveraged buyouts to take companies private, the Democratic financiers of the 1990s worked to help record numbers of companies go public and become open to ordinary investors. He pictured a new kind of boom: Arrogant Capital—the leveraged buyout crowd, hotshot hedge fund managers, CEOs overfattened on options, and rich politicians who promoted tax benefits for their own brackets—giving way to Humble Capital, the democratic (and Democratic) assemblage of folksy billionaire investor Warren Buffett, state and municipal pension funds, brokerage firms pricing Internet trades at $8.95 apiece, companies giving *all* employees options, and billionaires like George Soros, who faulted capitalism and conveyed huge sums to charity.

Humble Capital was also informal. The new wealthy, especially from the Internet or high technology, forswore the Savile Row suits favored by the 1980s nouveaux riches. Open-necked shirts and ponytails did convey lack of hierarchy. However, other wealth-holders, liberal or conservative, hid or hushed their luxury consumption out of political caution. One late-1990s glossary included "stealth wealth," born of how "the backlash against the excesses of the 1980s sensitized the rich to the outrage of the middle class, and to the danger from kidnappers, carjackers, tax collectors and Rolex bandits. Conspicuous consumption has thus gone underground, and the rich have begun to choose four-wheel-drive vehicles over Rolls-Royces and industrial-grade brown diamonds over ostentatious sparklers."

In 1997, *U.S. News & World Report,* after disclosing that Wall Streeters were making even more hay in the 1980s, added that "after being portrayed as greedy pigs during the Roaring '80s, fewer folks are, well, roaring about their pay. Indeed, firms now enforce strict policies intended to keep that kind of information under wraps. Just look at what happened to 25-year-old Philip Potter, until recently an analyst at Morgan Stanley. The day after the *New York Times* in October published his boasts about buying a 50-inch TV and a $3,500 Rolex watch, he was forced to resign."

The Millionaire Next Door, a best-selling book, spread its own camouflage netting with descriptions of how many lesser millionaires drank beer, ate middle-class cheeseburgers, and drove four-year-old Pontiacs, even though nineties data showed the purchases of luxuries rising three times faster than the total of consumer outlays. Another confusion lay in how many new fortune-holders had communications-based vocations—fashion designer, movie producer, pop singer, or publishing tycoon—or backgrounds that steered them away from the old money in Santa Barbara, Jupiter Island, or Southampton toward unpedigreed glitterati or celebrities. Ordinary Americans were used to celebrity extravagance.

Because books and articles of the nineties about playgrounds like Beverly Hills, Malibu, Aspen, or East Hampton ignored ninth-generation Beekmans and Brevoorts and emphasized the sort of celebrities—Steven Spielberg, Martha Stewart, Calvin Klein, et al.—entertaining to the masses since Gatsby and Garbo, the important distributional watershed went unappreciated. Whereas in, say, 1936, steel, coal, and railroad wealth had probably outweighed communications-based holdings by ten-to-one, by 2000 communications or TMT (technology, media, and telecommunications) wealth had jumped ahead by something on the order of twenty-to-one. This was a stealth realignment, a transformation partly disguised by its deceiving familiarity.

Conservatives, for somewhat different purposes, also sought to confuse the old cleavages between populist "have nots" and rich "haves." The political right had portrayed the wealthy liberal media and communications hierarchy as a rival elite for decades, but in the 1990s this argument took new twists, with the Internet and on-line trading being held up alongside talk radio as vehicles of populist empowerment. Generation X and younger baby boomers were offered the electronic marketplace as the ultimate democracy and populist tool for simultaneously outflanking Wall Street *and* CBS News. Business entrepreneurs, economic libertarians, and Internet pioneers became the good guys, however, bulging their wallets. Liberals or progressives who defended government and criticized market unfairness became the "elitists."

One observer summed up the message: In contrast to cruel mill owners and bankers in pinstripes, "this plutocracy was cool. They were flooding into bohemian neighborhoods like San Francisco's Mission District, chatting with the guys in the band and working on their poetry at

Starbucks . . . they were abjuring stodgy ties and suits for 24/7 casual; they were leaping on their trampolines, typing out a few last lines on the laptops before heading off to go paragliding, riding their bicycles to work, listening to Steppenwolf while they traded. And when they weren't being cool, they were being just like us, only more so," which included hard work and long hours.

For all these reasons—or so acolytes said—the new marketplace, far from being an institutional extension of existing wealth, was the ultimate economic battleground on which entrepreneurial America could defeat stagnating old family money. Market Darwinism was democracy; House speaker Newt Gingrich and author George Gilder said so. That was quite a promotion for the markets-cum-fairs that the Church had originally authorized as safety valves for sinful behavior, but much of its underlying premise was a mirage.

At the 1998 and 1999 peak of the stock market, vanity and consumption moved toward a new post-Veblen fulfillment. The portraiture by *Forbes* magazine in 1999 of the four hundred richest Americans began with an acknowledgment that "the extraordinary growth in net worth that began when the market took off in 1982 has produced opulence and ostentation on a scale that previous generations never dreamed possible," but went on to hedge that "there is still plenty of lavish consumption and display on the part of today's Overclass. Only it's kept, as much as possible, hidden from public view." Veblenesque behavior, in short, was itself being privatized.

Behind an increasingly Latin American array of gates, guards, walls, and distance, the scarcely visible displays included helicopter delivery of meals from one's favorite Manhattan, Los Angeles, or Florida restaurant. By 2000, moreover, a dozen U.S. hospitals had luxury wings, some with antiques, designer fabrics, catered meals, and prices to match.

The Hamptons, where roadside vegetable stands sell Osaka purple mustard and Romanian wax peppers, developed a particular case of arboreal chic. Crimson king maples and golden honey locusts costing tens of thousands of dollars apiece became status symbols along with weeping copper beeches, according to one local *Baedeker.* They had to look like they had been there since the first settler: "Size, rarity, and the difficulty of transportation add to the cachet of some trees, but in the end, it comes down to expense. Some trees now gracing Hamptons estates have been driven down from the Pacific Northwest in refrigerated tractor-trailers, and some have been planted with the aid of military-size Sikorsky helicopters to obviate the necessity of rutting the lawns with wheel tracks." These were hardly new psychologies.

Debt, too, left conflicting tracks. Americans were comforted by word from Washington that its perilous excesses of the eighties and early nineties—expressed in the federal budget deficit and the national debt—were being rolled back. The shrinkage, however, involved only that one aspect of debt, ignoring others from mortgage and credit card debt to international borrowing and the rapidly expanding current national account deficit.

The distinction is vital. Reduction of the federal budget deficit actually buoyed fin de siècle speculation by freeing private credit and by giving the money-supply controllers at the Federal Reserve the wherewithal to cut interest rates, as they did three times in 1998 to ease the international currency and debt crises. It also let them flood the U.S. financial system with liquidity, as they did in November and December 1999 to meet the supposed millennial Y2K threat. Both easings pumped air into the speculative bubble, monetarily but also psychologically as investors increasingly perceived the Federal Reserve as a New Era safety net and guarantor.

Alas, previous speculative buildups in the nineteenth and twentieth centuries had fed on just this availability and ballooning of *private* credit. During the Gilded Age and the 1920s the credit expansion in the new sectors of the economy had accelerated as budget deficits shrank and the U.S. national debt was paid down. Less public borrowing meant more private credit. So, too, in the 1990s, when the reduction of annual U.S. budget deficits, suggesting a new Washington commitment to thrift, abetted the surge in private debt displayed in Chart 3.12.

From here, however, we cannot move to the public's postspeculative repentance and disenchantment without examining a last, recurrent web of financial gossamer: the exaggeration of expanded middle-class participation in the boom and speculative buildup into a new "democratization" of money, investment, and finance. While there was some limited truth, this, too, had been a prop of New Era reassurances past.

4. THE DEMOCRATIZATION OF FINANCE: TWO MILLENNIA OF MYTHMAKING

Flattery of the middle class has not been confined to politicians and elected officeholders. Financiers, touts, and financial writers have joined in, especially in the expansive stages of a boom when the self-interest of marketmakers lies with participation by the thinner wallets but larger flocks of middle-class self-interest. Thus the many beckoning voices and advertisements.

To enlist middle-class pride and ambition, propagation of confidence in the 1990s promised self-fulfillment, empowerment, and the type of retirement "you had worked hard for." Themes stressed by financial advertisers of the nineties ranged from seizing your destiny, and fulfilling your dreams to a chance to trade with real-time quotes or tools hitherto reserved for professionals (the onetime big boys now being shouldered aside by you, the people).

Besides the tomes dispensing advice on becoming a millionaire in real estate or doubling your money in six months through options, others extended semipolitical congratulations. Financial journalist Joseph Nocera published *A Piece of the Action: How the Middle Class Joined the Money Class.* Daniel Gross, the youthful Democratic writer, praised his party for democratizing money, wealth, and Wall Street and empowering "the monied interests of the 1990s—the mass of individual investors."

If only history books could chuckle. The middle class has often been pulled into the "money class," but frequently to be relieved of some of its savings. All of the great speculative evanescences—seventeenth-century tulip mania, the South Sea and Mississippi bubbles, the British and American railway manias of the nineteenth century, the 1920s and the conjoined 1980s and 1990s—achieved that dubious distinction by reaching far below the top 1 percent of the population, the usual owner of 50 to 70 percent of national financial assets, and luring investment from the next 5, 10, or 20 percent.

As chapter 3 has detailed, Federal Reserve and private data showed that wealth *concentrated* between 1983 and 1997. Median households stagnated. At the annual symposium convened in 1998 in Jackson Hole, Wyoming, by the Kansas City Federal Reserve Bank, Chairman Greenspan himself admitted that the soaring Dow, instead of yielding "a rise in the share of stock and mutual fund assets owned by the bottom 90 percent of the wealth distribution," had "produced an apparent rise in the share of wealth held by the wealthiest families." In place of wealth data, he said, it might be appropriate to emphasize "trends in the dispersion of actual consumption"—dishwashers, clothes dryers, microwaves, and motor vehicles.

The numbers were stark. The top 1 percent pocketed 42 percent of the stock market gains between 1989 and 1997, while the top 10 percent of the population took 86 percent. "There was almost no trickle-down of growth to the average family," said New York University economist Edward Wolff. "Almost all the growth in household income and wealth has accrued to the richest twenty percent."

Before reviewing the participation and democratization ratios of the previous booms, let us capsule again the circumstances of the fin de siècle United States. In 1995, although statistics showed 40 percent of Americans owning stock directly or through pension funds, mutual funds, or 401(k) plans, over half had only a minor involvement, often worth less than their cars. One study by M.I.T. economist James Poterba showed that 71 percent of families individually owned no shares or held less than $2,000 worth.

Economist Wolff calculated that between 1989 and 1997 the average stockholdings of the middle quintile, adjusted for inflation, doubled from $4,000 to $8,000, but their net worth declined because of taking on debt. Estimates for 1998 and 1999 saw the dollar value of shareholdings climb higher among the 50th to 90th percentiles, but these were soon reduced by the 2000–2001 bear market.

Chart 9.1 shows the dream and the disillusionment of middle- and upper-middle-class participation in the 1990s bubble. As the mania crested, household discretionary portfolios regained and then surpassed their 1960s commitment to equities and equity mutual funds—at which point, the bubble popped.

Comparisons with the 1950s and 1960s are difficult because the earlier stock ownership data did not include those who owned stocks through pensions funds, retirement funds, or mutual funds. In his 1962 book *Wealth and Power in America,* Gabriel Kolko argued that even when the total number of shareholders increased, that made little difference to the concentration at the top, in which 1 to 2 percent of them owned 40 to 60 percent of the privately held stock. The 12.5 million shareowners of 1959, he said, actually represented a considerably smaller ratio of the total U.S. population than the 9 to 11 million shareholders of 1930. Sour memories lingered.

Obviously, by the 1990s, there were important aspects—credit cards and mutual funds were two—in which financial participation in the United States extended further down into the middle class than before. However, waves of middle-class participation are as old as speculation itself. The late 1630s Dutch tulip mania, according to one historian, overlapped a general boom in Dutch securities and large houses, and whereas these transactions were "reserved for the wealthy, tulip bulbs . . . lent

CHART 9.1 **The Dream and the Disillusionment**
The Nasdaq Bubble and Its Victims,
1996–2001

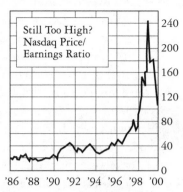

Sweat Equity
Hours of work needed for a
manufacturing employee to
purchase one S&P 500 share

1) As the stock indexes soared, pumped up
by stockbrokers and analysts

Still Too High?
Nasdaq Price/
Earnings Ratio

2) the price-to-earnings ratio of
Nasdaq stocks left sober precedent far
behind

Stocking Up

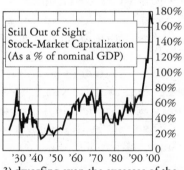

Still Out of Sight
Stock-Market Capitalization
(As a % of nominal GDP)

3) dwarfing even the excesses of the
late 1920s

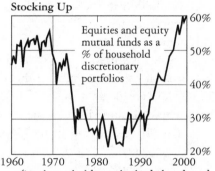

Equities and equity
mutual funds as a
% of household
discretionary
portfolios

4) as householders who had abandoned
stocks during the Silent Crash of
1966–82 were lured back in

What Did They Know . . .
And When Did They Know It?

Time Bomb
Customer Margin Debt
(billions)

5) not just by putting their money in
equities but by taking on record levels
of margin debt

In Billions

Insider Sells

Buys

6) while the insiders sold out to Mr.
and Ms. J. Q. Public, leaving the
ordinary citizens holding the bag.

Source: Separately published charts in Barron's national financial weekly, with sequential
arrangement and commentaries by the author.

themselves to widespread local speculation and became the mania of small-town dealers, tavernkeepers and horticulturists, what has aptly been described as a 'pastiche form of stockbroking'."

The Mississippi, Darien, and South Sea bubbles of the early eighteenth century marked a wider distribution of stock ownership. The secretary of state for Scotland, Sir John Dalrymple, observed that "the frenzy of the Scots nation to sign the Solemn League and Covenant never exceeded the rapidity with which they ran to subscribe to the Darien Company." England, however, kept actual shareholding records, which showed the owners of government and related stock (by 1719 including South Sea Company shares) expanding from 5,000 in 1694 to 10,000 in 1709 and 40,000 in 1719. By the time of the bubble in 1720 the number might have been 60,000, a level regained by 1752.

Shareholders in the Bank of England, many of whom would also have held government paper, rose from 1,272 in 1694 to 4,419 in 1712. Adding a half dozen other major companies—East India, Royal Africa, et al.—as well as scores of smaller local and fly-by-night ventures, the shareholder total could well have climbed from 10,000 in 1694 to 60,000 in 1719 and considerably more in 1720. While some of these would have been investors from Holland, the large majority were drawn from the mercantile, commercial, and financial classes of London. The disdainful nobility and gentry took little part—at least until the bubbling lure of the South Sea scheme.

With the population of England and Wales over five million in 1700 and six and one-half million in 1750, the shareowning population was roughly 1 percent by 1719, probably including the bulk of the London commercial middle class. In his *Wealth of England, 1496–1750,* the economic historian Sir George Clark concluded that "after the South Sea Bubble, the law and ethics of businessmen kept Stock Exchange dealings on the whole to such a level of responsibility that the habit of buying and holding Government securities and those of the greater companies spread all through the upper and middle strata."

At the height of the South Sea bubble, the farm journals of 1720 reported ambitious countrymen clogging the roads to London, and a Dutch correspondent told of more than one hundred ships moored along the Thames being for sale because owners of capital "prefer to speculate on shares than to work at their normal business." In France, the more or less contemporary "Mississippi" boom and bubble took on an even grander scale. According to one account, "around 200,000 (some put it as high as

500,000) people from Venice, Genoa, Geneva, Germany, England, Holland, and Spain, as well as vast numbers from the provinces, gravitated to the city [Paris] to play the markets."

The mid-nineteenth-century British railway mania, said one history, "brought into being a vastly enlarged share-owning class, people who had hitherto been considered 'uncommercial' (to use the contemporary description), whose investments had been in government stock. Duchesses, widows, spinsters, clergy, army officers, tailors and gentlemen now purchased railway shares. . . ." There was also a watershed inclusion of shop-keeping, mechanical, and commercial Britain, this time from beyond London. Of Scotland, the poet William Wordsworth said, "From Edinburgh to Inverness, the whole people are mad about railways. The country is an asylum of railway fanatics."

New stock exchanges sprang up in Bristol, Birmingham, Manchester, Liverpool, Glasgow, Edinburgh, and elsewhere during the 1840s, principally to trade in railway shares. Industrial Leeds, a Yorkshire railroad hub, actually had three competing stock exchanges, with three thousand stock-brokers processing half a million trades daily. Perhaps their flyers boasted of offering investment opportunities hitherto reserved for the few.

Estimates of the number of Britons who owned railway stock in the mania years go as high as 2 to 3 million out of a population (excluding Ireland) of 27 million, but the numbers were vague estimates. What could be said with certainty was that the bulk of the ownership and profit went to Britain's top 1 percent, whose share of the nation's wealth seems to have spent most of the nineteenth century in the 60 to 70 percent range.

As for the larger phenomenon of financial "democratization," a few broader perspectives are in order. The history of finance has recorded almost as many "democratizations" as swindles and bubbles. Throughout the Middle Ages, gold and silver was the money of aristocrats and the small wealthy portion of the bourgeoisie. But gradually in the fifteenth and sixteenth centuries, because of the spread of industry and commerce, use and access to money became "democratized"—the phrase of modern historians—and small coinage climbed. In England, at least, the seventeenth century brought a retrospective "democratization of business" with the collapse of royal monopolies. Karl Marx in the mid-nineteenth century theorized that the bourgeoisie had taken control of Britain through purchasing the bulk of the national debt. None of these democratizations changed human nature; nor did they have much effect in moving the financial assets concentration out of the top few percentiles.

Speculative upheavals commonly involve a second alleged "democratization": a conspicuous infusion of unpedigreed individuals often described as threatening or replacing a previous elite of aristocrats now reduced to cowering in their exclusive clubs. In this respect, much was made in the 1980s of the new blood at the Bear Stearns trading desks, in the corporate raider orbit, and in Michael Milken's Drexel Burnham junk bond orbit.* In the 1990s, technology maven George Gilder proclaimed his own vista of the "declining rich" being shown to the exits—barred from Bessemer Trust?—by "immigrants and outcasts, toughs and science wonks, nerds and boffins . . . the pony-tailed and the punk, accented from Britain and Madras, from Israel and Malaya."

As we have seen, the outsiderism of the new moneymen of early-eighteenth-century London—many were also Quakers, Huguenots, Jews, Presbyterians, and Anabaptists—made them fodder for playwrights, like the city of London's cruelly nicknamed "barrow boys" of the 1980s. The new nineteenth-century railroad money had no more couth—it was joked of Henry Gassaway Davis, the railroad millionaire turned U.S. senator from West Virginia, that being awakened one day at his Senate desk by a loud sneeze, he grabbed for the brake he had once applied as a brakeman on the Baltimore & Ohio.

During the 1920s, in turn, the new Wall Street money was thought by the Old Guard to have a distasteful disproportion of automobile arrivistes—the Fisher brothers and William Crapo Durant, with his unfortunate middle name—as well as Jews and Irish Catholics. The latter ranged from Charles Mitchell, the brash bond salesman who ran National City Bank, to stock pool operator Michael Meehan and Joseph P. Kennedy, half bootlegger and half speculator. Each wave in the end was not only absorbed with little moral or historical disquietude but left the concentration of wealth (and more recently, of trust funds and family offices) essentially undiminished.

Such changes led to talk about how wealth was "democratizing" and how ordinary citizens were "taking control" of their finances in some bold and unprecedented fashion, but in fact these needs were also recurrent. One has merely to cite the easterners or Europeans taking up land on America's nineteenth-century moving frontier, who faced their own daunting challenges. Although land speculation had been a pastime since

---

* Milken and corporate raiders like T. Boone Pickens liked to paint themselves as agents of the "democratization of capital," claiming that they were opposing the "corpocracy."

the first colonists, it was the 1820s and the 1830s that put "doing a land office business" into the national vocabulary.

So great was the volume of land speculation that U.S. economic historians have identified its excesses as the precursors of economic downturns in 1819 and (along with railroads) in 1837. In 1836, federal revenue from the sale of public lands was so large that for just that one peak year, it exceeded tariff receipts. Foreign visitors were startled and amazed. Michel Chevalier found speculation rampant in the 1830s, principally in "those subjects which chiefly occupy the Americans, that is to say, cotton, land, city and town lots, banks and railroads." Harriet Martineau found the dusty streets of Chicago swarming with speculators, while a black man dressed in scarlet and riding a snow-white horse cried land sales and storekeepers touted deals to passersby.

New small purchasers either swam financially or drowned. Up until 1820, public land could be bought on credit, often using notes from "wildcat" state banks. This was tricky because the wildcat paper currency was volatile, which made land values unstable. Federal legislation in 1820 reduced the maximum price of public land to $1.25 an acre and the minimum size of a lot to eighty acres, with this availability of farms for $100 becoming a historic milestone. According to one historian of Jacksonian America, "cheap land, virtually free at first, not only elevated the mass but imposed a limit on wealth by making labor expensive . . . a few years of high wages financed enough cheap land to yield a comfort and independence inconceivable to poor Europeans." To succeed, though, one had to navigate the rocks of volatility in both paper banknote and land values.

In the backcountry and along the frontier of that era, testimony to a relatively large "democratization of wealth" came from an expanding landowning yeomanry in the millions. In burgeoning cities like Cincinnati and Chicago, huge fortunes were made in real estate by Nicholas Longworth and a few others. However, hundreds of thousands of lesser landowners gained as the price of city real estate went up 40, 60, or 80 percent a decade—or lost, on occasion, when it plummeted. The depression from 1837 to 1843 pulled the worth of land in Chicago down to just 14 percent of its value at the peak in 1836. The impact on prices, families, vocations, and futures was devastating.

Even the small farmer—and 85 percent of Americans lived in the country—had to be a small businessman, able to judge crop prospects, land values, mortgage rates, bank practices, and the ups and downs of local banknotes, wildcat or otherwise. When William Jennings Bryan told the Democratic National Convention of 1896 that farmers were businessmen, too, he spoke a nineteenth-century truth.

Thus the fact that 48 percent of Americans, at least indirectly, held some stock in 2000 may not tell us a whole lot more than the likelihood that 30 or 40 percent of the farmers in 1840 counted a small net worth grouped around a land office receipt, maybe a few shares in a canal or turnpike, a payable or two, and a note of indebtedness to a state bank. Opportunity did exist, but the concentration of riches and power was elsewhere.

The history of the United States, in short, is full of money and wealth-related democratizations. Some were brief. A few stood the test of time and became pillars of American society. But as even Federal Reserve chairman Greenspan admitted, they have not, for more than brief periods or wave crests, notably changed the concentration of wealth in general or the concentration of financial assets in the hands of the top 1 percent.

5. SPECULATIVE COLLAPSES AND THE RHYTHM OF REFORM AND REALIGNMENT

Perhaps because the United States has been among the most speculative of nations, it also seems to be especially affected by the cultural and political rhythms attendant on speculative cycles. Neither Holland nor Britain was so much influenced over so much of history, although this must also reflect America's coming of age in the nineteenth and twentieth centuries when finance grew so much in importance and indulgence.

At any rate, the entirety of America's independent existence has overlapped the period identified by Kindleberger, Chancellor, and others as that during which global economic crises and downturns were at least partly linked to speculation. The connection began in the 1690s, and by 1819 and 1825 speculation was getting considerable blame. Indeed, Kindleberger, in his well-known dissection of manias, panics, and crashes, included within those categories virtually all of the significant U.S. downturns from independence up through 1975 (when he wrote): 1819, 1837, 1857, 1873, 1893, 1907, 1929, 1974. Few countries, in short, have had an economy so much influenced by speculation.

The people of the low countries, Flanders and Holland, felt some similar pressures in the sixteenth and seventeenth centuries when Antwerp and Amsterdam were the commercial capitals of Europe. Catholic, mid-sixteenth-century Antwerp dramatized the struggle between fear and greed, between Bible and sin, with occasional processions devoted to the *circulum vissitudinous rerum humanorum*—the fatal cycle of worldly fortune. Engravings of a procession in 1561 show the second triumphal vehicle holding Opulentia astride Fame, accompanied by the undesirable traits: Guile, Fraud, Vulpine, Usury, Betrayal, and Lust. In the rear, standing next to Idle Pleasure, the figure of False Joy was blowing her bubbles, which stood for the evanescence of human life. They have since reemerged in modern Anglo-American capitalism as symbols of speculation.

Following the collapse of Tulipmania in 1637 and the Mississippi Bubble in 1720, Protestant Dutch artists and printmakers published engravings that followed in the sinfully aware footsteps of Antwerp's Catholic processions. The subjects included Flora (of the tulips) dressed as a courtesan, cherubs or devils blowing bubbles, naked Fortuna bestowing stock, the rats of bankruptcy, and so on. Several were remade for English audiences, substituting a London background, with Exchange Alley and Bedlam instead of the Amsterdam Bourse and madhouse. The English artist William Hogarth mocked the South Sea Bubble with "Who'll Ride?"—a portrait of "The Carousel of Fools."

The subsequent, more secular and modern English approach was to revisit periods of intense speculation as "golden dreams" in which individuals—or for that matter, herds—surrendered their rationality to a vision, and then awoke disgusted at their folly and avarice. Scarcely a bubble has escaped the dream analogy, employed by so diverse a list as Alexander Pope, Edward Gibbon, and Charles Mackay in his book *Extraordinary Popular Delusions and the Madness of Crowds* (1841).

The approach in the United States, arguably, has been even more secular. In 1933, as we have seen, Franklin D. Roosevelt reached for a biblical phrase, "throwing the moneychangers out of the temple" to coalesce repentance and reform. But the general result of the American bubble-burstings, those that have led into real economic hardship, has been to generate political and financial reforms without any biblical parallels. The British, after the South Sea Bubble, tried various punishments and reforms and by the late nineteenth century concluded that legislation tended to make things worse. Reform in the United States has found more scope.

Not only was the United States the more manic of the two societies and devoid of any hereditary aristocracy to curb the moneymen, but speculation also flourished in the huge gaps or crosscurrents between federal and state regulation of money and banking.* In addition, the United States was the bigger innovator in communications—the telephone caught on much faster in the U.S. than in Britain, as did radios (and later, personal computers). When World War I made the United States the world's leading creditor as well as industrial power, primacy in technological and financial innovation again combined under one roof—and the great technology bubbles of 1925–29 and 1995–2000 were at least partial consequences.

Because speculation played a significant role in so many of the major U.S. economic crises and downturns, a follow-up often came in moods or waves of post-Crash securities or financial reform. The most stark example came with the New Deal securities, banking, and holding company laws of 1933–35. Other responses included the reforms in state incorporation processes after 1837, the pressures for a financial lender of last resort that built up after 1907, and the restrictions on securities program trading imposed after 1987.

Beyond these topical reforms however, the major economic downturns—perhaps we should say "post-bubble repentance"—often led to a wider range of upheavals dealing with taxes, the conduct of elections, and corporate behavior. Indeed, as we have seen, the Populist-Progressive years that followed the depression of 1893 and the New Deal era launched after the Crash of 1929 stand among the great reform periods of U.S. history. Each marked a major turn from the increasingly discredited politics of private interest to the beckoning causes of public interest.

In this sense, the United States has been a nation in which politics has justified the "creative destruction" theories of Joseph Schumpeter. Periodic watershed elections have led to reforms that cleared out the incompetent, reckless bankers, corporate executives, and government officials, the failed political party, and everyone else who might be blamed for the miscarriage of another economic cycle or bubble. Besides the reform

---

* No one should understate the speculative importance of federal-state differences. Prior to the Panic of 1819, land speculation had been bubbled by federal land offices accepting the cheap paper money of wildcat state banks that were in almost open disregard of federal specie requirements. In 1873, in the months leading up to the railroad debt-related panic, some railroad stocks were hurt by state Granger (partial railroad regulation) laws that exposed their flimsy structures and dubious profitability. In 1929, speculation soared beyond restraint partly because the Federal Reserve wouldn't act (until August) through its interest-rate jurisdiction while regulation of the New York Stock Exchange was a matter for New York State law, and Governor Franklin D. Roosevelt chose to leave the monkey on Washington's back.

eras that developed after the economic watersheds of 1896 and 1932, it is possible to take other national political watersheds, 1860 and 1968–72, and also find bubbles and bear markets nearby (1857, 1974). These economic connections, however, were less substantial.

For this discussion, what stands out about the precedents of the 1890s and especially the early 1930s is that they followed a level of speculation touched with myth and dream, the assurances of social Darwinism and the recurrence of what might be called conservative Market Utopianism. The utopia of American liberal or progressive politics has been the perfectibility of man or the achievability of justice and equality. The equally unachievable utopia of economic conservatism has been laissez-faire or the perfectibility and enthronement of the market.

The peril of any utopianism, of course, is how it suspends rationality and pursues a dream. In the case of millennial American conservatism, the political dream, for all its responsiveness to the tangible self-interest of rich constituencies, has been the illusion of markets as potential parliaments rather than descendants of carnivals, as rational decision-makers rather than precarious litmuses of human nature. Small wonder that when such exaggerated and irrational dreams implode speculatively, popular regret and remonstration have taken over—the Flemish and Dutch fatal cycle of worldly fortune.

During the summer of 1998 in the Hamptons, a speculative epicenter, *Business Week* described a growing edginess: " 'When will it all end?' is heard as much as 'Is that Martha Stewart?' No one actually says it out loud, but the question is always there. If the market goes, how in the world will I pay for that enormous house? The cars? The lessons? The clubs? So people bravely party on . . . it's splendid. It's exciting. It's like that other Long Island party that Gatsby threw in the '20s, waiting to end badly."

And, of course, it did. Twice before, in the Gilded Age and in the cataclysm leading to 1932, the failure of laissez-faire, a too-great reliance on markets, and the insistence of False Joy on blowing her disastrous bubbles had turned ideology and government in the United States back in the direction of democracy and reform. The cycle of worldly fortune so troubling to bygone centuries is hardly likely to worry cyber-markets that have long since forgotten their carnival past. Human nature, however, has also turned to a very different realm of politics to express its frustrations.

CHAPTER TEN

GREAT ECONOMIC POWER DECLINE AND THE POLITICS OF RESENTMENT

The disparity of fortune between the rich and the poor had reached its height, so that the city seemed to be in a dangerous condition and no other means for freeing it from disturbance seemed possible but despotic power.

—Plutarch, on the Athens of 594 B.C.

While merchants can recoup themselves by speculations, those for whom the work of their hands scarcely furnishes a livelihood are crushed beneath the burden.

—Libanius, fourth-century Roman historian

The concentration of wealth is natural and inevitable, and is periodically alleviated by violent or peaceable partial redistribution. In this view all economic history is the slow heartbeat of the social organism, a vast systole and diastole of concentrating wealth and compulsive recirculation.

—Historians Will and Ariel Durant, 1968

The wealthiest peoples of the last five hundred years have been among the most speculative—Americans, British, Dutch. We have seen how a late stage of luxuriating in finance was clearly an important element in the Dutch and then British decline.

However, history also shows a much broader vulnerability of great riches. In searching for what was common to twenty-one past civilizations that had failed, the historian Arnold J. Toynbee identified "concentrated ownership" and the inflexibility of elites in dealing with it. In short, greed, arrogance, and pride are ageless phenomena, as are the politics of wealth redistribution—Solon the Lawgiver of Athens anticipated by twenty-five hundred years the politics of Franklin D. Roosevelt.

Leading world economic powers, as we have seen, do not lose their preeminence overnight or even in one generation. From the cracks in the

Dutch Golden Age visible by the late 1600s to the polarization, speculative finance, and incipient revolution of the 1760s and 1770s was a matter of seven or eight decades. For the British the time lapse from their peak share of world manufacturing around 1865 to the Edwardian golden sunset and unmistakable economic decline of the late 1930s and 1940s took a bit longer. If we locate the absolute global peak of the United States in the late 1940s, with an onset of luxury and polarization into the eighties, nineties, and a millennial crest, the period to examine for early signs of popular reaction and political resentment runs more or less from Vietnam and the sixties.

First, however, it is time to pick up the leading economic power thread where chapter 4 left off, by recalling the popular politics of disillusionment and recrimination in the Netherlands of the 1760s, 1770s, and 1780s and then in the Britain of the first half of the twentieth century.

1. POMP AND POLARIZATION: THE GROWTH OF DUTCH AND BRITISH REVOLUTIONARY SENTIMENT

Mid to late-eighteenth-century Holland, behind its monied facade, was a land of declining industry and rising gin consumption, of impoverished agriculture and wandering gangs of beggars and banditti. Merchant bankers, speculators, and rentiers lived in splendor while much of the peasantry slid into a potato diet. Preachers and writers recalled the republic that had fought free of Spain two centuries earlier and wondered why the God of Zutphen, Flushing, and Breda had turned away. By the 1770s the decay of the Dutch Republic was symbolized, or so "economic patriots" insisted, by the gin manufacturers of Schiedam, the money changers of Amsterdam, and the indolent aristocrats of The Hague. "Antipecuniary diatribes," wrote one chronicler, "were a stock in trade of the increasing number of publicists specializing in nostalgic revivalism and extolling the virtues of ship and sail, loom and bobbin, against the depraved hoarding of filthy lucre."

Historian Simon Schama penned the best capsule:

> To its critics, Dutch society in the later eighteenth century was evolving towards a situation in which displays of conspicuous affluence by the relatively few were being indulged amid conditions of increasing impoverishment for the relatively many. The process was held to be all the more offensive for sinning against the cherished self-

image of a robust commonwealth of burgher-brothers where the distinctions of rank, fortune and status were less formally marked out than in more aristocratic societies. By seeming to become more socially stratified, the Republic was, by the same token, becoming less Dutch. The elaborately beautified Hague [the capital], where in 1777, the tax roll recorded the stabling of between 40,000 and 50,000 "pleasure" and carriage horses, was seen by the upholders of the traditional virtues of plain thrift and honest toil as a cesspool of luxury and foreign manners.

By then, middle-class frustration—the anger of shopkeepers, guildsmen, artisans, or merchants losing income and caste—was edging toward upheaval. The abandonment of industry, the growth of plutocracy and hereditary office, the rise of an attendant servant class, and the prominence of money changing and graft were all blamed for the decline in national fortune.

The Dutch "Patriot Revolt" of 1781–87, reflecting these provocations, foreshadowed the wave of revolution that then spread across Europe in the 1790s. Calvinist disdain for vanity and greed colored portions of Dutch revolutionary sentiment, as exemplified by a young theology professor, Isjbrand Van Hamelsveld. His book, *The Moral Condition of the Dutch Nation at the End of the 18th Century,* held corruption of character and the love of luxury to be hand in glove with men's abandonment of thrift and industry for the false gods of speculative finance. On the secular side, in 1785, Patriot faction delegates and journalists put together the Leiden Draft, a forerunner of several Dutch constitutions, which called for popular sovereignty and the abolition of aristocracy and purchasable offices, appending a heartfelt complaint about the rise of rentier finance at the expense of trade and industry. Although the Patriot Revolt was suppressed by Prussian and British intervention, another revolution during the 1790s, supported by France, for a decade turned the United Provinces into the Batavian Republic, partly on the French model.

More than a century later, even Britain at least flirted with revolution. During the decade leading to 1914, champagne corks were popping in Mayfair and Belgravia and the British upper classes directed two-thirds of their investment overseas while factories obsolesced in Birmingham and wages shrank in London's East End. The Dutch writers who had noted that many humbler folk of the late eighteenth century could no longer afford a meat, wheat bread, and dairy diet now had successors in British commentators struck by the significant 1900–1914 decline in working-class home consumption of meat and sugar. Both conditions stirred domestic upheaval.

For all that British tensions had many origins, an important turn had come in 1900–1901 with the Boer War fought in South Africa. The huge outlays needed for a slow British victory were a poor omen, albeit the flag-waving after several final successes enabled the Conservative government to win a large parliamentary majority in the "Khaki Election" of 1900 and keep power five more years. With prices rising sharply while employers declined to raise wages, labor restiveness grew—and it was increased by worker resentment of the judicial Taff Vale decision of 1901, which handcuffed strikes.

The Conservative government, favorable to Taff Vale, also proposed tariffs to protect British industry against growing foreign competition. Ordinary Britons, especially workers obliged to spend half their pay packets on food, feared that tariffs would only raise living costs even more. By opposing tariffs and promising to overturn Taff Vale, the Liberals won the general election of 1906 in a landslide.

This victory, in turn, set the scene for confrontation. The new government soon pushed through legislation reaffirming labor's right to strike as well as several minimum wage measures and old age pensions financed out of general revenues. The clash came slowly—some old-line Liberals were as conservative as Tories—becoming inevitable only in 1909 when Lloyd George, the feisty Welsh chancellor of the exchequer, provoked the House of Lords, which still had an effective legislative veto, into rejecting his "land tax" budget. His fiscal program included a duty on undeveloped land, a tax on coal and mineral royalties, and a supertax on incomes of over £5,000 a year, all calculated to infuriate the peers. Their angry rejection, in turn, committed the Liberal Party to curb the power of the upper house, which received narrow national support in the twin general elections of January and December 1910.

The Liberal Party, with its long-standing ties to industrial capitalism, lost some of this old backing in fighting elections over emerging, class-tinged issues. British workers, for their part, not only launched a wave of strikes between 1910 and 1914 but pushed aside moderate leaders to speak in a new idiom of distrust, socialism, and confrontation. This posture expanded the membership and aggressiveness of British labor unions so that by the early 1920s an increasingly powerful Labor Party, not the Liberal Party, would head a British coalition government.

Women, too, caught the new mood as the suffragette movement entered a violent phase that would last until war broke out in August 1914. Finally, the elections of 1910 had made (Catholic) Irish Nationalist members the swing bloc of Parliament, enabling them to force the issue of home rule for Ireland. This aroused the Conservatives, already furious over the emasculation of the Lords, to mobilize against home rule. In the spring of 1914 they incited the British army to commit to mutiny rather than impose Catholic-dominated Irish home rule on the Ulster Protestants of Northern Ireland.

These convulsions, defused only by the surprise outbreak of the world war, have been described, most famously, in George Dangerfield's book *The Strange Death of Liberal England, 1910–1914,* published in 1935. "Liberal England," was, of course, the old Victorian England of class tensions muted by golden-age prosperity and nationalism as well as by a Liberal-Conservative party system built around the nineteenth-century controversies of landowners versus industrialists and Anglicans versus nonconformists, most of which had less and less relevance. Dangerfield may have overstated his case about revolution hanging in the mid-1914 air, but there was no proving or disproving him. At least for a while the guns of August preempted all others. The great general strike scheduled for the autumn of 1914 never took place; nor, of course, did the army mutiny. Civil war in Ireland came later, by itself, with minimal spillover into England.

The new Britain of the twenties and thirties had much increased ratios of both voters and leftists. The social and economic assumptions of 1910–14 were no longer acceptable. In most industrial and working-class districts, the Liberals had been replaced by the socialist Labor Party. Its first prime minister, Ramsay McDonald, chosen in 1924, had even penned a book in 1913, *The Social Unrest,* predicting "angry class conflict" if British society continued to develop in the "plutocratic" form which he blamed on "the age of the financier" and a new type of wealth that "did not command the moral respect which tones down class hatreds, nor the intellectual respect which preserves a sense of equality even under a regime of considerable social differences, nor even the commercial respect which recognizes obligation to great wealth fairly earned." A decade earlier, Joseph Chamberlain, the Conservative, had himself suggested that the shift to finance involved an undependable economics, not genuine wealth creation.

Few upper-class Britons of 1906 would have dreamed that within two decades a Socialist prime minister would head a party of the labor unions, committed to a considerable program of income and wealth redistribution. The violent Dutch revolutions came before the age of detailed income statistics, but the arrival of the welfare state in Britain has been well-documented. Higher taxation allowed a sixfold increase in annual spending on social services between 1913 and 1938; this plus collective bargaining, wage gains, and the rising income tax increased the incomes of the working classes by 8 to 14 percent and reduced those of the middle and upper classes by 10 to 18 percent. Just before the Second World War, per capita food consumption had risen by 30–35 percent; working- and lower-middle-class Britons were clearly better off.

The greater tumble for upper-middle and upper-class Britons came during the 1939–49 period as war burdens and a growing welfare state further increased taxes, capped upper-income opportunities and consumed more of Britain's smaller overseas income and assets. One respected social historian cited findings that "the real, pre-tax income of the top 100,000 (£2,000 a year and up) fell by 64% between 1938 and 1949 and of the top half a million by 37%." High taxes further whittled the spendable portions. Well might the moderately successful sixty-five-year-old barrister of 1947, minding his shillings on £1,800 a year and in a 35–40 percent tax bracket, mourn the loss of the lifestyle, food, and servants he remembered on £800 a year in 1914. The top 1 percent's share of national wealth fell from 69 percent in 1911–13 to 60 percent in 1924–30, 55 percent in 1935–38, 50 percent in 1946–48, and just 42 percent in 1951–55.

Both the Dutch and British had the great wealth concentrations of their day, and these later outcomes both make a telling point: excessive late-stage wealth, taken like a champagne cork in the eye by the rest of the nation, tends to shape its own remedy.

2. MIDDLE AMERICAN RADICALISM IN THE UNITED STATES, 1970–2000

Frustration politics gathered in the United States during the last three decades of the twentieth century, especially during periods of reduced confidence in America's institutions and future in the world economy. For six or seven years—1972 to 1975 and 1988 to 1992—they were heated; otherwise, they were usually muted.

Until the late 1960s, by contrast, the splinter politics of the United States tended to hark back to the conflicts and issues of the New Deal coalition. One such was how Henry Wallace's 1948 Progressive campaign for the presidency recaptured the leftish naivete of the 1930s. The more powerful example was the insistence on states' rights and opposition to civil rights that guided South Carolina governor Strom Thurmond and his 1948 Dixiecrat movement and spurred Alabama governor George C. Wallace to run for president in 1964, 1968, and 1972, while in between promoting several Deep South slates of independent presidential electors in 1956 and 1960.

Gathering in the late sixties and early seventies, however, three over-lapping events—U.S. embarrassment and defeat in the Vietnam War, the trauma of the Watergate scandal, and the ability of the Organization of Petroleum Exporting Countries (OPEC) to impose a major oil price in-crease—combined to stir popular concern about the nation's seeming gov-ernmental and global incapacities. In 1974 a worn-out Richard Nixon had concurred with pundit Walter Lippmann's evaluation that his historical role had been "to liquidate, defuse, deflate the exaggerations of the ro-mantic period of American imperialism and American inflation. Inflation of promises, inflation of hopes, the Great Society, American supremacy—all that had to be deflated because it was all beyond our power. . . ."

Politically, however, Nixon shaped a mobilization of Middle American frustration over the events of the sixties. That coalition was renewed and extended between 1978 and 1980 around a kindred trio of issues—the treaties returning the Panama Canal, the second OPEC oil price hike in 1979, and the Iranian seizure of the U.S. embassy in Tehran. Once again the populace sensed the economic weakening of the American prospect.

Still another surge of frustration politics gathered in the late eighties and crested in the early 1990s. Some of its shapers were the 1987 stock market crash, the attention in 1988 and 1989 to books contending that the United States was in a decline like Britain's a century earlier and the growing national fear of Japanese economic rivalry. Others included the 1990 debate over the eighties as a "decade of greed," and the 1991–92 disquiet over high deficits and the economy—1990 had ushered in America's first white-collar recession—and the weak aspects of the Gulf War. These were the failure to dislodge Iraqi leader Saddam Hussein and the U.S. budget difficulties that required Washington to pass the hat for allied financial support of U.S. military operations.

Although the discontents of the early seventies, 1978–80, and the early nineties are not usually strung together, it makes sense to do so. They have a continuity. Each yielded an identifiable, though by no means similar, radicalization and frustration affecting a significant portion of the U.S. electorate: the so-called Middle American Radicals (MARs) of the 1970s, the vital working-class and lower-middle-class increment of the Reagan coalition of 1980, and the worried Perot, Buchanan, and Clinton electorates of 1990–92. More than economics was involved, but each of these periods did overlap one or more recessions.

The next subsection of this chapter will examine specific issues—trade and globalization, corporate practices and CEO salaries, the domination of politics by big money, anger at the rich and their consumption, the Federal Reserve Board, and the international financial agencies as well as Wall Street, speculation, and insider practices—that voters and ideological activists have taken up in response to uncertain economic horizons. The quarter-century thread of "middle American radical" politics, however, provides a starting framework. In contrast to Holland and Britain, the United States had an especially prominent populist heritage; its stirrings have been a frequent electoral litmus.

Political scientist Donald Warren in his 1976 book, *The Radical Center: Middle Americans and the Politics of Alienation,* used polling data to measure the anger and volatility that had swept through non-elite Americans back to the 1968 election. The George Wallace phenomenon, half about the familiar politics of race, a Southern persistence, was almost as much about an emerging politics of economic and cultural disappointment, visible in surprising support for Wallace in the North and even portions of the rural West. Warren estimated that there were some 25 million of these voters, alienated from government, unions, and corporations alike. He named them "Middle American Radicals."

He had set out an important amplification in a 1973 article:

> For many white Americans, the rejection of the blacks and poor is only part of a larger rejection of government and the rich. Preliminary data from a national cross-section probability sampling of 1690 white Americans indicate that 30 percent of the population thought that the blacks had too much political power; 63 percent said that about the rich. Approximately 30 percent said that poor blacks were getting more than their fair share of government aid; 56 percent said the same thing about the rich. Eighteen percent said that blacks have a better chance than whites to get fair treatment from the courts, while 42 percent said that about the rich. In other words, hostility towards the rich is extensive; it may equal or even exceed, hostility toward blacks.

Late in 1974, when Watergate was fresh in the U.S. psyche and unemployment was reaching post-Depression highs, Patrick Caddell—George McGovern's pollster in 1972 and Jimmy Carter's from 1976 to 1980—employed a survey using two-and-one-half-hour interviews to surface political beliefs and pathologies missed by more superficial inquiries. In his 1972 election samplings, 18 percent of Americans had been willing to back Wallace for president. By late 1974 that had doubled to 35 percent—18 percent wanting actually to elect him, 17 percent inclined to a protest vote. Voter ideology was churning. Many simultaneously favored radical socialistic economic solutions while taking a hard-line position on cultural issues.

"The people smack in the middle—the people who are the least ideological—are the most volatile," Caddell argued. "Forty-one percent thought that the American way of life is disappearing so fast that we may have to use force to save it." "The middle class," he said, "is coming unhinged. 'Center extremism' is correct as a description."

These views quieted by 1976, remaining subdued until 1978, when inflation was rising, OPEC was on the cusp of another oil price increase, and the Carter administration had reopened Vietnam-era psychological wounds over U.S. global retreat through a pair of treaties to convey the Panama Canal to Panama. The measures' strong support by U.S. banks and corporations seeking Panamanian and Latin American goodwill for their regional operations became a side issue. One activist later recalled the charges that certain large banks were holding IOUs that could not be redeemed unless canal revenues became available to Panama. Conservative populist leader Richard Viguerie called the treaties "a bail-out of David Rockefeller" and the Chase Manhattan Bank.

Liberals and corporation executives unacquainted with the dynamics of Middle American Radicalism found this opposition quaint and crude. However, as one historian of U.S. conservatism later noted, the New Right targeted treaty backers in 1978 and 1980. Of the 68 senators who had voted for ratification, 20 were denied renomination or reelection in those two years.

By 1980 the canal fight, the second OPEC oil price hike, surging inflation, and the Iran hostage crisis had heightened a climate that Walter Dean Burnham, a leading scholar of U.S. political realignments, put in a context involving the end of the 1945–65 "golden age," a crisis of the economy, empire, culture, and state, and a politics of a "middle class under stress." The immediate result was the election of Ronald Reagan by a

coalition much like Richard Nixon's of 1972: most of the usual GOP electorate with a notable increment of white working-class, Northern ethnic,
and Southern religious fundamentalist voters.

What Burnham found unnerving about the Reagan coalition—his
thesis that the early-stage crisis of the American "empire" and regime was
producing a "reactionary revitalization movement"—rested on multiple
foundations. Beyond the broad conservative revivalism, the United States
of the sixties and seventies, like London in the 1890s and Weimar
Germany in the 1920s, had a prominent and affluent intelligentsia deplored by many ordinary folk and regarded by some as a symptom of national decay. In the Britain of the 1890s, this mood, together with concern
about the industrial threats of the United States and Germany, added to
the John Bull nationalism and Boer War imperialism promulgated by the
Conservatives, giving them their crowning election victory in 1900.

Indeed, the Republicans of the Nixon and Reagan eras, deploring radicals, the avant-garde, and troublesome minorities (blacks) while praising
the patriotism of Merle Haggard's ballad "Okie from Muskogee" and defending overseas military involvement, were more than a little like the
British Conservative governments of the late Victorian years. These
Conservatives had deplored Bloody Sunday, Fabians, Oscar Wilde, the
Decadence movement, and troublesome minorities (Irish) while praising
Rudyard Kipling and defending overseas military involvement. The stage
of British disillusionment represented by economic radicalization, as we
have seen, came later.

The Dutch of the 1780s, as previously noted, had their own "reactionary
revitalization" in the Patriot Movement, which called for overthrowing
both aristocrats and plutocrats, ending corruption, and promoting hard
work and industry over finance. Like Donald Warren's Middle American
Radicals of the 1970s, the angry Dutch middle class distrusted both the
rich and the unruly poor.

In the United States of the Reagan era, the frustration so visible in
1980 had cooled by the 1984 election, which Reagan won with 59 percent of the vote, closely replicating the Nixon coalition of 1972 (61 percent). In 1986, however, a sharp regional downturn hit the agricultural
and energy states, and the Republicans lost the Senate they had controlled
since 1980. Frustration politics began regrouping after October 1987
when the stock market took its huge one-day drop. Through the summer
of 1988 it looked like the Republican nominee, George Bush, might lose
the November presidential race.

Luckily for Bush, the Democratic nominee was Massachusetts governor Michael Dukakis, a humorless Harvard intellectual disdainful of the Middle American Radical stream who by October was himself under fierce Republican cultural attack. Democratic strategists complained that, "They're running a class war against us, saying we're a bunch of Cambridge-Brookline eccentric literature professors. We've got to fight back and say they're the party of privilege, the party of the rich folks." Dukakis made some populist remarks in the final days, which helped him, but it was too late. Bush's campaign manager, Lee Atwater, as we have seen, privately observed that Dukakis had missed the boat by failing, until the end, to develop the class issue and divide the haves and have-nots.

In the meantime the stock market crash had sown doubts about the strength of the U.S. economy, and these were reinforced in 1988 by analyses such as Yale historian Paul Kennedy's *The Rise and Decline of the Great Powers,* suggesting that the United States might be going the way of Britain. Whereas in 1981, Ronald Reagan had proclaimed "morning again in America," in 1988, Senate Republican leader Robert Dole, Bush's nomination rival, called it "high noon." The economic showdown, many thought, would come with Japan, pictured as overtaking the United States in both technology and the valuation of its stock market.

The reason for citizen concern about apparent global retreat was less interest in foreign policy than in standards of living. Because the global supremacy ushered in by World War II brought the U.S. golden age, a major decline could further erode what already seemed threatened. Polls taken for the various foreign policy organizations in the seventies and eighties made the point well enough. When asked what should be the priority of U.S. foreign policy, the public answered quite simply: jobs. Good jobs in the United States.

Periods of Middle American Radicalism invariably touched this nerve. In 1990, with sensitivity to decline running high even before the recession, Congress considered some vehicles of economic nationalism: proposals to tighten laws regulating foreign takeovers of U.S. companies, to target the lobbying activities and alleged tax evasion of foreign corporations in the United States, and to attach new "Buy American" requirements to U.S. foreign aid and promote exports in the face of German and Japanese advances. The publication in June 1990 of *The Politics of Rich and Poor* marshaled statistics indicting the eighties as a decade of greed and wealth concentration. Taking that argument into the midterm election, Democrats blocked the Republicans' hoped-for gains. Autumn's preelection debate turned to new taxes, Bush's preoccupation with capital gains rate cuts, and alleged favoritism to the rich; and by late October reports had the GOP in "free fall." Some party identification polling reported a ten-point Republican drop—until the Republicans managed to partially refocus the public on the confrontation developing in the Persian Gulf.

When the recession seemed to worsen in 1991, even as official score-keepers judged it as being over, public anger wiped away President Bush's huge gains from the seemingly successful Gulf War. By the end of 1991 the Democrats had won a surprise victory in a special Pennsylvania U.S. Senate election conducted on economic frustration issues, and right-wing populist and extremist David Duke had carried a statewide nomination contest in economically dissatisfied Louisiana. The president in turn had a combative populist Republican opponent already stumping in the snows of New Hampshire, where the first 1992 presidential primary was just two months away.

By several yardsticks the public was angrier than in 1973–74 or during the hostage crisis. Whereas back in 1964 just 29 percent had told poll-takers that government was run for the benefit of a few big interests, that had climbed to 66 percent after Watergate and reached 70 percent in 1980 after popular disillusionment with Jimmy Carter. By 1992 fully 80 percent said government favored the rich and powerful. Unprecedented numbers also believed "quite a few" of the people running the government were crooked. Just 24 percent had said so in 1958, 45 percent in 1976, and 49 percent in 1980. In 1992, for the first time, a 65 percent majority agreed. Political analyst William Schneider combined these testiness measurements with three others to create what he called "P.O. Index." The conclusion, he said, was unmistakable: postwar Americans had never been so angry.

Middle American Radicalism was in full force, and by the time the November general election rolled around, three contenders had thrust taps into it: Bush's Republican nomination challenger Patrick Buchanan, the ultimate Democratic winner, Bill Clinton, and independent Ross Perot. The uncertainty of four years earlier was gone. After the 1988 election, Vincent Breglio, director of the Republican National Committee's polling, had admitted that even Dukakis's belated comments had made them nervous: "Going into the last week of the campaign, we clearly saw the populist message of Dukakis was having an effect. It was cutting." On the Democratic side, a preelection poll in 1988 by Stanley Greenberg and Celinda Lake found 70 percent of Reagan Democrats and other swing voters giving their highest priority to the populist agenda Dukakis had not wanted to embrace: making sure "the wealthy and big corporations pay their fair share of taxes."

"I want a revolution," Patrick Buchanan shouted in 1992 New Hampshire, "where the working class and the middle class take back control of the Republican Party." Earlier he had taken aim at George Bush by saying, in the matter of minority preferences, that it was "the sons of Middle America," in the factories and offices, who were being betrayed by "the Exeter-Yale GOP club . . . the scions of Yale and Harvard . . . the Walker's Point GOP." He even likened his supporters to the New England Minutemen who had gathered during the Revolution to fight the forces of George III.

Ross Perot, the Texas billionaire who entered the 1992 presidential race, withdrew, and then reentered before getting his 19 percent, was given to dismissing Bush and Secretary of State James Baker III as "country-clubbers" and "preppies." He thought the United States had to reverse its decline through fiscal frugality and economic nationalism. "The American people can't afford it themselves," Perot volunteered, "so I'm buying the country back for them."

Of Bill Clinton's Democratic 1992 primary opponents, Massachusetts senator Paul Tsongas talked of competitiveness, exaggerating that "the Cold War is over—Germany and Japan won." Former California governor Jerry Brown blistered the elite, charging that, "The ruling class has lost touch with the American people. They have lost touch because they swim in a world of privilege, power and wealth." Clinton himself was said to have become furious after reading a *New York Times* analysis that the top 1 percent had received over half of the additional income generated in the United States between 1977 and 1989. In his July 15 acceptance speech at the Democratic convention, he said, "In the name of all the people who do the work, pay the taxes, raise the kids and play by the rules—the hard-working Americans who make up our forgotten middle class—I accept your nomination for the presidency of the United States of America. I am a product of the middle class. And when I am president you will be forgotten no more."

The race between Clinton, Perot, and Bush sparked a five-point jump in the percentage of eligible-age Americans voting—up to 55 percent in 1992 from a meager 50 percent in 1988. At least temporarily, this suspended the argument that nonvoters had become the nation's most important party as turnout kept sinking among low and middle-income

Americans whose previous inclinations, at least, had been Democratic. But in 1996, when Perot had become old hat, turnout dropped back to 50 percent.

Clinton's first years in office seemed to worsen the disillusionment. He retracted his middle-income tax-cut promise and, by 1994, the scandals touching the White House and his personal life together with ongoing weakness in the economy—median household income was stagnant—made him an albatross for Democrats in the midterm elections. "Washington" itself by this point had become a focus of public contempt, with trust in the capital gang dropping to record (19 percent) lows. Some 57 percent told pollsters that "lobbyists and special interests" controlled Washington, not the president or Congress. In 1993, polling for the Boston-based Americans Talk Issues Foundation reported the citizenry so contemptuous of Congress that one-third of those sampled thought the offices might as well be auctioned to the highest bidders. Half thought Congress could be chosen randomly from a list of eligible voters. The emergence of rightwing "militias" in states from Michigan to Montana was still another sign of popular frustration.

This time it was Republican congressional candidates who tapped popular anger. The GOP captured both houses of Congress for the first time in forty years, although voters soon lost some confidence in them, which gave Clinton a convenient punching bag to win reelection two years later.

Middle American Radicalism had one more late-twentieth-century moment in the sun. As populist insurgent Buchanan beat the eventual nominee, Senator Robert Dole, in the 1996 Republican primary in New Hampshire, one issue particularly caught hold—Buchanan's appeal to the middle class with criticism of corporate chieftains whose pay had risen to two hundred times that of workers. Even Dole started speaking about "greedy CEOs" and Clinton called together a hundred of them to discuss the matter. But as the left-leaning *Mother Jones* magazine said a half year later, "after Pat Buchanan shocked the political establishment by prying open the Pandora's box of slow growth, wage stagnation, globalization, and increasing inequality, the lid is back on." After New Hampshire, Buchanan faded, and although Dole and some Republicans made desultory comments about how median family income had stagnated in 1993–94 while male earnings had continued to fall, their counterpoint hardly mattered. By mid-1996 the economy in general and the stock market in particular were visibly on the rise.

This time, it was no pleasing but routine cyclical peak as in 1976–77 and 1984–86. By 1997 and 1998 the economy had caught strong tail-winds: watershed technological innovation, tandem productivity gains, strong growth, and supportive consumer confidence. Many people started to believe in prospects they had scarcely credited since the late sixties and seventies (and perhaps for a short period after the 1980 election): a new economic era and rekindling prosperity that might last, an enduring American renewal. That mood, as we have seen, also came to include de-ification of technology, secular worship of the Federal Reserve, and confidence in the New Era sustainability of the soaring stock market.

In the seventies and eighties, each time Middle American Radicals had demobilized as economic horizons brightened, they returned, glummer and angrier, when the business cycle turned down again. The late nineties struck a new chord, defusing old explosives. The two more conservative populists, Perot and Buchanan, had become tired figures as economic recovery rolled through 1996 into 1998 and then even into 2000. Millennialism, the belief in a coming period of joy and prosperity, took over again in a nation with an old millennialist tendency.

After falling to 8 percent of the national vote after a disinterested campaign in 1996, Perot had even less interest in running again. Buchanan's attempt to get the Reform nomination against Perot's wishes succeeded, but the onetime New Hampshire winner, who committed himself to religious and cultural issues, wound up with a worthless nomination and an inconsequential candidacy. In the end he barely attacked George W. Bush, to whom the Religious Right flocked due to the candidate's campaign closeness to icons like religious broadcaster Pat Robertson and Bob Jones University. As a result, for the first time in at least fifty years, the weight of serious third-party politics failed on the right and emerged on the left through the presidential campaign of Ralph Nader and the Green Party.

Nader had run in 1996, but he had not been on a number of state ballots and had campaigned lackadaisically. In 2000, by contrast, he fought hard, drumming on corrupt election finance, a two-party system controlled by corporations, globalization, corporate welfare, outsourcing of production to China and Mexico, the financial bailouts orchestrated by the treasury, the Federal Reserve Board, and the IMF—discontents also shared by center and right-leaning Middle American Radicals. To these he added emphases on the environment and civil rights, issues usually skipped by right and even centrist populists. Hoping for 5 percent of the total vote, Nader got slightly under 3 percent. He probably would have made his 5 percent save for the extreme tightness of the Republican-Democratic race.

Postelection national polls showed 6, 7, and even 8 percent of the electorate saying they had supported Nader, a postelection behavior usually reflective of underlying sympathies.

Levels of dissatisfaction like those seen in the United States between 1968 and 1994 rarely dissolve in anything less than a truly new economic and political era. The extent to which large numbers of Americans thought one was materializing in 1997, 1998, and 1999 helps explain why the intensity of minor-party dissatisfaction collapsed in its previous framework and then reemerged in autumn 2000 on the left. Voters of the Religious Right liked the born-again Bush; November's new minor-party dissidence—the Nader vote—took shape around the distaste of a considerable minority of left-progressive voters for a "New Democratic" Clinton-Gore administration that appeared caught up in fundraising and corporate, technological, and financial triumphalism.

Despite the onset of disarray in the stock market, much of this triumphalism and new era conviction remained operative in November 2000. National confidence did not dip significantly until the election had turned into a persisting stalemate, and the first hints of a recession in the real economy emerged in late November and December. Election Day's reformist message was limited to the McCain, Bradley, and Nader attack on money politics.

What the election of 2000 did was to rearrange political and economic responsibility just as a period of renewed stress was about to unfold. The victory of George W. Bush, secured by a U.S. Supreme Court ruling and in the face of a Democratic popular vote margin of 500,000, followed a campaign in which he had substantial support from the erstwhile populist right. Bare-bones victory, then, empowered a Republican coalition unusually vulnerable to the sort of major economic downturn that might rekindle perceptions in the Middle American Radical mold. By contrast, the Democrats, who likely would have won the 2000 presidential election without Nader in the race, were shorn of institutional responsibility—until they regained hairbreadth control of the Senate in May 2001—and placed under pressure to pick up a number of Nader's populist themes. Then the attack on the World Trade Center created a new set of fears and a new patriotic context.

The shape of a new radicalism was critical. The lines between Republican and Democratic populists had been fluid in the 1890s and again between Republican and Democratic progressives in the collaboration-minded 1920s and 1930s. But whether a similar politics could gestate in the early twenty-first century depended on something new: a connection between decline, polarization, and unfairness.

3. THE ISSUES OF U.S. ECONOMIC DECLINE

Louis Hartz, the historian best known for his discourse on the liberal tradition in America, pointedly wondered back in the middle of the twentieth century what would become of American exceptionalism—and the optimism of the electorate—if the United States was forced to rejoin world history after a 150-year vacation from it. In the seventies, eighties, and early nineties, many scholars and pundits were convinced that this Hartzian hour was at hand.

Attention to decline, whether in Europe or the United States, has had its own rhythm. Each nation's early worriers, reacting to decline from an absolute zenith in share of world trade or manufacturing, have been premature, in practical terms, by some four or five decades. Yet their analyses are a useful jumping-off point. The stage at which considerable popular concern has developed—in the 1890s, for Britain, in the 1980s for the U.S.—has usually involved a stalling of previous advances for the working class while the upper classes, as we have seen, enjoy a glittering cosmopolitan zenith: Britain in 1900–1914, the United States of the 1980s, 1990s, and millennium.

Indeed, the wave of books assessing decline in Holland and Britain published in Europe and North America during the 1980s and 1990s suggests that full, open, and informed retrospect may even require the passage of fifty (or 150) years. Even then, the disagreement among scholars can be fierce. Volumes published during a leading power's sunset have to be indirect or oblique, like Paul Kennedy's *The Rise and Decline of the Great Powers,* or limited to one evident dimension, like the English books of the 1890s sounding alarm bells about the American or German economic threats.

Nevertheless, for U.S. purposes, the record of the three decades between 1970 and 2000 was replete with American moods, circumstances, and debates familiar from the later trajectory of two previous leading world economic powers. The sullenness of the workforce, especially men. The concern with globalization and hitherto domestic investment flowing overseas. The growing awareness of the rich and conspicuous consumption, and the hints of plutocracy. Other parallels include anger at the corruption of officeholders and anxiousness to democratize politics and increase popular electoral participation as well as a finger-pointing at financiers and incipient attention to increasing taxes on the rich to pay for popular social programs, pensions, health insurance, and the like.

The Dutch and British precedents that follow can be put alongside the short chronology of U.S. popular frustration and off-and-on Middle American Radicalism. And we can begin with the broadest frustration: the desire for institutional, moral, and economic revitalization.

In either a reactionary, democratic, or some mixed form of government, "revitalization" has been a common agenda in leading economic powers once the public starts to identify national decline or the corruption of formerly vital political institutions. In ancient Greece and Rome, Plato and Plutarch wrote of a need to escape plutocracy.

The Dutch revolutions of the 1780s and 1790s hummed with talk of "the people" and demand for universal male suffrage, although there were also vague hopes of somehow restoring the greatness of the long-ago Dutch nation that had broken free of Spain. The revolution of the 1790s broadened electoral participation. Catholics were given the vote, and the middle class dominated the membership of the legislature of the new "Batavian Republic." Hereditary and multiple offices were banned, striking at venality. However, as the Napoleonic Wars and their costs became ever more of a burden the first decade of the nineteenth century, the republic flagged and Napoleon established his brother as king of Holland.

In Britain, the democracy and enfranchisement debates were part of a reform tide that swept over the reluctant British upper classes in the first quarter of the twentieth century. Although the Reform Act of 1884 had enfranchised the majority of adult male Britons, the Representation of the People Act of 1918 established universal adult male suffrage and gave the vote to women over age thirty. This expansion of the electorate from 7 million in 1910 to 20.5 million in 1922, in turn, cemented the two-decade realignment of power between the old Liberal and new Labor parties and the accelerating rise of the welfare state. The House of Lords lost its effective veto in 1911, Ireland got the equivalent of Home Rule in 1922, and women of legal age but under thirty received the vote in 1928.

The United States of the eighties and nineties bred similar concerns about declining voter turnout, the Washington entrenchment of special interests, and the monied corruption of the election process. By 2000 these interwoven predicaments were fusing into a major topic of books, articles, broadcasts, and national discussions, as we have seen in chapter 8. In the major early 2001 debate over the corruption of election finance, reform passed the Senate but was narrowly defeated in the House.

Expansion of the shrinking U.S. electorate, in turn, was more a banner of reformers than popular opinion. The percentage of eligible Americans actually voting had declined from 65% in 1960 to 63% in 1964, 62% in 1968, 57% in 1972, 55% in 1976, 54% in 1980, 55% in 1984, 50% in 1988, 55% in 1992, 50% in 1996, and 49% in 2000. Easier registration seemed to make little difference. Walter Dean Burnham, describing the growing ranks of absentees as the "party of the non-voters," noted that most came from less prosperous, previously Democratic ranks. He hypothesized that it might take a European-style Social Democratic Party to lure them back.

Fordham University professor Thomas DeLuca explained how this lower-income, nonvoting pattern underpinned the rising Index of Political Inequality. Citing Census Bureau surveys showing that 38.7 percent of the bottom fifth had voted in the 1996 presidential election versus 72.6 percent of the top fifth, he posited that "the lower the turnout, the greater the class and education gap in voting." The less responsive the government—up to a point—the more the less educated and less affluent stopped voting.

Still others contended that amid the U.S. culture of success, economic disheartenment and individual joblessness worked to *decrease* rather than *increase* the likelihood of those affected deciding to vote. The heart of the decline—a lower share of eligible men casting ballots in 1996 than at any time since the Civil War—paralleled the downturn in the percentage of men actively seeking work, which dropped from 87 percent in 1948 to 75 percent in 1996. The brief uptick in voting participation, especially among males, brought by Perot's candidacy of 1992 with its Middle American Radical overtones, seemed the exception that proved the glum and disinterested rule.

Amid the new-era Millennialism of 2000, liberal-labor theorists Joel Rogers and Ruy Texiera, boldly identified "the forgotten majority" of white working-class voters—the non-college-graduate whites (about 55 percent of the electorate)—as the key to early-twenty-first-century U.S. politics. The males of these voting streams, having pulled away from the center-left during the cultural and nationalist contests beginning in 1968, had become frequent participants in the conservative coalition. Economics, however, could move them once again—and with them their nonvoting brothers, cousins, and aunts.

Inheritance is another issue that heats up as reaction against economic polarization sets in. The ability of the rich to pass along their estates relatively intact was sharply curtailed in both revolutionary Holland and the aroused British politics of the first half of the twentieth century. In Holland, emphasis on the *successie* (death duty) was increased during the revolution of the 1790s, in part to make up for revenues lost by reductions in regressive taxes. In Britain, the one Liberal government of the 1890s began graduated duties on large estates, which rose for the next half century, obliging manors, great houses, and lands to be sold in waves at the beginning of the twenties (after death duties climbed to 40 percent on estates worth over £2 million in 1919) and then after 1945 (with the over-90-percent peak in top death-duty rates). These postwar burdens produced the stories of dukes and earls opening their castles to admissions-paying tourists in order to be able to keep them.

The United States in turn entered the new century with the Republican Party having begun the elimination of federal estate and gift taxes in order to let the great wealth accumulations of the late twentieth century pass minimally hindered to the next generation. However, the complicated phase-ins of the legislation allowed the changes to be revisited.

Which brings us to another common thread: reversal of a regressive tax structure. In the Holland of late eighteenth century and first decade of the nineteenth, the revolutionary thrust was to shift the burden away from levies on staples like fish, butter, grits, oil, potatoes, candles, linen, and fuel that fell on the ordinary Hollander. As Professor Schama explains, "A great deal of Patriot anger had been expended at the continuous style of patrician ostentation while more frugal burghers were forced to pay inflated prices for items of necessity." More than a brief capsule of the tortuous emergence of a new tax system in Holland between 1798 and 1805 would be excessive, but in short, reliance was put on a land and property tax, a rents tax, a turnover tax on commercial, legal, financial, and official transactions (related to the value of the transaction), death duties, and levies on servants, horses, and pleasure coaches.

Isaac Gogel, the Patriot journalist who rose to finance minister and was the guiding hand of the revised tax structure, left comments in an autobiography on principles of fairness, the attempted evasions of the rich, and his own belief that "rich men, and above all proprietors of tenanted estates and holders of stock who practice no profession than what the price of their money can raise, are incomparably less worthy citizens than a trading or working man . . . especially when the [large] proprietor enjoys that income in the great towns."

The records of British parliamentary debate for the four decades after

1909 illustrated the slow prevalence of similar viewpoints, especially under Labor governments. In 1909 the chancellor of the exchequer proposed to raise the maximum income tax to 8 percent on the largest unearned incomes. The rate on the several thousand largest incomes climbed to 40 percent in World War I, dropped in the 1920s, then rose again to some 60 percent in the late thirties. By the late 1940s the highest British combined income and surtax brackets took some 95 percent of incomes over £20,000. A successful upper-middle-class professional, whose taxes would have been light in 1914, by 1938 was paying 35 to 40 percent of income and by 1955, roughly a half. On average the country's hundred thousand wealthiest households lost large sums—a redistribution amounting to roughly 5 percent of the national income—so that poorer Britons could have better education, health, social services, and old-age pensions.

Tax policy in the United States of the eighties and nineties, mostly dominated by politicians who spoke for lowered rates on $1 million and $100 million incomes, may be another conservative high-water mark. In 1990 even *Fortune* magazine had noted public support for higher taxes on the rich. And by the end of the decade, as congressional Republicans were mobilizing to cut the 39.6 percent rate on upper incomes—nonmillionaire incomes actually paid the highest effective rates, as chapter 5 detailed—a surprising selection of Americans, albeit not in Congress, called for the United States to adopt some version of the wealth tax that had been used off and on in twentieth-century France, Germany, and Italy.

Revealingly, this urging came principally among persons who had studied the subject enough to comprehend both the great fortunes and the inequality ratios: former U.S. secretary of labor Robert Reich; wealth and incomes scholar Edward Wolff; Vance Packard, author of *The Ultra Rich;* shared-capitalism advocate Jeff Gates, author of *Democracy at Risk,* and others. The most prominent billionaire supporter, real estate magnate Donald Trump, in 1999 suggested a onetime levy of 14.25 percent on net worths of $10 million or more, enough to pay off the national debt.

Sustenance of the welfare state only became an issue in the twentieth century, which makes previous comparison difficult. Part of the demand for higher taxes in the Britain of 1910–14 was to fund social assistance, pensions, and health insurance. In the Holland of the 1790s, pensions tended to be for upper-income officeholders, a very different controversy, but some social outlays were at stake. The twentieth-century British example, by far the more important, can be summed up as a Labor Party–led use of welfare mechanisms to achieve the income redistribution previously blocked by upper-class rejection of wage increases, labor organizations, strikes and higher income, estate, and royalties taxes.

A similar conflict gathered in the United States of the 1980s and 1990s over how to fund—or not fund—the future costs of expensive support programs like Social Security and Medicare. The first resort, keynoted by a bipartisan commission in 1984, had been to escalate the regressive FICA (Social Security and Medicare) taxes that fell on low-income and middle-class households but left the top several percentiles of taxpayers virtually unscathed. As the twenty-first century opened, the assumption was that an increasingly nonwhite (Hispanic, black, and Asian) young workforce of the 2010s, 2020s, and 2030s would balk at paying FICA taxes to support the pensions and medical expenses of largely white retirees. Groups representing corporate and financial interests generally favored reducing benefits and costs. Labor and lower-income groups, however, favored removing the income ceilings on FICA taxation and imposing a much larger share of the FICA burden on the rich, a course of action more in keeping with the Dutch and British transformations.

Despite the resentments of finance writ large in the speeches of Dutch Patriot movement leaders or British Laborites, little effort was made to dismantle their nations' finance or banking per se. Restoration of sacrificed or outdated industry was impossible, although some attempts were made in Britain through nationalization, subsidies, and regional support programs. Similarly, the Dutch revolutionaries committed themselves to upholding and servicing the Dutch debt, as did British Labor when its turn came. Financial services were too important to cripple.

What did weigh on the financial sector, especially in Britain, was the slow demise of hitherto helpful biases. One that wavered was official willingness to maintain a strong currency even when the process was expensive, vain, and damaging to manufacturing. A second lessened commitment was to budget curbs and suppression of inflation. A third retreat came in slackening opposition to tariffs, capital restrictions, and other interferences with free economic movement. The fourth to shrink, of course, was support for upper-class enjoyment of the fruits of finance through a tax system friendly to luxury, capital assets, and estates. By 1796 in Holland and 1946 in England it is fair to say that many stockbrokers and financiers were no longer enjoying the stables, estates, and yachts that had provoked excoriation by the Dutch Patriot press in 1780 and George Bernard Shaw in 1908.

Two economic institutions not arousing Britons in the early 1900s but an obvious bone of U.S. contention a century later were corporations—their tax breaks and subsidies, employee mass firings, and the sky-high compensation of corporate leaders—and the unelected Federal Reserve Board with its unprecedented influence over the U.S. economy. In late 2001 and early 2002, some observers suggested that the misbehavior and collapse of Enron would become a political and economic symbol.

Both eighteenth-century Holland and early-twentieth-century Britain did offer a preview of sorts—a popular sense of vague betrayal over how Dutch and British investors had sent their money to foreign shores while jobs and opportunity shrank at home. In the United States, resentment of large multinational corporations for moving production, jobs, and institutional loyalty out of the United States flared up in December 1999. Street demonstrations at that year's annual meeting of the World Trade Organization in Seattle sparked a mobilization of activists and a new sense of left-leaning opportunity that carried over into enthusiasm for Ralph Nader's 2000 presidential candidacy.

Indignation at the compensation and practices of corporate chief executives, briefly incendiary in New Hampshire's 1996 presidential primary, kept its edge as the ratio of CEO-to-worker pay rose ever higher—to 419:1 in 1999 and 460:1 in 2000. It started to decline in 2001, although even the stock market crash applied no great restraint. As the data had heated in the nineties, foes profiled the modern American CEO as a cross between the ancient pharaohs and Louis XIV. Print critics noted J. P. Morgan's stricture that chief executives of his companies should be paid no more than twenty times the lowest worker's pay; academicians pointed out that Plato had said that a five-to-one ratio was about right. Graef Crystal, a leading U.S. compensation consultant, ended his book *In Search of Excess* with the concern that "the widening gap between CEO and worker pay may even inspire a new Marx and a new Lenin, but with American names, and all this at a time when the original Marx and the original Lenin have been so discredited."

The Federal Reserve, even before its expanded 1990s role, had enemies on the ideological right and left alike, including an occasional president. Ronald Reagan, as we have seen, had discussed the board's possible abolition with Treasury Secretary Donald Regan, and one of Bill Clinton's radio addresses in 1995 blamed an "unelected Federal Reserve" for raising interest rates seven times. The Federal Reserve had been a prominent Depression whipping post for its monetary mismanagement before and after the 1929 stock market crash. Thus, by the time the 2000–2001 crash reached its own first birthday, Alan Greenspan's Fed was receiving a growing ratio of brickbats to kudos, although most economists stuck to the common wisdom that Fed rate cuts were bound to revive the economy.

For three or four years in the late nineties, as a culture of renewed economic optimism overcame the earlier concern, the nation's bookshelves paraded titles like *Dow 36,000, Dare To Be Rich, Telecosm, Being Digital,* and *The Long Boom.* The radical or reformist isotope was still traceable, albeit marginally, through such serious volumes as *Class War in America: How Economic and Political Conservatives are Exploiting Low- and Middle-Income Americans* (2000), *American Democracy in Peril* (1995), *The Great Betrayal: How American Sovereignty and Social Justice Are Being Sacrificed to the Gods of the Global Economy* (1998), *The Coming Class War and How to Avoid It* (1999), *America's Middle Class: From Subsidy to Abandonment* (1997), and *Democracy at Risk: Rescuing Main Street from Wall Street* (2000).

Those inclined to scoff must consider the data set out in Chart 10.1, taken from a 2001 publication of the Congressional Budget Office. No previous two decades in U.S. history have seen anything similar.

CHART 10.1 *Apres Nous, Le Deluge?* The Collapse of the American Social and Economic Compact

Average household cash income, 1979–1997, as calculated by the Congressional Budget Office.

(IN THOUSANDS OF AFTER-TAX 1997 DOLLARS)

INCOME CATEGORY	1979	1981	1983	1985	1987	1989	1991	1993	1995	1997
Lowest quintile	9.3	8.7	8.0	8.5	8.8	9.1	8.6	8.2	8.6	8.7
Middle quintile	31.7	30.3	29.9	31.2	32.0	32.6	31.7	31.1	31.8	33.2
Top 1 percent	256.4	278.4	364.0	444.2	421.5	506.8	438.2	433.7	447.1	644.3

Source: *Effective Federal Tax Rates, 1979–97,* Congressional Budget Office, Washington, October 2001, Table 1.2c, p. 134.

At the same time, the frustration politics that began in the late 1960s unmistakably went beyond paychecks and job layoffs; it also had a parallel track in the cultural and patriotic expression of public unhappiness with perceived American global retreat. Embarrassment over departure from Vietnam ultimately yielded psychologies from bitter opposition to the treaties giving up the Panama Canal in 1978 to cheers for 1980s gunboat diplomacy and the 1991 Gulf War, capped by enthusiastic 2001 support for bombing Afghanistan and disposing of the terrorist Osama Bin

Laden. Such preoccupations have a considerable history of diverting economic anger and postponing reform, not least in great powers caught up in growing uncertainty.

4. WAR, PATRIOTISM, AND ECONOMIC REFORM

The U.S. declaration of war against terrorism that followed the September 11, 2001, attack on the World Trade Center and the Pentagon, like so many previous trumpet calls, pushed economic and governmental reform agendas to the sidelines. The reverse side of the coin, also widely remarked upon by historians, is that wars, especially ones with bold new dimensions of geography, expense, and technology, have played critical negative roles in the ebb of the previous leading world economic powers. Reform then returns.

Almost by definition, leading economic powers have been triumphalist at the peak—or somewhat past the peak—of their financial and imperial prowess. Spain, for example, had been embarrassed in the late sixteenth century by the failure of the Armada sent against England and the deepening revolution in the Spanish-held Netherlands as well as by King Philip's 1596 bankruptcy. Nevertheless, in the years after 1618, Spanish leaders committed their soldiery to what we remember as the Thirty Years' War (1618–48), with its endless, enormously expensive campaigns in Italy, Germany, and the Low Countries. Reform proposals withered on the vine—the famous Articles of Reformation (1623)—and by the time the Treaty of Westphalia was signed in 1648, Spain was exhausted both militarily and economically.

The Dutch in turn helped dig the grave of their own world economic leadership in the sequence of European conflicts known as the Nine Years War (1688–97) and the War of the Spanish Succession (1702–13). These began after the United Provinces, at the peak of their power, sent a fleet four times the size of the Spanish Armada to carry a large army across the English Channel to depose the unpopular English king, James II, in favor of the Dutch Protestant prince, William of Orange, who became King William III. France promptly declared war, and that nine-year conflict, together with the one that followed between 1702 and 1713, drained the Dutch financially. Their national debt quadrupled, principally because of paying for a large army, and the resulting taxes and higher interest rates made their industries less competitive. The war at sea cost them control of important trade routes and transferred maritime supremacy to Great Britain.

The extent to which Britain, in turn, was bled by the First and Second World Wars needs no further repetition. Its financial and economic downfall completed the set of precedents so relevant to the twenty-first-century United States: Over four centuries, leading economic power decline has been catalyzed by an unexpectedly long war entered into with unwarranted hubris.

J. R. Hobson, a radical British economist, theorized in 1902 that, "It has become a commonplace of history how governments use national animosities, foreign wars and the glamor of empire-making, in order to bemuse the popular mind and divert rising sentiment against domestic abuses." As an explanation of the wars that undercut the Spanish, Dutch, and British, however, Hobson's analysis is too sweeping. Hubris and triumphalism can gestate from history and culture, not just through government manipulation.

From the late 1600s through the late 1700s, Dutch secular reformist politics was often countered by so-called Orangism—the support of tradition-minded Dutch Reformed churchmen and large portions of the urban mob for the House of Orange and its glorious antecedents in the Dutch Revolution. In Britain the readiness of crowds to cheer themselves hoarse as troops marched off to the Boer War in 1899 and to Belgium and France in 1914 had more to do with the spirit of the times—from Kipling's rough couplets to the patriotic stanzas of the pubs and the imperial pomp of Queen Victoria's several jubilees—than the skill of Whitehall rhetoric or manipulation.

Nervousness and triumphalism sometimes seemed to go together. One analysis of the dynamics of war, peace, and social change in Britain after 1900 set forth a theory of rising "bellicosity" and "jingoism"; "Charles Booth stressed the patriotic content of the music hall songs of the people of London; the hysteria which accompanied the Boer War yielded a new synonym for patriotic jubilation, 'Mafficking' [after Mafeking, a British success] and the naval race with Germany produced the doggerel cry for more battleships: 'We want eight and we won't wait.' A wealth of popular literature visualized the nature of the coming war."

The analogy to the United States of 2000 and 2001 is considerable. After the trauma of the "imperial presidency" and the frustration of the Johnson and Nixon administrations in the Vietnamese quagmire, the United States worked off its "Vietnam complex" with defeats of senators who supported the Panama Canal treaties and then of President Jimmy Carter himself in November 1980 on the one-year anniversary of the taking as hostages of the U.S. embassy staff in Iran. The Reagan administration thereupon embraced several flamboyant sequels to the gunboat diplomacy of the 1920s and 1930s: the invasion of Grenada and the bombing of Libya. Both were crowd-pleasing precedents in 1990 when President George H. W. Bush embarked on a more ambitious venture: putting together an American-led global coalition to successfully recapture the oil-rich sheikhdom of Kuwait after its seizure that summer by Iraqi dictator Saddam Hussein. Democrat Bill Clinton extended the pattern by using bomb and missile strikes to chasten Iraq for violations of the peace agreement and to eliminate supposed terrorist facilities in the Sudan and Afghanistan.

By the millennium, not a few American officials, commentators, and strategic thinkers had regained the heights of confidence occupied by Britons a century earlier. Swift justice for Libya, Iraq, Syria, and even Iran was only a guided-missile switch away. Why—they complained in the wake of the September 11 terrorist attack on New York—stop with Afghanistan, Bin Laden, and the Taliban? Some of the great conflicts, leading into never-intended ultimate consequences, have begun with less—and clearly a hypothetical, terror-linked world war centered in the ten-thousand-mile Muslim corridor from North Africa through the Middle East to Indonesia would have the historical stature, including energy supply and financial disruption, to undo yet another leading world power.

The interplay of politics and wartime economics in the United States, meanwhile, had been transformed during the last three decades of the twentieth century. The century's first four wars—World Wars I and II, Korea, and Vietnam—had all begun during Democratic presidencies, and some Republicans charged their opposition with using wars to create prosperity. The Republican vulnerability lay in presiding over most of the major economic downturns and stock market crashes. However, the two rarely overlapped, because in the days when serious wars still involved large-scale economic and military mobilization, bugle calls tended to shrink unemployment lines.

Dominant control of the White House then passed to the Republican Party at more or less the same point in American history when overseas military engagement—first under Nixon during the later Vietnam years, then under George H. W. Bush in the Persian Gulf in 1990–91—began turning into a diversion from and burden on the U.S. domestic economy. Symptoms and circumstances included currency crises, oil supply threats, inflation vulnerability, debt and deficits, vulnerable U.S. stock markets, eroding U.S. manufacturing, and white-collar job loss. The Republican recessions of 1970–71 and 1990–91 arguably rank as the first U.S. wartime recessions—certainly the only wartime recessions of the twentieth century.

Overseas conflicts diverted both presidents, Nixon and Bush, from domestic affairs. Nixon dealt only superficially with inflation and the dollar crisis, and was too caught up in Indochina and then Watergate to focus on U.S. energy supply problems and the early stage (1970–72) of price aggressiveness on the part of the Organization of Petroleum Exporting Countries. Bush, during his tenure, was too preoccupied with the Gulf crisis and later too smug over its outcome to appreciate the accelerating job losses of what became the first white-collar recession in the annals of the U.S. economy.

The other problem, less true of Nixon back in the sixties and early seventies, is that Republican presidents since the eighties—Reagan, Bush Senior, and Bush the Younger—have seen federal economic policy largely as a chessboard on which to win investment, profit, tax, and trade incentives for their corporate, financial, big-donor, and upper-income constituencies. These biases have given the GOP a much, much higher ratio of U.S. recessions than Democratic administrations—Carter had one, but Kennedy, Johnson, and Clinton had none—although the pivotal party economic interests have thrived.

Hawkish foreign policy, in turn, has been a Republican asset, especially with working-class and lower-middle-class male adherents of the several waves of Middle American Radicalism. Such voters subordinated economic complaints in the early seventies, responding to Nixon's themes of the "Silent Majority," liberal establishment "betrayal," and "peace with honor," and in 1990 when George H. W. Bush and the GOP stemmed some of the Democrats' economic gains in the midterm congressional elections with last-minute efforts to make the election a referendum on standing up to Saddam Hussein. George W. Bush's strong military reply to the September 11 terrorist attacks quickly created a kindred counterforce to economic issues in late 2001.

What changed in 2001, even compared with 1990–91, was the Republican aggressiveness in using the patriotic mood set off by the terrorist attacks, under the guise of "stimulus," to enact controversial legislation on behalf of corporations and the top income percentiles: The tax cut passed by the House of Representatives—not only repealing the

Corporate Alternative Minimum Tax, but giving corporations like IBM and General Motors a total of $25 billion in rebates for past AMT payments—produced a backlash that included analogies to war profiteering. Earlier wartime Democratic administrations, instead of advancing this kind of policy, had imposed high wartime income tax rates, excess-profits taxes, wage and price controls, war labor boards, and other mechanisms to promote equity and shared sacrifice.

Indeed, part of the Bush administration's context was the president's own subsequent claim that the September 11 attack was aimed at U.S. and world financial markets, in which he identified trade, globalization, and the financial markets with American "values" and prosperity, all but wrapping them in red, white, and blue bunting. While this is a logical extension of the market-oriented U.S. financial mercantilism discussed earlier as well as an obvious recognition of why the terrorists targeted the World Trade Center, it also gives new credence to a growing twenty-first-century controversy: the perils of U.S. overdependence on finance.

The precarious politics of this partial commingling of patriotism and private profit stand alongside a precarious economics. If Spain could be bled dry on the battlefields of Germany and Italy, the Dutch critically shorn of their trade routes, and British financial hegemony strangled by war debt, the extent to which the United States has let its economy become financialized stands to be a twenty-first-century Achilles' heel.

The interests behind that transformation, in turn, stand to fuel an inevitably fierce debate. Patriotism and *rage militaire* are a second track along which Middle American Radicalism and frustration can vent itself. But the economics will out.

PART IV
THINKING AHEAD

WEALTH AND DEMOCRACY: THE UNITED STATES AND THE NEW CENTURY

The fact that free enterprise remains the most successful method of stimulating economic growth does not mean it requires a reward system that creates and sustains increasingly grotesque accumulations of family wealth. The accumulations are starting to have a negative influence on the efficient operation of our economy. They have the potential of being hazardous politically. And in a democratic society, they are becoming inexcusable socially.

—Vance Packard, *The Ultra-Rich* (1989)

Money not only determines who is elected, it determines who runs for office. Ultimately, it determines what government accomplishes—or fails to accomplish. Congress, except in unusual moments, will listen to the 900,000 Americans who give $200 or more to their campaigns ahead of the 259,600,000 who don't. Real reform of democracy, reform as radical as those of the Progressive era and deep enough to get government moving again, must begin by completely breaking the connection between money and politics.

—U.S. senator Bill Bradley, 1996

How else to describe the new (2001) administration's legislative agenda—elimination of the inheritance tax, revision of the bankruptcy laws, the repeal of safety regulations in the workplace, easing of restriction on monopoly, etc.—except as an act of class warfare? Not the aggression that Karl Marx and maybe Ralph Nader had in mind, not the angry poor sacking the mansions of the rich, but the aggrieved rich burning down the huts of the presumptuous and troublemaking poor.

—Lewis Lapham, *Harper's* (2001)

N ew centuries have often been stress points in the psychology, if not the immediate fortunes, of the world's leading economic powers. Like its predecessors, the United States found its uncertainties rising sharply as the calendar turned.

Pollyanna views of a New Economy crashed with the drawn-out collapse of Nasdaq and technology stock valuations accompanied by downturns in productivity, corporate profits, and business activity. The hung presidential election of 2000, for its part, fed skepticism about the U.S. electoral system. September 11 added a grave concern about the future of American domestic and international security.

Before then, a prominent subtext of the 2000 election—the sharp criticisms of corruption and corporate wealth excesses by the defeated reformist Republican and Democratic nomination seekers, McCain and Bradley, and the principal third-party nominee, Nader—had hinted at one gathering brand of reform. That a third of the electorate had supported one of these three critics struck some observers as an augury of a greater tide still to come.

Absent explosive catalysts like Fort Sumter and Pearl Harbor, the mobilization of U.S. public opinion has been slow. The only explosive catalyst of 2000–2001 was the terrorist attack, which stirred a very different mobilization: half patriotism, half fear. Reactions against corporations, finance, and the rich have generally followed stock market collapses and severe economic downturns. Otherwise, they have been hard to focus.

This slowness has been remarked upon. The American Revolution and the supporting political "revolution" of 1800 left a mind-set that over several generations dismissed the prospect of aristocracy of wealth. The legacy of 1776 and the abolition of British laws of entail and primogeniture had seemed protection enough until the public's slow awakening after the Civil War. Only then did voters begin to understand how war profits, railroad power, corrupt government, the rise of corporations, and a Vanderbilt fortune swollen to almost five times Astor's $20 million record of 1848 had marked off a whole new playing field.

Even after Mark Twain coined the term "Gilded Age" in 1873, it took until the 1880s for journalists and reformers to draw connecting lines between excessive wealth, the rise of the corporation, monumental graft, and the essential irrelevance of century-old inheritance reforms. In 1880, Gen. James B. Weaver—Civil War hero, Greenbacker, and future Populist presidential nominee—observed that the nation's founders had ended primogeniture and entail "so that the wealth of the country should diffuse itself among the people according to natural and beneficent laws. They did not contemplate the creation of these corporations that are as real entities as are individuals." Through the 1890s and early 1900s, public concern grew to critical mass.

Another century later we can fairly link the slowness of public arousal of the 1980s and 1990s to another lingering belief: that the New Deal and World War II had secured the democratic ethos for the foreseeable future. By 2000, however, these achievements under Franklin D. Roosevelt were a half century old and the persistence of that comforting ethos more and more of an illusion.

1. Reveries of Progressivism

Tackling new concentrations of wealth and power has been tricky business. However, the success of Theodore Roosevelt in the early 1900s, following on the failure of Bryan's prairie radicalism, had over the years risen from history to legend, and during the 2000 campaign these themes appeared again as inspiration in the paragraphs and punch lines of McCain, Bradley, Nader, and their allies.

Bradley, the second-finishing contender for the Democratic nomination, described the renewed corruption of the 1990s as "a story Americans have heard before. It's the story of the late 19th century, the era of the spoils system and recurrent scandals, when politics became hostage to the money power of Wall Street financiers, railroads and industrialists, when each Senator was virtually the property of whatever magnate had engineered his appointment. . . . The theologian Walter Rauschenbach wrote of that time that 'In political life one can constantly see the cause of human life pleading long and vainly for redress, like the widow before the unjust judge. Then suddenly comes the voice of property, and all men stand with hat in hand.' "

McCain, runner-up for the Republican nomination, openly modeled his own combativeness on TR's. Descriptions became battle cries. Besides condemning the U.S. system of election finance as "an elaborate influence-peddling scheme in which both parties conspire to stay in office by selling the country to the highest bidder," the Arizona senator, as we have seen, condemned his party's 1999 tax bill in Congress for repudiating a pledge to eliminate corporate welfare and offering "another cornucopia for the special interests and a chamber of horrors for the taxpayers."

Like the first Roosevelt, McCain promised to use the White House as a kind of public woodshed for wayward corporate executives. He talked of calling in the nation's broadcasters "and saying you are the guys that got $70 billion worth of free spectrum—one of the greatest rip-offs since the Teapot Dome scandal," and then urging them to come up with a uniform

system for rating television programs. He also promised to tell pharmaceutical company chief executives that "we've got seniors out there who
can't afford their drugs, and we've got to work out some way" to help
them.

Ralph Nader, the Green Party nominee, more closely resembled
Wisconsin's Robert La Follette, the Peck's bad boy of the early-twentieth-
century GOP, whose verbal whiplash made business and industrial titans
more forgiving of TR. In Iowa, where Nader contended that "the two parties have morphed together into one corporate party with two heads wearing different make-up," he was introduced by longtime progressive
Democratic activist and former Federal Communications commissioner
Nicholas Johnson, who excused his own bolt by saying that "The corporate corruption that engulfs both parties has now reached the stage where
we cannot afford to wait any longer." Nader's campus rallies, more than
any others, recaptured the mood of the muckrakers a hundred years earlier.

What Republican McCain and Democrat Bradley did not do was draw
connecting lines, directly and boldly, between tainted government, corrupted politics, corporate venality, and the unprecedented two-decade
buildup of wealth itself. The shared top-bracket status of speculators, corporate raiders, $100,000-soft-money political donors, inside traders,
chainsaw-wielding corporate CEOs, and Washington megalobbyists never
became a talking point. How the top 1 percent garnered over half of
late-twentieth-century U.S. income gains went essentially unremarked
upon; the expansion of the combined assets of the *Forbes* 400 from several
hundred billion dollars in 1982 to $3 trillion in 2000 remained disem-
bodied, a ghostly aggrandizement almost never tied to the donations,
dealings, and purged workforces.

Careful, hedged statements, as chapter 7 has shown, had also been
common with both Roosevelts and even Bryan. Politicians rarely pick
unnecessary-seeming fights. Part of the confusion lay in the faux populism
of the nineties: Internet billionaires with open collars, autocratic global
bankers hailing the democracy of the markets, and House speaker Newt
Gingrich and other business-financial spokesmen in Congress proclaiming
themselves antiestablishment populists. The stock market crash of
2000–2001 brought a sharper focus.

In the previous Progressive example, a compelling clarity emerged between 1906 and 1912 when TR and others turned to indicting the excesses of wealth itself and endorsing curbs like graduated inheritance and

income taxes. The ideological watershed followed in 1912, four decades after Mark Twain gave the Gilded Age its name. But appropriate as these remembrances seemed in 2000, new circumstances from globalization to terrorism gave them the appearance of reveries.

2. THE UNCERTAINTY OF AMERICAN-LED GLOBALIZATION

The Roman god of beginnings—Janus, for whom January is named—had two faces so that he might look in two directions. The same could be said of the millennial United States after more than a half century of global dominance. Its domestic face, looking inward, was seen by workaday Americans—the profile of a worried middle class, churches and shopping malls, and the mixed First and Third World economies of cities like New York and Los Angeles. The second, presented internationally, was the aging visage of the leading world economic power—purple-veined with years of high living, lips curled with the insolence of great wealth, eyes bloodshot with the late vigils of increasingly frequent financial crises.

Most Americans knew the inward face; few considered the global one. But many foreigners did—and some even hypnotized themselves with ex-aggeration, including those who blueprinted terrorist strikes against U.S. financial and governmental institutions.

Unfortunately, the global face, realistically examined, is the more re-vealing. Even as the triumphalist expressions of the 1990s faded in 2000 and 2001, the flushed American outward visage called to mind the late-stage excesses seen of earlier powers. This resemblance, in contrast to the Gilded Age correction by reformers, is less open to purely national solu-tion. The memory of Theodore Roosevelt is, in one sense, irrelevant. What is newly relevant—the slow ebb and sinking trajectory of a leading world economic power—is not familiar to Americans, whatever distant recollec-tion may still exist in Amsterdam or London.

Not that trajectories are easily judged. In the late 1980s the United States was seen as slipping, in part because many Americans regarded Japan as the coming economic force. But instead of passing the United States, as the U.S. had passed Britain, Japan began a slow descent after the 1990 implosion of its stock and property market bubbles. Fear of Japan cooled in 1993 and 1994 and then vanished in 1996 just as a new U.S. boom gathered. Triumphalism resumed its old American accent, and U.S. concern over possible national decline retreated to academe (save for mild worry as the U.S. current account deficit grew to dimensions that matched

Britain's worst). Crying wolf in 1988 and 1989 inhibited discussion a decade later.

Instead, debate locked in on globalization, a term that became a Rorschach blot for both admirers and detractors. Labor and left-liberal activists criticized just what many multinational corporations and banks sought—the transfer of some economic, financial, and trade regulation away from local and national governments to the sympathetic mandarinates of transnational entities like the North American Free Trade Agreement and the World Trade Organization. Despite Nader's attentions, the Republican and Democratic presidential nominees of 2000 ignored a whole complex of related issues—the increasing gap between the Western elites who thrived on globalization and the less-favored billions losing ground, the income slippage of the masses across much of Africa, South Asia, and Latin America, the financialization and income polarization of the United States, and the "democratic deficit" or erosions of popular sovereignty touched on in chapter 5.

Grassroots apprehension in the United States was something to be circumvented, not seriously debated. *Wall Street Journal* polling in 1999, for example, showed that even in relatively good times, 58 percent of Americans regarded foreign trade as "bad for the U.S. economy because cheap imports hurt wages." The highest-income tenth of Americans, by contrast, would have disagreed by two-to-one, the top 1 percent probably by five-to-one, which spoke more loudly in a system increasingly attuned to wealth. Controversial trade proposals frequently became law during the nineties through debate-limiting methods like "fast track" and holding votes during postelection lame-duck sessions of Congress.

Economic historians could have shed some relevant light on the divisions. In 1999 the *New York Times* published a provocative truth. "Perhaps the greatest myth about globalization is that it is new," its report noted. "By some measures, the peak occurred a century ago." Indeed, trade and international capital mobility were only regaining their late-Victorian and Edwardian levels in the 1980s and 1990s. Thus, "although it is often said today that globalization is irreversible, it proved very reversible early in this century."

Far from being "irreversible," globalization has come in waves. As chapter 4 elaborated, its crest in the late-Victorian and Edwardian periods was supported by the self-interest and ideology of Britain during its economic heyday. The previous openness of European commerce from 1649 to 1690 in turn reflected the Dutch zenith. The repetition in the late twentieth century depended on a similar peak influence of the dominant wealth elites in the United States and among their allies.

Leading economic powers become cocksure in ways that breed both domestic and foreign resentment. By 2000 the great majority of the high incomes and major fortunes in the United States were directly or indirectly tied to global sway—in professions like law, accounting, engineering, and economics and in sectors like oil, pharmaceuticals, technology, aerospace, chemicals, tobacco, communications, entertainment, banking, and finance. The bottom 60 or 70 percent of Americans, by contrast, had closer ties to the globalization casualty lists, a connection confirmed by opinion polls, by male job loss, and by the persisting inability of real disposable wages among nonsupervisory workers to regain late-sixties heights, especially in manufacturing.

Twenty-first-century Washington insistences on U.S. global economic virtue are likely to be shrugged off by Asians just as European rivals shrugged off Dutch and British insistences. Britain and the United States, after all, had both built their own early industrial momentum with generations of government support and economic protection.

As for domestic politics, these same controversial priorities could be wrapped in the U.S. flag when foreign terrorists destroyed the World Trade Center—trade and "open" economics are good, it was implied, because their opponents are narrow and evil. On the other hand, critics pointed out the vulnerabilities that financial dependence and globalization have imposed on the United States—vulnerabilities that simply did not exist in the halcyon days of the 1950s.

3. The Changing Politics of Corporate Ascendancy

Turn-of-the-millennium efforts by the U.S. economic and opinion-molding elites to build a new global governmental and legal system pushed far beyond the previous high-water marks of transnationalism—the expansions resting on the maritime, naval, and colonial frameworks of the Spanish, Dutch, and British. Under the American flag, by contrast, corporations have been out in front because, since the nineteenth century, it has been their lot—as the ultimate vehicles of U.S. ingenuity and acquisitiveness—to play many of the expansionist roles previously associated with the Spanish church, the Dutch merchant marine, and the British navy. This may slight the quasi-governmental importance of the Dutch and British East India companies, but no other major nation has matched the United States for the overall centrality of private corporations (including banks) in its economic growth and political life.

That corporations have taken the spotlight as latter-day English-speaking conquistadores—Magellans of technology, Cortéses of consumer goods, and Pizarros of entertainment—reflected the cosmopolitanizing of their profits, a cousinship to earlier Dutch and then British cosmopolitanizing of investment. By the late 1990s, many of the *Fortune* 500 companies were one-third, one-half, or two-thirds tied to international sales, earnings, plants, and employees. Some managements hoped to no longer process or manufacture anything in the United States, but merely to import and distribute goods, much like the ill-fated Enron transformation from producing company to financial trader.

The corollary—and equally the political provocation—lay in their declining contribution to the employment base and community welfare of the United States. Management theorists enthused over virtual corporations that were all head—for finance, legal, marketing, design, and research and development functions—and little or no body, in the sense of fixed manufacturing capacity. That head might be in the United States, filled with two or three thousand upper- and upper-middle-bracket professionals (by no means all American). The employment of ordinary wage earners, however, was moving elsewhere, as the data in chapter 3 illustrate. Sales of the world's five hundred largest companies increased sevenfold between 1980 and 2000, but during that time their employment within the United States shrank by roughly one-third.

Ballooning corporate profits flowed to capital and shareowners at the expense of workers and communities. In 2000 some 40 percent of the U.S.-owned individual shares were held by the top 1 percent, representing a parochial and narrow enrichment alongside the wider employment, community benefit, and U.S. national commitment of the democratic capitalism of the 1950s.

In the wake of the Enron collapse, corporations are going to have to explain these transformations. Their political liability is that the emergence of the modern corporation in the United States has always depended on politics. Markets might be worshiped or laissez-faire speeches applauded, but only government could change statutes. Many of America's most famous presidents, as we have seen, tried to thwart corporations. Some succeeded. Corporate growth and momentum after the Civil War occurred not because of laissez-faire, but in considerable measure because railroads and other behemoths were big enough to methodically take over and dominate state legislatures, thereby taking control of the U.S. Senate and much of the federal and state judiciary.

Corporate power retreated during the Progressive and New Deal eras, as we have seen, and then again between the mid-1960s and late 1970s. The early twenty-first century should see another struggle because corporate aggrandizement in the 1980s and 1990s went beyond that of the Gilded Age—the parallels of political corruption and concentrated wealth—to frame issues of abandoning American workers, communities, and loyalties. It is not hard to imagine a twenty-first-century debate over a more sophisticated economic version of the old East German offense of *republikflugt*—flight from the nation.

The erosion within the United States of popular and national sovereignty, some of it tied to corporate behavior, also crystallized as a concern between 1995 and 2000. Public influence shrank as unelected experts became ever more prominent in national decision-making. Judges and the Federal Reserve Board enlarged their roles while corporate and bank influence over Congress and the White House climbed in tandem with the dollar totals of huge federal campaign contributions and lobbying outlays. Voters began to understand themselves to be on a seesaw—popular influence fell as that of the economic elites rose.

Loss of national sovereignty has become a popular concern. The small bits of jurisdiction given to international organizations before the 1990s never became a national issue, save to the political fringe. That changed between 1993 and 1995 as the enactment and implementation first of the North American Free Trade Agreement and then of the framework and mechanics of the World Trade Organization seemed to push democratic precepts aside. As noted earlier, the term "democratic deficit" emerged in scholarly articles and press coverage as the transnational deliberations of NAFTA, the WTO, and the European Union began to yield rulings that set aside local and national legislation and regulatory decisions from North America to Southeast Asia. In Washington the well-established Center for Strategic and International Studies questioned the full legitimacy of rules promulgated by elites "quite removed from the political process."

Rearranging layers of government to suit themselves, as U.S. corporations did during the Gilded Age, helped trigger the Progressive response and era. It confirmed how corporations, allowed to grow too big and powerful, could become what Henry Demarest Lloyd assailed in his book *Wealth Against Commonwealth*. A century later, corporate-keynoted globalization was becoming the new social Darwinism. Survival of the fittest had jumped onto an international stage. This time, *global* law and regulation, not domestic overinterpretation of the U.S. Constitution, was expected to favor the economic lions and suppress social and environmental priorities—a startling reenactment of the techniques damned a century earlier by Progressive critics.

Parallel late-1990s public arousal came as a shock just weeks before the century's end. The many trade officials and corporate executives gathering for the WTO "Millennial Round" of meetings in Seattle in December 1999 were stunned as thousands of activists blocked meeting hall entrances chanting, "We don't want you. We didn't elect you. And we don't want your rules."

The "democratic deficit" debate touches a particular chord in the United States and Europe. However, both the movement toward government by unelected experts and the anxieties it creates are global.

4. THE DEMOCRATIC DEFICIT AND THE RISE OF THE UNELECTED

The winter of 2000–2001, when Americans watched the U.S. Supreme Court determine the outcome of the November presidential election as the Federal Reserve Board made its critical judgments on the fate of the U.S. economy, threw the migration of political authority into bold relief. Two unelected branches of government, the judiciary and the central bankers of the Federal Reserve System, were taking up ever more vital decisionmaking. Public acquiescence or challenging response would reveal something about democracy's evolutions.

And not just in the United States. The worldwide rise during the 1980s and 1990s of central bankers, all unelected and operating through elite staffs, drew growing attention, especially in Europe, Japan, Taiwan, Singapore, Canada, and Brazil. The so-called Concert of Europe, which maintained the European balance of power after the Napoleonic Wars, had been an orchestration of great-power diplomats; the Concert of the West in the economic crises surrounding the millennium was an ensemble of central bankers, its leader the American that one book of 2000 christened *Maestro*: Alan Greenspan.

Growing central bank independence, it should be emphasized, was of elected *national* (or in the case of the European Central Bank, *supranational*) regimes. In short, independence from politicians. No one was foolish enough to think the central bankers of Washington, London, Brussels, or Tokyo independent of the sprawling, boundaryless international—and equally self-serving—networks of bankers, securities firms, hedge funds, economists, central bank and treasury bureaucracies, and international economic agencies. These hundred thousand honeybees, elite among the world's human billions, collectively shaped money supplies, stock markets, growth patterns, and recessions, yet central bankers, the heads of the financial hive, operated outside election processes.

Simply put, voters in the West were losing political and popular governance of the economy. If the twentieth had been the century of democracy, the twenty-first bid to be something different. The "democratization" of money in the United States alleged in the growth of mutual funds and 401(k) plans could be restated as "de-democratization" in terms of control over the money supply passing to the unelected Federal Reserve and its financial constituency. Under their aegis, liquidity—the tangible bounty of money supply expansion—tended to find its way to the financial sector rather than to commodities or goods production. And on a more mundane level, even sympathetic chroniclers wondered about the "extent to which we are relying for the prosperity of the free world economy—and ultimately the stability of the democratic society—on a handful of expert technocrats."

Politicians of the eighties and early nineties, for their part, had occasionally been unnerved by the shift. As we have seen, presidents Reagan and Clinton groused, and a group of Senate Democrats proposed in 1993 to end the participation in Federal Reserve Board money-supply decisions by the regional Federal Reserve Bank presidents, who were "accountable not to the people or their elected representatives, but to their boards of directors, which are dominated by commercial banks."

In 2000–2001, however, most political candidates, like most investors, were holding their breath to see if Greenspan could achieve his goal of a soft landing for the national economy and stock market indexes. The Fed's repute hung on the new decade's outcomes; the more pain, the closer the scrutiny and the more far-reaching the debate.

Eight years earlier the Fed chairman stated that he had a bias to limiting growth to avoid the sort of financial assets liquidation seen in recessions before World War II. Back then, "In effect, wealth moved into other hands. We can't socially and politically accept such a situation today. We have automatic stabilizers that put a floor under economic activity levels. But we can't eliminate the need to reduce the imbalances. So we try to unwind them without a sharp contraction. But nonetheless this creates slow economic growth."

The "wealth effect" implicit in these policies more than matched the other wealth consequence of the late nineties that preoccupied Greenspan—the spur given to spending, economic growth, and inflation by the $1–3 trillion-a-year gains in stock market valuation between 1996 and 1999. His choice to protect accumulated wealth through slow growth, which requires minimizing wage increases, has been a formula for favoring holders of financial assets and accepting a concomitant steady increase in economic inequality and polarization.

Politically, this marked something of a return to the alignment and bias of Nicholas Biddle and the Second Bank of the United States in the late 1820s and 1830s. Biddle was beaten by Andrew Jackson, and some of Jackson's indictments in his famous veto message of 1832 match the later belligerence of Theodore Roosevelt in their potential relevance for twenty-first-century political debate.

In addition to governance of trade and finance being globalized and moved into the hands of the unelected, another such transfer of power involved the escalating judicial and administrative determination of political and social issues once decided by popularly elected legislatures. Here again the United States, with its vivid displays of vigorous policymaking by judges, has set the example. Other nations followed suit in the nineties, particularly Europe and the European Union.

Earlier waves of judicial activism and assumptions of power in the early United States generally reflected the lag-effects of national party transitions—judges and justices appointed by Federalists did violence to new Jeffersonian objectives; those appointed by pre–Civil War Democratic presidents thwarted Lincoln; and a Republican-picked federal judiciary threw out large chunks of Franklin Roosevelt's New Deal. By contrast, the expanding reach of judicial power at the turn of the twenty-first century reflected the spread of legalistic procedures to deal with specialized subject matter.

The ascendancy of judges, while less examined than the parallel rise of central bankers, was cataloged in a 1995 survey, *The Global Expansion of Judicial Power,* that detailed the judicialization of governance in Britain, Australia, Canada, Israel, Italy, Sweden, and even France and Germany. Because judicial power tended to serve elite purposes, a significant minority of contributors expressed concern about the inroads on democracy.

In Britain, where skepticism of the European Union abounded, one of the most popular books of the millennial year, *Democracy in Europe,* by Oxford lecturer Larry Siedentop, charged that regulation from European Community headquarters in Brussels—strongest in the areas of multilateral trade, central banking, budget stingency, antitrust enforcement, and constitutional adjudication—threatened bureaucratic despotism while the "triumph of economic language" had "impoverished" European political discourse. British Euroskeptics seized on the burgeoning legitimacy gap to connect public alienation and the sharp decline in British voter turnout on how EU authority and practice was accelerating the decline of national parliamentary sovereignty and prestige.

Of these unelected rulers, be they transnational bureaucracies, powerful and independent central banks, EU and IMF economic inspectors, and even more policymakers in the judiciary, a considerable part of their evolution seems to overlap—and possibly reflect—the financialization, globalization, and wealth polarization of the eighties and nineties. Which came first is hard to say. Certainly some of the strongest support for such developments seems to come from the financial and multinational corporate communities.

The simultaneous erosion of national sovereignty, decline in Western voter participation, and rise in popular alienation from politics—summed up as the "democratic deficit" or legitimacy gap—would have bred a popular counterforce in the United States of 1950 or 1970. In fact, it did even in 1992, witness the direct democracy components of the Perot third-party presidential campaign. Whether that is still true is an important twenty-first-century litmus in its own right.

5. MARKETS AND DEMOCRACY: A TWENTY-FIRST-CENTURY TENSION?

We can begin with a simple premise: *Democracy and market economics are not the same thing.* Worse, the attempts to confuse and conflate them in pretended equivalence stood out at the millennium as a destructive aspect of U.S. politics. As noted, the rollbacks of democracy sketched in these chapters have accompanied the elevation of markets—the fulfillment of the North American Free Trade Agreement, the European Union (launched as a common market) and the World Trade Organization, and the ascent of the Federal Reserve Board as the protector and liquidity provider of financial and securities markets.

Washington, Jefferson, Lincoln, and the two Roosevelts would probably have been appalled. Politics and government down through the ages, while often brutal or grossly deficient, have been the subject matter of Plato and Aristotle, Aquinas and Machiavelli, Locke, and a few of

America's own great names. Markets, by contrast, descend from the fairs of late medieval Europe, church-permitted safety valves for gambling, money-lending, and other forms of license. The idea that they have turned into a vehicle for human governance lacks any base beyond the occasional financial publication.

Wealth has been a product of both: markets *and* politics. To historians Will and Ariel Durant, "Concentration of wealth is a natural result of concentration of ability, and regularly recurs in history. The rate of concentration varies (other factors being equal) with the economic freedom permitted by morals and the law. . . . democracy, allowing the most liberty, accelerates it." But just as inevitably, they added, wealth is partially redistributed, whether violently or peaceably. Thus the innate tensions between wealth laudation, which favors concentration, and democracy, which promotes distribution.

In the United States of the turn of the century, the wealth has concentrated with the help of the corruption of politics on one hand and the suasion of market idolatry and economic Darwinism on the other. The saving grace is that societies seem to have their own related rhythm, their larger pattern of rise and fall, as Toynbee and other historians have suggested.

Politics in the United States has been more cyclical than elsewhere, and Arthur Schlesinger has offered a philosophic interpretation—the necessary alternation of cycles of public purpose with those of private interest. Others have emphasized the inevitable strains between the values of capitalization—property, profits, and markets—and the emphases of democracy on equality, freedom, social responsibility, and the general welfare. Survey research was "unequivocal," said political scientists John Zaller and Herbert McClosky in 1984, that while neither side openly sought to abolish the other, those most supportive of the democratic values were least supportive of capitalist tenets and vice versa.

The merit of the alternating cycles recorded in the United States lies in enabling the nation to have both, wealth *and* democracy, the ability to move from one wave to the other being a genius of American politics. Thus the flaw in the Progressive era insistence by future Supreme Court justice Louis Brandeis: that "We can have a democratic society or we can have great concentrated wealth in the hands of a few. We cannot have both." At transition points, we have had both.

To be sure, the same cyclicality has mocked market absolutism. The "invisible hand" beloved of market theologians periodically sprains its theoretical wrist in speculative collapses, gluts of oversupply, or private monopolistic distortions.

Thus the prerequisite that capitalism and democracy, while easily overlapping and allied, must be kept separate. They cannot be confused. Candidate Bradley, in the early stages of his presidential campaign, worried that the inability to free U.S. politics from money rose out of this confusion—out of "a failure to understand that democracy and capitalism are separate parts of the American dream, and that keeping that dream alive depends on keeping one from corrupting the other."

Much of the late-twentieth-century failure, of course, was deliberate: the continued and heavily funded effort, over two decades of private interest exaltation, to displace the founders' republican arena of civic virtue and political engagement with the marketplace of economic self-interest. We have seen the speeches and metaphors of conservative politicians, bankers, and journalists hailing markets as economic voting machines and corporations as the democratic selectees of the marketplace. One notable Republican called politics underfunded (by private contributions) because Americans spent more on antacids alone.

Such choruses swelled during the 1990s like an economic version of Handel's *Messiah*. The market and the people are one and the same. *Hallelujah.* Buying, selling, and consuming is true democracy. *Hallelujah.* Popular will is expressed through the law of supply and demand. *Hallelujah.* Populism is market economics. *Hallelujah.* Opposition to the verdict of the market is elitism. *Hallelujah.* The Nations and Peoples shall rejoice. *Hallelujah, Hallelujah.*

In such a climate, market insistence began to encroach on representative government. The World Trade Organization, for example, in laying down enforceable legal standards that emphasized uninhibited flow of capital and goods, exalted markets over legislative criteria, including local democratic priorities.

Ultimately, the guideposts of a market-based society never seem to progress beyond tautology: policies that advance markets are good and efficient because they advance markets. The raw logic of a blurring between marketplace and polity, however, boils down to a disturbing simplicity: *one dollar, one vote.* Inequality is the natural law of the cash-driven marketplace. The more you have, the more you can buy. Buying is good. The more you can buy, the more validating your acts.

The next jump is the more perverse. Merge politics with the marketplace and buying becomes the game: one dollar, one vote, *ten* dollars *ten* votes. Even in America, nineteenth-century voting often had a property qualification. No holdings, no ballots. Property owners sometimes had a plural franchise—the right to vote in several places. Texas billionaire

H. L. Hunt published a book in the 1950s advocating that citizens' voting power be proportionate to the taxes they paid.

Absurd as this sounds, morphing politics into a marketplace is simply a back door to the house Hunt hoped to build. If the essence of democracy is to buy, sell, own, or consume, then political contributions are protected expressions (not far off some of the insistences in 2000–2001 congressional debate). However, as Charles Lindblom wrote in *Politics and Markets* (1977), because purchasing is the critical act of the marketplace, business enjoys a privileged position, as does wealth. Democratic politics, by contrast, provides the framework in which ordinary people—*voting* is their critical act, not *purchasing*—make up for the disproportionate power represented by organized money.

Which brings us back to where this chapter began: the analogy between today's market Darwinism and the social Darwinism of the Gilded Age. "There is absolutely nothing to be said," Theodore Roosevelt observed, "for government by a plutocracy, for government by men very powerful in certain lines and gifted with 'a money touch,' but with ideals which in their essence are merely those of so many glorified pawnbrokers."

Whether twenty-first-century Americans can again revitalize politics, stymie plutocracy, and confine market theory to commerce depends on how successfully the critical distinctions between capitalism and democracy can be brought back into focus. Markets, in short, must be reestablished as adjuncts, not criteria, of democracy and representative government.

6. A RENEWAL OF POLITICS OR THE END OF AMERICAN EXCEPTIONALISM?

The Progressive analogies so appealing to a minority in the 2000 elections tapped, at their root, a basic optimism that American democracy and exceptionalism would continue, that our civic culture was not in some global or historical peril. Doubters saw gloomier possibilities: the gathering of an undemocratic age, the global entrenchment of wealth elites, and even the possibility of U.S. capitalism—unrepentant at home and cocksure internationally—becoming another example of elite inflexibility and vulnerability.

On the surface, and given the parallels, another Rooseveltian-type mobilization was plausible. By mobilizing against corruption, polarization, and market Darwinism—living specifics, not gray abstractions—politics might be able to regain the relevance and popular support it had lost in the late twentieth century. Part of that would have to include a more democratic approach to taxation, money, and banking. Successful reform would not only prolong the rhythm so essential to U.S. politics, the alternation between public and private purpose, but it would prolong the case for American exceptionalism by proving a continuing national ability to return to vital roots.

None of the previous powers could. Indeed, the popular reactions in mid-eighteenth-century Holland and early-twentieth-century Britain against opulent aristocratic and financial elites raise a different possibility: the emergence during the first third of the twenty-first century of a U.S. radicalism seeded by economic and political pessimism. We have seen how a portion of the Dutch people, seeking a return to lost values, mounted a "Patriot Revolution." Major elements of the British population, seething against wealth and unfairness, used the new Labor Party to build a British welfare state—worker and lower-middle-income circumstances improved markedly—around the much higher tax rates imposed by war and politics on the upper and upper middle classes.

In *Globalization and History*, economists Kevin O'Rourke and Jeffrey Williamson make the point that pre-1914 globalization came to an end when "a political backlash developed in response to the actual or perceived distributional effects of globalization." A gathering trend toward capital controls, immigration restraints, tariffs, and abandonment of the gold standard, together with democratic enfranchisement and the rise of the welfare state, operated to tilt economics toward "deglobalization" and increased emphasis on equality for some three to four decades after 1918. Inequality did reverse in the rich nations, and the two men suggest that such forces may be building again: "The record suggests that unless politicians worry about who gains and who loses, they may be forced by the electorate to stop efforts to strengthen global economy links, and perhaps even to dismantle them."

Belief that Americans faced with the onset of decline would not be radical ignores both the polarization and wealth concentration of the eighties and nineties and the vein of recurring hostilities noted in chapter 10. The crash of 2000–2001 added a new layer of potential popular recrimination: that of individuals against corporations and the financial sector alike for insider dealings and false assurances, accompanied by a new politics of personal finance that demands recompense and regulatory safeguards. Abuses were identifiable well before the stock market implosion.

Beyond proposals for wealth taxes and curbs on corporate salaries, also noted in chapter 10, potential radicalism could respond to several peculiarly American situations. To begin with, high taxes on the assets, incomes, or consumption patterns of the rich—or all three—could be used in the twenty-first century to fund the late-twentieth-century promises of entitlements like Social Security and Medicare. Inheritance taxation, rather than being ended, could be rearranged to diminish wealth concentration in a new way: by taxing individuals on their cumulative inheritances over a certain amount rather than collecting from decedents' estates. Some left-leaning groups have urged federal rather than state chartering of corporations as well as an end to interpretations that entitle corporations to the protection of individual persons under the U.S. Constitution. In Britain, changes that seemed impossible in 1902 or 1904 became serious discussions in 1909, law in 1913, and were supplanted by even tougher statutes in 1919 or 1938.

Economic nationalism, in turn, could be pursued to make the United States more self-sufficient again, imposing import duties to recapture the U.S. internal market for domestic producers and workers. Despite the poor prospects for long-term success, attempts could find reward at the ballot box. The United States, as a dominant continental power with a large and rich domestic market, is better placed to follow such a strategy than maritime-periphery nations like the Dutch and British ever were.

If economic trauma has stimulated radicalism, so has war, both directly and indirectly. The immediate effects have usually been to divert reform, to submerge divisions in patriotism and temporary unity. But at a certain point in each leading world economic power's history, as we have seen, some major war proves too burdensome, economic prospects and divisions worsen, and the politics of frustration takes a critical leap forward.

As the twenty-first century gets underway, the imbalance of wealth and democracy in the United States is unsustainable, at least by traditional yardsticks. Market theology and unelected leadership have been displacing politics and elections. Either democracy must be renewed, with politics brought back to life, or wealth is likely to cement a new and less democratic regime—plutocracy by some other name. Over the coming decades, American exceptionalism may face its greatest test simply in convincing the American people to continue to believe in its comfort and reassurance.

U.S. Historical Price Indexes, 1790–1991

Composite Consumer Price Index, 1790–1991
Taylor-Hoover Wholesale Price Index, 1790–1958

Both indexes have been computed to use 1860 as a base (1860 equals 100). The Composite Consumer Price Index splices the U.S. government Consumer Price Index to the computations of economists Paul David and Peter Solar taking the index back to colonial times. The Taylor-Hoover Wholesale Price Index is included (through 1958) to illustrate the greater effects of inflation and deflation on agricultural commodities.

YEAR (BASE =)	TAYLOR-HOOVER (1859–60)	COMPOSITE CONSUMER PRICE INDEX (1860)	YEAR (BASE =)	TAYLOR-HOOVER (1859–60)	COMPOSITE CONSUMER PRICE INDEX (1860)
1790	99.9	110	1805	148.4	141
1791	98.1	113	1806	139.8	147
1792	101.3	115	1807	135.3	139
1793	109.3	119	1808	122.0	151
1794	121.7	132	1809	134.2	148
1795	146.2	151	1810	136.9	148
1796	158.0	159	1811	132.7	158
1797	143.4	153	1812	136.9	160
1798	139.2	148	1813	161.3	192
1799	141.9	148	1814	184.4	211
1800	140.6	151	1815	182.5	185
1801	151.1	153	1816	176.9	169
1802	128.8	129	1817	172.9	160
1803	128.3	136	1818	168.6	153
1804	136.0	142	1819	141.2	153

YEAR (BASE =)	TAYLOR-HOOVER (1859–60)	COMPOSITE CONSUMER PRICE INDEX (1860)	YEAR (BASE =)	TAYLOR-HOOVER (1859–60)	COMPOSITE CONSUMER PRICE INDEX (1860)
1820	116.5	141	1855	109.6	104
1821	106.7	136	1856	109.5	102
1822	112.7	141	1857	118.5	105
1823	105.2	126	1858	98.2	99
1824	102.4	116	1859	101.3	100
1825	111.9	119	1860	99.6	100
1826	99.5	119	1861	102.9	106
1827	96.5	120	1862	119.5	121
1828	95.6	114	1863	152.3	151
1829	94.7	112	1864	220.9	189
1830	90.6	111	1865	210.9	196
1831	91.7	104	1866	197.4	191
1832	95.0	103	1867	182.7	178
1833	98.1	101	1868	177.3	171
1834	94.6	103	1869	168.4	164
1835	109.1	106	1870	149.1	157
1836	122.2	112	1871	142.5	147
1837	113.9	115	1872	151.6	147
1838	110.1	112	1873	145.8	144
1839	115.0	112	1874	138.0	137
1840	94.9	104	1875	130.6	132
1841	92.7	105	1876	120.3	129
1842	80.8	98	1877	117.2	126
1843	75.1	89	1878	100.0	120
1844	78.0	90	1879	98.3	120
1845	81.8	91	1880	109.6	123
1846	82.5	92	1881	111.5	123
1847	92.5	99	1882	116.3	123
1848	78.4	95	1883	107.6	121
1849	81.5	92	1884	99.9	118
1850	90.6	94	1885	92.2	116
1851	86.5	92	1886	88.8	113
1852	87.6	93	1887	92.4	114
1853	95.9	93	1888	94.2	114
1854	102.7	101	1889	89.9	111

YEAR (BASE =)	TAYLOR-HOOVER (1859–60)	COMPOSITE CONSUMER PRICE INDEX (1860)	YEAR (BASE =)	TAYLOR-HOOVER (1859–60)	COMPOSITE CONSUMER PRICE INDEX (1860)
1890	90.8	109	1925	167.1	210
1891	90.1	109	1926	161.5	211
1892	84.3	109	1927	154.1	208
1893	86.2	108	1928	156.2	205
1894	77.4	103	1929	153.9	205
1895	78.8	101	1930	139.5	200
1896	75.1	101	1931	117.9	182
1897	75.3	100	1932	104.6	163
1898	78.3	100	1933	106.4	155
1899	84.3	100	1934	121.0	160
1900	90.6	101	1935	129.2	164
1901	89.3	102	1936	130.5	166
1902	95.1	103	1937	139.4	172
1903	96.2	106	1938	126.9	169
1904	96.4	107	1939	124.5	166
1905	97.1	106	1940	126.9	168
1906	99.8	108	1941	141.0	176
1907	105.3	113	1942	159.6	195
1908	101.6	111	1943	166.5	207
1909	109.2	109	1944	167.9	210
1910	113.7	114	1945	170.9	215
1911	104.8	114	1946	195.6	233
1912	111.6	117	1947	239.5	267
1913	112.7	119	1948	259.4	288
1914	110.0	120	1949	246.5	285
1915	112.2	121	1950	256.2	288
1916	138.1	130	1951	285.3	310
1917	189.8	153	1952	277.3	317
1918	212.0	180	1953	273.6	320
1919	223.8	207	1954	274.1	321
1920	249.3	240	1955	275.1	320
1921	157.6	214	1956	284.0	325
1922	156.2	200	1957	292.2	336
1923	162.5	204	1958	296.2	346
1924	158.4	204	1959		348

YEAR (BASE =)	COMPOSITE CONSUMER PRICE INDEX (1860)	YEAR (BASE =)	COMPOSITE CONSUMER PRICE INDEX (1860)
1960	354	1981	1,087
1961	358	1982	1,154
1962	362	1983	1,191
1963	366	1984	1,243
1964	371	1985	1,287
1965	377	1986	1,311
1966	388	1987	1,359
1967	399	1988	1,415
1968	416	1989	1,483
1969	438	1990	1,563
1970	464	1991	1,629
1971	484	1992	1,678
1972	500	1993	1,728
1973	531	1994	1,773
1974	590	1995	1,822
1975	643	1996	1,876
1976	680	1997	1,920
1977	725	1998	1,949
1978	780	1999	1,992
1979	868	2000	2,059
1980	985		

Source: John J. McCusker, *How Much Is That in Real Money?: A Historical Commodity Price Index for Use as a Deflator of Money Values in the Economy of the United States.* Second Edition, Revised and Enlarged. (Worcester, Mass.: American Antiquarian Society, 2001).

1929 REVISITED: THE RISING TOP ONE PERCENT SHARE OF TOTAL U.S. INCOME

A. Top 1/2 of 1% Share of Adjusted Gross Income (including full capital gains), 1960–1995					
1960	*1970*	*1980*	*1985*	*1990*	*1995*
7.55	6.36	7.00	9.34	10.75	11.25

Source: Daniel Feenberg and James M. Poterba, "The Income and Tax Share of Very High Income Households, 1960–1995," National Bureau of Economic Research, Feb. 2000.

B. Top 1% Share of U.S. Personal Income (not including capital gains), 1914–1948					
Year	*1914*	*1919*	*1928**	*1940*	*1948*
Top One Percent Share	13.1	12.8	14.94	11.89	8.38

Source: Simon Kuznets series in Williamson and Lindert, *American Inequality,* p. 316.

*Because of the impact of the autumn 1929 Crash, the peak income share of the top one percent during the 1920s came in 1928.

C. Top 1% Share of U.S. Income (including capital gains), 1979–1997									
Year	*1979*	*1981*	*1985*	*1987*	*1989*	*1991*	*1993*	*1995*	*1997*
Top One Percent Share	9.3	9.3	11.3	11.3	12.5	11.1	11.8	12.5	15.8

Source: Calculations from Congressional Budget Office data by Lawrence Mishel of the Economic Policy Institute.

D. Top 1% Share of U.S. Personal Income (including capital gains), 1983–1998					
	1982	1988	1991	1994	1997
Top 1% share	12.8%	16.6%	15.7%	14.4%	16.6%

Source: Table 3C, Edward Wolff, "Recent Trends in Wealth Ownership, 1983–1998," Jerome Levy Economics Institute, April 2000, p. 18. Wolff's computations were made from the 1983, 1989, 1992, 1995 and 1998 Federal Reserve Board Surveys of Consumer Finances.

E. Three Top-Tier Shares of All-Taxpayer Adjusted Gross Income (including capital gains), 1995–1997					
Taxpayer share of AGI	1993	1994	1995	1996	1997
$200,000 AGI and above	14.4	14.6	15.8	18.1	19.9
$500,000 AGI and above	7.6	7.6	8.6	10.3	11.8
$1 million AGI and above	4.9	4.9	5.6	7.0	8.2

Note: Taxpayer households with $200,000 AGI or higher would be 1.2% to 1.4% of the population, slightly broader than the top 1% category; $500,000 AGI or more would be slightly broader than the top one-half of one percent.

Source: *The Economic and Budget Outlook, Fiscal Years 2000–2009,* Congressional Budget Office, January, 1999, p. 50.

NOTES

Chapter 1: The Eighteenth and Nineteenth Centuries
PAGE

3   *"one of the harshest"* De Tocqueville quoted in Sellers, *The Market Revolution,* p. 238.

6   *During the same period* Schultz, *The Republic of Labor,* p. 39.

6   *This was bold talk* Rappoport, *Stability and Change in Revolutionary Pennsylvania,* p. 119.

7   *Estimates from rent rolls* Rubenstein, *Men of Property,* pp. 41–45.

10   *In 1756, only a year after* Burrows and Wallace, *Gotham,* p. 168.

10   *Historians Edwin Burrows and Mike Wallace* Ibid., pp. 168–70.

11   *Drake's own haul* Kindleberger, *World Economic Primacy,* p. 75.

11   *Much of the £100,000 estate* Rankin, *The Pirates of Colonial North Carolina,* p. 19.

11   *As Chart 1.1 has shown* Wattenberg, *The Statistical History of the United States,* p. 1175.

12   *Such was the hole* Jones, *Wealth of a Nation to Be,* p. 82.

12   *It is certainly possible* E. James Ferguson, *The Power of the Purse,* p. 76.

13   *Three of the most successful* *Salem National Maritime Park Guide,* p. 46.

14   *The five with the highest* Tyler, "Persistence and Change," *Entrepreneurs,* pp. 110–17.

14   *Neglecting Philadelphia* Myers, *The History of the Great American Fortunes,* p. 62.

14   *Two others, just below* Tyler, op. cit., pp. 104–15.

14   *Nathan Appleton, who would* Ibid., p. 117.

15   *This political shake-up* Bruchey, *The Wealth of the Nation,* p. 20.

15   *Wartime data* Miller, *Stealing from America,* p. 80.

17   *A group of New York investors* Burrows and Wallace, op. cit., p. 302.

17   *Massachusetts alone* Charles, *The Origins of the American Party System,* p. 18.

17   *Of the overall $40–$60 million* Burrows and Wallace, op. cit., p. 307.

18 *By 1794, "speculators"* Stewart, *The Opposition Press of the Federalist Period,* p. 64.

18 *"Archimedes"* Ibid., p. 60.

19 *Critics called him* Alberts, *Golden Voyage,* pp. 213, 217.

19 *Bingham may have been* Ibid., p. 429.

20 *To gain allies* Hofstadter, *The American Political Tradition,* p. 36.

20 *The trustees liquidating* Myers, op. cit., p. 77.

21 *Then governor of Michigan* Ibid., p. 103.

21 *Of the average Deep South slave owner's* Wright, *Old South, New South,* p. 19.

22 *Somewhat more broadly* Jones, op. cit., p. 276.

22 *The richest southerner* Hintz, *Ethnic New Orleans,* p. 115.

23 *So, too, in Boston* Pessen, *Riches, Class, and Power Before the Civil War,* pp. 33–39.

24 *As the Erie Canal* Carmer, *The Tavern Lights Are Burning,* p. 64.

26 *The reason, he argued* Myers, op. cit., p. 148.

26 *Taking real estate as determinative* Pessen, op. cit., p. 72.

29 *In New York and Philadelphia* Gronowicz, *Race and Class Politics in New York City Before the Civil War,* pp. 99–105.

30 *When the new Know-Nothing legislature convened* Mulkern, *The Know-Nothing Party in Massachusetts,* p. 184.

31 *Even so, the principal historian* Mulkern, op. cit., p. 113.

32 *The abolition of slavery* Moore, "One Hundred Years of Reconstruction of the South," *Journal of Southern History,* May 1943: pp. 153–80.

32 *According to historian* C. Vann Woodward, *Reunion and Reaction,* p. 246.

33 *Economic historian Robert Russel* Russel, *A History of the American Economic System,* pp. 273–74.

33 *Things here at the North* Burrows and Wallace, op. cit., p. 877.

34 *Calculated in 1860 dollars* McCusker, *How Much Is That in Real Money?* pp. 328–29.

35 *Railroad freight and* Wattenberg, op. cit., pp. 594 and 600.

36 *John D. Rockefeller* Josephson, *The Robber Barons,* p. 116.

39 *He added that* Ibid., p. vi.

40 *Members of the "shoddy aristocracy"* Burrows and Wallace, op. cit., pp. 875–78.

40 *One historian has estimated* Shannon, *The Organization and Administration of the Union Army,* p. 71.

41 *The daily wages* Wattenberg, op. cit., p. 165.

42 *This is also the* Rubenstein, op. cit., p. 45.

43 *One analysis in 1890* Groner and the editors of American Heritage, *The History of American Business and Industry,* p. 216.

43   *In Massachusetts* Huston, *Securing the Fruits of Labor,* p. 347.

43   *Thomas G. Sherman* Ibid.

44   *The per capita money supply* Shannon, *American Farmers' Movements,* p. 50.

46   *They were, in the words* Rienow and Rienow, *Of Snuff, Sin, and the Senate,* p. 22.

CHAPTER 2: SERIOUS MONEY

48   *They talked about* Hofstadter, op. cit., p. 220.

48   *Years later* Ibid., p. 199.

53   *Elsewhere on the ledger* Ruscavage, *Income Inequality in America,* p. 142.

53   *Economic historians* Williamson and Lindert, *American Inequality,* p. 77.

53   *Indeed, the NICB series* Kolko, *Wealth and Power in America,* p. 14.

55   *Successful stock* Brandes, *War Hogs,* pp. 135–36.

55   *War, the reformers complained* Lundberg, *America's Sixty Families,* p. 195.

55   *In 1935* Brandes, op. cit., p. 140.

59   *business profits buckled* Perrett, *America in the Twenties,* p. 50.

61   *Of twenty-six working-class families* Chase, *Prosperity: Fact or Myth?* p. 72.

61   *The average year-to-year increase* Wattenberg, op. cit., p. 950.

61   *So many family businesses* Perrett, op. cit., p. 336.

61   *So enlarged* Ibid., p. 339.

61   *According to the New York Stock Exchange* Groner, op. cit., p. 281.

62   *New offerings* Perrett, op. cit., p. 369.

62   *Near the peak* Lundberg, op. cit., p. 221.

63   *The 15 percent of national income* Ilicks, op. cit., p. 18.

64   *The AFL-CIO* Perrett, op. cit., p. 322.

64   *Instead, it was* Chase, op. cit., p. 177.

64   *The two spent almost* Ibid., p. 286.

64   *Jitters increased* Ibid., p. 375.

65   *Even the Republican Congress* Ibid., p. 376.

65   *In 1932* Perkins and Perkins, *The Internet Bubble,* p. 177.

66   *The economist J. Kenneth Galbraith* Galbraith, *The Great Crash, 1929,* pp. 186–88.

67   *The market value* Hicks, op. cit., p. 224.

68   *So extraordinary, so golden* Kolko, op. cit., p. 24.

68   *In terms of holdings* Lundberg, op. cit., p. 46.

69   *With so many erstwhile* Smolensky and Plotnick, *Inequality and Poverty in the United States, 1900 to 1990,* University of California, Berkeley, July 1992 (unpublished paper).

71   *The real truth* Leuchtenberg, *Franklin D. Roosevelt and the New Deal,* p. 80.

73   *"The percentage of living millionaires"* 2 Lundberg, op. cit., p. 21.

74   *A decade later* Ibid., p. 48.

74   *Recovery came fastest* Blum, *V Was for Victory,* p. 92.

75   *The pay of women* Ibid., p. 95.

75   *Many families had their first discretionary income* Ibid., p. 94, and Goulden, *The Best Years, 1945–1950,* p. 92.

75   *By one estimate* Goulden, op. cit., pp. 92–94.

76   *Economists Claudia Goldin and* Claudia Goldin and Robert A. Margo, "The Great Compression," *The Quarterly Journal of Economics* (February 1992): 1–34.

76   *By 1949* Ruscavage, op. cit., p. 148.

76   *Frederick Lewis* Allen, *The Big Change,* pp. 188–89.

77   *Business expense accounts* Ibid., p. 190.

77   *In 1955* Kolko, op. cit., p. 42.

77   *During the 1923–29 period* Ibid., p. 23.

78   *General Motors bestirred* Goldman, *Crucial Decade,* pp. 291, 303.

78   *That same year the Democats* Kolko, op. cit., p. 124.

78   *Capital gains* Lundberg, *The Rich and the Super-Rich,* pp. 8–11.

81   *That same year* Ruscavage, op. cit., p. 54.

83   *For ordinary citizens* The 10 percent median family income shrinkage from 1970 to 1982 is calculated as follows: In *Dollars and Dreams,* Frank Levy set out a 7 percent real decline for the 1973–80 period. The 1981–82 period yielded another 4 percent decline, while the years from 1970 to 1972 saw a slight net gain.

83   *A sampling of 1,844* Vogel, *Fluctuating Fortunes,* p. 145.

83   *At a series* Ibid.

83   *Ronald Reagan briefly* Greider, *Secrets of the Temple,* p. 378.

92   *Much of the money* Kindleberger, *World Economic Primacy,* p. 179.

92   *Economist Edward Wolff* Wolff, *Top Heavy,* p. 21.

95   *Milton Friedman* Greider, op. cit., p. 93.

95   *James Grant, an* The Trouble With Prosperity (New York, 1996), pp. 2, 309–15.

98   *The* Philadelphia Inquirer Phillips, *Boiling Point,* p. 85.

100   *One stalwart regretted* Greider, *The Nation,* February 14, 2000, p. 12.

101   *As late as* Dean Baker, "Bull Market Keynesianism," *The American Prospect,* January-February 1999, p. 78.

103   New York Times *correspondent Thomas Friedman* "Stock Market Diplomacy," *New York Time*s, April 6, 1994, p. 1.

103   *Steven Gaines, author* Gross, *Bull Run,* p. 142.

104   *"Stockmarket Keynesianism"* "Bull Market Keynesianism," p. 8.

104   *One political pundit* Friedman, "The New Soulmates," *Los Angeles Times,* May 7, 2000, p. M1.

CHAPTER 3: MILLENNIAL PLUTOGRAPHICS

109   *The stock market, caught*   Shiller, *Irrational Exuberance,* pp. 8, 99–103.

109   *The value of stocks*   "Marketplace," *New York Times,* June 28, 2001, p. C9.

111   *With federal taxes as well as inflation*   CBO data from CBPP analysis.

113   *The Bureau of Labor Statistics*   Gates, *Democracy Under Siege,* p. 144.

116   *By pooling their money*   Forbes, October 12, 1998, p. 47.

117   *A captive trust company solved*   "Trust Yourself," *Forbes,* October 12, 1988, pp. 62–64.

117   *One chronicler of the 1990s*   Klepper and Gunther, *The Wealthy 100,* p. 16.

117   *Strange, because*   Lundberg, op. cit., pp. 23–27.

117   *Below this, national wealth portraiture*   "Wealth: Happy Ending Is Illusive," *Los Angeles Times,* March 14, 2000.

119   *A second flawed premise*   Hacker, *Money,* p. 99.

119   *Staid Bessemer*   advertisement *Wall Street Journal,* January 21, 2001.

125   *In late September 2001*   "Going Downhill," *The Economist,* September 29, 2001, pp. 86 and 116.

129   *"The revolution in office technology"*   "What's Behind America's Trend Towards Widened Income Inequality," *Barron's,* October 26, 1998, p. 25.

129   *"What's happening," explained* Business Week   *Business Week,* September 27, 1999, p. 92.

132   *Between 1977 and 1999*   Shapiro and Greenstein, CBPP, September 4, 1999.

132   *These changes raised*   Phillips, *Boiling Point,* p. 117.

133   *For mid-range employees*   "Benefits Dwindle," *New York Times,* June 14, 1998.

135   *Between 1992 and the decade's end*   "Equity Shrivels as Homeowners Borrow and Buy," *New York Times,* January 19, 2001, p. 1.

138   *"Since the mid-1980s"*   Phillips, *Arrogant Capital,* p. 81.

141   *In reaching $2.6 trillion*   Gross, op. cit., p. 5.

142   *"For all the talk"*   "Wealth Gap," *Wall Street Journal,* September 13, 1999, p. 1.

143   *Enron, the Houston-based energy firm*   Business Week, February 12, 2001.

146   *In a startling portrait*   "Greed and Spin," *Los Angeles Times,* September 6, 1998, p. M6.

146   *The upsurge of the*   Perkins and Perkins, op. cit., p. 25.

148   *Boeing CEO Philip Condit*   Buchanan, *The Great Betrayal,* pp. 100–105.

148   *In 1961*   Brouwer, *Sharing the Pie,* p. 48.

148   *General Motors, having*   "Rich Comparison," *Wall Street Journal,* July 30, 1999, p. 1.

148   *Peter Capelli, professor* Brouwer, op. cit., p. 58.

148   *One well-rewarded strategy* Economic Report of the President, 1993 for 1960–1990.

149   *If that money had been earned* Lewis and Allison, *The Cheating of America*, pp. 135–37.

150   *Reduction at the state level* Korten, *The Post-Corporate World*, p. 97.

150   *In 1996, the Democratic Policy Committee* House Democratic Policy Committee, "Who Is Downsizing the American Dream?" pp. 14–15.

151   *Based on an examination* Ibid., p. 18.

153   *Corporate profits, by contrast* "49th Annual Executive Pay Survey," *Business Week*, April 19, 1999.

155   *Preoccupation with personal option–related* "A Benefit for the Few Weighs on Many," *New York Times*, February 25, 2001, section 3, p. 1.

155   *Dell, in some fiscal quarters* "Microsoft's Other Business," *Barron's*, May 1, 2000, p. 14.

155   *Business buyers of technology* "Growth Companies Feel Pressure to Book Sales," *Wall Street Journal*, September 16, 1997.

159   *It was claims like* Chancellor, *Devil Take the Hindmost*, p. 150.

161   *Technology publishers* Perkins and Perkins, op. cit., p. 184.

161   *Michael Moritz* Kaplan, *The Silicon Boys*, p. 321.

162   *In Atlanta* "Nation in a Jam," *New York Times*, May 13, 2001, WK13.

162   *Survey data showed* Gates, op. cit., p. 80.

164   *A similar pattern in the UK* "The Rise of the Inactive Man," *Financial Times*, June 21, 2001, p. 13.

168   *"Extra spending at the top"* *Wall Street Journal*, September 13, 1999, p. A1.

CHAPTER 4: THE WORLD IS OUR OYSTER

172   Details of these circumstances can be found in the works of Braudel, Elliott, Schama, Israel, Boxer, Cole, Dangerfield, and Thompson listed below.

173   *Theodore Roosevelt, reviewing* Adams, *The Law of Civilization and Decay*, p. 45.

173   *Fernand Braudel and others* Braudel, *On History*, p. 88.

174   *One eighteenth-century Dutch burgomaster* Schama, *Embarrassment of Riches*, p. 599.

177   *In the words of one* Schama, Ibid., p. 323.

179   *In the words of* Kindleberger, op. cit., p. 32.

179   *Historians have generally* Elliott, *Imperial Spain, 1479–1716*, p. 192.

180   *"The result," according to* Ibid., p. 313.

180   *Merchants and successful artisans* Ibid., p. 201.

180   *Their principal voice* Ibid., p. 306.

180   *Then, speaking from* Ibid., p. 313.

181   *Meanwhile, the* Thompson and Casalilla, *The Castilian Crisis of the Seventeenth Century,* pp. 115–35.

181   *Output in* Israel, *The Dutch Republic,* p. 624.

181   *One index* Landes, *The Wealth and Poverty of Nations,* p. 445.

181   *As early as the 1650s* Boxer, *The Dutch Seaborne Empire,* p. 34.

181   *By 1688, the English consul* Ibid., p. 42.

181   *Jonathan Israel, in his* Israel, op. cit., p. 618.

182   *Dutch interest rates* Boxer, op. cit., p. 118.

183   *Certainly, by 1730* Schama, op. cit., p. 286.

183   *The typical mid-eighteenth-century family* Israel, op. cit., p. 1007.

183   *"A further symptom"* Ibid., p. 1003.

183   *As a measure of Dutch* Braudel, *The Perspective of the World,* p. 245.

183   *The mass of Dutch* Boxer, op. cit., p. 329.

183   *However, the unacceptable* Boxer, p. 124.

184   *In 1865, Matthew Arnold* Phillips, *Boiling Point,* p. 204.

185   *Then a second publication* Friedberg, *The Weary Titan,* p. 238.

185   *Between 1899 and 1913* Cole and Postgate, *The British Common People,* p. 497.

185   *George Dangerfield* Dangerfield, *The Strange Death of Liberal England,* p. 259.

186   *During the prewar half decade* Cole, op. cit., p. 498.

186   *Some 43 percent* Thompson, *The Edwardians,* p. 154.

186   *The nation, he insisted* Friedberg, op. cit., pp. 72–76.

187   *According to L. H. Jenks* Thomson, *England in the Nineteenth Century,* p. 166.

187   *One European historian* Dominico Sella, quoted in Olson, *The Rise and Decline of Nations,* p. 123.

188   *This hope was reinforced* Stevenson, *British Society, 1914–1945,* p. 387.

188   *Measured as a percentage* Hobsbawm, *Industry and Empire,* pp. 152–53.

188   *The share of British* Thompson, *The Edwardians,* p. 273.

190   *As barriers went up* Israel, *Dutch Primacy in World Trade,* pp. 383–84.

191   *So did the value* "Economic Beat," *Barron's,* December 4, 2000, p. 32.

195   *Historians cite* Landes, op. cit., p. 172.

195   *The most conspicuous Dutch boast* Schama, op. cit., p. 224.

196   *How could London* Hobsbawm, op. cit., p. 192.

196   *Indeed, Park Lane* Briggs, *Victorian Cities,* pp. 316–17.

197   *Americans played a significant role* Hobsbawm, op. cit., p. 180.

197   *Firms like Hope & Company* Braudel, op. cit., pp. 245–48 and 266–73.

198   *Technological skills* Israel, op. cit., pp. 1012–13.

198   *Nineteenth century U.S.*   Misa, *A Nation of Steel,* p. 125.

199   *Rare are the Spanish*   Hobsbawm, op. cit., pp. 191–92.

199   *By then, most*   Landes, op. cit., p. 445.

199   *Economic historian E. J. Hobsbawm*   Hobsbawn, op. cit., p. 191.

CHAPTER 5: FRIENDS IN HIGH PLACES

207   *These boons ranged from*   Myers, op. cit., pp. 115–18, 139–40, 166–69.

207   *Astor and Girard themselves*   Taylor, *The Transportation Revolution,* p. 98.

208   *The jobs included*   Friedman, *The History of American Law,* pp. 158, 169.

208   *Daniel Raymond, in his*   Ibid., p. 242.

208   *William Leggett, of the*   Burrows and Wallace, op. cit., 607.

210   *The most-quoted American*   Beard, *The Economic Basis of Politics,* p. 6.

210   *Realignments, in this scheme*   Ferguson, *Golden Rule,* p. 23.

215   *Well-acquainted with the theory,*   Sloan *Principle and Interest,* p. 96.

215   *The first American*   Burrows and Wallace, op. cit., p. 308.

216   *Banks that bought*   Carruthers, op. cit., p. 203.

218   *Adam Smith had warned*   Sloan, *Principle and Interest,* p. 96.

219   *One critic estimated*   Lundberg, *Sixty Families,* p. 166.

220   *Thousands of lawyers*   Ibid., pp. 166–69.

221   *General Electric, according to*   Vogel, op. cit., pp. 245, 252–54.

221   *The sum of corporate-claimed*   Gates, op. cit., p. 166.

222   The Economist *of London*   *The Economist,* January 20, 1990, p. 8.

223   *Now we're going to see* "Business Gets Big Breaks in Tax Bills," *Washington Post,* July 24, 1999, p. A1.

228   *Writer Bob Woodward*   Woodward, *Maestro,* p. 37.

228   *E. Gerald Corrigan*   Ibid., p. 43.

228   *Ironically,* Forbes *magazine* "Stocks and the Economy," *Forbes,* June 12, 2000, p. 308.

230   *"Governments have largely ceded"* "O Brave New World," *Barron's,* Sep. 25, 2000, p. MW14.

230   *The U.S. Treasury Department* "Stiglitz and the Limits of Reform," The Nation, Oct. 2, 2000, p. 22.

231   *The broader WTO* "The Battle in Seattle," *The Nation,* December 6, 1999, p. 20.

231   *Critics in the* "The Battle in Seattle," *The Nation,* December 6, 1999, p. 21.

232   *"The WTO aspires"* "The Battle Beyond Seattle," *The Nation,* December 27, 1999, p. 5.

232   *Democratic U.S. senator Fritz Hollings* "Unto The Breach," *Harper's,* May 2000, p. 20.

233   *Half of all the Dutch patents*   Kindleberger, op. cit., p. 95.

233   *As for the British* Ibid., pp. 130–31.

233   *The acerbic Charles Dickens* Bruce, *Lincoln and the Tools of War,* pp. 60–63.

233   *To make them, Whitney* J. W. Roe, in Russel, op. cit., p. 178.

234   *In a late 1815 message* Watts, *The Republic Reborn,* p. 311.

235   *Of the $23 million* Taylor, op. cit., p. 96.

235   *Prior to 1861* Ibid., pp. 94–96.

235   *The U.S. Military Academy* Temin, *Engines of Enterprise,* p. 267.

235   *Of the 2,218 graduates* Ibid., p. 268.

235   *This meant huge* Myers, op. cit., p. 73.

236   *By 1864, the* McPherson, *Battle Cry of Freedom,* pp. 449, 819–20.

236   *To neutralize such threats* Hofstadter, *Social Darwinism in American Thought,* pp. 44–45.

237   *Then between 1885* Friedman, op. cit., p. 311.

237   *The judicial inventions* Jackson, *The Struggle for Judicial Supremacy,* pp. 55–56.

237   *Holmes also pointed* Ibid., p. 54.

237   *Angry Populists charged* Faulkner, *Politics, Reform, and Expansion,* p. 129.

238   *Henry Demarest Lloyd* Destler, *American Radicalism, 1865–1901,* p. 217.

238   *One chronicler* Misa, op. cit., p. 267.

238   *Robert and Leona Rienow* Rienow and Rienow, op. cit., p. xvi.

239   *This produced the half-reformism* Josephson, *The Politicos,* p. 153.

239   *Samuel Eliot Morison* Morison and Commager, *The Growth of the American Republic,* Vol. 2.

239   *He had warned* Rienow and Rienow, op. cit., p. 12.

240   *Satchels were filled* Ibid., p. 124.

241   *This prompted Sen.* Ibid., 110.

241   *Over a ten-year span* Ibid., 143.

241   *Lamenting his actions* Ibid., p. 283.

242   *To maximize* Ibid., 247.

243   *The famous Kansas editor* Ibid., p. 124.

243   *Iowa Governor* Ibid., p. 164.

243   *Then in the 1917–18 war years* Rhodes, *Visions of Technology,* p. 66.

243   *Between 1919 and 1929* Mowery and Rosenberg, *Paths of Innovation,* p. 116.

243   *During the twenties and thirties* Ibid., p. 106.

244   *World War II* Ibid., pp. 60, 61, and 66.

244   *In the words of one* Sloat, *1929: America Before the Crash,* p. 98.

245   *Besides which* Temin, op. cit., p. 273.

245   *Completed in 1945* Rhodes, op. cit., p. 178.

245   *The next group of* Mowery and Rosenberg, op. cit., pp. 135–38.

247   *Compliance meant that firms*   Ibid., p. 134.

247   *Mowery and Rosenberg*   Ibid., pp. 160–61.

247   *He correctly predicted*   Rhodes, op. cit., pp. 164–67.

248   *"The free distribution"*   McChesny, *Rich Media, Poor Democracy,* p. 142.

CHAPTER 6: TECHNOLOGY

251   *Historians agree*   Israel, op. cit., p. 998.

251   *Textiles led*   Kennedy, *The Rise and Fall of the Great Powers,* p. 148.

251   *American exhibits*   Groner, *History of American Business and Industry,* op. cit., p. 174.

252   *The richest among them*   Ferguson, *The House of Rothschild,* p. 482.

253   *Two of the least disreputable*   Chancellor, op. cit., pp. 34–73.

253   *Even during the Napoleonic*   George, *England in Transition,* p. 112.

253   *On both sides*   Hobsbawm, op. cit., p. 111.

254   *As a measure*   Ibid., p. 112.

254   *Standard Oil of Ohio*   Russel, op. cit., p. 365.

256   *The Austrian economist*   Chancellor, op. cit., p. 92.

258   *In the words of Sir Walter Raleigh*   Padfield, *Maritime Supremacy,* p. 2.

258   *Treviso itself*   Swetz, *Capitalism and Arithmetic,* pp. 1–12.

258   *The most sweeping economic theses*   Warsh, *The Idea of Economic Complexity,* pp. 114–22.

259   *High English prices*   Braudel, *The Wheels of Commerce,* vol. 2, p. 171.

259   *Professor David Hackett Fischer*   Fischer, *The Great Wave,* p. 79.

259   *For all that the Medici Bank*   O'Connell, *The Counter Reformation,* p. 202.

259   *Braudel concluded*   Braudel, *Civilization and Capitalism,* p. 87.

260   *Few historians disagree*   E. P. Thompson, *The Making of the English Working Class,* pp. 189–212.

260   *In the coal industry*   Ibid., p. 211.

262   *Some 200,000 workers*   Chase, op. cit., pp. 156–57.

264   *A Cornell University study*   "Ten Myths About Globalization," *The Nation,* December 6, 1999, p. 26.

264   *Perhaps the most intriguing*   O'Rourke and Williamson, *The History of Globalization,* pp. 165–72, 182–83, 285–87.

266   *Per capita income*   United Nations Human Development Report, 1999, p. 28.

267   *Tax policy also conformed*   "Tradition of Equality Is Fading in the New Japan," *New York Times,* January 4, 2000, p. A6.

268   *According to research*   "New Wireless Valhalla," *New York Times,* July 13, 2000, p. G7.

268   *Most wealth in Finland*   Reuters, *Palm Beach Post,* December 5, 2000.

268   *Their wealth*   Ibid.

268   *London's Millennial boom*   "Britain's Home-Help Market," *Wall Street Journal,* December 4, 2000.

269   *Two of the major Internet* Barron's, May 1, 2000, pp. 20–22.

269   *Of ten industrial countries* "The New Israel," *New York Times,* April 16, 2001, p. BUS1, 12.

269   *Shali Tshuva* Ibid., p. 12.

270   *A survey by McKinsey & Co.* Forbes, March 20 and June 12, 2000.

270   *John Wall* Ibid.

270   *In wealth distribution* "India's Unwired Villages," *New York Times,* March 19, 2000, p. 14.

270   *Software engineers* "The World Continues to Court Silicon Valley," *USA Today,* June 26, 2001, p. 7A.

272   *"The technological elite"* "California Grapples with Growing Income Gap," *Christian Science Monitor,* September 26, 1996, p. 4.

272   *In 1969, twenty states* Ibid.

272   *Incomes for the top fifth* David Friedman, "The Dark Side of the High-Tech Religion," *Los Angeles Times,* January 31, 1999, p. M1.

273   *By 2000, part-time workers* Kotkin, "Grassroots Business," *New York Times,* September 26, 1999.

273   *A senior research scholar* Alex Pang, "Creative Destruction," *Los Angeles Times Book Review,* October 31, 1999, p. 2.

273   *At the peak* "California Becoming a Hard Place to Call Home," *Washington Post,* January 29, 2000, p. 1.

273   *Another dimension* Friedman, op. cit., *Los Angeles Times,* January 31, 1999, p. M1.

273   *In the busy domestic service sector* "Britain's Home-Help Market," *Wall Street Journal,* December 4, 2000.

273   *Wages and work conditions* David Friedman, "The Jackpot Economy," *Los Angeles Times,* May 9, 1999, p. M1.

274   *Included were more families* "Poverty Found to Be Rising," *New York Times,* April 20, 2000, p. B1.

275   *"There may be enough poetry"* Sloat., op. cit., p. 93.

276   *Machinery is accomplishing* Ibid., pp. 132–33.

276   *Author Warren Sloat* Ibid., p. 87.

276   *The powers of the secretary* Burrows and Wallace, op. cit., p. 1022.

276   *The heady boom* Chancellor, p. 192.

276   *By 1929* Shiller, op. cit., p. 105.

277   *The speaker of the U.S. House* Frank, *One Market Under God,* p. 59.

278   *As for the repetitive implosions* Kindleberger, *Manias, Panics, and Crashes,* p. 253–59.

279   *Total volume* Burrows and Wallace, op. cit., pp. 567–69.

279   *Then in the second wave* Taylor, op. cit., p. 345.

279   *Briggs published* Burrows and Wallace, op. cit., p. 616.

279   *Dozens of railroads* Ibid., p. 616.

279   *By the summer of 1857*   Groner, *The History of American Business and Industry,* p. 138.

280   *The latter could no longer sell*   Kindleberger, op. cit., pp. 39, 110.

281   *"All about the failure"*   Josephson, *Robber Barons,* p. 170.

281   *Many "went from nowhere"*   Burrows and Wallace, op. cit., p. 1021.

281   *The biographer of railroad king*   Josephson, op. cit., p. 152.

281   *Economist Thorstein Veblen*   Ibid., p. 191.

281   *This convinced J. P. Morgan*   Burrows and Wallace, op. cit., p. 1044.

284   *Economist Paul Krugman*   Krugman, "For Sale: America," *Time,* September 14, 1987.

284   *An economist at New York's*   "With Assets Pumped Up, Few Worry About Inflation," *New York Times,* May 23, 1999.

286   *These cumulatively devastated*   Boxer, op. cit., p. 325.

288   *Take Britain's loss*   Landes, op. cit., p. 290.

288   *Harvard economist*   Ibid.

288   *One scholar*   Van Vugt, *Britain to America,* p. 11.

288   *By 1914, the development*   Misa, op. cit., pp. 175–257.

288   *The latter and its implications*   "The Big Question," *Red Herring,* June 11, 2001, p. 44.

289   *An economist at the University*   "Trolling for Brains in International Waters," *New York Times,* April 1, 2001.

289   *"The defining character"*   "The Venture Capitalist in My Bedroom," *New York Times Magazine,* May 28, 2000, pp. 32–59.

290   *The upshot was*   "These Days, Made in Taiwan Often Means Made in China," *New York Times,* May 29, 2001, p. A1.

CHAPTER 7: WEALTH AND POLITICS

293   *From the 1780s on*   Tucker, *Mugwumps,* p. 12.

298   *Abraham Lincoln*   Borritt, *Lincoln and the Economics of the American Dream,* p. 175.

299   *He warned in 1869*   Josephson, *The Robber Barons,* p. 60.

299   *Many years later*   Brinkley, *Voices of Discontent,* p. 326.

301   *Alexander McDougall*   Tiedemann, *Reluctant Revolutionaries,* p. 176.

301   *Virginians in turn*   Holton, *Forced Founders,* pp. 51–56.

301   *Thomas Jefferson later*   Breen, *Tobacco Culture,* p. 141.

302   *In the words of*   Ibid., p. 199.

302   *George Washington, himself*   Robson, *The American Revolution,* p. 52.

302   *So, too, for Jefferson's*   Rouse, *Planters and Pioneers,* p. 126.

302   *According to one historian*   Sellers, op. cit., p. 35.

303   *Virginians like Jefferson*   Watts, op. cit., p. 38.

303   *Harrison had also favored*   Sellers, op. cit., p. 167.

304   *Pennsylvania had antibank riots*   Ibid., pp. 162–71.

304   *By the early 1870s*   Chancellor, p. 175.

305   *Edward G. Ryan*   Rienow and Rienow, p. 168.

305   *Charles Francis Adams*   Stiles, *In Their Own Words,* p. 133.

305   *And a huge railroad*   Hofstadter, *Age of Reform,* p. 229.

306   *TR held out the possibility*   Koenig, *Bryan,* pp. 414–16.

306   *Former general James B. Weaver*   Huston, op. cit., p. 355.

307   *Thomas Shearman*   Ibid., pp. 346–47.

307   *"By 1890"*   Rienow and Rienow, op. cit., p. 168.

307   *"I believe in corporations"*   "Liberty, Community, and the National Idea," *American Prospect* (November–December 1996): p. 58.

308   *In 1890 the Populist firebrand*   Faulkner, op. cit., p. 115.

308   *Two years later*   McKenna, *American Populism,* p. 96.

308   *The whole inter-related problem*   Nye, *Midwestern Progressive Politics,* p. 44.

309   *Kansas Senator William Peffer*   Hofstadter, *Age of Reform,* p. 65.

309   *The Morgan interests*   Ibid., p. 218.

309   *This single network*   Ibid., p. 230.

309   *Wilson worried*   Wilson, *The New Freedom,* p. 177.

311   *He spoke about*   Manley, "The Significance of Class in American History and Politics," p. 20.

311   *Woodrow Wilson*   Hofstadter, *Age of Reform,* p. 225.

312   *His newly acquired mission*   Koenig, op. cit., p. 416.

312   *In 1912, still seeking*   Kelly, *The Fight for the White House,* p. 23.

312   *In his 1936 message*   Morris, *Encyclopedia of American History,* pp. 417–18.

312   *Roosevelt replied*   Binkley, *American Political Parties,* p. 383.

313   *"As the 1936 campaign got underway"*   Leuchtenberg, op. cit., p. 53–54.

315   *Churchill's worry*   Winokur, *The Rich Are Different,* p. 195.

CHAPTER 8: WEALTH, MONEY-CULTURE ETHICS, AND CORRUPTION

318   *Many, many books*   "Green With Envy," *Wall Street Journal,* October 14, 1999, p. A1.

318   *From Kindleberger's research*   Kindleberger, op. cit., p. 10.

319   *Parliament expelled*   Chancellor, op. cit., pp. 49, 88, 91.

319   *The old Commodore*   Ibid., p. 176.

319   *By 1892*   McKenna, op. cit., p. 90.

320   *"The two parties"*   *The Nation,* November 20, 2000, p. 6.

320   *Richard N. Goodwin*   "The Selling of Government," *Los Angeles Times,* January 30, 1997, p. A12.

321   *In 1865, 165*   Vaughn, *Railwaymen, Politics, and Money,* p. 354.

321   *Lyndon Johnson had* Schlesinger, *Cycles of History,* p. 41.

321   *In* Devil Take the Hindmost Chancellor, p. 187.

322   *In 1873 the speculator* Josephson, *Robber Barons,* p. 132.

322   *The S&L scandals* Chancellor, op. cit., p. 271.

324   *In the sixty House districts* "Democracy Versus Dollars," *American Prospect* (March–April 1997).

325   *Former New Jersey senator* "Presidential Bidding," *The Nation,* August 23, 1999, p. 3.

325   *Charging that it broke* "Business Gets Big Breaks in Tax Bills," *Washington Post,* July 24, 1999, p. A1.

330   *One modern scholar* Jardine, *Worldly Goods,* p. 436.

330   *We Amsterdammers* Landes, op. cit., p. 137.

330   *One English political thinker* Wood, *A Trumpet of Sedition,* p. 43.

331   *A century later* Chancellor, op. cit., p. 33.

331   *At the peak of regency-period amorality* Murray, *An Elegant Madness,* p. 74.

331   *According to historian Richard Hofstadter* Hofstadter, *Social Darwinism in American Thought,* p. 201.

331   *Thinkers in the United States* Hofstadter, op. cit., p. 44.

332   *Dismissing egalitarianism* Ibid., p. 58.

332   *Albert Jay Nock* Nock, *Memoirs of a Superfluous Man,* quoted in Lewis Lapham, *Money and Class in America,* p. 39.

332   *Oliver Wendell Holmes* Hofstadter, op. cit., p. 121.

332   *A few years earlier* Cumings, "The American Ascendancy," *The Nation,* May 8, 2000, p. 15.

332–33 *Sinclair Lewis* Sinclair Lewis, *Babbitt,* p. 143.

333   *His treasury secretary* "Reagan's Economics: Throwback to Coolidge," Knight-Ridder News Service, *Hartford Courant,* April 26, 1981.

333   *Risk arbitrageur Ivan Boesky* Winokur, op. cit., p. 172.

333   *Vreeland herself* Silverman, *Selling Culture,* p. 3.

334   *"The seven deadly sins"* Phillips, *The Politics of Rich and Poor,* p. 59.

335   *To Friedman, greed was* Chancellor, op. cit., p. 241.

335   *One such was Chicago* "Law and Economics: A New Order in the Court?" *Business Week,* November 16, 1987, p. 93.

337   *Political scientists at UCLA* Kuttner, *Everything for Sale,* p. 338.

337   *"The evolution of government"* Ibid., p. 330.

338   *Former House speaker Newt Gingrich* Frank, *One Market under God,* pp. 50–64.

338   *Baptist minister Russell Conwell* O'Toole, *Money and Morals,* pp. 151–52.

338   *President Calvin* Bruce Shulman "Entrepreneurs," *The Los Angeles Times,* April 3, 2000 p. M1.

339   *"That isn't an issue"* "The 400 Richest Americans," *Forbes,* October 11, 1999, p. 170.

339   *In the mid-1980s*   Schlesinger, op. cit., p. 38.

340   *They were reassured*   Nevins, *Grover Cleveland*, pp. 195, 481.

341   *"Cleveland," remarked Wilson*   Hofstadter, *American Political Tradition*, p. 220.

341   *Historian David Burner*   Burner, *The Politics of Provincialism*, p. 167.

341   *Liberal historian*   Schlesinger, op. cit., p. 241.

342   *David Friedman*   Friedman, "The Jackpot Economy," *Los Angeles Times*, May 9, 1999.

342   *This commitment, he explained*   "Bill's Backers," *Mother Jones*, November–December 1996, p. 63.

342   *"Unfortunately, we've been cowed"*   Ibid.

343   *The author, Professor Jeffery Berry*   Berry, *The New Liberalism*.

343   *Until then*   See Perrett, op. cit., pp. 321–22, and Garraty, *The Great Depression*, pp. 100–102.

345   *Then as per capita GDP*   Greider, *One World Ready or Not*, pp. 451–55.

345   *The Department of Labor admits*   "The Fed's Approach Isn't Working," *Wall Street Journal*, May 23, 2000, p. A26.

CHAPTER 9: THE CUP ALWAYS RUNNETH OVER

347   *Simon Schama*   Schama, op. cit., pp. 348–49.

347   *"Blue chip"*   Chancellor, op. cit., pp. 25–31.

348   *"Speculation," Chancellor concluded*   Ibid., p. 27.

349   *Milton Friedman*   Ibid., p. 242.

349   *The business of wagering*   Grant, *The Trouble with Prosperity*, p. 215.

349   *A local Connecticut billboard*   Shiller, op. cit., p. 42.

349   *The* Reader's Guide   Ibid., p. 241.

349   *Richard Canfield, himself*   Grant, op. cit., pp. 232–34.

350   *"Wagers," said historian*   Schama, op. cit., p. 347.

350   *Financial writer James Grant*   Grant, op. cit., p. 220.

351   *Before their rise*   Carruthers, op. cit., p. 8.

351   *The longer-term costs*   See especially Vaughan, op. cit., and Hobsbawm, op. cit.

352   *Unprecedented new financial or managerial*   Chancellor, op. cit., p. 191.

352   *A leading British*   Vaughan, op. cit., pp. 121–47.

352   *In the United States of 1873*   See Chancellor, op. cit., p. 182, and Kindleberger, op. cit., p. 168.

352   *He recalled 1901*   Chancellor, op. cit., p. 192.

353   *In late 1999, J. Kenneth Galbraith*   Galbraith interview, *Los Angeles Times*, Opinion section, December 12, 1999.

355   *Chauncey Depew*   Hofstadter, op. cit., pp. 44–45.

355   *"On $50,000 a year"*   Winokur, op. cit., p. 7.

355   *In 1894 the U.S. Supreme Court*   Faulkner, op. cit., p. 185.

355   *Multimillionaires of the twenties* Lundberg, *Sixty Families,* p. 470.

356   *Edgar Allan Poe* Winokur, op. cit., p. 50.

356   *With every sumptuous detail* Ibid., p. 140.

356   *Novelist F. Scott Fitzgerald* Chancellor, op. cit., p. 224.

357   *He pictured* Gross, op. cit., p. 194.

357   *One late-1990s glossary* Winokur, op. cit., p. 235.

357   *In 1997, U.S. News* *U.S. News & World Report,* December 15, 1997, p. 60.

358   *One observer summed up* Frank, op. cit., pp. 10–11.

359   *The portraiture by Forbes* *Forbes,* October 11, 1999.

359   *They had to look like* Fearon, *Hamptons Babylon,* pp. 246–48.

361   *In place of wealth data* "Jackson Hole Round-Up," *Federal Open Market Committee Alert,* September 29, 1998, p. 6.

361–62 *The top 1 percent* "U.S. Stock Holdings Rose 20%," *Wall Street Journal,* March 15, 1999.

362   *"There was almost no trickle-down"* Gates, op. cit., p. 58.

362   *Economist Wolff* "A Sinking Tide," *Business Week,* September 14, 1998.

362   *The 12.5 million shareholders* Kolko, op. cit., pp. 50–54.

362   *The late 1630s Dutch* Israel, *Dutch Republic,* p. 533.

364   *The secretary of state* Chancellor, op. cit., p. 51.

364   *The disdainful nobility and gentry* Carruthers, op. cit., pp. 83–86.

364   *In his* Wealth of England, 1496–1750 Clark, *Wealth of England, 1496–1750,* p. 184.

364   *At the height of* Chancellor, op. cit., pp. 76–77.

364–65 *According to one account* Gleeson, *Millionaire,* p. 57.

365   *The mid-nineteenth-century British railway mania* Vaughan, op. cit., p. 115.

365   *Of Scotland, the poet* Chancellor, op. cit., p. 184.

365   *Industrial Leeds* Ibid., p. 134.

365   *But gradually in the fifteenth* Swetz, op. cit., pp. 271–72.

365   *Karl Marx in the* Carruthers, op. cit., p. 204.

366   *As we have seen* See especially ibid., p. 85–89.

367   *Michael Chevalier found* Chancellor, op. cit., p. 153.

367   *Harriet Martineau* Sellers, op. cit., p. 54, and Remini, *The Revolutionary Age of Andrew Jackson,* p. 12.

367   *According to one history* Sellers, p. 149.

368   *At any rate* Kindleberger, op. cit., p. 6, and Chancellor, op. cit., pp. 52–118.

368   *Catholic, mid-sixteenth-century* Schama, op. cit., p. 327.

369   *The subjects included* Ibid., pp. 363–68.

369   *Scarcely a bubble* Chancellor, op. cit., pp. 84–86.

371   *During the summer of 1998*   "The Summer of Wretched Excess," *Business Week,* August 3, 1998, p. 35.

CHAPTER 10: GREAT ECONOMIC POWER DECLINE AND THE POLITICS
     OF RESENTMENT

374   *"Anti-pecuniary diatribes"*   Schama, *Patriots and Liberators,* p. 3.

374   *Historian Simon Schama*   Ibid., p. 45.

375   *His book,*   The Moral Condition Ibid., p. 72.

375   *On the secular side*   Ibid., p. 95.

375–76 *The Dutch writers*   Ibid., p. 43; Cole, op. cit., p. 497.

377   *Its first prime minister*   Dangerfield, op. cit., pp. 391, 394–97.

378   *Higher taxation*   Stevenson, op. cit., p. 119.

378   *One respected social historian*   Ibid., p. 123.

378   *The top 1 percent's*   Ibid., p. 330.

379   *In 1974 a worn-out*   Collins, *More,* p. 10.

380   *He had set out*   Phillips, *Post-Conservative America,* p. 199.

381   *"The middle class," he said*   Ibid., p. 198.

381   *One activist later recalled*   Rusher, *Rise of the Right,* p. 299.

381   *Conservative populist leader*   Hodgson, *The World Turned Right Side Up,* p. 229.

381   *By 1980 the canal fight*   Burnham, *The Current Crisis in American Politics,* pp. 268–307.

383   *Democratic strategists complained*   Phillips, *The Politics of Rich and Poor,* op. cit., p. 42.

384   *Political analyst William Schneider*   Phillips, *Boiling Point,* op. cit., pp. xix–xx.

384   *Vincent Breglio*   "To Broaden Political Base, Bush Must Keep Running," *Christian Science Monitor,* November 18, 1998.

384–85 *On the Democratic side*   Phillips, *Boiling Point,* op. cit., pp. 74–75.

385   *"I want a revolution"*   Ibid., pp. 19, 242.

385   *Former California governor Jerry Brown*   Ibid., p. xix.

386   *In 1993*   Phillips, *Arrogant Capital,* op. cit., p. 6.

386   *But as the left-leaning*   "Bill's Big Backers," *Mother Jones,* November–December 1996, p. 60.

391   *Fordham University professor Thomas DeLuca*   "The Voting Class Gap," *American Prospect* (May–June 1999).

392   *In Holland, emphasis*   Schama, op. cit., p. 386.

392   *As Professor Schama explains*   Ibid., p. 386.

392   *Isaac Gogel, the Patriot journalist*   Ibid., p. 506.

393   *By the late 1940s*   G. D. H. Cole, op. cit., pp. 290–91.

393   *A successful, upper-middle-class*   Ibid., pp. 290–92.

395   *Graef Crystal* Crystal, *In Search of Excess,* p. 292.

395   *Ronald Reagan, as we have seen* Gross, op. cit., p. 94.

398   *J. R. Hobson, a radical* Hobson, "Imperialism: A Study," in Beckson, *London in the 1890s: A Cultural History,* p. 348.

398   *One analysis of the* Marwick, *Britain in the Century of Total War: War, Peace, and Social Change, 1900–1967,* pp. 47–48.

401   *Indeed, part of the* "Bush Says Terrorists Sought Markets' Ruin," *Washington Post,* October 21, 2001, p. A25.

AFTERWORD: WEALTH AND DEMOCRACY

407   *Bradley, the second-finishing* Senator Bill Bradley, speech to John F. Kennedy School of Government, Harvard, January 16, 1996, p. 5.

407   *McCain, runner-up* "Business Gets Big Break in Tax Bills," *Washington Post,* July 24, 1999, p. A1.

408   *He also promised* "The Outlook," *Wall Street Journal,* February 14, 2000, p. 1.

408   *In Iowa, where* The Nation, November 20, 2000, p. 6.

410   *Wall Street Journal polling* "The Global Turning," *The Nation,* July 19, 1999.

410   *In 1999* "At This Rate, We'll All Be Global in Another Hundred Years," *New York Times,* May 23, 1999, p. WK5.

413   *In Washington* "Dialogue Won't Calm Global Protests," *International Herald Tribune,* June 25, 2001, p. 9.

414   *The many trade officials* The Nation, December 20, 1999, p. 3.

415   *Back then* Steven Solomon, *The Confidence Game* (New York, 1995).

416   *The ascendancy of judges* C. Neal Tate and Torbjorn Vallinder, eds., *The Global Expansion of Judicial Power* (New York, 1995).

416   *In Britain* "Despotism in Brussels?" *Foreign Affairs* (May–June 2001): pp. 114–22.

417   *British Euroskeptics* "From Disenchantment Back to Democracy," *Financial Times,* June 22, 2001, p. 13.

418   *To historians* Will and Ariel Durant, *The Lessons of History* (New York, 1968).

420   *However, as Charles Lindblom* Charles Lindblom, *Politics and Markets* (New York, 1977).

421   *In Globalization and History* O'Rourke and Williamson, op. cit., p. 287.

SELECT BIBLIOGRAPHY

The following are references cited in the text:

CHAPTER I

Charles Sellers, *The Market Revolution* (New York, 1991).

Ronald Schultz, *The Republic of Labor* (New York, 1993).

George Rappoport, *Stability and Change in Revolutionary Pennsylvania* (University Park, Pa.: 1996).

William Rubenstein, *Men of Property* (New Brunswick, 1981).

Edwin Burrows and Mike Wallace, *Gotham* (New York, 1998).

Charles Kindleberger, *World Economic Primacy* (New York, 1996).

Hugh Rankin, *The Pirates of Colonial North Carolina* (Raleigh, 1996).

Ben Wattenberg, *The Statistical History of the United States* (New York, 1976).

Alice Jones, *Wealth of a Nation to Be* (New York, 1980).

E. James Ferguson, *The Power of the Purse* (Chapel Hill, 1961).

Salem National Maritime Park Guide (Washington, D.C.: 1987).

John Tyler, "Persistence and Change," in *Entrepreneurs* (Boston, 1997).

Gustavus Myers, *The History of the Great American Fortunes* (New York, 1936).

Stuart Bruchey, *The Wealth of the Nation* (New York, 1988).

Nathan Miller, *Stealing from America* (New York, 1996).

Joseph Charles, *The Origins of the American Party System* (New York, 1961).

Daniel Stewart, *The Opposition Press of the Federalist Period* (Albany, N.Y.: 1961).

Robert Alberts, *Golden Voyage* (Boston, 1969).

Richard Hofstadter, *The American Political Tradition* (New York, 1948).

Gavin Wright, *Old South, New South* (Baton Rouge, 1986).

Martin Hintz, *Ethnic New Orleans* (Lincolnwood, 1995).

Edward Pessen, *Riches, Class, and Power Before the Civil War* (New Brunswick, N.J.: 1990).

Carl Carmer, *The Tavern Lights Are Burning* (New York, 1964).

Anthony Gronowicz, *Race and Class Politics in New York City Before the Civil War* (Boston, 1998).

John Mulkern, *The Know-Nothing Party in Massachusetts* (Boston, 1990).

Moore, "One Hundred Years of Reconstruction of the South," *Journal of Southern History* (May 1943): pp. 153–80.

C. Vann Woodward, *Reunion and Reaction* (Garden City, N.Y.: 1956).

Robert Russel, *A History of the American Economic System* (New York, 1964).

John McCusker, *How Much Is That in Real Money?* (Worcester, Mass.: 1992).

Matthew Josephson, *The Robber Barons* (New York, 1962).

Fred Shannon, *The Organization and Administration of the Union Army* (Cleveland, 1928).

Alex Groner and the editors of American Heritage, *The History of American Business and Industry* (New York, 1972).

James Huston, *Securing the Fruits of Labor* (Baton Rouge, 1998).

Fred Shannon, *American Farmers' Movements* (Princeton, N.J.: 1957).

Robert Rienow and Leona Rienow, *Of Snuff, Sin, and the Senate* (Chicago, 1965).

CHAPTER 2

Margaret Leech, *In the Days of McKinley* (New York, 1959).

Paul Ruscavage, *Income Inequality in America* (Armonk, N.Y.: 1999).

Jeffrey Williamson and Peter Lindert, *American Inequality* (New York, 1980).

Gabriel Kolko, *Wealth and Power in America* (New York, 1972).

Stuart Brandes, *War Hogs* (Lexington, Ky.: 1997).

Ferdinand Lundberg, *America's Sixty Families* (New York, 1937).

Geoffrey Perrett, *America in the Twenties* (New York, 1985).

John Hicks, *Republican Ascendancy* (New York, 1963).

Stuart Chase, *Prosperity: Fact or Myth?* (New York, 1929).

Anthony Perkins and Michael Perkins, *The Internet Bubble* (New York, 1999).

J. Kenneth Galbraith, *The Great Crash, 1929* (Boston, 1988).

Smolensky and Plotnick, "Inequality and Poverty in The United States, 1900–1990," University of California (Berkeley), July 1992 (unpublished paper).

William Leuchtenberg, *Franklin D. Roosevelt and the New Deal* (New York, 1963).

John Blum, *V Was for Victory* (New York, 1976).

Joseph Goulden, *The Best Years, 1945–1950* (New York, 1976).

Frederick Lewis Allen, *The Big Change* (New York, 1963).

Eric Goldman, *Crucial Decade* (New York, 1956).

Ferdinand Lundberg, *The Rich and the Super-Rich* (New York, 1957).

David Vogel, *Fluctuating Fortunes* (New York, 1989).

Thomas Friedman, "Stock Market Diplomacy," *New York Times*, April 6, 1994, p. 1.

William Greider, *Secrets of the Temple* (New York, 1987).

Edward Wolff, *Top Heavy* (New York, 1998).

Kevin Phillips, *Boiling Point* (New York, 1993).

William Greider, *The Nation,* February 14, 2000, p. 12.

Dean Baker, "Bull Market Keynesianism," *The American Prospect*, January–February 1999, p. 78.

Daniel Gross, *Bull Run* (New York, 2000).

David Friedman, "The New Soulmates," *Los Angeles Times,* May 7, 2000, p. M1.

CHAPTER 3

Robert Shiller, *Irrational Exuberance* (Princeton, N.J.: 2000).

"Marketplace," *New York Times,* June 28, 2001, p. C9.

CBO data from CBPP analysis.

Jeff Gates, *Democracy Under Siege* (New York, 2000).

Forbes, October 12, 1998, p. 47.

Michael Klepper and Robert Gunther, *The Wealthy 100* (Secaucus, N.J.: 1996).

"Wealth: Happy Ending Is Illusive," *Los Angeles Times,* March 14, 2000.

Andrew Hacker, *Money* (New York, 1997).

"Going Downhill," *The Economist,* September 29, 2001.

"What's Behind America's Trend Towards Widened Income Inequality," *Barron's,* October 26, 1998.

Business Week, September 27, 1999.

Shapiro and Greenstein, CBPP, September 4, 1999.

"Benefits Dwindle," *New York Times,* June 14, 1998.

"Equity Shrivels as Homeowners Borrow and Buy," *New York Times,* January 19, 2001, p. 1.

Kevin Phillips, *Arrogant Capital* (New York, 1994).

"Wealth Gap," *Wall Street Journal,* September 13, 1999, p. 1.

Business Week, February 12, 2001.

"Greed and Spin," *Los Angeles Times,* September 6, 1998, p. M6.

Steve Brouwer, *Sharing the Pie* (New York, 1998).

"Rich Comparison," *Wall Street Journal,* July 30, 1999.

Economic Report of the President, 1993, Washington, D.C., 1993.

David Korten, *The Post-Corporate World* (Berkeley, 1999).

House Democratic Policy Committee, "Who Is Downsizing the American Dream?" (Washington, D.C.: 1996).

49th Annual Executive Pay Survey, *Business Week,* April 19, 1999.

"A Benefit for the Few Weighs on Many," *New York Times,* February 25, 2001.

"Microsoft's Other Business," *Barron's,* May 1, 2000.

"Growth Companies Feel Pressure to Book Sales," *Wall Street Journal,* September 16, 1997.

Edward Chancellor, *Devil Take the Hindmost* (New York, 1999).

David Kaplan, *The Silicon Boys* (New York, 1999).

"Nation in a Jam," *New York Times,* May 13, 2001, WK13.

"The Rise of the Inactive Man," *Financial Times,* June 21, 2001.

"Extra Spending at the Top," *Wall Street Journal,* September 13, 1999, A1.

CHAPTER 4

Brooks Adams, *The Law of Civilization and Decay* (New York, 1943).

Fernand Braudel, *On History* (Chicago, 1980).

Simon Schama, *Embarrassment of Riches* (Berkeley, 1988).

J. H. Elliott, *Imperial Spain, 1479–1716* (New York, 1966).

I. Thompson and B. Casalilla, *The Castilian Crisis of the Seventeenth Century* (Cambridge, UK, 1994).

Jonathan Israel, *The Dutch Republic* (New York, 1995).

David Landes, *The Wealth and Poverty of Nations* (New York, 1998).

Boxer, *The Dutch Seaborne Empire* (New York, 1985).

Fernand Braudel, *The Perspective of the World* (New York, 1984).

Aaron Friedberg, *The Weary Titan* (Princeton, 1988).

G. D. H. Cole and Raymond Postgate, *The British Common People* (New York, 1961).

George Dangerfield, *The Strange Death of Liberal England* (New York, 1961).

Paul Thompson, *The Edwardians* (New York, 1992).

David Thomson, *England in the Nineteenth Century* (London, 1950).

Mancur Olson, *The Rise and Decline of Nations* (New Haven, 1982).

John Stevenson, *British Society, 1914–1945* (New York, 1984).

E. J. Hobsbawm, *Industry and Empire* (Baltimore, 1969).

Jonathan Israel, *Dutch Primacy in World Trade* (Oxford, 1989).

"Economic Beat," *Barron's,* December 4, 2000, p. 32.

Asa Briggs, *Victorian Cities* (Berkeley, 1993).

Thomas Misa, *A Nation of Steel* (Baltimore, 1995).

CHAPTER 5

George Taylor, *The Transportation Revolution* (New York, 1968).

Lawrence Friedman, *The History of American Law* (New York, 1973).

Charles Beard, *The Economic Basis of Politics* (New York, 1957).

Thomas Ferguson, *Golden Rule* (Chicago, 1995).

Bruce Carruthers, *City of Capital* (Princeton, N.J.: 1996).

Herbert Sloan, *Principle and Interest* (New York, 1995).

"Business Gets Big Breaks in Tax Bills," *Washington Post,* July 24, 1999, p. A1.

Bob Woodward, *Maestro* (New York, 2000).

"Stocks and the Economy," *Forbes,* June 12, 2000, p. 308.

"O Brave New World," *Barron's,* September 25, 2000, p. MW14.

"Stiglitz and the Limits of Reform," *The Nation,* December 6, 1999, p. 20.

"The Battle in Seattle," *The Nation,* December 6, 1999, p. 20.

"Unto the Breach," *Harper's,* May 2000, p. 20.

Robert Bruce, *Lincoln and the Tools of War* (Urbana, 1989).

Steven Watts, *The Republic Reborn* (Baltimore, 1987).

Peter Temin, *Engines of Enterprise* (Cambridge, Mass.: 2000).

James McPherson, *Battle Cry of Freedom* (New York, 1988).

Richard Hofstadter, *Social Darwinism in American Thought* (Boston, 1955).

Robert Jackson, *The Struggle for Judicial Supremacy* (New York, 1941).

Harold Faulkner, *Politics, Reform, and Expansion* (New York, 1963).

Chester Destler, *American Radicalism, 1865–1901* (Chicago, 1966).

Matthew Josephson, *The Politicos* (New York, 1938).

Samuel Eliot Morison and Henry S. Commager, *The Growth of the American Republic,* Volume 2 (New York, 1950).

Richard Rhodes, ed., *Visions of Technology* (New York, 1999).

David Mowery and Nathan Rosenberg, *Paths of Innovation* (New York, 1999).

Warren Sloat, *1929: America Before the Crash* (New York, 1979).

Robert McChesny, *Rich Media, Poor Democracy* (Urbana, 1989).

CHAPTER 6

Paul Kennedy, *The Rise and Fall of the Great Powers* (New York, 1987).

Niall Ferguson, *The House of Rothschild* (New York, 1998).

Dorothy George, *England in Transition* (London, 1953).

Peter Padfield, *Maritime Supremacy* (Woodstock, N.Y.: 2000).

Fred Swetz, *Capitalism and Arithmetic* (LaSalle, Ill.: 1987).

David Warsh, *The Idea of Economic Complexity* (New York, 1984).

Fernand Braudel, *The Wheels of Commerce* (New York, 1982).

David Hackett Fischer, *The Great Wave* (New York, 1996).

Marvin O'Connell, *The Counter Reformation* (New York, 1974).

Fernand Braudel, *Civilization and Capitalism* (New York, 1984).

E. P. Thompson, *The Making of the English Working Class* (New York, 1966).

United Nations Human Development Report, 1999, p. 28.

"Tradition of Equality Is Fading in the New Japan," *New York Times,* January 4, 2000, p. A6.

"New Wireless Valhalla," *New York Times,* July 13, 2000, p. G7.

Reuters, *Palm Beach Post,* December 5, 2000.

"Britain's Home-Help Market," *Wall Street Journal,* December 4, 2000.

"India's Unwired Villages," *New York Times,* March 19, 2000, p. 14.

"The World Continues to Court Silicon Valley," *USA Today,* June 26, 2001, p. 7A.

"California Grapples with Growing Income Gap," *Christian Science Monitor,* September 26, 1996, p. 4.

"The Dark Side of the High-Tech Religion," David Friedman, *Los Angeles Times,* January 31, 1999.

Joel Kotkin, "Grassroots Business," *New York Times,* September 26, 1999.

Alex Pang, "Creative Destruction," *Los Angeles Times Book Review,* October 31, 1999, p. 2.

"California Becoming a Hard Place to Call Home," *Washington Post,* January 29, 2000, p. 1.

David Friedman, "The Jackpot Economy," *Los Angeles Times,* May 9, 1999.

"Poverty Found Rising," *New York Times,* April 20, 2000, p. B1.

Kevin O'Rourke and Jeffrey Williamson, *Globalization and History* (Cambridge, Mass.: 1999).

Thomas Frank, *One Market under God* (New York, 2000).

Charles Kindleberger, *Manias, Panics, and Crashes* (New York, 1978).

Alex Groner, ed., *The History of American Business and Industry* (New York, 1972).

Paul Krugman, "For Sale: America," *Time,* September 14, 1987.

"With Assets Pumped Up, Few Worry About Inflation," *New York Times,* May 23, 1999.

William Van Vugt, *Britain to America* (Urbana, Ill.: 1999).

"The Big Question," *Red Herring,* June 11, 2001, p. 44.

"Trolling for Brains in International Waters," *New York Times,* April 1, 2001.

"The Venture Capitalist in My Bedroom," *New York Times Magazine,* May 28, 2000, pp. 32–59.

"These Days, Made in Taiwan Often Means Made in China," *New York Times,* May 29, 2001, p. A1.

CHAPTER 7

David Tucker, *Mugwumps* (Columbia, Mo.: 1998).

Gabor Borritt, *Lincoln and the Economics of the American Dream* (Urbana, Ill.: 1994).

Alan Brinkley, *Voices of Discontent* (New York, 1982).

Joseph Tiedemann, *Reluctant Revolutionaries* (Ithaca, N.Y.: 1997).

Woody Holton, *Forced Founders* (Chapel Hill, N.C.: 1949).

T. H. Breen, *Tobacco Culture* (Princeton, N.J.: 1985).

Eric Robson, *The American Revolution* (London, 1955).

Parke Rouse, *Planters and Pioneers* (New York, 1968).

T. J. Stiles, ed., *In Their Own Words* (New York, 1997).

Richard Hofstadter, *The Age of Reform* (New York, 1956).

Samuel Koenig, *Bryan* (New York, 1971).

"Liberty, Community, and the National Idea," *American Prospect* (November–December 1996): p. 58.

George McKenna, *American Populism* (New York, 1974).

Russell Nye, *Midwestern Progressive Politics* (New York, 1959).

Woodrow Wilson, *The New Freedom* (New York, 1913).

John Manley, "The Significance of Class in American History and Politics" draft paper, Stanford University, 1990.

Frank Kelly, *The Fight for the White House* (New York, 1961).

Richard B. Morris, *Encyclopedia of American History* (New York, 1976).

Wilfred Binkley, *American Political Parties* (New York, 1943).

Jon Winokur, *The Rich Are Different* (New York, 1996).

CHAPTER 8

"Green With Envy," *Wall Street Journal,* October 14, 1999.

Richard Goodwin, "The Selling of Government," *Los Angeles Times,* January 30, 1997, p. A12.

Adrian Vaughan, *Railwaymen, Politics, and Money* (London, 1997).

Arthur Schlesinger Jr., *Cycles of History* (Boston, 1986).

"Democracy Versus Dollars," *American Prospect* (March–April 1997).

"Presidential Bidding," *The Nation,* August 23, 1999.

"Business Gets Big Breaks in Tax Bills," *Washington Post,* July 24, 1999, p. A1.

Lisa Jardine, *Worldly Goods* (New York, 1996).

Ellen Wood and Neal Wood, *A Trumpet of Sedition* (New York, 1997).

Venetia Murray, *An Elegant Madness* (New York, 1999).

Lewis Lapham, *Money and Class in America* (New York, 1989).

Bruce Cumings, "The American Ascendancy," *The Nation,* May 8, 2000, p. 15.

Sinclair Lewis, *Babbitt* (New York, 1922).

"Reagan's Economics: Throwback to Coolidge," Knight-Ridder News Service, *Hartford Courant,* April 26, 1981.

Deborah Silverman, *Selling Culture* (New York, 1986).

Kevin Phillips, *The Politics of Rich and Poor* (New York, 1990).

"Law and Economics: A New Order in the Court?" *Business Week,* November 16, 1987.

Robert Kuttner, *Everything for Sale* (New York, 1998).

Patricia O'Toole, *Money and Morals* (New York, 1998).

"The 400 Richest Americans," *Forbes,* October 11, 1999, p. 170.

Allan Nevins, *Grover Cleveland* (New York, 1933).

David Burner, *The Politics of Provincialism* (New York, 1968).

David Friedman, "The Jackpot Economy," *Los Angeles Times,* May 9, 1999.

"Bill's Backers," *Mother Jones,* November–December 1996, p. 63.

Jeffrey Berry, *The New Liberalism* (Washington, 1999).

John Garraty, *The Great Depression* (New York, 1986).

William Greider, *One World Ready or Not* (New York, 1997).

"The Fed's Approach Isn't Working," *Wall Street Journal,* May 23, 2000, p. A26.

CHAPTER 9

James Grant, *The Trouble with Prosperity* (New York, 1996).

J. Kenneth Galbraith, interview, *Los Angeles Times,* Opinion, December 12, 1999.

"The 400 Richest Americans," *Forbes,* October 11, 1999.

Peter Fearon, *Hamptons Babylon* (Secaucus, N.J.: 1998).

"Jackson Hole Round-Up," *Federal Open Market Committee Alert,* September 29, 1998, p. 6.

"U.S. Stock Holdings Rose 20%," *Wall Street Journal,* March 15, 1999.

"A Sinking Tide," *Business Week,* September 14, 1998.

Sir George Clark, *Wealth of England, 1496–1750* (London, 1946).

Janet Gleeson, *Millionaire* (New York, 1999).

Robert Remini, *The Revolutionary Age of Andrew Jackson* (New York, 1976).

"The Summer of Wretched Excess," *Business Week,* August 3, 1998, p. 35.

CHAPTER 10

Simon Schama, *Patriots and Liberators* (New York, 1977).

Robert Collins, *More* (New York, 2000).

Kevin Phillips, *Post-Conservative America* (New York, 1982).

William Rusher, *Rise of the Right* (New York, 1984).

Godfrey Hodgson, *The World Turned Right Side Up* (New York, 1996).

Walter Dean Burnham, *The Current Crisis in American Politics* (New York, 1982).

"To Broaden Political Base, Bush Must Keep Running," *Christian Science Monitor,* November 18, 1998.

"Bill's Big Backers," *Mother Jones,* November–December 1996, p. 60.

Thomas DeLuca, "The Voting Class Gap," *American Prospect* (May–June 1999).

Graef Crystal, *In Search of Excess* (New York, 1991).

William E. Hudson, *American Democracy in Peril* (Chatham, N.J.: 1995).

Frederick R. Strobel and Wallace E. Peterson, *The Coming Class War and How to Avoid It* (Armonk, N.Y.: 1999).

Charles M. Kelly, *Class War in America* (Santa Barbara, Cal.: 2000).

Patrick J. Buchanan, *The Great Betrayal* (New York, 1998).

William J. Quirk and R. Randall Bridwell, *Abandoned: The Betrayal of the American Middle Class* (Chatham, N.J.: 1992).

William P. Kreml, *America's Middle Class: From Subsidy to Abandonment* (Durham, N.C.: 1997).

Jeff Gates, *Democracy At Risk: Rescuing Main Street From Wall Street* (New York, 2000).

CHAPTER 11

Senator Bill Bradley, speech to John F. Kennedy School of Government, Harvard, January 16, 1996, p. 5.

"Business Gets Big Breaks in Tax Bills," *Washington Post,* July 24, 1999, p. A1.

"The Outlook," *Wall Street Journal,* February 14, 2000, p. 1.

"Nader: Fast in the Stretch," *The Nation,* November 20, 2000, p. 6.

Robert Borosage, "The Global Turning," *The Nation,* July 19, 1999, p. 19.

"At This Rate, We'll All Be Global in Another Hundred Years," *New York Times,* May 23, 1999, p. WK5.

"Dialogue Won't Calm Global Protests," *International Herald Tribune,* June 25, 2001, p. 9.

Steven Solomon, *The Confidence Game* (New York, 1995).

C. Neal Tate and Torbjorn Vallinder, eds., *The Global Expansion of Judicial Power* (New York, 1995).

"Despotism in Brussels?" *Foreign Affairs* (May–June 2001): pp. 114–22.

"From Disenchantment Back to Democracy," *Financial Times,* June 22, 2001, p. 13.

Will and Ariel Durant, *The Lessons of History* (New York, 1968).

Charles Lindblom, *Politics and Markets* (New York, 1977).

INDEX

ACKNOWLEDGMENTS

For the research on the book, I have many debts. Bill Fowler and Peter Drummey of the Massachusetts Historical Society and John Van Horne of the Library Company of Philadelphia provided useful material on wealth and commerce in New England and Pennsylvania during the eighteenth and nineteenth centuries. The Office of the Historian of the U.S. Senate helped with information on the turn-of-the-twentieth-century millionaires who sat in the Senate. Lawrence Mishel of the Economic Policy Institute provided the recent economic data in a number of charts. The best recent wealth and net worth data, in turn, comes from New York University Professor Edward Wolff. The material on the richest people in America and the world published by *Forbes* magazine is another great resource. In a different vein, I appreciate the help given by Charles Lewis of the Center for Public Integrity, and by Micah Sifry and Nancy Watsman of Public Campaign.

On the literary front, thanks to Bill Leigh of the Leigh Bureau for his agenting; to my sons, Andrew and Alec; and my wife, Martha, for her Web site and research help. At Broadway Books, my thanks go to editor-in-chief Gerry Howard; to my two fine editors, Suzanne Oaks and Kristine Puopolo; and to their indefatigable assistants, Claire Johnson and Beth Haymaker.

ABOUT THE AUTHOR

Kevin Phillips is a contributing columnist to the *Los Angeles Times* and a regular contributor to National Public Radio. He is also a periodic contributor to *Time* and *Harper's*. Phillips was the chief political analyst for the 1968 Republican presidential campaign, and in 1969 published his landmark book *The Emerging Republican Majority*. From 1971 to 1998, he was the editor-publisher of the *American Political Report* and from 1984 to 1996, he was an elections commentator for CBS Television News. He lives in Connecticut.

His national bestseller *The Politics of Rich and Poor*—the 1990 predecessor to *Wealth and Democracy*—sparked a political firestorm and was described as a "founding document" of the 1992 presidential election.